Type 2
DIABETES
COOKBOOK

1000+ EASY AND TASTY DIABETIC-FRIENDLY RECIPES FOR THE NEWLY DIAGNOSED | INCLUDES A 4-WEEK MEAL PLAN FOR BEGINNER AND ADVANCED USERS

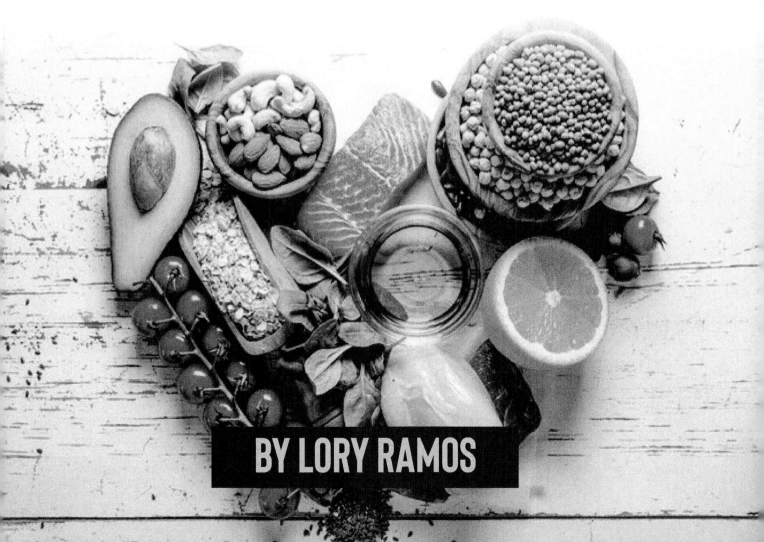

BY LORY RAMOS

Contents

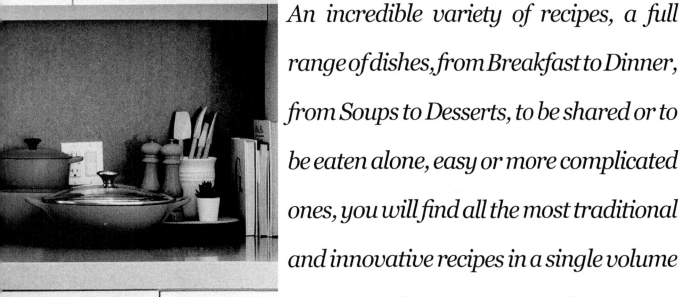

Introduction

An incredible variety of recipes, a full range of dishes, from Breakfast to Dinner, from Soups to Desserts, to be shared or to be eaten alone, easy or more complicated ones, you will find all the most traditional and innovative recipes in a single volume with more than one thousand recipes!

All the steps are explained, the nutritional values specified, all the ingredients are ready, so let's begin cooking now!

TYPE 2 DIABETES

Type 2 diabetes is the most common form of diabetes. When a person has diabetes, they cannot properly control the amount of sugar in their blood. The pancreas doesn't produce enough insulin, or the body's cells do not react to insulin, and glucose stays in the blood. The result of this condition is high blood sugar. High blood sugar is the leading cause of Type 2 diabetes.

It is also called adult-onset diabetes or non-insulin-dependent diabetes. Children with Type 1 diabetes are typically diagnosticated before they turn five. Children with Type 2 diabetes are diagnosed at any age, but most are diagnosed between 30 and 60 years old.

TYPE 2 DIABETES SIGNS AND SYMPTOMS

The symptoms of type 2 diabetes depend on whether your body produces enough insulin or not. In some cases, the only way to diagnose diabetes is to check your blood sugar level. If your blood sugar levels are high, the following signs and symptoms may occur:

» Excess thirst and urination
» Hunger and loss of weight
» Frequent urination, especially at night
» Sudden weight loss
» Mild to severe itching in the skin or eyes
» Fatigue
» Blurred vision
» Sluggishness or fatigue
» Vision problems, especially with blood
» Cold intolerance
» Worsening of existing eye disease

CAUSES OF TYPE 2 DIABETES

A variety of factors can cause diabetes. Some people are prone to diabetes genetically.; others may develop the syndrome due to potentially fatal illnesses or trauma.

There are many types of causes of diabetes. The following are some common causes of diabetes:

AGE

Diabetes is often due to old age. The body becomes less able to function as it ages, and it can no longer produce insulin properly. If a person lives a long time, the body will eventually have enough insulin to control the amount of glucose in the blood. Still, in some cases, the body does not have enough insulin, or the body's cells do not react to insulin. This causes high blood sugar levels.

HYPERTENSION

High blood pressure is an important risk factor for the development of diabetes. High blood pressure makes it more difficult for the body to produce and use insulin properly. If blood sugar levels are controlled, it will be less likely to develop diabetes.

SMOKING

Smoking is one of the most common risk factors for type 2 diabetes. Smoking causes high blood sugar levels to become more common. If a person quits smoking, it is easier to control their diabetes.

LACK OF EXERCISE

According to the American Diabetes Association, people who do not get the recommended amount of exercise or do not engage in regular exercise have a greater risk of developing type 2 diabetes. This happens in particular if a person has high blood pressure.

The risk of developing diabetes increases with age. However, young adults can develop diabetes at any age.

OBESITY

People who are obese have a greater risk of developing diabetes. Obesity can occur for many reasons, including weight gain from illness, not losing weight after the infection, overcompensation to deal with an illness, weight gain from gaining muscle, or loss of bone mass.

MEDICATIONS

Certain medications may cause diabetes. This can happen when a medication blocks the insulin from being appropriately produced or when a drug that lowers blood sugar levels affects insulin production. Medicines for high blood pressure or treating pain can be to blame. Other medications can also cause diabetes. These include some antidepressants, some antiseizure medications, and some antiviral medications.

FAMILY HISTORY

The risk of developing diabetes increases if you are close to the condition. There is some evidence that this risk can be lowered by having a good diet and regular physical activity.

GENETICS

Certain types of diabetes are inherited from parents. The same risk factor applies to Type 2 diabetes. For this type of diabetes, the gene that determines whether or not a person will develop Type 2 diabetes strongly influences the risk. If you have a family history of diabetes, you may also be at increased risk of developing the condition.

LIFESTYLE

Lifestyle changes can often reduce the risk of developing type 2 diabetes. Some good examples are being physically active and eating a healthy, balanced diet.

POOR DIET

The foods we eat tend to have more or fewer carbohydrates and fat, affecting how the body processes glucose. Glucose is the primary source of energy for our body, and this is needed to control the levels of sugar in the blood.

HOW IS TYPE 2 DIABETES DIAGNOSED

Diagnosing Type 2 diabetes is usually done using a blood test.

The most common tests used are blood sugar and blood glucose measurement tests.

A blood sugar test measures the level of glucose in the blood. A blood glucose measurement test can also detect the percentage of sugar in the blood.

The test involves pricking a person's finger, then taking a drop of blood from this drop, mixing it with chemicals, and watching how long it takes for it to change colour. Other tests may also be executed if the person's glucose level is not well controlled or if they have many different symptoms of diabetes. These include a urine glucose test, urinalysis test, or a sweat test.

TYPE 2 DIABETES GUIDE

Having a good diet and regular physical activity can help people with diabetes to reduce the risk of developing the condition. Having a good diet and regular physical exercise can help people with diabetes to reduce the risk of developing the disease. Some people believe that type 2 diabetes cannot be prevented, but research suggests that making some lifestyle changes may help prevent and delay type 2 diabetes.

MAKE PHYSICAL ACTIVITY A PRIORITY

Regular physical activity can help keep a person's blood sugar levels in control. Regular physical activity can help keep a person's blood sugar levels in control.

The most effective way to prevent type 2 diabetes is to start exercising as soon as possible and regularly.

EAT A HEALTHY DIET

Healthy diets are one of the best ways to prevent type 2 diabetes. People with type 2 diabetes should eat more fruit and vegetables and less animal and dairy foods, but they can still eat the foods they like in moderation.

AVOID ALCOHOL

Drinking alcohol is related to a higher risk of diabetes, mainly consumed regularly. People with type 2 diabetes should reduce the amount of alcoholic beverages or, if they are not in a condition to do so, they should be aware of the health effects of alcohol.

REDUCE OR ELIMINATE FOODS CONTAINING TRANS FAT

When a food contains trans-fat, it has been artificially created by adding hydrogenated oils. Trans fats have been related to an increased risk of type 2 diabetes and heart disease.

Foods that may contain high levels of trans fat include:

- Deep-fried foods, such as French fries
- Pre-cooked potato products
- Lunch meat and bacon
- Pretzels

REDUCE CONSUMPTION OF SALT

Sodium is another nutrient that causes blood sugar to rise quickly. Too much sodium increases a person's blood pressure, increasing the risk of heart disease, stroke, and kidney problems. According to the American Heart Association, people should cut down on sodium intake to help prevent and delay type 2 diabetes.

LIMIT FOODS CONTAINING HIGH LEVELS OF SUGAR

The common American diet is high in carbohydrates, which causes a person's blood sugar to rise quickly. When blood sugar levels rise quickly, a person can get the symptoms of type 2 diabetes, including blurred vision and trouble talking.

According to the American Diabetes Association, people should have no more than 100 grams (g) of sugar a day.

THE DIFFERENCE BETWEEN TYPE 1 AND TYPE 2 DIABETES

Both types of diabetes affect people in different ways. Types 1 and 2 diabetes are both forms of the condition, but they are not the same.

People with type 2 diabetes develop when their immune system destroys the insulin cells. In some cases, the immune system mistakes insulin for a toxin, which prevents the cells from doing their job.

As a result, a person may experience low blood sugar levels. When this happens, people with type 2 diabetes may experience the following symptoms:

◊ Severe thirst

◊ Difficulty thinking or concentrating

◊ Fatigue

◊ Anxiety or depression

◊ Pregnancy complications

People with type 1 diabetes develop when their bodies do not produce enough insulin. The body needs insulin to take the glucose from the bloodstream into the cells to make energy. Without insulin, blood sugar levels can build up and cause problems. Type 1 and 2 diabetes do not have the same symptoms. Still, a person's risk of developing the condition is increased if they have certain genetic traits, including a family history of the state of gestational diabetes.

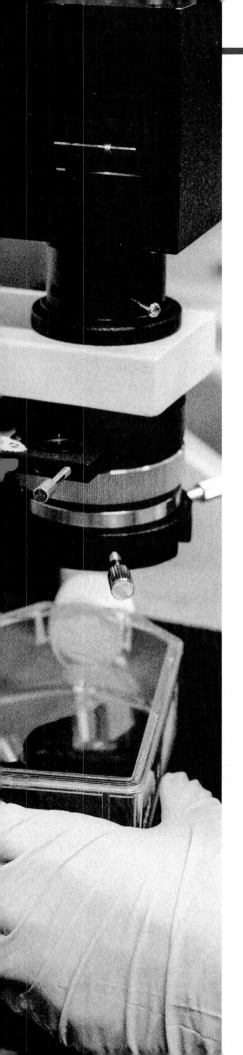

Both types of diabetes can be managed, but people may need to take additional medications and closely follow a healthy diet to manage type 2 diabetes. However, people with type 2 diabetes are more likely to develop complications, such as vision loss and kidney problems. They may also need to use insulin to manage their condition, which may increase the risk of complications.

OUTLOOK

The outlook for people with type 2 diabetes can change with their lifestyle choices and the treatments they receive.

Because a person's diabetes can be more serious, it is vital to manage the condition well by:

◊ Eating a healthy diet

◊ Monitoring blood sugar levels

◊ Managing blood pressure

◊ Taking medication

While a healthy diet and regular blood sugar monitoring can lower a person's risk of developing diabetes complications, diet and lifestyle changes are not enough on their own to prevent diabetes.

Some people may need to take medication to manage their type 2 diabetes, but they can also control their condition through lifestyle changes.

MEDITERRANEAN DIET FOR TYPE 2 DIABETES.

A Mediterranean diet decreases type 2 diabetes risk by 60 percent.

Mediterranean diet, which is a diet that includes more fish and olive oil, is a simple and healthy approach to maintaining good health. The Mediterranean diet is a balanced diet, therefore, it may be more accessible for the management of people with type 2 diabetes.

For people with type 2 diabetes, a large amount of research supports the benefits of a Mediterranean-style diet. The diet was initially developed to prevent type 2 diabetes and has been shown to improve blood sugar levels and reduce the risk of diabetes complications, such as heart disease and blindness.

The Mediterranean diet is very varied and it is rich in vegetables, fruits, nuts, olive oil and other healthy foods. Fruits, vegetables, and whole grains are lower in sugar, containing higher antioxidants. A recent study comparing a Mediterranean-style diet with other diets found that participants who ate the Mediterranean diet scored better on several common diabetes risk factors, including insulin resistance and high blood pressure.

Before trying a new diet to manage type 2 diabetes, people should talk to a doctor. A doctor can help them assess how well a diet will work for them and advise on changes they may need to make.

MEDITERRANEAN DIET PLAN FOR TYPE 2 DIABETES.

Eating healthy can help you to prevent Type 2 Diabetes.

Eating healthy is a big thing for your body, and it should be done regularly. But it becomes difficult to know what healthy food is? Then, you can find out about the Mediterranean diet plan for Type 2 Diabetes by simply following some easy steps. There are many

benefits of the Mediterranean diet for your health. So, it would help if you tried to learn how to make your Mediterranean diet plan for Type 2 Diabetes at home.

◊ Eating healthy food has many health benefits. It helps to lose weight. You can lose more weight by cutting down on your intake of unhealthy foods. It can also help to keep your blood glucose under control. Eating healthy food can lower your blood sugar levels.

◊ Mediterranean diet plan helps you to keep your blood glucose under control. You can also prevent and reduce inflammation in your body. It is a healthy diet that can reduce your risk of getting Type 2 diabetes. It is rich in antioxidants and antioxidants. These are the properties that help you fight against inflammation and oxidative stress. This plan can be effective in preventing and treating Type 2 Diabetes.

◊ Regular exercise is also a fundamental part of this plan. If you do not exercise regularly, your body starts using its glucose for energy. But when you have regular exercise, your body can do without using glucose from your body. It helps to burn fat. And this can help to prevent and treat Type 2 Diabetes.

◊ Always include vegetables and fruits in your diet plan. These can help you improve the body's cholesterol levels and fight against Type 2 Diabetes. Fruits are healthy. They are rich in nutrients, vitamins, and antioxidants. It contains fiber which is beneficial for your health. It can reduce your weight. And it can protect your blood glucose levels from high glucose levels.

THE LINK BETWEEN TYPE 1 AND TYPE 2

While type 1 and type 2 diabetes are both forms of diabetes, they're not the same.

Type 1 diabetes is an autoimmune disease in which the body mistakenly attacks the insulin-producing cells in the pancreas, leading to symptoms like frequent infections, nerve damage, kidney problems, and mental problems.

Type 2 diabetes, on the other side, is a result of metabolic diseases like obesity and a bad diet. Both have the same symptoms: increased thirst, frequent urination, increased hunger, and fatigue, but type 1 diabetes is usually diagnosed after a person is above the age of 40 and has had symptoms for more than ten years, while type 2 diabetes is generally diagnosed in adults and is usually diagnosed after 20 years of age. Both types can be managed with lifestyle changes, like adopting a healthy diet and exercising.

Conversion Tables

EQUIVALENTS

U.S.	U.S.
16 tablespoons	1 cup
12 tablespoons	¾ cup
10 tablespoons + 2 teaspoons	⅔ cup
8 tablespoons	½ cup
6 tablespoons	⅜ cup
5 tablespoons + 1 teaspoon	⅓ cup
4 tablespoons	¼ cup
2 tablespoons	⅛ cup
1 tablespoon	1/16 cup
1 pint	2 cups
1 quart	2 pints
1 tablespoon	3 teaspoons
1 cup	48 teaspoons
1 cup	16 tablespoons

WEIGHT

U.S.	METRIC
.035 oz.	1 gram
0.5 oz.	14 grams
1 oz.	28 grams
¼ pound (lb)	113 grams
⅓ pound (lb)	151 grams
½ pound (lb)	227 grams
1 pound (lb)	454 grams
1.10 pounds (lbs)	500 grams
2.205 pounds (lbs)	1 kilogram
35 oz.	1 kilogram

CAPACITY

U.S.	METRIC
¼ teaspoon	1 ml
1 teaspoon (tsp)	5 ml
1 tablespoon (tbsp)	15 ml
1 fluid oz.	30 ml
¼ cup	50 ml
¼ cup	60 ml
⅓ cup	80 ml
3.4 fluid oz.	100 ml
½ cup	120 ml
⅔ cup	160 ml
¾ cup	180 ml
1 cup	240 ml
1 pint (2 cups)	480 ml
1 quart (4 cups)	.95 liter
34 fluid oz.	1 liter
4.2 cups	1 liter
2.1 pints	1 liter
1.06 quarts	1 liter
.26 gallon	1 liter
4 quarts (1 gallon)	3.8 liters

MEASUREMENT CONVERSIONS

US STANDARD	US STANDARD (OUNCES)	METRIC (APPROXIMATE)
2 tablespoons	1 fl. oz.	30 mL
¼ cup	2 fl. oz.	60 mL
½ cup	4 fl. oz.	120 mL
1 cup	8 fl. oz.	240 mL
1½ cups	12 fl. oz.	355 mL
2 cups and 1 pint	16 fl. oz.	475 mL
4 cups and 1 quart	32 fl. oz.	1 L
1 gallon	128 fl. oz.	4 L

OVEN TEMPERATURES

FAHRENHEIT (F)	CELSIUS (C) (APPROXIMATE)
250 °F	120 °C
300 °F	150 °C
325 °F	165 °C
350 °F	180 °C
375 °F	190 °C
400 °F	200°C
425 °F	220 °C
450 °F	230 °C

BREAKFAST

1) *Berry-Oat Breakfast Bars*

Ingredients:

- 2 cups fresh raspberries or blueberries
- 2 tablespoons sugar
- 2 tablespoons freshly squeezed lemon juice
- 1 tablespoon cornstarch
- 1/2 cups rolled oats
- 1/2 cup whole-wheat flour
- 1/2 cup walnuts
- ¼ cup chia seeds
- ¼ cup extra-virgin olive oil
- ¼ cup honey
- 1 large egg

Direction: Preparation Time: 10 minutes Cooking Time: 25 minutes Servings: 12

- ✓ Preheat the oven to 350F.
- ✓ Stir together the berries, sugar, lemon juice, and cornstarch in a small saucepan over medium heat. Bring to a simmer. Lower the heat and let it simmer for only 2 or 3 minutes, or until the mixture thickens. Combine the oats, flour, walnuts, and chia seeds in a food processor or high-speed blender. Process until powdered. Add the olive oil, honey, and egg. Press half of the mixture into a 9-inch square baking dish.
- ✓ Spread the berry filling over the oat mixture. Add the remaining oat mixture on top of the berries. Bake for 25 minutes, until browned.
- ✓ Let cool, then cut into 12 pieces and serve. Store in a covered container for up to 5 days.

Nutrition: Calories: 201; Total fat: 10g; Saturated fat: 1g; Protein: 5g; Carbs: 26g; Sugar: 9g; Fiber: 5g; Cholesterol: 16mg; Sodium: 8mg

2) *Whole-Grain Breakfast Cookies*

Ingredients:

- cups rolled oats
- 1/2 cup whole-wheat flour
- ¼ cup ground flaxseed
- 1 teaspoon baking powder
- 1 cup unsweetened applesauce
- 2 large eggs
- 2 tablespoons vegetable oil
- 2 teaspoons vanilla extract
- 1 teaspoon ground cinnamon
- 1/2 cup dried cherries
- ¼ cup unsweetened shredded coconut
- 2 ounces dark chocolate, chopped

Direction: Preparation time: 20 minutes cooking time: 10 minutes Servings: 18 cookies

- ✓ Preheat the oven to 350F.
- ✓ In a large bowl, combine the oats, flour, flaxseed, and baking powder. Stir well to mix.
- ✓ Whisk the applesauce, eggs, vegetable oil, vanilla, and cinnamon in a medium bowl. Pour the wet mixture into the dry mixture, and stir until just combined.
- ✓ Fold in cherries, coconut, and chocolate. Drop tablespoon-size balls of dough onto a baking sheet. Bake for 10 to 12 minutes, until browned and cooked through.
- ✓ Let cool for about 3 minutes, remove from the baking sheet, and cool completely before serving. Keep using an airtight container for up to 1 week.

Nutrition: Calories: 136; Total fat: 7g; Saturated fat: 3g; Protein: 4g; Carbs: 14g; Sugar: 4g; Fiber: 3g; Cholesterol: 21mg; Sodium: 11mg

3) *Blueberry Breakfast Cake*

Ingredients:

- FOR THE TOPPING
- ¼ cup finely chopped walnuts
- 1/2 teaspoon ground cinnamon
- 2 tablespoons butter, chopped into small pieces
- 2 tablespoons sugar
- FOR THE CAKE
- Non-stick cooking spray
- 1 cup whole-wheat pastry flour
- 1 cup oat flour
- ¼ cup sugar
- 2 teaspoons baking powder
- 1 large egg, beaten
- 1/2 cup skim milk
- 2 tablespoons butter, melted
- 1 teaspoon grated lemon peel
- 2 cups fresh or frozen blueberries

Direction: Preparation time: 15 minutes; cooking time: 45 minutes; servings: 12

- ✓ TO MAKE THE TOPPING

✓ *Stir together the walnuts, cinnamon, butter, and sugar in a small bowl. Set aside.*

✓ *TO MAKE THE CAKE*

✓ *Preheat the oven to 350F. Spray a 9-inch square pan with cooking spray. Set aside.*

✓ *Stir together the pastry flour, oat flour, sugar, and baking powder in a large bowl.*

✓ *Add the egg, milk, butter, and lemon peel, and stir until there are no dry spots.*

✓ *Stir in the blueberries and gently mix until incorporated. Press the batter into the prepared pan, using a spoon to flatten it into the dish.*

✓ *Sprinkle the topping over the cake.*

✓ *Bake for 40-45 minutes and use a toothpick, inserting it into the cake to check if it comes out clean and served.*

Nutrition: Calories: 177; Total fat: 7g; Saturated fat: 3g; Protein: 4g; Carbs: 26g; Sugar: 9g; Fiber: 3g; Cholesterol: 26mg; Sodium: 39mg

4) *Buckwheat Grouts Breakfast Bowl*

Ingredients:

- *3 cups skim milk*
- *1 cup buckwheat grouts*
- *¼ cup chia seeds*
- *2 teaspoons vanilla extract*
- *1/2 teaspoon ground cinnamon*
- *Pinch salt*
- *1 cup water*
- *1/2 cup unsalted pistachios*
- *2 cups sliced fresh strawberries*
- *¼ cup cacao nibs (optional)*

Direction: Preparation time: 5 minutes, plus overnight to soak Cooking time: 10 to 12 minutes; Servings: 4

✓ *Stir together the milk, groats, chia seeds, vanilla, cinnamon, and salt in a large bowl. Cover and refrigerate overnight.*

✓ *Transfer the wet mixture to a medium pot and add the water the next morning. Bring to a boil over medium-high heat, lower the heat to maintain a simmer, and cook for 10 to 12 minutes until the buckwheat becomes tender and thickened.*

✓ *Transfer to bowls and serve, topped with the pistachios, strawberries, and cacao nibs (if using).*

Nutrition: Calories: 340; Total fat: 8g; Saturated fat: 1g; Protein: 15g; Carbs: 52g; Sugar: 14g; Fiber:

10g;
Cholesterol: 4mg; Sodium: 140mg

5) *Peach Muesli Bake*

Ingredients:

- *Non-stick cooking spray*
- *2 cups skim milk*
- *1 1/2 cups rolled oats 1/2 cup chopped walnuts*
- *1 large egg*
- *2 tablespoons maple syrup*
- *1 teaspoon ground cinnamon*
- *1 teaspoon baking powder*
- *1/2 teaspoon salt*
- *2 to 3 peaches, sliced*

Direction: Preparation time: 10 minutes; cooking time: 40 minutes; servings: 8

✓ *Preheat the oven to 375F. Spray a 9-inch square pan with cooking spray. Set aside.*

✓ *Stir together the milk, oats, walnuts, egg, maple syrup, cinnamon, baking powder, and salt in a large bowl. Spread half the mixture in the prepared baking dish.*

✓ *Place half the peaches in a single layer across the oat mixture.*

✓ *Spread the remaining oat mixture over the top. Add the remaining peaches in a thin layer over the oats. Bake for 35 to 40 minutes, uncovered until thickened and browned.*

✓ *Cut into 8 squares and serve warm.*

Nutrition: Calories: 138; Total fat: 3g; Saturated fat: 1g; Protein: 6g; Carbs: 22g; Sugar: 10g; Fiber: 3g; Cholesterol: 24mg; Sodium: 191mg

6) *Steel-Cut Oatmeal Bowl with Fruit and Nuts*

Ingredients:

- *1 cup steel-cut oats*
- *2 cups almond milk*
- *¾ cup water*
- *1 teaspoon ground cinnamon*
- *¼ teaspoon salt*
- *2 cups chopped fresh fruit, such as blueberries, strawberries, raspberries, or peaches*
- *1/2 cup chopped walnuts*
- *¼ cup chia seeds*

Direction: Preparation time: 5 minutes;
Cooking time: 20 minutes; Servings: 4

✓ *Combine the oats, almond milk, water, cinnamon, and salt in a medium saucepan over medium-high heat. Bring to a boil, then lower the heat and simmer for about 15-20 minutes and wait until the oats have softened and thickened.*

✓ *Top each bowl with 1/2 cup of fresh fruit, 2 tablespoons of walnuts, and 1 tablespoon of chia seeds before serving.*

Nutrition: Calories: 288; Total fat: 11g; Saturated fat: 1g; Protein: 10g; Carbs: 38g; Sugar: 7g; Fiber: 10g; Cholesterol: 0mg; Sodium: 329mg

7) *Fruited Granola*

15 minutes for preparation Time Required for Cooking: 35 minutes 6 portions
Ingredients:

- *3 cups fast cooking oats*
- *1 cup sliced almonds*
- *1/2 cup wheat germ*
- *3 tablespoons butter*
- *1 teaspoon crushed cinnamon*
- *1 cup honey*
- *3 cups whole-grain cereal flakes*
- *1/2 cup raisins*
- *1/2 cup dried cranberries*

Directions:

✓ *Preheat the oven to 325 degrees Fahrenheit.*

✓ *Dispose the almonds in a single layer on a baking sheet.*

✓ *Bake at 350°F for 15 minutes.*

✓ *In a bowl, combine the wheat germ, butter, cinnamon, and honey.*

✓ *Stir in the almonds and oats.*

✓ *Combine thoroughly.*

✓ *Spread evenly on the prepared baking sheet.*

✓ *Bake at 350°F for 20 minutes.*

✓ *Combine with the remaining ingredients.*

✓ *Allow cooling before serving.*

Nutrition: 210 Nutrition: Calories 7g saturated fat 2g cholesterol 5 mg sodium 58 mg Carbohydrates in Total 36 g Dietary Fiber 4 g Sugars in Total Protein: 2 g

8) *Apple & Cinnamon Pancakes*

Time Required for Preparation: 15 minutes Time

Required for Cooking: 10 minutes 4 portions
Ingredients:

- *1/4 tsp powdered cinnamon*
- *1 3/4 tbsp Better Baking Mix*
- *1 tbsp oil*
- *1 cup water*
- *2 egg whites*
- *1/2 tbsp. sugar-free applesauce*
- *cooking spray Substitute for sugar*

Directions:

✓ *In a mixing basin, combine the cinnamon and baking mix.*

✓ *In the center, create a hole then add: oil, water, egg, and applesauce.*

✓ *Combine thoroughly.*

✓ *Coat the pan with oil.*

✓ *Place it over a medium heat source.*

✓ *Distribute 14 cups of batter.*

✓ *Cook until golden on the other side.*

✓ *Garnish with yogurt and sugar substitute if desired.*

Nutrition: Calories 231 6 g Saturated Fat Sodium 545 mg 1 g Cholesterol 54 mg Carbohydrates in total 37 g Dietary Fiber 4 g Sugars in Total 1 gram of protein 8 g 750 mg potassium

9) *Scrambled Spinach*

Time Required for Preparation: 5 minutes Time Required for Cooking: 15 minutes 2 portions

- *14 cups liquid egg substitute 14 cups skim milk*
- *Season with salt and pepper to taste*
- *two tablespoons of crumbled bacon*
- *13 12 oz. canned spinach, drained*

Directions:

✓ *In a large mixing basin, put together all of the ingredients.*

✓ *Transfer the mixture to a skillet that has been coated with oil and set over medium heat.*

✓ *Continue stirring until thoroughly cooked.*

Nutrition: Calories 70 2 g Total Fat 1 g Saturated Fat 25 mg Sodium 700 mg Carbohydrates in Total 5 g Dietary Fiber 2 g Sugars in Total 1 gram of protein 8 g 564 mg potassium

10) *Omelet of Asparagus and Cheese*

Preparation Time: 10 minutes required for Cooking: 10 minutes 2 portions Ingredients:

- Non-stick cooking spray
- 4 spears asparagus, cut
- Salt and pepper to taste
- 3 egg whites 1/2 tbsps
- olive oil 1 oz. spreadable cheese, sliced

Directions:

✓ Coat your pan with oil spray.

✓ Cook asparagus for 5 to 7 minutes in a skillet over medium-high heat.

✓ Wrap in aluminium foil and set aside.

✓ In a mixing dish, combine the pepper and egg whites.

✓ Deglaze the pan with olive oil.

✓ Stir in the egg whites.

✓ When the edges begin to form, top with the asparagus and cheese.

✓ Before serving, sprinkle parsley over the top.

Nutrition: Calories 119 Total Fatty Acids 5 g Saturated Fatty Acids 2 g 10 mg cholesterol 427 mg sodium Carbohydrates in Total 5 g Dietary Fiber 2 g Sugars in Total Protein 3 g Potassium 308 mg

11) Potatoes, Sausage, and Egg

15 minutes for preparation Time Required for Cooking: 10 hours and 10 minutes 6 Servings

- Cooking spray 12 oz.
- sliced chicken sausage links
- 1 onion, chopped into wedges
- 2 red sweet peppers, sliced into strips
- 12 lb. sliced potatoes
- 1/4 cups low-sodium chicken broth
- Black pepper to taste
- 1/2 teaspoon crushed dry thyme
- 6 eggs
- 1/2 cup shredded low-fat cheddar cheese

Direction

✓ Spray oil onto a hefty foil sheet.

✓ Arrange the sausage, onion, sweet peppers, and potatoes in a single layer on the foil.

✓ Drizzle chicken broth over the top.

✓ Season with pepper and thyme to taste.

✓ Seal with a fold.

✓ Insert the packet into the cooker.

✓ Cook on low for ten hours.

✓ Boil the egg until fully cooked in the meantime.

✓ Combine eggs and sausage mixture in a serving dish.

Nutrition: Calories 281 12 g Saturated Fat 4 g Cholesterol 262 mg Sodium 485 mg Carbohydrates Total 23 g Fiber 3 g Sugars in Total 3 g protein; 21 g potassium; 262 mg potassium

12) Yogurt & Cucumber

Time Required for Preparation: 5 minutes 0 minute cooking time one portion

- 1 cup low-fat yogurt
- 1/2 cups diced cucumber
- 1/4 teaspoon lemon zest
- 1/4 teaspoon lemon juice
- 1/4 teaspoon fresh mint, chopped

Direction

✓ In a jar, merge all of the ingredients.

✓ Refrigerate until ready to serve.

Nutrition: Calories 164 4 g Saturated Fat Sodium 318 mg 2 g Cholesterol 15 mg Carbohydrates in total 19 g Dietary Fiber 1 g Sugars Total Protein: 18 g Potassium 13 g 683 mg

13) Yogurt Breakfast Pudding

Preparation Time for Yogurt Breakfast Pudding: 8 hours and 10 minutes 0 minute cooking time two servings

- 1/2 cups rolled oat
- 6 oz. low-fat yogurt
- 1/4 cups canned pineapple
- 1/2 tsp vanilla extract
- 1/8 tsp crushed cinnamon
- 1 tbsp flaxseed meal
- 4 tablespoons toasted and sliced almonds1/2 cup apple, chopped

Directions:

✓ Put together all ingredients except the almonds and apple in a large mixing bowl.

✓ Transfer the mixture to a container that is completely sealed.

✓ Cover with a lid and refrigerate for 8 hours.

✓ Before serving, garnish with almonds and apple.

Nutrition: Calories 255 7 g Total Fat 1 g Saturated Fat 5 mg Sodium: 84 mg Carbohydrates: 38 g Dietary Fiber: 5 g Sugars: 38 g Protein: 21 g

14) Vegetable Omelet

Time Required for Preparation: 5 minutes Time Required for Cooking: 25 minutes 4 portions

- *1/2 cups yellow summer squash, chopped*
- *1/2 cup canned diced tomatoes with herbs, drained*
- *1/2 ripe avocado, pitted and chopped*
- *1/2 cup cucumber, sliced*
- *2 eggs*
- *2 tablespoons water*
- *Salt and pepper to taste*
- *1 teaspoon dry basil, crushed*

Direction

✓ *Combine the squash, tomatoes, avocado, and cucumber in a large bowl.*

✓ *Separately, whisk together the eggs, water, salt, pepper, and basil in a separate bowl.*

✓ *Spray oil onto a skillet set over medium heat.*

✓ *Pour the egg mixture into the prepared pan.*

✓ *Scatter the veggie mixture over the egg.*

✓ *Raise and collapse.*

✓ *Continue cooking until the egg is set.*

✓ *Garnish with cheese and chives.*

Nutrition: Calories 128 Fat Total 6 g Saturated Fat 2 g Cholesterol 97 mg Sodium 357 mg Carbohydrates Total 7 g Dietary Fiber 3 g Sugars in Total Protein: 4 g

15) *Almond and Berry Smoothie*

Time Required for Preparation: 10 minutes 0 minute cooking time one portion

- *2/3 cup frozen raspberries*
- *1/2 cups frozen banana, diced*
- *1/2 cups unsweetened almond milk*
- *3 tablespoons sliced almonds*
- *1/4 teaspoon ground cinnamon*
- *1/8 teaspoon vanilla extract*
- *1/4 cup blueberries*
- *1 tablespoon coconut flakes (unsweetened)*

Direction

✓ *In a blender, combine all ingredients except the coconut flakes. Pulse until completely smooth.*

✓ *Before serving, sprinkle the coconut flakes on top.*

Nutrition: 360 Nutrition: Calories 19 g Total Fat 3 g Saturated Fat 0 mg Sodium 89 mg Carbohydrates 46 g Dietary Fiber 14 g Sugars Potassium 9 g 736 mg

16) *Smoothie Bowl with Bananas and Spinach*

Preparation Time: 10 minutes Required for Cooking: 10 minutes 3 servings

- *2 small ripe frozen bananas, peeled and sliced*
- *1/2 cup frozen blueberries*
- *1 cup frozen spinach*
- *1 cup cauliflower*
- *1 1/2 scoops of unsweetened vegan protein powder*
- *3 tablespoons peanut butter*
- *2 tablespoons hemp seeds*
- *1 teaspoon maca powder*
- *1 teaspoon spirulina*

Directions:

✓ *In a high-speed blender, combine all ingredients and pulse until smooth.*

✓ *Divide among three serving bowls and immediately top with your preferred topping.*

Nutrition: Calories 400 23 g total fat 12 g saturated fat 0 mg cholesterol 216 mg sodium Carbohydrates in total 36 g Fiber 9 g Sugar 17.4 g Protein 20.2 g

17) *Combination of Berries*

Preparation Time for Smoothie Bowl: 10 minutes Required for Cooking: 10 minutes 2 portions

Ingredients:

- *two large peeled and sliced frozen bananas*
- *1 cup frozen mixed berries*
- *1 scoop unsweetened vegan protein powder*

Directions:

✓ *Place all ingredients in a high-speed blender and pulse until smooth.*

✓ *Divide between two serving bowls and top with your preferred topping.*

Nutrition: Calories 242 2 g total fat 9 g saturated fat 0 mg cholesterol Total Carbohydrates 38.6 g Fiber 6 g Sugar 21 g Protein 17 g Sodium 77 mg

18) *Bulgur Porridge*

Time Required for Preparation: 10 minutes Time required for cooking: 15 minutes 2 portions

- *2/3 cup unsweetened soy milk*
- *1/3 cup washed bulgur*
- *one peeled and smashed ripe banana*
- *2 peeled and sliced kiwis*

Direction

✓ *Bring the soy milk, bulgur, and salt to a boil in a saucepan over medium-high heat.*

✓ *Reduce to low heat and simmer for approximately 10 minutes.*

✓ *Immediately remove the pan of bulgur from the heat and toss in the smashed banana.*

✓ *Garnish with kiwi slices and serve warm.*

Nutrition: 223 Calories Cholesterol 0 mg Total Fat 3 g Saturated Fat 0.3 g 126 mg sodium Carbohydrates in total 47.5 g 8.6 g Fiber 17.4 g Sugar 7.1 g Protein

19) *Buckwheat Porridge*

Time Required for Preparation: 10 minutes Time required for cooking: 15 minutes 2 portions

- *1 1/2 cups water*
- *1 cup rinsed buckwheat groats*
- *3/4 teaspoons vanilla extract*
- *1/2 teaspoon crushed cinnamon*
- *1/4 teaspoon salt*
- *2 tablespoons maple syrup*
- *1 ripe banana, peeled and smashed*
- *1 1/2 cups unsweetened soy milk*
- *1 tablespoon peanut butter*
- *1/3 cup hulled and chopped fresh strawberries*

Direction

✓ *Bring the water, buckwheat, vanilla essence, cinnamon, and salt to a boil in a saucepan.*

✓ *Lower heat and simmer for about 6 minutes, stirring occasionally.*

✓ *Stir in maple syrup, banana, and soy milk; cover and cook for approximately 6 minutes.*

✓ *Take the porridge pan from the heat and toss in the peanut butter.*

✓ *Garnish with strawberry slices and serve warm.*

Nutrition: Calories 453 9.4 g total fat 7 g saturated fat 0 mg cholesterol 374 mg sodium Carbohydrates in total 88 g Fiber 9.4 g Sugar 28.8 g Protein 16.2 g

20) *Pancakes with Oatmeal and Blueberries*

Time Required for Preparation: 10 minutes Time required for cooking: 40 minutes

Ingredients: 4 Servings

- *1/2 cups rolled oats*
- *1/2 cup unsweetened almond milk*
- *1/4 cup unsweetened applesauce*
- *1/4 cups unsweetened vegan protein powder*
- *1/2 tbsp flax meal*

Directions:

✓ *Pulse all ingredients (except the blueberries) in a food processor until smooth.*

✓ *In a bowl, transfer the mixture and leave aside for 5 minutes.*

✓ *Fold in blueberries gently.*

✓ *Heat a medium skillet with a light oil coating over medium heat until hot.*

✓ *Cook desired amount of mixture for approximately 3–5 minutes per side.*

✓ *Continue with the remainder of the mixture.*

✓ *Serve immediately.*

Nutrition: Calories 105 8 g Total Fat 0.2 g Saturated Fat 0 mg Sodium 204 mg Carbohydrates 14 g Fiber 2 g Sugar 2 g Protein 8 g

21) *Black Bean Tacos Breakfast*

Ingredients:

- *½ cup red onion, diced*
- *86-inch white soft corn tortillas, warmed*
- *1 garlic clove, minced*
- *1 tsp. avocado oil*
- *¼ cup chopped fresh cilantro*
- *1(15 oz.) can black beans, rinsed and drained*
- *1 small avocado, diced*
- *¼ tsp. ground chipotle powder*
- *½ cup fresh or your favorite jarred salsa*
- *4 eggs*

Direction: Preparation Time: 9 minutes Cooking Time: 13 minutes Servings: 4

✓ *Scramble the Eggs. You know how it can be done. Make them as you would usually make them. Here's a guide if you need a reminder, maybe!*

✓ *Sauté the beans: Heat the avocado oil over moderate heat in a large skillet. Sauté the onion for about 3 minutes until it is tender.*

✓ *Add the garlic and beans and heat until fully cooked, about 2–5 minutes. Blister the tortillas or heat them in a dry skillet over an open fire on the range. Put aside, wrapped to keep them warm, in a cloth napkin.*

✓ *Layer the beans, then slice each tortilla with the eggs. Maintain to only*

✓ *¼ cup beans per taco. You may be tempted, but try not to overstuff the tortillas. Top up as needed with salsa, avocado, and cilantro.*

Nutrition: Calories: 349 Protein: 11.5g Fat: 15g

22)   **Strawberry Coconut Bake**
Ingredients:

- ½ cup chopped walnuts
- cups unsweetened coconut flakes
- 1 tsp. cinnamon
- ¼ cup chia seeds
- 2 cups diced strawberries
- 1 ripe banana mashed
- 1 tsp. baking soda 4 large eggs
- ¼ tsp. salt
- 1 cup unsweetened nut milk
- 2 tbsp. coconut oil, melted

Direction: Preparation Time: 11 minutes Cooking Time: 41 minutes Servings: 2

✓ Preheat your oven to 375°F. Grease a square 8-inch pan and set it aside.

✓ Combine the dried ingredients in a big bowl: walnuts, chia seeds, cinnamon, salt, and baking soda.

✓ Whisk the eggs and milk together in a smaller dish. Now, add mashed banana and coconut oil to the mixture. To dry, add the wet ingredients and blend properly. Fold the strawberries in.

✓ Bake for about 40 minutes, or until the top is golden and solid.

✓ And serve hot!

Nutrition: Calories: 395 Fat: 40g Protein: 7.5g

23)   **Paleo Breakfast Hash**
Ingredients:

- Eight oz. white mushroom, quartered
- 1 lb. Brussels sprout, quartered Everything bagel seasoning
- 1 tbsp. olive oil or avocado oil
- 3 garlic cloves, minced
- 1 small onion diced
Crushed red pepper, optional
- Eight slices of nitrate-free bacon sugar-free, for Whole 30, cut into pieces
- Sea salt and pepper to taste 6 large eggs

Direction: Preparation Time: 7 minutes Cooking Time: 33 minutes Servings: 5

✓ Preheat to 425°F in your oven. Arrange the mushrooms and Brussels sprouts in a single layer on a sheet tray, drizzle with the olive oil and add salt and pepper. Sprinkle the onions on the end and place the strips of bacon equally over the vegetables.

✓ Roast for 15 mins in the preheated oven, then sprinkle with the garlic and stir gently. Roast for 10 mins or until the bacon and vegetables are crisp and fluffy. Extract from the stove.
For each egg, make tiny gaps in the hash, gently smash one at a time into a space, careful not to

'split' the yolk. Sprinkle all the bagel seasoning and crushed red pepper over the bacon, eggs, and vegetables as you wished.

✓ Return the baking tray to the oven and bake for another 5–10 minutes or until the eggs are ideally fried. For me, for solid whites and light yolks, it was 7 minutes. Remove from the oven and quickly serve. Enjoy!

Nutrition: Calories: 250 Protein: 14g Fat: 18g

24)   **Omelet with Chickpea Flour**
Ingredients:

- ½ tsp. Onion powder
- ¼ tsp. black pepper 1 cup, chickpea flour
- ½ tsp. garlic powder
- ½ tsp. baking soda
- ¼ tsp. white pepper
- 1/3 cup nutritional yeast
- 3 finely chopped green onions
- 4 oz. sautéed mushrooms

Direction: Preparation Time: 10 minutes Cooking Time: 20 minutes Servings: 1

✓ Combine the onion powder, white pepper, chickpea flour, garlic powder, black and white pepper, baking soda, and nutritional yeast.

✓ Add 1 cup water and create a smooth batter. On medium heat, put a frying pan and add the batter just like the way you would cook pancakes. On the batter, sprinkle some green onion and mushrooms. Flip the omelet and cook evenly on both sides.

✓ Once both sides are cooked, serve the omelet with spinach, tomatoes, hot sauce, and salsa.

Nutrition: Calories: 150 Fats: 1.9g Carbohydrates: 24.4g Proteins:10.2g

25)   **White Sandwich Bread**
Preparation Time: 10 minutes Cooking Time: 20 minutes Servings: 16
Ingredients:

- 1 cup warm water
- 2 tbsp. active dry yeast
- 4 tbsp. oil
- 2 ½ tsp. salt
- 2 tbsp. raw sugar or 4 tbsp. maple syrup/agave nectar
- cup warm almond milk or any other non-dairy milk of your choice
- 6 cups all-purpose flour

Direction:

✓ Add warm water, yeast, and sugar into a bowl and stir. Set aside for 5 minutes or until lots of tiny bubbles are formed, sort of bubbly.

✓ Add flour and salt into a mixing bowl and stir. Pour the oil, yeast mix, and milk and mix into the dough.

If the dough is too hard, add a little water, a tbsp. at a time and mix well each time. If the dough is too sticky, add more flour, a tbsp at a time. Knead the dough until soft and supple. Use hands or hook attachment of the stand mixer.

✓*Now spray some water on top of the dough. Keep the bowl covered with a towel. Let it rest until it doubles in size.*

✓*Remove the dough from the bowl and place it on your countertop. Punch the dough.*
Line a loaf pan with parchment paper. You can also grease with some oil if you prefer.

✓*Place the dough in the loaf pan. Now spray some more water on top of the dough. Keep the loaf pan covered with a towel. Let it rest until the dough doubles in size.*

✓*Bake in a preheated oven at 370°F for about 40–50 minutes.*

✓*Let it cool to room temperature. Cut into 16 equal slices and use as required. Store in a breadbox at room temperature.*
Nutrition: Cal: 209 Fat: 4g Carbs: 35g Protein: 1g

26) *Sprouted Toast with Creamy Avocado and Sprouts*
Ingredients:

- 2 tiny sized bread sprouts
- 1 cup finely cut tomatoes
- 2 moderate size avocados
- 1 small cup alfalfa
- Pure sea salt and bell pepper

Direction: Preparation Time: 10 minutes Cooking Time: 15 minutes Servings: 3

✓*Add the avocado, alfalfa, and tomatoes to the bread and season to taste with pure sea salt and pepper.*
. Have a sumptuous breakfast with any freshly extracted juice of your choice.
Nutrition: Calories: 82 Fiber: 15g Protein: 30g Sugar: 7g

27) *Scrambled Turmeric Tofu*
Ingredients:

- 1 crumbled serve of tofu
- 1 small cup finely chopped onions
- 1 tsp. the fresh parsley
- 1 tsp. coconut oil
- 1 cup soft spinach
- small tsp. Turmeric
- avocado serves 75g tomatoes
- 1 small spoon roasted paprika

Direction: Preparation Time: 5 minutes Cooking Time: 15 minutes Servings: 4

✓*Make tofu crumbs with your hands and keep them separately. Sauté diced onions in oil till it softens. Put your tofu, tomatoes, and other seasonings and*

combine till tofu is well prepared. Add veggies and stir. Serve in a bowl alongside some avocado.
Nutrition: Calories: 91 Fiber: 12g Protein: 30g Sugar: 8g

28) *Breakfast Salad*
Ingredients:

- 1 cup finely diced kale
- 1 cup cabbage, red and Chinese
- 2 tbsp. coconut oil
- 1 cup spinach
- 2 moderate avocados
- 1.2kg chickpeas sprout
- tbsp. sunflower seed sprouts Pure sea salt (seasoning)
- Bell pepper (seasoning)
- Lemon juice (seasoning)

Direction: Preparation Time: 5 minutes Cooking Time: 15 minutes Servings: 3

✓*Add spinach, Chinese and red cabbage, kale, coconut oil, to a container*
Add seasoning to taste and mix adequately.

✓*Add other ingredients ad mix.*
Nutrition: Calories: 112 Protein: 28g Fiber: 10g Sugar: 1g

29) *Green Goddess Bowl with Avocado Cumin Dressing*
Ingredients:

- heaping cups finely sliced kale
- 1 small cup diced broccoli florets
- ½ cup zucchini spiralized noodles
- ½ cup soaked Kelp noodles
- 3 cups tomatoes
- 2 tbsp. hemp seeds
- 1 tbsp. olive oil Bell pepper
- 1 tbsp. powdered cumin
- Tahini dressing ingredients:
- 1 small cup sesame butter
- 1 cup alkaline water
- cup freshly extracted lemon
- 1 garlic, finely chopped clove
- ¾ tbsp. pure sea salt
- 1 tbsp. olive oil Bell pepper
- Avocado Dressing Ingredients:
- 1 big avocado
- freshly extracted lime 1 cup alkaline water

Direction: Preparation Time: 10 minutes Cooking Time: 20 minutes Servings: 4

✓*Simmer veggies—kale and broccoli for about 4 minutes.*

✓ Combine noodles and add avocado cumin dressing. Toss for a while. Add tomatoes and combine well.

✓ Put the cooked kale and broccoli on a plate, add Tahini dressing, add noodles and tomatoes.

✓ Add a couple of hemp seeds to the whole dish and enjoy it.

Nutrition: Calories: 109 Protein: 25g Fiber: 17g Sugar: 8g

30) Quinoa Burrito
Ingredients:

- 1 cup quinoa
- 2 cups black beans
- 4 finely chopped onions, green
- 4 finely chopped garlic
- 2 freshly cut limes
- 1 big tbsp. cumin
- 2 beautifully diced avocado
- 1 small cup beautifully diced cilantro

Direction: Preparation Time: 15 minutes Cooking Time: 10 minutes Servings: 1

✓ Boil quinoa. During this process, put the beans in low heat.

✓ Add other ingredients to the bean pot and let it mix well for about 15 minutes.

✓ Serve quinoa and add the prepared beans.

Nutrition: Calories: 117 Protein: 27g Fiber: 10g

31) Baked Banana-Nut Oatmeal Cups
Ingredients:

- 3 cups rolled oats.
- 1 ½ cups low-fat milk
- 2 ripe bananas
- ¼ cup packed brown sugar
- 2 larges lightly beaten eggs.
- 1 tsp. Baking powder
- tsp. ground cinnamon
- 1 tsp. vanilla extract
- ½ tsp. salt
- ½ cup toasted chopped pecans

Direction: Preparation Time: 17 minutes Cooking Time: 40 minutes Servings: 4

✓ Preheat the cooking appliance to 375°F. Coat a gem tin with a change of state spray.

✓ Combine oats, milk, bananas, refined sugar, eggs, leaven, cinnamon, vanilla, and salt during a giant bowl. Fold in pecans. Divide the mixture among the gem cups (about ⅓ cup each). Bake till a pick inserted within the center comes out clean, within twenty-five minutes.

✓ Cool within the pan for ten minutes, then end up on a wire rack.

✓ Serve heat or at temperature.

Nutrition: Calories: 178 Protein: 5.3g Fat 6.3g

32) Veggie Breakfast Wrap
Ingredients:

- tsp. olive oil or other
- 1 cup sliced mushrooms
- 2 eggs
- ½ cup egg white or egg replacement
- 1 cup firmly packed spinach or other greens
- 2 tbsp. sliced scallions
- cooking nonstick spray
- whole wheat and low-carb flour tortillas
- 2 tbsp. salsa

Direction: Preparation Time: 12 minutes Cooking Time: 13 minutes Servings: 2

✓ Add oil to the frying pan over medium heat. Add mushrooms and sauté till nicely brown at edges (about 3 minutes), set aside.

✓ Beat eggs with egg whites or egg substitute in a medium-sized bowl, employing a mixer or by hand, till emulsified. Stir in cut spinach, and scallions. you'll additionally further recent or dried herbs like basil or parsley for Moe flavor.
Begin heating medium/large frying pan over medium-low heat—coat pan munificently with a change of state spray. Pour in the egg mixture and still scramble the mixture because it cooks employing a spatula. once eggs area unit broiled to your feeling, close up the warmth and stir in mushrooms.

✓ Unfold ½ the egg mixture down the middle of every battercake. high every with 1 tbsp. recent condiment or alternative e sauce of your alternative. Garnish with additional toppings like avocado slices, bell pepper, or tomato if desired, then roll it up to form a wrap.

Nutrition: Calories: 220 Fat: 11g Protein: 19g

33) Breakfast Egg and Ham Burrito
Ingredients:

- 4 eggs
- egg whites
- 1 dash hot pepper sauce
- ¼ tsp. black pepper
- 2 tbsp. cheddar cheese
- 2 tbsp. margarine
- 4 slices deli
- ¼ cup sliced onion
- ¼ cup diced green pepper.
- 4 heated corn tortilla Salsa

Direction: Preparation Time: 21 minutes Cooking Time: 13 minutes Servings: 3

✓ Using a medium bowl, whisk along the eggs, egg whites, hot Poivrade, black pepper, and cheese. Heat the spread during a medium non-stick pan over medium heat. Add the ham and sauté for 2–3 minutes. Take away the ham from the pan.

✓ Add the onions and fresh peppers to the recent pan, and cook for 5 minutes. Add the ham back to the pan.

✓ Scale back the warmth to low and add the eggs to the pan. Gently stir the eggs with a spoon or spatula and gently change the state over low heat until the eggs area unit is broiled and set.

✓ Equally, divide the egg mixture into 4 servings. Spoon every portion of the egg mixture into a battercake and high every with 1 tsp. Salsa. Fold the battercake to shut.

Nutrition: Calories: 210 Fat: 9g Carbohydrate: 16g

34) *Breakfast Cups for Meat Lover*
Ingredients:

- 1 tbsp. light sour cream
- 2 pre-cooked defrosted and diced turkey breakfast sausage patties
- 1 clove of minced garlic
- 2 tbsp. thinly sliced onion
- 1 ½ cup frozen hash browns
- 1 tsp. canola oil
- ¼ tsp. salt
- A pinch of black pepper
- 1 cup egg substitute
- 2 tbsp. turkey bacon
- 2 tbsp. Monterey jack cheese

Direction: Preparation Time: 12 minutes Cooking Time: 13 minutes Servings: 4

✓ Heat the kitchen appliance to 400°F. Coat a 6-cup quick bread tin with sloppy preparation spray. Equally, divide the hash browns among the quick bread cups and press firmly into the lowest and up the perimeters of every cup.

✓ In an exceedingly giant frying pan, heat the oil over medium heat. Sauté the onion till tender. Add the garlic and sausage; cook for 1 minute additional. Take away the frying pan from the heat; stir within the soured cream.

✓ In an exceedingly medium bowl, beat the egg substitute with the salt and black pepper, then pour it equally into the potato-lined quick bread cups. High every cup with a number of the sausage mixture, bacon, and cheese.

✓ Bake 15 to 19 minutes, or till the eggs area is set. Serve instantly, or freeze for later.

Nutrition: Calories: 120 Fat 4g Carbohydrate: 10g

35) *Breakfast Quesadilla*
Ingredients:

- 1 cooking spray
- ¼ cup canned green chiles
- 4 beaten eggs
- ¼ tsp. black pepper
- 2 10-inch of whole wheat flour tortillas
- 1 ½ cup cheddar cheese (reduced fat)
- 4 slices of turkey bacon (cooked crisp and crumbled)

Direction: Preparation Time: 13 minutes Cooking Time: 16 minutes Servings: 4

✓ Lightly brush a small skillet with cooking oil.

✓ Sauté the green chilies over medium-low heat for 1–2 minutes. Attach beaten eggs and cook until scrambled and set, stirring. Season with some pepper.

✓ Lightly brush a second large skillet with cooking oil. Place 1 tortilla in the skillet and cook over medium heat for about 1 minute, until the air bubbles begin to form. Flip the tortilla and cook for another 1 minute (don't let the tortilla get crispy).

✓ Layer half of the cheese thinly over the tortilla, protecting the corners.

✓ Reduce heat to minimum temperatures. Arrange half of the fried bacon and half of the egg mixture over the cheese quickly. Cook until the cheese begins to melt for about 1 minute.

✓ To make a half-moon shape, fold the tortilla in half. Flip the folded tortilla over and cook for 1–2 minutes, until lightly toasted and the cheese filling is fully melted.

Nutrition: Calories: 160 Fat: 19g Carbohydrate: 8g

36) *Toasts with Egg and Avocado*
Ingredients:

- 4 eggs
- 4 slices hearty wholegrain bread
- 1 avocado (mashed)
- ½ tsp. salt (optional)
- ¼ tsp. black pepper
- ¼ cup Greek yogurt (nonfat)

Direction: Preparation Time: 17 minutes Cooking Time: 0 minutes Servings: 4

✓ To poach each egg, fill ½ cup water with a 1 cup microwaveable bowl or teacup. Crack an egg into the water softly, make sure it's fully submerged. Cover on high for around 1 minute with a saucer and microwave, or before the white is set and the yolk starts to set, but still fluffy (not runny).

✓ Toast the bread and use ¼ of the mashed avocado to scatter each slice.

✓ Sprinkle the salt with avocado (optional) and pepper. Top with a poached egg on each piece. Top the egg with 1 tbsp. Greek yogurt.

Nutrition: Calories: 230 Fat: 13g Carbohydrate: 26g

37) Turkey Sausages and Egg Casserole

Ingredients:

- ½ cup green chopped onions
- 2 cups nonfat milk
- 1 nonstick cooking spray
- ½ tsp. mustard powder
- ¼ tsp. salt
- ¼ tsp. black pepper egg substitute
- 4 slices of whole wheat bread (cut into ½–inch cubes)
- 3 precooked (diced turkey breakfast sausage patties
- ¼ cup cheddar cheese (reduced-fat, shredded)

Direction: Preparation Time: 13 minutes Cooking Time: 13 minutes Servings: 5

✓ Preheat oven to 350°F. Coat a 9x13 baking dish with cooking spray.

✓ In a medium bowl, whisk together nonfat milk, green onions, dry mustard, salt (optional), pepper, and egg substitute.

✓ Place bread cubes and sausage on the bottom of the baking dish, pour egg mixture evenly over bread and sausage. Top with cheddar cheese.

✓ Cover pan with aluminum foil and bake for 20 minutes. Remove foil and bake for an additional 40 minutes.

Nutrition: Calories: 120 Fat: 3g Carbohydrate: 9g

38) Apple-Walnut French Toast

Ingredients:

- 4 slices multigrain Italian bread 6 oz.
- 1 cup egg substitute
- 4 tsp. pure maple syrup
- 1 cup diced apple
- walnuts (chopped)

Direction: Preparation Time: 12 minutes Cooking Time: 14 minutes Servings: 4

✓ Preheat your oven to 450°F. Meanwhile, put the bread in a baking pan of 13 to 9 inches, pour over all the egg substitutes, and turn several times until the bread slices are thoroughly coated and the egg mixture is used. (Stand in the baking pan when preheating the oven.) Put bread slices coated with cooking spray on the baking sheet.
Bake for 6 minutes, turn, and bake for 5 minutes or until the bottom is golden. Serve with similar proportions of syrup, apples, and nuts in the mixture.

Nutrition: Calories: 276 Fat: 12g Carbs: 33.56

39) Summer Smoothie Fruit

Ingredients:

- 1 cup fresh blueberries
- 1 cup fresh strawberries, chopped
- 2 peaches, peeled, seeded, and chopped
- Peach flavored Greek-style yogurt (nonfat)
- 1 cup unsweetened almond milk
- 2 tbsp. ground flax seed
- ½ cup ice

Direction: Preparation Time: 12 minutes Cooking Time: 0 minutes Servings: 4

✓ Combine in a blender and puree all ingredients until creamy.

✓ Serve

Nutrition: Calories: 130 Fat: 4g Carbohydrate: 23g

40) Chicken and Egg Salad

Ingredients:

- 2 cooked chicken breasts
- 3 hard-boiled eggs
- 2 tbsp. fat-free mayo
- 1 tbsp. curry powder
- Chives or basil (optional)
- Salt (optional)

Direction: Preparation Time: 5 minutes Cooking Time: 25 minutes Servings: 2

✓ .Bake the chicken for maybe 15 minutes in the oven around 360°F (confirm with just a knife that now the meat is cooked all the through).

✓ For 8 minutes, cook the eggs. Cut the eggs and chicken into a small- sized piece.

✓ Combine the cream cheese with curry powder In a large bowl, combine everything and mix.

✓ Allow a minimum of 10 minutes to chill in the refrigerator (it gets even better if you leave it overnight in the refrigerator).

✓ Serve with chives on toast or muffins and a bit of salt on top.

Nutrition: Calories: 139 Fat 9g Carbohydrate: 23g

41) Nicoise Salad Tuna

Ingredients:

- 4 oz. Ahi tuna steak
- 1 whole egg
- 2 cups baby spinach (3oz)
- 2 oz. green beans
- 1 ½ oz. broccoli
- Half red bell peppers
- 3 and a half oz. cucumber
- 1 radish
- 3 large black olives
- Handful of parsley
- 1 tsp. olive oil
- 1 tsp. balsamic vinegar

- ½ tsp. Dijon mustard
- ½ tsp. pepper

Direction: Preparation Time: 12 minutes Cooking Time: 5 minutes Servings: 1

✓ Cook the egg, and place it aside to cool.

✓ Steam beans and broccoli, then set aside. 2–3 mins of a little water in the microwave or 3 minutes in a kettle of hot water does the trick.

✓ In a tub, heat a bit of oil over high heat.

✓ On all sides, season the seafood using pepper, then place it there in the heat and stir on each edge for about 2 minutes.

✓ To the salad bowl or pan, add the spinach Chopped the red pepper, grapefruit as well as egg into pieces that are bite-sized. Add the spinach on top.

✓ Cut the radish into slices and mix the broccoli, beans, and olives. Add the spinach salad on top.

✓ Break the tuna into strips and add it to the salad.

✓ Toss the olive oil, balsamic vinegar, mustard, salt, and pepper together.

✓ The parsley is chopped and added to the vinaigrette.

✓ For drizzling the vinaigrette over a salad, use a spoon.

Nutrition: Calories: 149 Fat: 6g Carbohydrate: 21g

42) *Rolls with Spinach*

Ingredients:

- 16 oz. frozen spinach leaves
- 3 eggs
- 2 ½ oz. onion
- 2 oz. carrot
- 1 oz. low-fat mozzarella cheese
- 4 oz. fat-free cottage cheese
- 1 garlic clove
- 1 tsp. curry powder
- ¼ tsp. chili flakes Salt
- 1 tsp. pepper Cooking spray
- ½ cup parsley

Direction: Preparation Time: 15 minutes Cooking Time: 40 minutes Servings: 4

✓ Preheat the oven to 200ºC (400º F).

✓ Thaw the spinach and squeeze the water out (you can use a filter). In order to accelerate the thawing process, you can microwave the spinach for a few minutes.

✓ Mix the spinach, 2 eggs, mozzarella, ginger, half the salt, and pepper together in a baking bowl.

✓ Place parchment paper on a baking sheet and coat it with cooking spray. Move the spinach mixture, about half an inch thick and about 10 to 12 inches in height, to the sheet and press it down.

✓ Bake for 15 minutes and then set aside to cool on a

rack. Don't turn the oven off.

✓ Finely chop the onion and parsley. Grate the carrots.
In a pan with a bit of cooking oil, fry the onions for about a minute. Add the carrots and parsley to the pan and let it cook for about 2 minutes.

✓ Add cottage cheese, curry, chili, salt, and pepper to the other half. Briefly mix.

✓ Remove the fire from the pan, add an egg, and mix it all together.

✓ Spread the filling over the spinach that has been cooled. Do not stretch it all the way to the corners or as you fold it out, it will fall out.

✓ Roll the spinach mat carefully and fill it, then bake for 25 minutes.

✓ Take out the roll once the time is up, and let it cool for 5–10 minutes before cutting it into slices and serving.

Nutrition: Calories: 149 Fat: 11g Carbohydrate: 26g

43) *Balanced Turkey Meatballs*

Ingredients:

- 20 oz. ground turkey
- 3 ½ fresh or frozen spinach
- ¼ cup oats
- 2 egg whites
- Celery sticks
- 3 garlic cloves
- ½ green bell peppers
- Half red onion
- ½ cup parsley
- ½ tsp. cumin
- 1 tsp. mustard powder
- 1 tsp. thyme
- ½ tsp. turmeric
- ½ tsp. chipotle pepper
- 1 tsp. salt
- A pinch pepper

Direction: Preparation Time: 12 minutes Cooking Time: 26 minutes Servings: 2

✓ Preheat the oven to 350ºF (175ºC).

✓ Chop the onion, garlic, and celery very finely (or use a food processor), and add to a large mixing cup.

✓ In the dish, add the ham, egg whites, oats, and spices and combine well. Make sure the mix contains no pockets of spices or oats.

✓ Spinach, green peppers (stalked and seeded), and parsley are chopped. The bits need to be about a dime's size.
To the tub, add the vegetables and mix them until well-combined.

✓ Line the parchment paper with a baking sheet.

✓ Roll the turkey mixture (about the size of golf balls)

into 15 balls and put them on the baking sheet.

✓ Bake for 25 minutes, until fully baked.
Nutrition: Calories: 129 Fat: 9g Carbohydrate: 22g

44) *Curried Chicken with Apples*
Ingredients:

- 1lb. cooked, diced chicken breast
- 1 Granny Smith diced apple
- celery stalks, diced
- 2 green onions, diced
- ½ cup sliced cashew
- 1 cup plain Greek yogurt
- 1 tbsp. tahini
- 4 tsp. curry powder
- 1 tsp. ground cinnamon

Direction: Preparation Time: 12 minutes Cooking Time: 13 minutes Servings: 3

✓ In a big mixing cup, add the milk, tahini, curry powder, and cinnamon.

✓ Add the chicken, apple, celery, cashews, and green onions. Stir to blend.

✓ To offer it ever something of a tropical feel, this salad can be eaten on its own, as a snack, or in plucked-out papaya.
Nutrition: Calories: 139 Fat: 8g Carbohydrate: 19g

45) *Homemade Chicken Nuggets*
Ingredients:

- ½ cup almond flour
- 1tbsp. Italian seasoning
- 2tbsp. extra virgin olive oil
- ½ tsp. salt
- ½ tsp. pepper

Direction: Preparation Time: 15 minutes Cooking Time: 23 minutes Servings: 2

✓ Preheat the oven to 200ºC (400ºF), Use parchment paper to arrange a large baking dish.

✓ Whisk the Italian seasoning, almond flour, pepper, and salt together in a dish.

✓ Start cutting and remove any fat from the chicken breasts, after which slice into 1-inch-thick bits. Sprinkle the extra virgin olive oil to the chicken.

✓ Place each chicken piece in the flour bowl and toss until thoroughly covered, then move the chicken to the baking sheet that has been prepared.

✓ Roast for 20 minutes.

✓ To get exterior crispy, toggle the broiler and put the chicken nuggets underneath the broiler for 3–4 minutes.
Nutrition: Calories: 149 Fat: 9gCarbohydrate: 29g

46) *Beef Fajitas*
Ingredients:

- 1 lb. beef stir-fry strips
- 1 medium red onion
- 1 red bell pepper
- 1 yellow bell pepper
- ½ tsp. cumin
- ½ tsp. chili powder
- Splash oil
- Salt Pepper
- ½ lime, juiced
- Freshly chopped cilantro (also called coriander)
- 1 avocado

Direction: Preparation Time: 6 minutes Cooking Time: 19 minutes Servings: 4

✓ Over medium fire, steam a cast-iron pan.

✓ Clean and dress bell peppers, cut them into long strips of 0.5cm thick and then Set aside.

✓ Clean and cut the red onion into strips. Set aside.

✓ Add a little bit of oil once the skillet is heated. Add 2–3 packets of stir-fry strips while the oil is hot. Please ensure the strips wouldn't hit 1 another.

✓ Inside the pan, stir-fry each beef batch thoroughly with salt and pepper. Cook on each side for around 1 minute, set aside on a plate, and cover to stay warm.
Introduce chopped onion as well as ringer peppers to the residual meat juice when all the beef is finished cooking and set aside. Sweetened with chili powder and cumin, then simmer-fry till the preferred consistency is achieved.

✓ Move the stir-fry strips of vegetables and beef to just a plate and eat alongside a chopped avocado, a sprinkling of lemon juice, and a spray of fresh cilantro.

✓ Serve.
Nutrition: Calories: 151 Fat: 6g Carbohydrate: 27g

47) *Keto Salad*
Ingredients:

- 4 cherry tomatoes
- Half avocado
- 1 hard-boiled egg
- 2 cups mixed green salad
- 2 oz. chicken breast, shredded
- 1 oz. feta cheese, crumbled
- ¼ cup cooked bacon, crumbled

Direction: Preparation Time: 11 minutes Cooking Time: 0 minutes Servings: 2

✓ Slice the avocado and tomatoes. Slice the hard-boiled egg.

✓ On a large plate, put the mixed greens. Quantify the pulverized chicken breast, crushed bacon, and feta cheese.

✓ Position the tomatoes, egg, chicken, avocado, feta, and bacon on top of the greens in horizontal rows.
Nutrition: Calories: 152 Fat: 9g Carbohydrate: 24g

48) **Instant Pot Chicken Chili**

Ingredients:

- 1 tbsp. vegetable oil
- 1 yellow diced onion
- 4 minced garlic cloves
- 1 tsp. ground cumin
- 1tsp. oregano
- 2½ lb. chicken breasts, boneless and skinless
- 16 oz. salsa Verde

For Toppings

- 2 packages of queso fresco (crumbled) or sour cream
- 2 diced avocados
- Finely chopped radishes
- Eight springs cilantro (optional)

Direction: (Cooking Time:) Preparation Time: 6 minutes Cooking Time: 21 minutes Servings: 2

✓ Set the Instant Pot to a medium sauté setting.

✓ Add the oil to the vegetables.

✓ Attach the onion and simmer for 3 mins till the onion starts to melt, stirring regularly.

✓ Apply the garlic, then stir for a minute.

✓ Add the oregano and cumin and simmer for the next minute.

✓ Through the pot, add ½ of the salsa Verde. Finish only with the breasts of the chicken and spill over the chicken mostly with leftover salsa Verde. Position the cover on the Instant Pot, switch the nozzle to "seal," and choose "manual." set the timer to 10 minutes.

✓ Then let the pressure release naturally when the timer is up.

✓ Lift the cover, move the chicken to a small bowl just after pressure has dropped, and slice it with a fork.

✓ To mix mainly with remaining ingredients, transfer the meat to the pot and stir.

Nutrition: Calories: 144 Fat: 7g Carbohydrate: 20g

49) **Smoked Cheese Wraps with Salmon and Cream**

Ingredients:

- 18-inch low carb flour tortilla
- 2 oz. smoked salmon
- 2tsp. low-fat cream cheese
- 1 ½ oz. red onion
- Handful arugulas

- ½ tsp. fresh or dried basil
- A pinch pepper

Direction: Preparation Time: 12 minutes Cooking Time: 15 minutes Servings: 2

✓ In the oven or microwave, warm the tortilla (pro tip: to prevent it from drying out, warm it between 2 pieces of moist paper towel).

✓ The cream cheese, basil, and pepper are mixed and then scattered over the tortilla.
With the salmon, arugula, and finely sliced onion, finish it off. Roll it up and enjoy the wrap!

Nutrition: Calories: 138 Fat: 6g Carbohydrate: 19g

50) **Cheese Yogurt**

Ingredients:

- 1 thick and Creamy Yogurt or store-bought yogurt
- ½ tsp. kosher salt

Direction: Preparation Time: 12 minutes Cooking Time: 15 minutes Servings: 2

✓ Line a strainer of twice the normal or plastic cheesecloth thickness.

✓ Place the strainer on top of a bowl and apply the yogurt.
Cover and refrigerate for 2 hours. Stir in the salt and continue to drip for another 2 hours until the yogurt cheese is ready to spread.

Nutrition: Calories: 83 Protein: 5g Fat: 5.4g

51) **Muffins of Savory Egg**

Ingredients:

- 1½ cups water
- 2tbsp. unsalted butter
- 1 (6 oz.) package Stove, Top lower-sodium Stuffing Mix for chicken
- 3 oz. bulk pork sausage
- Cooking spray
- 6 eggs, beaten
- ½ cup (1.5 oz.) Monterey Jack cheese, shredded
- ½ cup finely chopped red bell pepper
- ¼ cup sliced green onions

Direction: Preparation Time: 12 minutes Cooking Time: 33 minutes Servings: 6

✓ Preheat oven to 400°F.

✓ In a medium saucepan, put 1 ½ cups water and butter to a boil. Stir in the blend of stuffing. Cover, and leave to stand for 5 minutes; use a fork to fluff. Let stand 10 minutes or before cool enough to hold, uncovered.

✓ Cook the sausage in a small skillet over medium-high heat until browned while the stuffing is cooling; stir to crumble. Coat the fingers with a mist for frying.
Press approximately ¼ cup stuffing into the bottom and sides of each of the 12 deeply coated muffin

cups with cooking oil. Pour the egg uniformly into the cups stuffing. Layer cheese, ham, bell pepper, and green onions equally over the egg if desired.

✓ Bake for 18 to 20 minutes at 400°F or until the centers are centered. Let it stand before serving for 5 minutes. Run a thin, sharp knife along the edges to loosen the muffin cups. Delete from the casseroles. Immediately serve.

Nutrition: Calories: 292 Fat: 16.7g Protein: 14.6g

52) *Parfaits of Yogurt, Honey, and Walnut*
Ingredients:

- cups Greek-style plain yogurt (don't use nonfat)
- ½ tsp. vanilla extract
½ cup honey

Direction: Preparation Time: 25 minutes Cooking Time: 15 minutes Servings: 6

✓ Preheat the oven to 375°F. Brush with the molten butter on a rimmed baking dish. Lay a tray of pastry on top.

✓ Sprinkle with more honey, then add sugar and nuts. Repeat with the remaining sheets of pastry, butter, sugar, and nuts.
Bake 10 to 15 minutes until golden brown and crisp. Enable it to cool on a wire rack on a baking sheet. Break the pastry into chunks.

✓ Mix the yogurt and vanilla in a tub. There are alternating layers of yogurt, honey, and phyllo bits in 4 glasses. Immediately serve.

Nutrition: Calories: 420 Fat: 22g Protein: 14g

53) *Greek-Yogurt Style*
Ingredients:

- 1 thick and Creamy Yogurt
or store-bought yogurt

Direction: Preparation Time: 12 minutes Cooking Time: 15 minutes Servings: 2

✓ Line a double thickness strainer with standard or synthetic cheesecloth
Place the strainer on top of a bowl and apply the yogurt.

✓ Chill and cover. Depending on how dense you want it, let it drain for 1 to 2 ½ hours.

Nutrition: Calories: 240 Protein: 14g Fat: 14g

54) *Shrimp and Grits Cajun-Style*
Ingredients:

- 1 tbsp. olive oil
- ½ cups (2 oz.) Tasso ham, minced
- 1 cup chopped onion 1 garlic clove, minced
- Thirty-6 medium shrimp, peeled (about 1 ¼ lb.)
- 1 tsp. Cajun seasoning
- 2½ cups water, divided
- 1 tbsp. unsalted butter

- 1 cup fat-free milk
- ¼ tsp. salt
- 1 cup uncooked quick-cooking grits
- 1 cup (4 oz.) of sharp cheddar cheese, shredded
- ½ cup sliced green onions

Direction: Preparation Time: 12 minutes Cooking Time: 20 minutes Servings: 6

✓ Heat the olive oil over medium-high heat in a large skillet. Add Tasso; sauté for 2 minutes or until golden on the edges. Stir in the onion; sauté for 2 minutes. Stir in garlic; sauté for 1 minute.

✓ Sprinkle with Cajun seasoning, add the shrimp to the grill, and cook for 3 minutes, rotating once. Apply ¼ cup water to loosen the browned pieces, scratching the pan. Remove from heat; mix with butter, stirring until melted. Cover yourself and stay warm.
On medium-high heat, put milk, salt, and 2 cups of water to a boil—heat elimination. Add the grits steadily, and cook until thick and sparkling (about 5 minutes), stirring continuously with a whisk. Drop the grits from the high temperatures; add the cheese and stir until the cheese melts, with a whisk.

✓ On 6 plates, the spoon grates evenly. Using seafood, ham combination, and green onions to finish uniformly.

Nutrition: Calories: 346 Fat: 14g Protein: 24g

55) *Scramble for Lox, Eggs, and Onion*
Ingredients:

- 6 eggs
- 4 egg whites
- 1 tsp. canola oil
- ¹/3 cup sliced green onions
- 4 oz. smoked salmon, cut into ½-inch pieces
- ¼ cup reduced-fat cream
- cheese, cut into 12 pieces
- ¼ tsp. freshly ground black pepper
- 4 slices pumpernickel bread, toasted

Direction: Preparation Time: 12 minutes Cooking Time: 15 minutes Servings: 4

✓ Place the eggs and egg whites in a bowl; stir until mixed with a whisk.

✓ Over medium-high prepare, heat a medium nonstick skillet. In a bath, apply oil; swirl to coat. In the pan, add the green onions; sauté for 2 minutes or until tender. Attach a tray of the egg mixture. Until the mixture settles on the rim, cook without stirring.
Draw a spatula to form curds over the bottom of the tub. Add the cream cheese and salmon. Continue to draw the spatula across the bottom of the pan until the egg mixture is somewhat thick but still moist; do not continuously stir.

✓ Remove directly from the pan. Sprinkle the pepper

with the egg mixture. Serve the toast of
pumpernickel.
Nutrition: Calories: 297 Fat: 14.5g Protein: 22.8g

56) *Peach and Pancakes with Blueberry*
Ingredients:

- 1½ cups all-purpose flour 2 tbsp. sugar
- 2tbsp. flaxseed (optional)
- 1 tbsp. Baking powder
- ½ tsp. kosher salt
- 1½ cups nonfat buttermilk
- 1 tsp. grated lemon rind
- 2eggs
- 1 cup fresh or frozen blueberries, thawed
- 1 cup chopped fresh or frozen peaches, thawed
- 2 tbsp. unsalted butter
- Fresh blueberries (optional)

Direction: Preparation Time: 12 minutes Cooking Time: 16 minutes Servings: 6

✓ Weigh or spoon the flour gently into dry measuring cups; level it with a knife. In a large cup, mix the flour, sugar, flaxseed, baking powder, and salt if necessary, and stir with a fork.

✓ In a medium cup, mix the buttermilk, lemon rind, and eggs and stir with a fork. To the flour mixture, apply the buttermilk mixture, stirring only, so it is moist. Fold in the blueberries and peaches kindly. Heat a nonstick griddle or nonstick skillet over medium heat. Pour $1/3$ of a cup flour into the pan per pancake. Cook for 2 to 3 minutes over medium heat or until bubbles cover the tops and the edges appear fried. Switch the cakes over gently; cook for 2–3 mins or until the bottoms become golden brown.
Nutrition: Calories: 238 Fat 2.8g Protein: 8.1g

57)Omelet with Turmeric, Tomato, and Onions
Ingredients:

- 4 large eggs
- Kosher salt
- 1 tbsp. olive oil
- ¼ tsp. brown mustard seeds Turmeric powder
- 2 green onions, finely chopped
- ¼ cup diced plum tomato
- Dash black pepper

Direction: Preparation Time: 8 minutes Cooking Time: 15 minutes Servings: 2

✓ Whisk the eggs and salt together.

✓ Heat oil over medium-high heat in a large cast-iron skillet. Apply the mustard and turmeric seeds; simmer for 30 seconds or until the seeds pop up,

stirring regularly. Add onions; simmer for 30 seconds or until tender, stirring regularly. Add the tomato; simmer for 1 minute or until very tender, stirring regularly.
Pour the plate with the egg mixture; scatter uniformly. Cook until the edges are set (about 2 minutes). Slide the spatula's front edge between the omelet edge and the plate. Raise the omelet edge softly, tilting the pan to allow the pan to come into contact with any uncooked egg mixture.

✓ Procedure to replicate on the opposite edge. Continue to cook till the center is really just set (about 2 minutes). Loosen the omelet and fold it in half with a spatula. Slide the omelet carefully onto a platter. Halve the omelet and dust it with black pepper.
Nutrition: Calories: 216 Fat: 16.9g Protein: 13.3g

58) *Breakfast Bowl of Yogurt*
Ingredients:

- 1 tsp. tandoori spice or curry powder
- ¼ cup honey
- 2 cups 2% plain Greek yogurt
- ½ cup all-natural granola
- 1 cup fresh berries
- 1 cup freeze-dried mango, pineapple, and/or berries
- Small sprigs of fresh cilantro

Direction: Preparation Time: 8 minutes Cooking Time: 15 minutes Servings: 4

✓ Toast the spices on low in a small skillet, stirring, until very fragrant, for about 2 minutes. Take it out of the oven, add honey and, stir.
Break the yogurt into 4 cups. Drizzle with spiced honey; finish with cilantro, granola, and mango. Just serve.
Nutrition: Calories: 227 Fat: 3.1g Protein: 11g

59) *Tex-Mex Migas*
Ingredients:

- 3 large eggs
- 3 egg whites
- 1 tbsp. canola oil
- 4 corn tortillas, cut into ½-inch-wide strips
- ½ cup chopped onion
- 2 large seeded jalapeño peppers
- 2-third cup lower-sodium salsa
- ½ cup Monterey Jack cheese, shredded
- ½ cup sliced green onions
- Hot sauce (optional)
- Lower-sodium red salsa (optional)
- Lower-sodium green salsa (optional)

Direction: Preparation Time: 9 minutes Cooking Time: 15 minutes Servings: 4

✓ *Place the eggs and egg whites in a bowl; stir until mixed with a whisk.*

✓ *Over medium-high prepare, heat a medium nonstick skillet. In a bath, apply oil; swirl to coat. Apply tortilla strips to the skillet and cook, stirring constantly, for 3 minutes or until brown. In a sauce, add the onion and jalapeño peppers; sauté for 2 minutes or until tender. Stir in 2/3 of a cup salsa, and simmer for 1 minute, stirring continuously.*

✓ *Add the mixture of eggs; simmer for 2 minutes or until the eggs are tender, stirring periodically. Sprinkle the cheese with the egg mixture. Cook for thirty seconds or until the cheese is molten. Cover with the green onions, then serve right away. If preferred, serve with hot sauce, red salsa, or green salsa.*

Nutrition: Calories: 193 Fat: 10.4g Protein: 10.2g

60) **Barley Breakfast with Banana &Sunflower Breakfast Bowl of Yogurt Seeds**

Ingredients:

- -third cup water
- 1 third cup uncooked quick- Cooking pearl barley
- 1 banana, sliced
- 1 tsp. honey
- 1 tbsp. unsalted sunflower seeds

Direction: Preparation Time: 5 minutes Cooking Time: 11 minutes Servings: 1

✓ *In a shallow microwave-safe cup, mix water and barley a high 6-minute microwave.*

✓ *Delete and leave to stand for 2 minutes.*

✓ *Cover with slices of banana, sunflower seeds, and honey.*

Nutrition: Calories: 410 Fat: 6g Protein: 10g

61)**Banana Smoothie for Breakfast**

Ingredients:

- ½ cup 1% low-fat milk
- ½ cup crushed ice
- 1 tbsp. honey
- ½ tsp. ground nutmeg
- 1 frozen sliced ripe large banana
- 1 cup plain 2% reduced-fat Greek yogurt

Direction: Preparation Time: 12 minutes Cooking Time: 0 minute Servings: 2

✓ *In a blender, combine the first 5 ingredients; mix for 2 minutes or until smooth. Add the yogurt; just process until it's blended. Immediately serve.*

Nutrition: Calories: 212 Fat: 3.6g Protein: 14.2g

62) **Blackberry-Mango Shake**

Ingredients:

- 1 cup orange juice
- 1 cup refrigerated bottled mango slices
- ¼ cup light firm silken tofu 3 tbsp. honey
- 1 ½ cups frozen blackberries

Direction: Preparation Time: 12 minutes Cooking Time: 0 minutes Servings: 4

✓ *In a blender, place all ingredients in the order given; process until smooth*

Nutrition: Calories: 162 Fat: 0.6g Protein: 3.7g

63) **Bulgur Porridge Breakfast**

Ingredients:

- 4 cups 1% low-fat milk
- 1 cup bulgur
- $^1/_3$ cup dried cherries
- ¼ tbsp. salt
- $^1/_3$ cup dried apricots, coarsely chopped
- ½ cup sliced almonds

Direction: Preparation Time: 5 minutes Cooking Time: 15 minutes Servings: 4

✓ *Combine the milk, bulgur, dried cherries, and salt in a medium saucepan; bring it to a boil. Reduce heat to low and simmer, stirring regularly, until tender and the oatmeal consistency of the bulgur is tender (10–15 minutes). Divide into 4 bowls of hot porridge; top with the apricots and almonds.*

Nutrition: Calories: 340 Fat: 6.7g Protein: 15g

64) **Turkey Meatballs**

Ingredients:

- 20 oz. ground turkey
- 4 oz. fresh or frozen spinach ¼ cup oats
- 2 egg whites
- 2 celery sticks
- 3 garlic cloves
- Half green bell peppers Half red onion
- ½ cup parsley
- ½ tsp. cumin
- 1 tsp. mustard powder 1
- tsp. Thyme
- ½ tbsp. Turmeric
- ½ tsp. chipotle pepper
- 1 tsp. salt
- Pinch pepper

Direction: Preparation Time: 16 minutes Cooking Time: 25 minutes Servings: 5

✓ *Preheat the oven to 350°F (175°C).*

✓ *Chop very finely (or use a food processor) the onion, garlic, and celery, and add to a large mixing cup.*

✓ *In the dish, add the ham, egg whites, oats, and spices and combine well. Make sure the blend has no pockets of spices or oats.*

✓ *Spinach, green peppers (stalked and seeded), and parsley are chopped. The bits need to be about a dime's size.*
To the tub, add the vegetables and mix them until well-combined.

✓ *Line the parchment paper with a baking sheet.*

✓ *Roll the turkey mixture (about the size of golf balls) into 15 balls and put them on the baking sheet.*

✓ *Bake for 25 minutes, until fully baked.*
Nutrition: Calories: 349 Fat: 7g Protein: 19g

65) *Berry Avocado Smoothie*
Ingredients:

- Half an avocado
- 1 cup strawberries
- ¼ cup blueberries
- ½ cup low-fat milk
- ½ cup 2% Greek yogurt
- 1 tsp. raw honey, optional

Direction: Preparation Time: 7 minutes Cooking Time: 20 minutes Servings: 2

✓ *Fill the blender with avocado, strawberries, blueberries, and milk.*

✓ *Blend until perfectly smooth.*

✓ *Taste, then, if using honey, you can add.*

✓ *Serve or put in a refrigerator for up to 2 days.*
Nutrition: Calories: 350 Fat: 17g Protein: 24g

66) *Bagel Hummus Toast*
Ingredients:

- soft boiled egg halved
- 6 tbsp. plain hummus
- 2 pieces' gluten-free bread, toasted
- Pinch paprika
- 2 tsp. Everything Bagel Spice
- Drizzle olive oil

Direction: Preparation Time: 30 minutes Cooking Time: 4 hours Servings: 2

✓ *Spread each bread piece with 3 tbsp. Hummus.*

✓ *Attach a slice of halved egg and finish with 1 tsp. of 'Bagel' spice each.*

✓ *Sprinkle a small amount of paprika, muzzle with olive oil, and serve at once.*
Nutrition: Calories: 213 Fat 11.6g Protein: 6.5g

67) *Cinnamon Apple Chips*
Ingredients:

- 1 medium apple, sliced thin
- ¼ tsp. cinnamon
- ¼ tsp. nutmeg Nonstick cooking spray

Direction: Preparation Time: 6 minutes Cooking Time: 11 minutes Servings: 2

✓ *Heat oven to 375°F. Spray a baking sheet with cooking spray.*

✓ *Place apples in a mixing bowl and add spices. Toss to coat.*
Arrange apples, in a single layer, on the prepared pan. Bake 4 minutes, turn apples over and bake 4 minutes more.

✓ *Serve immediately or store in an airtight container.*
Nutrition: Calories: 58 Protein: 0.1g Fat 0.3g

68) *Whole-Grain Breakfast Cookies*
Ingredients:

- cups rolled oats
- 1/2 cup whole-wheat flour
- ¼ cup ground flaxseed
- 1 teaspoon baking powder
- 1 cup unsweetened applesauce
- 2 large eggs
- 2 tablespoons vegetable oil
- 2 teaspoons vanilla extract
- 1 teaspoon ground cinnamon
- 1/2 cup dried cherries
- ¼ cup unsweetened shredded coconut
- 2 ounces dark chocolate, chopped

Direction: Preparation time: 20 minutesCooking time: 10 minutes Servings: 18 cookies

✓ *Preheat the oven to 350F.*

✓ *In a large bowl, combine the oats, flour, flaxseed, and baking powder. Stir well to mix.*

✓ *In a medium bowl, whisk the applesauce, eggs, vegetable oil, vanilla, and cinnamon. Pour the wet mixture into the dry mixture, and stir until just combined.*

✓ *Fold in cherries, coconut, and chocolate. Drop tablespoon-size balls of dough onto a baking sheet. Bake for 10 to 12 minutes, until browned and cooked through.*

✓ *Let cool for about 3 minutes, remove from the baking sheet, and cool completely before serving. Store in an airtight container for up to 1 week.*
Nutrition: Calories: 136; Total fat: 7g; Protein: 4g; Carbs: 14g;

69) *Hash of Tempeh and Veggies*

15 minutes for preparation Time required for cooking: 25 minutes 3 portions
Ingredients:

- 2 1/2 cups peeled and diced sweet potato
- 1/3 cup finely chopped red onion
- 1 cup cubed tempeh
- 1 cup quartered Brussels sprouts
- 2 minced garlic cloves

- *1 1/2 cups fresh kale, tough ribs removed and diced*

Direction

✓ *Place the sweet potato cubes in a pan of boiling water and simmer for approximately 8 minutes.*

✓ *Completely drain the sweet potato cubes.*

✓ *Heat the canola oil and sauté the onion for approximately 4–5 minutes in a skillet over medium-high heat.*

✓ *Add the remaining ingredients (except the spinach) and simmer, occasionally stirring, for approximately 6–7 minutes.*

✓ *Cook for approximately 5 minutes, stirring twice, adding cooked sweet potato and greens.*

✓ *Serve immediately.*

Nutrition: Calories 298 6.5 g Total Fat 3 g Saturated Fat 0 mg Sodium 139 mg Carbohydrates 48.2 g Fiber 7.6 g Sugar 11 g Protein 16 g

70) *Muffins with Tofu and Zucchini*

15 minutes for preparation Time required for cooking: 40 minutes 6 portions

Ingredients:

- *1/2 ounces extra-firm silken tofu, drained and pressed*
- *2 tbsp canola oil*
- *1 tbsp apple cider vinegar*
- *1 cup whole-wheat pastry flour*
- *1/2 tbsp chickpea flour*
- *1 tsp baking powder*
- *1/2 tbsp baking soda 1 tsp smoked paprika*
- *1 tsp onion powder*
- *1 tsp salt*
- *1/2 tbsp zucchini, diced*

Directions:

✓ *Preheat the oven to 400 degrees Fahrenheit.*

✓ *Prepare a 12-cup muffin tray by lining it with paper liners.*

✓ *Place tofu in a bowl and press it with a fork until smooth.*

✓ *In a mixing bowl, combine the tofu, almond milk, oil, and vinegar until slightly soft.*

✓ *In a separate large mixing bowl, merge the flours, baking powder, baking soda, spices, and salt.*

✓ *Pour the mixture evenly over among the*

muffin cups.

✓ *Bake 35–40 minutes, or until a toothpick inserted in the center comes out clean.*

✓ *Remove the muffin tray from the oven and cool for approximately 10 minutes on a wire rack.*

✓ *Invert the muffins carefully onto a serving platter and serve warm.*

Nutrition: 237 Nutrition: Calories 9 grams saturated fat 1 gram Cholesterol 0 mg sodium 520 mg Carbohydrates in total 2293 g Fiber 9 g Sucrose Protein: 7 g 11 gram

71) *Smoothie with Strawberries and Spinach*

Preparation Time: 10 minutes Required for Cooking: 15 minutes 2 servings

Ingredients:

- *1 1/2 cup fresh strawberries, hulled and sliced*
- *1 cup almond milk, unsweetened*
- *1/4 cup cubes d' ice*

Direction

✓ *In a high-powered blender, merge all the ingredients and process until smooth.*

✓ *Immediately pour into serving glasses and serve.*

Nutrition: Calories 96 3 g total fat 0.2 g saturated fat 1 mg cholesterol Carbohydrates in total 13 g 7.7 g sugar 9 g fiber 144 mg potassium 8.1 g protein

72) *Waffles with Sweet Potatoes*

Time Required for Preparation: 10 minutes Time Required for Cooking: 20 minutes 2 portions

- *one big sweet potato, peeled, grated, and pressed*
- *1 teaspoon minced fresh thyme*
- *1 teaspoon minced fresh rosemary*
- *1/8 teaspoon crushed red pepper flakes*

Directions:

✓ *Preheat and oil the waffle iron.*

✓ *In a large mixing basin, blend all ingredients until well incorporated.*

✓ *Cook for approximately 8-10 minutes or until golden brown, half of the sweet potato mixture in a preheated waffle iron.*

✓ *Continue with the remainder of the mixture.*

✓ *Serve immediately.*

Nutrition: 72 Nutrition: Calories Cholesterol 0 mg Total Fat 0.3 g Saturated Fat 0.1 Carbohydrates 16.3 g Sodium 28 mg Potassium 369 mg 6 g protein

73) <u>Apple Omelet</u>

Time Required to Prepare: 10 minutes Time Required for Cooking: 10 minutes 3 portions

- *4 tbsp olive oil, split*
- *2 small green apples, cored and finely sliced*
- *1/4 tbsp crushed cinnamon*
- *pinch ground cloves*
- *pinch ground nutmeg*
- *4 large eggs*
- *1/4 tbsp organic vanilla essence*
- *pinch salt*

Direction

- ✓ *In a frying pan over medium-low heat, cook one teaspoon*
- ✓ *Arrange the apple slices in a single layer and season with spices.*
- ✓ *Cook for approximately 4-5 minutes, turning halfway through.*
- ✓ *Meanwhile, in a separate dish, whisk together the eggs, vanilla extract, and salt until frothy.*
- ✓ *Add the remaining oil to the pan and bring to a full boil.*
- ✓ *Evenly distribute the egg mixture over the apple slices and cook for approximately 3-5 minutes, or until the desired doneness is achieved.*
- ✓ *Invert the pan onto a serving plate, fold the omelet immediately.*
- ✓ *Immediately serve.*

Nutrition: Calories 228 Cholesterol 248 mg Total Fat 12 g Saturated Fat 3 g 23 g Carbohydrates, 16.1 g Sugar, 8 g fiber, 145 mg Sodium, 251 mg Potassium, 8.8 g Protein

74) <u>Vegetable Frittata</u>

Time Required for Preparation: 15 minutes Time Required for Cooking: 25 minutes 6 portions

Ingredients:

- *one tablespoon olive oil*
- *1 large sweet potato, cut and peeled into thin slices*
- *1 yellow squash, sliced*
- *1 zucchini, sliced*
- *1/2 red bell peppers, seeded and sliced*
- *1/2 yellow bell peppers, seeded and sliced*

Directions:

- ✓ *Preheat the oven to the broiler.*
- ✓ *Oven medium-low heat, cook the sweet potato for about 6-7 minutes.*
- ✓ *Add the yellow squash, zucchini, and bell peppers and cook for about 3-4 minutes.*
- ✓ *Meanwhile, in a bowl, add the eggs, salt, and black pepper and beat until well combined.*
- ✓ *Pour egg mixture over vegetable mixture.*
- ✓ *Transfer the skillet to the oven and broil for about 3-4 minutes or until the top becomes golden brown.*
- ✓ *With a sharp knife, cut the frittata in desired size slices and serve with the garnishing of cilantro.*

Nutrition: Calories 143 Total Fat 8.4 g Saturated Fat 2 g Cholesterol 218 mg Total Carbs 9.3 g Sugar 2 g Fiber 1 g Sodium 98 mg Protein 8.9 g

75) <u>Chicken & Sweet Potato Hash</u>

Preparation Time: 15 minutes Required for Cooking: 35 minutes Servings: 8

Ingredients:

- *2 tablespoons olive oil, divided*
- *1½ pounds boneless, skinless chicken breasts, cubed*
- *Salt and ground black pepper, as required*
- *two celery stalks, chopped*
- *one medium white onion, chopped*
- *four garlic cloves, minced*
- *one tablespoon fresh oregano, chopped*
- *1 tablespoon fresh thyme, chopped*
- *two large sweet potatoes, peeled and cubed*
- *1 cup low-sodium chicken broth*
- *1 cup scallion, chopped*
- *two tablespoons fresh lime juice*

Directions:

- ✓ *Heat one tablespoon of oil over medium heat and cook the chicken with a bit of salt and black pepper for about 4-5 minutes.*
- ✓ *Transfer the chicken into a bowl.*
- ✓ *Heat the remaining oil over medium heat and sauté celery and onion in the same skillet for about 3-4 minutes.*
- ✓ *Add the garlic and herbs and sauté for about 1 minute.*
- ✓ *Add the sweet potato and cook for about 8-10 minutes.*
- ✓ *Add the broth and cook for about 8-10 minutes.*

✓ *Add the cooked chicken and scallion and cook for about 5 minutes.*

✓ *Stir in lemon juice, salt and serve.*

Nutrition: Calories 253 Total Fat 10 g Saturated Fat 3 g Cholesterol 76 mg Total Carbs 14 g Sugar 2 g Fiber 6 g Sodium 92 mg Potassium 597 mg Protein 26 g

76) Pancakes

Time Required for Preparation: 5 minutes Time Required for Cooking: 10 minutes 2 portions

Ingredients:

- *2 tbsp coconut oil*
- *1 tsp maple extract*
- *2 tbsp cashew milk*
- *2 eggs*

Directions:

✓ *Add the oil to a skillet.*

✓ *Add a quarter-cup of the batter and fry until golden on each side.*

✓ *Continue adding the remaining batter.*

Nutrition: 260 cal.23g fat 7g protein 3g carbs

77) Breakfast Sandwich

Preparation Time: 10 minutes Cooking Time: 0 minutes 2 portions

Ingredients:

- *260g cheddar cheese*
- *1/6 30g smoked ham*
- *2 tbsp butter*
- *4 eggs*

Directions:

✓ *Fry all the eggs and sprinkle the pepper and salt on them.*

✓ *Place an egg down as the sandwich base. Top with the ham and cheese and a drop or two of Tabasco.*

✓ *Place the other egg on top and enjoy.*

Nutrition: 600 cal.50g fat 12g protein 7g carbs.

78) Egg Muffins

Time Required for Preparation: 10 minutes Time Required for Cooking: 20 minutes 6 portions

Ingredients:

- *1 tbsp green pesto*
- *3 oz/75g shredded cheese*
- *5 oz/150g cooked bacon*
- *1 scallion, chopped*
- *6 eggs*

Directions:

✓ *You should set your oven to 350°F/175°C.*

✓ *Place liners in a regular cupcake tin.*

✓ *Beat the eggs with pepper, salt, and pesto. Mix in the cheese.*

✓ *Pour the eggs into the cupcake tin and top with the bacon and scallion.*

✓ *Cook for 15-20 minutes*

Nutrition: 190 cal.15g fat 7g protein 4g carbs.

79) Bacon & Eggs

Preparation Time: 2 minutes Cooking Time: 3 minutes 4 portions

Ingredients:

- *Parsley*
- *Cherry tomatoes*
- *5 1/3 oz/150g bacon*
- *8 eggs*

Directions:

✓ *Fry up the bacon and put it to the side.*

✓ *Scramble the eggs in the bacon grease with some pepper and salt*

✓ *If you want, scramble in some cherry tomatoes. Sprinkle with some parsley and enjoy.*

Nutrition: 80 cal 7g fat 14g protein 2g carbs.

80) Eggs on the Go

Time Required for Preparation: 5 minutes Cooking Time: 5 minutes 4 portions

Ingredients:

- *4 oz/110g bacon, cooked*
- *Pepper*
- *Salt*
- *12 eggs*

Directions:

✓ *You should set your oven to 200°C.*

✓ *Place liners in a regular cupcake tin.*

✓ *This will help with easy removal and storage.*

✓ *Break one egg into each cup and sprinkle them with some bacon. Season with some pepper and salt.*

✓ *Bake until the eggs are set.*

Nutrition: 75 cal. 6g fat 8g protein 1g carbs.

81) Cream Cheese Pancakes

Time Required for Preparation: 5 minutes Cooking Time: 5 minutes Servings: 1

Ingredients:

- 2 oz cream cheese
- 2 eggs
- ½ tsp cinnamon
- 1 tbsp keto coconut flour
- ½ to 1 packet of Stevia

Directions:

- ✓ Skillet with butter in the pan or coconut oil on medium-high.
- ✓ Make them as you would normal pancakes.
- ✓ Cook and flip one side to cook the other side!
- ✓ Top with some butter and sugar-free syrup.

Nutrition: 340 cal.30g fat 7g protein 3g carbs

82) *Breakfast Mix*

Preparation Time: 10 minutes Cooking Time: 5 minutes Servings: 1

Ingredients:

- 5 tbsp coconut flakes, unsweetened
- 7 tbsp hemp seeds
- 5 tbsp flaxseed, ground
- 2 tbsp. sesame, ground
- 2 tbsp cocoa, dark, unsweetened

Directions:

- ✓ 1 Grind the sesame and flaxseed.
- ✓ Only grind the sesame seeds for a short period.
- ✓ Using a jar, mix all the ingredients, then shake it.
- ✓ Keep refrigerated until ready to eat.
- ✓ Serve softened with black coffee or even with plain water. Add coconut oil which serves to increase the fat content. It also blends well with cream or with mascarpone cheese.

Nutrition: 150 cal.9g fat 8g protein 4g carbs.

83) *Breakfast Muffins*

Time Required for Preparation: 10 minutes Cooking Time: 5 minutes 1 portion

Ingredients:

- 1 medium egg
- ¼ cup heavy cream
- one slice of cooked bacon (cured, pan-fried, cooked)
- 1 oz cheddar cheese

- Salt and black pepper (to taste)

Directions:

- ✓ Preheat the oven to 350°F.
- ✓ Mix the eggs with cream, salt, and pepper in a bowl.
- ✓ Spread into muffin tins and fill the cups half full.
- ✓ Place one slice of bacon into each muffin hole and half an ounce of cheese on top of each muffin.
- ✓ Bake for around 15-20 minutes or until slightly browned.
- ✓ Add another ½ oz of cheese onto each muffin and broil until the cheese is slightly browned. Serve!

Nutrition: 150 cal 11g fat 7g protein 2g carbs

84) *Porridge of Eggs*

Time Required for Preparation: 10 minutes Time Required for Cooking: 10 minutes 1 portion

- 2 organic free-range eggs
- 1/3 cup organic heavy cream without added sugar
- 2 tbsp grass-fed butter, ground organic cinnamon to taste

Directions:

- ✓ Combine the eggs, cream, and sweetener in a mixing dish.
- ✓ In a saucepan over medium heat, melt the butter. Once the butter has melted, reduce the heat to low.
- ✓ Combine the egg and cream mixture in a separate bowl.
- ✓ Continue mixing while cooking until the mixture thickens and curdles.
- ✓ When the first traces of curdling appear, immediately remove the saucepan from the heat.
- ✓ Transfer the porridge to a serving bowl. Serve immediately with cinnamon sprinkled over the top.

604 Nutrition: Calories 45g fat 8g protein 8g carbohydrates

85) *Eggs Florentine*

Time Required for Preparation: 10 minutes Time Required for Cooking: 10 minutes 2 portions

- 1 cup freshly washed spinach leaves
- 2 tbsp freshly grated parmesan cheese
- sea salt and pepper

- *1 tbsp white vinegar*

Direction

✓ *Microwave or steam the spinach until wilted.*

✓ *Sprinkle with parmesan cheese and spice with salt and pepper.*

✓ *Using a sharp knife, cut into bite-size pieces.*

✓ *Bring a pan of water to a boil and add the vinegar. With a spoon, quickly stir.*

✓ *In the center, crack an egg. Remove from the heat and cover it until set.*

✓ *Do the same thing with the second egg.*

✓ *To serve, arrange the eggs on top of the spinach.*

180 Nutrition: Calories.10g fat Protein: 7 g 5g carbohydrate.

86) **_Eggplant Omelet_**

Time Required for Preparation: 10 minutes Time Required for Cooking: 5 minutes 2 servings

- *1 large eggplant*

- *1 tbsp melted coconut oil*

- *1 tbsp unsalted butter*

- *2 eggs*

- *2 tbsp chopped green onions*

Direction

✓ *Preheat the grill on the highest setting.*

✓ *In the meantime, prepare the eggplant by cutting two slices about 1-inch thick from the eggplant and reserving the remaining eggplant for later use.*

✓ *Take the eggplant slices and brush them on both sides with oil, then season with salt. Place the slices on the grill and cook for 3 to 4 minutes per side.*

✓ *Transfer grilled eggplant to a cutting board, cool for 5 minutes, and then use a cookie cutter to create a house in the center of each slice.*

✓ *Heat a frying pan over medium heat and add the butter. Add the eggplant slices and crack an egg into each hole when the butter melts.*

✓ *Allow the eggs to cook for 3 minutes before carefully flipping the eggplant slice and cooking for another 3 minutes, or until the egg is well cooked.*

✓ *Season eggs with salt and black pepper, transfer to a serving plate and garnish with green onions.*

184 Nutrition: Calories 11 g Fatty Acids 7.8 g Protein 3 g Carbohydrates Fiber 5 g

87) **_Keto Egg Scramble_**

Preparation Time: 2 minutes 3 minutes cooking time two portions

- *1/4 tsp salt*

- *1 tbsp. softened unsalted butter*

- *1/8 tsp crushed black pepper*

- *2 tbsp cold unsalted butter*

- *three eggs*

Directions:

✓ *In a bowl, whisk cracked eggs until well combined, and then stir in diced cold butter until well incorporated.*

✓ *Heat a skillet pan over medium-low heat, add butter, and when it melts, pour in the egg mixture and simmer, without stirring, for 1 minute.*

✓ *Cook, occasionally stirring, for 1 to 2 minutes, or until the omelet is properly cooked and scrambled to the desired level.*

✓ *Season scrambled eggs with salt and freshly ground black pepper before serving.*

85 Nutrition: Calories 75 g Fats 75 g Protein 0.25 g Carbohydrates 0.25 g Fiber

88) **_Pancakes with Low Carbohydrates and Cheese_**

2 minutes for preparation 3 minutes cooking time two portions

- *1/2 teaspoons cinnamon*

- *1 teaspoon unsalted butter*

- *2 eggs*

- *2 ounces cream cheese*

Direction

✓ *In a blender, combine cream cheese, eggs, and cinnamon; pulse for 1 minute or smooth. Let the batter rest for 5 minutes.*

✓ *Heat a frying pan over medium heat and add butter. When the butter melts, drop one-fourth of the batter into the pan, spread evenly, and cook the pancakes for 2 minutes per side until done.*

✓ *Transfer pancakes to a serving platter and serve.*

97.8 Nutrition: Calories 8.4 g Fatty Acids Protein: 4 g 1 g Carbohydrates Net 0.2 g Fiber

89)   _Scrambled Eggs and Veggies_

2 minutes for preparation 3 minutes cooking time two portions

- 1/4 tsp salt
- 1 tbsp unsalted butter
- 1/8 tsp powdered black pepper
- 4 ounces spinach

Direction

- ✓ Heat a frying pan over medium heat. Add butter and sauté until melted.
- ✓ Add spinach and cook for 5 minutes, or until leaves wilt.
- ✓ Add eggs, season with salt and pepper, and cook for 3 minutes, or until scrambled to the desired level.

90 Nutrition: Calories 7 g lipids 6 g Protein; 0.7 g Carbohydrate Fiber 0.6 g

90)   _In a Pan, Egg "Dough."_

Time Required for Preparation: 4 minutes Time Required for Cooking: 4 minutes 2 servings

- 1/4 tsp salt
- 1/2 medium red bell peppers, diced
- 1/8 tsp crushed black pepper
- 2 eggs
- 2 tbsp chopped chives

Direction

- ✓ Turn on the oven and set the temperature to 350 degrees F. Allow the oven to Preheat.
- ✓ Meanwhile, crack eggs into a bowl and mix in the remaining ingredients until incorporated.
- ✓ Remove a small heatproof dish from the refrigerator, pour in the egg mixture, and bake for 5 to 8 minutes, or until set.
- ✓ Once finished, cut it into two squares and serve.

87 Nutrition: Calories 4 grams fat Protein 7.2 g 7 g Carbohydrates Net 0.7 g Fiber

91)_Savory Keto Pancakes_

3 minutes to prepare time Required for Cooking: 2 minutes 2 servings

Ingredients:

- 14 cups almond flour
- 1/2 tbsp unsalted butter
- two eggs
- 2 ounces softened cream cheese

Direction

- ✓ In a large mixing bowl, crack eggs, slam vigorously until frothy. Add flour and cream cheese and whisk until thoroughly blended.
- ✓ Heat a frying pan over medium heat, add butter, and when it melts, drop the pancake batter in four pieces, distribute evenly, and cook for 2 minutes per side, or until golden brown.

166.8 Nutrition: Calories 15 g Fats Protein 8 g 8 g Carbohydrates 0.8 g Fiber

92)   _Combine Vegetable Fritters_

Time Required for Preparation: 4 minutes

- 3 minutes cooking time two portions
- 1/2 tsp nutritional yeast
- 1 oz chopped broccoli
- 1 oz grated, squeezed zucchini
- 2 eggs
- 2 tbsp almond flour

Direction

- ✓ Wrap shredded zucchini in cheesecloth and twist it tightly to remove excess liquid. In a bowl, combine zucchini.
- ✓ Whisk in the remaining ingredients, except the oil, until completely blended.
- ✓ Heat a skillet over medium heat, add oil, and when heated, drop zucchini mixture in four sections, shape into flat patties, and cook for 4 minutes per side, or until well cooked.

191 Nutrition: Calories 16.6 g Fats Protein 9.6 g Carbohydrates 0.8 g Net Carbohydrates 0.2 g Fiber

93)   _Cheese Rolls Keto_

Time Required for Preparation: 5 minutes Time Required for Cooking: 0 minutes Servings: 2

Ingredients:

- 1 oz unsalted butter
- 2 oz sliced full-fat mozzarella cheese

Directions:

- ✓ Slice the cheese and then the butter into thin slices.
- ✓ Place a slice of butter on top of each cheese slice, roll it up, and serve.

Nutrition: 166 Nutrition: Calories 15 g lipids Protein 6.5 g 2 g Carb Fiber 0 g

94) <u>Creamed Coconut Curry Spinach</u>

30 minutes to prepare Time Required for Cooking: 1 hour 6 portions

- *1 pound thawed and drained frozen spinach*
- *2 tsp yellow curry paste*
- *1 tsp lemon zest*

Directions:

✓ *Preheat a medium-sized skillet over medium-high heat and add the curry paste—Cook for 30 seconds. Stir, add a tiny amount of coconut milk, and heat until the paste is fragrant.*

✓ *Stir in the spinach and season with salt and pepper. Add the remaining ingredients, except the cashews, and allow the sauce to decrease slightly.*

✓ *Maintain a creamy sauce but reduce it slightly to coat the spinach nicely. Serve with cashews that have been chopped.*

Nutrition: 3g net carbohydrates, 4g protein, 18g fat, 191kcal.

95) <u>Tasty Cauliflower Risotto</u>

Preparation Time: 20 minutes Required for Cooking: 1 hour 4 portions

- *4 cups raw cauliflower riced*
- *2 tbsp butter*
- *1/2 tsp kosher salt*
- *1/8 tsp black pepper*
- *1/4 tsp garlic powder*
- *1/3 cup mascarpone cheese*
- *2 tbsp. parmesan cheese*

Directions:

✓ *In a microwave-safe bowl, mix all ingredients except the cheeses and pesto and cook on high for 6-7 minutes, or until the cauliflower is soft.*

✓ *Stir in the mascarpone cheese and simmer for 2 minutes—season with salt and pepper.*

✓ *Stir in the parmesan cheese until well mixed into the risotto. To maintain the green hue, add the pesto immediately before serving. Serve immediately.*

Nutrition: 4g net carbohydrates, 6g protein, 21g fat, 225kcal Nutrition: Calories.

96) <u>Cauliflower Mash with Garlic and Chives</u>

Preparation Time: 20 minutes Required for Cooking: 1 hour 5 portions

Ingredients:

4 cups cauliflower

- *1/3 cup vegetarian mayonnaise*
- *1 garlic clove*
- *1/2 teaspoon kosher salt*
- *1 tbsp. water*
- *1/8 teaspoon pepper*
- *1/4 teaspoon lemon juice*
- *1/2 teaspoon lemon zest*

Directions:

✓ *In a microwave-safe bowl, combine the cauliflower, mayonnaise, garlic, water, and salt/pepper until the cauliflower is well covered. Cook for 15-18 minutes on high or until the cauliflower is nearly mushy.*

✓ *Using a strong blender, blend the ingredients until totally smooth, adding additional water if the liquid is too thick. Serve garnished with the remaining ingredients.*

Nutrition: 3g net carbohydrates, 2g protein, 18g fat, 178kcal Nutrition: Calories.

97) <u>Wilted Beet Greens with Feta and Pine Nuts</u>

Time Required for Preparation: 25 minutes Time Required for Cooking: 30 minutes 3 servings

Ingredients:

- *4 cups washed and roughly sliced beet tops*
- *1 tsp EVO olive oil*
- *1 tbsp. Unsweetened balsamic vinegar*
- *2 oz. Crumbled dry goat cheese*
- *2 tbsps. Toasted pine nuts*

Directions:

✓ *In a large skillet, heat the oil over medium-high heat and sauté the beet greens until they shed their liquid. Allow simmering until nearly soft. Remove from fire and season with salt and pepper.*

✓ *Toss the greens in balsamic vinegar and olive oil mixture, then sprinkle with nuts and cheese. Serve immediately.*

Nutrition: 5g net carbs, 10g protein, 18g fat, 215kcal.

98) <u>*Parmesan Eggplant*</u>

Time Required for Preparation: 1 hour and 20 minutes Time Required for Cooking: 30 minutes 4 portions

Ingredients:

- *1 large eggplant*
- *1/2 teaspoon salt*
- *1 large egg*
- *1 tbsp almond milk*
- *1/2 cup almond flour*
- *1/2 cup coconut flour*
- *1 tsp Italian seasoning*

Directions:

- ✓ *Prepare the eggplant by cutting it into 1/4" rounds. Sprinkle them with salt and set them aside for 45=60 minutes*
- ✓ *Set up a normal breading station: whisk the eggs in one dish and season with salt, place the parmesan cheese in another bowl, combine the flours and Italian seasoning in a separate bowl, and season with salt.*
- ✓ *Pat the eggplant slices dry and then dip them in the egg, followed by the cheese and finally the flour. Then, in a heavy-bottomed pot, heat the frying oil.*
- ✓ *When the oil is hot, add the eggplant slices and fry until both sides are golden brown. Turn the eggplant once a ring of golden brown appears at the bottom edge. Each side should cook for around 3-5 minutes.*
- ✓ *Pat dry with paper towels and season with salt to taste. Serve immediately.*

Nutrition: 7.3g net carbohydrates, 16.2g protein, 32g fat, 405kcal Nutrition: Calories.

99) <u>*Fresh Herbs and Roasted Radish*</u>

15 minutes for preparation Time Required for Cooking: 30 minutes 4 portions

- *one tablespoon coconut oil*
- *1 bunch of radishes*
- *2 tablespoons chopped chives*
- *1 tablespoon minced rosemary*
- *1 tablespoon minced thyme*

Direction

- ✓ *Rinse the radishes and cut off the tops and stems. Quarter them and set them aside.*
- ✓ *In a cast-iron skillet, heat the oil over medium heat. Season with salt and pepper and add the radishes. Simmer for 6-8*

minutes, or until almost cooked, then add the herbs and cook until the herbs are wilted.

- ✓ *Serve the radishes heated with meats or cold with salads.*

Nutritional information per serving: 8g net carbs, 9g protein, 13g fat, 133kcal Nutrition: Calories.

100) <u>*Bruschetta de Verano*</u>

15 minutes for preparation Time Required for Cooking: 30 minutes 4 portions

- *Six basil leaves (chopped) 12 artichoke hearts (quartered)*
- *14 cups Kalamata olives (halved)*
- *1/4 cup capers*
- *4 Roma tomatoes, diced*
- *3 tbsp balsamic vinegar*
- *3 tbsp avocado oil*
- *34 teaspoons onion powder*
- *34 teaspoons sea salt*
- *1/2 teaspoon s black pepper*
- *2 tbsp. minced garlic*

Directions:

- ✓ *In a slow cooker, mix all ingredients and stir well.*
- ✓ *Cook on high for 3 hours, stirring the mixture after each hour.*

Nutrition: 152 Nutrition: Calories, 13 grams total fat, 7.5 grams net carbs, and 1 gram protein.

101) <u>*Garlic Herbed Mushrooms*</u>

Time Required for Preparation: 10 minutes Time Required for Cooking: 3-4 hours 4 portions

- *24 oz. cremini mushrooms*
- *4 minced garlic cloves*
- *1/2 teaspoon dried basil*
- *1/2 teaspoon dried oregano*
- *1/4 teaspoon dried thyme*
- *2 bay leaves*
- *1 cup vegetable broth*
- *2 tbsp unsalted butter*
- *two tablespoons of fresh parsley leaves (chopped)*
- *Kosher salt and freshly ground black pepper, to taste*

Directions:

- ✓ *In a slow cooker, mix all ingredients except the butter, half & half, and fresh parsley.*

✓ *Cook covered on low heat for 3-4 hours.*

✓ *Add the butter and half-and-half 20 minutes before the cooking time expires.*

✓ *Serve garnished with parsley.*

Nutrition: 120 Nutrition: Calories, 8 g fat, 20 mg cholesterol, 450 mg sodium, 7 g net carbohydrate, 2 g fiber, 6 g protein

102) *Brussels Sprouts with a Cashew Dipping Sauce*

Time Required for Preparation: 20 minutes Time Required for Cooking: 15 minutes 10 portions

Ingredients:

- *2 tbsp extra-virgin olive oil*
- *1 pound Brussels sprouts (trimmed ends)*
- *1/4 teaspoon pepper*
- *1 cup Silk Cashew milk (unsweetened)*
- *1 chopped garlic clove 3 tablespoons lemon juice*
- *1 12 cups unsweetened cashew butter*
- *1/2 teaspoon s coarse sea salt*
- *2 tsp. black pepper*

Directions:

✓ *Toss the sprouts in a bowl with salt, pepper, and oil.*

✓ *Roast for 12-15 minutes at 400 degrees Fahrenheit in a preheated oven and set aside.*

✓ *Add all the cashew dip ingredients in a blender and blend until smooth.*

✓ *Arrange the sprouts alongside the dip.*

Nutrition: 221 Nutrition: Calories, 17 g total fat (3 g saturated fat), 0 mg cholesterol, 241 mg sodium, 19 g carbohydrate, 3 g fiber, 7.4 g protein.

103) *Spaghetti Squash Mash*

Time Required for Preparation: 5 minutes Time Required for Cooking: 1 hour 4 portions

Ingredients:

- *1 spaghetti squash (halved and seeds removed)*
- *2 tablespoons olive oil*
- *1 teaspoon garlic powder*
- *1 teaspoon dried rosemary*
- *1 teaspoon dried parsley*
- *1 teaspoon dried thyme*
- *1/2 teaspoon dried sage*
- *1 teaspoon salt*

- *1/2 teaspoon cracked pepper*

Directions:

✓ *Fill a baking pan halfway with water and set the squash halves cut side down in it.*

✓ *Roast for 45–60 minutes at 350 degrees Fahrenheit in a preheated oven.*

✓ *Remove from the heat, allow to cool somewhat, and then scoop out all of the meat.*

✓ *In a bowl, mix the squash and the remaining ingredients.*

✓ *Return to the oven and bake for an additional 15 minutes.*

Nutrition: 91 Nutrition: Calories, 7 g total fat, 5 g net carbohydrate, 5 g fiber, 3 g protein

104) *Avocado Hummus*

Time Required for Preparation: 10 minutes Time Required for Cooking: 30 minutes 4 portions

- *Zucchini (peeled and cubed) - 1*
- *Lemon (juice) – ½*
- *1 avocado (peeled, pitted, and diced)*
- *1/4 cup creamy roasted tahini (seasoned)*
- *1 tablespoon olive oil*
- *3 chopped garlic cloves 1 teaspoon cumin*
- *1 teaspoon sea salt*

Directions:

✓ *In a food processor, combine all of the ingredients.*

✓ *Process until completely smooth.*

✓ *Refrigerate for 3-4 hours before serving.*

Nutrition: 80 Nutrition: Calories, 7.2 g total fat, 4 g net carbs, and 2 g protein

105) *Roasted Broccoli*

Time Required for Preparation: 5 minutes Time Required for Cooking: 15 minutes 4 portions

Ingredients:

- *Broccoli (florets removed) - 2*
- *Extra-virgin olive oil – 1/4 cup*
- *2 chopped garlic cloves*
- *2 tablespoons lemon juice*
- *1/2 teaspoon salt*

Direction

✓ *Mix ingredients in a large mixing bowl and transfer to a baking dish.*

✓ *Roast for 12-15 minutes until crispy tender in a 450 degree Fahrenheit oven.*

179 Nutrition: Calories, 13 grams total fat (8.3 g sat. fat) Carbohydrates: 10.9 g, Fiber: 9 g, Protein: 3 g.

106) *Hummus with Avocado and Cauliflower*

Time Required for Preparation: 20 minutes Time Required for Cooking: 20 minutes 2 portions

- 1 medium cauliflower (stem removed and cut)
- 1 large Hass avocado (peeled, pitted, and chopped)
- large carrots (peeled and sliced into fries, or use store-bought raw carrot fries)
- optional: 14 cups fresh cilantro (chopped)

Direction

✓ Preheat the oven to 450 F/220 degrees Celsius and line a baking tray with aluminum foil.

✓ Dispose the cauliflower in a single layer on the baking dish and drizzle with 2 tablespoons olive oil.

✓ Roast the cauliflower, chopped, for 20-25 minutes, or until gently browned.

✓ Remove the tray from the oven and set it aside to cool the cauliflower.

✓ In a food processor or blender, combine all ingredients—except the carrots and optional fresh cilantro—and process until a smooth hummus forms.

✓ Move the hummus to a medium-sized bowl, cover, and chill for at least 30 minutes before serving.

✓ Remove the hummus from the refrigerator and, if preferred, garnish with chopped cilantro and additional salt and pepper to taste; serve alongside the carrot fries and enjoy!

✓ Alternatively, store it in the refrigerator in an airtight container for up to 2 days and consume it during that period.

Nutrition: 416 kcal 8.4 g Net Carbohydrates 40.3 g fat 3 g protein 10.3 g fiber 7.1 g sugar

107) *Rice with Peppers*

Time Required for Preparation: 10 minutes Time Required for Cooking: 25 minutes 4 portions

- 1 yellow bell pepper, chopped
- 1 red bell pepper, chopped
- 1 green bell pepper, chopped
- scallions, chopped

- 1 tablespoon olive oil
- 1 teaspoon coriander, powdered
- 1 teaspoon cumin, ground
- 1 teaspoon basil, dried
- 1 teaspoon oregano, dried
- 1 tablespoon chopped chives

Directions:

✓ Heat the oil in a medium-sized sauté pan over medium heat. Add the scallions and peppers and sauté for 5 minutes.

✓ Toss in the cauliflower rice and remaining ingredients; simmer for 20 minutes over medium heat; divide into plates, and serve as a side dish.

Nutrition: Calories 69 Fat 4 Fiber 3 Carbohydrates Protein 8.9 3

108) *Cauliflower and Chives Mash*

Time Required for Preparation: 10 minutes Time Required for Cooking: 20 minutes 4 portions

- 1 pound cauliflower florets
- 3 cups water
- 1 teaspoon dried thyme
- 1 teaspoon dried cumin
- 1 cup coconut cream
- 2 minced garlic cloves
- A teaspoon of salt and freshly ground black pepper

Directions:

✓ In a medium saucepan, combine the cauliflower florets, water, and all ingredients except the cream. Bring to a simmer and cook for 20 minutes over medium heat.

✓ Drain the cauliflower, add the cream, mash everything together with a potato masher, whisk until smooth, divide among plates, and serve.

Nutrition: Nutrition: Calories 200 Fat 17 Fiber 7.2 Carbohydrates 16.3 Protein 6.1

109) *Scallions of Orange with Brussels Sprouts*

Time Required for Preparation: 10 minutes Time Required for Cooking: 25 minutes 4 servings

Ingredients:

- 1 pound trimmed and halved Brussels sprouts
- 1 cup chopped scallions

- *1 tbsp grated lime zest*
- *1 tbsp olive oil*
- *1/4 tbsp orange juice*
- *2 tbsp. stevia*

Direction

✓ *Heat the oil in a medium saucepan over medium heat. Add the scallions and sauté for 5 minutes.*

✓ *Toss in the sprouts and remaining ingredients; simmer for an additional 20 minutes over medium heat; divide the mixture amongst plates and serve.*

Nutrition: Calories 193 Fat 4 Fiber 1 Carbohydrates 8 Protein 10 72

110) *Roasted Artichokes with a Creamy Sauce*

Time Required for Preparation: 10 minutes Time Required for Cooking: 30 minutes 4 portions

- *trimmed and halved large artichokes*
- *tablespoons avocado oil*
- *lime juice*
- *teaspoon turmeric powder*
- *1 cup coconut cream*
- *a sprinkle of salt and black pepper*
- *1/2 teaspoons onion powder*
- *1/4 tsp sweet paprika*
- *1 tsp ground cumin*

Directions:

✓ *In a roasting pan, combine the artichokes, oil, lime juice, and remaining ingredients; toss and bake for 30 minutes at 390 degrees F.*

✓ *Distribute the artichokes and sauce among serving plates.*

Nutrition: Nutrition: Calories 190 Fat 6 Fiber 8 Carbohydrates 10 Protein 9 7

111) *Risotto di Zucchini*

Time Required for Preparation: 10 minutes Time Required for Cooking: 30 minutes 4 portions

- *1/2 cup chopped shallots*
- *4 tablespoons olive oil*
- *4 minced garlic cloves*
- *6 cups cauliflower rice*
- *6 cups cubed zucchini*
- *6 cups veggie stock*
- *1/2 cup chopped white mushrooms*

- *1/2 teaspoon ground coriander*
- *A pinch of salt and black pepper*
- *1/4 teaspoon dried oregano*
- *4 tablespoons chopped parsley*

Direction

✓ *Heat the oil in a large sauté pan over medium heat. Add the shallots, garlic, mushrooms, coriander, oregano, and sauté for 10 minutes, stirring occasionally.*

✓ *Toss in the cauliflower rice and remaining ingredients, cook for a further 20 minutes, divide across plates, and serve.*

Nutrition: Calories 231 fat 5 fiber 3 carbohydrates 9 protein 1

112) *Cauliflower with Rice*

Time Required for Preparation: 10 minutes Time Required for Cooking: 30 minutes 4 portions

- *1 cup shredded green cabbage*
- *2 tablespoons olive oil*
- *2 tablespoons tomato passata*
- *spring onions, diced*
- *2 teaspoons balsamic vinegar*
- *pinch of salt and black pepper*
- *2 teaspoons crushed fennel seeds*
- *1 teaspoon ground coriander*

Directions:

✓ *Heat the oil in a medium saucepan over medium heat. Add the spring onions, fennel, and coriander and simmer, occasionally stirring, for 5 minutes.*

✓ *Toss in the cabbage, cauliflower rice, and remaining ingredients; simmer for an additional 25 minutes over medium heat; divide amongst plates and serve.*

Nutrition: Calories 200 fat 4 1 carbohydrate 8 protein 7

113) *Tomato Risotto*

Time Required to Prepare: 10 minutes Time Required for Cooking: 30 minutes 4 portions

- *1 cup chopped shallots*
- *1 cup cauliflower rice*
- *3 tablespoons olive oil*
- *1 cup smashed tomatoes*
- *1/4 cup chopped cilantro*
- *1/2 teaspoon chili powder*
- *1 teaspoon ground cumin*

- *1 teaspoon ground coriander*

Direction

✓ *Heat the oil in a medium saucepan over medium heat. Add the shallots and sauté for 5 minutes.*

✓ *Toss in the cauliflower rice, tomatoes, and remaining ingredients; simmer for an additional 25 minutes over medium heat; divide amongst plates and serve.*

Nutrition: Calories 200 Fat 4 Fiber 3 Carbohydrates 6 Protein 8

114) *Risotto with Herbs*

Preparation Time: 10 minutes Time Required for Cooking: 25 minutes 4 portions

Ingredients:

- *1 cup cauliflower rice*
- *1 tablespoon scallions, chopped*
- *1 tablespoon avocado oil*
- *1 cup vegetable stock*
- *1 lime juice*
- *1 tablespoon parsley, chopped*
- *1 tablespoon cilantro, chopped*
- *1 tablespoon basil, chopped*
- *1 tablespoon oregano, chopped*
- *A teaspoon of salt and freshly ground black pepper*

Directions:

✓ *Heat the oil in a medium saucepan over medium heat. Add the scallions and cook for 5 minutes.*

✓ *Toss in the cauliflower rice, stock, and remaining ingredients; simmer for 20 minutes over medium heat; divide into plates and serve as a side dish.*

Nutrition: Calories 182 calorie fat 4 calorie fiber 2 calorie carbohydrate 8 calorie protein 10

115) *Broccoli and Radish*

Time Required for Preparation: 10 minutes Time Required for Cooking: 30 minutes 4 servings

Ingredients:

- *1 pound broccoli florets*
- *2 tablespoons olive oil*
- *chopped scallions*
- *12 pounds halved radishes*
- *minced garlic cloves*
- *tsp ground cumin*
- *4 tbsp tomato passata*

- *1/2 tbsp vegetable stock*
- *A dash of salt and freshly ground black pepper*

Directions:

✓ *Heat the oil in a medium saucepan over medium heat. Add the scallions and cook for 5 minutes.*

✓ *Toss in the broccoli, radishes, and remaining ingredients; simmer for an additional 25 minutes over medium heat; divide amongst plates and serve.*

Nutrition: Calories 261 fat 5 fiber 4 carbohydrate 9 protein 12

116) *Mushrooms and Radishes Incorporated*

Time Required for Preparation: 10 minutes Time Required for Cooking: 25 minutes 4 portions

- *1 pound halved white mushrooms*
- *1/2 pounds halved radishes*
- *1/2 scallions, chopped*
- *1 garlic cloves, minced*
- *2 tablespoons olive oil*
- *1/2 cup veggie stock*
- *2 tablespoons parsley, chopped*
- *1 teaspoon crushed coriander*
- *1 teaspoon dried rosemary*

Direction

✓ *Heat the oil in a medium saucepan over medium heat. Add the scallions, garlic, coriander, and rosemary and simmer, occasionally stirring, for 5 minutes.*

✓ *Toss in the mushrooms, radishes, and remaining ingredients; simmer for 20 minutes over medium heat; divide amongst plates and serve as a side dish.*

Nutrition: Nutrition: Calories 182 Fat 4 Fiber 2 Carbohydrates 6 Protein 8

117) *Summertime Chicken Wraps with Vegetables*

15 minutes for preparation Time Required for Cooking: 0 minutes 4 portions

- *2 cups cooked chicken, chopped*
- *1/2 English cucumbers, diced*
- *1/2 red bell pepper, diced*
- *1/2 cup carrot, shredded*
- *1 tablespoon freshly squeezed lemon juice*
- *1/2 teaspoons chopped fresh thyme*

- *pinch salt*
- *pinch crushed black pepper*

Directions:

✓ *Combine chicken, red bell pepper, cucumber, carrot, yogurt, scallion, lemon juice, thyme, sea salt, and pepper in a medium bowl.*

✓ *Combine thoroughly.*

✓ *Spoon a quarter of the chicken mixture into the center of the tortilla and fold the tortilla's opposing sides over the contents.*

✓ *From the side, roll the tortilla to make a snug pocket.*

✓ *Continue with the remainder of the ingredients and serve.*

✓ *Enjoy!*

Nutrition: 278 Nutrition: Calories 4g fat 28g Carbohydrates 27g protein

118) *Baby Potatoes Roasted to Perfection*

Time Required for Preparation: 10 Minutes to Cook: 35 minutes

- *2 pounds young yellow potatoes, cleaned and cut into wedges*
- *2 tbsp extra virgin olive oil*
- *2 tbsp fresh rosemary, chopped*
- *1 tsp paprika dulce*
- *1/2 tsp sea salt*
- *1/2 tsp freshly crushed black pepper*

Directions:

✓ *Preheat the oven to 400°F.*

✓ *Prepare a baking sheet by lining it with aluminum foil and setting it aside.*

✓ *Combine potatoes, olive oil, garlic, rosemary, paprika, sea salt, and freshly ground pepper in a large mixing bowl.*

✓ *Arrange potatoes on a baking sheet in a single layer and bake for 35 minutes.*

✓ *Distribute and enjoy!*

Nutrition: 225 Calories 7g fat 37g Carbohydrates 5 g protein

119) *Linguine Pasta with Feta Cheese and Cherry Tomatoes*

Time Required for Preparation: 10 minutes Time Required for Cooking: 15 minutes 4 portions

Ingredients:

- *2-pound cherry tomatoes*

- *3 tbsp extra virgin olive oil*
- *2 tbsp balsamic vinegar*
- *2 tsp minced garlic*
- *1 pinch freshly ground black pepper*
- *34-pound whole-wheat linguine pasta*
- *1 tablespoon minced fresh oregano*
- *1/4 cup crumbled feta cheese*

Directions:

✓ *Preheat the oven to 350°F.*

✓ *Prepare a baking sheet by lining it with parchment paper and setting it aside.*

✓ *Toss cherry tomatoes, 2 tablespoons olive oil, balsamic vinegar, garlic, and pepper in a large bowl.*

✓ *Evenly distribute tomatoes on a baking sheet and roast for 15 minutes.*

✓ *Cook the pasta according to the package directions and strain the paste into a wide basin while the tomatoes roast.*

✓ *Combine pasta and 1 tablespoon olive oil in a large mixing bowl.*

✓ *Toss in roasted tomatoes (with juice).*

✓ *Garnish with oregano and feta cheese.*

✓ *Enjoy!*

Nutrition: 397 Nutrition: Calories 15g fat 55g carbohydrates 13g protein

120) *Mediterranean Zucchini Mushroom Pasta*

10 minutes to prepare Time Required for Cooking: 10 minutes 4 servings

- *12-pound pasta*
- *2 tablespoons olive oil*
- *6 crushed garlic cloves*
- *1 teaspoon red chili powder*
- *2 sliced spring onions*
- *3 teaspoons chopped rosemary*
- *1 large zucchini, cut in half lengthwise, and sliced*
- *5 large portabella mushrooms*
- *1 can tomatoes*
- *4 tablespoons Parmesan cheese*
- *Fresh ground black pepper*

Directions:

✓ *Cook the pasta until al dente in boiling water.*

✓ *Preheat a large frying pan over medium*

heat.

✓ Add oil and let it come to a boil.

✓ Sauté the garlic, onion, and chili for a few minutes, or until golden.

✓ Cook for a few minutes before adding the zucchini, rosemary, and mushroom.

✓ Increase the heat to medium-high and whisk in the tinned tomatoes until smooth.

✓ Transfer drained pasta to a serving plate.

✓ Spoon the tomato mixture over the top and toss with tongs.

✓ Sprinkle with Parmesan cheese and freshly ground black pepper.

✓ 10. Enjoy!

Nutrition: 361 Calories 12g fat 47g Carbohydrates 14g protein

121) *Fettucine with Lemon and Garlic*

Time Required for Preparation: 5 minutes Time Required for Cooking: 15 minutes 5 portions

Ingredients:

- 8 ounces whole-wheat fettuccine
- 4 tablespoons extra virgin olive oil
- 4 minced garlic cloves
- 1 cup fresh breadcrumbs
- 1/4 cup lemon juice
- 1 teaspoon freshly ground pepper
- 1/2 teaspoon salt
- 2 cans 4 ounce boneless and skinless sardines (dipped in tomato sauce)

Direction

✓ Bring a big saucepan of water to a boil.

✓ Cook pasta in boiling salted water for 10 minutes or al dente.

✓ Heat a small skillet over medium heat.

✓ Add 2 tbsp. Oil and allow to heat.

✓ Cook for 20 seconds before adding the garlic.

✓ Place the garlic in a medium-sized mixing bowl.

✓ Cook breadcrumbs in a heated skillet for 5-6 minutes or until they become brown.

✓ In the garlic bowl, whisk in the lemon juice, pepper, and salt.

✓ To the bowl, add the pasta (garlic), sardines, parsley, and Parmesan.

✓ 10. Combine thoroughly and sprinkle with

bread crumbs

✓ 1 Enjoy!

Nutrition: 480 Nutrition: Calories 21g fat 53g Carbohydrates 23g protein

122) *Broccoli Roasted with Parmesan*

Time Required for Preparation: 10 minutes Time Required for Cooking: 10 minutes 4 portions

- two head broccoli, chopped into florets
- 2 tablespoons extra-virgin olive oil
- 2 teaspoons minced garlic
- 1 lemon zest
- pinch of salt
- 1/2 cup grated Parmesan cheese

Direction

✓ Preheat the oven to 400 degrees Fahrenheit.

✓ Grease a baking sheet lightly with olive oil and set it aside.

✓ In a large mixing bowl, combine broccoli, 2 tbsp olive oil, lemon zest, garlic, lemon juice, and salt.

✓ Spread the mixture in a single layer on the baking sheet and sprinkle with Parmesan cheese.

✓ Bake for 10 minutes or until the vegetables are soft.

✓ Arrange broccoli in a serving dish.

✓ Finally, serve and enjoy!

Nutrition: 154 Calories 11g fat 10g Carbohydrates 9g protein

123) *Spinach and Feta Bread*

Preparation Time: 10 minutes Time Required for Cooking: 12 minutes 6 portions

- 6 ounces sun-dried tomato pesto
- 6-inch whole-wheat pita bread
- 2 chopped Roma plum tomatoes
- 1 bunch rinsed and chopped spinach
- 4 sliced fresh mushrooms
- 1/2 cups crumbled feta cheese
- 2 teaspoons grated Parmesan cheese
- 3 tablespoons olive oil

Directions:

✓ Preheat the oven to 350 degrees Fahrenheit.

✓ Spread tomato pesto on one side of the pita bread and arrange it on a baking sheet *(with the pesto side up).*

✓ *Pile spinach, tomatoes, feta cheese, mushrooms, and Parmesan cheese on top of the pitas.*

✓ *Sprinkle with olive oil and season with freshly ground pepper.*

✓ *Bake for approximately 12 minutes or until the bread is crispy.*

✓ *Quarter the pita and serve!*

Nutrition: 350 Calories 17g fat 41g Carbohydrates Protein:11g

124) *Quick Zucchini Bowl*

Time Required for Preparation: 10 minutes Time Required for Cooking: 10 minutes 4 portions

Ingredients:

- *1/2-pound pasta*
- *2 tablespoons olive oil*
- *6 smashed garlic cloves*
- *1 teaspoon red chili powder*
- *2 finely sliced spring onions*
- *3 teaspoons chopped rosemary*
- *1 large zucchini cut in half lengthwise and sliced*
- *5 large portabella mushrooms*
- *1 container tomatoes*

Directions:

✓ *Cook the pasta until al dente in boiling water.*

✓ *Preheat a large frying pan over medium heat.*

✓ *Add oil and let it come to a boil.*

✓ *Sauté the garlic, onion, and chili for a few minutes, or until golden.*

✓ *Cook for a few minutes before adding the zucchini, rosemary, and mushroom.*

✓ *Increase the heat to medium-high and whisk in the tinned tomatoes until smooth.*

✓ *Transfer the drained pasta to a serving plate.*

✓ *Spoon the tomato mixture over the top and toss with tongs.*

✓ *Sprinkle Parmesan cheese and freshly ground black pepper.*

✓ *10. Enjoy!*

Nutrition: 361 Calories 12g fat 47g Carbohydrates 14g protein

125) *Healthy Basil Platter*

Time Required for Preparation: 25 minutes Time Required for Cooking: 15 minutes 4 portions

Ingredients:

- *2 red peppers, seeded and cut into chunks*
- *2 red onions, cut into wedges*
- *2 mild red chilies, diced and seeded*
- *3 coarsely chopped garlic cloves*
- *1 teaspoon golden caster sugar*
- *2 tablespoons olive oil (plus more for serving)*
- *2 pounds small ripe tomatoes, quartered*

Directions:

✓ *Preheat the oven to 392°F.*

✓ *Arrange pepper, red onion, garlic, and chilies in a large roasting tray.*

✓ *Scatter sugar on top.*

✓ *Drizzle with olive oil and season with salt and pepper.*

✓ *Roast the vegetables for 15 minutes in the oven.*

✓ *In a large saucepan, cook the pasta until al dente in boiling, salted water.*

✓ *Empty them.*

✓ *Remove the vegetables from the oven and mix them with the pasta.*

✓ *Toss thoroughly and sprinkle with basil leaves.*

✓ *10. Garnish with Parmesan and serve!*

Nutrition: 452 Calories 8g fat 88g Carbohydrates Protein: 14g

126) *Herbed Up Bruschetta*

Time Required for Preparation: 12 minutes 0 minute cooking time 12 portions

- *16 thinly sliced toasted French bread*
- *2 cups quartered cherry tomatoes*
- *1 roughly chopped medium-sized white onion*
- *As desired, freshly ground black pepper*
- *Fresh sweet basil*
- *For the dressing*
- *1/4 cups olive oil*
- *2 tbsp balsamic vinegar*
- *1 tbsp lemon juice*
- *1 tbsp Dijon mustard*
- *2 tbsp chopped fresh herbs*

- *1 tbsp minced garlic*

Directions:

- ✓ *In a medium-sized bowl, whisk together the olive oil, lemon juice, balsamic vinegar, Dijon mustard, garlic, and mixed herbs.*
- ✓ *Combine the onion and cherry tomatoes in a medium bowl.*
- ✓ *Toss lightly to coat.*
- ✓ *Season with pepper and salt to taste.*
- ✓ *Spread the tomato mixture on top of each bread toast.*
- ✓ *Drizzle with additional dressing if desired.*
- ✓ *Garnish with fresh basil leaves.*
- ✓ *Serve.*

Nutrition: 118 Calories 4g fat 18g Carbohydrates 4 g protein

127) *Homemade Almond Biscotti*

Time Required for Preparation: 10 minutes Time Required for Cooking: 35 minutes 30 portions

- *2/3 cup unsalted butter*
- *3/4 cup and 2 tablespoons granulated sugar*
- *1 teaspoon crushed anise seed*
- *2 whole eggs*
- *2 tablespoons amaretto liqueur*
- *1 teaspoon vanilla extract*
- *2 1/4 cup all-purpose flour*
- *1 teaspoon baking powder*
- *1 teaspoon baking soda*
- *1/2 teaspoon salt*
- *3/4 cup roasted almonds, diced*

Direction

- ✓ *Preheat the oven to 325 degrees Fahrenheit.*
- ✓ *Preheat the oven to 350°F. Line a cookie sheet with parchment paper.*
- ✓ *Cream your butter with an electric mixer.*
- ✓ *Add the sugar progressively and continue mixing until light and fluffy.*
- ✓ *Stir in the aniseed.*
- ✓ *Add the eggs one at a time, mixing well between additions.*
- ✓ *Combine the amaretto liqueur and vanilla essence in a mixing bowl.*
- ✓ *Add the flour, baking soda, and baking powder in a slow, steady stream.*
- ✓ *Gently fold in the almonds.*

- ✓ *10. Using floured dusted hands, divide the dough in half and shape each half into a rough 12 x 2 and a 12-inch log.*
- ✓ *1 Bake the logs for 25 minutes, or until they have a delicate golden-brown texture.*
- ✓ *1 Place those on a wire rack to cool.*
- ✓ *1 Cut your logs diagonally into 12-inch broad pieces using a serrated knife.*
- ✓ *1 Arrange them in a single layer on your baking sheet.*
- ✓ *1 Place them back in the oven and bake for an additional 7 minutes, or until the sides are browned.*
- ✓ *1 Serve.*

Nutrition: 111 Calories 6 g fat 13g Carbohydrates 2 g protein

128) *Garlic Lemon Beans, green*

Time Required for Preparation: 5 minutes Time Required for Cooking: 10 minutes 6 portions

Ingredients:

- *12 pounds trimmed green beans*
- *2 tablespoons olive oil*
- *1 teaspoon fresh lemon juice*
- *2 minced garlic cloves*

Directions:

- ✓ *Prepare a large bowl of ice water by filling it halfway with water.*
- ✓ *Bring a kettle of salted water to a boil, add the green beans, and cook for 2 minutes.*
- ✓ *Cook for 3 minutes and immediately drain and immerse in icy water.*
- ✓ *Allow the beans to cool completely before draining thoroughly.*
- ✓ *Heat the oil in a large pan over medium-high heat.*
- ✓ *Toss in the green beans, followed by lemon juice, garlic, salt, and pepper.*
- ✓ *Cook for 3 minutes, or until the beans are tender-crisp, and serve immediately.*

Nutrition: 75 Calories 8g Total Fat 0.7g Saturated Fat 8.5g Total Carbohydrates 8.5g Net Carbs Protein: 6g 1 g sugar 7 g dietary fiber 9g

129) *Salad of Brown Rice and Lentils*

Time Required for Preparation: 10 minutes Time Required for Cooking: 10 minutes 4 portions

- *1 cup water*
- *1/2 cup instant brown rice*

- 2 tablespoons olive oil
- 2 tablespoons red wine vinegar
- 1 tablespoon Dijon mustard
- 1 tablespoon minced onion
- 1/2 teaspoon paprika
- Salt and pepper
- 1 (15-ounce) can brown lentils, rinsed and drained

Directions:

✓ Combine the water and instant brown rice in a medium saucepan.

✓ Bring to a boil and then reduce to low heat and cover for 10 minutes.

✓ Take the pan from the heat and set it aside to cool while preparing the salad.

✓ In a medium bowl, whisk together the olive oil, vinegar, Dijon mustard, onion, paprika, salt, and pepper.

✓ Combine the cooked rice, lentils, carrots, and parsley in a large mixing bowl.

✓ Season with salt and pepper, then whisk thoroughly and serve warm.

Nutrition: Calories 1455 8g Total Fat 0.7g Saturated Fat 8.5g Carbohydrates 8.5g Net Carbohydrates 6g Protein 1g Carbohydrates 7g Fiber 9g Sodium 75mg

130) *Mashed Butternut Squash*

Time Required for Preparation: 5 minutes Time Required for Cooking: 25 minutes 6 portions

- 3 pounds whole butternut squash (about 2 medium)
- 2 teaspoons olive oil

Directions:

✓ Preheat the oven to 400 degrees Fahrenheit and line a baking sheet with parchment paper.

✓ Cut the squash in half and remove the seeds.

✓ Cube the squash and stir with the oil before spreading it on the baking sheet.

✓ Roast for 25 minutes, or until soft, before transferring to a food processor.

✓ Puree until smooth and season to taste with salt and pepper.

Nutrition: Calories 90 8g Total Fat 0.7g Saturated Fat 8.5g Carbohydrates 8.5g Net Carbohydrates 6g Protein 1g Carbohydrates 7g Fiber 9g Sodium 4mg

131) *Quinoa with Cilantro and Lime*

Preparation Time: 5 minutes Time Required for Cooking: 25 minutes 6 portions

- 1 cup uncooked quinoa
- 1 teaspoon olive oil
- 1 medium yellow onion, diced
- 2 garlic cloves minced
- 1 (4-ounce) can diced green chilis, drained
- Season with salt and pepper

Directions:

✓ Thoroughly rinse the quinoa in cool water using a fine mesh screen.

✓ Heat the oil In a large pan over medium heat.

✓ Add the onion and sauté for 2 minutes, then add the chili and garlic and stir to combine.

✓ Cook for 1 minute, then combine the quinoa and chicken broth.

✓ Bring to a boil, then reduce to low heat and cover and simmer for about 20 to 25 minutes, or until the quinoa absorbs the liquid.

✓ Take the pan off the heat and add the cilantro, green onions, and lime juice.

✓ Season to taste with salt and pepper and serve immediately.

Nutrition: 150 Nutrition: Calories 8g Total Fat 0.7g Saturated Fat 8.5g Total Carbohydrates 8.5g Net Carbohydrates Protein: 6g 1g Sucrose 7 grams fiber 9g 179mg sodium

132) *Veggies Roasted in the Oven*

Time Required for Preparation: 5 minutes Time Required for Cooking: 25 minutes 6 portions

- 1 pound cauliflower florets
- 1/2 pound broccoli florets
- 1 large yellow onion, cut into bits
- 1 large red pepper, cored and diced
- 2 medium carrots, peeled and sliced

Directions:

✓ Preheat the oven to 425 F, line a large rimmed baking sheet with parchment paper.

✓ Arrange the vegetables in a single layer on the baking sheet and sprinkle them with oil and vinegar.

✓ Season with salt and pepper and toss well.

✓ Arrange the vegetables in a single layer on the prepared baking sheet and roast for 20 to 25 minutes, stirring every 10 minutes, until soft.

✓ Season to taste and serve immediately.

Nutrition: Calories 100 Total Carbohydrates 8.5g Net Carbohydrates 6g Protein 1g Sugar 7g Fiber 9g

133) <u>*Rice Pilaf with Vegetables*</u>

Time Required for Preparation: 5 minutes Time Required for Cooking: 25 minutes 6 portions

Ingredients:

- *1 tablespoon olive oil*
- *12 medium yellow onions, chopped*
- *1 cup uncooked long-grain brown rice*
- *2 garlic cloves minced*
- *1/2 teaspoon dried basil*
- *Salt and pepper*

Directions:

- ✓ *In a large skillet over medium heat, heat the oil.*
- ✓ *Add the onion and cook, occasionally stirring, for 3 minutes, or transparent.*
- ✓ *Add the rice and cook, occasionally stirring, until gently toasted.*
- ✓ *Stir in the garlic, basil, salt, and pepper.*
- ✓ *Add the chicken broth and return to a boil.*
- ✓ *Reduce to low heat and cover for 10 minutes.*
- ✓ *Stir in the frozen vegetables and simmer, covered, for an additional 10 minutes, or until heated through. Serve immediately.*

Nutrition: Calories 75 Total Carbohydrates 8.5g Net Carbohydrates 6g Protein 1g Sugar 7g Fiber 9g Sodium 7mg

134) <u>*Roasted Cauliflower Florets in Curry*</u>

Time Required for Preparation: 5 minutes Time Required for Cooking: 25 minutes 6 portions

- *8 cups cauliflower florets*
- *2 tbsp olive oil*
- *1 tbsp curry powder*
- *1/2 tbsp garlic powder*
- *Season with salt and pepper*

Directions:

- ✓ *Preheat the oven to 425°F and line a baking sheet with foil.*
- ✓ *Coat the cauliflower in olive oil and spread it out on the baking pan.*
- ✓ *Add curry powder, garlic powder, salt, and pepper to taste.*
- ✓ *Roast for 25 minutes or until the vegetables are barely soft. Serve immediately.*

Nutrition: 75 Calories 8g Total Fat 0.7g Saturated Fat 8.5g Total Carbohydrates 8.5g Net Carbohydrates Protein: 6g 1 g Sucrose 7 g Fiber 40mg Sodium 9g

135) <u>*Risotto with Mushrooms and Barley*</u>

Preparation Time: 5 minutes Time Required for Cooking: 25 minutes 8 portions

- *4 cups fat-free beef broth*
- *2 tablespoons olive oil*
- *1 small onion, finely chopped*
- *2 garlic cloves minced*
- *8 ounces thinly sliced mushrooms*
- *1/4 tsp dried thyme*
- *Salt and pepper*
- *1 cup pearled barley*

Directions:

- ✓ *In a medium saucepan, heat the beef broth and keep it warm.*
- ✓ *In a big, deep skillet, heat the oil over medium heat.*
- ✓ *Sauté the onions and garlic for 2 minutes before stirring in the mushrooms and thyme.*
- ✓ *Season with salt and pepper and sauté for 2 minutes.*
- ✓ *Stir in the barley and cook for 1 minute before adding the wine.*
- ✓ *Carefully ladle approximately 12 cups of beef broth into the skillet and stir to mix.*
- ✓ *Cook until the broth has been absorbed in its entirety, then add another ladle.*
- ✓ *Continue until all of the liquid has been used and the barley is al dente.*
- ✓ *Season with salt and pepper to taste and serve immediately.*

Nutrition: Calories 1555 8g Total Fat 0.7g Saturated Fat 8.5g Carbohydrates Net 6g Protein 1 g sugar 7 g dietary fiber 9g 445mg sodium

136) <u>*Smoothie with Peaches and Cream*</u>

Time required for preparation: 5 minutes Time Required for Cooking: 0 minutes 1 portion

- *1 cup frozen peach slices*
- *1 cup Greek yogurt*
- *1/4 cup oats*
- *1/4 teaspoon vanilla extract*
- *1 cup almond milk*

Directions:

- ✓ *In a blender, combine all ingredients and blend until smooth.*

Nutrition: Cal: 331 fat 46 g carbs 29g

137) *Jicama & Ham Hash*

15 Minutes Cooking Servings4

- 6 beaten eggs
- 2 cups shredded jicama
- 1 cup grated low-fat cheddar cheese
- 1 cup diced ham
- What you'll need from your pantry:
- Salt and pepper to taste

Directions:

✓ Preheat a large nonstick skillet over medium-high heat and spray with cooking spray. Cook, occasionally stirring, until the jicama begins to brown, about 5 minutes.

✓ Reduce heat to medium-low and add remaining ingredients. Cook for approximately 3 minutes, then flip over and cook for an additional 3-5 minutes, or until eggs are set. Serve with salt & pepper.

Nutrition: Calories 221 Carbs 8g Carbohydrates Net 5g Protein 21g Fat 11g Sugar 2 g Fiber 3g

138) *Breakfast in Italy 8 Baked Servings*

Time Required for Cooking: 1 Hour

- 1 yellow onion, chopped
- 8 eggs
- 2 cups half-and-half
- 2 cups reduced-fat cheddar cheese, grated
- 1/4 cup fresh parsley, diced
- What you'll need from your pantry:
- 1/2 loaf bread cubed
- 1 teaspoon salt
- 1/4 teaspoon pepper
- 1/4 teaspoon red pepper flakes
- Cooking spray with non-stick properties

Directions:

✓ Cooking spray a 9x13-inch baking dish.

✓ In a pan over medium heat, melt 1 tablespoon butter. Cook, breaking up the sausage with a spatula until no longer pink. Transfer the mixture to a large bowl.

✓ Cook the remaining tablespoon butter in the skillet with the onion for 3-5 minutes, or until tender. Combine the cheese and bread cubes with the sausage.

✓ Whisk together eggs, half-n-half, and seasonings in a separate bowl. Pour over the sausage mixture and toss to combine.

Fill prepared baking dish halfway with batter, cover, and chill for 2 hours or overnight.

✓ Preheat the oven to 350 degrees Fahrenheit. Bake for 50-60 minutes, or until a knife inserted in the center comes out clean. Garnish with parsley and serve immediately.

Nutrition: 300 Nutrition: Calories Total Carbohydrates 6g Net Carbohydrates 5g Protein 22g Fatty Acids 20g Sucrose 4g Fiber 1g

139) *Incorrect Quente*

4 portions Time Required for Cooking: 10 Minutes

- 4 slices unwrapped bread
- 4 slices turkey breast
- 4 slices cheese
- 2 tbsp cream cheese
- 2 tsp butter

Direction

✓ Preheat the air fryer. Set a 5-minute timer and a temperature of 200C.

✓ Spread butter on one side of the bread slice and cream cheese on the other.

✓ Assemble the sandwiches by sandwiching two slices of turkey breast and two pieces of cheese between the slices of bread, cream cheese on the inside, and butter on the outside.

✓ Arrange the sandwiches in the air fryer's basket. Set the timer for 5 minutes on the air fryer and push the power button.

Nutrition: 340 Nutrition: Calories 15g fat 32g Carbohydrates 15 g protein 0g sugar 0mg cholesterol

140) *Bread with Zucchini*

8 portions Time Required for Cooking: 40 Minutes

- 3/4 cup shredded zucchini
- 1/2 cup almond flour
- 1/4 teaspoon salt
- 1/4 cup unsweetened cocoa powder
- 1/2 cup unsweetened chocolate chips, divided
- 6 tablespoons erythritol sweetener
- 1/2 teaspoon baking soda
- 2 tablespoons olive oil
- 1/2 teaspoon unsweetened vanilla extract
- 2 tablespoons unsalted butter, melted

Directions:

✓ Turn on the air fryer, insert the fryer basket, coat it with olive oil, cover it with the lid, and preheat for 10 minutes at 310 degrees F.

✓ In the meantime, combine flour, salt, cocoa powder, and baking soda in a mixing dish.

✓ In a separate dish, crack the eggs and whisk in the sweetener, egg, oil, butter, and vanilla extract until smooth.

✓ Fold in zucchini and 1/3 cup chocolate chips until just combined.

✓ Grease a mini loaf pan large enough to fit inside the air fryer with olive oil, then pour in the prepared batter and sprinkle with the remaining chocolate chips.

✓ Preheat the fryer to 310 degrees F. Place the loaf pan in the fryer and cover with the lid. Cook for 30 minutes, or until a toothpick inserted into the bread comes out clean.

✓ When the air fryer whistles, remove the loaf pan and set it on a wire rack to cool for 20 minutes.

✓ Remove the bread from the oven and cool completely before cutting it into slices and serving.

Nutrition: 356 Nutrition: Calories Carbohydrates: 2 g 10 g fat 8 g protein 5 g fiber

141) **Grits & Poached Eggs**

4 Servings 10 Minutes to Cook

• 4 poached eggs
• 3 cups skim milk
• 1/4 cup grated Colby cheese What you'll require from your pantry:
• 1 cup grits
• 2 tsp grated reduced-fat parmesan cheese

Directions:

✓ In a large microwave-safe bowl, combine the grits and most of the milk, reserving a small amount to stir in afterward. Cook for 8-10 minutes, stirring occasionally.

✓ Poach the eggs in a large pot of boiling water in the meantime.

✓ When the grits are done, add the cheese and stir until smooth and melted. Add the remaining milk if they appear too stiff.

✓ Ladle into four dishes and garnish each with a poached egg.

Nutrition: Calories 180 Carbohydrates Total 15g Carbohydrates Net Protein: 14 g 13 g Fat 6 g Sucrose

ten grams fiber 1 g

142) **French toast stuffed**

1 portion Time Required for Cooking: 10 Minutes

• 1 slice brioche bread, 64 mm thick, preferably rotten
• 113g cream cheese
• 2 eggs
• 15 ml milk
• 30 ml whipped cream
• 38g sugar
• 3g cinnamon
• 2 ml vanilla extract
• Nonstick Spray Oil
• Pistachios sliced to cover

Direction

✓ Preheat the air fryer to 175°C.
✓ Make a slit down the center of the muffin.
✓ Stuff the slit with cream cheese. Set aside.
✓ In a separate bowl, whisk together the eggs, milk, whipping cream, sugar, cinnamon, and vanilla extract.
✓ Soak the stuffed French toast for 10 seconds on each side in the egg mixture.
✓ Lightly coat both sides of the French toast with oil spray.
✓ Cook the French toast for 10 minutes at 175°C in the preheated air fryer.
✓ When the French toast is finished cooking, carefully stir it with a spatula.

Nutrition: Calories: 1597.5g fat 22g Carbohydrates 14g protein 0g sugar Cholesterol: 90mg

143) **Smoothies for the Sunrise**

3 portions Time Required for Cooking: 10 Minutes

• 1 frozen and sliced banana
• 3/4 cup ruby red grapefruit juice
• 1/2 cup cubed fresh pineapple
• 1/2 cup unsweetened peach segments
• What you'll require from your pantry:
• 1 tbsp.
• 4 ice cubes Splenda

Directions:

✓ In a blender, combine all ingredients. Process until completely smooth. Serve in cold glasses.

Nutrition: 97 Nutrition: Calories Total Carbohydrates 24g Net Carbohydrates 22g Protein 1

gram fat 0 gram sugar 18 gram fiber 2g

144) *Crepes de Framboise et de Ricotta*

4 portions 15 Minutes Cooking

- *8 eggs*
- *1 cup sliced strawberries*
- *1 cup low-fat ricotta cheese*
- *What you'll need from your pantry:*
- *2 tsp Splenda*
- *2 tsp vanilla*

Directions:

- ✓ *Place strawberries in a small bowl and sprinkle with 1 teaspoon Splenda; leave aside.*
- ✓ *Whisk together 12 cups ricotta cheese and additional ingredients in a large mixing basin.*
- ✓ *Heat a small non-stick skillet over medium heat sprayed with cooking spray.*
- ✓ *Pour 14 cups of batter into the hot pan one at a time, stirring the pan to coat the bottom. Cook for approximately 1-2 minutes, or until the bottom is golden. Cook for an additional minute on the other side.*
- ✓ *Add 2 tablespoons ricotta cheese on each crepe and fold over to serve. Strawberries should be placed on top.*

Nutrition: Calories 230 Total Carbohydrates 10g Net Carbohydrates 8g Protein 17g Fat 14g Sugar 9 g

145) *Scones de fraise et de coco*

8 portions time Required for Cooking: 40 Minutes

Ingredients:

- *1/2 cup sliced strawberries*
- *1 big egg What you'll require from your pantry:*
- *1/2 cup almond flour*
- *1/4 cup melted coconut oil*
- *1/4 cup Splenda*
- *1/4 cup grated unsweetened coconut*
- *2 tbsp cornstarch*
- *1 tsp vanilla extract*
- *1 tsp baking powder*

Direction

- ✓ *Preheat the oven to 350°F. Line a 9-inch round baking dish with parchment paper.*
- ✓ *In a large mixing bowl, whisk together the*

egg, oil, Splenda, and vanilla extract until smooth. Scrape the sides as necessary.

- ✓ *Reduce mixer speed to low and gradually add flour, cornstarch, coconut, and baking powder.*
- ✓ *Fold strawberries into the mixture. Evenly distribute the batter in a prepared pan. 35-40 minutes in the oven.*
- ✓ *Allow 15 minutes for cooling before removing from pan. Cut into eight pieces.*

Nutrition: 225 Calories 14g Net Carbohydrates 11g Protein 5g Fat 17g Sugar 8g Fiber 3g

146) *Blueberry Loaf of English Muffins*

12 portions time Required for Cooking: 1 Hour

- *6 beaten eggs*
- *1/2 cup unsweetened almond milk*
- *1/2 cup blueberries What you'll need from your pantry:*
- *1/2 cup cashew butter*
- *1/2 cup almond flour*
- *1/4 cup coconut oil*
- *2 tsp baking powder*
- *1/2 tsp salt*

Directions:

- ✓ *Preheat the oven to 350 degrees Fahrenheit. Prepare a loaf pan by lining it with parchment paper and lightly spraying it with cooking spray.*
- ✓ *Microwave cashew butter and oil for 30 seconds in a small glass bowl. Stir well until completely blended.*
- ✓ *In a large mixing basin, combine the dry ingredients. Stir in cashew butter mixture thoroughly.*
- ✓ *In a separate dish, whisk together the milk and eggs. Combine with the flour mixture and whisk well. Blueberries should be folded in.*
- ✓ *Pour into the prepared pan and bake for 45 minutes, or until a toothpick inserted in the center comes out clean.*
- ✓ *Cook for 30 minutes before removing from the pan and slicing.*

Nutrition: 162 Calories Carbohydrates Total 5g Carbohydrates Net 4g Protein 6g Fat 14g Sugar 1g Fiber 1g

147) *Waffles with Cheese and Spinach*

4 portions Time Required for Cooking: 20 Minutes

- 2 cooked and crumbled bacon strips
- 2 softly beaten eggs
- 1/2 cup grated cauliflower
- 1/2 cup frozen spinach, diced (squeeze out any water first)
- 1/2 cup grated low-fat mozzarella cheese
- 1/2 cup grated low-fat cheddar cheese
- What you'll require from your pantry:
- 1/4 cup reduced-fat Parmesan cheese, grated
- 1 teaspoon powdered garlic
- Cooking spray with nonstick properties

Directions:

✓ Defrost spinach and wring out as much water as possible; transfer to a big bowl.

✓ Spray your waffle iron with cooking spray and preheat it.

✓ Combine the remaining ingredients with spinach.

✓ Spoon tiny amounts onto the waffle iron and fry as you normally would. Serve immediately.

Nutrition: 186 Calories 2g protein 14g fat 14g sugar 1g fiber

148) *Strawberries and Kiwi Smoothies*

4 portions 3 Minutes Cooking

- 2 kiwis, peeled and quartered
- 1 cup frozen strawberries
- 1/2 cup unsweetened skim milk
- What you'll need from your pantry:
- 2 tablespoons honey

Direction

✓ In a blender, combine all ingredients and pulse until smooth.

✓ Immediately pour into glasses and serve.

Nutrition: 120 Calories Total Carbohydrates 26g Net Carbohydrates 24g Protein 3 g fat 1 g sugar 23 g dietary fiber 2 g

149) *Breakfast in Hawaii Bake*

6 portions Time Required for Cooking: 20 Minutes

- 6 thinly sliced ham slices
- 6 eggs
- 1/4 cup grated reduced-fat cheddar cheese
- What you'll need from your pantry:
- 6 pineapple slices
- 2 tbsp. salsa
- 1/2 tsp salt-free spice blend

Direction

✓ Preheat the oven to 350 degrees.

✓ Arrange sliced ham in six muffin cups or ramekins. Stack cheese, salsa, and pineapple on top.

✓ In each cup, crack one egg and sprinkle with a seasoning blend.

✓ Place ramekins on a baking sheet and bake for 20-25 minutes, or until the egg whites are totally set, but the yolks are still soft. Serve right away.

Nutrition: Calories 135 Total Carbohydrates 5g Net Carbohydrates 4 gram protein 12 gram fat 8 gram sugar 3 gram fiber 1 gram apple

150) *French Toast with a Topping*

Servings: 2 Time Required for Cooking: 10 Minutes

- 1 apple, peeled and thinly sliced
- 1/4 cup skim milk
- 2 tbsp. margarine, split

Directions:

✓ In a large skillet over medium-high heat, melt 1 tablespoon margarine. Cook, stirring regularly until apples are soft.

✓ Whisk together the egg, milk, and vanilla extract in a shallow bowl.

✓ In a separate skillet over medium-high heat, melt the remaining margarine. Each piece of bread should be dipped in the egg mixture and cooked on both sides until golden brown.

✓ Arrange two slices of French toast on individual dishes and garnish with apples. Serve right away.

Nutrition: 394 Calories Total Carbohydrates 27g Net Carbohydrates 22g Protein 10g Fatty Acids 23g Sucrose 19g Fiber 5g

151) *Pancakes with Pecans and Oatmeal*

6 portions 15 Minutes Cooking

- 1 cup quick-cooking oats
- 11/2 teaspoon baking powder
- 2 eggs

- *1/3 cup smashed banana (about 12 big bananas)*
- *1/3 cup skim milk*
- *1/2 teaspoon vanilla extract*
- *2 tablespoons chopped pecans*

Directions:

✓ *Blend the oats until they reach a powder-like consistency.*

✓ *Combine the ground oats and baking powder in a small bowl. Combine thoroughly.*

✓ *In a separate bowl, whisk together the eggs, smashed banana, skim milk and vanilla extract. Pour into the dry ingredients bowl and whisk with a spatula until just combined, then add the chopped pecans and stir thoroughly.*

✓ *Heat the canola oil in a large no-stick skillet over medium heat.*

✓ *Scoop 14 cups of batter for each pancake onto a hot skillet, rotating the pan to coat the bottom evenly with batter. Cook for 1–2 minutes, or until bubbles appear on the surface of the pancake. Cook for a further 1 to 2 minutes on the other side, or until the pancake is golden and cooked through. Rep with the remainder of the batter.*

✓ *Remove from the heat and transfer to a serving platter.*

Nutrition: (1 Pancake) 131 Calories; 6.9g protein; 11g carbohydrate; 0g sugar; 9g sodium; 120mg

152) __Breakfast Bake with Tex-Mex Flavors__

9 portions time Required for Cooking: 40 Minutes

Ingredients:

- *2 cups egg substitute*
- *4 sliced scallions*
- *1 cup reduced-fat Monterey Jack cheese, grated and divided*
- *3/4 cup chopped bell pepper*
- *1/2 cup fat-free milk*
- *1/2 cup salsa,*
- *10 slices light whole-grain bread, sliced into 1-inch pieces*
- *1 (4-ounce) can diced and drained green chiles*
- *Cooking spray with nonstick properties*

Directions:

✓ *Cooking spray a 9x13-inch baking dish.*

Distribute bread equally across the bottom.

✓ *Coat a small skillet with cooking spray and set aside on a medium heat setting. Cook until bell pepper is soft, about 5 minutes.*

✓ *Whisk together remaining ingredients in a medium basin, reserving 12 cups cheese.*

✓ *Arrange the sautéed peppers on top of the toast, followed by the egg mixture. Refrigerate for at least 2 hours or overnight.*

✓ *Preheat the oven to 350 degrees Fahrenheit. Cover the dish with the reserved 12 cheese and bake for 20 minutes, covered. Remove the lid and continue baking for a further 15–20 minutes, or until the eggs are hard in the center.*

✓ *Serve immediately with salsa on top.*

Nutrition: Calories 197 Carbohydrates 25g Net Carbohydrates Protein: 19 g 16g Fatty Acids 4g

153) __Muffins with Blueberries__

14 portions 30 Minutes Cooking

- *1 cup almond flour*
- *1 cup frozen blueberries*
- *2 teaspoons baking powder*
- *1/3 cup erythritol sweetener*
- *1 teaspoon unsweetened vanilla extract*
- *1/2 teaspoon salt*
- *1/4 cup heated coconut oil*
- *1 pastured egg*

Directions:

✓ *Turn on the air fryer, insert the fryer basket, coat it with olive oil, cover it with the lid, and preheat for 10 minutes at 360 degrees F.*

✓ *In the meantime, in a large mixing basin, blend flour, berries, salt, sweetener, and baking powder until thoroughly incorporated.*

✓ *In a separate dish, crack the eggs and whisk in the vanilla, milk, and applesauce until blended.*

✓ *Grease 14 silicone muffin cups with oil and fill them evenly with the prepared batter.*

✓ *Remove the cover from the fryer and stack the muffin cups inside. Cook for 10 minutes, or until the muffins are pleasantly golden brown and firm.*

✓ *When the air fryer whistles, open the cover and transfer the first muffin to a serving*

platter. Repeat with the other muffins.
Nutrition: 201 Calories 27.3 g Carbohydrates 8.8 g Fat 3 g protein

154) *Blueberry Croissants*

6 portions 12 Minutes Cooking

- 240 g all-purpose flour
- 50 g granulated sugar
- 8 g baking powder
- 2 g salt
- 85 g cold butter
- 85 g fresh blueberries
- 3 g shredded fresh ginger
- 113 ml whipping cream
- 2 big eggs
- 4 ml vanilla extract
- 5 ml water

Directions:

✓ Combine sugar, flour, baking powder, and salt in a large mixing basin.

✓ Using a blender or your hands, combine the butter and flour until the mixture resembles thick crumbs.

✓ Combine the blueberries and ginger with the flour mixture and leave them aside.

✓ Combine the whipped cream, 1 egg, and vanilla extract in a separate container.

✓ Combine the cream mixture and flour mixture until well blended.

✓ Roll out the dough to a thickness of about 38 mm and cut it into eighths.

✓ Spread the buns with an egg and water mixture. Reserving preheat the air fryer to 180 degrees Celsius.

✓ Line the inner basket with baking paper and arrange the buns on top. Cook at 180°C for 12 minutes or until golden brown.

Nutrition: 105 Calories 64g fat 20.09g Carbohydrates 43g protein 1g sugar 0mg cholesterol

155) *Smoothies au café mocha*

3 portions Time Required for Cooking: 5 Minutes

- 1 avocado, pit removed and sliced in half
- 1/2 cup unsweetened almond milk
- 1/2 cup canned coconut milk
- What you'll require from your pantry:
- 3 tbsp. splenda

- 3 tbsp unsweetened cocoa powder

Directions:

✓ Mix all the ingredients in a blender except the avocado. Process until completely smooth.

✓ Add the avocado and mix until completely smooth and without chunks.

✓ Transfer to glasses and serve.

Nutrition: Total Carbohydrates: 109 Nutrition: Calories 15g Protein 6g Fat 1g Sugar 13g

156) *Hard-Boiled Eggs*

2 portions Time Required for Cooking: 17 Minutes

- 2 tbsp thawed frozen spinach
- 1/2 tbsp salt
- 1/4 tbsp powdered black pepper
- 2 pastured eggs
- 3 tbsp shredded parmesan cheese, reduced-fat

Direction

✓ Turn on the air fryer, enter the frying basket, grease it with olive oil, then cover it with the lid. Preheat the fryer to 330 degrees F for 5 minutes.

✓ In the meantime, grease two silicon muffin cups with oil, crack an egg into each cup, and evenly distribute the cheese, spinach, and milk.

✓ Season the egg with salt and freshly ground black pepper and gently beat the ingredients. Be careful not to break the egg yolk.

✓ Preheat the fryer, add the muffin cups, cover, and cook for 8 to 12 minutes, or until the eggs are cooked to desired doneness.

✓ When the air fryer whistles, open the cover and remove the muffin cups.

Nutrition: 161 Calories Carbohydrates: 3 g 14 g fat 11 g protein 1 g fiber

157) *French Toast with Blueberries*

8 portions Time Required for Cooking: 20 Minutes

- 4 eggs
- 1/2 cup blueberries
- 1/2 cup orange juice
- 1 teaspoon orange zest
- What you'll require from your pantry:
- sixteen slices of bread
- 3 tbsp. Splenda, split

- *Cooking spray with no-stick properties*

Directions:

✓ *Preheat the oven to 400 degrees Fahrenheit. Cooking spray a big baking sheet.*

✓ *Combine berries and 2 tablespoons Splenda in a small bowl.*

✓ *Arrange eight pieces of bread on the work surface. Add approximately 3 tablespoons of berries and top with the second slice of bread. Slightly flatten.*

✓ *In a small bowl, stir together the remaining ingredients. Bread should be carefully dipped on both sides in an egg mixture and placed on a preheated pan.*

✓ *Bake for 7-12 minutes on each side, or until the chicken is lightly browned.*

✓ *Bring dessert sauce to low heat and keep warm. Arrange the French toast on a serving plate and drizzle with 1-2 teaspoons of the sauce. Serve.*

Nutrition: 208 Nutrition: Calories Total Carbohydrates 20g Net Carbohydrates 18g Protein 7g Fat 10g 14g sugar 2g fiber

158) *Pancakes with Cottage Cheese*

2 portions Time Required for Cooking: 5 Minutes

- *1 cup low-fat cottage cheese*

- *4 egg whites*

- *What you'll need from the pantry*

- *1/2 cup oats*

- *1 tbsp. raw Stevia, optional*

- *Cooking spray with nonstick properties*

Directions:

✓ *Mix all ingredients in a blender and pulse until smooth.*

✓ *Coat a medium skillet with cooking spray and set aside.*

✓ *Pour approximately 14 cups of batter onto a heated pan and cook until both sides are golden brown.*

✓ *Garnish with sugar-free syrup, fresh berries, or other desired garnish.*

Nutrition: 250 Calories 25g carbohydrate total 23g carbohydrate net 25g protein 25g fat 4g sugar 7g fiber 2g

159) *Breakfast Pizza*

8 pcs. 30 Minutes Cooking

- *12 eggs*

- *12 lb. breakfast sausage*

- *1 cup sliced bell pepper*

- *1 cup sliced red pepper*

- *1 cup shredded cheddar cheese*

- *What you'll require from your pantry:*

- *1/2 teaspoon   salt*

- *1/4 teaspoon   pepper*

Directions:

✓ *Preheat the oven to 350 degrees Fahrenheit.*

✓ *Brown sausage in a big cast-iron skillet. Transfer to a serving bowl.*

✓ *Add peppers and simmer, occasionally stirring, for 3-5 minutes, or until they begin to soften. Transfer the mixture to a bowl.*

✓ *Whisk together the eggs, cream, salt, and pepper in a small bowl. Transfer to a skillet. Cook for 5 minutes, or until the sides begin to firm up.*

✓ *Bake 15 minutes at 350 degrees.*

✓ *Turn off the oven and preheat to broil. Sausage, peppers, and cheese should be layered on top of the "crust." 3 minutes in broiler, or until cheese is melted and beginning to color.*

✓ *Allow 5 minutes for resting before slicing and serving.*

Nutrition: 230 Nutrition: Calories 230 Carbohydrates 16g Fat 4g Sugar 2g Fiber 0g

160) *Sticks of French Toast*

4 portions Time Required for Cooking: 10 Minutes

- *4 slices of white bread, 38 mm thick, preferably hard*

- *2 ml extract de vanilla*

- *Spray Oil for Nonstick Surfaces*

- *38g sugar*

- *3g cinnamon powder*

- *Maple syrup (for serving) Sugar (for sprinkling)*

Directions:

✓ *Cut each bread slice in thirds to get 12 pieces. Place in a horizontal position*

✓ *In a separate bowl, whisk: the eggs, milk, maple syrup, vanilla extract.*

✓ *Preheat the air fryer to 175 degrees Celsius.*

✓ *Coat the bread slices in the egg mixture and drop them in the preheated air fryer. Generously spray French toast with oil* spray.

✓ *Preheat the oven to 175°C and cook French toast for 10 minutes. Halfway through cooking, turn the toast.*

✓ *In a bowl, combine the sugar and cinnamon.*

✓ *When the French toast has finished cooking, cover it with the sugar and cinnamon mixture.*

Nutrition: 128 Calories, 6.2 g fat, 16.3 g carbohydrate, 3 g sugar, 2 g protein, 17 mg cholesterol

161) <u>**Smoothies with mango and strawberries**</u>

2 portions Time Required for Cooking: 10 Minutes

- *12 mango, peeled and diced*
- *3/4 cup halved strawberries*
- *1/2 cup skim milk*
- *1/4 cup vanilla yogurt*
- *From the store cupboard, you'll require the following:*
- *3 ice cubes 2 teaspoons Splenda*

Directions:

✓ *In a blender, combine all ingredients. Process until completely smooth. Serve immediately in cold glasses.*

Nutrition: 132 Calories 26g Net Carbohydrates 24g Protein 5g Fat 1g Sugar 23g Fiber 2g

162) <u>**fried egg**</u>

Time Required for Cooking: 4 Minutes

- *1 pastured egg*
- *1/8 teaspoon salt*
- *1/8 teaspoon cracked black pepper*

Directions:

✓ *Grease the fryer pan with olive oil and add the egg.*

✓ *Turn on the air fryer, insert the frying pan, cover it, and set the temperature to 370 degrees F.*

✓ *Set the frying timer to 3 minutes; when the air fryer beeps, lift the lid and check the egg; if the egg needs additional cooking, continue frying it for another minute.*

✓ *Transfer the egg to a serving plate and season generously with salt and black pepper.*

Nutrition: 90 Calories 0.6 g Carbohydrates 7 g Fat 6.3 g protein 0 g fiber

163) <u>**Scrambled Tofu**</u>

18 Minutes Cooking Servings: 3

- *12 ounces extra-firm tofu, drained, sliced into 12-inch cubes*
- *1 teaspoon garlic powder*
- *1 teaspoon onion powder*
- *1 teaspoon paprika*
- *1/2 teaspoon powdered black pepper*
- *1/2 teaspoon salt*
- *1 tablespoon olive oil*

Directions:

✓ *Turn on the air fryer, insert the frying basket, coat it with olive oil, cover it with the lid, and preheat for 5 minutes at 220 degrees F.*

✓ *Meanwhile, in a bowl, combine tofu pieces, oil, and xanthan gum and mix until completely coated.*

✓ *Toss the tofu with the remaining ingredients until completely coated.*

✓ *Uncover the frying, add the tofu, and cook for 13 minutes, shaking the basket every 5 minutes until pleasantly golden and crispy.*

✓ *When the air fryer whistles, open the cover and transfer the tofu to a serving plate.*

Nutrition: 94 Nutrition: Calories Carbohydrates: 5 g 5 g fat 6 g protein 0 g fiber

164) <u>**Orange Muffins That Are Simply Delectable**</u>

8 portions 15 Minutes Cooking

- *Dry Ingredients*
- *212 c. coarsely crushed almond flour*
- *1/2 tsp baking powder*
- *1/2 tsp ground cardamom*
- *34 tsp ground cinnamon*
- *1/4 tsp salt*
- *2 large eggs*
- *4 tbsp avocado or coconut oil*
- *1 tbsp raw honey*
- *1/4 tsp vanilla essence*
- *1 medium orange, grated zest, and juice*
- *Equipment Exceptional:*
- *Muffin tin with eight cups*

Directions:

✓ *Preheat the oven to 375 degrees Fahrenheit (190 degrees Celsius) and line an 8-cup muffin tray with paper liners.*

✓ *In a large mixing bowl, mix: almond flour, baking powder, cardamom, cinnamon, and salt. Place aside.*

✓ *Mix the eggs, oil, honey, vanilla, zest, and juice. Pour the wet ingredients into the dry ingredients bowl and whisk with a spatula just until merged.*

✓ *Pour the batter into the muffin cups, about three-quarters of the way filled.*

✓ *Bake for 15 minutes, or until golden on top and a toothpick inserted in the center comes out clean.*

✓ *Wait 10 minutes for the muffins to cool before serving.*

Nutrition: Calories: 287 fat: 25g protein: 7.9g carbs: 18g fiber: 8g sugar: 9.8g sodium: 96mg

165) Cauliflower Hash Browns

6 portions Time Required for Cooking: 25 Minutes
Ingredients:

- *1/4 cup chickpea flour*
- *4 cups cauliflower rice*
- *1/2 medium white onion, peeled and chopped*
- *1/2 teaspoon garlic powder*
- *1-tablespoon xanthan gum*
- *1/2 teaspoon salt*
- *1-tablespoon nutritional yeast flakes*
- *1-teaspoon ground paprika*

Directions:

✓ *Switch on the air fryer, insert fryer basket, grease it with olive oil, then shut with its lid, set the fryer at 375 degrees F and preheat for 10 minutes.*

✓ *Meanwhile, pour all the ingredients in a basin, whisk until well mixed and then shape the mixture into six rectangular disks, each about ½-inch thick.*

✓ *Open the fryer, pour hash browns in it in a single layer, close with its lid and cook for 25 minutes at 375 degrees F until perfectly golden and crispy, turning halfway through the cooking.*

✓ *When the air fryer whistles, remove the lid and transfer the hash browns to a serving plate.*

Nutrition: 112 Calories Carbohydrates: 6.2 g 7.3 g fat 7.4 g protein 2 g fiber

166) Sandwich Grilled With Three Different Types Of Cheese

Two portions Time Required for Cooking: 8 Minutes

- *2 tbsp. mayonnaise*
- *18 tsp. dried basil*
- *18 tsp. dry oregano*
- *4 slices whole-wheat bread*
- *2 slices 12 to 1 oz. cheddar cheese*
- *2 slices Monterey Jack cheese*
- *12 to 1 oz. Butter that is still soft*

Directions:

✓ *Mix mayonnaise, basil, and oregano; distribute the mixture on both sides of the slice. Each piece should be topped with a slice of cheese and a slice of tomato, followed by the other slice of bread.*

✓ *Brush each side of the sandwich lightly with the brush and arrange the sandwiches in the basket. Cook for 8 minutes at 400°F, flipping halfway through.*

Nutrition: 141 Calories 01g fat 68g Carbohydrates 08g protein 0.25 g sugar 33mg cholesterol

167) Strata de Navidad

Time Required for Cooking: 1 Hour Servings: 8

- *8 eggs*
- *6 sliced bacon slices*
- *4 breakfast sausages, casings removed, and flesh crumbled*
- *1-pint cherry tomatoes*
- *4 cups spinach*
- *3 cups skim milk*
- *What you'll require from your pantry:*
- *12 Italian loaf bread, sliced into 2-inch cubes*
- *2 tsp Dijon mustard*
- *1 tsp salt*
- *1/4 tsp pepper*

Directions:

✓ *Cooking spray a 13x9-inch baking dish.*

✓ *In a large non-stick skillet, heat the oil over medium heat. Cook until the bacon is crisp and the sausage is cooked for about 5-7 minutes. Transfer to a paper towel lined plate. Using a strainer, remove all except 1 tablespoon of grease from the pan.*

✓ *Add onion and sauté for about 6 minutes, or until tender and golden brown.*

✓ Add tomatoes and spinach and heat for about 2 minutes, or until tomatoes begin to soften and spinach wilts. Take the pan from the heat and set it aside to cool.

✓ In a large mixing bowl, whisk together eggs, milk, Dijon, salt, and pepper. Combine cheese, bread, bacon, sausage, and spinach combination in a large mixing bowl. Cover with plastic wrap and pour into prepared pan.

✓ Refrigerate for at least two hours, preferably overnight.

✓ Preheat the oven to 359 degrees Fahrenheit. Uncover and bake for 1 hour or until the middle is set. Allow to cool slightly before serving.

Nutrition: 343 Calories Total Carbohydrates 24g Net Carbohydrates 22g Protein 25g Fat 16g 7g sugar 2g fiber

168) *Muffins with Blueberries and Cinnamon*

10 portions 30 Minutes Cooking

- 3 eggs
- 1 cup blueberries
- 1/3 cup half-and-half
- 1/4 cup melted margarine
- What you'll require from your pantry:
- 11/2 cup almond flour
- 1/3 cup Splenda
- 1 tsp baking powder

Directions:

✓ Preheat the oven to 350 degrees Fahrenheit. Ten muffin cups should be lined with paper liners.

✓ Combine dry ingredients in a large mixing bowl.

✓ Stir in wet ingredients until well combined.

✓ Gently stir in the blueberries and pour them into the prepared muffin cups.

✓ Bake for 25-30 minutes, or until a toothpick inserted in the center comes out clean.

Nutrition: 194 Calories 12g Carbohydrates Total 12g Carbohydrates Net 10g Protein 5g Fat 14g Sugar 9g Fiber 2g

169) *Frittata with crab and spinach*

30 Minutes Cooking Servings: 10

- 34 pounds crabmeat
- 8 eggs
- 10 ounces spinach, frozen and thawed, squeeze dry
- 2 celery stalks, diced
- 2 cup half-n-half
- 1 cup Swiss cheese
- 1/2 cup onion, chopped
- 1/2 cup red pepper, diced
- What you'll require from your pantry:
- 1 cup bread crumbs
- 1/2 teaspoon salt
- 1/4 teaspoon pepper
- 1/4 teaspoon nutmeg
- Cooking spray with nonstick properties

Directions:

✓ Preheat the oven to 375 degrees Fahrenheit. Cooking spray a big casserole or baking dish.

✓ In a large mixing bowl, whisk together eggs and half-n-half. Combine crab, spinach, bread crumbs, cheese, and seasonings in a large mixing bowl.

✓ In a large skillet over medium heat, melt butter. Celery, onion, red pepper, and mushrooms should all be included. Cook, stirring periodically, for approximately 5 minutes, or until vegetables are soft. Combine with egg mixture.

✓ Pour the mixture into the prepared pan and cook for 30-35 minutes, or until the eggs have set and the surface is slightly golden. Wait 10 minutes for cooling before serving.

Nutrition: 261 Calories 18g Carbohydrates Total 18g Carbohydrates Net 16g Protein 14g Fat 15g Sugar 4g Fiber 2g

170) *Swedish Pancake with Apple Filling*

6 portions Time Required for Cooking: 20 Minutes

- 2 cored and thinly sliced apples
- 3/4 cupegg substitute
- 1/2 cup fat-free milk
- 1/2 cup sugar-free caramel sauce
- 1 tbsp. reduced-calorie margarine
- 1/2 cup flour
- 1 tbsp brown sugar replacement
- 2 tsp water
- 1/4 tsp cinnamon

- *1/8 tsp cloves*
- *1/8 tsp salt*

Directions:

✓ *Preheat the oven to 400 degrees Fahrenheit. Place margarine in a cast iron or ovenproof skillet and heat until melted.*

✓ *Whisk together flour, milk, egg substitute, cinnamon, cloves, and salt in a medium basin until smooth.*

✓ *Pour batter into heated skillet and bake for 20–25 minutes, or until golden brown and puffy.*

✓ *Using cooking spray, coat a medium pot. Preheat over a medium heat source.*

✓ *Combine apples, brown sugar, and water in a medium bowl. Cook, turning periodically, for approximately 4 – 6 minutes, or until apples are soft and golden brown.*

✓ *In a microwave-safe measuring glass, pour the caramel sauce and heat for 30 – 45 seconds, or until warmed through.*

✓ *Spoon apples into pancakes and drizzle with caramel to serve. Slicing into wedges*

Nutrition: Calories 193 Carbohydrates 25g Net Carbohydrates 23g Protein 6g Fatty Acids 2g Sucrose 12g dietary fiber 2g

171) *Muffins with Apples and Cinnamon*

12 portions Time Required for Cooking: 25 Minutes

- *1 cup apple, finely diced*
- *2/3 cup skim milk*
- *1/4 cup melted reduced-calorie margarine*
- *1 lightly beaten egg*
- *What you'll need from the pantry*
- *1 tbsp. stevia*
- *2 1/2 tsp. baking powder*
- *1 tsp cinnamon*
- *1/2 tsp. sea salt*
- *1/4 tsp. nutmeg*
- *Cooking spray with nonstick properties*

Directions:

✓ *Preheat the oven to 400 degrees Fahrenheit. Cooking spray a 12-cup muffin tray.*

✓ *In a large mixing basin, whisk together the dry ingredients.*

✓ *In a separate bowl, combine milk,*

margarine, and egg.

✓ *Combine wet and dry ingredients in a bowl and whisk just until moistened. Gently incorporate apples into the mixture.*

✓ *Spoon into muffin tins that have been prepared. Bake for 25 minutes, or until the tops of the muffins are gently browned.*

Nutrition: 119 Calories 17g Carbohydrates Total 17g Carbohydrates Net 16g Protein 3g Fat 4g Sugar 3g Fiber 1g

172) *Pizza in the Santa Fe Style*

Two portions Time Required for Cooking: 10 Minutes

- *1 tsp. vegetable oil*
- *1/2 tsp. ground cumin*
- *2 tortillas 7 to 8 inches in diameter*
- *1/4 cup prepared black bean sauce*
- *4 oz cooked chicken, cut into strips or grated*
- *1 tbsp taco spices*
- *2 oz premade chipotle sauce or preferred sauce*
- *1/4 cup plus 2 tbsp corn kernels, fresh or frozen (thawed)*
- *1 tbsp sliced scallions*
- *1 tbsp chopped cilantro*

Directions:

✓ *In a small bowl, combine the oil and cumin; sprinkle the mixture on both tortillas. Then, evenly distribute the black bean sauce between the two tortillas. Combine the chicken pieces and taco seasonings; stir until the chicken is evenly coated. Combine the sauce with the covered chicken.*

✓ *Remove half of the chicken and layer it in one of the tortillas over the bean sauce. Distribute half of the corn, chives, and cilantro evenly over the tortilla, followed by half of the cheese. Place the pizza in the basket and bake for 10 minutes at 400°F. After removing the first tortilla, prepare the second tortilla and cook it.*

Nutrition: 41 Calories 01g fat 6.68g Carbohydrates 08g protein 0.25 g sugar 0mg cholesterol

173) *With Fried Eggs on Brussels Sprouts*

4 portions 15 Minutes Cooking

- *3 tbsp extra-virgin olive oil, split*

- *1 pound (454 g) chopped Brussels sprouts*
- *2 garlic cloves, finely sliced*
- *1/4 tsp salt*
- *1 lemon's juice*

Directions:

✓ *In a large skillet over medium heat, heat 11/2 tbsps olive oil.*

✓ *Add the Brussels sprouts and sauté for 6 to 8 minutes, turning regularly until crispy and tender.*

✓ *Add the garlic and simmer for approximately 1 minute, or until fragrant. Season with salt and lemon juice to taste.*

✓ *Transfer the skillet contents to a plate and set them aside.*

✓ *In a skillet over medium-high heat, heat the remaining oil. Crack the eggs into the skillet one at a time and fry for approximately 3 minutes. Continue cooking the eggs until the egg whites are set and the yolks are cooked to your satisfaction, or until the egg whites are set, and the yolks are cooked to your liking.*

✓ *Arrange the fried eggs on top of the roasted Brussels sprouts.*

Nutrition: 157 Calories; 8.9g protein; 18g carbohydrate; 1g fiber; 0g sugar; 233mg sodium

174) *Breakfast Hash with Cauliflower*

2 portions Time Required for Cooking: 20 Minutes

- *4 cups shredded cauliflower*
- *1 cup chopped mushrooms*
- *3/4 cup diced onion 3 slices bacon*
- *1/4 cup grated sharp cheddar cheese*

Directions:

✓ *Fry bacon in a medium skillet over medium-high heat until crisp; set aside.*

✓ *Cook, stirring regularly until the veggies are golden brown.*

✓ *Chop bacon into small pieces and add to skillet.*

✓ *Sprinkle cheese on top and let it melt. Serve right away.*

Nutrition: 155 Calories 16g Carbohydrates Net Carbohydrates 10g Protein 10g Fat 7g Sugar 7g Fiber 6g

175) *Oatmeal With Peanut Butter And Berries*

2 portions 15 Minutes Cooking

- *1/2 cup unsweetened vanilla almond milk*
- *3/4 cup rolled oats*
- *1 tablespoon chia seeds*
- *1/4 cup divided fresh berries (optional)*
- *2 teaspoons divided walnut bits (optional)*

Directions:

✓ *In a small saucepan, bring the almond milk, oats, and chia seeds to a boil.*

✓ *Cook, covered, for approximately 10 minutes, stirring frequently, or until the oats have absorbed the milk.*

✓ *Stir in the peanut butter until the oats are thick and creamy.*

✓ *Distribute the oatmeal evenly between two serving bowls. If desired, garnish with berries and walnut pieces.*

Nutrition: 260 Calories; 19g protein; 26.9g carbohydrates; 7.1g fiber; 0g sugar; 130mg sodium

176) *Yogurt Sundae Quick Breakfast*

1 portion 0 Minutes Cooking

- *3/4 cup plain Greek yogurt*
- *1/4 cup mixed berries (blueberries, strawberries, and blackberries)*
- *2 tbsp cashew, walnut, or almond pieces*
- *1 tbsp ground flaxseed*

Directions:

✓ *In a large parfait glass, pour the yogurt and top with the berries, cashew pieces, and flaxseed.*

✓ *Garnish with mint leaves and serve cold.*

Nutrition: 238 Calories: 12g fat; 20.9g carbohydrate: 18g fiber; 1g sugar; 8.9g sodium: 63mg

177) *Frittata with Olives and Mushrooms*

Time Required for Cooking: 20 Minutes Servings: 4

- *2 cups chopped fresh spinach*
- *1 cup sliced cremini mushrooms*
- *4 eggs*
- *2 egg whites*
- *1/3 cup grated reduced-fat Parmesan cheese*

- 1/4 cup pitted and sliced thin Kalamata olives
- 1 large shallot, sliced thin What you'll require from the pantry
- 1 tablespoon olive oil
- 1/2 teaspoon   rosemary
- 1/4 teaspoon   black pepper
- 1/8 teaspoon salt

Directions:

✓ Preheat the oven to broil.

✓ Heat oil in a nonstick, broiler-safe skillet over medium heat. Cook for 3 minutes, stirring occasionally. Cook, occasionally stirring, until mushrooms and spinach are soft, about 5 minutes.

✓ Whisk together eggs and spices in a medium bowl. Fill skillet halfway with egg mixture. While cooking, run a spatula over the edge of the skillet, raising the frittata to allow raw eggs to drain beneath. Cook, occasionally stirring, until the eggs are almost set.

✓ Scatter the olives and cheese on top. Grill 4 inches from the heat source for about 2 minutes or until the top is lightly browned. Allow 5 minutes before slicing into 4 wedges and serving.

Nutrition: Calories 146 Carbohydrates Protein 3 g 10g Fatty Acids 11g 0g sugar 0g fiber

178)   *Muffins de Pommes*

10 portions Time Required for Cooking: 20 Minutes

- 2 eggs
- 1/4 cup melted butter
- What you'll require from your pantry:
- 2 cup almond flour
- 3/4 cup pumpkin
- 1/3 cup Splenda
- 2 tbsp pumpkin seeds

Directions:

✓ Preheat the oven to 400 degrees Fahrenheit. Prepare a muffin mold by lining it with paper cups.

✓ In a large mixing bowl, whisk together butter, pumpkin, eggs, and vanilla extract. Whisk until completely smooth.

✓ Whisk flour, Splenda, baking powder, cinnamon, and salt. Combine with pumpkin mixture. Distribute evenly among muffin cups.

✓ Sprinkle the pumpkin seeds on top and bake for 20 minutes, or until a toothpick inserted in the center comes out clean.

✓ Allow 10 minutes for cooling before serving.

Nutrition: 212 Calories Total Carbohydrates 13g Net Carbohydrates 10g Protein 6g Fat 16g 8g sugar 3g fiber

179)   *Smoothies with Vanilla and Mango*

3 portions Time Required for Cooking: 5 Minutes

- 1 cup mango chunks, frozen
- 6 oz. plain yogurt
- 1/2 cup unsweetened orange juice
- What you'll require from your pantry:
- 1 tablespoon honey

Directions:

✓ In a blender, combine all ingredients. Process until completely smooth. Serve in cold glasses.

Nutrition: 112 Calories 22g Net Carbohydrates 21g Protein 4g Fat 1g Sugar 21g Fiber 1g

180)   *Casserole De Spinach Et D'eggs Cheesy*

8 portions Time Required for Cooking: 35 Minutes

- 1 (10-ounce / 284-g) box thawed and drained frozen spinach
- 1 (14-ounce / 397-g) can drained artichoke hearts
- 1/4 cup finely chopped red bell pepper
- 8 lightly beaten eggs
- 1/4 cup unsweetened plain almond milk
- 2 minced garlic cloves
- 1/2 teaspoon   salt
- 1/2 teaspoon   freshly ground black pepper

Directions:

✓ Preheat the oven to 375 degrees Fahrenheit (190 degrees Celsius). Prepare a baking dish by spraying it with nonstick cooking spray and setting it aside.

✓ In a large mixing bowl, mix: spinach, artichoke hearts, bell peppers, beaten eggs, almond milk, garlic, salt, pepper.

✓ Transfer the mixture to a greased pan and sprinkle with the goat cheese.

✓ Bake for 35 minutes, or until the top is lightly brown and the eggs are set.

✓ *Remove from oven and serve immediately.*
Nutrition: Calories: 105 fat: 8 g protein: 8.9 g carbohydrates: 6.1 g fiber: 7 g sugar: 0 g sodium: 486mg

181) *Smoothie with Pumpkin Pie*

2 portions Time Required for Cooking: 5 Minutes

- *1/2 cup unsweetened almond milk*
- *4 oz. softened reduced-fat cream cheese*
- *1/2 cup plain Greek yogurt*
- *What you'll require from your pantry:*
- *1/4 cup pumpkin puree*
- *2 tbsp. splenda*
- *1/8 tsp cinnamon*

Directions:

✓ *In a blender, combine all ingredients. Proceed until smooth and all the ingredients are well blended..*

✓ *Divide between two glasses and garnish with a pinch of ginger.*

Nutrition: 220 Calories 27g Carbohydrates Net Carbohydrates 25g Protein 13g Fat 5g Sugar 15g Fiber 2g

182) *Berry Breakfast Bark*

Servings: 6 Cooking Time: 2 Hours
Ingredients:

- *3-4 strawberries, sliced*
- *1 ½ cup plain Greek yogurt*
- *½ cup blueberries*
- *What you'll need from the store cupboard:*
- *½ cup low-fat granola*
- *3 tbsp. sugar-free maple syrup*

Directions:

✓ *Line a baking sheet with parchment paper.*

✓ *In a medium bowl, mix yogurt and syrup until combined. Pour into prepared pan and spread in a thin, even layer.*

✓ *Top with remaining Ingredients. Cover with foil and freeze for two hours or overnight.*

✓ *To serve: slice into squares and serve immediately. If bark thaws too much, it will lose its shape. Store any remaining bark in an airtight container in the freezer.*

Nutrition: Calories 69 Total Carbs 18g Net Carbs 16g Protein 7g Fat 6g Sugar 7g Fiber 2g

183) *Lean Lamb And Turkey Meatballs With Yogurt*

Servings: 4 Cooking Time: 10 Minutes
Ingredients:

- *1 egg white*
- *4 ounces ground lean turkey*
- *1 pound of ground lean lamb*
- *1 teaspoon each of cayenne pepper, ground coriander, red chili paste, salt, and ground cumin*
- *2 garlic cloves, minced*
- *1 1/2 tablespoons parsley, chopped*
- *1 tablespoon mint, chopped*
- *1/4 cup of olive oil*
- *For the yogurt*
- *2 tablespoons of buttermilk*
- *1 garlic clove, minced*
- *1/4 cup mint, chopped*
- *1/2 cup of Greek yogurt, non-fat*
- *Salt to taste*

Directions:

✓ *Set the Air Fryer to 390 degrees.*

✓ *Mix all the ingredients for the meatballs in a bowl. Roll and mold them into golf-size round pieces. Arrange in the cooking basket. Cook for 8 minutes.*

✓ *While you wait, in a bowl, combine all the ingredients for the mint yogurt and mix thoroughly.*

Nutrition: Calorie: 154 Carbohydrate: 9g Fat: 5g Protein: 8.6g Fiber: 4g

184) *Cocotte Eggs*

Servings: 1 Cooking Time: 15 Minutes
Ingredients:

- *1 tbsp. olive oil soup*
- *2 tbsp. crumbly ricotta*
- *1 tbsp. parmesan cheese soup*
- *1 slice of gorgonzola cheese*
- *1 slice of Brie cheese*
- *1 tbsp. cream soup*
- *1 egg*
- *Nutmeg and salt to taste*
- *Butternut to taste*

Directions:

✓ *Spread with olive oil in the bottom of a*

small glass refractory. Place the cheese in the bottom and season with nutmeg and salt. Add the cream.

✓ Break the egg into a cup and add it gently to the mixture.

✓ Preheat the air fryer for the time of 5 minutes and the temperature at 200C. Put the refractory in the basket of the air fryer, set the time to 10 minutes, and press the power button. Remove and serve still hot.

Nutrition: Nutrition: Calories: 138 Cal Carbs: 3 g Fat: 33 g Protein: 7.4 g Fiber: 2 g

185) *Cream Buns With Strawberries*

Servings: 6 Cooking Time: 12 Minutes
Ingredients:

- 240g all-purpose flour
- 50g granulated sugar
- 8g baking powder
- 1g of salt
- 85g chopped cold butter
- 84g chopped fresh strawberries
- 120 ml whipping cream
- 2 large eggs
- 10 ml vanilla extract
- 5 ml of water

Directions:

✓ Sift flour, sugar, baking powder, and salt in a large bowl. Put the butter with the flour using a blender or your hands until the mixture resembles thick crumbs.

✓ Mix the strawberries in the flour mixture. Set aside for the mixture to stand. Beat the whipping cream, 1 egg, and the vanilla extract in a separate bowl.

✓ Put the cream mixture in the flour mixture until they are homogeneous, then spread the mixture to a thickness of 38 mm.

✓ Use a round cookie cutter to cut the buns. Spread the buns with a combination of egg and water. Set aside

✓ Preheat the air fryer, set it to 180°C.

✓ Place baking paper in the preheated inner basket.

✓ Place the buns on top of the baking paper and cook for 12 minutes at 180°C, until golden brown.

Nutrition: Calories: 150Fat: 14g Carbohydrates: 3g Protein: 11g Sugar: 8g Cholesterol: 0mg

186) *Yogurt & Granola Breakfast Popsicles*

Servings: 6 Cooking Time: 8 Hours
Ingredients:

- 1 ½ cups fresh berries, chopped
- 1 ¼ cups plain low-fat yogurt
- What you'll need from the store cupboard
- 6 tbsp. granola, crumbled
- 4 tsp sugar-free maple syrup, divided
- 1 tsp vanilla
- 6 3-oz Popsicle molds

Directions:

✓ In a medium bowl, stir together yogurt, berries, 2 teaspoons maple syrup, and vanilla together.

✓ Pour evenly into Popsicle molds.

✓ In a small bowl, mix the remaining syrup and granola. Top each Popsicle with 1 tablespoon of the granola mixture. Insert sticks and freeze 8 hours, or overnight. Popsicles can be stored in the freezer for up to 1 week.

Nutrition: Nutrition: Calories 73 Total Carbs 20g Net Carbs 18g Protein 5g Fat 4g Sugar 7g Fiber 2g

187) *Spinach Cheddar Squares*

Servings: 4 Cooking Time: 40 Minutes Ingredients:

- 10 oz. spinach, frozen, thaw and squeeze dry
- 1 ½ cupegg substitute
- ¾ cup skim milk
- ¾ cup reduced-fat cheddar cheese, grated
- ¼ cup red pepper, diced
- What you'll need from the store cupboard:
- 2 tbsp. reduced-fat parmesan cheese
- 1 tbsp. bread crumbs
- ½ tsp minced onion, dried
- ½ tsp salt
- ¼ tsp garlic powder
- ¼ tsp pepper
- Nonstick cooking spray

Directions:

✓ Heat oven to 350 degrees. Spray an 8-inch square baking dish with cooking spray.

✓ Sprinkle bread crumbs over the bottom of the prepared dish. Top with ½ cup cheese, spinach, and red pepper.

✓ In a small bowl, whisk together the remaining ingredients. Pour over vegetables.

✓ Bake 35 minutes. Now, sprinkle with the remaining cheese and cook for another 2-3 minutes, or check that the cheese is melted using a knife inserted in the center and comes out clean.

✓ Let cool 15 minutes before cutting and serving.

Nutrition: Calories 159 Total Carbs 7g Net Carbs 5g Protein 22g Fat 5g Sugar 4g Fiber 2g

188) *Peanut Butter Waffles*

Servings: 4 Cooking Time: 10 Minutes
Ingredients:

- 4 eggs
- ½ cup low-fat cream cheese
- ½ cup half-n-half
- 2 tbsp. margarine
- What you'll need from the store cupboard:
- 2/3 cup low-fat peanut butter
- 2 tsp Splenda
- 1 tsp baking powder
- Nonstick cooking spray

Directions:

✓ Lightly spray waffle iron with cooking spray and preheat.

✓ In a medium glass bowl, place peanut butter, margarine, and cream cheese. Microwave 30 seconds and stir to combine.

✓ Stir in the cream, baking powder, and Splenda and mix until all the ingredients are combined. Stir in eggs and mix well.

✓ Pour into the waffle iron and cook until golden brown and crisp on the outside. Serve.

Nutrition: Calories 214 Total Carbs 9g Net Carbs 8g Protein 9g Fat 15g Sugar 2g Fiber 1g

189) *Bruschetta*

Servings: 2 Cooking Time: 10 Minutes
Ingredients:

- 4 slices of Italian bread
- 1 cup chopped tomato tea
- 1 cup grated mozzarella tea
- Olive oil
- Oregano, salt, and pepper

- 4 fresh basil leaves

Directions:

✓ Preheat the air fryer. Set the timer of 5 minutes and the temperature to 2000C.

✓ Sprinkle the slices of Italian bread with olive oil. Divide the chopped tomatoes and mozzarella between the slices. Season with salt, pepper, and oregano.

✓ Put oil in the filling. Place a basil leaf on top of each slice.

✓ Put the bruschetta in the basket of the air fryer, being careful not to spill the filling. Set the timer of 5 minutes, set the temperature to 180C, and press the power button.

✓ Transfer the bruschetta to a plate and serve.

Nutrition: Calories: 434 Fat: 14g Carbohydrates: 63g Protein: 11g Sugar: 8g Cholesterol: 0mg

190) *Garlic Bread*

Servings: 4-5 Cooking Time: 15 Minutes
Ingredients:

- 2 stale French rolls
- 4 tbsp. crushed or crumpled garlic
- 1 cup of mayonnaise
- Powdered grated Parmesan
- 1 tbsp. olive oil

Directions:

✓ Preheat the air fryer. Set the time of 5 minutes and the temperature to 200 C.

✓ Mix mayonnaise with garlic and set aside.

✓ Cut the baguettes into slices, but without separating them completely.

✓ Fill the cavities of equals. Brush with olive oil and sprinkle with grated cheese.

✓ Place in the basket of the air fryer. Set the timer to 10 minutes, adjust the temperature to 1800C, and press the power button.

Nutrition: Calories: 340 Fat: 15g Carbohydrates: 32g Protein: 15g Sugar: 0g Cholesterol: 0mg

191) *Coconut Breakfast Porridge*

Servings: 4 Cooking Time: 10 Minutes
Ingredients:

- 4 cup vanilla almond milk, unsweetened
- What you'll need from the store cupboard:
- 1 cup unsweetened coconut, grated
- 8 tsp coconut flour

Directions:

✓ *Add coconut to a saucepan and cook over med-high heat until it is lightly toasted. Be careful not to let it burn.*

✓ *Add milk and bring to a boil. While stirring, slowly add flour, cook, and stir until mixture starts to thicken about 5 minutes.*

✓ *Remove from heat. The mixture will thicken more as it cools. Ladle into bowls, add blueberries, or drizzle with a little honey if desired.*

Nutrition: Calories 231 Total Carbs 21g Net Carbs 8g Protein 6g Fat 14g Sugar 4g Fiber 13g

192) *Coconut Porridge for Breakfast*

4 portions Time Required for Cooking: 10 Minutes

- *4 cup unsweetened vanilla almond milk*
- *What you'll require from your pantry:*
- *1 cup grated unsweetened coconut*
- *8 tablespoons coconut flour*

Directions:

✓ *In a saucepan, combine coconut and cook over medium-high heat until lightly toasted. Take care not to allow it to burn.*

✓ *Bring milk to a boil and add. Slowly add flour while stirring; cook and stir until mixture begins to thicken about 5 minutes.*

✓ *Take the pan from the heat; the mixture will continue to thicken as it cools. Ladle into bowls and top with blueberries or a drizzle of honey, if desired.*

Nutrition: Calories 231 Carbohydrates Total 21g Carbohydrates Net 8g Protein 6g Fat 14g Sugar 4g Fiber 13g

193) *Bacon Bbq*

Servings: 2 Cooking Time: 8 Minutes

Ingredients:

- *13g dark brown sugar*
- *5g chili powder*
- *1g ground cumin*
- *1g cayenne pepper*
- *4 slices of bacon, cut in half*

Directions:

✓ *Mix seasonings until well combined.*

✓ *Dip the bacon in the dressing until it is completely covered. Leave aside.*

✓ *Preheat the air fryer, set it to 160°C.*

✓ *4 Place the bacon in the preheated air fryer*

✓ *Select Bacon and press Start/Pause.*

Nutrition: Calories: 1124 Fat: 72g Carbohydrates: 59g Protein: 49g Sugar: 11g Cholesterol: 77mg

194) *Almond Cheesecake Bites*

Prep time: 5 minutes, chill time: 30 minutes, Serves: 6

Ingredients:

- *½ cup reduced-fat cream cheese, soft What you'll need from store cupboard:*
- *½ cup almonds, ground fine*
- *¼ cup almond butter*
- *2 drops liquid stevia*

Instructions:

✓ *In a large bowl, beat cream cheese, almond butter, and stevia on high speed until the mixture is smooth and creamy. Cover and chill for 30 minutes.*

✓ *Use your hands to shape the mixture into 12 balls.*

✓ *Place the ground almonds on a shallow plate. Roll the balls in the nuts, completely covering all sides. Store in an airtight container in the refrigerator.*

Nutrition: Calories 68 Total Carbs 3g Net Carbs 2 Protein 5g Fat 5g Sugar 0g Fiber 1g

195) *Almond Coconut Biscotti*

Prep time: 5 minutes, Cook time: 50 minutes, Serves: 16

Ingredients:

- *1 egg, room temperature*
- *1 egg white, room temperature ½ cup margarine, melted*
- *What you'll need from the store cupboard: 2 ½ cups flour*
- *1 1/3 cup unsweetened coconut, grated ¾ cup almonds, sliced*
- *2/3 cup Splenda*
- *2 tsp baking powder*
- *1 tsp vanilla*
- *½ tsp salt*

Instructions:

✓ *Heat oven to 350 degrees. Line a baking sheet with parchment paper.*

✓ *In a large bowl, combine dry ingredients.*

✓ *In a separate mixing bowl, beat other Ingredients together. Add to dry ingredients and mix until thoroughly combined.*

✓ *Divide dough in half. Shape each half into a loaf measuring 8x2 ¾-inches. Place loaves on pan 3 inches apart.*

✓ *Bake 25-30 minutes or until set and golden brown. Cool on wire rack 10 minutes.*

✓ *With a serrated knife, cut loaf diagonally into ½-inch slices. Place the cookies, cut side down, back on the pan, and bake another 20 minutes, or until firm and nicely browned. Store in an airtight container. The serving size is 2 cookies.*

Nutrition: Calories 234 Total Carbs 13g Net Carbs 10g Protein 5g Fat 18g Sugar 9g Fiber 3g

196)   *Almond Flour Crackers*

Prep time: 5 minutes, Cook time: 15 minutes, Serves: 8

Ingredients:

- *½ cup coconut oil, melted*
- *What you'll need from the store cupboard 1 ½ cups almond flour*
- *¼ cup Stevia*

Instructions:

✓ *Heat oven to 350 degrees. Line a cookie sheet with parchment paper.*

✓ *In a mixing bowl, combine all ingredients and mix well.*

✓ *Spread dough onto prepared cookie sheet, ¼-inch thick. Use a paring knife to score into 24 crackers.*

✓ *Bake 10 – 15 minutes or until golden brown.*

✓ *Separate and store in an air-tight container.*

Nutrition Facts Per Serving Nutrition: Calories 281 Total Carbs 16g Net Carbs 14g Protein 4g Fat 23g Sugar 13g Fiber 2g

197)   *Asian Chicken Wings*

Prep time: 5 minutes, Cook time: 30 minutes, Serves: 3

Ingredients:

- *24 chicken wings*
- *What you'll need from the store cupboard: 6 tbsp. soy sauce*
- *6 tbsp. Chinese 5 spice*
- *Salt & pepper*
- *Nonstick cooking spray*

Instructions:

✓ *Heat oven to 350 degrees. Spray a baking sheet with cooking spray.*

✓ *Combine the soy sauce, 5 spices, salt, and*

pepper in a large bowl. Add the wings and toss to coat.

✓ *Pour the wings onto the prepared pan. Bake 15 minutes. Turn the chicken over and cook another 15 minutes until the chicken is cooked through.*

✓ *Serve with your favorite low carb dipping sauce.*

Nutrition: Calories 178 Total Carbs 8g Protein 12g Fat 11g Sugar 1g Fiber 0g

198)   *Banana Nut Cookies*

Prep time: 10 minutes, Cook time: 15 minutes, Serves: 18

Ingredients:

- *1 ½ cup banana, mashed*
- *What you'll need from the store cupboard: 2 cups of oats*
- *1 cup raisins*
- *1 cup walnuts*
- *1/3 cup sunflower oil*
- *1 tsp vanilla*
- *½ tsp salt*

Instructions:

✓ *Heat oven to 350 degrees.*

✓ *In a large bowl, combine oats, raisins, walnuts, and salt.*

✓ *In a medium bowl, mix banana, oil, and vanilla. Stir into oat mixture until combined. Let rest 15 minutes.*

✓ *Drop by rounded tablespoonful onto 2 ungreased cookie sheets. Bake 15 minutes, or until a light golden brown. Cool and store in an airtight container. The serving size is 2 cookies.*

Nutrition Facts Per Serving Nutrition: Calories 148 Total Carbs 16g Net Carbs 14g Protein 3g Fat 9g Sugar 6g Fiber 2g

199)   *BLT Stuffed Cucumbers*

Prep time: 15 minutes, Serves: 4

Ingredients:

- *3 slices bacon, cooked crisp and crumbled 1 large cucumber*
- *½ cup lettuce, diced fine*
- *½ cup baby spinach, diced fine*
- *¼ cup tomato, diced fine*
- *What you'll need from the store cupboard: 1 tbsp. + ½ tsp fat-free mayonnaise ¼ tsp black pepper*

- *1/8 tsp salt*

Instructions:

✓ *Peel the cucumber and slice it in half lengthwise. Use a spoon to remove the seeds.*

✓ *In a medium bowl, combine the remaining ingredients and stir well.*

✓ *Spoon the bacon mixture into the cucumber halves. Cut into 2-inch pieces and serve.*

Nutrition: Calories 95 Total Carbs 4g Net Carbs 3g Protein 6g Fat 6g Sugar 2g Fiber

200) *Buffalo Bites*

Prep time: 5 minutes, Cook time: 10 minutes, Serves: 4

Ingredients:

- *1 egg*
- *½ head of cauliflower, separated into florets*
- *What you'll need from the store cupboard: 1 cup panko bread crumbs*
- *1 cup low-fat ranch dressing*
- *½ cup hot sauce*
- *½ tsp salt*
- *½ tsp garlic powder*
- *Black pepper*
- *Nonstick cooking spray*

Instructions:

✓ *Heat oven to 400 degrees. Spray a baking sheet with cooking spray.*

✓ *Place the egg in a medium bowl and mix in the salt, pepper, and garlic. Place the panko crumbs into a small bowl.*

✓ *Dip the florets first in the egg then into the panko crumbs. Place in a single layer on prepared pan.*

✓ *Bake 8-10 minutes, stirring halfway through until cauliflower is golden brown and crisp on the outside.*

✓ *In a small bowl, stir the dressing and hot sauce together. Use for dipping.*

Nutrition: Calories 132 Total Carbs 15g Net Carbs 14g Protein 6g Fat 5g Sugar 4g Fiber 1g

201) *Candied Pecans*

Prep time: 5 minutes, Cook time: 10 minutes, Serves: 6

Ingredients:

- *1 ½ tsp butter*
- *What you'll need from the store cupboard: 1*
- *½ cup pecan halves*
- *2 ½ tbsp. Splenda divided 1 tsp cinnamon*
- *¼ tsp ginger*
- *1/8 tsp cardamom*
- *1/8 tsp salt*

Instructions:

✓ *In a small bowl, stir together 1 1/2 teaspoons Splenda, cinnamon, ginger, cardamom, and salt. Set aside.*

✓ *Melt butter in a medium skillet over med-low heat. Add pecans and two tablespoons Splenda. Reduce heat to low and cook, occasionally stirring, until sweetener melts, about 5 to 8 minutes.*

✓ *Add spice mixture to the skillet and stir to coat pecans. Spread mixture to parchment paper and let cool for 10-15 minutes. Store in an airtight container. The serving size is ¼ cup.*

Nutrition: Calories 173 Total Carbs 8g Net Carbs 6g Protein 2g Fat 16g Sugar 6g Fiber 2g

202) *Cauliflower Hummus*

Prep time: 5 minutes, Cook time: 15 minutes, serves 6

Ingredients:

- *3 cup cauliflower florets*
- *3 tbsp. fresh lemon juice*
- *What you'll need from the store cupboard: 5 cloves garlic, divided*
- *5 tbsp. olive oil, divided*
- *2 tbsp. water*
- *1 ½ tbsp. Tahini paste*
- *1 ¼ tsp salt, divided*

Instructions

✓ *Smoked paprika and extra olive oil for serving:*

✓ *In a microwave-safe bowl, combine cauliflower, water, 2 tablespoons oil, ½ teaspoon salt, and 3 whole cloves garlic. Microwave on high for 15 minutes or until cauliflower is soft and darkened.*

✓ *Transfer mixture to a food processor or blender and process until almost smooth. Add tahini paste, lemon juice, remaining garlic cloves, remaining oil, and salt. Blend until almost smooth.*

✓ *Place the hummus in a bowl and drizzle lightly with olive oil and a sprinkle or two of paprika. Serve with your favorite raw vegetables.*

Nutrition: Calories 107 Total Carbs 5g Net Carbs 3g

Protein 2g Fat 10g Sugar 1g Fiber 2g

203) *Cheese Crisp Crackers*

Prep time: 5 minutes, Cook time: 10 minutes, Serves: 4
Ingredients:

- 4 slices pepper Jack cheese, quartered
- 4 slices Colby Jack cheese, quartered
- 4 slices cheddar cheese, quartered

Instructions:

- ✓ Heat oven to 400 degrees. Line a cooking sheet with parchment paper.
- ✓ Place cheese in a single layer on a prepared pan and bake 10 minutes, or until cheese gets firm.
- ✓ Transfer to paper towel line surface to absorb excess oil. Let cool, and cheese will crisp up more as it cools.
- ✓ Store in an airtight container or Ziploc bag. Serve with your favorite dip or salsa.

Nutrition: Calories 253 Total Carbs 1g Protein 15g Fat 20g Sugar 0g Fiber 0g

204) *Breakfast Bark with Berries*

Time Required for Cooking: 2 Hours

- 3-4 chopped strawberries
- 1/2 cup plain Greek yogurt
- 1/2 tbsp. blueberries
- What you'll require from your pantry:
- 1/2 cup granola reduced in fat
- 3 tbsp sugar-free maple syrup

Directions:

- ✓ Preheat the oven to 350°F. Line a baking sheet with parchment paper.
- ✓ In a medium bowl, whisk together yogurt and syrup until smooth.
- ✓ Fill prepared pan halfway with batter and spread in a thin, equal layer.
- ✓ Sprinkle remaining ingredients on top.
- ✓ Wrap in foil and place in the freezer for two hours or overnight.
- ✓ To serve, cut the squares in half and serve immediately.
- ✓ If the bark is allowed to thaw excessively, it will lose its shape.
- ✓ Any residual bark should be frozen in an airtight container.

Nutrition: 69 Nutrition: Calories 18g Carbohydrates 18g Net Carbohydrates 16g Protein 7 g fat 6 g sugar 7 g dietary fiber 2 g

205) *Eggs Cocotte*

15 Minutes Cooking

- 1 tbsp. olive oil soup
- 2 tbsp. crumbled ricotta soup
- 1 tbsp. parmesan cheese soup
- 1 slice gorgonzola cheese
- 1 slice Brie cheese
- Nutmeg and salt to taste

Directions:

- ✓ Coat the bottom of a small glass refractory with olive oil. Season the cheese with nutmeg and salt on the bottom. Incorporate the cream.
- ✓ Gently add the egg to the refractory mixture in a cup.
- ✓ Preheat the air fryer for 5 minutes at 200C. In the basket of the air fryer, place the refractory, set the timer to 10 minutes, and push the power button. Remove from heat and serve immediately.

Nutrition: 138 Calories Carbohydrates: 3 g 33 g fat 7.4 g protein 2 g fiber

206) *Strawberries and Cream Buns*

6 portions 12 Minutes Cooking

- 240 g all-purpose flour
- 50 g granulated sugar
- 8 g baking powder
- 1 g salt
- 85 g chilled butter
- 84 g fresh strawberries
- 120 ml whipping cream
- 2 big eggs
- 10 ml vanilla extract 5 ml water

Directions:

- ✓ In a large mixing basin, sift flour, sugar, baking powder, and salt.
- ✓ Using a blender or your hands, combine the butter and flour until the mixture resembles thick crumbs.
- ✓ Combine the strawberries and flour mixture in a medium bowl.
- ✓ Allow the mixture to stand for 10 minutes.
- ✓ In a separate dish, whisk together the whipped cream, 1 egg, and vanilla extract.
- ✓ Stir the cream mixture into the flour mixture until smooth, then spread the mixture to a 38 mm thickness.

- ✓ Cut the buns with a round cookie cutter.
- ✓ Spread the buns with an egg and water mixture.
- ✓ Reserving
- ✓ Preheat the air fryer to 180 degrees Celsius.
- ✓ Line the warmed inside basket with baking paper.
- ✓ Arrange the buns on the baking paper and bake at 180°C for 12 minutes, or until golden brown.

Nutrition: 150 Calories 14g fat 3g Carbohydrates 11g protein 8 g sugar 0mg cholesterol

207) *Breakfast Popsicles with Yogurt and Granola*

6 portions Time Required for Cooking: 8 Hours

- 1/2 cup chopped fresh berries
- 1/4 cup plain low-fat yogurt
- What you'll need from the pantry
- 6 tbsp. crumbled granola
- 4 tbsp. divided sugar-free maple syrup
- 1 tsp vanilla

Directions:

- ✓ In a medium mixing bowl, combine yogurt, berries, 2 tbsp maple syrup, and vanilla extract.
- ✓ Distribute evenly among Popsicle molds.
- ✓ In a small mixing bowl, combine the remaining syrup and granola.
- ✓ 1 tablespoon of the granola mixture on top of each Popsicle
- ✓ Insert sticks and freeze for at least 8 hours, preferably overnight.
- ✓ Popsicles can be frozen for up to a week.

Nutritional Information:73 Nutrition: Calories Carbohydrates in total: 20g Carbohydrates in net: 18g Protein: 5g Fat: 4g Sugar: 7g Fiber: 2g

208) *Squares of Spinach and Cheddar*

4 portions Time Required for Cooking: 40 Minutes

- 10 oz. frozen spinach, thawed and squeezed dry
- 1/2 cup-egg substitute
- 3/4 cup skim milk
- 3/4 cup grated reduced-fat cheddar cheese
- What you'll need from your pantry:
- 2 tbsp. reduced-fat parmesan cheese

- 1 tbsp. bread crumbs
- 1/2 tsp. dried chopped onion
- 1/2 tsp. salt
- 1/4 ts garlic powder
- 1/4 tsp pepper

Directions:

- ✓ Preheat the oven to 350 degrees Fahrenheit.
- ✓ Cooking spray an 8-inch square baking dish.
- ✓ Bread crumbs should be sprinkled over the bottom of the prepared dish.
- ✓ Add 12 cups of cheese, spinach, and red pepper to the top.
- ✓ Whisk together the remaining ingredients in a small dish.
- ✓ Distribute over veggies.
- ✓ 35 minutes in the oven.
- ✓ Sprinkle remaining cheese on top and bake for an additional 2-3 minutes, or until cheese is melted and a knife inserted in the center comes out clean.
- ✓ Allow 15 minutes for cooling before cutting and serving.

Nutrition: Cals 159 Carbohydrates 7g Carbohydrates Net Protein 5 g 22 g fat 5 g sugar 4 g dietary fiber 2g

209) *Nutella Waffles*

4 portions Time Required for Cooking: 10 Minutes

- 4 eggs
- 1/2 cuplow-fat cream cheese
- 1/2 cup half-and-half
- 2 tbsp. margarine
- 2 tsp Splenda
- 1 tsp baking powder

Directions:

- ✓ Coat waffle iron lightly with cooking spray and preheat.
- ✓ Combine peanut butter, margarine, and cream cheese in a medium glass bowl.
- ✓ 30 seconds in the microwave and mix to blend.
- ✓ Stir in the cream, baking powder, and Splenda until blended.
- ✓ Add eggs and whisk well.
- ✓ Cook until golden brown and crisp on the outside, ladle onto waffle iron.
- ✓ Serve.

Nutrition: 214 Calories 9g Carbohydrates Net Carbs 8g Protein 9g Fat 15g Sugar 2g Fiber 1g

210) <u>*Bruschetta*</u>

Time Required for Cooking: 10 Minutes

- 4 pieces Italian bread
- 1 cup chopped tomato tea
- 1 cup shredded mozzarella tea
- Olive oil
- Oregano, salt, and pepper

Directions:

✓ Preheat the air fryer to high.

✓ Set a 5-minute timer and the temperature to 2000C.

✓ Drizzle olive oil over the slices of Italian bread.

✓ Between the pieces, divide the chopped tomatoes and mozzarella.

✓ Add salt, pepper, and oregano to taste.

✓ Fill the filler with oil.

✓ Each slice should be topped with a basil leaf.

✓ Carefully place the bruschetta in the air fryer basket, taking care not to spill the contents.

✓ Set a 5-minute timer, adjust the temperature to 180C, and power on the oven.

✓ Arrange the bruschetta on a serving platter.

Nutrition: 434 Calories 14g fat 63g Carbohydrates 11g protein 8 g sugar 0mg cholesterol

211) <u>*Tasty Garlic Bread*</u>

15 Minutes Cooking

- 2 stale French rolls
- 4 tbsp crushed or crumbled garlic
- 1 tbsp. grated Parmesan cheese

Directions:

✓ Preheat the air fryer to high.

✓ Set a 5-minute timer and a temperature of 2000C.

✓ Combine mayonnaise and garlic in a small bowl and set aside.

✓ Slice the baguettes but do not entirely separate them.

✓ Equally fill the cavities.

✓ Sprinkle with grated cheese and brush with olive oil.

✓ Place in the air fryer's basket.

✓ Set the timer for ten minutes, the

temperature to 1800C, and power on the oven.

Nutrition: 340 Calories 15g fat 32g Carbohydrates 15 g protein 0g sugar 0mg cholesterol

212) <u>*Coconut Porridge for Breakfast*</u>

4 portions Time Required for Cooking: 10 Minutes

- 4 cup unsweetened vanilla almond milk
- What you'll require from your pantry:
- 1 cup grated unsweetened coconut
- 8 tablespoons coconut flour

Directions:

✓ In a saucepan, combine coconut and cook over medium-high heat until lightly toasted.

✓ Take care not to allow it to burn.

✓ Bring milk to a boil and add.

✓ Slowly add flour while stirring; cook and stir until mixture begins to thicken about 5 minutes.

✓ Take the pan from the heat; the mixture will continue to thicken as it cools.

✓ Ladle into bowls and top with blueberries or a drizzle of honey, if desired.

Nutrition: Calories 231 Carbohydrates Total 21g Carbohydrates Net 8g Protein 6g Fat 14g Sugar 4g Fiber 13g

213) <u>*Breakfast Popsicles with Yogurt and Granola*</u>

6 portions Time Required for Cooking: 8 Hours

- 1/2 cup chopped fresh berries
- 1/4 cup plain low-fat yogurt
- What you'll need from the pantry
- 6 tbsp. crumbled granola
- 4 tbsp. divided sugar-free maple syrup
- 1 tsp vanilla

Directions:

✓ In a medium mixing bowl, combine yogurt, berries, 2 tbsp maple syrup, and vanilla extract.

✓ Distribute evenly among Popsicle molds.

✓ In a small mixing bowl, combine the remaining syrup and granola. 1 tablespoon of the granola mixture on top of each Popsicle Insert sticks and freeze for at least 8 hours, preferably overnight. Popsicles can be frozen for up to a week.

Nutrition: 73 Calories Carbs in total: 20g Protein: 5g Fat: 4g Sugar: 7g Fiber: 2g

SALAD

214) *Salad de tuna*

Time Required for Preparation: 10 minutes required for cooking: none 3 servings

- 1 can tuna (6 oz)
- 1/3 cups fresh cucumber, diced
- 1/3 cup fresh tomato, chopped
- 1/3 cup avocado, chopped
- 1/3 cup celery, chopped
- 4 tbsp olive oil
- 2 tbsp lime juice

Directions:

- ✓ To make the dressing, whisk together olive oil, lime juice, minced garlic, and freshly ground black pepper.
- ✓ In a salad bowl, combine the salad ingredients and sprinkle with the dressing.

Nutrition: 8 g Carbohydrates 13 g Protein Sugars in total: 1 g 212 g Nutrition: Calories

215) *Salad with Roasted Portobello Mushrooms*

Time Required for Preparation: 10 minutes Time required for cooking: none 4 portions

- 1 1/2-pound Portobello mushrooms, stems removed
- 3 heads sliced Belgian endive
- 1 small sliced red onion
- 4 oz blue cheese
- 8 oz mixed salad greens

Dressing:

- 3 tbsp red wine vinegar
- 1 tbsp Dijon mustard
- 23 cup olive oil

Direction

- ✓ Preheat the oven to 450°F.
- ✓ Whisk vinegar, mustard, salt, and pepper to make the dressing. Add olive oil in a slow, steady stream while whisking.
- ✓ Cut the mushrooms in half and lay them stem-side up on a baking pan. Prepare the mushrooms by coating them with dressing and baking for 15 minutes.
- ✓ Toss the salad greens with the onion, endive, and cheese in a salad dish. She was dressing to taste.
- ✓ To the salad bowl, add mushrooms.

Nutrition: 23 g Carbohydrates 19 g Protein 1 g sugars in total 501

216) *Calories Salad with Shredded Chicken*

Time Required for Preparation: 5 minutes Time required for cooking: 10 minutes 6 portions

- 2 boneless, skinless chicken breasts
- 1 head iceberg lettuce, cut into strips
- 2 bell peppers, cut into strips
- 1 fresh cucumber, quartered, sliced
- 3 scallions, sliced

Directions:

- ✓ Bring 1 cup of salted water to a boil in a skillet.
- ✓ Cover and cook the chicken breasts over low heat for 5 minutes. Take off the cover. Then, using a fork, remove the chicken from the skillet.
- ✓ Combine the veggies and cooled chicken in a salad dish, season with salt, and top with peanut vinaigrette and chopped peanuts.

Nutrition: 9 g Carbohydrates 16 g Protein Sugars in total: 2 g 117

217) *Calories Broccoli Salad*

Time Required for Preparation: 10 minutes required for cooking: none 6 servings

- 1 medium head broccoli, raw, florets only
- 1/2 cup red onion, chopped
- 1/2 oz turkey bacon, diced and fried till crisp
- 1/2 cup cherry tomatoes, halved
- 1/4 cup sunflower kernels
- 3/4 cup raisins
- 3/4 cups mayonnaise

Direction

- ✓ Combine the broccoli, tomatoes, and onion in a salad dish.
- ✓ Combine mayo and vinegar in a small bowl and drizzle over the broccoli.
- ✓ Toss in the sunflower seeds, raisins, and bacon.

Nutrition: 17.3 g Carbohydrates 11 g Protein 10 g sugars in total 220 Nutrition: Calories

218) *Salad of Cherry Tomatoes*

Time Required for Preparation: 10 minutes Time required for cooking: none six portions

- 40 cherry tomatoes, halved
- 1 cup halved mozzarella balls
- 1 cup sliced green olives

- *1 can (6 oz) sliced black olives*
- *2 chopped green onions*
- *3 oz roasted pine nuts*
- *12 cups olive oil*
- *2 tablespoons red wine vinegar*
- *1 teaspoon dried oregano*
- *Season with salt and pepper to taste*

Direction

✓ *Combine the tomatoes, olives, and onions in a salad dish.*

✓ *Combine olive oil, red wine vinegar, dried oregano, salt, and pepper to make the dressing.*

✓ *Drizzle with dressing and garnish with nuts.*

✓ *Refrigerate for 1 hour to marinate.*

Nutrition: Carbohydrates: 10.7 g Protein: 4 g Carbohydrates: 10.7 g Sugars in total: 6 g

219) *Salad with ground turkey*

Time Required for Preparation: 10 minutes Time required for cooking: 35 minutes 6 portions

- *1 pound lean meat turkey*
- *1/2 inch minced ginger*
- *2 minced garlic cloves*
- *1 chopped onion*
- *1 tbsp olive oil*
- *1 bag lettuce leaves (for serving)*
- *1 tsp cayenne pepper*
- *1 tsp powdered turmeric*
- *Season with salt to taste*
- *4 cups water*
- *2 tbsp fat-free yogurt*
- *1 tbsp nonfat sour cream*
- *one tablespoon reduced-fat mayonnaise*
- *1 squeezed lemon*
- *1 tsp red chili flakes*
- *Season with salt and pepper to taste*

Directions:

✓ *In a skillet, heat the olive oil and sauté the garlic and ginger for 1 minute—season with salt and pepper. Cook, occasionally stirring, for 10 minutes over medium heat.*

✓ *Add the ground turkey and cook for an additional 3 minutes. Combine the spices (turmeric, red chili powder, and coriander powder).*

✓ *Add 4 cups water and simmer, covered, for 30 minutes.*

✓ *Combine yogurt, sour cream, mayonnaise, lemon juice, chili flakes, salt, and pepper to make the dressing.*

✓ *To assemble the salad, put the salad leaves on serving plates and top with cooked ground turkey. I was dressing on top.*

Nutrition: 9.1 g Carbohydrates 17.8 g Protein 5 g sugars in total 176

220) *Salad with Asian Cucumbers*

Time Required for Preparation: 10 minutes required for cooking: none six servings

Ingredients:

- *1 pound sliced cucumbers*
- *2 scallions*
- *2 tbsp sliced pickled ginger, minced*
- *1/4 cup cilantro*
- *1/2 sliced red jalapeno*
- *3 tbsp rice wine vinegar*
- *1 tbsp. sesame oil*
- *1 tbsp. sesame seeds*

Directions:

1. *Toss all ingredients together in a salad dish.*

Nutrition: 7 g Carbohydrates 1 g Protein Sugars in total: 1 g 52 Nutrition: Calories

221) *Salad with Cauliflower and Tofu*

Time required for preparation: ten minutes Time required for cooking: 15 minutes 4 portions

- *2 cups blended cauliflower florets*
- *1 diced fresh cucumber*
- *1/2 cup diced green olives*
- *13 cups diced red onion*
- *2 tbsp toasted pine nuts*
- *2 tbsp raisins*
- *1/3 cups crumbled feta*
- *1/2 cup pomegranate seeds*
- *2 lemons (juiced, zest grated)*
- *8 oz tofu*
- *2 tsp oregano*
- *2 minced garlic cloves*
- *1/2 tsp red chili*

Directions:

✓ *Season the cauliflower with salt and drain*

it in a colander.

✓ Combine 2 tbsp lemon juice, 5 tbsp olive oil, minced garlic, chili flakes, oregano, and salt and pepper in a small bowl. To begin, coat the tofu with the marinade and put it aside.

✓ Preheat the oven to 450 degrees Fahrenheit.

✓ Bake tofu for 12 minutes on a baking sheet.

✓ Combine the remaining marinade with the onions, cucumber, cauliflower, olives, and raisins in a salad dish. Combine the remaining olive oil and lemon zest in a small bowl.

✓ Garnish with a sprinkle of tofu, pine nuts, feta, and pomegranate seeds.

Nutrition: 31 g carbohydrate 11 g protein Sugars in total: 15 g 328 Nutrition: Calories

222) *Scallop Caesar Salad*

Time Required for Preparation: 5 minutes Time Required for Cooking: 2 minutes 8 sea scallops

- 4 cups romaine lettuce
- 2 tsp olive oil
- 3 tbsp Caesar Salad Dressing
- 1 tablespoon lemon juice
- Season with salt and pepper to taste

Direction

✓ In a frying pan, heat the olive oil and cook the scallops in a single layer for no more than 2 minutes on each side—season to taste with salt and pepper.

✓ Arrange lettuce on serving dishes and top with scallops.

✓ Drizzle the Caesar dressing and lemon juice over the top.

Carbohydrates: 14 g 30.7 g protein 2 g sugars in total 340 g Nutrition: Calories

223) *Chicken Avocado Salad*

Time Required for Preparation: 30 minutes Time required for cooking: 15 minutes 4 portions

- 1 pound cooked, shredded chicken breast
- 1 avocado, pitted, peeled, sliced
- 2 tomatoes, diced
- 1 cucumber, peeled, sliced
- 1 head lettuce, chopped
- 3 tbsp olive oil
- 2 tbsp lime juice
- 1 tbsp cilantro, chopped

Direction

✓ Whisk together the oil, lime juice, cilantro, salt, and a pinch of pepper in a bowl.

✓ In a salad dish, combine lettuce, tomatoes, and cucumber; toss with half of the dressing.

✓ Toss remaining dressing with chicken and add with vegetable mixture.

✓ Garnish with avocado.

Nutrition: 10 g Carbohydrates 38 g Protein Sugars in total: 15 g 380 Nutrition: Calories

224) *California Wraps*

Time Required for Preparation: 5 minutes Time Required for Cooking: 15 minutes 4 portions

- 4 cooked turkey breast pieces
- 4 cooked ham slices
- 4 lettuce leaves
- 4 slices tomato
- 4 slices avocado
- 1 tablespoon lime juice
- A handful of watercress leaves
- 4 tbsp sugar-free ranch dressing

Directions:

✓ Arrange turkey, ham, and tomato slices on a lettuce leaf.

✓ Combine avocado and lime juice in a bowl and spoon over tomatoes. Add watercress and dressing to the top.

✓ Repeat with the remaining ingredients for 4, adding a turkey slice, ham slice, tomato, and dressing to each lettuce leaf.

Carbohydrates: 4g Protein: 9g Sugars in total: 0.5 g 140 Nutrition: Calories

225) *Cucumber Cup Salad with Chicken*

Time Required for Preparation: 5 minutes Time Required for Cooking: 15 minutes 4 portions

- 12 skinless chicken breasts, boiled and shredded
- 2 long cucumbers, chopped into 8 thick rounds, scooped out
- 1 teaspoon chopped ginger
- 1 teaspoon grated lime zest
- 4 teaspoon olive oil
- 1 teaspoon sesame oil
- 1 teaspoon lime juice

- *Season with salt and pepper to taste*

Directions:

✓ *Whisk together lime zest, lime juice, olive and sesame oils, ginger, and salt in a bowl.*

✓ *Toss the chicken with the dressing and spoon the salad into the cucumber cups.*

Nutrition: 4 g Carbohydrates 12 g Protein Sugars in total: 0.5 g Nutrition: Calories in total: 116 g

226) *Sunflower Seeds with Arugula Salad*

Time required for preparation: 5 minutes Time required for cooking: 10 minutes 6 portions

- *1/4 tsp black pepper*
- *1/4 tsp salt*
- *1 tsp fresh thyme, chopped*
- *2 tbsp toasted sunflower seeds*
- *2 cups halved red grapes*
- *7 cups loosely packed baby arugula*
- *1 tbsp coconut oil*
- *2 tsp honey*
- *3 tbsp red wine vinegar*
- *1/2 tsp stone-ground mustard*

Directions:

✓ *Whisk mustard, honey, and vinegar in a small bowl. Pour oil slowly while whisking.*

✓ *Combine thyme, seeds, grapes, and arugula in a large salad dish.*

✓ *Drizzle with vinaigrette and serve.*

Nutrition: 86.7g Nutrition: Calories 6g protein Carbohydrates: 11g 1g fat

227) *Caesar Salad Supreme*

Time required for preparation: 5 minutes Time required for cooking: 10 minutes 4 portions

- *1/4 cup olive oil*
- *3/4 cups mayonnaise*
- *1 head romaine lettuce, chopped into bite-size pieces*
- *1 tbsp lemon juice*
- *1 teaspoon Dijon mustard*
- *1 teaspoon Worcestershire sauce*
- *3 garlic cloves, peeled and minced*
- *3 garlic cloves, peeled and quartered*
- *4 cups day-old bread, diced five anchovy filets, minced*
- *6 tbsp grated parmesan cheese, divided*

Directions:

✓ *Whisk together lemon juice, mustard, Worcestershire sauce, 2 tbsp. Parmesan cheese, anchovies, mayonnaise, and minced garlic in a small bowl. Season with freshly ground pepper and sea salt to taste. Keep refrigerated.*

✓ *Heat oil in a big nonstick saucepan over medium heat.*

✓ *Sauté quartered garlic in olive oil until lightly browned, perhaps a minute or two. Eliminate and dispose of.*

✓ *In the same pan, sauté bread cubes until gently browned. Season with salt and pepper to taste. Transfer to a serving dish.*

✓ *In a large dish, combine lettuce and dressing. To coat, toss thoroughly. Sprinkle leftover parmesan cheese on top.*

✓ *Garnish with bread cubes and serve.*

Nutrition: 443 kcal 31g fat 16g protein Carbohydrates: 27 g

228) *Salad Tabouleh-Arabian*

Time required for preparation: 5 minutes Time required for cooking: 10 minutes 6 portions

- *1/4 cup chopped fresh mint*
- *1 2/3 cup boiling water*
- *1 peeled, seeded, and diced cucumber*
- *1 cup bulgur*
- *1 cup chopped fresh parsley*
- *1 cup chopped green onions*
- *1 tsp salt*
- *1/3 cup lemon juice*
- *1/3 cup olive oil*
- *3 chopped tomatoes*

Directions:

✓ *In a large mixing bowl, combine boiling water and bulgur. Allow soaking for an hour, covered.*

✓ *Toss in cucumber, tomatoes, mint, parsley, onions, lemon juice, and oil after one hour. Season with freshly ground black pepper and salt to taste. Toss well and refrigerate for an additional hour covered in the refrigerator before serving.*

Nutrition: 185g Nutrition: Calories 11g fat 1g protein Carbohydrates: 18 g

229) *Salad of Tangy Citrus and Grilled Cod*

Time required for preparation: 5 minutes required

for cooking: 10 minutes

- 1/2 cup orange segments
- 3/4 cups chopped red bell pepper
- 1/2 cups shredded carrot
- 1/2 cup shredded kohlrabi
- 1/2 cup shredded spinach
- 1/2 tbsp. Olive oil
- 1 cup grapefruit segments
- 1 cup shredded celery
- 1 tbsp. Minced garlic
- 1 tbsp. shredded fresh basil
- 1 tsp black pepper
- 6 oz baked or broiled cod
- 1 orange's zest and juice

Direction

✓ Coat the grill grate with cooking spray and Preheat to a medium-high heat setting. Grill cod until flaky, about 5 minutes per side, once the grate is hot.

✓ In the meantime, in a large salad bowl, combine all remaining ingredients except the citrus pieces and toss well to blend.

✓ To serve, split salad evenly between two plates and top with 12 grilled cod and citrus pieces.

Nutrition: 389g Calories 22g protein Carbs: 47.6g 15g fat.

230) *Salad Thai with Cilantro and Lime Dressing*

Time required for preparation: ten minutes Time required for cooking: 20 minutes 2 portions

- 1/4 cup cashews
- 1/4 cup fresh mint leaves
- 1/4 cup fresh Thai basil leaves
- 1/4 teaspoon fish sauce
- 1/2 cup julienned green papaya
- 1/2 teaspoon honey
- 1 head chopped green leaf lettuce
- 1 loose handful of fresh cilantro
- 1 tablespoon lime juice
- 1 teaspoon coconut amines
- 3 tablespoons olive oil

Direction

✓ Combine honey, fresh cilantro, fish sauce, coconut amino acids, lime juice, and oil in a mixing bowl. Combine and set aside.

✓ Combine the remaining six ingredients for the salad. Toss everything together to ensure even distribution of the ingredients.

✓ Toss the vegetables with the salad dressing.

✓ Chill before serving.

Calorie count: 649.8g fat: 57.4g Protein: 7.5g Carbohydrates: 28 g

231) *Salad with Truffle Oil, Mushrooms, and Cauliflower*

Time required for preparation: ten minutes Time required for cooking: 25 minutes 4 portions

Ingredients:

- 1/4 tsp freshly ground black pepper
- 1/4 tsp salt
- one 15-oz BPA-free can of unsalted cannellini beans, drained and rinsed
- 1 cup low-sodium chicken broth
- 1 large head cauliflower, chopped into florets
- 1 yellow onion, chopped
- 1/3 cup chopped fresh flat-leaf parsley leaves
- 2 tbsp fresh lemon juice
- 3 minced garlic cloves
- 4 teaspoon truffle oil
- 8 oz cremini mushrooms, sliced

Directions:

✓ Divide cauliflower into three batches and pulse till the size of a rice grain in a food processor. Continue until all batches are complete.

✓ Next, combine broth and beans in a blender for a minute or until smooth.

✓ Place a big pan over medium-low heat and coat with cooking spray.

✓ Add onions and mushrooms and stir-fry for approximately 5-7 minutes, or until liquid is nearly completely evaporated.

✓ Season with pepper, salt, and garlic powder. Cook for an additional minute.

✓ Raise the heat to a medium-high setting and add the lemon juice. Cook and stir for approximately one minute or until liquid has evaporated.

✓ Stir in pureed beans and cook to low heat. Once the sauce is simmering, add the cauliflower and stir well. Cover, decrease the heat to a medium-low setting, and stir regularly while cooking cauliflower until soft, approximately 8-10 minutes.

✓ Once the cauliflower is tender, remove it from the fire.

✓ Stir in the truffle oil, parsley, and 34 ounces of cheese. Combine thoroughly.

✓ 10. Divide evenly among bowls, garnish with remaining cheese, and serve.

Nutrition: Calories: 506.1g 19.3g protein Carbohydrates: 76.4g 17g fat

232) *Salad with Tuna and Avocado*

Time required for preparation: 5 minutes Time required for cooking: 0 minutes 4 portions

- 1 avocado, pit removed, and sliced
- 1 lemon, juiced
- 1 tablespoon minced onion
- 5 ounces cooked or canned tuna

Directions:

✓ Combine the avocado and lime juice in a mixing dish. Combine the avocado and tuna in a masher.

✓ Season to taste with salt and pepper.

✓ Chill before serving.

Nutrition: Calories: 695g 50.7 g fat 45 g protein Carbohydrates: 18.3 g

233) *Salad of Tuna and Mediterranean*

15 minutes for preparation Time required for cooking: 0 minutes 6 portions

- 1/4 cup pitted ripe olives, diced
- 1/4 cup roasted red peppers, drained and chopped
- 1/4 cup mayonnaise dressing with olive oil
- 1 tbsp. Rinsed and drained small capers
- 2 sliced green onions
- 2 x 6 oz. cans tuna drained and flaked

Directions:

✓ In a bowl, combine all ingredients except the salad leaves and bread. You can lay it on top of salad leaves or serve it with toast if preferred.

Nutrition: 197.1g Calories 6.9g protein 7g fat Carbohydrates: 16.3g

234) *Salad With Southwestern Beans and Peppers.*

Time Required for Preparation: 6 minutes Time Required for Cooking: 0 minutes 4 portions

- 1 (15-ounce) can drain and rinsed pinto beans
- 2 cored and sliced bell peppers
- 1 cup corn kernels (cut from 1 to 2 ears or frozen and thawed)
- 1 tbsp. Freshly crushed black pepper
- 2 tbsp. Lime juice
- 1 tbsp. Olive oil
- 1 tbsp. avocado, chopped

Directions:

✓ Combine beans, peppers, corn, salt, and pepper in a large bowl. To taste, squeeze fresh lime juice and whisk in olive oil. Refrigerate the mixture for 30 minutes.

✓ Just before serving, add avocado.

✓ Money-saving tip: Avocado costs fluctuate significantly based on their availability. Additionally, while avocado adds a lot of flavor and satiation to salads, you can make an equally excellent salad by adding a cup of cooked and chopped sweet potatoes and 1 to 2 teaspoons of sunflower seeds.

Nutrition: 245 Nutrition: Calories in total 11g total fat 2g saturated fat 0mg cholesterol Sodium content: 97mg 380mg potassium Carbohydrates in total: 32g 10g dietary fiber 4 g sugars 8g protein

235) *Cauliflower Mashed "Potatoes"*

Time Required for Cooking: 10 minutes 4 portions

Ingredients:

- 1/6 cups water (enough to cover cauliflower)
- 1 head cauliflower (about 3 pounds), trimmed and sliced into florets four garlic cloves
- one tablespoon olive oil
- 1/4 teaspoons salt
- 1/8 teaspoons freshly ground black pepper

Directions:

✓ Bring a big pot of water to a boil on the stovetop. Combine the cauliflower and garlic in a medium bowl. Cook for approximately 10 minutes, or until the cauliflower is soft when pierced with a fork. Drain, reintroduce it to the heated pan, and cover for 2 to 3 minutes.

✓ In a food processor or blender, combine the cauliflower and garlic. Purée the olive oil, salt, and pepper until smooth.

✓ Season with salt and pepper. Transfer to a

serving bowl, stir in the parsley until mixed.

✓ *If preferred, garnish with additional olive oil. Serve right away.*

✓ *If you do not have a food processor or blender, you can make this recipe using a potato masher or hand blender.*

Nutrition: Calories in total: 87g 4g total fat 1 g saturated fat omg cholesterol 210mg sodium 654mg potassium Carbohydrates in total: 12g 5 g fiber 0g sugars 4 g protein

236) *Brussel sprouts roasted*

Time required for preparation: 5 minutes Time required for cooking: 20 minutes 4 portions

Ingredients:

- *1 1/2 pounds trimmed and halved Brussels sprouts*
- *2 tablespoons olive oil*
- *1/4 teaspoon salt*
- *1/2 teaspoons freshly ground black pepper*

Directions:

✓ *Preheat the oven to 400 degrees Fahrenheit.*

✓ *In a large mixing bowl, combine the Brussels sprouts and olive oil and toss until evenly coated.*

✓ *Arrange the Brussels sprouts cut-side down on a large baking sheet, with the flat part touching the baking sheet. Season with salt and pepper to taste.*

✓ *Bake for 20–30 minutes, or until the Brussels sprouts are lightly charred and crisp on the outside and slightly toasted on the bottom. Additionally, the outer leaves will be extra dark.*

✓ *Immediately serve.*

✓ *When selecting Brussels sprouts, look for bright green heads that are firm and heavy in proportion to their size. The leaves should be packed tightly. Avoid sprouts with yellowing leaves—a sign of aging—or sprouts with black spots—a sign of fungus.*

Nutrition: Calories in total: 134 8g total fat 1 grams saturated fat omg cholesterol Sodium: 189 milligrams 665mg potassium Carbohydrates in total: 15g 7g fiber; 4g sugars 6 g protein

237) *Green Salad with Blackberries, Goat Cheese, and Sweet Potatoes*

Preparation Time: 15 minutes Cooking Time: 20 minutes 4 portions

Ingredients:

FOR THE VINAIGRETTE

- *1-pint blackberries*
- *two tablespoons red wine vinegar*
- *one tablespoon honey*
- *three tablespoons extra-virgin olive oil*
- *¼ teaspoon salt*
- *Freshly ground black pepper*

FOR THE SALAD

- *1 sweet potato, cubed*
- *one teaspoon extra-virgin olive oil*
- *8 cups salad greens (baby spinach, spicy greens, romaine)*
- *½ red onion, sliced*
- *¼ cup crumbled goat cheese*

Directions:

✓ *TO MAKE THE VINAIGRETTE*

✓ *In a blender jar, combine the blackberries, vinegar, honey, oil, salt, and pepper, and process until smooth. Set aside.*

✓ *TO MAKE THE SALAD*

✓ *Preheat the oven to 425°F. Line a baking sheet with parchment paper.*

✓ *In a medium mixing bowl, toss the sweet potato with olive oil. Transfer to the Prepare baking sheet and roast for 20 minutes, stirring once halfway through, until tender. Remove and cool for a few minutes.*

✓ *In a large bowl, toss the greens with the red onion and cooled sweet potato, and drizzle with the vinaigrette. Serve topped with one tablespoon of goat cheese per serving.*

Nutrition: Calories: 196 Total Fat: 12g Protein: 3g Carbohydrates: 21g Sugars: 10g Fiber: 6g Sodium: 184mg

238) *Salad of Warm Barley and Squash with Balsamic Vinaigrette.*

Time Required for Preparation: 20 minutes Time Required for Cooking: 40 minutes 8 portions

Ingredients:

- *1 small butternut squash*
- *3 teaspoons plus*
- *two tablespoons extra-virgin olive oil, divided*
- *2 cups broccoli florets*
- *1 cup pearl barley*
- *1 cup toasted chopped walnuts*

- *2 cups baby kale*

Directions:

✓ *Preheat the oven to 400 degrees Fahrenheit. Preheat the oven to 350°F. Line a baking sheet with parchment paper.*

✓ *Peel and seed the squash, then dice it. Toss the squash with two tablespoons of olive oil in a large basin—roast for 20 minutes on the prepared baking sheet.*

✓ *While the squash roasts, mix the broccoli with 1 teaspoon olive oil in the same bowl. After 20 minutes, rotate and push the squash to one side of the oven sheet. Continue roasting the broccoli on the other side for an additional 20 minutes or until tender.*

✓ *While the vegetable roast, cover the barley with several inches of water in a medium saucepan. Bring to a boil, lower to low heat, cover, and cook for 30 minutes, or until the soft vegetables. Drain and rinse thoroughly.*

✓ *Combine the barley, cooked squash and broccoli, walnuts, kale, and onion in a large mixing bowl.*

✓ *Combine the remaining 2 tablespoons of olive oil, balsamic vinegar, garlic, salt, and pepper in a small bowl. To serve, toss the salad with the dressing.*

Nutrition: 274 Calories 15g total fat 6 g protein 32g Carbohydrates 3 g sugars 7g dietary fiber 144mg sodium

239) *Salad with Salmon, Quinoa, and Avocado*

Time Required for Cooking: 20 minutes 4 portions

Ingredients:

- *1/2 cups quinoa*
- *1 cup water*
- *4 (4-ounce) salmon fillets*
- *1-pound trimmed asparagus*
- *1 teaspoon extra-virgin olive oil, plus*
- *2 tablespoons*
- *1/2 teaspoon salt, divided*
- *1/2 teaspoons freshly ground black pepper, divided*
- *1/4 teaspoon red pepper flakes*
- *1 avocado, chopped*
- *1 lime juice*

Direction

✓ *In a small saucepan over medium-high heat, combine the quinoa and water and bring to a boil. Cover, lower the heat to a low level, and simmer for 15 minutes.*

✓ *Preheat the oven to 425 degrees Fahrenheit. Preheat the oven to 350°F. Line a large baking sheet with parchment paper.*

✓ *Arrange the salmon on one side of the baking sheet that has been prepared. Arrange the asparagus on the other side of the baking sheet, tossing it with 1 teaspoon olive oil, 1/4 teaspoon salt, 1/4 teaspoon pepper, and red pepper flakes. Season the salmon and asparagus with 1/4 teaspoon salt, 1/4 teaspoon pepper, and red pepper flakes—roast for 12 minutes, or until browned and tender.*

✓ *While the fish and asparagus are cooking, carefully toss the cooked quinoa, avocado, onions, cilantro, and oregano in a large mixing bowl. Season with the remaining 1/4 teaspoon salt and 1/4 teaspoon pepper. Add the remaining two tablespoons of olive oil and lime juice.*

✓ *Remove the fish's skin and bones and slice the asparagus into bite-size pieces. Serve heated or at room temperature, folded into the quinoa.*

Nutrition: 397 Calories 22g total fat 29g protein 23g Carbohydrates 3 g sugars 8g fiber 292mg sodium

240) *Salad with Cucumber, Tomato, and Avocado*

Time Required for Preparation: 10 minutes Time Required for Cooking: 0 minutes 4 portions

- *1 cup halved cherry tomatoes*
- *1 large chopped cucumber*
- *1 small thinly sliced red onion*
- *1 diced avocado*
- *2 tablespoons chopped fresh dill*
- *2 tablespoons extra-virgin olive oil*
- *1 lemon juice*
- *1/4 teaspoon salt*
- *1/4 teaspoons freshly ground black pepper*

Directions

✓ *Combine the tomatoes, cucumber, onion, avocado, and dill in a large mixing basin.*

✓ *In a small bowl, whisk together the oil, lemon juice, salt, and pepper.*

✓ *Drizzle the dressing over the veggies and toss to coat evenly with the dressing. Serve.*

Nutrition: 151 Calories 12g total fat 2 g protein 11g

Carbohydrates 4 g sugars 4g fiber 128mg sodium

241) *Cabbage Slaw Salad*

Time Required for Preparation: 15 minutes Time Required for Cooking: 0 minutes 6 portions

- *2 cups finely chopped green cabbage*
- *2 cups finely chopped red cabbage*
- *2 cups shredded carrots*
- *three sliced scallions, white and green sections*
- *2 tablespoons extra-virgin olive oil*
- *2 tablespoons rice vinegar*
- *1 teaspoon honey*
- *1 minced garlic clove*

Directions:
- ✓ *Toss the green and red cabbage, carrots, and onions in a large basin.*
- ✓ *Whisk the oil, vinegar, honey, garlic, and salt in a small basin.*
- ✓ *Drizzle the dressing over the vegetables and toss to coat.*
- ✓ *Serve immediately or refrigerate for several hours before serving.*

Nutrition: 80 Calories 5g total fat 1 gram protein 10g Carbohydrates 6 g sugars 3 g fiber 126mg sodium

242) *Salad with Winter Chicken and Citrus*

Time Required for Preparation: 10 minutes Time Required for Cooking: 0 minutes 4 portions

- *4 cups baby spinach*
- *2 tablespoons extra-virgin olive oil*
- *1 tablespoon freshly squeezed lemon juice*
- *1/8 teaspoon salt*
- *freshly crushed black pepper*
- *2 cups chopped cooked chicken*

Directions:
- ✓ *Toss the spinach with olive oil, lemon juice, salt, and pepper in a large mixing bowl.*
- ✓ *In a large mixing bowl, combine the chicken, oranges, grapefruit, and almonds. Gently toss.*
- ✓ *Arrange on four individual platters and serve.*

Nutrition: Calories: 249 12g total fat 24g protein 11g Carbohydrates 7g sugars 3 g fiber 135mg sodium

243) *Salad with Blueberries and Chicken on a Bed of Greens*

Time Required for Preparation: 10 minutes Time Required for Cooking: 0 minutes 4 portions

- *2 cups chopped cooked chicken*
- *1 cup fresh blueberries*
- *1/4 cup finely chopped almonds*
- *1 celery stalk, finely chopped*
- *1/4 cups finely chopped red onion*
- *1 tablespoon chopped fresh basil*
- *1 tablespoon chopped fresh cilantro*
- *1/2 cups plain, nonfat Greek yogurt or vegan mayonnaise (baby spinach, spicy greens, romaine)*

Direction
- ✓ *Combine the chicken, blueberries, almonds, celery, onion, basil, and cilantro in a large mixing bowl. Gently toss to combine.*
- ✓ *Combine the yogurt, salt, and pepper in a small bowl. Combine with the chicken salad.*
- ✓ *Arrange 2 cups of salad greens on each of the four serving plates and divide the chicken salad evenly among them.*

Nutrition: Calories: 207 6g total fat 28g protein 11g Carbohydrates 6 g sugars 3 g fiber 235mg sodium

244) *Salad with Cauliflower and Apple*

Time Required for Preparation: 25 minutes Time Required for Cooking: 0 minutes 4 portions

- *3 Cups Chopped Cauliflower*
- *2 Cups Baby Kale*
- *1 Sweet Apple, cored and chopped*
- *1/4 Cup Basil, fresh and chopped*
- *1/4 Cup Mint, fresh and chopped*
- *1/4 Cup Parsley, fresh and chopped*
- *1/3 Cup Scallions, thinly sliced*
- *2 Tablespoons Yellow Raisins*
- *1 Tablespoon Sun-Dried Tomatoes, chopped*

Directions:
- ✓ *Combine all ingredients in a mixing bowl, tossing before serving.*
- ✓ *Interesting Facts: This vegetable is a good source of vitamin A, vitamin B1, vitamin B2, and vitamin B*

Nutrition: 198 Nutrition: Calories 7 grams protein 8 grams of fat Carbohydrates: 32 g

245) <u>Salad with Corn and Black Beans</u>

Time Required for Preparation: 10 minutes Time Required for Cooking: 0 minutes 6 portions

- *1/4 Cup Cilantro, Fresh and Chopped*
- *1 Can Corn, Drained (10 Ounces)*
- *1/8 Cup Red Onion, Chopped*
- *1 Can Black Beans, Drained (15 Ounces)*
- *1 Tomato, Chopped*
- *3 Tablespoons Fresh Lemon Juice*
- *2 Tablespoons Olive Oil*

Direction

- ✓ *Combine all ingredients in a mixing bowl and chill until cool. Serve at room temperature.*
- ✓ *Interesting Facts: Whole corn contains a high concentration of phosphate, magnesium, and B vitamins. Additionally, it aids healthy digestion and includes antioxidants beneficial to the heart. It is critical to seek out organic maize to avoid genetically engineered products.*

Nutrition: 159 Calories 6.4 grams protein 6 Grams of fat Carbohydrates: 27 grams

246) <u>Salad with Spinach and Orange</u>

15 minutes for preparation Time Required for Cooking: 0 minutes 6 portions

- *1/4 -1/3 Cup Vegan Dressing*
- *3 medium oranges, peeled, seeded, and sectioned*
- *34 oz. fresh and torn spinach*
- *1 medium red onion, sliced and separated into rings*

Direction

- ✓ *Toss all ingredients together and serve with dressing.*
- ✓ *Fascinating Facts: Spinach is one of the most delicious green vegetables available. Each serving contains 3 grams of protein and is an excellent addition to a plant-based diet.*

Nutrition: 99 Calories 5 grams protein 5-gram fat Carbohydrates: 11 grams

247) <u>Salad with Red Peppers and Broccoli</u>

15 minutes for preparation Time Required for Cooking: 0 minutes 2 portions

- *1 oz. Lettuce Salad Mix*
- *1 head broccoli, chopped into florets*
- *1 seeded and chopped red pepper*
- *Dressing: 3 tbsp.*
- *White wine vinegar;*
- *1 tbsp. Dijon mustard;*
- *1 clove garlic, peeled and finely chopped;*
- *1/2 tbsp. Black pepper;*
- *1/2 tbsp. Sea salt, finely chopped;*
- *2 tbsp. Olive oil*
- *1 tbsp. parsley, chopped*

Direction

- ✓ *Drain the broccoli in boiling water onto a paper towel.*
- ✓ *In a separate bowl, whisk together all dressing ingredients.*
- ✓ *Toss together ingredients just before serving.*
- ✓ *Interesting Facts: In various diets, this oil is the primary source of dietary fat. It contains various vitamins and minerals that contribute to lowering the risk of stroke, lowering cholesterol and blood pressure, and aiding in weight loss. It is best consumed cold since it loses part of its nutritional value when heated (though it is still excellent for cooking: the extra virgin is preferable).*
- ✓ *Many recommend taking a shot of cold oil olive every day! Additionally, if you dislike the flavor or texture, you can add a shot to your smoothie.*

Nutrition: 185 Calories 4 grams protein 14 grams of fat Carbohydrates: 8 g

248) <u>Lentil Potato Salad</u>

Time Required for Preparation: 35 minutes Time Required for Cooking: 25 minutes 2 portions

Ingredients:

- *1/2 Cup Beluga Lentils*
- *8 Fingerling Potatoes*
- *1 Cup Scallions, Thinly Sliced*
- *1/4 Cup Cherry Tomatoes, Halved*
- *1/4 Cup Lemon Vinaigrette*

Directions:

- ✓ *Bring two cups of water to a boil in a saucepan and add the lentils—Cook for around twenty to twenty-five minutes before draining. Your lentils should be cooked through.*

✓ Reduce to low heat and cook for fifteen minutes. Drain. Once the potatoes are cold enough to touch, halve them.

✓ Arrange lentils on a serving plate and scatter onions, potatoes, and tomatoes on top. Drizzle the vinaigrette over the salad and season with salt and pepper.

✓ Fascinating Facts Lemons are well-known for their high vitamin C content, containing significant amounts of folate, fiber, and antioxidants. Additionally, it aids with cholesterol reduction. Double Bonus: Lowers risk of cancer and hypertension.

Nutrition: Calories: 400 7 grams protein 26 Grams of fat Carbohydrates: 39 g

249) *Salad with Black Beans and Corn with Avocado*

Time Required for Preparation: 20 minutes Time Required for Cooking: 15 minutes 6 portions

Ingredients:

- 1 and 1/2 cup cooked & frozen or canned corn kernels
- 1/2 cupolive oil
- 1 minced garlic clove
- 1/3 cup fresh lime juice
- 1 avocado (peeled, pitted, and diced)
- 18 teaspoons cayenne pepper
- 2 cans black beans (about 15 oz.)
- 6 thinly sliced green onions
- 1/2 cup fresh cilantro
- 2 chopped tomatoes
- 1 chopped red bell pepper
- 1/2 teaspoon salt

Directions:

✓ Combine the olive oil, lime juice, garlic, cayenne pepper, and salt in a small jar.

✓ Replace the top and shake vigorously until all of the contents in the container are thoroughly blended.

✓ In a large dish or covered plastic container, combine the green onions, corn, beans, bell pepper, avocado, tomatoes, and cilantro.

✓ Reshake the lime dressing and pour it over the salad components.

✓ Toss salad to coat beans and vegetables in dressing; cover and chill.

✓ Allow this to settle for a moment or two to mix the flavors properly.

✓ Regularly take the container out of the refrigerator and gently flip it upside down and backward several times to reorganize the dressing.

Nutrition: Calories: 448 0 mg Total Fat 23 g 50.8 g Cholesterol 13 g Carbohydrates Protein: 12 g

250) *Salad with Chickpeas in the Summer*

15 minutes for preparation Time Required for Cooking: 15 minutes 4 portions

- 1/2 Cups Halved Cherry Tomatoes
- 1 Cup English Cucumber, Sliced
- 1 cup canned chickpeas, unsalted, drained and rinsed
- 1/4 cup slivered red onion
- 2 tbsp olive oil
- 1/2 tbsp fresh lemon juice
- Season with salt and ground black pepper to taste

Directions:

✓ Incorporate all ingredients in a mixing bowl and toss to combine before serving.

Nutrition: Calories: 145 4 gram protein 7.5 grams fat Carbohydrates: 16 g

251) *Edamame Salad*

Time Required for Preparation: 15 minutes Time Required for Cooking: 0 minutes 1 portion

- ¼ cups chopped red onion
- 1 cup fresh corn kernels
- 1 Cup Shelled & Thawed Edamame Beans
- 1 Red Bell Pepper, Chopped
- 2-3 Tablespoons Fresh Lime Juice
- 5-6 Fresh & Sliced Basil Leaves
- 5-6 Fresh & Sliced Mint Leaves
- Sea Salt & Black Pepper to Taste

Directions:

✓ Combine all ingredients in a Mason jar and carefully seal. Before serving, shake vigorously.

✓ Fascinating Facts Corn in its entirety is an excellent source of phosphate, magnesium, and B vitamins. Additionally, it aids healthy digestion and includes antioxidants beneficial to the heart. It is critical to seek out organic maize to avoid genetically engineered products.

Nutrition: Calories: 299 20 grams protein 9 grams of fat Carbohydrates: 38 g

252) *Fruity Kale Salad*

Time Required for Preparation: 30 minutes Time Required for Cooking: 0 minutes 4 portions

Ingredients:

- *Salad:*
- *10 oz. Baby Kale;*
- *12 oz. Pomegranate Arils;*
- *1 tbsp. Olive Oil;*
- *1 sliced apple*
- *Dressing:*
- *3 tbsp. Apple cider vinegar*
- *3 tbsp. Olive oil*
- *1 tbsp. tahini sauce (optional)*
- *sea salt and freshly ground black pepper to taste*

Direction

✓ *Thoroughly wash and dry the kale. Suppose kale is prohibitively expensive; substitute lettuce, arugula, or spinach. Remove the stems and cut the leaves.*

✓ *Combine all salad ingredients in a large mixing bowl.*

✓ *Whisk together all dressing ingredients until smooth before spreading it over the salad just before serving.*

Nutrition: 220 Calories 4-gram protein 17 Grams of fat Carbohydrates: 16 g

253) *Salad with Olives and Fennel*

Preparation Time: 5 minutes Required for Cooking: 0 minutes 3 portions

- *6 Tablespoons Olive Oil*
- *3 Fennel Bulbs, Trimmed, Cored, and Quartered*
- *2 Tablespoons, Parsley, Fresh & Chopped*
- *1 Lemon, Juiced & Zesty*
- *½ Cup of black olives*

Direction

✓ *Take Black Olives, Sea Salt & Black Pepper to Taste Ascertain that the cut side is facing upward.*

✓ *Combine the lemon zest, lemon juice, salt, pepper, and oil in a mixing bowl and pour over the fennel.*

✓ *Sprinkle your olives on top and bake at 400 degrees for 15 minutes.*

✓ *Serve garnished with parsley.*

✓ *Fascinating Facts In a number of diets, this oil provides the primary source of dietary*

fat. It contains various vitamins and minerals that contribute to lowering the risk of stroke, lowering cholesterol and blood pressure, and aiding in weight loss. It is best consumed cold since it loses part of its nutritional value when heated (though it is still excellent for cooking: the extra virgin is preferable). Many recommend taking a shot of cold oil olive every day! Bonus: if you're not a fan of the flavor or texture, simply add a shot to your smoothie.

Nutrition: 331 Calories 3 grams protein 29 Grams of fat Carbohydrates: 15 g

254) *Gazpacho de Tomas*

Time Required for Preparation: 2 hours and 25 minutes Time Required for Cooking: 0 minutes 6 portions

- *2 tbsp. + 1 tbsp. Red wine vinegar, divided*
- *1/2 tbsp. Pepper*
- *1 tbsp. sea salt*
- *1/4 cup Fresh Basil, Chopped*
- *3 Tablespoons + 2 Teaspoons Olive Oil, Divided*
- *1 Clove Garlic, crushed*
- *1 Red Bell Pepper, Sliced & Seeded*
- *1 Cucumber, Chunked*

Directions:

✓ *Cover half of the cucumber, bell pepper, and 14 cups of each tomato in a dish. Place it in the frying pan.*

✓ *Puree the remaining tomatoes, cucumber, and bell pepper in a blender with the garlic, three tablespoons oil, two teaspoons vinegar, sea salt, and black pepper until smooth. Transfer the mixture to a bowl and refrigerate for two hours.*

✓ *Chop the avocado and combine it with the remaining oil, vinegar, salt, pepper, and basil.*

✓ *Ladle the tomato puree mixture into dishes and serve as a salad with chopped veggies.*

Nutrition: Calories: 181 3 grams protein 14 grams of fat Carbohydrates: 14 g

255) *Salad with Snow Whites*

Time Required for Preparation: 10 minutes Time Required for Cooking: 5 minutes 4 portions

- *2 Cups Greek yogurt*
- *1 large or two small cucumbers, fresh or pickled*

- *1/2 cup crumbled walnuts*
- *2-3 smashed garlic cloves*
- *12 bunch dill*
- *season with salt to taste*
- *2 tbsps Olive oil*

Directions:

✓ *Using a piece of cheesecloth or a clean white dishtowel, strain the yogurt. It can be hung over a bowl or a sink.*

✓ *In a large bowl, lay the cucumbers, peeled and diced. Combine the smashed walnuts and garlic, the oil, and the finely chopped dill in a medium bowl. Scoop the drained yogurt into a mixing basin and whisk vigorously.*

✓ *Season with salt to taste, cover with cling film, and chill for at least an hour to allow the flavors to meld.*

Nutrition: Calories: 523; Fat total: 50g; Carbohydrates total: 9g; Fiber total: 4g; Sugar total: 2g; Protein total: 13g; Sodium total: 366mg

256) *Green Salad*

Preparation Time: 10 minutes Time Required for Cooking: 5 minutes 4 portions

- *1 head of green lettuce, cleaned and drained*
- *1 cucumber, sliced*
- *a bunch of radishes, sliced*
- *a bunch of spring onions, finely chopped*
- *season with salt to taste*

Direction

✓ *Thinly slice the lettuce. Cucumber and radishes should be sliced as thinly as possible, and spring onions should be chopped.*

✓ *In a large salad bowl, combine all of the salad ingredients; add the lemon juice and oil, and season with salt to taste.*

Nutrition: Calories: 242; Fat total: 9g; Carbohydrates total: 35g; Fiber total: 10g; Sugar total: 8g; Protein total: 9g; Sodium total: 688mg

257) *Pepper Dip with Roasted Eggplant*

Time Required for Preparation: 10 minutes Time Required for Cooking: 5 minutes 4 portions

- *2 medium eggplants*
- *2 red or green bell peppers*
- *2 tomatoes*

- *3 crushed garlic cloves*
- *fresh parsley*
- *1-2 tbsp red wine vinegar*
- *olive oil, to taste*

Direction

✓ *Wash and dry the vegetables. Prick the eggplants' skins. Bake the eggplants, tomatoes, and peppers for about 40 minutes, or until the skins are well burned. Remove from the oven and set aside for approximately 10 minutes in a closed container.*

✓ *Remove the skins and wring off any excess fluids. Remove the seeds from the peppers. All vegetables should be cut into small bits. Combine the garlic with a fork or in a food processor until well combined.*

✓ *Stir in the olive oil, vinegar, and season with salt to taste. Restir. Serve chilled, garnished with parsley.*

Nutrition: 476 Calories; 40g total fat; 26g total carbohydrate; 11g fiber; 10g sugar; 9g protein; 655mg sodium

258) *Salad Russe*

15 minutes for preparation Time Required for Cooking: 5 minutes 4 portions

- *3 potatoes*
- *2 carrots*
- *1 cup cooked, drained green peas*
- *1 cup mayonnaise*
- *5-6 chopped pickled gherkins*
- *salt to taste*
- *6-7 black olives, to serve*

Directions:

✓ *Cook the potatoes and carrots in salted water until tender, then slice them into tiny pieces. Combine all ingredients, except the mayonnaise, in a serving bowl. Season with salt and pepper to taste, then whisk in the mayonnaise.*

✓ *Sprinkle parsley and olives over the top. Serve at room temperature.*

Nutrition: 326 Calories; 24g total fat; 22g total carbohydrate; 4g fiber; 7g sugar; 8g protein; 573mg sodium

259) *Yogurt-Fried Zucchinis*

Time Required for Preparation: 10 minutes Time Required for Cooking: 5 minutes 4 portions

- *4 medium zucchinis*

- 1/2 cup yogurt
- 3 crushed garlic cloves
- a handful of minced fresh dill
- 1 cup all-purpose flour
- salt, to taste

Direction

✓ In a bowl, combine the garlic and chopped dill with the yogurt—season with salt to taste and place in the refrigerator.

✓ Wash and peel the zucchinis, then slice them thinly diagonally or in 0.20-inch-thick rings. Season with salt and place them in a good basin, angled to drain away any juices.

✓ Coat the zucchinis with flour and cook, occasionally turning, until golden brown (about 3 minutes on each side). Transfer to paper towels and pat dry with a paper towel. Serve the zucchinis hot or cold with a side of garlic yogurt.

Nutrition: 499 Nutrition: Calories; 41g total fat; 26g total carbohydrate; 8g fiber; 9g sugar; 12g protein; 859mg sodium

260) *Lyutenitsa-Bulgarian Tomato Dip*

Preparation Time: 10 minutes Time Required for Cooking: 5 minutes 4 portions

Ingredients:

- 5 lb red peppers
- 4 lb Roma tomatoes
- 3 lb eggplant
- 2 lb carrots
- 6-7 crushed garlic cloves
- 1/3 cup sugar
- 3-4 tsp salt
- 2/3 cup sunflower oil (optional)

Directions:

✓ Wash and roast the eggplants and peppers in a preheated oven set to 480 degrees Fahrenheit until the skins are slightly blackened. Remove from the oven and set aside approximately 5 minutes in a closed container. Remove the skins and wring out any excess fluids. In a blender, combine all ingredients.

✓ Rinse the tomatoes thoroughly, chop them into quarters, and blend on the lowest setting until they are chunky but not too much.

✓ Bring the vegetables to a boil.

✓ In a big pot, combine all vegetables. Add the garlic, sugar, salt, and oil and cook over medium-high heat, frequently stirring, for approximately 3-4 hours, or until the liquid evaporates and the lutenists thicken. You can also bake the lyutenitsa in the oven.

✓ Check to see if the lyutenitsa is finished by placing a spoonful on a clean, dry plate; if a wide "watery ring" forms around the thicker mixture, it is not finished yet.

✓ Ladle into hot jars when finished. Invert or process for 10 minutes in boiling water.

Nutrition: Calories: 306; Fat total: 20g; Carbohydrates total: 24g; Fiber total: 6g; Sugar total: 7g; Protein total: 11g; Sodium total: 706mg

261) *Potato Salad*

Preparation Time: 10 minutes Time Required for Cooking: 5 minutes 4 portions

- 4-5 big potatoes
- 2-3 spring onions, coarsely chopped
- 5 tbsp sunflower or olive oil
- season with salt and pepper to taste

Directions:

- Peel and boil the potatoes for approximately 20-25 minutes, then drain and chill.

- In a salad bowl, carefully combine the finely chopped spring onions, lemon juice, salt, pepper, and olive oil. Cube the potatoes and place them in the salad bowl. Gently combine and garnish with parsley. Serve at room temperature.

Nutrition: Calories: 238; Fat total: 1g; Carbohydrates total: 46g; Fiber total: 7g; Sugar total: 29g; Protein total: 16g; Sodium total: 15mg

262) *Salad with White Beans*

Time Required for Preparation: 5 minutes Time Required for Cooking: 10 minutes

- 1 cup white beans
- 1 onion
- 3 tbsp white vinegar
- a handful of fresh parsley
- salt and pepper

Directions:

✓ Rinse the beans and soak them in cold water overnight to swell—Cook in the same water as the onion that has been peeled. Once tender, drain and transfer to a larger bowl. Take out the onion.

✓ *Combine oil, vinegar, salt, and pepper well. Pour over still-warm beans and allow to cool for approximately 30-40 minutes.*

✓ *Chop the onion and parsley, combine with the beans, and set aside for at least 40 minutes to cool. Serve at room temperature.*

Nutrition: Calories: 450; Fat total: 13g; Carbohydrate total: 68g; Fiber total: 12g; Sugar total: 7g; Protein total: 17g; Sodium total: 791mg

263) *Ginger Broccoli Chili*

5 Servings 15 Minutes to Cook
Ingredients:

- *8 cup florets de broccoli*
- *1/2 cup extra virgin olive oil*
- *2 freshly squeezed lime juice*
- *2 tbsp grated fresh ginger*
- *2 tsp chopped chili pepper*

Directions:

✓ *Steam broccoli florets for 8 minutes in a steamer.*

✓ *Meanwhile, make the dressing by combining lime juice, oil, ginger, and chili pepper in a small bowl.*

✓ *In a large bowl, combine steamed broccoli and dressing. Toss carefully.*

Nutrition: Calories: 239 Fat: 20.8 g Carbohydrates: 17 g Sugar: 3 g Protein: 3 g 5 g 0 mg cholesterol

264) *Chicken Salad*

6 portions 30 Minutes Cooking
Ingredients:

- *1 kg chicken breast*
- *125 ml chicken broth*
- *1 teaspoon salt*
- *½ teaspoon black pepper*

Directions:

✓ *Add all of the ingredients to the Instant Pot.*

✓ *Secure the lid, close the pressure valve and cook for 20 minutes at high pressure.*

✓ *Quick-release pressure.*

✓ *Shred the chicken. Store in an air-tight container with the liquid to help keep the meat moist.*

Nutrition: Calories 356 Carbohydrates 27.2 g 16 g Sugar 3 g Protein 9 g Cholesterol 5 mg

265) *"Pasta" de Zucchini Salad*

5 portions Time Required for Cooking: 1 Hour

- *5 oz. spiralized zucchini*
- *1 avocado, peeled and sliced*
- *1/3 cup crumbled feta cheese*
- *1/4 cup diced tomatoes*
- *1/4 cup diced black olives*
- *1/3 cup Salad Dressing Green Goddess*
- *1 teaspoon olive oil*
- *1 teaspoon basil Season with salt and pepper to taste*

Directions:

✓ *Arrange zucchini on a cutting board lined with paper towels. Sprinkle with a pinch of salt and set aside for 30 minutes to absorb any extra moisture. Gently squeeze.*

✓ *In a medium skillet, heat the oil over medium-high heat. Cook, constantly stirring, until zucchini is tender, about 3 – 4 minutes.*

✓ *In a large mixing basin, combine zucchini and the remaining ingredients, except the avocado. Wrap in plastic wrap and chill for 1 hour.*

✓ *Garnish with avocado.*

Nutrition: Calories 200 Carbohydrates Total 7g Carbohydrates Net 4g Protein 3 g Fatty Acids 18 g Sucrose 2 g Fiber 3 g

266) *Salad with Broccoli and Mushrooms*

4 portions Time Required for Cooking: 10 Minutes

- *4 sun-dried tomatoes, halved*
- *3 cup torn leaf lettuce*
- *1/2 cupbroccoli florets*
- *1 cup sliced mushrooms*
- *1/3 cup sliced radishes*
- *What you'll need from your pantry:*
- *2 tbsp water*
- *1 tbsp balsamic vinegar*
- *1 tbsp vegetable oil*
- *1/4 tbsp chicken bouillon granules*
- *1/4 tbsp parsley*
- *1/4 tbsp dry mustard*
- *1/8 tsp cayenne pepper*

Directions:

✓ *Place tomatoes in a small bowl and cover with boiling water. Allow 5 minutes before draining.*

✓ *Chop tomatoes into small pieces and*

arrange them in a big bowl. Combine lettuce, broccoli, mushrooms, and radishes in a large bowl.

✓ *Combine remaining ingredients in a jar with a tight-fitting cover and shake vigorously. Toss salad to coat with dressing. Serve.*

Nutrition: 54 Calories, 9g net carbs, 3g protein, 2g fat, 2g sugar, 2g fiber

267) *Salad with Baked "Potatoes"*

8 portions 15 Minutes Cooking

- *2 lb. cauliflower, split into small florets*
- *6-8 slices bacon, chopped and cooked crisp*
- *6 hard-boiled eggs, chilled, peeled, and chopped*
- *1 cup grated sharp cheddar cheese*
- *1/2 cupsliced green onion*
- *1 cup reduced-fat mayonnaise*
- *2 teaspoon yellow mustard*
- *1/2 teaspoon onion powder, split*

Directions:

✓ *Steam cauliflower for 5-6 minutes in a vegetable steamer or a saucepan with a steamer insert.*

✓ *Drain and set aside the cauliflower.*

✓ *Whisk together mayonnaise, mustard, 1 teaspoon onion powder, salt, and pepper in a small bowl.*

✓ *Using paper towels, pat cauliflower dry and place in a large mixing basin. Then add the eggs, salt, pepper, and the remaining 1/2 teaspoon onion powder, followed by the dressing. Gently mix ingredients.*

✓ *Combine the bacon, cheese, and green onion in a large mixing bowl. Serve immediately or cover and chill until ready to serve.*

Nutrition: 247 Calories 8g Carbohydrates Net Carbohydrates 5g Protein 17g Fat 17g Sugar 3g

268) *Salad with Broccoli and Bacon*

Servings: 4

- *2 cups broccoli, divided into florets*
- *4 slices bacon, diced and cooked crisp*
- *1/2 cup cheddar cheese, cubed*
- *1/8 cup finely diced red onion*
- *1/8 cup sliced almonds*
- *What you'll require from the pantry*

- *1/4 cup reduced-fat mayonnaise*
- *1 tablespoon lemon juice*
- *1 tablespoon apple cider vinegar*
- *1 tablespoon granulated sugar replacement*

Directions:

✓ *Combine broccoli, onion, cheese, bacon, and almonds in a large mixing basin.*

✓ *In a separate bowl, whisk together the remaining ingredients until incorporated.*

✓ *Drizzle dressing over broccoli mixture and toss to coat. Refrigerate for at least 1 hour prior to serving.*

Nutrition: 217 Calories 12g Carbohydrates Net Carbohydrates 10g Protein 11g Fat 14g Sugar 6g Fiber 2g

269) *Salad with Watermelon and Arugula*

6 portions Time Required for Cooking: 1 Hour

- *4 cups watermelon, sliced into 1-inch cubes*
- *3 cup arugula*
- *1 lemon, zested*
- *1/2 cup crumbled feta cheese*
- *1/4 cup fresh mint, chopped*
- *From the pantry, gather the following:*
- *3 tbsp. olive oil*
- *Fresh ground black pepper*
- *Salt to taste*

Directions:

✓ *In a large mixing bowl, combine the oil, zest, juice, and mint. Combine thoroughly.*

✓ *Toss in watermelon lightly to coat. Toss in the remaining ingredients. Season with salt and pepper to taste.*

✓ *Wrap in plastic wrap and chill for at least 1 hour before serving.*

Nutrition: Calories 148 Carbohydrates 10g Net Carbohydrates 9g Protein 4 g triglycerides 11 g fructose 7 g Fiber 1g

270) *Salad of Lobster Rolls with Bacon Vinaigrette*

6 portions Time Required for Cooking: 35 Minutes

- *6 slices bacon*
- *2 whole-grain ciabatta bread, halved horizontally*
- *2 (8 oz.) fresh or frozen spiny lobster tails*
- *2 cups fresh baby spinach*

- *2 cups torn romaine lettuce*
- *1 cup chopped seeded cucumber*
- *1 cup diced red sweet peppers*
- *2 teaspoons finely diced shallot*
- *2 tablespoons finely diced fresh chives*
- *What you'll require from the pantry*
- *2 garlic cloves, finely chopped*
- *3 tbsp. white wine vinegar*

Directions:

✓ *Preheat a grill or use medium heat charcoals.*

✓ *Rinse and pat lobster dry. Lobster tails shaped like butterflies Cover and cook for 25–30 minutes, or until the meat is opaque.*

✓ *Remove lobster from heat and set aside to cool.*

✓ *Whisk together 2 tablespoons of olive oil and garlic in a small bowl. Brush the oil mixture on the cut sides of the rolls. Cook, cut side down, until crisp, about 2 minutes. Remove to a chopping board.*

✓ *While the lobster is cooking, cut the bacon and sauté until crisp in a medium skillet. Transfer to paper towels and pat dry. 1 tablespoon bacon grease should be reserved.*

✓ *To create the vinaigrette, in a glass jar fitted with an airtight cover, combine saved bacon grease, vinegar, shallot, remaining 1 tablespoon oil, and chives. Screw the lid on and shake vigorously to mix.*

✓ *Carefully detach the lobster from its shells and cut it into 12-inch chunks. Rolls should be cut into 1-inch pieces.*

✓ *To create the salad, add spinach, romaine, tomatoes, cucumber, peppers, lobster, and bread cubes in a big bowl. To blend, toss. Drizzle with vinaigrette and transfer to a serving dish. Serve with bacon on top.*

Nutrition: 255 Calories 18g Carbohydrates Net Carbohydrates 16g Protein 20g Fat 11g Sugar 3g

271) *Salad with Strawberries and Avocado*

6 portions Time Required for Cooking: 10 Minutes

- *6 oz. baby spinach*
- *2 avocados, diced*
- *1/4 cup crumbled feta cheese*
- *What you'll require from your pantry:*
- *1/4 cup chopped almonds*

- *Creamy Poppy Seed Dressing*

Directions:

✓ *Toss spinach, berries, avocado, almonds, and cheese together in a large bowl.*

✓ *Toss salad with 12 recipes of Creamy Poppy Seed Dressing. If desired, add additional dressing. Serve.*

Nutrition: 253 Calories 19g Net Carbohydrates 13g Protein 4g Fat 19g Sugar 9g Fiber 6g

272) *Salad with Shrimp and Avocado*

4 portions Time Required for Cooking: 5 Minutes

- *12-pound raw shrimp, peeled and deveined*
- *3 cups chopped romaine lettuce*
- *1 cup chopped napa cabbage*
- *1 avocado, pit removed, and sliced*
- *1/4 cup chopped red cabbage*
- *1/4 cucumber, julienned*
- *What you'll require from the pantry*
- *2 tbsp coconut oil*
- *1 tbsp. sesame seeds*
- *Ranch dressing made without fat*

Directions:

✓ *In a medium skillet over medium heat, toast sesame seeds. Shake the skillet frequently to avoid them scorching. Cook for approximately 2 minutes, or until they begin to brown. Place aside.*

✓ *In a skillet, heat the coconut oil. Using a paper towel, pat the shrimp dry and season with the five spices. Combine with heated oil. Cook for 2 minutes on each side or until they begin to turn pink. Place aside.*

✓ *Arrange lettuce and cabbage in a circular pattern on a serving plate. Green onions, cucumber, and cilantro should be sprinkled over the top. Combine the shrimp and avocado.*

✓ *Drizzle desired amount of dressing over the top and sprinkle sesame seeds. Serve.*

Nutrition: Calories 306 Carbohydrates 20g Carbohydrates Net 15 gram protein 15 gram fat 19 gram sugar 4 gram fiber 5 gram

273) *Salad for the Holidays*

8 portions Time Required for Cooking: 1 Hour

- *1 head broccoli, separated into florets*
- *1 head cauliflower, separated into florets*

- *1 red onion, thinly sliced*
- *2 cup cherry tomatoes, halved*
- *What you'll require from your pantry:*
- *1 cup lite mayonnaise Splenda*

Directions:

✓ *Combine vegetables in a large mixing bowl.*

✓ *Whisk together mayonnaise, sour cream, and Splenda in a small bowl. Distribute evenly over vegetables and toss to coat.*

✓ *Refrigerate covered for at least 1 hour before serving.*

Nutrition: 152 Calories 12g Carbohydrates Total 12g Carbohydrates Net 10g Protein 2g Fat 10g Sugar 5g Fiber 2g

274) *Salad with Grilled Vegetables and Noodles*

4 portions Time Required for Cooking: 10 Minutes

- *2 husked ears corn on the cob*
- *1 red onion, sliced into 12-inch thick slices*
- *1/3 cup sliced fresh basil*
- *1/3 cup crumbled feta cheese*
- *What you'll require from your pantry:*
- *1 homemade noodle recipe cook and drain*
- *4 tbsp. vinaigrette d'herbes*
- *Cooking spray with nonstick properties*

Directions:

✓ *Preheat the grill to a medium heat setting. Coat rack with nonstick frying spray.*

✓ *Place corn and onions on the grill and cook, occasionally rotating, for about 10 minutes, or until lightly browned and tender.*

✓ *Remove the corn kernels off the cob and place them in a medium basin. Add the onion, chopped, to the corn.*

✓ *Toss in the noodles, tomatoes, basil, and vinaigrette. Serve with a sprinkle of cheese on top.*

Nutrition: 330 Calories Total Carbohydrates 19g Net Carbohydrates 16g Protein 10g Fat 9g 5g sugar 3g fiber

275) *Salad with Asparagus and Bacon*

1 portion Time Required for Cooking: 5 Minutes

- *1 peeled and sliced hard-boiled egg*
- *1 2/3 cup chopped asparagus*
- *2 crisped and crumbled bacon slices*

- *What you'll require from your pantry:*
- *1 tbsp extra virgin olive oil*
- *1 tbsp red wine vinegar*
- *1/2 tbsp Dijon mustard*

Directions:

✓ *Bring a small saucepan of water to a boil. Cook for 2-3 minutes, or until the asparagus is tender-crisp. Drain and replace with cold water to bring the cooking process to a halt.*

✓ *In a small bowl, whisk together the mustard, oil, vinegar, and season to taste with salt and pepper.*

✓ *Arrange the asparagus in a single layer on a platter and top with the egg and bacon. Serve drizzled with vinaigrette.*

Nutrition: 356 Calories Carbohydrates in total 10g Carbohydrates in net 5g Protein 25g Fat 25g Sugar 5g Fiber 5g

276) *Salad with Apples and Cranberries for the Holidays*

10 portions 15 Minutes Cooking

- *12 oz. salad greens*
- *3 thinly sliced Honeycrisp apples*
- *1/2 cupcrumbled blue cheese*
- *What you'll require from your pantry:*
- *Apple Cider Vinaigrette*
- *1 cup toasted pecan halves*

Directions:

✓ *In a big plastic bag, place the apple slices and squeeze the half lemon over them. Shake the bag to coat.*

✓ *Layer greens, apples, pecans, cranberries, and blue cheese in a big bowl. Drizzle with enough vinaigrette just before serving to season the salad. Toss to evenly coat all ingredients.*

Nutrition: 291 Calories 19g Carbs Net Carbs 15g Protein 5g Fat 23g Sugar 13g Fiber 4g

277) *Salad with Cantaloupe and Prosciutto*

4 portions 15 Minutes Cooking

- *6 mozzarella balls, quartered*
- *1 medium cantaloupe, peeled and cubed*
- *4 oz. prosciutto, diced*
- *1 tbsp. fresh lime juice*
- *1 tbsp. fresh mint, chopped*

- *2 tbsp. extra virgin olive oil*

Directions:

✓ *Whisk together the oil, lime juice, honey, and mint in a large mixing basin. Season to taste with salt and pepper.*

✓ *Toss in the cantaloupe and mozzarella. Distribute the mixture evenly on a serving platter and top with prosciutto. Serve.*

Nutrition: 240 Calories, 6g protein, 18g fat, 16g sugar, 4g fiber

278) *Salad with Pecans and Pears*

8 portions 15 Minutes Cooking

- *10 oz. mixed greens*
- *3 sliced pears*
- *1/2 cup crumbled blue cheese*
- *What you'll require from your pantry:*
- *2 cup halved pecans*
- *1 cup dried cranberries*
- *1/2 cupolive oil*
- *6 tbsp champagne vinegar*
- *2 tbsp Dijon mustard*

Directions:

✓ *Combine greens, pears, cranberries, and pecans in a large mixing basin.*

✓ *In a separate bowl, whisk together the remaining ingredients, except the blue cheese. Toss salad to coat with dressing. Serve with blue cheese crumbles on top.*

Nutrition: 325 Calories 20g Carbohydrates Net Carbohydrates 14g Protein 5g Fat 26g Sugar 10g Fiber 6g

279) *Salad with Asian Noodles*

30 minutes prep time, 4 servings

Ingredients:

- *2 thinly sliced carrots*
- *2 thinly sliced radishes*
- *1 English cucumber, thinly sliced 1 julienned mango*
- *1 julienned bell pepper*
- *1 serrano pepper, seeded and thinly sliced 1 tofu bag Noodles Shirataki Fettuccini 1/4 tbsp lime juice*
- *1/4 cup chopped fresh basil*
- *1/4 cup chopped fresh cilantro*
- *2 tbsp. chopped fresh mint*
- *What you'll require from the pantry*

- *2 tbsp. vinegar de rice*
- *2 tbsp. sauce sweet chili*
- *2 tbsp. finely chopped roasted peanuts*
- *1 tbsp. Splenda*
- *1/2 teaspoon sesame oil*

Instructions:

✓ *Vegetables pickled: Combine radish, cucumbers, and carrots in a large basin. Stir in the vinegar, coconut sugar, and lime juice until the vegetables are well coated. Refrigerate covered for 15–20 minutes.*

✓ *Rinse the noodles under cold water after removing them from the packet. Reduce the size of the parts. Using paper towels, pat dry.*

✓ *To put the salad together. Remove the vegetables from the marinade and place them in a large mixing bowl, reserving the marinade. Combine noodles, mango, bell pepper, chile, and herbs in a medium bowl.*

✓ *Combine 2 tablespoons marinade, chili sauce, and sesame oil in a small bowl. Toss salad to coat with dressing. Serve garnished with peanuts.*

Nutrition: 158 Carbohydrates 30g Carbohydrates Net Protein: 24 g 4g Fatty Acids 4g Sucrose 19g dietary fiber 6g

280) *Slaw in the Asian Style*

5 minutes prep time, 2 hours chill time, 8 servings

Ingredients:

- *1 pound coleslaw mix*
- *5 sliced scallions*
- *What you'll require from your pantry: sunflower seeds, 1 cup*
- *1 cup sliced almonds*
- *3 oz. Ramen noodles, broken 3/4 cup oil de veg.*
- *12 c. Splenda*
- *1/3 cup distilled vinegar*

Instructions:

✓ *Combine coleslaw, sunflower seeds, almonds, and scallions in a large bowl.*

✓ *In a large measuring cup, whisk together the oil, vinegar, and Splenda. Pour dressing over salad and toss to mix.*

✓ *Stir in ramen noodles and refrigerate for 2 hours.*

Nutrition: Calories 354 Carbs 24g Protein 5g Fat 26g Sugar 10g Fiber

281) <u>*Salad with Asparagus and Bacon*</u>

5 minutes for preparation Time required for cooking: 5 minutes

- *1 hard-boiled egg, peeled and sliced*
- *1 2/3 cup chopped asparagus*
- *2 bacon pieces, crisped and crumbled*
- *What you'll require from your pantry:*
- *1 teaspoon olive oil extra virgin*
- *1 teaspoon vinaigrette de vinaigrette*
- *1/2 teaspoon mustard Dijon*
- *1 pinch salt and freshly ground pepper, to taste*

Instructions:

- ✓ *Bring a small saucepan of water to a boil. Cook for 2-3 minutes, or until the asparagus is tender-crisp. Drain and replace with cold water to bring the cooking process to a halt.*
- ✓ *Whisk together mustard, oil, vinegar, and salt & pepper to taste in a small bowl.*
- ✓ *Arrange the asparagus on a platter and sprinkle it with the egg and bacon. Serve drizzled with vinaigrette.*

Nutrition: Calories 356 Total Carbohydrates 10g Net Carbohydrates 5g Protein 25g Fat 25g Sugar 5 g Fiber

282) <u>*Autumn Slaw*</u>

15 minutes for preparation; 2 hours for 8 portions
Ingredients:

- *10 cup shredded cabbage*
- *12 red onion, finely chopped*
- *3/4 cup chopped fresh Italian parsley*
- *What you'll require from your pantry:*
- *3/4 cup sliced and toasted almonds*
- *3/4 cup cranberries, dry*
- *1/3 cup oil de veg*
- *1/4 cup apple cincinnati vinegar*
- *2 tbsp. maple syrup (sugar-free)*
- *4 teaspoon mustard Dijon*
- *1/2 tsp salt*
- *Season with salt and pepper to taste*

Instructions:

- ✓ *Whisk together vinegar, oil, syrup, Dijon, and 1/2 tsp salt in a large mixing basin. Stir in the onion. Allow 10 minutes for resting, or cover and chill until ready to use.*

- ✓ *After 10 minutes, whisk in the remaining ingredients and toss to coat. Season with salt and pepper to taste. 2 hours before serving, cover, and chill.*

Nutrition: Calories 133 Carbohydrates 12g Carbohydrates net 8g Protein 2 g fat 9 g sugar 5 g dietary fiber 4g

283) <u>*Salad with Avocado and Citrus Shrimp*</u>

Preparation time: ten minutes Time required for cooking: 5 minutes 4 portions
Ingredients:

- *1 pound medium shrimp, peeled and deveined; tails removed Salad greens, 8 cup*
- *ONE LEMON*
- *1 diced avocado*
- *1 shallot, finely chopped*
- *What you'll require from your pantry:*
- *1/2 cupsliced and toasted almonds*
- *1 tbsp. extra-virgin olive oil*
- *Season with salt and freshly ground black pepper to taste.*

Instructions:

- ✓ *Lemons should be cut in half, and the juice squeezed from both sides should be placed in a small basin and kept aside. Lemon wedges, thinly sliced*
- ✓ *In a skillet over medium heat, heat the oil. Add lemon wedges and simmer for approximately 1 minute to infuse the oil with lemon flavor.*
- ✓ *Cook, often stirring, until the prawns turn pink. Remove the lemon wedges and set them aside to cool.*
- ✓ *In a large bowl, combine the salad greens. Toss the shrimp in the pan juices to coat. Toss in the remaining ingredients. Serve.*

Nutrition: Calories Per Serving 425 Total Carbohydrates 17 Net Carbohydrates 8 g Protein 35 g Fat 26 g Sucrose 2 Fibrous 9

284) <u>*Salad with Baked "Potatoes"*</u>

15 minutes for preparation; 15 minutes for cooking 8 portions
Ingredients:

- *2 pound. cauliflower, florets separated*
- *6-8 bacon pieces, diced and cooked crisp*
- *6 chilled, peeled, and diced hard-boiled eggs*
- *1 cup shredded strong cheddar cheese*

- *1/2 cup chopped green onion*
- *What you'll require from the pantry*
- *1 cup mayonnaise with reduced-fat*
- *2 teaspoon mustard*
- *1 and a half teaspoon onion powder, divided*
- *To taste, season with salt and freshly ground black pepper.*

Instructions:

✓ *Steam cauliflower for 5-6 minutes in a vegetable steamer or a saucepan with a steamer element.*

✓ *Drain and set aside the cauliflower.*

✓ *Whisk together mayonnaise, mustard, 1 teaspoon onion powder, salt, and pepper in a small bowl.*

✓ *With paper towels, pat cauliflower dry and place in a large mixing basin. Then add the eggs, salt, pepper, and the remaining 1/2 teaspoon onion powder, followed by the dressing. Gently mix ingredients.*

✓ *Combine the bacon, cheese, and green onion in a large mixing bowl. Serve immediately or cover and chill until ready to serve.*

Nutrition 247 Calories Carbohydrates in Total 8g Carbohydrates Net Protein 5 g 17g Fatty Acids 17g Sucrose 3 g

285) *Bacon & Broccoli Salad*

10 minutes prep time, 4 servings
Ingredients:

- *2 cups broccoli, florets separated*
- *4 bacon pieces, diced and fried crisp*
- *1/2 cupcubed cheddar cheese*
- *1/4 cup nonfat Greek yogurt*
- *1/8 cup finely sliced red onion*
- *1/8 cup sliced almonds*
- *What you'll require from the pantry*
- *1/4 cup mayonnaise with reduced-fat*
- *1 tbsp. freshly squeezed lemon juice*
- *1 tbsp. vinegar de cidre apple*
- *1 tbsp. sugar replacement granulated*
- *1/4 teaspoon salt*
- *1/4 teaspoon pepper*

Direction

✓ *Combine broccoli, onion, cheese, bacon, and almonds in a large bowl.*

✓ *Whisk together the remaining ingredients*

in a small dish until incorporated.

✓ *Stir dressing into broccoli mixture. Refrigerate for at least 1 hour prior to serving.*

Nutrition: 217 Calories 12g Carbohydrates Total 12g Carbohydrates Net 10g Protein 11g Fat 14g Sugar 6g Fiber 2g

286) *Salad with Broccoli and Mushrooms*

Time allotted: ten minutes 4 portions
Ingredients:

- *4 halved sun-dried tomatoes*
- *3 cup shredded lettuce*
- *1/2 cupflorets de broccoli*
- *1 cup sliced mushrooms*
- *1/3 cup chopped radishes*
- *What you'll require from your pantry: 2 tablespoons water*
- *1 tablespoon balsamic vinaigrette*
- *1 teaspoon oil de veg.*
- *1/4 teaspoon granulated chicken bouillon*
- *1/4 teaspoon parsley*
- *1/4 teaspoon dried mustard*
- *1/8 teaspoon cayenne*

Instructions:

✓ *Place tomatoes in a small bowl and cover with boiling water. Allow 5 minutes before draining.*

✓ *Tomatoes should be chopped and placed in a large bowl. Combine lettuce, broccoli, mushrooms, and radishes in a large bowl.*

✓ *Combine remaining ingredients in a jar with a tight-fitting lid and shake well. Toss salad to coat with dressing. Serve.*

Nutrition: Calories 54, Carbohydrates 9g Net Carbohydrates 7g Protein 3 g fat 2 g sugar 2 g

287) *Salad with Cantaloupe and Prosciutto*

15 minutes total time, 4 servings

- *6 quartered mozzarella balls*
- *1 medium cantaloupe, peeled and cubed*
- *4 oz. chopped prosciutto*
- *1 tbsp. freshly squeezed lime juice*
- *1 tbsp. chopped fresh mint*
- *What you will require from your store cupboard 2 tbsp. olive oil extra virgin*
- *1 teaspoon honey*

Instructions:

✓ Whisk together the oil, lime juice, honey, and mint in a large mixing basin. Season to taste with salt and pepper.

✓ Toss in the cantaloupe and mozzarella. Distribute the mixture evenly on a serving platter and top with prosciutto. Serve.

Nutrition: Calories 240 Carbohydrates 6 g protein, 18 g fat, 16 g sugar, and 4 g dietary fiber 0g

288) *Salad Caprese*

10 minutes total time, 4 servings

- 3 medium tomatoes, sliced 2 (1-oz.) mozzarella cheese slices, cut in strips
- 1/4 cup thinly chopped fresh basil
- What you'll require from your pantry: 2 teaspoon olive oil extra-virgin
- 1/8 teaspoon sodium chloride
- Pinch freshly ground black pepper

Direction

✓ Distribute tomatoes and cheese evenly among serving dishes.

✓ Season with salt and pepper to taste.

✓ Drizzle oil over and sprinkle basil on top. Serve.

Nutrition: Calories 77 Total Carbohydrates Protein: 4 g 5g Fatty Acids 5g Sucrose 2 g Fiber

289) *Salad with Celery and Apples*

5 minutes prep time, 15 minutes total time, 4 servings

Ingredients:

- 2 diced green onions
- 2 pitted and finely chopped Medjool dates
- 1 thinly sliced honey crisp apple
- 2 cup sliced celery
- 1/2 cup diced celery leaves
- What you'll require from your pantry: 1/4 cup chopped walnuts, Maple Shallot Vinaigrette

Instructions:

✓ Preheat the oven to 375 degrees Fahrenheit. To toast walnuts, spread them out on a baking sheet and bake for 10 minutes, stirring every few minutes.

✓ Incorporate all ingredients in a large mixing bowl and toss to combine.

✓ Dress with vinaigrette and toss to coat. Serve right away.

✓ Nutritional Information Per Serving

171 Calories 25g Net Carbohydrates 21g Protein 3g Fat 8g Sugar 15g Fiber 4g

290) *Salad de Guacamole with Pollo*

Preparation time: ten minutes Time required for cooking: 20 minutes 6 portions

Ingredients:

- 1 pound boneless and skinless chicken breast Avocados, two
- 1-2 seeded and diced jalapeño peppers 1/3 cup diced onion
- 3 tbsp. chopped cilantro
- 2 tbsp. freshly squeezed lime juice
- What you'll require from your pantry: 2 minced garlic cloves
- 1 tbsp. extra-virgin olive oil
- Season with salt and pepper to taste

Instructions:

✓ Preheat the oven to 400 degrees Fahrenheit. Prepare a baking sheet by lining it with foil.

✓ Season chicken with salt and pepper and arrange in a single layer on the Preheated pan. Bake for 20 minutes, or until chicken is thoroughly done. Allow to cool completely before serving.

✓ Once the chicken has cooled slightly, shred or dice it and place it in a large mixing basin. Combine the remaining ingredients in a large mixing bowl, crushing the avocado as you go. Season with salt and pepper to taste. Serve right away.

Nutrition: Calories 324 Total Carbohydrates 12g Carbohydrates Net 5 g Protein 23 g Fat 22 g Sugar 1 g Fiber 7g

291) *Salad with Chopped Veggies*

15 minutes in total 4 portions

Ingredients:

- 1 chopped cucumber
- 1 pint halved cherry tomatoes 3 radishes, chopped
- 1 chopped yellow bell pepper
- 1/2 cup chopped fresh parsley
- What you'll require from your pantry: 3 tbsp. freshly squeezed lemon juice
- 1 tbsp. extra-virgin olive oil
- Season with salt to taste

Instructions:

✓ Toss together all ingredients in a large mixing bowl. Serve immediately or chill in

the refrigerator until ready to serve.
Nutrition: 70 Carbohydrates in total 9g Carbohydrates 7g Protein 2 g fat 4 g sugar 5 g dietary

292) *Crab Slaw with Cream*

Time required for preparation: ten minutes; time required for chilling: one hour. 4 portions

- *12 lb. shredded cabbage*
- *12 lb. shredded red cabbage*
- *2 hard-boiled eggs, chopped*
- *1/2 lemon juice*
- *What you'll require from your pantry: 2 6 oz. cans drained crabmeat 1/2 cup mayonnaise lite*
- *1 teaspoon seeds de celery*
- *Season with salt and pepper to taste*

Direction

- ✓ *Combine both types of cabbage in a big bowl.*
- ✓ *Combine mayonnaise, lemon juice, and celery seeds in a small bowl. Toss with cabbage to coat.*
- ✓ *Toss in crab and eggs and season with salt and pepper. 1 hour before serving, cover, and chill.*

Nutrition: Calories 380 Calories Per Serving 25g Carbohydrates Total Carbohydrates 17g Carbohydrates Net Carbohydrates 18g Protein 18g Fat 24g Sugar 13g Fiber 8g

293) *Salad for the Holidays*

Time required for preparation: ten minutes; time required for chilling: one hour. 8 portions

Ingredients:

- *1 head broccoli, florets separated*
- *1 head cauliflower, florets separated*
- *1 thinly chopped red onion*
- *2 cup halved cherry tomatoes*
- *1/2 cup fat-free sour cream*
- *What you'll require from your pantry: 1 cup mayonnaise, lite*
- *1 tablespoon Splenda*

Instructions:

- ✓ *Combine vegetables in a large bowl.*
- ✓ *Whisk together mayonnaise, sour cream, and Splenda in a small bowl. Distribute evenly over vegetables and toss to coat.*
- ✓ *Refrigerate covered for at least 1 hour before serving.*

Nutrition: 152 12g Carbohydrates Total 12g

Carbohydrates Net 10g Protein 2g Fat 10g Sugar 5g

294) *Salad with Grilled Vegetables and Noodles*

15 minutes for preparation Time required for cooking: ten minutes 4 portions

Ingredients:

- *2 husked ears corn on the cob*
- *1 red onion, quartered and sliced into 12-inch thick slices*
- *1 tomato, finely chopped*
- *1/3 cup chopped fresh basil*
- *1/3 cup crumbled feta cheese*
- *What you'll require from your pantry: a single recipe Cook and drain*
- *4 tbsp. homemade noodles Herb Dressing vinaigrette*
- *Cooking spray that is nonstick*

Instructions:

- ✓ *Preheat the grill to a medium heat setting. Coat rack with nonstick frying spray.*
- ✓ *Grill corn and onions, occasionally turning, until lightly browned and tender, about 10 minutes.*
- ✓ *Remove the corn kernels from the cob and place them in a medium basin. Add the onion, chopped, to the corn.*
- ✓ *Toss in the noodles, tomatoes, basil, and vinaigrette. Serve with a sprinkle of cheese on top.*
- ✓ *Nutritional Information Per Serving*

Nutrition: Calories 330 Carbohydrates Total 19g Carbohydrates Net 16g Protein 10g Fat 9g Sugar 5g

295) *Salad de récolte*

15 minutes preparation time, 25 minutes cooking time, 6 servings

Ingredients:

- *10 oz. deboned and chopped kale 1/2 cup fresh blackberries*
- *12 diced butternut squash*
- *1/4 cup crumbled goat cheese*
- *What you'll require from your pantry: Salad with Maple Mustard Adornment*
- *1 cup pecans, raw*
- *1/4 cup dried cranberries*
- *1/3 cup raw pumpkin seeds*
- *3 1/2 tbsp. extra-virgin olive oil*

- *1/2 tbsp . maple syrup without added sugar*
- *3/8 teaspoon sodium chloride, divided*
- *To taste, pepper*
- *Cooking spray that is nonstick*

Instructions:

✓ *Preheat the oven to 400 degrees Fahrenheit. Cooking spray a baking sheet.*

✓ *Spread squash on preheated pan and toss with 1/2 tbsps oil, 1/8 teaspoon salt, and pepper to coat evenly. 20-25 minutes in the oven.*

✓ *In a large bowl, place the kale. 2 tbsp oil and 1/2 tsp salt should be added and massaged into the kale with your hands for 3-4 minutes.*

✓ *Cooking spray a clean baking sheet. Combine pecans, pumpkin seeds, and maple syrup in a medium bowl until nuts are evenly coated. Pour onto a prepared baking sheet and bake for 8-10 minutes; they can be done concurrently with the squash.*

✓ *To assemble the salad in a large bowl, combine all of the ingredients. Toss in dressing to coat. Serve.*

Nutrition: Calories 436 Carbohydrates 24g Carbohydrates Net Protein 17g 9 g fat 37 g sugar 5 g dietary fiber 7g

296) *Salad de Tacos Nutritious*

15 minutes preparation time, 10 minutes cooking time, 4 servings

Ingredients:

- *2 whole Romaine hearts, chopped*
- *1 pound ground beef, lean*
- *1 full avocado, diced 3 ounces grape tomatoes, half 1/2 cup cheddar cheese, cubed 2 tbsp. red onion*
- *What you'll require from the pantry 1/2 batch Mexican Salad Dressing with a Tangy Flavour*
- *1 teaspoon cumin powder*
- *Season with salt and pepper to taste*

Instructions:

✓ *In a pan over medium heat, brown the ground meat. While the beef is cooking, break it up into little pieces. Stir in seasonings until well combined. Drain grease and set aside for approximately 5 minutes to cool.*

✓ *To begin, combine all ingredients in a big basin. Toss to combine, then drizzle with dressing and toss again. If desired, garnish*

with reduced-fat sour cream and/or salsa.
Nutrition: Calories 449 9g Carbohydrates Total 4g Carbohydrates Net 4g Protein 40g Fat 22g Sugar 3g Fiber 5g

297) *Salad with Apples and Cranberries for the Holidays*

15 minutes total time, 10 servings

Ingredients:

- *Salad greens, 12 oz.*
- *3 thinly sliced Honeycrisp apples*
- *1 teaspoon lemon*
- *1/2 cup crumbled blue cheese*
- *What you'll require from your pantry: Vinaigrette de Cidre d'Apple*
- *1 cup toasted pecan halves*
- *3/4 cup cranberries, dry*

Instructions:

✓ *Squeeze the 1/2 lemon over the apple slices in a big plastic bag. Shake the bag to coat.*

✓ *Layer greens, apples, pecans, cranberries, and blue cheese in a big bowl. Drizzle with enough vinaigrette just before serving to season the salad. Toss to evenly coat all ingredients.*

Nutrition: Calories 291 Total Carbohydrates 19g Net Carbohydrates Protein 15 g 5 g triglycerides 23 g sugar 13 g dietary fiber

298) *Salad with Layers*

Preparation time: ten minutes; servings: ten

- *6 bacon pieces, chopped and fried crisp*
- *2 diced tomatoes*
- *2 sliced celery stalks 1 diced romaine lettuce head*
- *1 chopped red bell pepper*
- *1 cup thawed frozen peas*
- *1 cup shredded strong cheddar cheese*
- *1/4 cup finely sliced red onion*
- *What you'll require from the pantry 1 cup ranch dressing (fat-free)*

Instructions:

✓ *Layer half of the lettuce, pepper, celery, tomatoes, peas, onion, cheese, bacon, and dressing in a 9x13-inch glass baking dish. Repeat. Serve immediately or cover and refrigerate until ready to serve.*

Nutrition: Calories 130 Total Carbohydrates 14g Net Carbohydrates 12g Protein 6g Fat 6g Sugar 5g Fiber 2g

299) <u>*Salad of Lobster Rolls with Bacon Vinaigrette*</u>

Time required for preparation: 10 minutes; time required for cooking: 35 minutes. 6 portions

Ingredients:

- *6 bacon slices*
- *2 ciabatta rolls, whole grain, halved horizontally 3 medium tomatoes, halved*
- *2 (8 oz.) fresh or frozen spiny lobster tails (thawed)*
- *2 cups baby spinach, fresh*
- *2 cups torn romaine lettuce*
- *1 cup chopped seeded cucumber*
- *1 cup chopped red sweet peppers*
- *2 tbsp shallot, finely chopped*
- *2 tablespoons finely diced fresh chives*
- *What you'll require from the pantry*
- *2 garlic cloves, finely chopped*
- *3 tbsp. vinegar de vinaigrette*
- *3 tbsp. extra virgin olive oil, divided*

Instructions:

✓ *Preheat a grill or use medium heat charcoals.*

✓ *Rinse and pat lobster dry. Lobster tails shaped like butterflies Cover and cook for 25–30 minutes, or until the meat is opaque.*

✓ *Remove lobster from heat and set aside to cool.*

✓ *Whisk together 2 tablespoons of olive oil and garlic in a small bowl. Brush the oil mixture on the cut sides of the rolls. Cook, cut side down, until crisp, about 2 minutes. Remove to a chopping board.*

✓ *While the lobster is cooking, cut the bacon and sauté until crisp in a medium skillet. Transfer to paper towels and pat dry. 1 tablespoon bacon grease should be reserved.*

✓ *To create the vinaigrette, in a glass jar fitted with an airtight lid, combine the saved bacon grease, vinegar, shallot, remaining 1 tablespoon oil, and chives. Screw the lid on and shake vigorously to mix.*

✓ *Cut the lobsters into 12-inch chunks after removing them from their shells. Rolls should be cut into 1-inch pieces.*

✓ *To create the salad, put spinach, romaine, tomatoes, cucumber, peppers, lobster, and bread cubes in a large mixing bowl. To*

blend, toss. Drizzle with vinaigrette and transfer to a serving dish. Serve with bacon on top.

Nutrition: Calories 255 per serving 18g Carbohydrates Total 18g Carbohydrates Net 16g Protein 20g Fat 11g Sugar 3g Fiber

300) <u>*Mustard, Salad with "Potatoes"*</u>

15 minutes for preparation, 5 minutes for cooking 8 portions

Ingredients:

- *2 pounds cauliflower, florets separated*
- *1 peeled and sliced hard-boiled egg*
- *1/2 cup diced celery*
- *1/4 cup diced red onion*
- *What you'll require from the pantry*
- *1/4 cup mayonnaise*
- *1 tbsp. relish de pickles*
- *1 tablespoon Mustard Dijon*
- *1/4 teaspoon   celery seeds*
- *1/4 teaspoon   black pepper*

Instructions:

✓ *Cook cauliflower for 5 minutes, or until almost soft, in a vegetable steamer. Drain and set aside to cool.*

✓ *Whisk together mayonnaise, relish, mustard, celery seed, and pepper in a small bowl.*

✓ *Once cauliflower has cooled to room temperature, towel dry and throw in a large mixing bowl. Combine the egg, celery, and onion.*

✓ *The dressing should be poured over vegetables and gently mixed to incorporate. Refrigerate for at least two hours before serving.*

Nutrition: Calories 71 Total Carbohydrates 9g Net Carbohydrates 6g Protein 3g Fat 3g Sugar 4g Fiber 3 gram

301) <u>*Pecan Salad with Pears*</u>

15 minutes total time, 8 servings

Ingredients:

- *10 oz. mixed greens*
- *3 chopped pears*
- *1/2 cup crumbled blue cheese What you'll require from your pantry: 2 cups halved pecans*
- *1 cup cranberries, dried*

- *1/2 cup extra virgin olive oil*
- *6 tbsp. vinaigrette de champagne*
- *2 tablespoons Dijon mustard*
- *1/4 teaspoon salt*

Instructions:

✓ *Combine greens, pears, cranberries, and pecans in a large bowl.*

✓ *In a small bowl, whisk together the remaining ingredients, except the blue cheese. Toss salad to coat with dressing. Serve with blue cheese crumbles on top.*

Nutrition: 325 Calories Carbohydrates in Total 20g Carbohydrates Net Protein: 14 g 5g Fatty Acids 26g Sucrose ten grams fiber

302) *Salad with Pickled Cucumber and Onion*

- *10 minutes total time, 2 servings*
- *12 cucumbers, peeled and sliced*
- *1/4 cup red onion, thinly sliced*
- *From the pantry, you'll need:*
- *1 tbsp. olive oil*
- *1 tbsp. distilled white vinegar*
- *1 teaspoon dill*

Direction

✓ *Toss all ingredients in a medium bowl to mix. Serve.*

Nutrition: Calories 79 Total Carbohydrates 4g Carbohydrates Net Protein 3 g 1 gram fat 7 gram sugar 2 g Fiber 1 gram

303) *Easy Pomegranate and Brussels sprouts Salad*

Time required for preparation: 10 minutes; total time required: 10 minutes, servings; 6

Ingredients:

- *3 bacon pieces, fried crisp and crumbled*
- *3 cup shredded Brussels sprouts*
- *3 cup shredded kale*
- *1/2 cup seeds de pomegranate*
- *What you'll require from your pantry:*
- *1/2 cup toasted and chopped almonds*
- *1/4 cup grated parmesan cheese Citrus Vinaigrette*

Instructions:

✓ *In a large mixing bowl, combine all ingredients.*

✓ *Dress the salad with vinaigrette and toss well to coat. Garnish with additional cheese*

if desired.

Nutrition: Calories 256 Carbohydrates Total 15g Carbohydrates Net Contains 10g protein, 9g fat, 18g sugar, and 5g fiber. 5g

304) *Salad with Shrimp and Avocado*

Time required for preparation: 20 minutes Time required for cooking: 5 minutes 4 portions

Ingredients:

- *12 pound. peeled and deveined raw shrimp*
- *3 cups chopped romaine lettuce;*
- *1 cup chopped napa cabbage;*
- *1 avocado, pit removed and sliced;*
- *1/4 cup chopped red cabbage;*
- *1/4 cucumber, julienned*
- *2 tbsp. finely sliced green onions*
- *2 tbsp. chopped fresh cilantro*
- *1 teaspoon fresh ginger, finely diced*
- *What you'll require from the pantry*
- *2 tbsp. unrefined coconut oil sesame seeds, 1 tbsp.*
- *1 teaspoon five-spice powder*
- *Ranch dressing made without fat*

Instructions:

✓ *In a medium skillet over medium heat, toast sesame seeds. Shake the skillet frequently to avoid them scorching. Cook for approximately 2 minutes, or until they begin to brown. Place aside.*

✓ *In a skillet, add coconut oil. Using a paper towel, pat the shrimp dry and season with the five spices. Combine with heated oil. Cook for 2 minutes on each side or until they begin to turn pink. Place aside.*

✓ *On a serving tray, arrange lettuce and cabbage. Green onions, cucumber, and cilantro should be sprinkled over the top. Combine the shrimp and avocado.*

✓ *Drizzle desired quantity of dressing over the top and sprinkle sesame seeds. Serve.*

Nutrition: Calories 306 Total Carbohydrates 20g Net Carbohydrates 15g Protein 15g Fatty Acids 19g Sucrose 4g Fiber 5g

305) *Salad with Southwest Chicken*

Preparation time: ten minutes, servings: six

- *2 cups cooked and shredded chicken*
- *1 tiny chopped red bell pepper*

- *1/4 cup finely sliced red onion*
- *What you'll require from the pantry*
- *1/4 cup mayonnaise, reduced in fat*
- *1/2 teaspoon   cumin powder*
- *1 teaspoon powdered garlic*
- *1 teaspoon coriander*

Direction

- ✓ *Season with salt and pepper to taste*
- ✓ *In a large mixing bowl, combine all ingredients and stir until well combined.*
- ✓ *Season with salt and pepper to taste. Refrigerate until ready to serve.*

Nutrition: Calories 117 Carbohydrates Total 4g Carbohydrates Net 0g Protein 14g Fat 5g Sugar 2g Fiber 0g

306) *Salad with Strawberries and Avocado*

10 minutes total time, 6 servings

- *6 oz. baby spinach*
- *2 avocados, quartered*
- *1 cup sliced strawberries*
- *1/4 cup crumbled feta cheese What you'll require from your pantry:*
- *Dressing of Creamy Poppy Seeds*
- *1/4 cup sliced almonds*
- ✓ *Toss spinach, berries, avocado, almonds, and cheese together in a large bowl.*
- ✓ *Toss salad with Creamy Poppy Seed Dressing. If desired, add additional dressing. Serve.*

Nutrition: Calories 253 Total Carbohydrates 19g Net Carbohydrates 13g Protein 4g Fat 19g Sugar 9 g

307) *Salad of Summer Corn*

Time required for preparation: ten minutes; time required for chilling: two hours. 8 portions

Ingredients:

- *2 avocados, peeled and cubed in 1/2-inch cubes*
- *1 quart cherry tomatoes, halved*
- *2 cups cooked fresh corn kernels*
- *1/2 cup finely chopped red onion*
- *1/4 cup chopped cilantro*
- *1 tbsp. freshly squeezed lime juice*
- *1/2 teaspoon   lime zest*
- *What you'll require from your pantry: 2 tablespoons olive oil*

- *1/4 teaspoon   salt*
- *1/4 teaspoon   pepper*

Instructions:

- ✓ *Combine corn, avocado, tomatoes, and onion in a large bowl.*
- ✓ *Whisk together the remaining ingredients in a small bowl until mixed. Toss salad to coat with dressing.*
- ✓ *Wrap in plastic wrap and chill for 2 hours. Serve.*
- ✓ *Nutritional Information Per Serving*

Nutrition: Calories 239 Carbohydrates 20g Carbohydrates Net 13g Protein 4 g fat 18 g sugar 4 g dietary fiber 7g

308) *Salad de Portobello*

5 minutes preparation time, 10 minutes cooking time, 4 servings

Ingredients:

- *6 cup salad greens, mixed*
- *1 cup sliced Portobello mushrooms 1 sliced green onion*
- *What you'll require from your pantry:*
- *Warm Bacon or Walnut Dressing vinaigrette*
- *1 tbsp. extra-virgin olive oil*
- *1/8 teaspoon freshly ground black pepper*

Instructions:

- ✓ *In a nonstick skillet, heat oil over medium-high heat. Cook, stirring periodically, for 10 minutes, or until the mushrooms are soft. Reduce heat to low and add onions.*
- ✓ *Arrange salad greens on serving dishes and sprinkle with mushrooms and pepper. Drizzle lightly with a vinaigrette of your choice.*

Nutrition: Calories 81 Total Carbohydrates 9g Protein 0g Fiber 4g Fat 4g Sugar 0g

309) *Salad with Watermelon and Arugula*

Ten minutes for preparation; one hour for chilling 6 servings

Ingredients:

- *4 cups watermelon, peeled and cubed into 1-inch cubes*
- *3 tbsp. arugula*
- *1 lemon, zested*
- *1/2 cup crumbled feta cheese*
- *1/4 cup chopped fresh mint*

- *1 tbsp. freshly squeezed lemon juice*
- *What you'll require from your pantry:*
- *3 tablespoons olive oil*
- *Black pepper, freshly ground*
- *Season with salt to taste*

Instructions:

- ✓ *In a large mixing bowl, combine the oil, zest, juice, and mint. Combine thoroughly.*
- ✓ *Toss in watermelon carefully to coat. Toss in the remaining ingredients. Season with salt and pepper to taste.*
- ✓ *Refrigerate for at least 1 hour prior to serving.*

Nutrition: Calories 148 Total Carbohydrates 10g Net Carbohydrates 9g Protein 4 g fat 11 g sugar 7 g dietary fiber 1g

310) *Salad with Zucchini "Pasta"*

45 minutes for preparation; 1 hour for chilling 5 servings

Ingredients:

- *5 oz. spiralized zucchini*
- *1 peeled and sliced avocado*
- *1/3 cup crumbled feta cheese*
- *1/4 cup chopped tomatoes*
- *1/4 cup diced black olives*
- *What you'll require from the pantry*
- *1/3 cup Salad de la Goddess Verde Dressing*
- *1 tablespoon olive oil*
- *1 teaspoon basil*
- *Season with salt and pepper to taste*

Instructions:

- ✓ *Arrange zucchini on a cutting board lined with paper towels. Sprinkle with a pinch of salt and set aside for 30 minutes to absorb any extra moisture. Gently squeeze.*
- ✓ *Heat oil in a medium skillet over medium-high heat. Cook, constantly stirring, until zucchini is tender, about 3 – 4 minutes.*
- ✓ *Transfer zucchini to a large mixing basin and combine with the remaining ingredients, excluding the avocado. Wrap in plastic wrap and chill for 1 hour.*
- ✓ *Serve with avocado on top.*

Nutrition: Calories Carbohydrates in Total 200 7g Carbohydrates Net 4 gram protein 3 gram fat 18 gram sugar 2 gram fiber 3 gram

PORK

311) **Pork Chops Stuffed with Nuts**

Time required for preparation: 20 minutes 30 minutes for cooking 4 portions

- 3 ounces goat cheese
- 1/2 cup chopped walnuts
- 14 cups toasted chopped almonds
- 1 teaspoon minced fresh thyme
- 4 center-cut pork chops, butterflied

Directions:

✓ Preheat the oven to 400 degrees Fahrenheit.

✓ In a small bowl, combine the goat cheese, walnuts, almonds, and thyme until well combined.

✓ Season the interior and outside of the pork chops with salt and pepper. Stuff each chop, ensuring that the filling extends to the bottom of the chopped area. Stuff the meat with the stuffing and secure it with toothpicks.

✓ Heat the olive oil in a large skillet over medium-high heat. Sear the pork chops in a hot pan until browned on all sides, about 10 minutes total.

✓ Transfer the pork chops to a baking tray and roast for about 20 minutes or until cooked through.

✓ Serve immediately after toothpicks are removed.

Nutrition: 481 Nutrition: Calories 38g fat 29g protein Carbohydrates: 5 g 3 g fiber Net Carbohydrates: 2 g 70% fat / 25% protein / 5% carbohydrate

312) **Pork Loin Roasted with Grainy Mustard Sauce**

Time required for preparation: ten minutes required for cooking: 70 minutes 8 portions

Ingredients:

- 1 boneless pork loin roast (2 pounds)
- Sea salt freshly ground black pepper
- 3 tablespoons olive oil
- 1 1/2 cup heavy (whipping) cream
- 3 tablespoons grainy mustard, such as Pommery

Directions:

✓ Preheat the oven to 375 degrees Fahrenheit.

✓ Season the pork roast well with sea salt and freshly ground pepper.

✓ Heat the olive oil in a large skillet over medium-high heat.

✓ In a skillet, brown the roast on all sides, about 6 minutes total, and transfer to a baking dish.

✓ Roast for approximately 1 hour, or until a meat thermometer inserted into the thickest portion of the roast registers 155°F.

✓ With approximately 15 minutes remaining in the roasting time, combine the heavy cream and mustard in a small saucepan over medium heat.

✓ Continue stirring the sauce until it comes to a simmer, then lower to low heat. Simmer the sauce for approximately 5 minutes, or until it is quite rich and thick. Turn off the heat and set the pan aside.

✓ Allow 10 minutes for the pork to rest before slicing and serving with the sauce.

Nutrition: 368 Nutrition: Calories 29g fat 25g protein Carbohydrates: 29 fat / 25% protein /

313) **Pork Loin**

Preparation Time: 10 minutes Time Required for Cooking: 20 minutes 6 portions

- 1/2 pound patted dry pork tenderloin
- Nonstick frying spray
- 2 tbsp. garlic scape pesto

Direction

✓ Preheat the Air Fryer to 3750F.

✓ Coat the tenderloin on all sides with nonstick frying spray.

✓ Season with pepper, garlic scape pesto, and salt to taste.

✓ Coat the Air Fryer basket with nonstick cooking spray.

✓ Preheat the Air Fryer and place the tenderloin in it.

✓ Cook the food for 10 minutes at 400°F.

✓ Flip over and cook for a further 10 minutes on the first side.

✓ Turn off the air fryer and remove the food.

Nutrition: 379 kcal 8.4g protein; 2g fat; 0g carbohydrate

314) **Pork Tenderloin**

Preparation Time: 10 minutes Time Required for Cooking: 30 minutes 6 portions

- 1 1/2 lbs. pork tenderloin

Direction

✓ *Preheat the Air Fryer to 3700F.*

✓ *Arrange the pork tenderloin in the Air Fryer basket.*

✓ *Cook at 4000F for approximately 30 minutes, flipping halfway through for an even cook.*

✓ *Serve.*

Nutrition: 419 kcal; 5g fat; 0g carbohydrate; 26g protein

315) *Removed Pork*

Time Required for Preparation: 10 minutes Time Required for Cooking: 212 hours 8 portions

- *2 tbsp chili powder*
- *1 tsp garlic powder*
- *1/2 tsp onion powder*
- *1/2 tsp powdered black pepper*
- *1/2 tsp cumin*

Directions:

✓ *1 pork shoulder (4 pounds)*

✓ *Combine chili powder, garlic powder, onion powder, pepper, and cumin in a small bowl. Rub the spice mixture all over the pork shoulder, making sure to get it into the skin. Pork shoulder should be placed in the air fryer basket.*

✓ *Preheat the oven to 350°F and set a timer for 150 minutes.*

✓ *When finished, the pork skin will be crispy, and the meat easily shredded with two forks. At a minimum, the interior temperature should be 145°F.*

Nutrition: Calories: 537 46 g protein 0.8 g fiber 0.7 g carbohydrate 0.7 g fat 35 g 180 mg sodium 5 g carbohydrate 0.2 g sugar

316) *Wrapped with Bacon Hot Dog*

Time Required for Preparation: 5 minutes Time Required for Cooking: 10 minutes 4 portions

- *4 beef hot dogs*
- *4 sugar-free bacon pieces*

Direction

✓ *Wrap a slice of bacon around each hot dog and fasten with a toothpick. Arrange in an air fryer basket.*

✓ *Preheat the oven to 370°F and set a timer for 10 minutes.*

✓ *Halfway through the cooking period, flip each hot dog. When bacon is thoroughly cooked, it will be crispy. Serve immediately.*

Nutrition: Calories: 197 9.2 g protein 0.0 g fiber

Carbohydrates: 3 g Carbohydrates: 10 g 571 mg sodium 3 g Carbohydrates 0.6 g Sugar

317) *Casserole de Bacon et de Cheddar*

Preparation Time: 15 minutes Required for Cooking: 20 minutes 4 portions

- *1 pound 80/20 ground beef*
- *14 medium peeled and chopped white onions*
- *1 cup shredded Cheddar cheese, divided*
- *1 big egg*
- *4 slices sugar-free bacon, cooked and crumbled*

Directions:

✓ *In a medium skillet over medium heat, brown the ground beef for about 7–10 minutes. Drain the fat when no pink remains. Take the pan from the heat and add the ground beef to a large mixing bowl.*

✓ *Combine the onion, 12 cups Cheddar, and egg in a bowl. Combine all ingredients thoroughly and add crumbled bacon.*

✓ *Transfer the mixture to a 4-cup round baking dish and sprinkle the top with the remaining Cheddar cheese. Arrange in an air fryer basket.*

✓ *Preheat the oven to 375°F and set a timer for 20 minutes.*

✓ *The casserole should be golden on top and firm in the center when fully cooked. Serve immediately, garnished with sliced pickles.*

Nutrition: Calories: 369 30 g protein 0.2 g fiber 0 g Carbohydrates 26 g fat 454 mg sodium 2 g carbohydrate 0.5 g sugar

318) *Easy Juicy Pork Chops*

Time Required for Preparation: 5 minutes Time Required for Cooking: 15 minutes 2 portions
Ingredients:

- *1 tsp chili powder*
- *1/2 tsp garlic powder*
- *1/2 tsp cumin*
- *1/4 tsp powdered black pepper*
- *1/4 tsp dried oregano*
- *2 boneless pork chops (4 oz)*
- *2 tbsp unsalted butter, divided*

Directions:

✓ *Combine chili powder, garlic powder, cumin, pepper, and oregano in a small bowl. On pork chops, rub dry rub. Pork chops should be placed in the air fryer basket.*

✓ *Preheat the oven to 400°F and set a timer for 15 minutes.*

✓ *When thoroughly cooked, the internal temperature should be at least 145°F. Serve warm, with 1 tablespoon butter on top of each serving.*

Nutrition: 313 Calories 24 g protein 0.7 g fiber 1 g carbohydrate 26 g fat Sodium: 117 milligrams 8 g carbohydrate 0.1 g sugar

319) Pork Roast

Time Required for Preparation: 10 minutes Time Required for Cooking: 3 hours 2 portions

Ingredients:

• *1 tbsp. Coconut oil*

• *1 tbsp. water (2 c)*

• *Portobello mushrooms (5 thinly sliced)*

• *Garlic (2 smashed cloves)*

• *Onion (.5 chopped) (1 rib)*

• *Pimento (.5 tsp.)*

• *Roasted pork (1 lb.)*

Directions:

✓ *Begin with adding the garlic, onion, and celery to the Instant Pot cooker pot, followed by the water, and then the roast— season with salt and pepper to taste.*

✓ *Insert the Instant Pot cooker pot and secure the cover. Set the pressure to high and the timer to 60 minutes.*

✓ *When the timer sounds, select the option for instant pressure release.*

✓ *Set aside the roast and puree the veggies and resulting broth in a blender.*

✓ *Return the roast to the Instant Pot cooker, seal it, and cook on high pressure for 2 hours; this will help render the fat and ensure the edges are crisp.*

✓ *When the timer sounds, immediately release the pressure and transfer the roast to a serving dish using the instant pressure release option.*

✓ *Select the sauté setting on the Instant Pot cooker before adding the coconut oil. Once hot, add the mushrooms and simmer for 5 minutes. Add the blender gravy and reduce until desired thickness is attained.*

✓ *Drizzle gravy over roast just before serving.*

Nutrition: 28 grams protein Carbohydrates: 12 g 9 g dietary fiber 2 grams sugar 5 grams fat 360

320) Children's Back Ribs

Time Required for Preparation: 5 minutes Time Required for Cooking: 25 minutes 4 portions

• *2 pounds baby back ribs*

• *2 tsp chili powder*

• *1 tsp paprika*

• *1/2 tsp onion powder*

• *1/2 tsp garlic powder*

• *1/4 tsp ground cayenne pepper*

• *1/2 tbsp. sugar-free, low-carb barbecue sauce*

Direction

✓ *Rub the ribs with all ingredients except the barbecue sauce. Arrange in an air fryer basket.*

✓ *Preheat the oven to 400°F and set a timer for 25 minutes.*

✓ *When finished, the ribs should be dark and charred on the outside and have an interior temperature of at least 190°F. Brush ribs liberally with barbecue sauce and serve immediately.*

Nutrition: Calories: 650 40.1 g protein 0.8 g Fiber 8 g Carbohydrates 55 g fat 332 mg sodium 6 g carbohydrate 0.2 g sugar

321) Pork Curry

Time Required for Preparation: 10 minutes Time Required for Cooking: 20 minutes 2 portions

Ingredients:

• *Cauliflower (2 sliced)*

• *Curcumin (.25 tsp.)*

• *5 teaspoons garam masala (4 oz.)*

• *Zucchini (.25 chopped)*

• *Ghee (1 tbsp) (1 pinch)*

• *Coconut milk (.5 c) (.5 diced)*

• *Juice of a lime (.5 limes)*

• *Ginseng (1 inch grated)*

• *Onion (2 cloves minced)*

• *Pork (1 lb.)*

Directions:

✓ *Place the meat in a sealable container before adding the coconut milk, garlic, lime juice, and ginger and thoroughly combining. For optimal results, marinate the meat overnight.*

✓ *In the Instant Pot cooking pot, mix the onions, carrots, garam masala, ghee, tomatoes, and meat completely.*

✓ Insert the Instant Pot cooker pot and secure the cover. Select the high-pressure setting and a timer for 20 minutes.

✓ Select the natural pressure release option and set the timer for ten minutes when the timer sounds.

✓ After opening the lid, set the Instant Pot cooker to sauté and add the zucchini—Cook for 5 minutes.

✓ Serve immediately with shirataki rice.

Nutrition: Calories 38 g protein Carbohydrates: 29 g 23 grams dietary fiber 5 grams sugar 33 grams fat 520

322) *Pork Fillet with Serrano Ham*

Time Required for Preparation: 10 minutes Time Required for Cooking: 20 minutes 4 portions

• 400g extremely thinly sliced pork fillets

• 2 boiled and chopped eggs

• 100g chopped Serrano ham

• 1 beaten egg

Direction

✓ Form a roll with the pork fillets. Bring a half-cooked egg and Serrano ham to the table. Secure the roll with a string or chopsticks to prevent it from losing its shape.

✓ Roll the rolls in the beaten egg and then in the breadcrumbs until a good layer appears.

✓ Preheat the air fryer to 180° C for a few minutes.

✓ Place the rolls in the basket and set the timer for approximately 8 minutes at 180 degrees Celsius.

✓ Serve.

Nutrition: 424 kcal 115g fat 37.47g Carbohydrates 384g Protein

323) *Pork Wrapped in a Blanket*

Time Required for Preparation: 5 minutes Time Required for Cooking: 10 minutes 4 portions

• 1/2 puff pastry sheet defrosted

• 16 thick smoked sausages

Direction

✓ Preheat the air fryer to 200°C and set the timer for 5 minutes.

✓ Cut the puff pastry into strips measuring 64 x 38 mm.

✓ Place a cocktail sausage at the end of the puff pastry and roll the pastry around the

sausage, moistening the dough with water to seal.

✓ Brush the tops of the milk-wrapped sausages with a brush and drop them in the preheated air fryer.

✓ Bake for 10 minutes at 200°C or until golden brown.

Nutrition: Calories: 242 kcal 14g fat Carbohydrates: 0g 27g protein

324) *Ribs de Provençal*

Time Required for Preparation: 10 minutes Time Required for Cooking: 20 minutes 4 portions

• 500g pork ribs

• Provencal herbs

• Salt

• Ground pepper

• Oil

Direction:

✓ In a bowl, combine the ribs with the oil, Provencal herbs, salt, and freshly ground pepper.

✓ Stir well and chill for at least 1 hour.

✓ Place the ribs in the air fryer basket and set the temperature to 200OC for 20 minutes.

✓ Shake the basket occasionally to remove the ribs.

Nutrition: Calories: 296 kcal 263g fat Carbohydrates: 0g 271g protein

325) *Loin Potatoes Marinated*

Time Required for Preparation: 20 minutes Time Required for Cooking: 1 hour 4 portions

• 2 medium potatoes

• 4 marinated loin fillets

• A drizzle of extra virgin olive oil

• Salt

Direction

✓ Peel and chop the potatoes. Cut mandolins the size of matchsticks, potatoes with a cane but very thinly sliced.

✓ Rinse and soak in water for 30 minutes.

✓ Drain and thoroughly dry.

✓ Add a drizzle of oil and swirl thoroughly to coat all potatoes with oil.

✓ Transfer to the basket of the air fryer and evenly distribute.

✓ Cook for 10 minutes at 160 c° C.

✓ Remove the basket and shake vigorously to

dislodge the potatoes. Allow the potato to become soft. If it is not, allow an additional five minutes.

✓ *Arrange the steaks atop the potatoes.*

✓ *Select 10 minutes, followed by another 5 minutes at 1800C.*

Nutrition: 136 kcal 1g fat Carbohydrates: 9g 20.7g protein

326) *Pork with Honey Mustard*

15 minutes for preparation Time required for cooking: 60 minutes 2 servings

- *5 pounds wrapped, trimmed pork joint*
- *1 cup low-carb honey mustard sauce*
- *season with salt and pepper*

Direction

✓ *In your Instant Pot, combine all of the ingredients.*

✓ *Cook for 60 minutes on Stew.*

✓ *Allow the pressure to dissipate naturally.*

Nutrition: Calories: 290 Carbohydrates: 9 Sugar: 8 Fat: 17 Protein: 39 Glycemic Index: 4

327) *Pork Bondiola Chop*

Time Required for Preparation: 5 minutes Time Required for Cooking: 20 minutes 4 servings

- *1-kilogram bondiola in pieces*
- *Breadcrumbs*
- *2 beaten eggs*
- *Season to taste*

Directions:

✓ *Roughly chop the bondiola.*

✓ *Season to taste with seasonings.*

✓ *Distribute the beaten eggs evenly over the seasoned bondiola.*

✓ *Gently fold in the breadcrumbs.*

✓ *Cook for 20 minutes in the air fryer, flipping halfway through.*

✓ *Serve*

Nutrition: 265 cal;20.36g fat; 8.7 g carbs; 19.14g pro;

328) *Roast Pork*

Time Required: 10 minutes Required for Cooking: 30 minutes 6 servings

- *2 lbs. pork loin*
- *1 tbsp. Olive oil*
- *1 tsp. salt*

Direction

✓ *Preheat the Air Fryer at 3600F.*

✓ *Rub the meat with the oil.*

✓ *Season with salt.*

✓ *Cook the pork for approximately 50 minutes on the Air Fryer. Halfway through the cooking process, shake the food.*

✓ *Remove the cooked meal from the Air Fryer and set it aside to cool.*

✓ *Serve*

Nutrition: 150 kcal 6g fat; 0g carbohydrate; 21g protein

329) *Wrapped in Ham, Pork Trinoza*

6 portions Time Required for Cooking: 20 Minutes Ingredients:

- *6 Serrano ham slices, thinly cut*
- *454g pork halves, butter, and crushed*
- *6 g sodium chloride*
- *1 teaspoon black pepper*
- *227g freshly split spinach leaves*
- *4 slices mozzarella cheese,*
- *18g sun-dried tomatoes, 10 ml olive oil,*

Directions:

✓ *Arrange three ham slices on baking paper, slightly overlapping one another. 12 of the pork should be placed in the ham. Rep with the remaining half.*

✓ *Salt and pepper the insides of the pork rolls.*

✓ *Top the pork loin with half of the spinach, cheese, and sun-dried tomatoes, leaving a 13 mm border on both sides.*

✓ *Roll the fillet tightly around the filling well and secure it with a kitchen cord.*

✓ *Rep with the remaining pork steaks and store them in the refrigerator.*

✓ *Select In the air fryer, Preheat and press Start/Pause.*

✓ *Each wrapped steak should be brushed with 5 ml olive oil and placed in the preheated air fryer.*

✓ *Choose a steak. Start/Pause the timer after setting it to 9 minutes.*

✓ *Allow 10 minutes for cooling before cutting.*

Nutrition: 282 Calories 241 g fat 16.59 grams protein 0g sugar 73gm cholesterol

330) *Pot Roast in the Style of Mississippi*

8 portions Time Required for Cooking: 8 Hours

Ingredients:

- *Chuck roast, 3 lb.*
- *six to eight pepperoncini*
- *1 envelope gravy mix au jus 1 sachet ranch dressing*

Directions:

- ✓ *Place roast in a slow cooker. Sprinkle the top with the contents of both envelopes of mixes. Arrange the peppers in a circle around the roast.*
- ✓ *Cook on low for 8 hours or on high for 4 hours, covered.*
- ✓ *Transfer to a large basin and shred the roast with two forks. Reintroduce it to the crock cooker and stir. Pepperoncini should be removed, chopped, and reintroduced to the roast. Serve.*

Nutrition: 379 Calories Carbohydrates in total 3g Protein 56g Fat 14g Sugar 1g Fiber 0g

331) *Rolls Stuffed With Cabbage And Pork Loin*

4 portions Time Required for Cooking: 25 Minutes
Ingredients:

- *500 g blanched cabbage*
- *a single onion*
- *8 tenderloin steaks de pork 2 carnations*
- *4 tablespoons soy sauce*
- *50g extra virgin olive oil*
- *Salt*
- *8 rice sheets*

Directions:

- ✓ *Combine the chopped cabbage, onion, and carrot in the Thermo mix glass.*
- ✓ *Choose 5 seconds at a speed. Combine the extra virgin olive oil and balsamic vinegar. Select the 5-minute timer, the Varoma temperature, the left turn, and the spoon speed.*
- ✓ *Thinly slice the tenderloin steaks. Fill the Thermomix glass halfway with meat. Select the 5-minute timer, the Varoma temperature, the left turn, and the spoon speed. Absent beaker, combine the soy sauce and sesame oil. Select the 5-minute timer, the Varoma temperature, the left turn, and the spoon speed. Salt should be rectified. Allow it to cool.*
- ✓ *Prepare the rice slices by hydrating them. Extend them and divide the filling evenly between them.*

- ✓ *Form the rolls, folding the edges tightly shut. Coat the rolls with oil and place them in the air fryer.*
- ✓ *Choose ten minutes at 1800C.*

Nutrition: 120 Calories 41g fat 0g Carbohydrates 20.99g protein 0g sugar 65mg cholesterol

332) *Flamingos Made at Home*

4 portions Time Required for Cooking: 20 Minutes
Ingredients:

- *400g pork fillets, very thinly cut c / n 2 boiled and chopped eggs*
- *100g Serrano ham, chopped*
- *1 egg, beaten*
- *Breadcrumbs*

Directions:

- ✓ *Roll the pork fillets. Bring a half-cooked egg and Serrano ham to the table. Secure the roll with a string or chopsticks to prevent it from losing its shape.*
- ✓ *Roll the rolls in beaten egg and then in breadcrumbs until a good layer appears.*
- ✓ *Preheat the air fryer to 180° C for a few minutes.*
- ✓ *Place the rolls in the basket and set the timer for approximately 8 minutes at 180 degrees Celsius.*

Nutrition: 482 Calories 241g fat 0g carbohydrate 16.59 grams protein 0g sugar 173gm cholesterol

LAMB

333) *Lamb Chops with Tapenade de Kalamata*

15 minutes for preparation Time required for cooking: 25 minutes 4 portions
Ingredients:

- 1 cup pitted Kalamata olives
- 2 tablespoons chopped fresh parsley
- 2 tablespoons extra-virgin olive oil
- 2 teaspoons minced garlic
- 2 teaspoons freshly squeezed lemon juice
- 2 (1-pound) racks French-cut lamb chops (8 bones each)
- 1 tbsp. Sea salt
- 1 tbsp. freshly ground black pepper

Directions:

- ✓ In a food processor, combine the olives, parsley, olive oil, garlic, and lemon juice and process until the mixture is smooth but still slightly chunky.
- ✓ Spoon the tapenade into a jar and refrigerate it until needed.
- ✓ HOW TO MAKE LAMB CHOPS
- ✓ Preheat the oven to 450 degrees Fahrenheit.
- ✓ Salt and pepper the lamb racks.
- ✓ Heat the olive oil in a large ovenproof skillet over medium-high heat.
- ✓ Sear all sides of the lamb racks in a pan until browned, about 5 minutes total.
- ✓ Arrange the racks upright in the skillet, bones interwoven, and roast for about 20 minutes for medium-rare or until the internal temperature reaches 125°F.
- ✓ Allow the lamb to rest for 10 minutes before slicing the racks into chops. Distribute four chops per person and top with the Kalamata tapenade.

Nutrition: 348 Calories 28g fat 21g protein Carbohydrates: 2 g 1 gram fiber Carbohydrates: 1 g 72% fat / 25% protein / 3% carbohydrate

334) *Lamb Racks with Rosemary and Garlic*

Time required for preparation: ten minutes, plus one hour for marinating Time required for cooking: 25 minutes 4 portions
Ingredients:

- 4 tbsp extra-virgin olive oil
- 2 tbsp finely chopped fresh rosemary
- 2 tbsp minced garlic
- pinch sea salt (8 bones each)

Direction

- ✓ Whisk the olive oil, rosemary, garlic, and salt in a small basin.
- ✓ Place the racks in a sealable freezer bag and fill the bag halfway with the olive oil mixture. Massage the meat in and out of the bag to coat it with the marinade. Seal the bag after pressing out the air.
- ✓ Refrigerate the lamb racks for 1 to 2 hours.
- ✓ Preheat the oven to 450 degrees Fahrenheit.
- ✓ Heat the oil to medium-high heat in a large ovenproof skillet. Remove the lamb racks from the bag and sear them on all sides in the skillet for about 5 minutes total.
- ✓ Roast the racks upright in the skillet, bones interwoven, for about 20 minutes for medium-rare or until the internal temperature reaches 125°F.
- ✓ Allow 10 minutes for the lamb to rest before slicing the racks into chops.
- ✓ Distribute four chops to each person.

Nutrition: 354 Calories 30g fat 21g protein Carbohydrates: 0g 0g fiber Net Carbohydrates: 0g 70% fat / 30% protein / 0% carbohydrate

335) *Leg of Lamb with Pesto of Sun-Dried Tomatoes*

15 minutes for preparation Time required for cooking: 70 minutes 8 portions
Ingredients:

- FOR THE PESTO:
- 1 cup sun-dried tomatoes packed in oil, drained
- 1/4 cup pine nuts
- 2 tablespoons extra-virgin olive oil
- 2 tablespoons chopped fresh basil
- 2 teaspoons minced garlic FOR THE LAMB LEG:
- 1 (2-pound) lamb leg

Directions: TO MANUFACTURE THE PESTO

- ✓ In a blender or food processor, combine the sun-dried tomatoes, pine nuts, olive oil, basil, and garlic; process until smooth.
- ✓ Reserve till required.
- ✓ TO FORM THE LEG OF THE LAMB
- ✓ Preheat the oven to 400 degrees Fahrenheit.
- ✓ Season both sides of the lamb leg with salt

and pepper.

✓ Heat the olive oil in a large ovenproof skillet over medium-high heat.

✓ Sear the lamb on all sides until well browned, approximately 6 minutes.

✓ Distribute the sun-dried tomato pesto evenly over the lamb and arrange it on a baking sheet. Roast for approximately 1 hour or until the meat achieves your preferred degree of doneness.

✓ Allow 10 minutes for the lamb to rest before slicing and serving.

Nutrition: 352 Calories 29g fat 17g protein Carbohydrates: 5 g 2g fiber; Carbohydrates net: 3 g 74% fat / 20% protein / 6% carbohydrate

336) *Diced lean lamb*

15 minutes for preparation Time required for cooking: 35 minutes

- *1 pound diced lean lamb*
- *1 quartered onion*
- *2 sliced carrots*
- *1 cup reduced-sodium broth*
- *0.5 cup mint sauce*

Direction

✓ Place the lamb in the Instant Pot.

✓ Surround it with the onion and carrots.

✓ Drizzle it with the sauce and broth.

✓ Cook for 35 minutes on Stew.

✓ Allow the pressure to dissipate naturally.

Nutrition: Calories: 400 Carbohydrates: 14 Sugars: 4 Fats: 20 Proteins: 37 GL: 6

337) *With Yogurt, Lean Lamb and Turkey Meatballs*

Time Required for Cooking: 10 Minutes 1 egg white

- *4 ounces ground lean turkey*
- *1 pound ground lean lamb*
- *1 teaspoon cayenne pepper,*
- *crushed coriander,*
- *red chili paste,*
- *salt, and ground cumin*
- *2 minced garlic cloves*
- *1 1/2 teaspoons parsley*
- *1 tablespoon mint*
- *1/4 cup olive oil*
- *2 tablespoons buttermilk*

- *1 minced garlic clove*
- *1/4 cup chopped mint*
- *1/2 cup fat-free Greek yogurt*

Directions:

✓ Preheat the Air Fryer to 390°F.

✓ In a mixing dish, combine all of the meatball ingredients. They should be rolled and molded into golf-size round pieces. Arrange the ingredients in the cooking basket. 8 minutes in the oven.

✓ While you wait, in a bowl, combine all of the ingredients for the mint yogurt. Combine thoroughly.

Nutrition: 154 Calories 9g Carbohydrates 5g fat 8.6g protein 4g fiber

MEAT

338) *Sirloin with Compound Blue Cheese Butter*

Time required for preparation: ten minutes plus one hour cooling Time required for cooking: 12 minutes 4 portions

Ingredients:

- 6 tbsp. Room temperature butter
- 4 oz. blue cheese, such as Stilton or Roquefort
- 4 (5-ounce) beef sirloin steaks
- 1 tablespoon olive oil

Directions:

- ✓ In a blender, pulse the butter until whipped for about 2 minutes.
- ✓ Pulse in the cheese until just integrated.
- ✓ Spoon the butter mixture onto a sheet of plastic wrap and roll it into a 12-inch diameter log by twisting both ends of the plastic wrap in opposite directions.
- ✓ Refrigerate the butter for approximately 1 hour or until thoroughly firm.
- ✓ Slice the butter into 12-inch disks and refrigerate until ready to serve the steaks. Refrigerate leftover butter for up to 1 week.
- ✓ Preheat a grill to a medium-high setting.
- ✓ Remove the steaks from the refrigerator and allow them to come to room temperature.
- ✓ Rub the olive oil all over the steaks and season with salt and pepper.
- ✓ Grill the steaks until the desired doneness is achieved, approximately 6 minutes per side for medium.
- ✓ 10. If you do not have a grill, broil the steaks for 7 minutes per side in a preheated oven.
- ✓ 1 Allow 10 minutes for the steaks to rest. Serve with a disk of the compound butter on top of each.

Nutrition: 544 Calories 44g fat 35g protein Carbohydrates: 0g fiber Net Carbohydrates: 0g 72 % fat / 28 % protein / 0 % carbs

339) *Short Ribs Braised in Garlic*

Time required for preparation: ten minutes 2 hours and 20 minutes for cooking 4 portions

Ingredients:

- 4 (4-ounce) short ribs de boeuf
- 1 tablespoon olive oil
- 2 tablespoons minced garlic
- 12 cups dry red wine
- 3 cups rich beef stock

Directions:

- ✓ Preheat the oven to 325 degrees Fahrenheit.
- ✓ Season both sides of the beef ribs with salt and pepper.
- ✓ Heat the olive oil in a large ovenproof skillet over medium-high heat.
- ✓ Sear the ribs on all sides until golden brown, approximately 6 minutes total. Transfer the ribs to a serving dish.
- ✓ Add the garlic to the skillet and sauté for about 3 minutes, or until transparent.
- ✓ Add the red wine and whisk to deglaze the pan. Scrape the bottom of the pan clean of any browned chunks of meat. Simmer the wine for approximately 2 minutes, or until it is somewhat reduced.
- ✓ Return the beef stock, ribs, and any juices remaining on the plate to the skillet and heat to a boil.
- ✓ Cover the skillet and place it in the oven to braise the ribs for about 2 hours, or until the meat falls off the bone tender.
- ✓ Drizzle a teaspoon of the cooking liquid over each plate of ribs.

Nutrition: 481 Calories 38g fat 29g protein Carbohydrates: 5 g 3 g fiber Net Carbohydrates: 2 g 70% fat / 25% protein / 5% carbohydrate

340) *Asian Peanut Sauce on Skirt Steak*

15 minutes for preparation, plus 30 minutes for chilling Time Required for Cooking: 15 minutes 4 portions

Ingredients:

- 13 cups light coconut milk
- 1 teaspoon curry powder
- 1 teaspoon soy sauce with reduced sodium
- 114-pound skirt steak
- 12 cups Asian Peanut Sauce

Directions:

- ✓ Whisk the coconut milk, curry powder, coriander powder, and soy sauce in a large mixing basin. Turn the steak to coat with the sauce. Refrigerate the bowl for at least 30 minutes and up to 24 hours.
- ✓ Preheat the grill or spray a grill pan with cooking spray and set the steak over a medium-high heat source—Grill the meat for approximately 3 minutes per side or

until it reaches an internal temperature of 145oF. Take the steak from the grill and set it aside for 5 minutes to rest. Serve the steak cut into 5-ounce chunks with 2 tablespoons of the Asian Peanut Sauce on the side.

✓ REFRIGERATE: For up to 1 week, store the cooled steak in a resealable container. Microwave each component for 1 minute.

Nutrition: 361 Calories 22g fat 7g Saturated Fat 36g protein Carbohydrates in total: 8g 2g dietary fiber

341) Burgers Tex-Mex

15 minutes for preparation Time Required for Cooking: 10 minutes 4 portions

- 1 pound lean ground beef (90 percent or leaner)
- 14 red onion, finely chopped
- 14 green bell pepper, finely chopped
- 1/4 cup chopped cilantro
- 2 garlic cloves, minced

Directions:

✓ Combine the ground beef, onion, bell pepper, cilantro, garlic, cumin, paprika, salt, black pepper, and allspice in a medium mixing bowl. Form the mixture into four patties using clean hands.

✓ Coat a grill pan or sauté pan with cooking spray and heat over a medium heat source. When the oil is shimmering, add the patties and fry for about 5 minutes per side, or until a thermometer put into the center of a burger reads 155oF.

✓ Before serving, drizzle each burger with 2 tablespoons of the Avocado Lime Mayonnaise.

✓ REFRIGERATE: For up to 1 week, store the cooled burgers and mayonnaise in separate resealable containers. Microwave the burgers for 1 to 2 minutes to reheat. Additionally, they can be warmed on the grill or a grill pan for approximately 4 minutes per side. Before eating, drizzle with mayonnaise.

✓ FREEZE: Freeze the chilled burgers for up to 2 months in a freezer-safe container. Thaw overnight in the refrigerator and reheat for 1 to 2 minutes in the microwave. Additionally, they can be warmed on the grill or a grill pan for approximately four minutes per side. Mayonnaise is not a good candidate for freezing.

Nutrition: 267 Calories 17g fat 5g Saturated Fat 24g protein Carbohydrates in total: 5g 3 g fiber 253mg sodium

342) Meatballs with Beef and Mushrooms

15 minutes for preparation Time Required for Cooking: 30 minutes 24 meatballs

Ingredients:

- 1 tablespoon canola or safflower oil
- 1 (8-ounce) container finely chopped Portobello mushrooms
- 1 pound lean ground beef (90 percent or higher)
- 3/4 cup unseasoned bread crumbs
- 1/2 cup chopped fresh parsley
- 2 minced garlic cloves
- 1 beaten egg

Directions:

✓ Heat the oil in a medium skillet over medium heat until it shimmers. Add the mushrooms and sauté for about 5 minutes, or until they soften. Allow 5 minutes to cool slightly.

✓ Preheat the oven to 350 degrees Fahrenheit. Coat the inside of a mini muffin tin with cooking spray.

✓ Combine the mushrooms, beef, bread crumbs, parsley, garlic, egg, salt, and pepper in a large mixing bowl. Mix until well combined, using clean hands.

✓ Form a 2-inch ball from 1 heaping teaspoon of the beef mixture. Fill a muffin cup halfway with it and continue forming meatballs.

✓ Bake for approximately 25 minutes, or until the golden brown meatballs. Allow cooling for 5 minutes before transferring each meatball to a storage container using a teaspoon.

✓ REFRIGERATE: Refrigerate the cooled meatballs for up to 1 week in a resealable container—microwave for 1 minute to reheat. The meatballs also can be reheated in a saucepan over medium heat along with the Speedy Tomato Sauce.

✓ FREEZE: Store the cooled meatballs in a freezer-safe container for up to 2 months. Thaw in the refrigerator overnight and reheat in the microwave for 1 minute. The meatballs also can be reheated in a saucepan over medium heat along with the Speedy Tomato Sauce.

Nutrition: Calories: 232 Fat: 12g Saturated Fat: 4g Protein: 19g Total Carbs: 12g Fiber: 1g Sodium: 276mg

343) *Lentil Beef Meatloaf*

Time Required for Preparation: 15 minutes Time
Required for Cooking: 1 hour 8 portions

Ingredients:

- Cooking spray
- 1 pound lean ground beef (90 percent lean or higher)
- 1 (8-ounce) container finely chopped mushrooms
- 12 onion, finely chopped
- 1 garlic clove, minced
- 1 (15-ounce) can low-sodium lentils, drained and rinsed
- 1/2 cup chopped fresh cilantro
- 1 large egg, beaten

Directions:

✓ Preheat the oven to 350 degrees Fahrenheit. Coat the bottom and sides of a 9-by-5-inch loaf pan with cooking spray.

✓ Combine the beef, mushrooms, onions, garlic, lentils, cilantro, egg, panko, salt, and pepper in a large mixing bowl. Combine until completely mixed.

✓ Spoon the meat mixture into the loaf pan, smoothing the surface. Distribute the tomato sauce evenly over the meatloaf.

✓ Bake for approximately 1 hour to 1 hour, 10 minutes, or until a thermometer inserted into the center of the meatloaf reads 1550F.

✓ Allow it to cool somewhat before slicing into 8 equal parts.

✓ REFRIGERATE: Refrigerate cooled meatloaf slices for up to 1 week in a resealable container—microwave for 1 to 12 minutes to reheat.

✓ FREEZE: Freeze the chilled meatloaf slices for up to 2 months in a freezer-safe container. Refrigerate overnight to defrost—microwave for 1 to 12 minutes to reheat.

Nutrition: 210 Calories 7g fat 3g Saturated Fat 19g protein Carbohydrates in total: 18g 5 g fiber 224

344) *Stuffed Mediterranean Peppers*

30 minutes for preparation, plus 30 minutes for chilling Time Required for Cooking: 1 hour and 40 minutes 8 portions

Ingredients:

- 3 cups water
- 1 cup farro
- Cooking spray
- 1 pound lean ground beef (90 percent lean or higher)
- 1 cup reduced-sodium canned chickpeas, drained and rinsed
- 1 cup cherry tomatoes, quartered
- 1 bunch parsley, chopped
- 12 small yellow onion, chopped
- 13 cups crumbled feta cheese

Directions:

✓ Bring the water to a boil in a medium saucepan over high heat. Stir in the farro, then reduce to medium-low heat and simmer for about 30 minutes, or until the water is absorbed and the grain is soft. Any surplus liquid should be drained. Allow cooling for approximately 10 minutes before transferring to a container, covering, and chilling for at least 30 minutes.

✓ Preheat the oven to 350 degrees Fahrenheit. I am using the cooking spray, coat a 9-by-13-inch baking dish.

✓ Combine the beef, chickpeas, tomatoes, parsley, and onion in a large mixing basin and toss until well combined. Stir in the chilled farro and feta cheese.

✓ Whisk the olive oil, lemon juice, salt, and black pepper in a small bowl. Stir this into the beef-farro mixture until well combined.

✓ Remove the peppers' tops. Remove the membranes and seeds from the inside of each pepper using a paring knife. Fill each pepper with 3/4 cups of the beef mixture and put the peppers in the baking dish, allowing approximately 2 inches to wrap aluminium foil around the dish.

✓ Bake at 350°F for 50 minutes. Then remove the foil and bake for a further 20 minutes.

✓ REFRIGERATE: Refrigerate the cooled peppers for up to 1 week in a resealable container—microwave one pepper for 1 to 2 minutes. To ensure an even reheating, halve the pepper.

✓ FREEZE: For up to 2 months, store cooled peppers in a freezer-safe container. Refrigerate overnight to defrost— microwave one pepper for 1 to 2 minutes. To ensure an even reheating, halve the pepper.

Nutrition: 320 Calories 14g fat 4g Saturated Fat 19g protein Carbohydrates in total: 30g 7g dietary fiber

345) *Mature Meatloaf in the Traditional Style*

Time Required for Preparation: 10 minutes Time Required for Cooking: 25 minutes 6 portions
Ingredients:

- 1 pound 80/20 ground beef
- 14 medium yellow onions, peeled and diced
- 12 medium green bell peppers, seeded and diced
- 1 large egg
- 3 tablespoons blanched finely ground almond flour
- 1 tablespoon Worcestershire sauce
- 1/2 teaspoon garlic powder
- 1 teaspoon dried parsley
- 2 tablespoons tomato paste

Directions:

- ✓ In a large mixing basin, combine ground beef, onion, pepper, egg, and almond flour. Add the Worcestershire sauce to the bowl and the garlic powder and parsley. Combine until completely mixed.
- ✓ Divide the mixture in half and divide equally between two (4") loaf baking tins.
- ✓ Combine the tomato paste, water, and erythritol in a small basin. Distribute half of the ingredients evenly among the loaves.
- ✓ If required, work in batches, insert loaf pans into the air fryer basket.
- ✓ Preheat the oven to 350°F and set a timer for 25 minutes, or until the internal temperature reaches 180°F.
- ✓ Serve immediately.

Nutrition: 170 Calories 19 g protein 0.9 g fiber 4 g fat 85 mg sodium 0 g Carbohydrates 5 g sugar

346) *Burger with Chorizo and Beef*

Preparation Time: 10 minutes Required for Cooking: 15 minutes 4 portions
Ingredients:

- ¾ pounds 80/20 ground beef
- ¼ -pound Mexican-style ground chorizo
- ¼ cups chopped onion
- 5 sliced pickled jalapenos, chopped

Directions:

- ✓ Combine all ingredients in a large mixing dish. Divide the ingredients into four equal portions and shape each portion into a burger patty.

- ✓ Working in batches if required, place burger patties in the air fryer basket.
- ✓ Preheat the oven to 375°F and set a timer for 15 minutes.
- ✓ Halfway through the cooking period, flip the patties. Serve immediately.

Nutrition: Calories: 291 26 g protein 0.9 g fiber 8 g carbohydrate 18.3 g fat 474 mg sodium 7 g carbohydrate 5 g sugar

347) *Snappy Brats*

Time Required for Preparation: 5 minutes Time Required for Cooking: 15 minutes 4 portions

- 4 (3-ounce) beef bratwursts

Directions:

- ✓ Arrange brats in the air fryer basket.
- ✓ Preheat the oven to 375°F and set a timer for 15 minutes.
- ✓ Serve immediately.

Nutrition: Calories: 286 18 g protein 0.0 g fiber 28 g fat 50 mg sodium 0.0 g Carbohydrates 0.0 g Sucrose 0.0 g

348) *Peppers Stuffed with Tacos*

15 minutes for preparation Time Required for Cooking: 15 minutes 4 portions

- 1 pound 80/20 ground beef
- 1 tablespoon chili powder
- 2 teaspoons cumin
- 1 teaspoon garlic powder
- 1 teaspoon salt
- 1/4 teaspoon s crushed black pepper
- 1 (10-ounce) can diced tomatoes and green chili, drained

Directions:

- ✓ Brown the ground beef in a medium skillet over medium heat for about 7–10 minutes. Drain the grease from the skillet once no pink remains.
- ✓ Return the skillet to the fire and season with chili powder, cumin, garlic powder, salt, and freshly ground black pepper. To the skillet, add the drained can of diced tomatoes and chilies. Cook for another 3–5 minutes.
- ✓ Halve each bell pepper while the mixture is simmering. Seeds and white membranes should be removed. Distribute the cooked mixture evenly among the bell peppers and sprinkle with 14 cups of cheese. Fill the air fryer basket halfway with stuffed peppers.

✓ *Preheat the oven to 350°F and set a timer for 15 minutes.*

✓ *When finished, the peppers should be fork soft and the cheese browned and bubbly. Serve immediately.*

Nutrition: 346 Calories 27.8 g protein 5 g Fiber 7.2 g Carbohydrates 19.1 g fat 991 mg sodium 10.7 g carbohydrate 9 g sugar

349) *Stuffed Italian Bell Peppers*

15 minutes for preparation Time Required for Cooking: 15 minutes 4 portions

- *1 pound ground pork Italian sausage*
- *1/2 teaspoon   garlic powder*
- *1/2 teaspoon s dried parsley*
- *1 medium Roma tomato, diced*
- *1/4 cup chopped onion*
- *4 medium green bell peppers*

Ingredients:

✓ *Brown the ground sausage in a medium skillet over medium heat for about 7–10 minutes, or until no pink remains. The skillet's fat should be drained.*

✓ *Place the skillet back on the burner and add the garlic powder, parsley, tomato, and onion; simmer for an additional 3–5 minutes.*

✓ *Halve the peppers and scrape off the seeds and white membrane.*

✓ *Remove the meat mixture from the heat and pour into pepper halves in an equal layer. Sprinkle mozzarella on top. Fill the air fryer basket halfway with pepper halves.*

✓ *Preheat the oven to 350°F and set a timer for 15 minutes.*

✓ *When finished, the peppers should be fork soft and the cheese browned. Serve immediately.*

Nutrition: 358 Calories 21 g protein 6 grams of fiber 8.7 g carbohydrate 21 g fat Sodium: 1,029 milligrams 13 g carbohydrate 8 g sugar

350) *Pork Glazed with Maple*

Time Required for Preparation: 10 minutes Time Required for Cooking: 15 minutes 2 servings

- *Maple syrup (.25 c)*
- *Honey (.25 c)*
- *Cinnamon (1 tsp)*
- *Brown sugar (.25 c)*

- *Orange juice (2 tsp)*
- *Nutmeg (1 tsp) (1 small)*

Directions:

✓ *In a saucepan over medium heat, combine all ingredients except the ham; stir well.*

✓ *Place the ham in the pressure cooker. Cook for 15 minutes and then use the quick release method.*

✓ *Arrange the ham in the prepared baking dish. Drizzle glaze over ham.*

✓ *Broil the ham to caramelize the sugars and create a slight char.*

Nutrition: 28 grams protein Carbohydrates: 37.5 g 38 grams fiber 18.2 grams sugar 42 g fat 540

351) *Roast Beef in the Air Fryer*

Time Required for Preparation: 5 minutes Time Required for Cooking: 45 minutes

- *3 tbsps. Olive oil*
- *1 tbsp. Rosemary*
- *1/2 tbsp. garlic powder*
- *1/2 tsp coarsely ground black pepper*

Directions:

✓ *Preheat the air fryer to 360°F.*

✓ *On a plate, combine herbs and oil. On the plate, roll the roast in the blend to coat the entire surface of the beef.*

✓ *Arrange the beef in a single layer in the air fryer basket. Set the timer for 45 minutes for tool-rare beef and 51 minutes for the tool. Check the beef with a meat thermometer to ensure it is cooked to your preference.*

✓ *Cook for additional 6-minute periods if desired. Bear in mind that the roast will almost certainly continue to cook while you are relaxing.*

✓ *Transfer the roast from the air fryer to a plate and tent with lightweight aluminium foil. Allow 10 minutes before serving.*

Nutrition: Calories: 666 kcal; Carbohydrates: 0.3 g; Fat: 54 g; Proteins: 43 g

352) *Beef Empanadas in the Air Fryer*

Time Required for Preparation: 10 minutes Time Required for Cooking: 20 minutes 3 servings

- *8 defrosted Goya empanada discs*
- *1 cup picadillo 1 blended egg white*
- *1 tsp. water*

- *Cooking spray*

Directions:

✓ *Preheat the air fryer to 325 degrees Fahrenheit.*

✓ *Coat the basket with cooking spray.*

✓ *Fill each disc space with 2 tbsp. Picadillo. Invert and secure using a fork. Repeat with the remaining dough.*

✓ *Combine the water and egg whites in a mixing bowl. Sprinkle on top of empanadas.*

✓ *Place three of them in your air fryer and bake for a few minutes. Set aside the reserved empanadas and repeat with the remaining empanadas.*

Nutrition: 183 kcal Carbohydrates: 22 g 11 g protein Fat:5g

353) *Air Fryer Steak*

Preparation Time: 5 minutes Time Required for Cooking: 10 minutes 2 portions

- *1 Ribeye Steak or 1 New York City Strip Steak*

- *Salt and Pepper*

- *Garlic Powder*

- *Paprika*

Direction

✓ *Place the meat in a bowl at room temperature.*

✓ *Coat both sides of the meat with olive oil.*

✓ *Season with salt and pepper to taste.*

✓ *Stir in the garlic powder and paprika.*

✓ *Preheat the air fryer to 400 degrees Fahrenheit.*

✓ *Cook the steak in the air fryer for 12 minutes, turning halfway through.*

✓ *When ready, drizzle it with butter and serve.*

Nutrition: Calories: 301 kcal 23g fat Carbohydrates: 0g 23g protein

354) *Roast Beef*

Time Required for Preparation: 5 minutes Time Required for Cooking: 45 minutes 4 Servings

- *1-kilogram Beef Joint*

- *1 tbsp. Extra Virgin Olive Oil*

- *Salt and Pepper*

Directions:

✓ *Rub extra virgin olive oil all over the beef.*

✓ *Season with salt and pepper to taste.*

✓ *Then, position the seasoned beef on the air*

fryer oven rotisserie.

✓ *Set the timer for 45 minutes and the temperature to 380 degrees Fahrenheit. Ascertain that the beef is rotated.*

✓ *After 45 minutes, check the roast beef's ready and slice it into pieces.*

✓ *Serve*

Nutrition: 666kcal Protein: 43g Fat: 54g

355) *Traditional Beef Stew*

Time Required for Preparation: 15 minutes Time Required for Cooking: 35 minutes 2 portions

- *1 pound diced stewing steak*

- *1 pound chopped veggies*

- *1 cup reduced-sodium beef broth*

- *1 tbsp black pepper*

Directions:

✓ *In your Instant Pot, combine all of the ingredients.*

✓ *Cook for 35 minutes on Stew.*

✓ *Allow the pressure to dissipate naturally.*

Nutrition: Calories: 300 Carbohydrates: 6 1 g sugar 9 g fat 43 g protein 2 g glycerol

356) *Steak and Kidney Stew*

Time Required for Preparation: 15 minutes required for cooking: 35 minutes

- *1 pound diced stewing steak*

- *0.5 pound diced kidneys*

- *1 pound chopped veggies*

- *1 cup low sodium beef broth*

- *0.5 cups low carb beer*

Direction

✓ *In your Instant Pot, combine all of the ingredients.*

✓ *Cook for 35 minutes on Stew.*

✓ *Allow the pressure to dissipate naturally.*

Nutrition: Calories: 380 Carbohydrates: 10 Sugar: 3 Fat: 12 Protein: 48 GL: 4

357) *Beef Shredded*

- *15 minutes for preparation Time required for cooking: 35 minutes 2 servings*

- *5-pound lean steak*

- *1 cup low sodium gravy*

- *2 tbsp mixed spices*

Direction

✓ *In your Instant Pot, combine all of the*

ingredients.

✓ *Cook for 35 minutes on Stew.*

✓ *Allow the pressure to dissipate naturally.*

✓ *Shred the beef using a fork.*

Nutrition: Calories: 200 Carbohydrates: 2 Sugar: 0 Fat: 5 Protein: 48 GL: 1

358) *Italian Sausage Casserole*

Time to Prepare: 15 minutes required for cooking: 5 minutes 1 pound cooked sausages

• *1 pound chopped Mediterranean vegetables*

• *1 cup low sodium broth*

• *1 tbsp mixed herbs*

Direction

✓ *In your Instant Pot, combine all of the ingredients.*

✓ *Cook for 5 minutes on Stew.*

✓ *Allow the pressure to dissipate naturally.*

Nutrition: Calories: 320 Carbohydrates: 8 Sugars: 2 Fats: 18 Proteins: 41 GL: 4

359) *Skillet with Beef and Broccoli*

4 portions Time Required for Cooking: 10 Minutes Ingredients:

• *1 pound ground beef, lean*

• *3 cups cooked cauliflower rice*

• *2 cups chopped broccoli*

• *4 sliced green onions*

• *1 teriyaki sauce cup*

Directions:

✓ *In a large skillet over med-high heat, brown the meat. Cook, stirring for 1 minute until the broccoli and white parts of the onion are tender.*

✓ *Continue heating the cauliflower and sauce until heated through and the broccoli is tender-crisp for about 3-5 minutes. Serve garnished with green onion segments.*

Nutrition: Calories 255 Carbohydrates total 9g Carbohydrates net 6g Protein 37g Fat 7g Sugar 3g Fiber 3g

360) *Steaks From Russia With Nuts And Cheese*

4 portions Time Required for Cooking: 20 Minutes Ingredients:

• *800 g pork mince*

• *Cream cheese, 200 g*

• *50g walnuts, peeled*

• *a single onion*

• *Salt*

• *Peppercorns, ground*

• *a single egg*

• *Breadcrumbs*

• *Olive oil extra virgin*

Directions:

✓ *In the Thermomix glass, place the quartered onion and select 5 seconds speed*

✓ *Combine the minced meat, cheese, egg, salt, and pepper in a medium bowl.*

✓ *Select ten seconds at a speed of five and turn left.*

✓ *Select 4 seconds, turn left, speed.*

✓ *Add the chopped and peeled walnuts.*

✓ *Transfer the dough to a mixing bowl.*

✓ *Construct Russian steaks and sift through the breadcrumbs.*

✓ *Brush both sides of the Russian fillets with extra virgin olive oil.*

✓ *Place the Russian fillets in the air fryer basket without stacking them.*

✓ *15 minutes at 1800C.*

Nutrition: 1232 Calories 41g fat 0g Carbohydrates 20.99g protein 0g sugar 63

361) *Beef with a Tangy Balsamic Glaze*

8 portions Time Required for Cooking: 6 – 8 Hours Ingredients:

• *3-4 pounds boneless beef roast 12 onion, finely diced*

• *1/2 cup balsamic vinegar*

• *1 container low sodium beef broth*

• *5 garlic cloves, finely chopped 3 tablespoons honey*

• *1 tablespoon light soy sauce*

• *Worcestershire sauce, 1 tbsp. 1 teaspoon flakes de chili Rojo*

Directions:

✓ *All ingredients, except the roast, should be placed in the crockpot. Stir thoroughly. Turn roast to cover with sauce.*

✓ *Cook covered on low for 6-8 hours. Remove the meat to a platter and shred using two forks. Reintroduce it to the sauce and serve.*

Nutrition: 410 Nutrition: Calories Carbohydrates in total 9g Protein 45g Fat 20g Sugar 7g Fiber 0g

362) _Strips of Sirloin & "rice"_

6 portions 30 Minutes Cooking
Ingredients:

- 12 pound prime sirloin steak, thinly sliced Cauliflower,
- 3 cup Cook rice
- 2 thinly sliced onions
- 14 12 oz. chopped, undrained tomatoes
- 1/2 cupbeef broth with a low sodium content
- 1/3 cup red wine, dry
- 1 minced garlic clove
- 1 leaf of bay
- 2 tbsp split olive oil
- 1 teaspoon salt
- 1/2 teaspoon   basil
- 1/2 teaspoon   thyme
- 1/4 teaspoon   pepper

Directions:

✓ Season beef strips with salt and pepper to taste.

✓ In a large skillet over medium heat, heat the oil. Cook, often stirring, until steak is browned. Transfer to a plate and cover with foil to keep warm.

✓ Cook until the onion is soft with the remaining oil in the skillet. Add the garlic and cook for a further 1 minute.

✓ Bring to a boil, stirring in the remaining ingredients, except the cauliflower. Reduce to low heat and continue simmering for 10 minutes.

✓ Reintroduce the steak to the skillet and cook for an additional 2-4 minutes, or until heated through and tender. Remove bay leaf before serving over cauliflower rice.

Nutrition: 278 Calories Carbohydrates in total 9g Carbohydrates in net 6 gram protein 37 gram fat 9 gram sugar 5 gram fiber 3 gram

363) _Beef Brisket Spicy Bbq_

14 portions Time Required for Cooking: 5 Hours
Ingredients:

- 3 ½ pound beef brisket
- 1/2 cup onion, finely diced
- 1 teaspoon freshly squeezed lemon juice
- 2 tablespoons barbecue sauce
- Chili seasoning, 1 pkt.

- Worcestershire sauce,
- 1 teaspoon garlic, finely chopped

Directions:

✓ The brisket should be cut in half and placed in a crock cooker.

✓ Combine the remaining ingredients in a small bowl and pour over beef. Cook, covered, for 5-6 hours on high heat, or until beef is fork-tender.

✓ The brisket should be transferred to a bowl. Shred using two forks. Reintroduce the meat to the crockpot and stir to re-heat. Serve plain or with buns.

Nutrition: Total Carbohydrates: 239 Nutrition: Calories 7g Protein 34g Fat 7g Sugar 4g Fiber 0g

364) _Beef Stew with a Twist_

6 portions Time Required for Cooking: 2 Hours
Ingredients:

- 2 tbsp unbleached all-purpose flour
- 1 tablespoon seasoning de Italie
- 2 lb (907 g) top circular, chopped into cubes of 34 inches
- 2 tbsp olive oil
- 12 pounds (680 g) cremini mushrooms, rinsed, stems removed, and quartered
- 1 big, finely chopped onion
- 3 minced garlic cloves
- 3 medium carrots, peeled and quartered 1 cup peas, frozen
- 1 tablespoon minced fresh thyme
- 1 tablespoon vinegar de vin rouge
- 1/2 tsp freshly ground black pepper 1/2 tsp

Directions:

✓ In a large mixing bowl, combine the flour and Italian spice. Coat the meat cubes thoroughly in the bowl.

✓ In a saucepan over medium heat, heat the olive oil until it shimmers.

✓ Cook in a single layer for 2 to 4 minutes, or until the meat is golden brown on all sides. Frequently turn the meat cubes.

✓ Remove and set aside the meat, then add 14 cups chicken broth to the pot.

✓ Sauté the mushrooms for 4 minutes, or until tender. Remove and set aside the mushrooms from the saucepan.

✓ Fill the pot with 14 cups chicken broth. Sauté the onions and garlic for 4 minutes, or until transparent.

✓ *Reintroduce the beef to the pot and add the remaining stock. Increase the heat to high and bring to a boil.*

✓ *Reduce to a low heat and cover. Reduce to a low heat and simmer for 45 minutes. Periodically stir.*

✓ *Simmer the carrots, mushroom, peas, and thyme in the pot for a further 45 minutes, or until the veggies are tender.*

✓ *Remove the cover and drizzle with red wine vinegar. Season with freshly ground black pepper. In a big bowl, combine all ingredients and serve.*

Nutrition: 250 Nutrition: Calories 7.0g fat; 20g protein; 20g carbohydrate; 0g fiber; 0g sugar 290mg sodium

FISH AND SEAFOOD

365) **Baked Salmon topped with Garlic Parmesan**

5 minutes for preparation; 20 minutes for cooking 4 portions

Ingredients:

- *1 pound filets of wild-caught salmon*
- *2 tbsp. margarine*
- *What you'll require from your pantry:*
- *14 cups grated parmesan cheese with reduced fat content*
- *¼ cups light mayonnaise*
- *2-3 garlic cloves, chopped 2 tbsp. parsley*

Directions:

- ✓ *Preheat the oven to 350 degrees Fahrenheit and line a baking sheet with parchment paper.*
- ✓ *Season salmon with salt and pepper and place in pan.*
- ✓ *Melt butter in a medium skillet over medium heat. Add garlic and simmer for 1 minute, stirring constantly.*
- ✓ *Reduce to low heat and stir in additional ingredients. Stir until all ingredients are melted and mixed.*
- ✓ *Spread evenly over salmon and bake for 15 minutes using frozen fish or 20 minutes using thawed fish. Salmon is cooked when it easily flakes with a fork. Serve.*

Nutrition: 408 Calories Carbohydrates in total 4g Protein 41g Fatty Acids 24g Sucrose 1 gram fiber 0 gram

366) **Tilapia Herb & Parmesan**

4 portions of fish 15 Minutes Cooking

Ingredients:

- *tilapia fillets 16 oz.*
- *1/3 cup sliced and chopped almonds*
- *1/2 teaspoon minced parsley*
- *1/4 cup bread crumbs*
- *1/2 teaspoon powdered garlic*
- *1/4 teaspoon ground black pepper*
- *1/2 tsp paprika*
- *3 tbsp grated Parmesan cheese Olive oil*

Directions:

- ✓ *Preheat the oven to 350 degrees Fahrenheit.*
- ✓ *In a bowl, combine the bread crumbs, almonds, spices, and Parmesan cheese.*
- ✓ *Brush a light coating of oil on the fish.*

- ✓ *Coat the almond mixture evenly with the coating.*
- ✓ *Maintain the fish on an oiled foil-lined baking sheet.*
- ✓ *10-12 minutes in the oven. Your fork should readily flake the fish.*

Nutrition: 225 calories, 7g carbohydrate, 1g fiber, 57mg cholesterol, 9g total fat, 29g protein, 202mg sodium

367) **Grilled Shrimp**

Time required for preparation: 5 minutes required for cooking: 5 minutes 4 servings

- *12 lb. shrimp, peeled and deveined*
- *4 lime wedges*
- *4 tbsp. Cilantro, chopped What you'll require from your pantry:*
- *4 minced garlic cloves*
- *1 tbsp chili powder*
- *1 tbsp paprika*
- *1 tbsp olive oil*
- *2 tbsp. splenda brown sugar*
- *1 tsp cumin*
- *1 tbsp oregano*
- *1 tbsp garlic powder*
- *1 tsp salt*
- *1/2 tsp pepper*

Direction

- ✓ *Whisk together seasonings and Splenda brown sugar in a small dish.*
- ✓ *In a skillet over medium-high heat, heat the oil. Cook shrimp in a single layer for 1-2 minutes on each side.*
- ✓ *Add seasonings and cook for 30 seconds, stirring constantly. Garnish with cilantro and a wedge of lime.*

Nutrition: Calories 252 7g Carbohydrates Total 7g Carbohydrates Net 6g Protein 39 g fat 7 g sugar 2 g dietary fiber 1g

368) **Cajun Catfish**

Time required for preparation: 5 minutes Time required for cooking: 15 minutes 4 portions

- *4 (8 oz.) catfish fillets*
- *What you'll need from your pantry: 2 tbsp olive oil*
- *2 tsp garlic salt*
- *2 tsp thyme*
- *2 tsp paprika*

- *1/2 tsp cayenne pepper*
- *1/2 tsp red hot sauce*
- *1/4 tsp black pepper*

Direction

✓ *Preheat the oven to 450 degrees. Cooking sprays a 9x13-inch baking dish.*

✓ *In a small bowl, whisk together all ingredients except the catfish. Brush both sides of the fillets with the spice mixture.*

✓ *Bake for 10-13 minutes, or until the fish easily flakes with a fork. Serve.*

Nutrition: Calories 366 Carbohydrates in total 0g Protein 35g Fat 24g Sugar 0g Fiber 0g

369) *Flounder Cajun & Tomatoes*

Time required for preparation: ten minutes Time required for cooking: 15 minutes 4 portions

- *4 flounder fillets*
- *2 1/2 cup chopped tomatoes*
- *3/4 cups diced onion*
- *3/4 cup diced green bell pepper*
- *What you'll require from your pantry:*
- *2 garlic cloves, finely chopped*
- *1 tbsp. seasoning Cajun*
- *1 tablespoon olive oil*

Directions:

✓ *In a large skillet, heat oil over medium-high heat. Cook for 2 minutes, or until the onion and garlic are tender. Cook for 2-3 minutes, or until tomatoes soften.*

✓ *Arrange fish on top. Cook, covered, for 5-8 minutes, or until salmon flakes easily with a fork. Transfer fish to serving dishes and spoon sauce over the top.*

Nutrition: Calories 194 8g Carbohydrates Total 8g Carbohydrates Net 6g Protein 32g Fat 3g Sugar 5g Fiber 2g

370) *Cajun Shrimp & Roasted Vegetables*

Time required for preparation: 5 minutes Time required for cooking: 15 minutes 4 portions

- *1 pound large peeled and deveined shrimp*
- *2 sliced zucchinis*
- *2 sliced yellow squash*
- *½ bunch asparagus, divided into thirds*
- *2 sliced red bell pepper*
- *What you'll require from your pantry:*
- *2 tbsp. olive oil*

- *Season with salt and pepper to taste*

Direction

✓ *Preheat the oven to 400 degrees.*

✓ *In a large mixing basin, combine shrimp and vegetables. Toss with the oil and seasonings.*

✓ *Spread vegetables equally on a large baking sheet and bake for 15-20 minutes, or until tender. Serve.*

Nutrition: Calories 251 Carbohydrates 13g Net Carbs 9g Protein 30g Fat 9g Sugar 6g Fiber 4g

371) *Grilled Shrimp with Cilantro and Lime*

Time required for preparation: 5 minutes Time required for cooking: 5 minutes 6 portions

- *12 lbs. big raw shrimp, peeled and deveined with tails on*
- *1 lime juice and zest*
- *What you'll require from your pantry:*
- *¼ cups olive oil*
- *2 garlic cloves, finely sliced*
- *1 teaspoon paprika, smoked*
- *1/4 tbsps cumin*
- *1/2 teaspoon salt*
- *1/4 tbsp cayenne pepper*

Directions:

✓ *In a big Ziploc bag, place the shrimp.*

✓ *In a separate bowl, combine remaining ingredients and pour over shrimp. Allow 20-30 minutes for marinating.*

✓ *Preheat the grill. Cook the shrimp on skewers for 2-3 minutes per side, or until they turn pink. Caution: Do not overcook them. Garnish with cilantro if desired.*

Nutrition: 317 Calories Carbohydrates in total 4g Protein 39g Fat 15g Sugar 0g Fiber 0g

372) *Frittata de Crab*

Time required for preparation: ten minutes required for cooking: 50 minutes 4 portions

- *4 eggs*
- *2 cups lump crabmeat*
- *1 cup half-n-half*
- *1 cup diced green onions*
- *What you'll need from your pantry:*
- *1 cup grated reduced-fat parmesan cheese*
- *1 teaspoon salt*

- *1 teaspoon pepper*
- *1 teaspoon smoked paprika*
- *1 tsp Italian seasoning*

Directions:

✓ *Preheat the oven to 350 degrees Fahrenheit. Cooking spray an 8-inch springform pan or pie plate.*

✓ *Whisk together the eggs and half-n-half in a large mixing dish. Stir in spices and parmesan cheese.*

✓ *Add the onions and crab meat and combine well. Bake 35-40 minutes, or until eggs are set, gently browned the top.*

✓ *Allow 10 minutes for cooling before slicing and serving warm or at room temperature.*

Nutrition: Calories 276 Carbohydrates 5g Net Carbohydrates 4g Protein 25g Fat 17g Sugar 1g Fiber 1g

373) *Lemon Shrimp Crunchy*

Time required for preparation: 5 minutes Time required for cooking: 10 minutes 4 portions

- *1 pound raw shrimp, peeled and deveined*
- *2 tbsp. Finely chopped Italian parsley*
- *2 tbsp. lemon juice, divided*
- *What you'll require from your pantry:*
- *2/3 cups panko bread crumbs*
- *Season with salt and pepper to taste*

Directions:

✓ *Preheat the oven to 400 degrees Fahrenheit.*

✓ *Evenly distribute the shrimp in a baking dish and season with salt and pepper. 1 tablespoon lemon juice and 1 tablespoon olive oil drizzled on top Place aside.*

✓ *Combine parsley, remaining lemon juice, bread crumbs, remaining olive oil, and 1/4 tsp salt and pepper in a larger bowl. Distribute the panko mixture evenly over the shrimp.*

✓ *Bake for 8-10 minutes, or until the shrimp are done and the panko is golden brown.*

Nutrition: Calories 283 Carbohydrates 15g Net Carbohydrates 14g Protein 28g Fat 12g Sugar 1g Fiber 1g

374) *Tuna Steaks Grilled*

Time required for preparation: 5 minutes Time required for cooking: 10 minutes 6 portions

- *6 6 oz. Tuna steaks*
- *3 tbsp. diced fresh basil*

- *What you'll require from your pantry:*
- *4 1/2 tbsp olive oil*
- *¾ tbsp salt*
- *1/4 tbsp pepper*

Directions:

✓ *Preheat the grill to a medium heat setting. Coat rack with nonstick frying spray.*

✓ *Drizzle oil on both sides of the tuna. Season with basil, salt, and pepper to taste.*

✓ *Grill for 5 minutes per side or until the tuna is slightly pink in the center. Serve.*

Nutrition: Calories 343 Carbohydrates in total 0g Protein 51g Fat 14g Sugar 0g Fiber 0g

375) *Pasta with Red Clam Sauce*

Time required for preparation: ten minutes 3 hours for cooking 4 portions

- *1 diced onion*
- *1/4 cup diced fresh parsley*
- *What you'll need from your pantry:*
- *½ oz. Cans chopped, undrained clams*
- *1/2 oz. Diced, undrained tomatoes*
- *6 oz. tomato paste*
- *2 garlic cloves, diced*
- *1 bay leaf*
- *1 tbsp sunflower oil*
- *1 tsp Splenda*
- *1 tsp basil*
- *1/2 tsp thyme Cook and drain pasta*

Directions:

✓ *In a small skillet over medium-high heat, heat the oil. Cook until the onion is soft. Add garlic and cook for an additional 1 minute. Transfer to a slow cooker.*

✓ *Stir in the remaining ingredients, except the pasta, and cook on low for 3-4 hours.*

✓ *Remove bay leaf and serve immediately over cooked spaghetti.*

Nutrition: Calories 223 Carbohydrates Total 32g Carbohydrates Net 27g Protein 12g Fat 6g Sugar 15g Fiber 5g

376) *Milano Salmon*

Time required for preparation: ten minutes Time required for cooking: 20 minutes 6 portions

- *2 ½ lb. salmon filets*
- *2 sliced tomatoes*
- *½ cup margarine*

- What you'll require from your pantry:
- ½ cup pesto Basilico (Basil pesto)

Directions:

✓ Preheat the oven to 400 degrees Fahrenheit. Line a 9x15-inch baking sheet with foil, ensuring that the foil extends all the way around. Arrange another large piece of foil on the baking sheet and top it with the salmon filet.

✓ In a blender or food processor, pulse the pesto and margarine until smooth. Distribute equally across salmon. On top, arrange tomato slices.

✓ Wrap the foil around the salmon, tenting the top to keep the foil as far away from the salmon as possible. Bake for 15-25 minutes, or until salmon easily flakes with a fork. Serve.

Nutrition: Calories 444 Carbohydrates in total: 2g Protein 55g Fat 24g Sugar 1g Fiber 0g

377) *Skillet with Shrimp and Artichokes*

Time required for preparation: 5 minutes Time required for cooking: 10 minutes 4 portions

- 12 cups peeled and deveined shrimp
- 2 shallots, chopped
- 1 tbsp. margarine
- 2 12 oz. jars artichoke hearts drained and rinsed
- 2 garlic cloves, finely chopped

Directions:

✓ In a large skillet over medium-high heat, melt margarine. Cook, turning regularly until shallot and garlic begin to brown.

✓ Cook for 5 minutes before adding the artichokes. Reduce the heat to low and add the wine. Cook, stirring periodically, for 3 minutes.

✓ Add the shrimp and cook for a few seconds more, or until they turn pink. Serve.

Nutrition: Calories 487 26g Total Carbohydrates 17g Net Carbohydrates 64g Protein 5g Sugar 3g Fiber 9g

378) *Carbonara Tuna*

Time required for preparation: 5 minutes Time required for cooking: 25 minutes 4 portions

Ingredients:

- 12-pound tuna fillet, chopped into pieces
- 2 eggs
- 4 tbsp. diced fresh parsley

- What you'll need from your pantry:
- 12 homemade pasta shells, cooked and drained
- 12 cups parmesan cheese, reduced in fat
- 2 peeled garlic cloves
- 2 tbsp. extra virgin olive oil
- Season with salt and pepper to taste

Directions:

✓ In a small mixing bowl, whisk together the eggs, parmesan, and a pinch of pepper.

✓ In a large skillet over medium-high heat, heat the oil. Cook until garlic is browned. Cook for 2-3 minutes, or until the tuna is almost cooked through. Remove the garlic.

✓ Add the spaghetti and reduce the heat to a low setting. Stir in egg mixture and cook for 2 minutes, stirring constantly. If the sauce is too thick, dilute it with water a tablespoon at a time until it reaches a creamy consistency.

✓ Season with salt and pepper to taste and sprinkle with parsley.

Nutrition: Calories 409 Carbohydrates 7g Net Carbohydrates 6g Protein 25g Fat 30g Sugar 3g Fiber 1g

379) *Fillets de poisson de la Méditerranée*

Time Required for Preparation: 10 minutes 3 minutes cooking time 4 portions

Ingredients:

- 4 cod fillets
- 1 pound halved grape tomatoes
- 1 cup pitted and sliced olives
- 2 tbsp capers
- 1 tsp dried thyme
- 2 tbsp olive oil
- 1 tsp minced garlic
- PEPPER

Directions:

✓ Fill the instant pot halfway with water and add the steamer rack.

✓ Coat the inside of a heat-safe baking dish with cooking spray.

✓ Season with pepper and salt half of the grape tomatoes in the dish.

✓ Arrange fillets of fish atop cherry tomatoes. Season with garlic, thyme, capers, pepper, and salt. Drizzle with oil and season with garlic, thyme, capers, pepper, and salt.

✓ Arrange the remaining olives and grape

tomatoes on top of the fish fillets.

✓ *In the saucepan, place the dish on top of the steamer rack.*

✓ *Cover the pot with a lid and cook on high for 3 minutes using the manual setting.*

✓ *Once completed, quickly remove the pressure. Take the cover off.*

✓ *Assemble and serve.*

Nutrition: 212 Calories 19 g fat 7.1 g Sucrose Protein 3 g 55 mg Cholesterol 24 g

380) *Flavors Cioppino*

Time Required for Preparation: 10 minutes Time Required for Cooking: 5 minutes 6 portions

Ingredients:

- *1 pound codfish, chunked*
- *1 1/2 pounds shrimp*
- *2/8 ounces chopped tomatoes*
- *1 cup dry white wine*
- *1 bay leaf*
- *1 tsp cayenne pepper*
- *1 tsp oregano*
- *1 shallot, diced*
- *1 tsp garlic, minced*

Direction

✓ *Place oil in the inner pot of the instant pot and turn it to sauté mode.*

✓ *Sauté the shallot and garlic for 2 minutes.*

✓ *Cook for 3 minutes before adding the wine, bay leaf, cayenne pepper, oregano, and salt.*

✓ *Stir in the other ingredients until completely combined.*

✓ *Cover the pot with a lid and simmer on low for 0 minutes using the manual setting.*

✓ *Once completed, quickly release pressure. Take the cover off.*

✓ *Assemble and serve.*

281 Nutrition: Calories 5 g fat 10.5 g carbohydrate 9 g protein 40.7 g cholesterol 266 mg

381) *Delicious Alfredo Shrimp*

Time Required for Preparation: 10 minutes 3 minutes cooking time 4 portions

- *12 shrimp, shells removed*
- *1 tbsp minced garlic*
- *1/4 cup parmesan cheese*
- *2 cups whole wheat rotini noodles — 1 cup*

fish stock

- *15 oz alfredo sauce*
- *1 onion, chopped*

Direction

✓ *In the instant pot, combine all ingredients except the parmesan cheese and whisk well.*

✓ *Cover the saucepan tightly with the cover and cook on high for 3 minutes.*

✓ *Once completed, quickly release pressure. Take the cover off.*

✓ *Remove from heat and stir in cheese.*

669 Nutrition: Calories, 21 g fat, 76 g carbohydrate, 4 g sugar, 37.8 g protein, 190 mg cholesterol

382) *Fish Fillets with Tomatoes and Olives*

Time Required for Preparation: 10 minutes Time Required for Cooking: 8 minutes 4 portions

- *2 pounds halibut fillets*
- *2 oregano sprigs*
- *2 rosemary sprigs*
- *2 tbsp fresh lime juice*
- *1 cup pitted olives*
- *28 oz can diced tomatoes*
- *1 tbsp minced garlic*
- *1 onion, sliced*

Direction

✓ *Place oil in the inner pot of the instant pot and turn it to sauté mode.*

✓ *Stir in onion and cook for 3 minutes.*

✓ *Add garlic and cook for a further minute.*

✓ *Stir in lime juice, olives, herb sprigs, and tomatoes.*

✓ *Cover the saucepan tightly with the cover and cook on high for 3 minutes.*

✓ *Once completed, quickly release pressure. Take the cover off.*

✓ *Add the salmon fillets, replace the cover, and cook on high for 2 minutes.*

✓ *Once completed, quickly remove the pressure. Take the cover off.*

✓ *Assemble and serve.*

Nutrition: Calories 333 19.1 g fat 38 g carbohydrate 8.4 g sugar 14 g protein 5 mg cholesterol

383) *Easy Salmon Stew*

Time Required for Preparation: 10 minutes Time Required for Cooking: 8 minutes 6 portions

- *2 lbs cubed salmon fillet*
- *1 onion, diced*
- *2 cups fish broth*
- *1 tbsp olive oil*

Direction

✓ *Place oil in the inner pot of the instant pot and turn it to sauté mode.*

✓ *Sauté onion for 2 minutes.*

✓ *Stir in the other ingredients until completely combined.*

✓ *Cover the saucepan tightly with the cover and cook on high for 6 minutes.*

✓ *Once completed, quickly release pressure. Take the cover off.*

✓ *Serve with a stir.*

Nutrition: 243 Calories 16 g fat 0.8 g sugar 0.3 g protein 31 g cholesterol 78 mg

384) *Italian Tuna Pasta*

Time Required for Preparation: 10 minutes Time Required for Cooking: 5 minutes 6 portions

- *15 oz whole wheat pasta*
- *2 tbsp capers*
- *3 oz tuna*
- *2 cups smashed can tomatoes*
- *2 anchovies*
- *1 tbsp chopped garlic*
- *1 tbsp olive oil*
- *Salt*

Direction

✓ *Place oil in the inner pot of the instant pot and turn it to sauté mode.*

✓ *Sauté the anchovies and garlic for 1 minute.*

✓ *Stir in the other ingredients until completely combined. Fill the saucepan halfway with enough water to cover the pasta.*

✓ *Cover the pot with a lid and simmer on low for 4 minutes on manual.*

✓ *Once completed, quickly release pressure. Take the cover off.*

✓ *Serve with a stir.*

Nutrition: 339 Calories, 6 g fat, 56.5 g carbohydrate, 2 g sugar, 12 g protein, 10 mg cholesterol

385) *Garlicky Clams*

Time Required for Preparation: 10 minutes Time Required for Cooking: 5 minutes 4 portions

- *3 pound clean clams*
- *4 garlic cloves*
- *1/4 cup olive oil*
- *1/2 cup freshly squeezed lemon juice*
- *PEPPER*

Direction

✓ *Place oil in the inner pot of the instant pot and turn it to sauté mode.*

✓ *Sauté garlic for 1 minute.*

✓ *Cook for 2 minutes before adding the wine.*

✓ *Stir in the other ingredients until completely combined.*

✓ *Cover the saucepan tightly with the cover and cook on high for 2 minutes.*

✓ *Once completed, allow pressure to dissipate naturally. Take the cover off.*

✓ *Assemble and serve.*

Nutrition: 332 Calories 15 g fat 40.5 g carbohydrate 14 g protein 5 g cholesterol 0 mg

386) *Fantastic Fish Tacos*

Time Required for Preparation: 10 minutes Time Required for Cooking: 8 minutes 8 portions

- *4 tilapia fillets*
- *1/4 cup chopped fresh cilantro*
- *1/4 cup fresh lime juice*
- *2 tbsp paprika*
- *1 tbsp olive oil*
- *Pepper*
- *Salt*

Directions:

✓ *Fill the instant pot halfway with water and add the steamer rack.*

✓ *Line a baking sheet with parchment paper and arrange fish fillets on it.*

✓ *Sprinkle paprika, pepper, and salt over fish fillets and sprinkle with oil and lime juice.*

✓ *Wrap the parchment paper around the fish fillets and place them in the pot on a steamer rack.*

✓ *Cover the saucepan tightly with the cover and cook on high for 8 minutes.*

✓ *Once completed, quickly release pressure. Take the cover off.*

✓ *Remove and open the fish packet from the pot.*

✓ *Using a fork, shred the fish and serve.*

Nutrition: 67 Calories 5 g fat Carbohydrates Sugar: 1 g Protein: 0.2 g Cholesterol 28 mg 10.8 g

387) *Pesto Fish Fillet*

Time Required for Preparation: 10 minutes Time Required for Cooking: 8 minutes 4 portions

- *4 halibut fillets*
- *1/2 cup water*
- *1 tbsp grated lemon zest*
- *1 tbsp capers*
- *1/2 cup basil, chopped*
- *1 tbsp garlic, minced*

Directions:

✓ *In a blender, combine the lemon zest, capers, basil, garlic, avocado, pepper, and salt until smooth.*

✓ *Arrange fish fillets on aluminium foil and distribute them with a mixed mixture.*

✓ *Wrap the foil tightly around the fish fillets.*

✓ *Fill the instant pot halfway with water and add the trivet.*

✓ *Arrange the foil packet of fish on the trivet.*

✓ *Cover the saucepan tightly with the cover and cook on high for 8 minutes.*

✓ *Once completed, let the pressure naturally dissipate. Take the cover off.*

✓ *Assemble and serve.*

Nutrition: Calories 426 16.6 g fat 5 g carbohydrate 0.4 g sugar 68 g protein 93 mg cholesterol

388) *Fillets de Salsa*

Time Required for Preparation: 10 minutes Time Required for Cooking: 2 minutes 4 portions

- *1 pound tilapia fillets*
- *1/2 cup salsa*
- *1 cup water*
- *Pepper*
- *Salt*

Directions:

✓ *Line aluminum foil with fish fillets and top with salsa. Season with pepper and salt to taste.*

✓ *Wrap the foil tightly around the fish fillets.*

✓ *Fill the instant pot halfway with water and add the trivet.*

✓ *Arrange the foil packet of fish on the trivet.*

✓ *Cover the saucepan tightly with the cover and cook on high for 2 minutes.*

✓ *Once completed, quickly release pressure. Take the cover off.*

✓ *Assemble and serve.*

Nutrition: Calories 342 10.5 g fat 45 g carbohydrate

9 g protein 18.9 g cholesterol 31 mg

389) *Croatian Coconut Clam Chowder*

Time Required for Preparation: 10 minutes Time Required for Cooking: 7 minutes 6 servings

Ingredients:

- *6 oz chopped clams*
- *1 cup heavy cream*
- *1/4 sliced onion*
- *1 cup chopped celery*
- *1 lb chopped cauliflower*
- *1 cup fish broth*
- *1 bay leaf*
- *2 cups coconut milk*
- *Salt*

Directions:

✓ *In a large mixing bowl, combine all ingredients except the clams and heavy cream.*

✓ *Cover the saucepan tightly with the lid and cook on high for 5 minutes.*

✓ *Once completed, quickly release pressure. Take the cover off.*

✓ *Add heavy cream and clams and simmer for 2 minutes on sauté mode.*

✓ *Serve immediately after a thorough stirring.*

Nutrition: 301 Calories Carbohydrates 27.2 g 16 g Sucrose Protein: 6 g Cholesterol 9 g 33 milligram

390) *Chili Mahi with Almond Crust*

Time Required for Preparation: 20 minutes Time Required for Cooking: 15 minutes 8 portions

Ingredients:

- *4 Mahi fillets*
- *1 lime*
- *2 tablespoons olive oil*
- *Salt and pepper to taste*
- *1/2 cup almond*
- *1/4 teaspoon   paprika*
- *1/4 teaspoon   onion powder*
- *34 teaspoon chili powder*

Directions:

✓ *Preheat the oven to 325 degrees Fahrenheit.*

✓ *Prepare your baking pan by lining it with parchment paper.*

✓ *Squeeze the lime to extract the juice.*

✓ *Zest the peel.*

✓ *In a bowl, combine the juice and zest.*

✓ *Add the oil, salt, and pepper to taste.*

✓ *In a separate bowl, combine the apples, paprika, onion powder, and chili powder.*

✓ *In a food processor, combine the almonds and sugar.*

✓ *Pulse until the mixture is powdery.*

✓ *Each fillet should be dipped in the oil mixture.*

✓ *1 Dredge with the mixture of almond and chili.*

✓ *1 Arrange in the oven in a single layer.*

✓ *1 Bake for 12 to 15 minutes, or until the pastry is completely cooked.*

✓ *1 Garnish with roasted red bell peppers, onion, and cilantro.*

Nutrition: 105 Nutrition: Calories Carbohydrates 27.2 g Protein 16 g 31 mg Cholesterol 3 g

391) *Swordfish with Salsa de Tomas*

Time Required for Preparation: 20 minutes Time Required for Cooking: 12 minutes 4 portions

Ingredients:

• *1 cup tomato, chopped*

• *1/4 cup tomatillo, chopped*

• *2 tablespoons fresh cilantro, chopped*

• *1/4 cup avocado, chopped*

• *1 clove garlic, minced*

• *1 jalapeno pepper, chopped – 1 tablespoon lime juice*

• *Salt and pepper to taste*

Directions:

✓ *Preheat your grill to high heat.*

✓ *Combine the tomato, tomatillo, cilantro, avocado, garlic, jalapeno, lime juice, salt, and pepper in a bowl.*

✓ *Wrap the bowl with foil and refrigerate.*

✓ *Rub swordfish steaks all over with sliced garlic.*

✓ *Drizzle both sides with lemon juice.*

✓ *Season with salt, pepper, and cayenne pepper to taste.*

✓ *Grill for 12 minutes or until the fish reaches an internal temperature of 145°F.*

✓ *Garnish with salsa.*

Nutrition: Calories 27.2 g Carbohydrates 125 g Fat

Protein 16 g Cholesterol: 7 g 31 mg

392) *Salmon & Asparagus*

Time Required for Preparation: 10 minutes Time Required for Cooking: 10 minutes 2 portions

Ingredients:

• *2 salmon fillets*

• *8 asparagus spears, trimmed*

• *2 tablespoons balsamic vinegar*

• *1 teaspoon olive oil*

• *1 teaspoon*

Directions:

✓ *Preheat the oven to 325 degrees Fahrenheit.*

✓ *Using paper towels, pat dry the salmon.*

✓ *Arrange the asparagus on a baking sheet around the salmon fillets.*

✓ *In a separate bowl, combine the remaining ingredients.*

✓ *Distribute the mixture evenly over the fish and vegetables.*

✓ *Bake for 10 minutes or until the fish is completely cooked.*

Nutrition: Calories 150 g Carbohydrates 22 g Fat Protein 16 g 7 g 20 mg cholesterol

393) *Halibut sauced in a spicy apricot sauce*

Time Required for Preparation: 20 minutes Time Required for Cooking: 17 minutes 4 portions

Ingredients:

• *4 pitted fresh apricots*

• *1/3 cup apricot preserves*

• *1/2 cup apricot nectar*

• *3 tbsp. scallion, slice*

• *1 tbsp. hot pepper sauce*

• *4 halibut steaks*

Directions:

✓ *In a saucepan, combine the apricots, preserves, nectar, oregano, scallion, hot pepper sauce, and salt.*

✓ *Bring to a boil and then reduce to low heat for 8 minutes.*

✓ *Drizzle olive oil over the halibut steaks.*

✓ *Grill for 7–9 minutes or until the salmon flakes easily.*

✓ *Brush 1 tbsp. sauce on both sides of the fish.*

✓ *Garnish with reserved sauce.*

✓ *Bake for 10 minutes or until the fish is completely cooked.*
Nutrition: Calories: 150 g Fat: 22 g Carbohydrates: 22 g Protein: 16 g 7 g Cholesterol: 20 mg

394) *Popcorn Shrimp*

Time Required for Preparation: 10 minutes Time Required for Cooking: 8 minutes 4 portions

Ingredients:

- *Nonstick cooking spray*
- *1/2 cup all-purpose flour*
- *2 beaten eggs*
- *2 tbsp water*
- *1/2 cup panko breadcrumbs*
- *1 tbsp garlic powder*
- *1 tbsp ground cumin*
- *1 lb. shrimp, peeled and deveined*
- *1/2 cup ketchup*
- *2 tbsp fresh cilantro, chopped*
- *2 tbsp lime juice*
- *Salt to taste*

Directions:

✓ *Coat the cooking basket of the air fryer with cooking spray.*

✓ *In an ish, place the flour.*

✓ *In a separate bowl, whisk together the eggs and water.*

✓ *In a three dish combine the breadcrumbs, garlic powder, and cinnamon.*

✓ *Dip each shrimp in one of the three dishes, starting with the flour, then the egg, and last, the breadcrumb combination.*

✓ *Arrange the shrimp in a single layer in the air fryer basket.*

✓ *Bake for 8 minutes at 360 degrees F, flipping halfway through.*

✓ *Combine the remaining ingredients to make a shrimp dipping sauce.*

Nutrition: Calories 200 g FAT 25 g CARBS 18 g PROTEIN 10 g CARBS 21 mg CHOLESTEROL

395) *Shrimp Lemon Kebab*

Time Required for Preparation: 10 minutes Time Required for Cooking: 4 minutes 5 portions

- *1/2 pound shrimp, peeled but with tails intact*
- *1/3 cup olive oil*
- *1/4 cup lemon juice*

- *2 tablespoons lemon zest*
- *1 tablespoon chopped fresh parsley*
- *8 cherry tomatoes, quartered*

Directions:

✓ *In a bowl, combine the olive oil, lemon juice, lemon zest, and parsley.*

✓ *Marinate the shrimp for 15 minutes in this mixture.*

✓ *Thread one shrimp at a time onto the skewers.*

✓ *Cook for 4 to 5 minutes on each side, rotating halfway through.*

✓ *Serve alongside tomatoes and scallions.*

Nutrition: Calories 180 g Carbohydrates 20 g Fat Protein: 15 g Cholesterol: 11 g 26 milligram

396) *Salmon Grilled Herb with Raspberry Sauce and Mayo*

Time Required for Preparation: 20 minutes Time Required for Cooking: 30 minutes 4 portions

- *½ cup Mayo made with salmon*
- *3 salmon fillets*
- *1 tablespoon olive oil*
- *Salt and pepper to taste*
- *1 teaspoon fresh sage, chopped*
- *1 tablespoon fresh parsley, chopped*
- *2 tablespoons apple juice*
- *1 teaspoon Worcestershire sauce*
- *1 cup cumber, chopped*

Directions:

✓ *Drizzle oil over the salmon fillets.*

✓ *Season with salt, pepper, parsley, sage, and thyme.*

✓ *Wrap the salmon with aluminum foil.*

✓ *Grill for approximately 20 minutes or until the fish is flaky.*

✓ *In the meantime, whisk together the apple juice, and Worcestershire sauce.*

✓ *Transfer the mixture to a sautépan set over medium heat.*

✓ *Bring to a boil and then reduce to low heat for 8 minutes.*

✓ *In a separate bowl, combine the remaining ingredients.*

✓ *Garnish fish with raspberry sauce and a fresh dip. Set mayo aside.*

Nutrition: 301 Calories 27.2 g fat 16 g carbohydrate 33 mg Cholesterol 9 g

397) *Scallops of Tarragon*

Time Required for Preparation: 20 minutes Time Required for Cooking: 15 minutes 4 portions

Ingredients:

- *1 cup water*
- *1 pound asparagus spears, trimmed*
- *2 lemons*
- *1 14 pound scallops*
- *Salt and pepper to taste*

Directions:

- ✓ *Fill a saucepan halfway with water.*
- ✓ *Increase heat to high and bring to a boil.*
- ✓ *A spear of asparagus*
- ✓ *Cook covered for 5 minutes.*
- ✓ *Drain and place on a plate.*
- ✓ *Squeeze 1 lemon into wedges.*
- ✓ *Squeeze the remaining lemon juice and shred the zest.*
- ✓ *Season with salt and pepper the scallops.*
- ✓ *Heat a skillet over medium heat.*
- ✓ *10. Add a tablespoon of oil to the pan.*
- ✓ *1 Cook the scallops until they are a golden brown colour.*
- ✓ *1 Arrange scallops alongside the asparagus on the same platter.*
- ✓ *1 To the pan, add lemon zest, juice, and tarragon.*
- ✓ *1 Continue cooking for 1 minute.*
- ✓ *1 Drizzle the tarragon sauce over the scalloped potatoes and asparagus spears.*

Nutrition: 250 Calories, 10 g fat, 30 g carbohydrate, 15 g protein, 24 mg cholesterol

398) *Garlic Shrimp & Spinach*

Time Required for Preparation: 20 minutes Time Required for Cooking: 30 minutes 4 portions

Ingredients:

- *3 tbsp. olive oil*
- *6 tbsp. garlic, sliced*
- *1 lb. spinach*
- *Salt to taste*
- *1 tbsp. lemon juice*
- *1 lb. shrimp, peeled and deveined*
- *1/4 tbsp . red pepper, crushed*
- *1 tbsp. parsley, chopped*

Directions:

- ✓ *In a medium saucepan, heat 1 tablespoon olive oil over medium heat.*
- ✓ *Cook for 1 minute the garlic.*

- ✓ *Arrange the spinach in a single layer and season with salt.*
- ✓ *Cook for a total of 3 minutes.*
- ✓ *Add the lemon juice.*
- ✓ *Spoon into a basin.*
- ✓ *Pour the remainder of the oil.*
- ✓ *A is for the shrimp.*
- ✓ *Season with salt and freshly ground pepper.*
- ✓ *Cook for a total of 5 minutes.*
- ✓ *1 Just before serving, sprinkle parsley and lemon zest over the shrimp.*

Nutrition: 280 Calories 10 g fat 35 g protein 15 g cholesterol 24 mg

399) *Ceviche de Watermelon Shrimp*

Time required for preparation: 20 minutes; time required for chilling: 1 hour 30 minutes; Serves: 14

Ingredients:

- *1 pound medium shrimp, peeled, deveined, and without tails 1 finely chopped jalapeno pepper*
- *1/2 cup seedless watermelon, finely diced 1/2 cup lime juice, split 12 cups jicama, finely diced 12 cups red onion, finely sliced*
- *1/2 cup chopped fresh cilantro*
- *What you'll need from the pantry: Salt and freshly ground pepper to taste*

Instructions:

- ✓ *Finely chop shrimp.*
- ✓ *Combine shrimp and 12 cups lime juice in a medium bowl. Refrigerate covered for 1 hour or until prawns turn pink. Squeeze out and discard juice.*
- ✓ *Combine all ingredients in a large mixing dish. Season with salt and pepper to taste. Refrigerate for at least 30 minutes.*
- ✓ *Serve alongside or on your preferred crackers. 1/4 cup is the serving size.*

Nutrition: Calories 47 Carbohydrates in Total 3 g protein, 8 g fat, 1 g sugar, and 1 g dietary fiber 0 g

400) *Tuna Steaks Grilled*

6 portions Time Required for Cooking: 10 Minutes,

Ingredients:

- *6 tuna steaks, 6 oz.*
- *3 tbsp. chopped fresh basil*
- *1/2 teaspoon olive oil*

- ¾ teaspoon salt
- 1/4 teaspoon pepper

Directions

✓ *Cooking spray that is nonstick*

✓ *Heat grill to a medium heat setting. Coat rack with nonstick frying spray.*

✓ *Drizzle oil on all sides of the tuna. Season with basil, salt, and pepper to taste.*

✓ *Cook for 5 minutes per side, or until the tuna is slightly pink in the center. Serve.*

Nutrition: 343 Calories Carbohydrates in total 0g Protein 51g Fat 14g Sugar 0g Fiber 0g

401) *Tacos de Pescado*

8 portions Time Required for Cooking: 8 Minutes
Ingredients:

- *4 tilapia fillets*
- *1/4 cup chopped fresh cilantro*
- *1/4 cup freshly squeezed lime juice*
- *2 tablespoons paprika*
- *1 tbsp extra-virgin olive oil*
- *Salt*
- *Pepper*

Directions

✓ *Fill the instant pot halfway with water and add the steamer rack.*

✓ *Arrange fillets of fish on parchment paper.*

✓ *Drizzle fish fillets with oil and lime juice and season with paprika, pepper, and salt.*

✓ *Wrap parchment paper around the fish fillets and arrange them in the pot on a steamer rack.*

✓ *Cook, covered, on high for 8 minutes.*

✓ *Once completed, quickly remove the pressure. Take the cover off.*

✓ *Remove and open the fish packet from the pot.*

✓ *Serve the fish shredded with a fork.*

Nutrition: 67 Calories 5 g fat Carbohydrates Sugar: 1 g Protein: 0.2 g Cholesterol 10.8 g 28 milligram

402) *Curry with Shrimp and Coconut*

2 portions Time Required for Cooking: 20 Minutes
Ingredients:

- *1 pound cooked shrimp*
- *1 onion, thinly sliced*
- *1 cup yogurt made with coconut*

- *3 tablespoons curry paste*
- *1 tbsp vegetable oil or ghee*

Directions:

✓ *Sauté the onion, oil, and curry paste in the Instant Pot.*

✓ *Add the other ingredients and close once the onion is tender.*

✓ *Cook for 20 minutes on Stew.*

✓ *Naturally, relieve the pressure.*

Nutrition: Calories: 380 Carbohydrates: 13; sugars: 4; fats: 22; protein: 40;

403) *Stew with Salmon and Shrimp*

6 portions Time Required for Cooking: 21 Minutes
Ingredients:

- *2 tbsp olive oil*
- *1/2 cup onion, finely chopped*
- *2 minced garlic cloves*
- *1 serrano pepper, peeled and chopped*
- *1 teaspoon paprika smoky*
- *4 cups diced fresh tomatoes*
- *4 cups chicken broth with reduced sodium*
- *1 pound cubed salmon 1 pound peeled and deveined shrimp*
- *2 tbsp. lime juice*
- *1/4 cup chopped fresh basil*
- *1/4 cup chopped fresh parsley*
- *Pepper, Ground, As Required*
- *2 sliced scallions*

Directions:

✓ *Melt coconut oil in a large soup pan over medium-high heat and sauté the onion for around 5-6 minutes.*

✓ *Sauté for approximately 1 minute with the garlic, Serrano pepper, and smoky paprika.*

✓ *Bring to a moderate simmer over medium heat with the tomatoes and broth.*

✓ *Cook for approximately 5 minutes.*

✓ *Cook for approximately 3-4 minutes before adding the salmon.*

✓ *Cook for a further 4-5 minutes, stirring in the remaining seafood.*

✓ *Remove from heat and stir in the lemon juice, basil, parsley, sea salt, and black pepper.*

✓ *Serve immediately with a scallion garnish.*

✓ *Transfer the stew to a large mixing bowl and leave aside to cool. Distribute the stew evenly across four containers. Refrigerate the containers for 1-2 days. Before serving, reheat in the microwave.*

Nutrition: Total Fat 11 g Saturated Fat 8 g Calories 271 mg Cholesterol 193 mg Carbohydrates in total 8.6 g Sugar 8 g Fiber 1 g 273 mg sodium 763 mg potassium Protein 37 g

404) *Swordfish With Tomatoes Salsa*

4 portions 12 Minutes Cooking
Ingredients:

- 1 cup tomato,
- 1/4 cup tomatillo,
- 2 tablespoons fresh cilantro,
- 1/4 cup avocado,
- 1 clove garlic, minced
- 1 jalapeno pepper,
- 1 tablespoon lime juice
- Season with salt and pepper to taste
- 4 steaks of swordfish
- 1 clove garlic, halved
- 2 tbsp lemon juice
- 1/2 tsp ground cumin

Directions:

✓ Preheat the grill to high.
✓ Combine the tomato, tomatillo, cilantro, avocado, garlic, jalapeno, lime juice, and salt and pepper in a bowl.
✓ Wrap the bowl with foil and refrigerate.
✓ Each swordfish steak should be rubbed with slice garlic.
✓ Drizzle both sides with lemon juice.
✓ Season with salt, pepper, and cayenne pepper to taste.
✓ Grill for 12 minutes or until the salmon reaches the desired degree of doneness.
✓ Serve alongside salsa.

Nutrition: Calories 27.2 g Carbohydrates 16 g Protein 125 g Fat Cholesterol 7 g 31 milligram

405) *Shrimp Boil*

4 portions 15 Minutes Cooking
Ingredients:

- 8 oz. unpeeled raw shrimp
- Chicken sausage, 8 oz.,
- small 1-inch squares Baby potatoes, 8 oz.
- 1 leek, sliced
- 2 corns, halved
- 3 tsp lemon juice
- ten cups water
- 1/4 teaspoon Old Bay seasoning
- Butter that has melted
- slices of lemon

Directions

✓ In a small saucepan, combine the lemon juice, Old Bay, and water. Boil.
✓ Cook potatoes for 5-7 minutes.
✓ Combine the sausage, shrimp, leek, and corn in a medium bowl. Cook for an additional 5 minutes while stirring. Vegetables and shrimp should be soft and pink.
✓ Now, using a spoon and tongs, divide the vegetables, sausage, and shrimp among the serving bowls.
✓ Drizzle the cooking liquid in an even distribution.
✓ Accompany with butter (optional).

Nutrition: 202 Calories, 22g carbohydrate, 2g fiber, 0g sugar, 109mg cholesterol, 5g total fat, 19g protein

406) *Artichoke & Shrimp Skillet*

4 portions
Time Required for Cooking: 10 Minutes
Ingredients:

- 1/2 cup peeled and deveined shrimp
- 2 shallots, peeled and diced
- 1 tbsp. lard
- 2 jars 12 oz. artichoke hearts drained and rinsed
- 2 c. wine blanc
- 2 garlic cloves, finely chopped

Directions

✓ In a large skillet over medium-high heat, melt margarine. Cook, turning regularly until shallot and garlic begin to brown.
✓ Cook for 5 minutes before adding the artichokes. Reduce the heat to low and add the wine. Cook, stirring periodically, for 3 minutes.
✓ Add the shrimp and cook for a few seconds longer, or until they turn pink. Serve.

Nutrition: 487 Calories 26g Carbohydrates Total 17g Carbohydrates Net 64g Fat 5g Sugar 3 g Fiber 9g

407) *Pasta with Red Clam Sauce*

4 portions
Time Required for Cooking: 3 Hours,
Ingredients:

- *1 chopped onion*
- *¼ cups diced fresh parsley*
- *2 12 oz. cans chopped, undrained clams*
- *¼ 12 oz. chopped, undrained tomatoes Tomato paste, 6 oz.*
- *2 minced garlic cloves*
- *1 leaf of bay*
- *Sunflower oil, 1 tbsp.*
- *1 tablespoon Splenda*
- *1 teaspoon basil*
- *1/2 teaspoon thyme*
- *12 Made-from-scratch pasta, cooked and drained*

Directions:

- ✓ *In a small skillet over medium-high heat, heat the oil. Cook until the onion is soft. Add garlic and cook for an additional 1 minute. Transfer to a slow cooker.*
- ✓ *Combine all remaining ingredients, except pasta, in a medium saucepan and simmer on low heat for 3-4 hours.*
- ✓ *Remove bay leaf before serving over cooked pasta.*

Nutrition: 223 Calories Total Carbohydrates 32g Net Carbohydrates 27g Protein 12g Fatty Acids 6g Sucrose 15g Fiber 5g

408) *Salmon Grilled with Herbs & Raspberry Sauce & Cucumber Dill Dip*

4 portions 30 Minutes Cooking
Ingredients:

- *3 fillets de salmon*
- *1 tsp olive oil*
- *Season with salt and pepper to taste*
- *1 teaspoon chopped fresh sage*
- *1 tablespoon chopped fresh parsley*
- *2 tsp apple juice*
- *1 cup raspberry preserves*
- *1 teaspoon sauce Worcestershire*
- *1 cup chopped cucumber*
- *2 tbsp. mayonnaise*
- *1/2 tsp dried dill*

Directions:

- ✓ *Oil the salmon fillets.*
- ✓ *Season with kosher salt, freshly ground pepper, sage, and parsley.*
- ✓ *Wrap the fish with aluminum foil.*
- ✓ *Grill for approximately 20 minutes or until the fish is flaky.*
- ✓ *While you wait, combine the apple juice, raspberries, and Worcestershire sauce in a small bowl.*
- ✓ *Combine the ingredients in a saucepan set over medium heat.*
- ✓ *Bring to a boil and then reduce to low heat for 8 minutes.*
- ✓ *In a separate bowl, combine the remaining ingredients.*
- ✓ *Salmon should be served with raspberry sauce and cucumber dip.*

Nutrition: 256 Calories 15 g Saturated Fat 3 g Cholesterol 68 mg Sodium 176 mg 6 g Fiber 1 g Sugars Total Protein 5 g Potassium 23 g

409) *Green Beans with Shrimp*

4 portions 2 Minutes Cooking
Ingredients:

- *¾ pound trimmed fresh green beans*
- *1 pound medium peeled and deveined frozen shrimp*
- *2 tbsp. freshly squeezed lemon juice*
- *2 tbsp olive oil*
- *Season with salt and freshly ground black pepper to taste.*

Directions

- ✓ *In the Instant Pot, place a steamer trivet and a cup of water.*
- ✓ *Arrange the green beans in a single layer on top of the trivet and sprinkle with shrimp.*
- ✓ *Drizzle with oil and freshly squeezed lemon juice.*
- ✓ *Season with salt and freshly ground black pepper to taste.*
- ✓ *Cover the container and set the pressure valve to the "Seal" position.*
- ✓ *Simply click "Steam" and stick with the default time of 2 minutes.*
- ✓ *Allow a "Natural" release by pressing "Cancel."*
- ✓ *Serve immediately after opening the lid.*

Nutrition: 223 Calories, 1g fat, 7.9g carbohydrate, 4g sugar, 27.4g protein, 322mg sodium

410) *Curry with Crab*

2 portions
Time Required for Cooking: 20 Minutes
Ingredients:

- 0.5 pound crab, chopped
- 1 red onion, thinly sliced
- 0.5 cup tomato, chopped
- 3 tablespoons curry paste
- 1 tbsp vegetable oil or ghee

Directions

✓ Set the Instant Pot's sauté function to high and add the onion, oil, and curry paste.

✓ Add the other ingredients and close once the onion is tender.

✓ Cook for 20 minutes on Stew.

✓ Naturally relieve the pressure.

Nutrition: Calories 2; Carbohydrates 11; Sugar 4; Fat 10; Protein 24; GL 9

411) *Mussels with Sauce Tomato*

4 portions 3 Minutes Cooking
Ingredients:

- 2 tomatoes, seeded and finely chopped
- 2 pound mussels, de-bearded and cleaned
- 1 cup chicken broth with a low sodium content
- 1 tbsp. lemon juice
- 2 minced garlic cloves

Directions:

✓ Combine tomatoes, garlic, wine, and bay leaf in the Instant Cooker pot.

✓ Arrange the mussels in a circular pattern on top.

✓ Cover the container and set the pressure valve to the "Seal" position.

✓ Press "Manual" and cook for approximately 3 minutes on "High Pressure."

✓ Press "Cancel" and allow a "Quick" release carefully.

✓ Serve immediately after opening the lid.

Nutrition: 213 Calories, 22g fat, 11g carbohydrate, 1g sugar 28.2g protein, 670mg sodium

412) *Shrimp Salad*

Portion: 6 Time Required for Cooking: 4 Minutes
Ingredients:

- Salad:
- 1 pound peeled and deveined shrimp
- Season with salt and freshly ground black pepper to taste.
- 1 teaspoon extra-virgin olive oil
- 1/2 cup peeled and julienned carrots
- 1/2 cup shredded red cabbage
- 1/2 cup julienned cucumber
- 5 tbsp. baby arugula
- 1/4 cup chopped fresh basil
- 1/4 cup chopped fresh cilantro
- 4 cups torn lettuce
- 1/4 cup chopped almonds
- Dressing:
- 2 tbsp. almond butter
- 1 smashed garlic clove
- 1 tablespoon chopped fresh cilantro
- 1 tbsp. lime juice
- 1 tbsp unsugared applesauce
- 2 tsp balsamic vinaigrette
- 1/2 tsp cayenne
- As necessary, salt
- 1 tbsp water
- 1/3 cup extra virgin olive oil

Directions

✓ Add the oil gradually, beating continuously until smooth.

✓ To make the salad, combine shrimp, salt, black pepper, and oil in a bowl and toss well to coat.

✓ Cook the shrimp for approximately 2 minutes per side in a pan over medium-high heat.

✓ Take the pan off the heat and allow it cool.

✓ Combine the shrimp and vegetables in a large mixing basin.

✓ To make the dressing, put all ingredients except the oil in a bowl and beat until well incorporated.

✓ Toss the shrimp mixture lightly with the dressing to coat well.

✓ Serve right away.

✓ Meal Prep Tip: Divide dressing evenly among six big mason jars. In the layers of carrots, put the remaining ingredients: cabbage, cucumber, arugula, basil, cilantro, shrimp, lettuce, and almonds. Refrigerate each jar tightly covered with the lid for approximately 1 day. Just before serving, *shake the jars vigorously.*

Nutrition: 274 Calories 17.7 g total fat 4 g saturated fat 159 mg cholesterol Carbohydrates in total 10 g Sugar 8 g Fiber 20.5 g Grille Herbe 9 g Sodium 242 mg Potassium 481 mg

413) *Salmon with raspberry sauce and cucumber-dill dipping sauce*

4 Servings 30 Minutes to Cook
Ingredients:

- *3 fillets de salmon*
- *1 tsp olive oil*
- *Season with salt and pepper to taste \1 teaspoon chopped fresh sage*
- *1 tablespoon chopped fresh parsley*
- *2 tbsp apple juice*
- *1 cup fresh raspberries*
- *1 tsp Worcestershire sauce*
- *1 tbsp cucumber, chopped*
- *2 tbsp. mayonnaise*

Directions:

- ✓ *Oil the salmon fillets.*
- ✓ *Season with kosher salt, freshly ground pepper, sage, and parsley.*
- ✓ *Wrap the fish with aluminium foil.*
- ✓ *Grill for approximately 20 minutes or until the fish is flaky.*
- ✓ *While you wait, combine the apple juice, raspberries, and Worcestershire sauce in a small bowl.*
- ✓ *Combine the ingredients in a sautépan set over medium heat.*
- ✓ *Bring to a boil and then reduce to low heat for 8 minutes.*
- ✓ *In a separate bowl, combine the remaining ingredients.*
- ✓ *Serve salmon with raspberry sauce and a slice of cucumber.*

Nutrition: 301 Calories Carbohydrates 27.2 g Protein 16 g 33 mg Cholesterol 9 g

414) *Shrimp Cajun & Roasted Vegetables*

4 portions15 Minutes Cooking
Ingredients:

- *1 pound large peeled and deveined shrimp*
- *2 sliced zucchinis*
- *2 sliced yellow squash*

- *12 bunch sliced asparagus*
- *2 red bell peppers, halved*
- *2 tablespoons olive oil*
- *2 tablespoons Cajun Seasoning*
- *Season with salt and pepper to taste*

Directions:

- ✓ *Preheat the oven to 400 degrees Fahrenheit.*
- ✓ *In a large bowl, combine shrimp and vegetables. Toss with the oil and seasonings.*
- ✓ *Bake for 15-20 minutes, or until vegetables are soft, on a large baking sheet. Serve.*

Nutrition: 251 Calories Carbohydrates in total 13g Carbohydrates in net Protein: 9 g 30g Fatty Acids 9g Sucrose 6 g Fiber 4 g

415) *Salmon with Lemon Juice*

Servings: 3 3 Minutes Cooking
Ingredients:

- *1 pound salmon fillet, sliced into three pieces*
- *3 tsp. fresh dill, diced*
- *5 tbsp. freshly squeezed lemon juice, divided*
- *Season with salt and freshly ground black pepper to taste.*

Directions:

- ✓ *In the Instant Pot, place a steamer trivet and 14 cups lemon juice.*
- ✓ *Season the salmon evenly with salt and freshly ground black pepper.*
- ✓ *Arrange the salmon pieces skin side down on the trivet and drizzle with the remaining lemon juice.*
- ✓ *Now evenly sprinkle dill over the fish chunks.*
- ✓ *Cover the container and set the pressure valve to the "Seal" position.*
- ✓ *Press "Steam" and set the timer to the default of three minutes.*
- ✓ *Allow a "Natural" release by pressing "Cancel."*
- ✓ *Serve immediately after opening the lid.*

Nutrition: 20 Calories 9.6g fat, 1g carbohydrate, 0.5g sugar, 29.7g protein, 74mg sodium

416) *Herring and Vegetables*

5 soup servings Time Required for Cooking: 25 Minutes
Ingredients:

- *2 tbsp olive oil*

- *1 chopped shallot*
- *2 minced tiny garlic cloves*
- *1 chopped jalapeno pepper*
- *1 chopped head cabbage*
- *1 seeded and coarsely chopped tiny red bell pepper*
- *1 seeded and finely chopped tiny yellow bell pepper*
- *5 cups chicken broth with a low salt content*
- *2 (4-ounce) diced boneless herring fillets 14 cups chopped fresh cilantro*
- *2 tbsp. freshly squeezed lemon juice*
- *Pepper, Ground, As Required*
- *2 sliced scallions*

Directions:

- ✓ *Heat the oil in a large soup pan over medium heat and sauté the shallot and garlic for 2-3 minutes.*
- ✓ *Sauté the cabbage and bell peppers for around 3-4 minutes.*
- ✓ *Bring the broth to a boil over high heat.*
- ✓ *Reduce to medium-low heat and simmer for approximately 10 minutes.*
- ✓ *Cook for approximately 5-6 minutes before adding the herring cubes.*
- ✓ *Cook for around 1-2 minutes, stirring in the cilantro, lemon juice, salt, and black pepper.*
- ✓ *Serve immediately with a scallion garnish.*
- ✓ *Transfer the soup to a large bowl and leave it aside to cool somewhat. Distribute the soup evenly among five containers. Refrigerate the containers for 1-2 days. Before serving, reheat in the microwave.*

Nutrition: 215 Calories 12 g total fat 1 g saturated fat Cholesterol 35 mg Carbohydrates: 17 g Carbohydrates: 7 g Fiber: 5 g Sodium: 152 mg Potassium: 574 mg Protein: 11 g

417) *Garlicky Clams*

4 portions Time Required for Cooking: 5 Minutes
Ingredients:

- *3 pound clean clams*
- *4 cloves of garlic*
- *1/4 cup extra virgin olive oil*
- *1/2 cup freshly squeezed lemon juice*
- *1 quart of white wine*
- *Salt*

- *Pepper*

Directions

- ✓ *In the inner pot of the instant pot, add the oil and turn the pot to sauté mode.*
- ✓ *Sauté garlic for 1 minute.*
- ✓ *Cook for 2 minutes before adding the wine.*
- ✓ *Stir in the other ingredients until completely combined.*
- ✓ *Cook, covered, on high for 2 minutes.*
- ✓ *Once completed, allow pressure to dissipate naturally. Take the cover off.*
- ✓ *Serve and take pleasure in.*

Nutrition: 332 Calories 15 grams fat 40.5 grams sugar 14 grams protein 5 grams

418) *Salad with Tuna*

2 portions
Ingredients:

- *2 (5-ounce) cans tuna in water, drained*
- *2 tbsp plain Greek yogurt*
- *Season with salt and freshly ground black pepper to taste.*
- *2 medium peeled and shredded carrots*
- *2 cored and cut apples*
- *2 cups torn fresh spinach*

Direction

- ✓ *In a large mixing bowl, combine the tuna, yogurt, salt, and black pepper with a gentle whisk.*
- ✓ *Stir in the carrots and apples.*
- ✓ *Serve right away.*
- ✓ *Meal Prep Tip: Divide tuna mixture evenly between two mason jars. In the layers of carrots, apples, and spinach, stack the additional ingredients. Refrigerate each jar tightly covered with the lid for approximately 1 day. Just before serving, shake the jars vigorously.*

Nutrition: 306 Calories 8g total fat 0g saturated fat 63 mg cholesterol 38 g Total Carbs 26 g Sugar 7.6 g Fiber 324 mg Sodium 602 mg Protein 38 g

419) *Grilled Tuna Salad*

4 portions 15 Minutes Cooking
Ingredients:

- *4 oz. tuna steaks*
- *34 lb. chopped red potatoes*
- *12 lb. trimmed green beans*
- *16 chopped kalamata olives*

- *4 tbsp. baby spinach*
- *2 tsp canola oil*
- *2 tbsp. vinegar de vino*
- *1/8 teaspoon sodium chloride*
- *1 tbsp water*
- *1/8 teaspoon crushed red pepper*

Directions:

✓ *To tenderize the green beans and potatoes, steam them.*

✓ *Drain and rinse to remove excess water.*

✓ *While the vegetables are cooking, combine the vinaigrette ingredients in your container. Close the lid and give it a good shake. Everything should be in harmony.*

✓ *Dress your fish with the vinaigrette.*

✓ *Coat your pan with canola oil. Heat to a moderate temperature.*

✓ *Grill the tuna for 3 minutes on each side.*

✓ *Distribute the greens evenly among your serving plates.*

✓ *Over the greens, arrange the green beans, olives, and potatoes.*

✓ *Dress the salad with the vinaigrette. Add tuna on the top.*

Nutrition: 345 Calories, 26g carbohydrate, 5g fiber, 40mg cholesterol, 14g total fat, 29g protein, 280mg sodium

420) *Fillets of Mediterranean Fish*

4 portions 3 Minutes Cooking

Ingredients:

- *4 cod fillets*
- *1 pound halved grape tomatoes 1 cup pitted and sliced olives 2 tablespoons capers*
- *1 teaspoon thyme, dry*
- *2 tablespoons olive oil*
- *1 teaspoon minced garlic*
- *Salt PEPPER*

Directions:

✓ *Fill the instant pot halfway with water and add the steamer rack.*

✓ *Coat a baking dish with cooking spray that is suitable for use in the oven.*

✓ *Season with pepper and salt half of the grape tomatoes into the dish.*

✓ *Arrange fillets de poisson atop cherry tomatoes. Season with garlic, thyme, capers, pepper, and salt. Drizzle with oil and season with garlic, thyme, capers,*

pepper, and salt.

✓ *Distribute the remaining olives and grape tomatoes on top of the fish fillets.*

✓ *In the saucepan, place the dish on top of the steamer rack.*

✓ *Cover the saucepan with a lid and cook on high for 3 minutes using the manual setting.*

✓ *Once completed, quickly remove the pressure. Take the cover off.*

✓ *Serve and take pleasure in.*

Nutrition: 212 Calories 19 g fat 7.1 g carbohydrate 3 g protein, 24 g fat, 55 mg cholesterol

421) *Salmon with Herbs*

4 portions 3 Minutes Cooking

Ingredients:

- *4 (4 oz.) salmon fillets*
- *1/4 cup olive oil*
- *2 tbsp. freshly squeezed lemon juice*
- *1 minced garlic clove*
- *1/4 teaspoon oregano, dry*
- *Season with salt and freshly ground black pepper to taste.*
- *4 sprigs of fresh rosemary*
- *4 slices of lemon*

Directions:

✓ *To dress: In a large mixing bowl, whisk together the oil, lemon juice, garlic, oregano, salt, and black pepper until thoroughly blended.*

✓ *In the Instant Pot, place a steamer trivet and 11/2 cups water.*

✓ *Arrange the salmon fillets in a single layer on top of the trivet and drizzle with the dressing.*

✓ *Each fillet should include 1 rosemary sprig and 1 lemon slice.*

✓ *Cover the container and set the pressure valve to the "Seal" position.*

✓ *Simply click "Steam" and stick with the default time of 3 minutes.*

✓ *Press "Cancel" and allow a "Quick" release carefully.*

✓ *Serve immediately after opening the lid.*

Nutrition: 262 Nutrition: Calories, 17g fat, 0.7g carbohydrate, 0.2g sugar, 21g protein, 91mg sodium

422) *Scallops de Tarragon*

4 portions 15 Minutes Cooking

Ingredients:

- *a cup of water*
- *1 pound asparagus spears, cleaned*
- *2 limes scallops*
- *Season with salt and pepper to taste*
- *1 tsp olive oil*
- *1 tablespoon chopped fresh tarragon*

Directions:

✓ *Fill a pot halfway with water.*
✓ *Increase the heat to high and bring it to a boil.*
✓ *A spear of asparagus.*
✓ *For 5 minutes, cover and cook.*
✓ *Transfer to a platter after draining.*
✓ *Squeeze 1 lemon into wedges.*
✓ *Squeeze the remaining lemon juice and shred the zest.*
✓ *Season with salt and pepper the scallops.*
✓ *Preheat a skillet over medium heat.*
✓ *Add a tablespoon of oil to the pan.*
✓ *Cook the scallops until they are a golden brown colour.*
✓ *Transfer to the same platter as the asparagus, placing the scallops alongside the asparagus.*
✓ *To the pan, add lemon zest, juice, and tarragon.*
✓ *1 minute cook time.*
✓ *Drizzle tarragon scallops and asparagus with tarragon sauce.*

Nutrition: 250 Calories 10 g fat Protein 30 g 15 grams Cholesterol 24 milligram

423) *Curry with Sardines*

2 portions Time Required for Cooking: 35 Minutes
Ingredients:

- *5 cans sardines in tomato sauce 1 pound veggies, chopped*
- *1 cup fish broth with a low sodium content*
- *3 tablespoons curry paste*

Directions:

✓ *In your Instant Pot, combine all of the ingredients.*
✓ *Cook for 35 minutes on Stew.*
✓ *Naturally relieve the pressure.*

Nutrition: Calories 320; Carbohydrates 8; Sugar 2; Fat 16; Protein GL 3

424) *Salmon Grilled with Ginger Sauce*

4 portions Time Required for Cooking: 8 Minutes
Ingredients:

- *1 tablespoon sesame oil, roasted*
- *1 tablespoon chopped fresh cilantro*
- *1 tsp lime juice*
- *1 tsp soy sauce*
- *1 crushed garlic clove*
- *1 teaspoon grated fresh ginger 1 teaspoon minced jalapeno pepper 4 fillets de salmon*
- *1 tsp olive oil*
- *Season with salt and pepper to taste*

Directions:

✓ *Sesame oil, cilantro, lime juice, fish sauce, garlic, ginger, and jalapeno pepper should all be combined in a bowl.*
✓ *Preheat the grill to high.*
✓ *Oil salmon with a brush.*
✓ *Season with salt and pepper on both sides.*
✓ *Salmon should be grilled for 6 to 8 minutes, rotating once or twice.*
✓ *Take 1 tablespoon of the oil mixture and set aside.*
✓ *While grilling the fish, brush with this mixture.*
✓ *Serve the remaining sauce alongside the grilled fish.*

Nutrition: 204 Calories Fat total 11 g Saturated fat 2 g Cholesterol 53 mg Sodium 320 mg Carbohydrates total 2 g Dietary Fiber 0 g Sugars in Total Protein: 2 g Potassium 437 mg 23 g

425) *Broccoli with Shrimp*

6 portions 12 Minutes Cooking
Ingredients:

- *2 tbsp olive oil, split*
- *4 cups chopped broccoli*
- *2-3 tbsp filtered water*
- *12 pounds large peeled and deveined shrimp*
- *2 minced garlic cloves 1 (1-inch) piece fresh ginger*

Directions

✓ *Season with salt and freshly ground black pepper to taste.*
✓ *In a large skillet over medium-high heat, heat 1 tablespoon of oil and sauté the broccoli for about 1-2 minutes, turning*

regularly.

✓ Cook, covered, for approximately 3-4 minutes, stirring periodically.

✓ Push the broccoli to one side of the pan using a spoon.

✓ Allow the remaining oil to heat.

✓ Cook for approximately 1-2 minutes, tossing occasionally.

✓ Sauté the remaining ingredients for approximately 2-3 minutes.

✓ Serve immediately.

Nutrition: 197 Calories 6.8 g Total Fat 3 g Saturated Fat 239 mg Cholesterol 6.1 g Carbohydrates, 1 g Sugar, 6 g Fiber, 324 mg Sodium, 389 mg Potassium, 27.6 g Protein

426) *Citrus Salmon*

4 portions 7 Minutes Cooking
Ingredients:

- 4 salmon fillets (4 oz.)

- 1 cup chicken broth with a low sodium content

- 1 teaspoon minced fresh ginger

- 2 tablespoons freshly grated orange zest 3 tbsp. freshly squeezed orange juice 1 tsp olive oil

- Pepper, Ground, As Required

Directions

✓ In an Instant Pot, combine all ingredients.

✓ Cover the container and set the pressure valve to the "Seal" position.

✓ Press "Manual" and cook for approximately 7 minutes on "High Pressure."

✓ Allow a "Natural" release by pressing "Cancel."

✓ Serve the salmon fillets with the cooking sauce drizzled on top.

Nutrition: Calories 190, Fat 10.5g, Carbohydrates 8g, Sugar 1g, Proteins 22g, Sodium 68mg

427) *Salmon Served With A Green Sauce*

4 portions 12 Minutes Cooking
Ingredients:

✓ 4 salmon fillets (6 oz.)

✓ 1 peeled, pitted, and chopped avocado

✓ 1/2 cup chopped fresh basil

✓ 3 minced garlic cloves

✓ 1 tablespoon freshly grated lemon zest

Directions:

✓ Grease a large sheet of foil with cooking spray.

✓ In a large mixing basin, combine all ingredients except the salmon and water and mash completely with a fork.

✓ Fillets should be placed in the center of the foil and equally topped with avocado mixture.

✓ To seal the fillets, fold the foil around them.

✓ In the Instant Pot, place a steamer trivet and 1/2 cup of water.

✓ On top of the trivet, place the foil packet.

✓ Cover the container and set the pressure valve to the "Seal" position.

✓ Press "Manual" and cook for about minutes under "High Pressure."

✓ In the meantime, preheat the oven to the broiler.

✓ Allow a "Natural" release by pressing "Cancel."

✓ Transfer the salmon fillets to a broiler pan after opening the cover.

✓ Broil for approximately 3–4 minutes.

✓ Serve immediately.

Nutrition: 333 Calories, 20.3g fat, 5g carbohydrate, 0.4g sugar, 32g protein, 79mg sodium

428) *Shrimp that has been blackened*

4 portions Time Required for Cooking: 5 Minutes
Ingredients:

- 12 pound shrimp, peeled and deveined

- 4 tbsp. chopped cilantro

- 4 minced garlic cloves

- 1 tbsp. cayenne pepper

- Paprika, 1 tbsp.

- 1 tbsp. extra-virgin olive oil

- 2 tsp brown Splenda sugar 1 teaspoon cumin

- 1 tablespoon oregano

- 1 teaspoon powdered garlic

- 1 teaspoon salt

- 1/2 teaspoon pepper

Directions

✓ Combine seasonings and Splenda brown sugar in a small bowl.

✓ In a skillet over medium-high heat, heat the oil. Cook shrimp in a single layer for 1-2 minutes on each side.

✓ Season with seasonings and cook for 30 seconds, stirring constantly. Garnish with cilantro and a wedge of lime.

Nutrition: Calories 252 Carbohydrates 7g Net Carbohydrates 6g Protein 39g Fatty Acids 7g Sucrose 2 g Fiber 1 gram

429) *Popcorn Shrimp*

4 portions Time Required for Cooking: 8 Minutes
Ingredients:

- Spray for cooking
- 1/2 cup unbleached all-purpose flour
- 2 beaten eggs
- 2 tbsp. water
- 1/2 cup panko bread
- 1 tbsp garlic powder
- 1 tsp ground cumin
- 1 pound peeled shrimp
- 1/2 tbsp ketchup
- 2 tbsp. fresh cilantro, chives
- 2 tbsp lime juice
- Season with salt to taste

Directions

✓ Coat the air fryer basket in cooking spray. Place the flour in a small bowl.

✓ In a separate bowl, beat the eggs and water.

✓ Put the breadcrumbs, garlic powder, and cilantro in three Different Containers.

✓ Each shrimp should be dipped starting with the flour, then the eggs, and last the breadcrumb combination

✓ In the air fryer basket, place the shrimp.

✓ Cook for 8 minutes at 360 degrees F, flipping halfway through.

✓ Combine the remaining ingredients to make a shrimp dipping sauce.

Nutrition: CALORIES 200 g FAT 25 g Protein 18 g Cholesterol 10 g 21 milligram

430) *Carbonara Tuna*

4 portions Time Required for Cooking: 25 Minutes
Ingredients:

- 12 lb. tuna fillet, sliced
- 2 Eggs
- 4 tbsp. chopped fresh parsley
- 12 Made-at-home pasta, cooked and drained

- 1/2 cup parmesan cheese, reduced fat
- 2 peeled garlic cloves
- 2 tbsp. olive oil extra virgin
- Season with salt and pepper to taste

Directions:

✓ In a small mixing bowl, whisk together the eggs, parmesan, and a pinch of pepper.

✓ In a large skillet over medium-high heat, heat the oil. Cook until garlic is browned. Cook for 2-3 minutes, or until the tuna is almost cooked through. Remove the garlic.

✓ Reduce heat to low and add the pasta. Stir in egg mixture and cook for 2 minutes, stirring constantly. If the sauce is too thick, dilute it with water a tablespoon at a time until it reaches a creamy consistency.

✓ Season with salt and pepper to taste and sprinkle with parsley.

Nutrition: 409 Calories Carbohydrates in Total 7g Carbohydrates Net 6 g protein, 25 g fat, 30 g sugar, and 3 g dietary fiber 1g

431) *Flavors Cioppino*

Portion Size: 6 Time Required for Cooking: 5 Minutes
Ingredients:

- 1 pound codfish, cut into portions
- 5 pound shrimp
- 28 oz can chopped tomatoes
- 1 cup unsweetened white wine
- 1 leaf of bay
- 1 tsp cayenne pepper
- 1 tablespoon oregano
- 1 chopped shallot
- 1 teaspoon minced garlic
- 1 tbsp extra-virgin olive oil
- 1 teaspoon salt

Directions

✓ In the inner pot of the instant pot, add the oil and turn the pot to sauté mode.

✓ Sauté the shallot and garlic for 2 minutes.

✓ Cook for 3 minutes before adding the wine, bay leaf, cayenne pepper, oregano, and salt.

✓ Stir in the other ingredients until completely combined.

✓ Cover the saucepan with a lid and cook on low for 0 minutes using the manual setting.

✓ Once completed, quickly remove the

pressure. Take the cover off.

✓ *Serve and take pleasure in.*

Nutrition: 281 Calories 5g fat 10.5g carbohydrate 9g protein 40.7g cholesterol 266 mg

432) *Delectable Shrimp Alfredo*

4 portions 3 Minutes Cooking

Ingredients

- *12 shrimp, shells removed*
- *1 tbsp minced garlic*
- *1/4 cup grated parmesan*
- *2 cup rotini noodles, whole wheat 1 cup broth de poisson*
- *15 oz sauce alfredo*
- *1 chopped onion*
- *Salt*

Directions

✓ *In the instant pot, combine all ingredients except the parmesan cheese and mix well.*

✓ *Cook, covered, on high for 3 minutes.*

✓ *Once completed, quickly remove the pressure. Take the cover off.*

✓ *Serve with cheese.*

Nutrition: 669 Calories 21 g fat 76 g carbohydrate 4 g protein 190 mg Cholesterol 37.8 g

433) *Asparagus & Salmon*

2 portions

Time Required for Cooking: 10 Minutes

Ingredients:

- *2 salmon fillets*
- *8 asparagus spears, trimmed*
- *2 tbsp balsamic vinegar*
- *1 teaspoon extra-virgin olive oil*
- *Season with salt and pepper to taste*

Directions:

✓ *Preheat the oven to 325 degrees Fahrenheit.*

✓ *Using paper towels, pat dry fish.*

✓ *Arrange the asparagus on a baking sheet around the salmon fillets.*

✓ *Combine the remaining ingredients in a bowl.*

✓ *Distribute the mixture evenly over the fish and vegetables.*

✓ *Bake for 10 minutes or until the fish is completely cooked.*

Nutrition: Calories 150 g Carbohydrates 22 g Fat 16 g Protein 7 g 20 mg cholesterol

434) *Tuna Casserole de Corn Sucre*

2 portionsTime Required for Cooking: 35 Minutes

Ingredients:

- *3 little tuna tins*
- *0.5 pound kernels of sweet corn*
- *1 pound veggies, chopped*
- *1 cup vegetarian broth with a low sodium content*
- *2 tbsp seasoning*

Directions

✓ *In your Instant Pot, combine all of the ingredients.*

✓ *Cook for 35 minutes on Stew.*

✓ *Naturally relieve the pressure.*

Nutrition: Calories: 300;Carbohydrates: 6;Sugar: 1;Fat: 9;Protein: ;GL: 2

435) *Salad with Tortilla Chips and Black Beans*

4 portions

Time Required for Cooking: 20 Minutes

Ingredients:

- *4 oz. white fish fillets, tortilla chips*
- *1/3 cup thawed frozen egg*
- *¼ red onion, diced*
- *1/4 teaspoon cumin, crushed*
- *1/2 cup halved cherry tomatoes*
- *2 tsp extra virgin olive oil*
- *1 tbsp lime juice*
- *1/4 tsp cayenne*
- *1/2 cup chopped green bell pepper*
- *1/4 teaspoon salt*
- *Spray for cooking*

Directions:

✓ *Preheat the oven to 350 degrees Fahrenheit. Line your baking sheet with foil.*

✓ *Coat the foil with cooking spray.*

✓ *In a food processor, combine the cayenne pepper and tortilla chips.*

✓ *Cover and continue crushing until it is finely crushed. Maintain in a dish.*

✓ *Pat dry with paper towels.*

✓ *In a second dish, pour the egg. Dip your fish in this, followed by your tortilla chips.*

✓ *Maintain the fish on the baking sheet at this point. Coat it lightly with cooking spray.*

✓ *8 minutes in the oven. The fish should flake*

readily when pierced with a fork.

✓ *Meanwhile, in a bowl, combine the tomatoes, onion, lemon juice, bell pepper, cumin, salt, and oil for the salad.*

✓ *Arrange fish atop the salad. On top, sprinkle some cheese.*

Nutrition: 361 Calories, 35g carbohydrate, 8g fiber, 0.3g sugar, 46mg cholesterol, 11g total fat, 28g protein

436) *Lemon Shrimp Crunchy*

4 portions Time Required for Cooking: 10 Minutes, Ingredients:

- *1 pound peeled and deveined raw shrimp*
- *2 tbsp. coarsely chopped Italian parsley*
- *2 tbsp. freshly squeezed lemon juice, split*
- *23 cup bread crumbs panko*
- *2 tbsp. olive oil*
- *Season with salt and pepper to taste*

Directions:

✓ *Preheat the oven to 400 degrees Fahrenheit.*

✓ *Evenly distribute the shrimp in a baking dish and season with salt and pepper. 1 tablespoon lemon juice and 1 tablespoon olive oil drizzled on top Place aside.*

✓ *Combine parsley, remaining lemon juice, bread crumbs, remaining olive oil, and 1/4 tsp salt and pepper in a medium bowl. Distribute the panko mixture evenly over the shrimp.*

✓ *Bake for 8-10 minutes, or until the shrimp are done, and the panko is golden brown.*

Nutrition: Calories 283 Carbohydrates 15g Net Carbohydrates 14g Protein 28g Fatty Acids 12g Sucrose 1 gram fiber 1 gram

437) *Fish Amandine*

4 portions 15 Minutes Cooking Ingredients:

- *4 oz. tilapia, halibut, or trout fillets, frozen or fresh (skinless, 1-inch size)*
- *1/8 teaspoon crushed red pepper*
- *1/4 cup chopped almonds*
- *1/2 cup crumbs de pâtisserie*
- *2 tbsp. chopped parsley*
- *1/2 teaspoon mustard powder*
- *1/4 tbsp. buttermilk*
- *1 tablespoon butter, melted*
- *2 tsp grated parmesan cheese*

- *1/4 teaspoon salt*

Directions:

✓ *Preheat the oven to 350 degrees Fahrenheit and butter a baking pan. It should be set aside.*

✓ *Rinse the fish thoroughly. Pat dry with paper towels.*

✓ *Fill a bowl halfway with buttermilk.*

✓ *In a separate dish, combine the parsley, breadcrumbs, salt, and dry mustard.*

✓ *In a bowl, combine the fish and buttermilk. Then incorporate it into your crumb mixture.*

✓ *Maintain the coated fish in the baking pan at this point.*

✓ *On the fish, sprinkle Parmesan cheese and nuts. Drizzle melted butter over the top.*

✓ *Additionally, sprinkle crushed red pepper.*

✓ *Preheat the oven to 4-6 minutes.*

Nutrition: 209 Calories, 7g carbohydrate, 1g fiber, 1g sugar, 67mg cholesterol, 9g total fat, 26g protein

438) *Shrimp and Vegetables Curry*

6 portions Time Required for Cooking: 20 Minutes Ingredients:

- *2 tsp extra virgin olive oil*
- *12 medium sliced white onions*
- *2 medium seeded and sliced green bell peppers*
- *3 medium peeled and sliced carrots*
- *3 garlic cloves, finely chopped*
- *1 tablespoon coarsely chopped fresh ginger*
- *2 tsp curry powder*
- *112 pound peeled and deveined shrimp*
- *1 cup distilled or filtered water*
- *2 tbsp. lime juice*
- *Season with salt and freshly ground black pepper to taste.*
- *2 tbsp. chopped fresh cilantro*

Directions

✓ *In a large skillet over medium-high heat, heat the oil and sauté the onion for about 4-5 minutes.*

✓ *Sauté the bell peppers and carrots for around 3-4 minutes.*

✓ *Sauté the garlic, ginger, and curry powder for approximately one minute.*

✓ *Sauté the shrimp for approximately 1 minute.*

✓ Stir in the water and simmer, occasionally stirring, for approximately 4-6 minutes.

✓ Remove from heat and stir in lime juice.

✓ Serve immediately with a sprinkle of cilantro.

✓ Transfer the curry to a large mixing bowl and leave aside to cool. Distribute the curry evenly among six containers. Refrigerate the containers for 1-2 days. Before serving, reheat in the microwave.

Nutrition: 193 Calories Cholesterol 239 mg Total Fat 8 g Saturated Fat 0.9 g Carbohydrates 12 g Sugar 7 g Fiber Protein 3 g Sodium 328 mg Potassium 437 mg 27.1 g

439) *Chowder de Clams de Coco*

6 portions 7 Minutes Cooking
Ingredients:

- 6 ounces sliced clams
- 1 cup heavy cream
- 1 cup celery, chopped
- 1 pound cauliflower, chopped
- 1 leaf of bay
- 2 oz. coconut milk
- Salt

Directions

✓ Stir up all ingredients except the clams and heavy cream.

✓ Cook, covered, on high for 5 minutes.

✓ Once completed, quickly remove the pressure. Take the cover off.

✓ Stir in heavy cream and clams and simmer for 2 minutes on sauté mode.

✓ Serve immediately after vigorously stirring.

Nutrition: Calories 301 27.2 g fat 16 g carbohydrate 6 g protein 33 mg Cholesterol 9 g

440) *Citrus Pepper Salmon*

4 portions Time Required for Cooking: 10 Minutes
Ingredients:

- 3 tbsp. ghee or avocado oil
- 1 pound salmon filet, skin on
- 1 red bell pepper, julienned
- 1 green zucchini, julienned
- 1 carrot, julienned
- 34 c. water
- Several sprigs of parsley, tarragon, dill, basil, or a combination of the above 1/2 lemon, sliced

- 1/2 teaspoon freshly ground black pepper
- 1/4 teaspoon sea salt

Directions:

✓ In the bottom of the Instant Pot, combine the water and herbs and insert a wire steamer rack, ensuring that the handles extend upward.

✓ Arrange the salmon filet on the wire rack, skin side down.

✓ Drizzle ghee over the salmon and season with black pepper and salt. Garnish with lemon wedges.

✓ Securely close and seal the Instant Pot, ensuring that the vent is set to "Sealing."

✓ Cook for 3 minutes on the "Steam" setting.

✓ Julienne the veggies and set aside while the salmon cooks.

✓ After completing the procedure, quickly release the pressure and then push the "Keep Warm/Cancel" button.

✓ Remove the cover and carefully remove the steamer rack containing the salmon while using oven mitts.

✓ Remove and discard the herbs.

✓ Reintroduce the vegetables to the saucepan and replace the cover.

✓ Cook for 1-2 minutes on the "Sauté" function.

✓ Serve the vegetables beside the fish and deglaze the pan with the remaining fat.

✓ If desired, drizzle a little of the sauce over the fish and vegetables.

Nutrition: 296 Calories, 8g carbohydrate, 15g fat, 31g protein, 1084 mg potassium, 284 mg sodium

441) *Fillets of Fish with Tomatoes and Olives*

4 portions Time Required for Cooking: 8 Minutes
Ingredients:

- 2 pound fillets of halibut
- 2 sprigs oregano
- 2 sprigs rosemary
- 2 tbsp freshly squeezed lime juice
- 1 cup pitted olives 28 oz chopped tomatoes
- 1 tbsp minced garlic
- 1 chopped onion
- 2 tablespoons olive oil

Directions:

✓ In the inner pot of the instant pot, add the

oil and turn the pot to sauté mode.

✓ Sauté onion for 3 minutes.

✓ Sauté garlic for 1 minute.

✓ Stir in lime juice, olives, herb sprigs, and tomatoes.

✓ Cook, covered, on high for 3 minutes.

✓ Once completed, quickly remove the pressure. Take the cover off.

✓ Seal the saucepan once again with the lid and cook on high for 2 minutes.

✓ Once completed, quickly remove the pressure. Take the cover off.

✓ Serve and take pleasure in.

Nutrition: 333 Calories 19.1 g Fat 38 g Carbohydrates 8.4 g Sugar Cholesterol 5 mg 14 g

442) *Almond Chili Crustd Baked Mahi Mahi*

4 portions 15 Minutes Cooking
Ingredients:

- 4 fillets of mahi mahi
- ONE LEMON
- 2 tsp extra virgin olive oil
- Season with salt and pepper to taste
- 12 c. almonds
- 1/4 tsp paprika
- 1/4 tsp onion powder
- 34 tsp chili powder
- 1/2 cup chopped red bell pepper
- 1/4 cup chopped onion
- 1/4 cup chopped fresh cilantro

Directions:

✓ Preheat the oven to 325 degrees Fahrenheit.

✓ Preheat the oven to 350°F. Line a baking tray with parchment paper.

✓ Lime juice should be squeezed.

✓ Grate the peel.

✓ In a bowl, combine the juice and zest.

✓ Combine the oil, salt, and pepper in a small bowl.

✓ Add the almonds, paprika, onion powder, and chili powder to a separate bowl.

✓ In a food processor, place the almond mixture.

✓ Pulse until the mixture is powdered.

✓ Each fillet should be dipped in the oil mixture.

✓ Dredge the chicken in the almond-chili mixture.

✓ Arrange in the oven in a single layer.

✓ Bake for 12–15 minutes, or until the chicken is fully done.

✓ Combine the red bell pepper, onion, and cilantro in a small bowl.

Nutrition: 322 Calories 12 g Total Fat 2 g Saturated Fat 83 mg Sodium 328 mg Carbohydrates in Total 28 g Dietary Fiber 4 g Sugars in Total Potassium 829 mg 10 g Protein 28 g

443) *Lemon Shrimp Kebab*

5 portions Time Required for Cooking: 4 Minutes
Ingredients:

- 12 pound shrimp, peeled but with tails intact
- 1/3 cup extra virgin olive oil
- 1/4 tbsp lemon juice
- 2 tbsp lemon zest
- 1 tablespoon chopped fresh parsley
- 8 cherry tomatoes, quartered;
- 2 scallions, slicing

Directions:

✓ In a bowl, combine the olive oil, lemon juice, lemon zest, and parsley.

✓ For 15 minutes, marinate the shrimp in this marinade.

✓ Each shrimp should be threaded onto the skewers.

✓ Grill for 4–5 minutes, flipping halfway.

✓ Serve with tomatoes and scallions on the side.

Nutrition: Calories 180 g Carbohydrates 20 g Fat Protein 15 g Cholesterol 11 g 26 milligram

444) *Salad with Turkish Tuna, Bulgur, and Chickpeas*

4 portions Time Required for Cooking: 20 Minutes
Ingredients:

- 16 oz. tuna, 4 steaks
- 12 c. bulgur
- Chickpeas, 12 oz.
- 4 teaspoons grated lemon zest
- ¼ cups chopped Italian parsley

What you'll need from the pantry:

- 1/4 cup olive oil extra-virgin
- 1/4 tsp freshly ground pepper

- *1/2 tsp salt*

Directions:

✓ *Bring water to a boil and place the bulgur in a bowl.*

✓ *2 inches of water*

✓ *Combine bulgur, 1 tablespoon oil, pepper, salt, and lemon zest in a mixing bowl.*

✓ *Combine the chickpeas and parsley in a medium bowl.*

✓ *Combine thoroughly.*

✓ *Now, in your skillet, heat the remaining oil over medium heat.*

✓ *Include the tuna. Both sides should be seared until brown.*

✓ *Your fork should easily flake the tuna. Transfer to a serving dish.*

✓ *Meanwhile, in a dish, combine 1/4 tsp salt and the remaining lemon zest.*

✓ *Transfer the tuna fish to a serving plate and set it aside.*

✓ *Garnish with lemon zest and serve alongside the bulgur.*

Nutrition: 459 Calories, 43g carbohydrate, 8g fiber, 0.2g sugar, 44mg cholesterol, 16g total fat, 36g protein

445) *Tomatoes & Cajun Flounder*

4 portions 15 Minutes Cooking

Ingredients:

- *4 fillets flounder*
- *2 1/2 cup chopped tomatoes 3/4 cups diced onion*
- *3/4 cup chopped green bell pepper*
- *2 garlic cloves, finely chopped*
- *1 tbsp. Seasonings de Cajun*
- *1 tablespoon olive oil*

Directions

✓ *In a large skillet, heat oil over medium-high heat. Cook for 2 minutes, or until the onion and garlic are tender. Cook for 2-3 minutes, or until tomatoes soften.*

✓ *Arrange fish on top. Cook, covered, for 5-8 minutes, or until salmon flakes easily with a fork. Transfer fish to serving dishes and spoon sauce over the top.*

Nutrition: Calories 194 Carbohydrates in total 8g 6 g Carbohydrates 32 g Fat 3 g Sugar 5 g Fiber 2 g

446) *Lime Sole*

2 portions Time Required for Cooking: 5 Minutes

Ingredients:

- *1 pound sole fillets, boned and skinned*
- *1 cup fish broth with a low sodium content*
- *2 shredded sweet onions*
- *lemon juice*
- *2 tbsp dried coriander*

Directions:

✓ *In your Instant Pot, combine all of the ingredients.*

✓ *Cook for 5 minutes on Stew.*

✓ *Naturally relieve the pressure.*

Nutrition: Calories 230; Carbohydrates 1; Fat 6; Protein 46; GL 1

447) *Trout Bake*

Servings: 2 Time Required for Cooking: 35 Minutes

Ingredients:

- *1 pound boneless trout fillets*
- *1 pound winter veggies, chopped*
- *1 cup fish broth with a low sodium content*
- *1 tbsp sprigs of mixed herbs*
- *sea salt to taste*

Directions:

✓ *In a foil pouch, combine all ingredients except the broth.*

✓ *Place the pouch in the Instant Pot's steamer basket.*

✓ *Fill the Instant Pot halfway with broth.*

✓ *Cook for 35 minutes on Steam.*

✓ *Naturally relieve the pressure.*

Nutrition: 310 Calories; 14 carbohydrate; 2 sugar; 12 fat; 40 protein; GL 5

448) *Spinach & Garlic Shrimp*

4 portions Time Required for Cooking: 10 Minutes

Ingredients:

- *3 tbsp. extra-virgin olive oil, split 6 garlic cloves, cut and divided 1 pound spinach*
- *Season with salt to taste*
- *1 tsp lemon juice*
- *1 pound peeled and deveined shrimp*
- *1/4 teaspoon crushed red pepper*
- *1 tablespoon chopped parsley*
- *1 teaspoon zest de limon*

Directions:

✓ *1 tablespoon olive oil in a medium saucepan over medium heat.*

✓ *For 1 minute, cook the garlic.*

✓ *Season with salt and pepper.*

✓ *3 minutes.*

✓ *Add lemon juice.*

✓ *Transfer the mixture to a bowl.*

✓ *Pour the remainder of the oil.*

✓ *Toss in the shrimp.*

✓ *Season with salt and freshly ground red pepper to taste.*

✓ *5 minutes.*

✓ *Before serving, sprinkle parsley and lemon zest over the shrimp.*

Nutrition: 226 Calories 12 g Total Fat 2 g Saturated Fat 183 mg Sodium 444 mg Carbohydrates 6 g Dietary Fiber 3 g Sugars in Total 1 gram of protein Potassium 963 mg 26 g

449) **With Salmon and Bell Peppers**

6 portions Time Required for Cooking: 20 Minutes
Ingredients:

- *6 salmon fillets (3 oz.)*

- *Squeeze of salt*

- *Pepper, Ground, As Required*

- *1 seeded and diced yellow bell pepper*

- *1 seeded and diced red bell pepper*

- *4 cubed plum tomatoes*

- *1 finely sliced tiny onion*

- *1/2 cup chopped fresh parsley*

- *1/4 cup olive oil*

- *2 tbsp. freshly squeezed lemon juice*

Directions:

✓ *Preheat the oven to 400 degrees Fahrenheit.*

✓ *Season each salmon fillet with a pinch of salt and freshly ground black pepper.*

✓ *Combine the bell peppers, tomato, and onion in a bowl.*

✓ *Arrange six foil squares on a flat surface.*

✓ *Sprinkle 1 salmon fillet with salt and black pepper over each foil paper.*

✓ *Distribute veggie mixture evenly over each fillet and garnish with parsley and capers.*

✓ *Drizzle with oil and freshly squeezed lemon juice.*

✓ *Seal each foil packet by folding it around the salmon mixture.*

✓ *Arrange the foil packets in a single layer on a large baking sheet.*

✓ *Preheat the oven to 200°F. Bake for*

approximately 20 minutes.

✓ *Serve immediately.*

✓ *Transfer the salmon mixture to a large bowl and set aside to cool somewhat.*

✓ *Distribute the salmon mixture evenly among six containers.*

✓ *Refrigerate the containers for 1 day.*

✓ *Before serving, reheat in the microwave.*
Nutrition: 220 Calories 14 g Total Fat 2 g Saturated Fat 38 mg Cholesterol Carbohydrates in total 7.7 g Sugar 8 g Fiber 2 g Sodium 74 mg Potassium 647 mg Tarragon 17.9 g

450) **Scallops**

4 portions 15 Minutes Cooking
Ingredients:

- *1 cup distilled water*

- *1 pound trimmed asparagus spears 2 limes*

- *Scallops 14 lb.*

- *Season with salt and pepper to taste*

- *1 tsp olive oil*

- *1 tablespoon chopped fresh tarragon*
Directions

✓ *Fill a pot halfway with water.*

✓ *Increase the heat to high and bring it to a boil.*

✓ *Arrange asparagus spears on top.*

✓ *Cook, covered, for 5 minutes.*

✓ *Transfer to a platter after draining.*

✓ *One lemon should be cut into wedges.*

✓ *Squeeze the remaining lemon juice and shred the zest.*

✓ *Season with salt and pepper the scallops.*

✓ *Preheat a skillet over medium heat.*

✓ *Oil the pan.*

✓ *Scallops should be cooked until golden brown.*

✓ *Transfer scallops and asparagus to the same plate.*

✓ *To the pan, add the lemon zest, juice, and tarragon.*

✓ *1 minute cook time.*

✓ *Drizzle the scallops and asparagus with the tarragon sauce.*
Nutrition: 253 Calories 12 g Total Fat 2 g Saturated Fat 47 mg Sodium 436 mg Carbohydrates 14 g Dietary Fiber 5 g Sugars in Total Protein 3 g Potassium 773 mg 27 g

451) *Curry with Salmon*

6 portions 30 Minutes Cooking
Ingredients:

- 6 salmon fillets (4 oz.)
- 1 teaspoon turmeric powder, divided As necessary, salt
- 3 tbsp olive oil
- 1 yellow onion, finely chopped
- 1 teaspoon paste de garlic
- 1 teaspoon freshly grated ginger
- 3-4 halved green chilies
- 1 teaspoon chili powder, red
- 1/2 teaspoon   cumin powder
- 1/2 teaspoon   cinnamon powder
- 3/4 cup whipped fat-free plain Greek yogurt
- 3/4 cups filtered water
- 3 tablespoons chopped fresh cilantro

Directions:

- ✓ Each salmon fillet should be seasoned with 1/2 teaspoons of turmeric and salt.
- ✓ Melt 1 tablespoon of the butter in a large skillet over medium heat and cook the salmon fillets for approximately 2 minutes per side.
- ✓ Arrange the salmon on a serving platter.
- ✓ Melt the remaining butter in the same skillet over medium heat and sauté the onion for about 4-5 minutes.
- ✓ Sauté for approximately 1 minute with the garlic paste, ginger paste, green chilies, remaining turmeric, and spices.
- ✓ Reduce the heat to a medium-low setting.
- ✓ Add the yogurt and water gradually, constantly stirring, until smooth.
- ✓ Cover the skillet and cook for approximately 10-15 minutes, or until the sauce reaches the desired consistency.
- ✓ Add the salmon fillets carefully and cook for approximately 5 minutes.
- ✓ Serve immediately with a sprinkle of cilantro.
- ✓ Transfer the curry to a large mixing bowl and leave aside to cool. Distribute the curry evenly among six containers. Refrigerate the containers for 1-2 days. Before serving, reheat in the microwave.

Nutrition: 242 Calories 13 g Total Fat 2 g Saturated Fat 51 mg Cholesterol Carbohydrates in total 1 g

Sugar 2 g cellulose Protein 0.8 g Sodium 98 mg Potassium 493 mg

452) *Halibut With Spicy Apricot Sauce*

4 portions Time Required for Cooking: 17 Minutes
Ingredients:

- 4 pitted fresh apricots
- 1/3 cup apricot preserves
- 1/2 cup nectar d'apricot
- 1/2 teaspoon   oregano, dry
- 3 tablespoons sliced scallion 1 tsp spicy pepper sauce
- Season with salt to taste
- 4 steaks of halibut
- 1 tsp olive oil

Directions

- ✓ In a saucepan, combine the apricots, preserves, nectar, oregano, scallion, hot pepper sauce, and salt.
- ✓ Bring to a boil and then reduce to low heat for 8 minutes.
- ✓ Place aside.
- ✓ Olive oil should be brushed on the halibut steaks.
- ✓ Grill for 7–9 minutes, or until the fish is opaque and flaky.
- ✓ One tablespoon of the sauce should be brushed on both sides of the fish.
- ✓ Serve with any remaining sauce.

Nutrition: 304 Calories 8 g Total Fat 1 g Saturated Fat 73 mg Sodium 260 mg Carbohydrates 27 g Dietary Fiber 2 g Sugars in Total Potassium 637 mg 16 g Protein 29 g

453) *Simple Salmon Stew*

6 portions Time Required for Cooking: 8 Minutes
Ingredients:

- 2 pound cubed salmon fillet
- 1 chopped onion
- 2 c. broth de poisson (Fish Stock)
- 1 tbsp extra-virgin olive oil
- Salt
- Pepper

Directions

- ✓ In the inner pot of the instant pot, add the oil and turn the pot to sauté mode.
- ✓ Sauté onion for 2 minutes.

✓ Stir in the other ingredients until completely combined.

✓ Cook, covered, on high for 6 minutes.

✓ Once completed, quickly remove the pressure. Take the cover off.

✓ Serve with a stir.

Nutrition: 243 Calories 16 g fat 0.8 g carbohydrate 0.3 g protein 31 g 78 mg cholesterol

454) *Grilled Shrimp with Cilantro and Lime*

6 portions Time Required for Cooking: 5 Minutes,
Ingredients:

- 12 lb. uncooked, peeled, deveined big shrimp with tails 1 lime juice and zest
- 2 tbsp. chopped fresh cilantro
- 1/4 cup extra virgin olive oil
- 2 garlic cloves, finely chopped
- 1 teaspoon paprika, smoked
- 1/4 teaspoon cumin
- 1 tsp salt
- 1/4 tsp cayenne

Directions

✓ Put the shrimp in a large Ziploc bag.

✓ In a small bowl, combine the remaining ingredients and pour over shrimp. Allow 20-30 minutes for marinating.

✓ Preheat the grill. Cook the shrimp on skewers for 2-3 minutes per side, or until they turn pink. Caution:

✓ Do not overcook them. Garnish with cilantro if desired.

Nutrition: 317 Calories Total Carbohydrates 0g Fiber 0g Protein 4g Fat 39g Carbohydrates 15g Sugar 0g

455) *Cajun Catfish*

4 portions 15 Minutes Cooking
Ingredients:

- 4 (8 oz.) catfish fillets
- 2 tablespoons olive oil
- 2 tsp salt de garlic
- 2 teaspoon thyme
- paprika, 2 tsp
- 1/2 tsp cayenne
- 1/2 teaspoon   spicy sauce
- 1/4 tsp ground black pepper
- Cooking spray that is nonstick

Directions:

✓ Preheat the oven to 450 degrees Fahrenheit. Cooking spray a 9x13-inch baking dish.

✓ In a small dish, whisk together all ingredients except the catfish. Brush both sides of the fillets with the spice mixture.

✓ Bake for 10-13 minutes, or until the fish easily flakes with a fork. Serve.

Nutrition: 366 Calories, 0g protein, 35g fat, 24g sugar, 0g fiber 0g

456) *Halibut Sauced in Spicy Apricot*

4 portions Time Required for Cooking: 17 Minutes
Ingredients:

- 4 pitted fresh apricots
- 1/3 cup apricot preserves
- 1/2 cup nectar de apricot
- 1/2 teaspoon oregano rie
- 3 tbsp scallion, mince
- 1 tsp cayenne pepper sauce
- Season with salt to taste
- 4 steaks of halibut
- 1 tsp olive oil

Directions:

✓ In a saucepan, combine the apricots, preserves, nectar, oregano, scallion, hot pepper sauce, and salt.

✓ Bring to a boil and then reduce to low heat for 8 minutes.

✓ Asie.

✓ Olive oil should be brushed on the halibut steaks.

✓ Grill for 7–9 minutes, or until the fish is opaque and flaky.

✓ One tablespoon of the sauce should be brushed on both sides of the fish.

✓ Serve immediately with the reserved sauce.

✓ Bake for 10 minutes or until the fish is completely cooked.

Nutrition: Calories 150 g Carbohydrates 22 g Fat Protein 16 g 7 g 20 mg cholesterol

457) *Mixed Chowder*

Servings: 2 Time Required for Cooking: 35 Minutes
Ingredients:

- 1 pound fish stew mix
- 2 tablespoons white sauce

- *3 tbsp seasoning with old bay*

Directions:

✓ *In your Instant Pot, combine all of the ingredients.*

✓ *Cook for 35 minutes on Stew.*

✓ *Naturally relieve the pressure.*

Nutrition: 320 Calories; 9 carbohydrates; 2 sugar; 16 fat; 4 g protein

458) *Zucchini Shrimp*

4 portions Time Required for Cooking: 8 Minutes
Ingredients:

- *3 tbsp olive oil*
- *1 pound peeled and deveined medium shrimp*
- *1 minced shallot*
- *4 minced garlic cloves*
- *1/4 teaspoon crushed red pepper flakes*
- *Season with salt and freshly ground black pepper to taste.*
- *1/4 cup chicken broth with a low sodium content*
- *2 tbsp. freshly squeezed lemon juice*
- *1 teaspoon fresh lemon zest, grated finely*
- *½ pound zucchini, spiralized with Blade*

Directions:

✓ *In a large skillet, heat the oil and butter over medium-high heat and sauté the shrimp, shallot, garlic, red pepper flakes, salt, and black pepper for about 2 minutes, turning regularly.*

✓ *Stir in the broth, lemon juice, and lemon zest and bring to a mild boil.*

✓ *Stir in zucchini noodles and simmer for about 1-2 minutes.*

✓ *Serve immediately.*

✓ *Meal Prep Tip: Transfer the shrimp mixture into a large bowl and leave aside to cool. Distribute the shrimp mixture evenly among four containers. Refrigerate the containers for approximately 1-2 days. Before serving, reheat in the microwave.*

Nutrition: 245 Calories 16 g total fat 2 g saturated fat 239 mg cholesterol 8 g sugar 2 g fiber Sodium: 289 mg Potassium: 381 mg Protein: 08 g 27 g

459) *Shrimp Braised*

4 portions Time Required for Cooking: 4 Minutes
Ingredients:

- *1 pound peeled and deveined frozen big shrimp*
- *2 shallots, chopped*
- *3/4 cup chicken broth, reduced in sodium*
- *2 tbsp. freshly squeezed lemon juice*
- *2 tbsp olive oil*
- *1 tablespoon crushed garlic*
- *pepper, ground, as required*

Directions

✓ *In the Instant Pot, add the oil and press "Sauté." Cook for approximately 2 minutes before adding the shallots.*

✓ *Cook for approximately 1 minute after adding the garlic.*

✓ *Select "Cancel" and add the shrimp, broth, lemon juice, and black pepper to taste.*

✓ *Cover the container and set the pressure valve to the "Seal" position.*

✓ *Press "Manual" and cook for approximately 1 minute under "High Pressure."*

✓ *Press "Cancel" and allow a "Quick" release carefully.*

✓ *Serve immediately after opening the lid.*

Nutrition: 209 Calories, 9g fat, 3g carbohydrate, 0.2g sugar, 26.6g protein, 293mg sodium

460) *Soup de saumon*

4 portions Time Required for Cooking: 20 Minutes
Ingredients:

- *1 tsp olive oil*
- *1 chopped yellow onion*
- *1 minced garlic clove*
- *4 cups chicken broth with a low salt content*
- *1 pound cubed boneless salmon*
- *2 tbsp chopped fresh cilantro*
- *Ground black pepper to taste*
- *1 tbsp. lime juice*

Directions

✓ *In a large skillet over medium heat, heat the oil and sauté the onion for about 5 minutes.*

✓ *Sauté the garlic for around 1 minute.*

✓ *Bring to a boil over high heat, stirring in the broth.*

✓ *Reduce to low heat and simmer for approximately 10 minutes.*

✓ *Cook for approximately 3-4 minutes before adding the fish and soy sauce.*

✓ *Serve immediately with black pepper, lime*

juice, and cilantro.

✓ Transfer the soup to a large bowl and leave it aside to cool somewhat. Distribute the soup evenly among four containers. Refrigerate the containers for 1-2 days. Before serving, reheat in the microwave.

Nutrition: Calories 208 10.5 g total fat 5 g saturated fat 50 mg cholesterol Carbohydrates 9 g Sugar 2 g

461) _With Pineapple-cilantro Salmon Salsa_

Portion Size: 4 15 Minutes Cooking
Ingredients:

- 1 pound skinless salmon fillets,
- 1 inch thick
- 2 tbsp chopped parsley or cilantro
- 2 cups chopped pineapple
- 1/4 cup chopped red onion
- 1/2 cup chopped green or red bell pepper
- 1/4 tsp salt
- 1/2 tsp chili powder
- 3 tsp lime juice
- Lime wedges, if desired
- 1 tsp cayenne pepper

Directions:

✓ Rinse the fish thoroughly. Pat dry with paper towels.

✓ To make the salsa, in a mixing bowl, combine the bell pepper, pineapple, lime juice, red onion, and 1 tablespoon parsley or cilantro. This should be set aside.

✓ Combine the lime juice, salt, and remaining parsley or cilantro in a medium bowl.

✓ This should be applied to both sides of your fish.

✓ Maintain the salmon on the grill and cook for 8 minutes. Twice.

✓ Cut the fish into four equal-sized servings. Distribute salsa on top.

✓ Serve alongside lettuce and lime wedges.

Nutrition: 257 Calories, 13g carbohydrate, 2g fiber, 1g sugar, 66mg cholesterol, 12g total fat, 23g protein

462) _Italian Pasta with Tuna_

Servings: 6 Time Required for Cooking: 5 Minutes
Ingredients:

- 15 oz pasta made with whole wheat 2 tablespoons capers
- 3 ounces tuna

- 2 cup smashed tomatoes from a can 2 sardines
- 1 teaspoon minced garlic
- 1 tbsp extra-virgin olive oil
- Salt

Directions:

✓ In the inner pot of the instant pot, add the oil and turn the pot to sauté mode.

✓ Sauté the anchovies and garlic for 1 minute.

✓ Stir in the other ingredients until completely combined. Fill the saucepan halfway with enough water to cover the pasta.

✓ Cover the saucepan with a lid and cook on low for 4 minutes using the manual setting.

✓ Once completed, quickly remove the pressure. Take the cover off.

✓ Serve with a stir.

Nutrition: Calories 339 6 g fat 56.5 g carbohydrate 2 g sugar 12 g protein

463) _Garlic-Baked Salmon Parmesan Topping_

4 portions 20 Minutes Cooking Time,
Ingredients:

- 1 pound filets of wild caught salmon 2 tablespoons margarine
- 1/4 cup grated parmesan cheese with reduced-fat
- 1/4 cup light mayonnaise
- 2-3 garlic cloves, diced
- 2 tablespoons parsley
- Season with salt & pepper

Directions:

✓ Preheat the oven to 350 degrees Fahrenheit and line a baking sheet with parchment paper.

✓ Season fish with salt and pepper.

✓ Melt butter in a medium skillet over medium heat. Add garlic and simmer for 1 minute, stirring constantly.

✓ Reduce to a low heat and stir in additional ingredients. Stir until all ingredients are melted and mixed.

✓ Spread evenly over salmon and bake for 15 minutes if using frozen fish or 20 minutes if using thawed fish. Salmon is cooked when it easily flakes with a fork. Serve.

Nutrition: Calories 408 Carbohydrates 4g Protein 41g Fat 24g Sugar 1g Fiber 0g

POULTRY

464) *Chicken Fajita Burritos in the Slow Cooker*

Time required for preparation: ten minutes Time Required for Cooking: 6 hrs. 8 portions

Ingredients:

* *1 tsp cumin*
* *1 cup cheddar cheese + 2 tbsp shredded reduced-fat*
* *1 pound skinless and boneless chicken strips*
* *8 large low-carb tortillas*
* *1 sliced green pepper*
* *1 can (15 oz) rinsed and drained black beans*
* *1 sliced red pepper*
* *1/3 cup water*
* *1 sliced medium onion*
* *1/2 cup salsa*
* *1 tablespoon chili powder*
* *1 teaspoon garlic powder*

Directions:

* ✓ *In a slow cooker, place strips of chicken breast.*
* ✓ *Arrange all of the ingredients listed above on top of the chicken, except the cheese and tortillas. Cook, covered, for roughly 6 hours, or until done.*
* ✓ *Using a fork, shred the chicken.*
* ✓ *Place a half cup of chicken and the bean mixture on each tortilla.*
* ✓ *Sprinkle tortilla with 2 tablespoons of shredded cheese and fold into a burrito.*

Nutrition: 250Calories; 7 g fat; 31 g carbohydrate total; 28 g protein

465) *Crock Pot Cacciatore de Pollo*

Time required for preparation: ten minutes Time required for cooking: 4 hours 6 servings

Ingredients:

* *1 can (15 oz) diced tomatoes*
* *6 medium skinless chicken thighs*
* *1 onion, sliced*
* *1 tablespoon Italian seasoning*
* *1 green bell pepper, seeded and sliced*
* *3 clove garlic, minced*

Directions:

* ✓ *Combine all ingredients in a Crock-Pot*

slow cooker and cook on High for 4 hours.

* ✓ *If desired, serve chicken cacciatore over whole wheat rotini pasta.*

Nutrition: 170 Calories; 5 g fat; 18 g carbohydrate total; 16 g protein

466) *Slow Cooker Chicken & Sweet Potatoes in the Crock-Pot*

Time required for preparation: ten minutes Time required for cooking: 5-7 hours 4 portions

* *1 1/2 cup low-sodium, low-fat chicken broth*
* *4 (4 ounces) skinless and boneless chicken thighs*
* *2 tablespoons Dijon mustard*
* *1 onion, diced*
* *1/4 teaspoon dried thyme*
* *2 large sweet potatoes, peeled and sliced into large rounds*

Directions:

* ✓ *In the Crock-Pot slow cooker, place 4 (4 oz) chicken thighs.*
* ✓ *Arrange sliced potatoes and chopped onions on top of chicken thighs.*
* ✓ *Now, combine all of the remaining ingredients in the Crock-Pot slow cooker. Cook on low for approximately 5-7 hours, or until chicken is thoroughly cooked.*
* ✓ *Once completed, remove the bay leaf from the slow cooker's Crock-Pot.*
* ✓ *Serve immediately.*

Nutrition: 75 Calories; 7 g fat; 32 g carbohydrate total; 21 g protein

467) *Tex-Mex Slow Cooker Crock-Pot Chicken*

Time required for preparation: ten minutes Time required for cooking: 4 hours 40 minutes 6 portions

* *4 tablespoons cup water*
* *1 teaspoon ground cumin*
* *1 pound boneless chicken thighs, visible fat removed, washed, and patted dry*
* *1 (10 ounces) can chopped tomatoes with green chiles*

Direction

* ✓ *Coat a skillet with cooking spray and turn on the heat.*
* ✓ *In a skillet over medium heat, sauté chicken thighs until browned on each side. Remove*

from the skillet once browned.

✓ *Add peppers and onions to the same skillet and sauté until soft.*

✓ *Place sauteed peppers and onions in the bottom of a 4- to 5-quart Crock-Pot slow cooker, followed by the chicken thighs.*

✓ *Distribute tomatoes and 4 tablespoons of water evenly over meat. Cook on low for approximately 4 hours.*

✓ *Add 1 teaspoon ground cumin and continue cooking for another half hour.*

✓ *Remove it from the oven and serve immediately!*

Nutrition: 121Calories; 2 g fat; 6.4 g carbohydrate total; 16 g protein

468) *Slow Cooker Ranch Chicken in the Crock-Pot*

Time required for preparation: ten minutes Time required for cooking: 4 hours 4 portions

• *1 cup cream cheese spread with chive and onion*

• *1/2 teaspoon freshly ground black pepper*

• *4 boneless chicken breasts*

• *1 1-oz packet ranch dressing and spice mix*

• *1/2 cup low sodium chicken stock*

Direction

✓ *Preheat the Crock-Pot slow cooker by spraying it with cooking spray.*

✓ *Using a paper towel, pat dry the chicken and transfer it to the Crock-Pot slow cooker.*

✓ *Cook for approximately 4-5 minutes on each side, or until chicken is browned.*

✓ *Combine 12 cups low sodium chicken stock, 1 oz. Ranch dressing and seasoning mix, 1 cup chive and onion cream cheese spread, and 1/2 teaspoon freshly ground black pepper in a medium bowl. Cover the slow cooker and simmer on low for approximately 4 hours, or until the internal temperature reaches 165 degrees, F. Remove it from the Crock-Pot slow cooker once it is cooked.*

✓ *Whisk the sauce in the slow cooker's Crock-Pot until smooth. If a thick sauce is desired, simmer for approximately 5-10 minutes, stirring frequently.*

✓ *Serve chicken garnished with sliced onions and bacon.*

Nutrition: 362 Calories; 18.5 g fat; 9.7 g carbohydrate total; 37.3 g protein

469) *Buffalo Chicken Dip in the Crock-Pot*

Time required for preparation: ten minutes 3 hours for cooking 10 portions

• *2 cups cooked chicken, cut into small pieces*

• *1 cup ranch dressing*

• *16 oz cream cheese, diced and softened*

Directions:

✓ *In a 3-quart Crock-Pot slow cooker, combine 5 oz hot sauce, 16 oz cubed cream cheese, and 1 cup ranch dressing. Cover and cook on low for approximately 2 hours, stirring occasionally.*

✓ *When the cheese has melted, stir in 2 cups cooked chicken. Cover the Crock-Pot slow cooker once more and simmer on low for another hour.*

✓ *Serve buffalo chicken with vegetables or any other chips of your choice.*

Nutrition: 344Calories; 29 g fat; 5 g carbohydrate total; 15 g protein

470) *Slow Cooker Mulligatawny Soup in the Crock-Pot*

Time required for preparation: ten minutes Time required for cooking: 6 hours 8 servings

• *2 whole cloves*

• *1/4 cup chopped green pepper*

• *1 carton (32 oz.) low-sodium chicken broth*

• *1/4 teaspoon pepper*

• *1 can (14 1/2 oz.) diced tomatoes*

• *1/2 teaspoon sugar*

• *2 cups cubed cooked chicken*

• *1 large tart green apple, peeled and diced*

• *1 teaspoon salt*

• *1/4 cup finely chopped onion*

• *2 teaspoon lemon juice*

• *1/4 cup carrot, chopped*

Direction

✓ *Combine all ingredients in a 3- or 4-quart Crock-Pot slow cooker. Cover the cooker and cook on Low for approximately 6-8 hours.*

✓ *Once finished, discard the cloves and serve.*

Nutrition: 107 Calories; 2 g fat; 10 g carbohydrate total; 12 g protein

471) *Greek Chicken*

Time required for preparation: ten minutes Time

required for cooking: 9-10 hours 4-6 portions

- *1 entire garlic bulb, chopped*
- *1 tablespoon olive oil*
- *4 potatoes, peeled and quartered*
- *1/2 teaspoon pepper*
- *2 pounds chicken parts, skin, and fat removed*
- *3/4 teaspoon salt*
- *2 large onions, quartered*

Direction

- ✓ *Place potatoes in the slow cooker, spreading them out evenly on the bottom.*
- ✓ *After that, add 2 pounds of chicken pieces, minced garlic, and quartered onions.*
- ✓ *Top with 3 tsp dried oregano, 3/4 tsp salt, and 1/2 tsp pepper.*
- ✓ *Drizzle 1 tablespoon olive oil on top.*
- ✓ *Cook on low for approximately 9-10 hours and on high for approximately 5-6 hours.*

Nutrition: 278Calories; 6 g fat; 29 g carbohydrate total; 27 g protein

472) *Chicken Polynesian*

Time required for preparation: ten minutes Time required for cooking: 4 hours 6 cup servings

- *3 minced garlic cloves*
- *2 bell peppers, cut into 1/2-inch strips — 1 (20-ounce) can pineapple chunks in juice, drained but with liquid kept*
- *1 1/2 pounds boneless chicken breasts, cut into 2-inch cubes*
- *1 teaspoon ginger powder*

Directions:

- ✓ *In a bowl, whisk together the saved pineapple juice, 3 tablespoons soy sauce, 1/3 cup honey, 1 teaspoon ground ginger, and 3 chopped garlic cloves. Then mix in 2 tablespoons tapioca flour until blended.*
- ✓ *In a slow cooker, combine chicken and pineapple chunks.*
- ✓ *Spoon the pineapple juice mixture over the chicken and cover the cooker.*
- ✓ *Cook on low heat for approximately 4-5 hours, or until chicken is completely cooked through.*
- ✓ *Finally, add bell pepper strips during the final hour of cooking. Serve and take pleasure in!*

Nutrition: 273 Calories; 26 g fat; 37 g carbohydrate total; 26 g protein

473) *Coconut Chicken*

10 minutes to prepare Time required for cooking: 4 hours 6 portions

Ingredients:

- *2 minced garlic cloves*
- *1/2 cup light coconut milk*
- *6 tablespoons sweetened coconut, shredded and toasted*
- *2 tablespoons brown sugar*
- *6 boneless skinless chicken thighs (about 1-1/2 pounds)*
- *2 teaspoons reduced-sodium soy sauce*
- *1/8 teaspoon ground cloves*

Directions:

- ✓ *In a large mixing bowl, combine brown sugar, 1/2 cup light coconut milk, 2 teaspoons soy sauce, 1/8 teaspoon ground cloves, and 2 minced garlic cloves.*
- ✓ *In a Crockpot, combine 6 boneless chicken thighs.*
- ✓ *Pour the coconut milk mixture over the chicken thighs. Cover the cooker and cook on low for approximately 4-5 hours.*
- ✓ *Garnish with cilantro and coconut; enjoy!*

Nutrition: 201 Calories; 10 g fat; 6 g carbohydrate total; 21 g protein

474) *Chicken with Spicy Lime*

Time required for preparation: ten minutes 3 hours for cooking 6 portions

Ingredients:

- *3 tablespoons lime juice*
- *Fresh cilantro leaves*
- *1 1/2 pounds (about 4) boneless skinless chicken breast halves*
- *1 teaspoon lime zest, grated*

Direction

- ✓ *In a slow cooker, combine chicken breast halves.*
- ✓ *In a separate bowl, combine 1 tablespoon chili powder, 3 tablespoons lime juice, and 2 cups chicken stock; whisk well and pour over chicken.*
- ✓ *Cover the cooker and cook on low for approximately 3 hours. Once cooked, remove the chicken from the cooker and allow to cool.*
- ✓ *Once the chicken has cooled, shred it with forks and return it to the Crockpot.*
- ✓ *Add 1 teaspoon grated lime zest and mix*

well. Enjoy spicy lime chicken with cilantro!
Nutrition: 132 Calories; 3 g fat; 2 g carbohydrate total; 23 g protein

475) *Cheese with Vegetables*

Time required for preparation: ten minutes Time required for cooking: 9 hours 2 portions
Ingredients:

- *1/4 cup dry red wine*
- *1/4 teaspoon salt*
- *8 oz boneless lean chuck roast*
- *1/4 teaspoon black pepper*
- *1 tsp Worcestershire*
- *8 oz. entire mushrooms*
- *1 1/4 cup trimmed fresh green beans*

Directions:

- ✓ *In a bowl, add all ingredients except the salt; stir well and then put to a slow cooker.*
- ✓ *Cover the cooker and simmer on low for approximately 9 hours or on high for approximately 4 1/2 hours, or until the meat is completely cooked through and tender.*
- ✓ *Gently stir in 1/4 teaspoon salt. Transfer the vegetables and beef to two shallow dishes.*
- ✓ *Pour liquid into the skillet; bring to a gentle boil and cook for approximately 1 1/2 minutes, or until the liquid reduces to 14 cups.*
- ✓ *Drizzle over vegetables and beef. Serve immediately after discarding the bay leaf.*

Nutrition: 215 Calories; 5 g fat; 17 g carbohydrate total; 26 g protein

476) *Chicken with Mustard and Basil*

Time Required for Preparation: 20 minutes Time Required for Cooking: 30 minutes 4 portions

- *1 tsp chicken stock*
- *2 chicken breasts, skinless and boneless; halves*
- *1 tbsp basil, chopped*
- *What you'll need from your pantry:*
- *Salt and black pepper*
- *1 tablespoon olive oil*
- *1/2 teaspoon garlic powder*
- *1/2 teaspoon onion powder*
- *1 teaspoon Dijon mustard*

Directions:

- ✓ *On the instant pot, press 'Sauté' and add the oil. Brown the chicken in the hot oil for 2-3 minutes.*
- ✓ *Stir in the remaining ingredients and cook at high pressure for 12 minutes.*
- ✓ *Allow 10 minutes for natural pressure release before dividing into plates and serving.*

Nutrition: Calories: 34, fat: 6, carbs: 0.7, protein: 0.3, fiber: 0.1

477) *Basil Chili Chicken*

Time Required for Cooking: 20 minutes 4 portions

- *1/2 cup chicken stock*
- *1 pound chicken breast*
- *2 teaspoon sweet paprika*
- *1 cup coconut cream*
- *2 tbsp basil (sliced)*
- *What you'll need from your pantry:*
- *Salt and freshly ground black pepper to taste*
- *1 tablespoon chili powder*

Directions:

- ✓ *In your instant pot, combine the chicken and remaining ingredients, stir briefly, cover, and cook on high for 20 minutes.*
- ✓ *Gently release the pressure for 10 minutes, then divide them across plates before eating.*

Nutrition: 364 Calories, 22g fat, 3g fiber, 1g carbohydrate, 34g protein

478) *Chicken with Garlic Chives*

Preparation Time: 20 minutes Time Required for Cooking: 10 minutes 4 portions

- *1 pound (skin and bones removed) chicken breast*
- *1 tablespoon chives*
- *1 cup chicken stock*
- *3 tbsp chopped garlic cloves*
- *What you'll need from your pantry:*
- *1 and a half tbsp balsamic vinegar*

Directions:

- ✓ *In the instant pot, combine the chicken and remaining ingredients, then cover and cook on high for 20 minutes.*
- ✓ *Gently release the pressure for 10 minutes, then divide them over your plates before*

eating.
Nutrition: 360Calories, 21g fat, 4g fiber, 1g carbs, 35g protein

479) *Mixture of Turkey with Spring Onions*

15 minutes for preparation Time Required for Cooking: 10 minutes 4 portions

Ingredients:

- ¼ Cup of Cilantro
- 4 spring onions (sliced)
- 1 spring onion (no skin and bones) Breast of turkey
- 1 cup tomato passata
- 2 tbsp avocado oil
- Season with salt and freshly ground black pepper to taste

Direction

- ✓ Select the Sauté option on the instant pot, then add the oil and cook. Following that, add the meat and heat for 5 minutes.
- ✓ Combine the remaining ingredients, then cover and simmer on high for 20 minutes.
- ✓ Gently release the pressure for 10 minutes, then divide them over your plates before eating.

Nutrition: Calories 222, Fat 6.7g, Fiber 6g, Carbohydrates 8g, Protein 34g

480) *Chicken with Peppered Broccoli*

Preparation Time: 20 minutes Time Required for Cooking: 30 minutes 4 portions

- 1 tbsp sage (sliced)
- 1 cup broccoli florets
- 1 lb (no bones and skin) Breast of chicken
- 3 garlic cloves
- 1 cup passata di tomato
- What you'll need from your pantry:
- Season with salt and freshly ground black pepper to taste
- 2 tbsp. olive oil

Directions:

- ✓ Select the Sauté option on the instant pot, then add the oil and cook. Following that, add the chicken and garlic and cook for 5 minutes.
- ✓ Combine the remaining ingredients, then cover and simmer on high for 25 minutes.

- ✓ Gently release the pressure for 10 minutes, then divide them over your plates before eating.

Nutrition: Calories: 217; Fat: 10.1g; Fiber: 8g; Carbohydrates: 9g; Protein: 24g.

481) *Turkey Coriander Dish*

Time Required for Preparation: 20 minutes Time Required for Cooking: 20 minutes 4 portions

- 1/2 bunch coriander (sliced)
- 1 cup chard (sliced)
- 1 turkey breast (boneless and skinless)
- 2 garlic cloves
- What you'll need from your pantry:
- 1 tbsp Ghee melted

Direction

- ✓ Select the Sauté option on the instant pot, then add the ghee and cook. Following that, add the garlic and meat and heat for 5 minutes.
- ✓ Combine the remaining ingredients, then cover and simmer on high for 25 minutes.
- ✓ Gently release the pressure for 10 minutes, then divide them over your plates before eating.

Nutrition: Calories: 225; Fat: 8.9g; Fiber: 0.2g; Carbohydrates: 0.8g; Protein: 35g

482) *Peppered Breast of Chicken with Basil*

Time Required for Preparation: 10 minutes Time Required for Cooking: 20 minutes 4 portions

Ingredients:

- 1/4 cup roasted red bell peppers
- 1 cup chicken stock
- 2 chicken breasts, skin and bones removed
- 4 garlic cloves (crushed)
- 1 1/2 tbsp Basil (crushed)
- What you'll need from your pantry:
- 1 tbsp cayenne pepper

Directions:

- ✓ In an instant pot, combine all ingredients and cook on high for 25 minutes.
- ✓ Quickly release the pressure for 5 minutes, then divide them across your plates before eating.

Nutrition: 230 Calories, 14g fat, 0.8g fiber, 7g carbs, 32g protein

483) Garlic Chicken with Soy Glaze

Time Required for Preparation: 10 minutes Time Required for Cooking: 25 minutes 6 servings

- 2 pounds boneless chicken thighs
- What you'll need from the pantry:
- Sea salt and freshly ground pepper
- 1 tablespoon minced garlic
- 1/4 tbsp soy sauce
- 3/4 cup fermented apple cider vinegar

Direction

- ✓ Season the chicken with salt and pepper and place it skin-side down in the Instant Pot.
- ✓ Combine the apple cider vinegar, soy sauce, and garlic in a small bowl and add to the pot.
- ✓ Once the lid is closed and locked, hit the Manual button and set the timer to 15 minutes.
- ✓ When the timer sounds, allow the pressure to naturally vent.
- ✓ Once the pressure in the pot has been released, remove the cover.
- ✓ Transfer the chicken to a baking sheet and broil for 3–5 minutes, or until the skin is crispy.
- ✓ In the meantime, set the Instant Pot to Sauté and cook, occasionally stirring, until the sauce thickens.
- ✓ Spoon the sauce over the chicken and serve.

Nutrition: Calories 335 calorie fat 23 calorie protein 27.5g carbohydrates 5g dietary fiber 0g carbohydrate net 5g

484) Coco Turkey in Tomato Pasta

Time Required for Preparation: 15 minutes Time Required for Cooking: 20 minutes 4 portions

- 1 large turkey, boneless and skinless
- 1 and a half cups coconut cream
- 2 tbsp garlic
- 1 tbsp basil
- 2 tbsp tomato spaghetti
- What you'll need from your pantry:
- Season with salt and freshly ground black pepper to taste
- 1 tbsp melted ghee

Directions:

- ✓ Select the Sauté option on the instant pot, then add the ghee and cook. Following that,

add the garlic and meat and heat for 5 minutes.

- ✓ Add the other ingredients, cover, and simmer on high for 20 minutes.
- ✓ Gently release the pressure for 10 minutes, then divide them over your plates before eating.

Nutrition: Calories: 229; Fat: 8.9g; Fiber: 0.2g; Carbohydrates: 8g; Protein: 36g.

485) Avocado with Cheesy Chicken in Tomato Sauce

Time Required for Preparation: 20 minutes Time Required for Cooking: 10 minutes 8 portions Ingredients:

- 1 cup shredded cheddar cheese
- 2 skinless, boneless chicken breasts halves
- 2 avocados pitted, skinned, and cubed
- 2 cups Tomato passata

Directions:

- ✓ On the instant pot, press 'Sauté' and add the oil. Brown the chicken for 5 minutes in the heated oil.
- ✓ Combine the passata, avocados, salt, and pepper in a medium mixing bowl.
- ✓ Spread the cheese evenly over the mixture and lock the lid to cook at high pressure for 12 minutes.
- ✓ Allow 10 minutes for natural pressure release before dividing into plates and serving.

Nutrition: Calories 198, fat 16.4, carbohydrates 6.6, protein 4, fiber 6

486) Chicken Olives with Oregano Flavor

15 minutes for preparation Time Required for Cooking: 15 minutes 4 portions

- 2 chicken breasts (without skin and bones)
- 2 eggplants
- 1 tbsp oregano
- 1 cup tomato passata
- What you'll need from your pantry:
- Salt and freshly ground black pepper to taste
- 2 tbsp olive oil

Direction

- ✓ In an instant pot, combine all of the ingredients, then cover and cook on high for 20 minutes.

✓ Gently release the pressure for 10 minutes, then divide them over your plates before eating.

Nutrition: Calories 362, Fat 16.1, Fiber 4g, Carbohydrates 4g, Protein 36.4g

487) *Sauce de Canard au Garlic et d'Onion*

Time Required for Preparation: 20 minutes Time Required for Cooking: 20 minutes 4 servings
Ingredients:

- 2 tbsp coriander
- 2 spring onions (no skin and bones)
- 2 duck legs
- 2 garlic cloves
- 2 tbsp tomato passata
- 2 tbsp Ghee melted

Direction

✓ Select the Sauté option on the instant pot, then add the ghee and cook. Following that, add the spring onions and all ingredients (excluding the tomato passata and meat) and heat for 5 minutes.

✓ Place the meat in the pan and cook for 5 minutes.

✓ Add the sauce, cover, and simmer on high for 25 minutes.

✓ Gently release the pressure for 10 minutes, then divide them over your plates before eating.

Nutrition: 263 Calories, 12g fat, 0.2g fiber, 1g carbs, 35g protein

488) *Chinese Stuffed Chicken*

Time Required for Preparation: 20 minutes Time Required for Cooking: 30 minutes 8 portions

- 1 entire chicken
- 10 wolfberries
- 2 chopped red chilies
- 4 ginger slices
- 1 cubed yam
- 1 tbsp. soy sauce
- 3 tbsp. sesame oil
- Salt and white pepper to taste

Direction

✓ Season chicken with salt and pepper and rub with soy sauce and sesame oil before stuffing with wolfberries, yam cubes, chiles, and ginger.

✓ Place in an air fryer and cook at 400

degrees Fahrenheit for 20 minutes, then at 360 degrees Fahrenheit for 15 minutes. Carve chicken and divide among plates.

Nutrition: Calories 320; Fat 12; Fiber 17; Carbohydrates 22; Protein 12

489) *Asparagus and chicken*

Time Required for Preparation: 20 minutes Time Required for Cooking: 10 minutes 4 portions

- 8 halved chicken wings
- 8 asparagus stalks
- 1 tbsp. chopped rosemary
- 1 tsp. ground cumin
- Season with salt and freshly ground black pepper to taste

Directions:

✓ Pat dry chicken wings, season with salt, pepper, cumin, and rosemary, place in the basket of your air fryer, and cook for 20 minutes at 360 °F.

✓ In the meantime, preheat a pan over medium heat, add asparagus, cover with water, and steam for a few minutes; move to a bowl of ice water, drain, and arrange on plates. Serve with chicken wings on the side.

Nutrition: 270 Calories; 8 grams fat; 12 grams fiber; 24 grams carbohydrates; 22
257 grams protein.

490) *Italian Chicken*

Time Required to Prepare Italian Chicken: 10 minutes Time Required for Cooking: 16 minutes 4 portions
Ingredients:

- 5 chicken thighs
- 1 tbsp. olive oil
- 1/4 cup grated parmesan
- 1/2 cup sun-dried tomatoes
- 2 minced garlic cloves
- 1 tbsp. chopped thyme
- 1/2 cup heavy cream
- 3/4 cup chicken stock
- 1 tsp crushed red pepper flakes
- 2 tbsp chopped basil
- Season with salt and freshly ground black pepper to taste

Direction

✓ Season chicken with salt and pepper, massage with half of the oil, and cook for 4 minutes in a preheated air fryer set to 350

°F.

✓ Meanwhile, heat the remaining oil in a saucepan over medium-high heat. Add the thyme, garlic, pepper flakes, sun-dried tomatoes, heavy cream, stock, parmesan, and salt and pepper; stir, bring to a simmer and remove from heat.

✓ Arrange chicken thighs on top, place in the air fryer, and cook for 12 minutes at 320 °F. Distribute among plates and garnish with basil.

Nutrition: 272 Calories; 9 grams fat; 12 grams fiber; 37 grams carbohydrates; 23 grams protein

491) *Chinese Chicken Wings*

Time Required for Preparation: 20 minutes Time Required for Cooking: 10 minutes 6 portions

- 16 chicken wings
- 2 tbsp honey
- 2 tbsp soy sauce
- Season with salt and freshly ground black pepper to taste
- 1/4 tsp. white pepper
- 3 tbsp. lime juice

Directions:

✓ In a bowl, whisk together honey, soy sauce, salt, black and white pepper, and lime juice. Add chicken pieces and toss to coat. Refrigerate for 2 hours.

✓ Transfer the chicken to an air fryer and cook for 6 minutes on each side at 370 °F. Increase heat to 400 °F and cook for an additional 3 minutes. Serve immediately.

Nutrition: 372 Calories; 9 grams fat; 10 grams fiber; 37 grams carbohydrates; 24 grams protein

492) *Rice, Peas, and Creamy Chicken*

Time Required for Preparation: 20 minutes Time Required for Cooking: 20 minutes 4 portions

- 1 pound skinless, boneless, and quartered chicken breasts
- 1 cup cooked white rice — 1 cup chicken stock
- 1/4 cup chopped parsley
- 2 cups frozen peas
- 12 cups grated parmesan
- 1 tbsp olive oil
- 3 minced garlic cloves
- 1 diced yellow onion

- 1/2 cup white wine
- 1/4 cup heavy cream
- Season with salt and freshly ground black pepper to taste

Directions:

✓ Season chicken breasts with salt and pepper, spray half of the oil over them, massage well, place in the basket of your air fryer, and cook for 6 minutes at 360 °F.

✓ Heat the remaining oil in a saucepan over medium-high heat and add the garlic, onion, wine, stock, salt, and pepper; stir, bring to a simmer and cook for 9 minutes.

✓ Transfer chicken breasts to a heatproof dish that fits your air fryer, stir with peas, rice, and cream mixture, sprinkle with parmesan and parsley, and set in the air fryer. Cook for 10 minutes at 420 °F. Distribute evenly across plates and serve immediately.

Nutrition: 313 Calories; 12 fat fiber carbs; 44

493) *Chicken with Green Onion Sauce*

Time Required for Preparation: 10 minutes Time Required for Cooking: 16 minutes 4 portions

- 10 green onions, roughly chopped
- 1 inch piece sliced ginger root
- 4 garlic cloves minced
- 2 tablespoons fish sauce
- 3 tablespoons soy sauce
- 1 tsp. five-spice powder
- 10 chicken drumsticks
- 1 cup coconut milk
- 1 tbsp. melted butter
- 1/4 cup chopped cilantro
- 1 tbsp. freshly squeezed lime juice
- Season with salt and freshly ground black pepper to taste

Direction

✓ In a food processor, pulse together green onions, ginger, garlic, soy sauce, fish sauce, five spices, salt, pepper, butter, and coconut milk.

✓ In a bowl, combine the chicken and green onion mixture; toss well. Transfer to a pan that fits your air fryer and cook for 16 minutes at 370 °F, shaking the fryer once. Distribute among plates, sprinkle with cilantro, pour with lime juice, and serve

alongside a side salad.
Nutrition: Calories 321; Fat 12; Fiber 12; Carbs 22; Protein 20

494) *Chicken Cacciatore*

Time Required for Preparation: 20 minutes Time Required for Cooking: 10 minutes 4 portions

- *8 bone-in chicken drumsticks*
- *1/2 cup pitted and sliced black olives*
- *1 bay leaf*
- *1 tsp garlic powder*
- *1 yellow onion; diced*
- *Season with salt and freshly ground black pepper to taste*

Directions:
- ✓ *In a heatproof dish large enough to fit your air fryer, combine chicken, salt, pepper, garlic powder, bay leaf, onion, tomatoes and juice, oregano, and olives; toss, add to the prepared air fryer, and cook for 20 minutes at 365 °F.*
- ✓ *Distribute evenly among plates and serve.*

Nutrition: Calories 300; Fat 12; Fiber 8; Carbohydrates 20; Protein 24

495) *Chicken with Herbs*

Time Required for Preparation: 20 minutes Time Required for Cooking: 50 minutes 4 portions

- *1 entire chicken*
- *1 teaspoon garlic powder*
- *1 teaspoon onion powder*
- *1/2 tsp. dried thyme*
- *1 tsp. dry rosemary*
- *1 tbsp. lemon juice*
- *2 tbsp. olive oil*

Directions:
- ✓ *Season chicken with salt and pepper, rub with thyme, rosemary, garlic powder, and onion powder, drizzle with lemon juice, and set aside for 30 minutes.*
- ✓ *Place chicken in an air fryer and cook for 20 minutes on each side at 360 °F. Allow chicken to cool somewhat before carving and serving.*

Nutrition: Calories 390; Fat 10; Fiber 5; Carbohydrates 22; Protein 20

496) *Honey and Lemon Glazed Chicken*

Time Required for Preparation: 50 minutes Time Required for Cooking: 50 minutes 4 portions

Ingredients:
- *The Filling:*
- *3 lb whole chicken*
- *2 red onions, peeled*
- *2 tbsp olive oil*
- *2 apricots*
- *1 zucchini*
- *1 apple*
- *2 garlic cloves, freshly chopped*
- *Fresh thyme, chopped*
- *5 oz honey for the marinade*
- *1 lemon's juice*
- *2 tbsp olive oil*
- *Salt and pepper*

Directions:
- ✓ *For the stuffing, finely chop all ingredients. Transfer the mixture to a large bowl and stir in the olive oil. Season with salt and freshly ground black pepper to taste. Stuff the cavity of the bird liberally with the stuffing.*
- ✓ *Cook the chicken in the Air Fryer for 35 minutes at 340 degrees F.*
- ✓ *In a large saucepan, warm the honey and lemon juice; season with salt and pepper.*
- ✓ *Reduce the Air Fryer's temperature to 320 F.*
- ✓ *Brush some of the honey-lemon marinade over the chicken and place it back in the fryer. Cook for a further 70 minutes, brushing the chicken with the marinade every 20-25 minutes.*
- ✓ *Serve garnished with parsley and accompanied by potatoes.*

Nutrition: Calories: 342; Carbohydrates: 68g; Fat: 28g; Protein: 33g

497) *Chicken with Spicy Honey Orange*

Time Required for Preparation: 10 minutes Time Required for Cooking: 10 minutes 4 portions

Ingredients:
- *½ pound washed and sliced chicken breast*
- *Parsley to taste*
- *1 cup shredded coconut*
- *3/4 cup breadcrumbs*
- *2 whole eggs, beaten*

- *1/2 cup flour*
- *1/2 tsp pepper*
- *Salt to taste*
- *1/2 cup orange marmalade*
- *1 tbsp red pepper flakes*
- *1/4 cup honey*
- *3 tbsp dijon mustard*

Direction

✓ *Preheat your Air Fryer to 400 degrees Fahrenheit. Combine coconut, flour, salt, parsley, and pepper in a mixing bowl. In a separate bowl, combine the beaten eggs. In a third bowl, combine breadcrumbs. Chicken should be dredged in egg mixture, flour, and finally breadcrumbs. Bake the chicken for 15 minutes in the Air Fryer cooking basket.*

✓ *Separately, combine honey, orange marmalade, mustard, and pepper flakes in a separate bowl. Cover chicken with marmalade mixture and continue cooking for 5 minutes longer. Enjoy!*

Nutrition: 246 Calories; 21g carbohydrates; 6g fat; 25g protein

498) *Chicken Fingers Crunchy*

Time Required for Preparation: 4 minutes Time Required for Cooking: 4 minutes 2 portions

- *2 medium-sized chicken breasts, striped*
- *3 tbsp parmesan cheese*
- *1/4 tbsp chopped fresh chives*
- *1/3 cup breadcrumbs*
- *1 egg white*
- *2 tbsp plum sauce, optional*
- *1/2 tbsp chopped fresh thyme*
- *1/2 tbsp black pepper*
- *1 tbsp water*

Directions:

✓ *Preheat the Air Fryer to 360 degrees Fahrenheit.*

✓ *Combine the chives, parmesan, thyme, pepper, and breadcrumbs in a medium mixing bowl.*

✓ *In a separate bowl, whisk the egg white and water together.*

✓ *Chicken strips should be dipped in both the egg mixture and the breadcrumb mixture.*

✓ *Cook the strips for 10 minutes in the air fryer basket. Accompany with plum sauce.*

Nutrition: 253 Calories; 31g carbohydrates; 18g fat;

28g protein

499) *Turkey Breast with Mustard and Maple*

Time Required for Preparation: 20 minutes Time Required for Cooking: 1 hour 6 portions

- *5 lb entire turkey breast*
- *1/4 cup maple syrup*
- *2 tbsp dijon mustard*
- *1/2 tbsp smoked paprika*
- *1 tbsp thyme*
- *2 tbsp olive oil*
- *1/2 tbsp sage*
- *1 tbsp melted butter*

Directions:

✓ *Preheat the oven to 350 degrees Fahrenheit and spray the turkey with olive oil. In a small bowl, combine all herbs and seasonings and rub the mixture all over the turkey. 25 minutes in the air fryer. Turn the turkey over and continue cooking for an additional 12 minutes.*

✓ *Now, flip the pan over and cook for an additional 12 minutes. In a small bowl, whisk together the butter, maple syrup, and mustard. When finished, brush the glaze over the entire turkey.*

✓ *Return to the air fryer and cook for a further 5 minutes, or until the chicken is nice and crispy.*

Nutrition: 529 Calories; 77g carbohydrates; 20g fat; 13g protein

500) *Breast of Chicken with Tarragon*

Time Required for Preparation: 20 minutes Time Required for Cooking: 15 minutes 3 portions

Ingredients:

- *1 boneless and skinless chicken breast*
- *1/2 tbsp butter*
- *1/4 tbsp kosher salt*
- *1/4 cup dried tarragon*

Direction

✓ *Preheat the Air Fryer to 380 F and line a 12x12 inch foil wrap with each chicken breast.*

✓ *Season the chicken with salt and pepper to taste and garnish with tarragon and butter.*

✓ *Wrap the foil loosely around the chicken breast to allow for air circulation.*

✓ *Cook for 15 minutes in the Air Fryer.*
✓ *Serve the chicken carefully unwrapped.*
Nutrition: Calories 493; Carbohydrates 36.5g; Fat 11g; Protein 57.5g

501) *Chicken with Cashew Nuts*

Time Required for Preparation: 20 minutes Time Required for Cooking: 30 minutes 4 portions

- *1 pound chicken cubes*
- *2 tbsp soy sauce*
- *1 tbsp cornflour 2 12 onion cubes*
- *1 carrot, diced*
- *1 chopped capsicum*
- *2 tbsp crushed garlic*
- *Salt and white pepper*

Direction

✓ *Marinate the chicken cubes in a mixture of 1/2 tbsp white pepper, 1/2 tbsp salt, 2 tbsp soy sauce, and 1 tbsp cornflour.*
✓ *Remove from heat and set aside for 25 minutes. Transfer the marinated chicken to the Air Fryer and preheat to 380 F.*
✓ *Fry for 5-6 minutes the garlic, onion, capsicum, and carrot. Before serving, roll it in cashew nuts.*

Nutrition: Calories: 425; Carbohydrates: 25g; Fat: 35g; Protein: 53g

502) *Curry of Chicken and Cabbage*

Time Required for Preparation: 20 minutes Time Required for Cooking: 30 minutes 4 portions

Ingredients:

- *1 kilogram boneless skinless chicken breast, chopped into little pieces*
- *2 cans coconut milk*
- *3 tbsp curry paste*
- *1 small onion, chopped*
- *1 medium red bell pepper*
- *1 medium green bell pepper*

Directions:

✓ *Stir the curry paste into the coconut milk until completely dissolved. Transfer to the Instant Pot.*
✓ *Combine the chicken and coconut curry paste in a large bowl.*
✓ *Cube both peppers and add them to the saucepan.*
✓ *Stir in the onion.*
✓ *Slice the cabbage and add to the saucepan.*

Assemble all components in a single layer of coconut milk.

✓ *Cover, secure, and cook on Low for 30 minutes.*
✓ *Once done, carefully open and serve immediately.*

Nutrition: 301 Calories 27.2 g fat 16 g carbohydrate 6 g protein 33 mg Cholesterol 9 g

503) *Chicken Salad*

Preparation Time: 20 minutes Time Required for Cooking: 30 minutes 6 portions

- *1 kilogram chicken breast*
- *125 mL chicken broth*
- *1 tsp salt*
- *1/2 tsp black pepper*

Directions:

✓ *In the Instant Pot, combine all of the ingredients.*
✓ *Secure the cover, close the pressure valve, and cook on High pressure for 20 minutes.*
✓ *Rapid release of pressure.*
✓ *Shred the chicken using a fork.*
✓ *Keep the meat wet by storing it in an airtight container with the liquid.*

Nutrition: Calories 356 27.2 g fat 16 g carbohydrate 3 g protein, 9 g fat, 5 mg cholesterol

504) *Lemon Chicken Casserole*

Time Required for Preparation: 20 minutes Time Required for Cooking: 30 minutes 4 portions

- *2 tbsp olive oil*
- *200 ml chicken broth*
- *1 tbsp lemon juice*
- *1 kilogram chicken thighs*
- *2-3 tbsp Dijon mustard*
- *2 tbsp Mediterranean seasoning*
- *800 g quartered red potatoes*

Direction

✓ *Add oil to Instant Pot.*
✓ *Add the chicken thighs to the Instant Pot and season with salt and pepper.*
✓ *In a separate bowl, whisk together chicken broth, lemon juice, and Dijon mustard; pour over chicken.*
✓ *Stir in quartered potatoes and season with salt and pepper.*
✓ *Cover the Instant Pot with the lid and cook on Manual for 15 minutes.*

✓ *Press the Quick Release button when the pot beeps.*

Nutrition: Calories 301 27.2 g fat 16 g carbohydrate 6 g sugar 9 g protein 33 mg cholesterol

505) *Chicken Tikka Masala*

Time Required for Preparation: 20 minutes Time Required for Cooking: 10 minutes 4 portions Ingredients:

- *2 tbsp olive oil*
- *1 small onion, chopped*
- *3 garlic cloves, minced*
- *1 (2-inch) piece fresh ginger, peeled and grated*
- *1 & 1/2 tbsp garam masala*
- *1 tsp paprika*
- *1/2 tsp turmeric powder*
- *1/2 tsp salt*
- *1/4 tsp cayenne pepper*
- *750 g boneless, skinless chicken flesh, chopped into small pieces*
- *Chopped fresh cilantro*

Directions:

✓ *Preheat the cooker to the Sauté setting. When the oil is hot, add the onion and sauté for about 3 minutes, or until softened. Cook until the garlic and ginger are tender.*

✓ *Combine half of the chicken broth with flour. Cook for a few minutes, stirring constantly. Stir in the garam masala, paprika, turmeric, salt, and cayenne pepper.*

✓ *Stir in the chicken, leftover chicken broth, and tomatoes.*

✓ *Secure the lid by closing and locking it. Cook at high pressure for 10 minutes. Once cooked, quickly release the pressure.*

✓ *Combine the coconut milk and sauce in a separate bowl.*

✓ *Suggestions for serving: Serve with cauliflower "rice" or cooked potatoes as a bed.*

Nutrition: 245 Calories 25 g fat Carbohydrates 16 g Sucrose Protein: 4 g Cholesterol 35 mg 5 g

506) *Juicy Whole Chicken*

Time Required to Prepare a: 10 minutes Time Required for Cooking: 30 minutes 6 portions Ingredients:

- *2 tbsp olive oil*
- *300 mL chicken broth*
- *3 red potatoes*
- *Your choice of spices, e.g., thyme, oregano, salt, garlic salt*

Direction

✓ *Set your Instant Pot to Saute, Low.*

✓ *When the olive oil is hot, add the chicken to the pot and cook, occasionally stirring, for about 2 minutes. Rep with the opposite side. By pressing Cancel, you can turn off the computer.*

✓ *Empty the Instant Pot of the browned meat and add the chicken stock, potatoes, and chicken (whole or in pieces). The chicken should be arranged atop the potatoes.*

✓ *Close lid, secure steam valve, and set the timer to 25 minutes on Poultry, regular setting. Once cooked, perform a fast release.*

Nutrition: 301 Calories Carbohydrates 27.2 g 16 g Sucrose Protein: 6 g 33 mg Cholesterol 9 g

507) *Chicken Breasts with a Spicy Lime Sauce*

Time Required for Preparation: 20 minutes Time Required for Cooking: 20 minutes 5 portions

- *2 tbsp lime zest*
- *2 tbsp honey*
- *1 tbsp lime juice*
- *3 tbsp minced garlic*
- *Salt and pepper to taste*
- *1/2 tbsp chili powder*
- *1/2 tbsp paprika*
- *1 tbsp crushed allspice*

Direction

✓ *Combine the lime zest, honey, lime juice, garlic, pepper, sea salt, chili powder, paprika, and allspice in a bowl. Coat chicken breasts with marinade.*

✓ *Pour broth into the Instant Pot, followed by the chicken.*

✓ *Secure the cover in place and seal the steam nozzle.*

✓ *Cook for 15 minutes on high pressure.*

✓ *Allow pressure to naturally release for 5 minutes before releasing any remaining pressure.*

✓ *Carefully open the Pot and serve.*

Nutrition: 325 Calories fat 27.2 g carbohydrate 16 g Sucrose Protein: 7 g Cholesterol 5 g 36 milligram

508) *Whole Roasted Chicken*

Time Required for Preparation: 20 minutes Time Required for Cooking: 10 minutes 6 portions

- 1 whole chicken (about 2 kg)
- 1 tablespoon chopped fresh rosemary
- 1 1/2-2 tablespoons olive oil, plus a bit more for pouring on a pan
- 4-6 garlic cloves
- Season with salt and pepper to taste
- Zest 1 lemon
- 1 cup chicken broth

Directions:

- ✓ Rinse and pat dry the chicken with cool water. Set aside in a baking pan.
- ✓ Set Instant Pot to Saute mode and preheat.
- ✓ Combine rosemary, olive oil, garlic, paprika, salt, pepper, and lemon zest in a small bowl. Lemons should be sliced in half and stuffed into the cavity of the chicken after the zest is removed. Spread the spice mixture evenly over the chicken. Drizzle a little olive oil into a heated pan and add the chicken breast-side down. 3-4 minutes, or until golden brown. Bake the chicken on the opposite side.
- ✓ Transfer chicken from pan to the baking dish where it was previously placed. Pour broth into the pan. Arrange onion in the bottom of the pan, followed by the chicken (breast-side up) and securing the lid.
- ✓ Cook for 6 minutes per pound on high pressure. Wait 10 minutes after it is cooked before releasing steam. Remove chicken and allow a minimum of 5 minutes before slicing.

Nutrition: Calories 301 27.2 g fat 16 g carbohydrate 6 g sugar 9 g protein 33 mg cholesterol

509) *Chicken Breast in the Italian Style*

Time Required for Preparation: 20 minutes Time Required for Cooking: 15 minutes 3 portions

Ingredients:

- 1 tbsp olive oil
- 3 boneless, skinless chicken breasts
- 1/4 tsp garlic powder and ordinary salt per breast
- dash black pepper
- 1/8 tsp dried oregano
- 1/8 tsp dried basil

Directions:

- ✓ Preheat the Instant Pot to Saute and add the oil.
- ✓ Season one side of the chicken breasts and carefully place the chicken breasts, seasoned side down, to the pot once the oil is hot.
- ✓ Season the second side in the meantime.
- ✓ Cook for approximately 3 to 4 minutes on each side and remove with tongs.
- ✓ Fill the saucepan halfway with 250 mL water, plus the trivet.
- ✓ Arrange the chicken breasts on the trivet.
- ✓ Secure the cover and cook for 5 minutes on manual high.
- ✓ Allow the chicken to release naturally for a few minutes before quickly releasing the remainder.
- ✓ Carefully remove from the heat and allow at least 5 minutes before slicing.

Nutrition: 202 Calories, 29 g fat, 16 g carbohydrate, 6 g sugar, 9 g protein, 33 mg cholesterol

510) *Rosemary Lemon Chicken*

20 minutes to prepare Time Required for Cooking: 14 minutes 4 portions

Ingredients:

- 1 kilogram halved chicken breasts
- 1 lemon, peeled and sliced into rounds
- 1/2 orange, peeled and sliced into rounds, or to taste
- 3 cloves roasted garlic, or to taste
- salt and freshly ground black pepper to taste (optional)
- 1/4 cup water
- 2 stemmed sprigs of fresh rosemary, or to taste

Direction

- ✓ Place the chicken in the Instant Pot. Season with salt and pepper. Add lemon, orange, and garlic. Drizzle the top with olive oil and agave syrup (if using). Combine the water and rosemary. Secure the lid of the cooker.
- ✓ Cook for 14 minutes on High pressure using the "Meat" and "Stew" settings. Allow approximately 20 minutes for pressure to dissipate naturally.

Nutrition: 325 Calories 5 g fat 20 g Sucrose Protein: 2 g Cholesterol 10 g 33 milligram

511) *Spicy Drumsticks de Cocunut*

Time Required for Preparation: 20 minutes Time Required for Cooking: 10 minutes 6 portions

- *1/2 cup ketchup*
- *1/4 cup dark brown sugar*
- *1/4 cup red wine vinegar*
- *3 tbsp soy sauce*
- *1 tbsp chicken spice*
- *Salt to taste*

Direction

- ✓ *In the Instant Pot, combine ketchup, brown sugar, red wine vinegar, soy sauce, spice, and salt. Stir in chicken pieces to coat.*
- ✓ *Secure the lid of the Instant Pot and ensure that the steam release handle is in the 'Sealing' position.*
- ✓ *Cook for 12 minutes on 'Manual' (or 'Pressure Cook').*
- ✓ *Perform a rapid pressure release and carefully remove the lid from the Instant Pot.*
- ✓ *Set aside chicken parts.*
- ✓ *Select 'Saute' and simmer until the sauce is slightly thickened, approximately 5 to 7 minutes.*

Nutrition: Calories 145 Fat 28 Carbohydrates 16 Carbohydrates 16 Carbohydrates 16 Carbohydrates 16 Carbohydrates 2 Carbohydrates Cholesterol 45 mg 9 g

512) *Ginger-Flavored Chicken*

Time Required for Preparation: 20 minutes Time Required for Cooking: 15 minutes

Ingredients: 6 Servings

- *1 kilogram boneless, skinless chicken breasts (frozen OR thawed)*
- *6 tbsp soy sauce*
- *3 tbsp rice vinegar*
- *1/2 tbsp honey*
- *2 tbsp. freshly sliced ginger*
- *6 minced garlic cloves*
- *3 tsp cornstarch*

Directions:

- ✓ *In an Instant Pot, place chicken breasts.*
- ✓ *Whisk together the vinegar, soy sauce, honey, water, ginger, and garlic in a small mixing basin. Distribute mixture evenly over chicken.*
- ✓ *Place the Instant Pot's lid on and cook on High pressure for 15 minutes. When the*

meat is done, let steam escape.

- ✓ *Transfer chicken breasts to a cutting board. Bring remaining sauce to a simmer in the pan (use the Saute feature on an electric cooker). Combine cornstarch and 3 tablespoons cold water in a small bowl and then pour into prepared pan. Simmer until sauce has thickened, then remove from heat.*
- ✓ *Return chicken to pot with sauce after shredding.*

Nutrition: 313 Calories, 26 g fat, 16 g carbohydrate, and 7 g protein Cholesterol: 8 g 36 mg

513) *Buffalo Chicken*

Time Required for Preparation: 20 minutes Time Required for Cooking: 30 minutes 8 portions Ingredients:

- *2 celery stalks, diced*
- *1 medium-sized onion, chopped*
- *100 mL chicken broth*
- *21 kilogram frozen chicken breasts*

Direction

- ✓ *In the Instant Pot, combine the celery, onions, wing sauce, chicken stock, and chicken. Cook frozen chicken for 20 minutes under high pressure. To completely relieve the pressure, set the pressure valve to "Vent."*
- ✓ *Remove the shredded chicken breasts from the pot.*
- ✓ *You may or may not drain the majority of the liquid from the pot.*

Nutrition: Calories: 197 8g fat 16g Carbohydrates 14g protein

514) *Breaded Chicken with Sunflower Seed Chips*

Time required for preparation: ten minutes Time required for cooking: 40 minutes 4 portions

- *12 chicken breast fillets*
- *Salt*
- *2 eggs*
- *Breadcrumbs*
- *Olive oil extra virgin*

Directions:

- ✓ *Season chicken fillets with salt.*
- ✓ *Finely crush the seed chips and combine them with the breadcrumbs.*
- ✓ *Whisk together the two eggs.*

✓ Dredge the chicken breast fillets in beaten egg and then in the seed chips tied with breadcrumbs.

✓ Once all of them are breaded, paint them with extra virgin olive oil using a brush.

✓ Arrange the fillets in a single layer in the air fryer basket.

✓ Preheat the oven to 170 degrees for 20 minutes.

✓ Remove one batch and replace it with another, maintaining the same temperature and duration. Thus, until all the steaks are consumed.

Nutrition: Calories: 242 13g fat 15g Carbohydrates 18g protein 0g sugar 42mg cholesterol

515) *Turkey Chops in Salted Biscuit Pie*

Time required for preparation: 5 minutes Time required for cooking: 20 minutes 4 portions

- 8 large turkey chops
- 300 g crackers
- 2 eggs
- Extra virgin olive oil
- Sea salt
- PEPPER, GROUND

Direction

✓ Arrange the turkey chops on the worktable and season with salt and pepper.

✓ In a separate bowl, beat the eggs.

✓ Using a few turbo strokes in the Thermomix or a blender, crush the cookies until they are gritted.

✓ In a bowl, combine the cookies.

✓ Dip the chops into the beaten egg and then into the broken cookies. Firmly press the empanada to ensure its perfection.

✓ Using a silicone brush and extra virgin olive oil, paint the empanada.

✓ Place the chops in the air fryer's basket; not all will fit. They will be completed in stages.

✓ Preheat the oven to 200 degrees for 15 minutes.

✓ Once all of the chops are prepared, serve.

Nutrition: 126 Nutrition: Calories 6 g fat 0g Carbohydrates 18g protein 0g sugar

516) *Lemon Chicken with Basil.*

Time required for preparation: ten minutes Time required for cooking: 1 hour 4 portions

- 1 kilogram chopped chicken

- 1 or 2 lemons
- Basil, salt, and freshly ground pepper

Direction

✓ Place the chicken in a bowl and drizzle with extra virgin olive oil.

✓ Combine salt, pepper, and basil in a small bowl.

✓ Thoroughly combine and set aside for at least 30 minutes, stirring occasionally.

✓ Place the chicken pieces in the air fryer basket and turn on the air fryer.

✓ Choose 30 minutes.

✓ Remove from time to time.

✓ Remove one batch and replace it with another.

✓ Repeat the operation.

Nutrition: 126 Nutrition: Calories 6 g fat 0g Carbohydrates 18g protein 0g sugar

517) *Tamari and Mustard Fried Chicken*

15 minutes for preparation Cooking time: 1 hour and twenty minutes 4 portions

- 1 kilogram very finely chopped chicken
- Tamari Sauce
- Original mustard
- Ground pepper
- 1 lemon
- Flour
- Extra virgin olive oil

Directions:

✓ Place the chicken in a bowl; you can serve it with or without the skin, depending on your preference.

✓ Whisk in a liberal stream of tamari, one or two tablespoons mustard, a pinch of freshly ground pepper, and a splash of lemon juice.

✓ Combine everything thoroughly and set aside for an hour to macerate.

✓ Lightly flour the chicken pieces and drop them in the air fryer basket.

✓ Preheat the oven to 200 degrees for 20 minutes. Remove the chicken from the basket at halftime.

✓ Avoid crushing the chicken; it is recommended to create two or three batches of chicken to allow the pieces to build up and not be fried thoroughly.

Nutrition: 100 Calories 6 g fat 0g Carbohydrates 18g protein 0g sugar

518) *Crispy Chicken Fillets*

Time required for preparation: ten minutes Time required for cooking: 25 minutes 4 portions

- 3 small chicken breasts or 2 large chicken breasts
- Salt Ground pepper
- 3 garlic cloves
- 1 lemon

Direction:

- ✓ Prepare the breasts by cutting them into fillets.
- ✓ Combine in a bowl with lemon juice, garlic cloves, and pepper.
- ✓ Flirt vigorously and then step away for ten minutes.
- ✓ On a separate plate, beat the eggs and spread the breadcrumbs.
- ✓ Gently dredge the chicken breast fillets in the beaten egg and breadcrumbs.
- ✓ Once all of them are breaded, begin frying.
- ✓ Using a silicone brush and extra virgin olive oil, paint the breaded breasts.
- ✓ Place a batch of fillets in the air fryer basket and set the timer to 10 minutes 180 degrees.
- ✓ Rotate 180 degrees and leave another 5 minutes.

Nutrition: Calories: 120 6g fat 0g carbohydrate 18g protein 0g sugar

519) *Chicken Wings with a Dry Rub*

Time required for preparation: 5 minutes 30 minutes for cooking 4 portions

- 9 g garlic powder
- 1 cube reduced-sodium chicken broth
- 5g salt
- 3g black pepper
- 1g smoked paprika
- 1 g cayenne pepper
- 3 g sodium-free Old Bay seasoning
- 3 g onion powder
- 1 g dried oregano
- 453 g chicken wings
- To serve, ranch sauce

Direction

- ✓ Preheat the air fryer. Preheat the oven to 180 °C.
- ✓ In a mixing basin, combine all ingredients.
- ✓ Season half of the chicken wings with the spice combination and liberally coat with oil spray.
- ✓ Preheat the air fryer and add the chicken wings.
- ✓ Make a selection of Chicken and set the timer for 30 minutes.
- ✓ Halfway through cooking, shake the baskets.

Calorie: 120 Fat content: 6g Carbohydrates: 0g 18g protein 0g sugar

520) *Chicken Soup*

Preparation Time: 20 minutes Time Required for Cooking: 30 minutes 6 Servings

Ingredients:

- 4 pound chicken, cut into pieces
- 5 carrots, sliced thickly
- 8 cups water
- 2 celery stalks, sliced 1 inch thick

Direction

- ✓ In a large saucepan, combine chicken, water, and salt. Bring to a rolling boil.
- ✓ In the same saucepan, add the celery and onion and stir well.
- ✓ Reduce to medium-low heat and continue simmering for 30 minutes.
- ✓ Stir in carrots and cover with a lid; cook for 40 minutes.
- ✓ Remove chicken from pot, discarding bones and slicing into bite-size pieces.
- ✓ Return chicken to the pot and give it a good stir.
- ✓ Assemble and serve.

Nutrition: Calories: 89 6.33g fat 0g Carbohydrates 7.56g protein 0g sugar 0mg cholesterol

521) *Ginger Chili Broccoli*

Time Required for Preparation: 10 minutes Time Required for Cooking: 15 minutes 5 portions

- 8 cups broccoli florets
- 1/2 cup olive oil
- 2 fresh lime juice
- 2 tbsp grated ginger
- 2 tsp minced chili pepper

Direction

- ✓ Steam broccoli florets for 8 minutes in a steamer.
- ✓ Meanwhile, in a small bowl, whisk together lime juice, oil, ginger, and chile pepper to make the dressing.

✓ *In a large bowl, combine steamed broccoli and dressing. Toss carefully.*

Nutrition: Calories: 239 Fat: 20.8 Carbohydrates: 17 g Sucrose Protein 3 g 5 g 0 mg cholesterol

522) *Garlic Parmesan Chicken Wings*

Time required for preparation: 5 minutes.

- *25 g cornstarch*
- *20 g grated Parmesan cheese*
- *Season with salt and pepper to taste*
- *680g chicken wings*

Direction

✓ *Press Start / Pause and select Preheat. Set the temperature to 200 °C.*

✓ *In a bowl, whisk together corn starch, Parmesan, garlic powder, salt, and pepper.*

✓ *Combine the spice with the chicken wings and dip until completely coated.*

✓ *Coat the baskets and air fryer with oil spray and add the wings, making sure to sprinkle the tops of the wings as well.*

✓ *Click Start/Pause and then select Chicken. Shake the baskets frequently throughout the cooking process.*

✓ *Garnish with the remaining Parmesan mixture and serve.*

Nutrition: 204 Calories 15g fat 1 gram carbohydrate 12g protein 0g sugar 63mg cholesterol

523) *Chicken Wings in the Jerk Style*

Time required for preparation: 5 minutes.

- *2-3 portions*
- *1 g crushed thyme*
- *1 g dried rosemary*
- *2 g allspice*
- *4 g ground ginger*
- *3 g garlic powder*
- *2 g onion powder*
- *1 g cinnamon*
- *2 g paprika*
- *2 g chili powder*
- *1 g nutmeg*
- *Salt to taste*

Direction

✓ *Press Start/Pause after selecting Preheat and setting the temperature to 200°C.*

✓ *In a bowl, combine all of the spices and oil to make a marinade.*

✓ *In a large mixing bowl, combine the chicken wings and marinade until completely coated.*

✓ *Preheat the air fryer and add the chicken wings.*

✓ *Click Start/Pause and then select Chicken. Shake the baskets frequently throughout the cooking process.*

✓ *Transfer the wings to a serving platter.*

✓ *Serve the wings with fresh lemon juice squeezed over them.*

Nutrition: 240 Calories 15g fat 5g Carbohydrates 19g protein 4 g sugars 60mg cholesterol

524) *Delicious Chicken Tenders*

Time required for preparation: 5 minutes. 4 portions

- *1 tbsp. extra virgin olive oil*
- *1 tsp. rotisserie chicken seasoning*
- *2 tbsp. BBQ sauce*

Directions:

✓ *In a zip-lock bag, combine all ingredients except the oil.*

✓ *Refrigerate bag for 2-3 hours.*

✓ *In a large skillet over medium heat, heat oil.*

✓ *In a skillet, sauté marinated chicken tenders until gently browned and done.*

Nutrition: 365 Calories 16.1 g fat, 8 g carbohydrate, 2 g sugar, 49.2 g protein, 151 mg cholesterol

525) *Yogurt Chicken Skewers*

Time required for preparation: 4 hours and 10 minutes.

- *2-4 portions*
- *123g plain whole-milk Greek yogurt*
- *20 ml olive oil*
- *2 g paprika*
- *1 g cumin*
- *1 g crushed red pepper*
- *1 lemon, juice, and peel*
- *5 g salt*
- *1 g freshly ground black pepper*
- *4 minced garlic cloves*

Direction:

✓ *In a large mixing bowl, combine the yogurt, olive oil, paprika, cumin, red paprika, lemon juice, lemon zest, salt, pepper, and garlic.*

✓ *Combine the chicken and marinate in the refrigerator for at least 4 hours.*

✓ *Press Start/Pause and then select Preheat.*

✓ *Skewer the marinated chicken thighs in 38 mm pieces.*

✓ *Preheat the air fryer and insert the skewers.*

✓ *Cook for 10 minutes at 200°C.*

Nutrition: 113 Calories 4 g fat 0g Carbs 20.6g protein

526) *Lime-Fried Chicken*

Time required for preparation: 5 minutes.

- *6 portions*
- *6 chicken thighs*
- *2 tbsp. olive oil*
- *2 tbsp. lemon juice*
- *1 teaspoon Celtic sea salt*
- *1 teaspoon freshly ground pepper*
- *1 lemon, thinly sliced*

Direction

✓ *In a bowl or bag, combine all ingredients except the sliced lemon; whisk to coat chicken.*

✓ *Allow 30 minutes to marinate overnight.*

✓ *Remove the chicken from the pan and let the leftover oil drain (it does not need to dry out, just do not drip with tons of excess oil).*

✓ *Arrange the chicken thighs and lemon slices in a single layer in the fryer basket, taking care not to crowd the chicken thighs together.*

✓ *Preheat the fryer to 200°F and cook for ten minutes.*

✓ *Carefully remove the basket from the pan and flip the chicken thighs over.*

✓ *Cook for an additional 10 minutes at 200 degrees.*

Nutrition: 215 Calories 13g fat 1 gram carbs 2 g protein 1 g sugar 130mg cholesterol

527) *Chicken Fingers Crunchy*

2 portions Time Required for Cooking: 4 Minutes
Ingredients:

- *2 chicken breasts, medium-sized, striped*
- *3 tbsp parmesan*
- *1/4 tbsp chopped fresh chives*

- *1/3 cup breadcrumbs 1 beaten egg white*
- *2 tbsp plum sauce, if desired*
- *1/2 tbsp chopped fresh thyme*
- *1/2 tbsp freshly ground black pepper*
- *1 tablespoon water*

Directions:

✓ *Preheat the Air Fryer to 360 degrees Fahrenheit. Combine the chives, parmesan, thyme, pepper, and breadcrumbs in a medium mixing bowl.*

✓ *In a separate bowl, whisk the egg white and water together.*

✓ *Chicken strips should be dipped in both the egg mixture and the breadcrumb mixture.*

✓ *Cook the strips for 10 minutes in the air fryer basket. Accompany with plum sauce.*

Nutrition: 253 Calories; 31g carbs; 18g fat; 28g protein

528) *Chicken from Polynesia*

6 Cups Time Required for Cooking: 4 Hours
Ingredients:

- *3 minced garlic cloves*
- *2 bell peppers, quartered*
- *1 can (20 oz.) pineapple chunks in juice, drained but with juice retained*
- *1 1/2 pounds boneless chicken breasts, cubed*
- *1/3 cup molasses*
- *2 tbsp tapioca starch*
- *3 tbsp reduced-sodium soy sauce*
- *1 teaspoon ginger powder*

Directions:

✓ *In a bowl, whisk together the saved pineapple juice, 3 tablespoons soy sauce, 1/3 cup honey, 1 teaspoon ground ginger, and 3 minced garlic cloves.*

✓ *Then mix in 2 tablespoons tapioca flour until blended.*

✓ *In a slow cooker, combine chicken and pineapple chunks.*

✓ *Cover the cooker and pour the pineapple juice mixture over the chicken.*

✓ *Cook on low heat for approximately 4-5 hours, or until chicken is completely cooked through.*

✓ *Then, during the final hour of simmering, add bell pepper strips. Serve and take pleasure in!*

Nutrition:273 Cal; 26g fat; 37g carbs; 26g protein

529) **Buffalo Chicken**

8 portions 30 Minutes Cooking
Ingredients:

- *2 celery stalks, peeled and chopped*
- *1 medium onion, peeled and sliced*
- *100 ml. BUFFALO WING SAUCE*
- *100 ml. chicken broth*
- *Chicken breasts, 2.100 kg, frozen*

Direction

✓ *In the Instant Pot, combine the celery, onions, wing sauce, chicken broth, and chicken. Cook frozen chicken for 20 minutes under high pressure. To completely relieve the pressure, set the pressure valve to "Vent."*

✓ *Shred the chicken breasts after removing them from the pot.*

✓ *You can either drain the majority of the liquid from the saucepan or leave it in.*

Nutrition: 197 Calories 8g fat 16g Carbs 14g protein

530) **Stir-fry of Chicken and Peanuts**

4 portions 15 Minutes Cooking
Ingredients:

- *3 tsp lime juice*
- *1/2 teaspoon lime zest 4 garlic cloves, minced*
- *2 tsp sauce chili bean*
- *1 tsp fish sauce*
- *1 tbsp water*
- *2 tbsp almond butter*
- *3 tsp. olive oil, divided*

Direction

✓ *1 pound chicken breast, cut 1 red sweet pepper, sliced 3 finely sliced green onions 2 cups shredded broccoli*

✓ *2 tbsp. chopped peanuts Combine the lime juice, lime zest, garlic, chili bean sauce, fish sauce, water, and peanut butter in a mixing bowl. Combine thoroughly.*

✓ *2 teaspoons of oil in a skillet over medium-high heat.*

✓ *Cook the chicken until both sides are brown. Pour in the remainder of the oil.*

✓ *Pepper and green onions should be added at this point. Combine the chicken, broccoli, and sauce in a medium bowl.*

✓ *2 minutes Before serving, sprinkle with peanuts.*

Nutrition: 368 Calories 11 g Total Fat 2 g Saturated Fat 66 mg Sodium 556 mg Carbohydrates 34 g Dietary Fiber 3 g Sugars in Total Protein: 4 g Potassium 482 mg 32 g

531) **Curry with Meatballs**

Time Required for Cooking: 25 Minutes Servings: 6
Ingredients:

- *To Make Meatballs:*
- *1 pound lean ground chicken*
- *1 tsp freshly grated ginger*
- *1 tsp paste de garlic*
- *1 finely chopped green chili*
- *1 tablespoon chopped fresh cilantro leaves*
- *1 teaspoon coriander, ground*
- *1/2 tsp cumin seeds*
- *1/2 teaspoon chili powder, red*
- *1/2 teaspoon turmeric powder*
- *1/8 teaspoon sodium chloride*
- *Curry:*
- *3 tbsp olive oil*
- *1/2 tsp cumin seeds*
- *1 cinnamon stick (1 inch)*
- *2 chopped onions*
- *1 teaspoon minced fresh ginger*
- *1 teaspoon minced garlic*
- *4 tomatoes, finely chopped*
- *2 tsp. coriander, ground*
- *1 tsp garam masala*
- *1/2 teaspoon freshly ground nutmeg*
- *1/2 teaspoon chili powder, red*
- *1/2 teaspoon turmeric powder*
- *As necessary, salt*
- *1 cup distilled or filtered water*
- *3 tbsp. chopped fresh cilantro*

Directions:

✓ *To make meatballs, combine all ingredients in a large mixing basin until well blended.*

✓ *Make little meatballs of equal size from the ingredients.*

✓ *Over medium heat, heat the oil in a big deep skillet and fry the meatballs for about 3-5 minutes, or until browned on both sides.*

✓ *In a bowl, place the meatballs.*

✓ *Sauté the cumin seeds and cinnamon stick*

in the same skillet for approximately 1 minute.

✓ Sauté the onions for approximately 4-5 minutes.

✓ Sauté the ginger and garlic paste for approximately 1 minute.

✓ Cook, mashing the tomato and spices with the back of a spoon, for approximately 2-3 minutes.

✓ Bring the water and meatballs to a boil.

✓ Reduce to low heat and simmer for approximately 10 minutes.

✓ Serve immediately with a garnish of cilantro.

✓ Transfer the curry to a large mixing bowl and set aside to cool. Distribute the curry evenly among five containers. Refrigerate the containers for 1-2 days. Before serving, reheat in the microwave.

Nutrition: 196 Calories 14 g Total Fat 4 g Saturated Fat 53 mg Cholesterol Carbohydrates in total: 7.9 g Sugar 9 g Fiber 1 g Sodium 143 mg Potassium 279 mg Protein 16.7 g

532) *Jerk Style Chicken Wings*

2-3 Servings 25 Minutes to Cook
Ingredients:

- 1 g dried thyme
- 1 g rosemary, dried
- 2 grams allspice
- 4 g ginger powder
- 3 g minced garlic
- 2g powdered onion
- 1 teaspoon cinnamon
- paprika, 2 g
- 2g cayenne pepper
- 1 gram nutmeg
- Season with salt to taste
- 30 milliliters vegetable oil Chicken wings, between 0.5 and 1 kg 1 lime, freshly squeezed

Directions:

✓ Select Preheat, set the temperature to 200°C, and press Start/Pause.

✓ Combine all spices and oil in a bowl to create a marinade.

✓ Mix the chicken wings in the marinade until they are well covered.

✓ Place the chicken wings in the preheated air fryer.

✓ Select Chicken and press Start/Pause. Be sure to shake the baskets in the middle of cooking.

✓ Remove the wings and place them on a serving plate.

✓ Squeeze fresh lemon juice over the wings and serve.

Nutrition: Calories: 240 Fat: 15g Carbohydrate: 5g Protein: 19g Sugars: 4g Cholesterol: 60mg

533) *Coconut Chicken*

Servings: 6 Time Required for Cooking: 4 Hours
Ingredients:

- 2 garlic cloves, minced
- Fresh cilantro, minced
- 1/2 cup light coconut milk
- 6 tablespoons sweetened coconut, shredded and toasted
- 2 tablespoons brown sugar
- 6 (about 1-1/2 pounds) boneless skinless chicken thighs
- 2 tablespoons reduced-sodium soy sauce
- 1/8 teaspoon ground cloves

Directions:

✓ Mix brown sugar, 1/2 cup light coconut milk, 2 tablespoons soy sauce, 1/8 teaspoon ground cloves, and 2 minced cloves of garlic in a bowl.

✓ Add 6 boneless chicken thighs into a Crockpot.

✓ Now pour the mixture of coconut milk over chicken thighs. Cover the cooker and cook for about 4-5 hours on low.

✓ Serve coconut chicken with cilantro and coconut; enjoy!

Nutrition: 201 Calories; 10 g fat; 6 g total carbs; 21 g protein

534) *Spicy Lime Chicken*

Servings: 6 Cooking Time: 3 Hours
Ingredients:

- 3 tsp lime juice
- Fresh cilantro leaves
- 1-1/2 pounds (about 4) (about 4) boneless skinless chicken breast halves
- 1 teaspoon lime zest, grated
- 2 cups chicken broth

- *1 tablespoon chili powder*

Directions:

✓ *Add chicken breast halves into a slow cooker.*

✓ *Add 1 tablespoon chili powder, 3 tablespoons lime juice, and 2 cups chicken broth in a small bowl; mix well and pour over chicken.*

✓ *Cover the cooker and cook for about 3 hours on low.*

✓ *Once cooled, shred chicken by using forks and transfer back to the Crockpot.*

✓ *Stir in 1 teaspoon grated lime zest. Serve spicy lime chicken with cilantro, and enjoy!*

Nutrition: 132 Calories; 3 g fat; 2 g total carbs; 23 g protein

535) *Crock-pot Slow Cooker Ranch Chicken*

4 portions Time Required for Cooking: 4 Hours
Ingredients:

- *1 cup chive and onion cream cheese spread*
- *½ teaspoon freshly ground black pepper*
- *4 boneless chicken breasts*
- *1 1-oz package ranch dressing and seasoning mix*
- *½ cup low sodium chicken stock*

Directions:

✓ *Spray the Crock-Pot slow cooker with cooking spray and preheat it.*

✓ *Dry chicken with a paper towel and transfer it to the Crock-Pot slow cooker.*

✓ *Cook each side until chicken is browned, for about 4-5 minutes.*

✓ *Add ½ cup low sodium chicken stock, 1 1-oz. package ranch dressing and seasoning mix, 1 cup chive and onion cream cheese spread, and ½ teaspoon freshly ground black pepper. Cover the Crock-Pot slow cooker and cook for about 4 hours on Low or until the internal temperature reaches 165 F. Once cooked, take it out from the Crock-Pot slow cooker.*

✓ *Whisk the sauce present in the Crock-Pot slow cooker until smooth. If you need thick sauce, then cook for about 5-10 minutes, with frequent stirring.*

✓ *Garnish chicken with sliced onions and bacon and serve.*

Nutrition: 362 Calories; 18.5 g fat; 9.7 g total carbs; 37.3 g protein

536) *Mustard Chicken With Basil*

4 portions 30 Minutes Cooking
Ingredients:

- *1 tsp Chicken stock*
- *2 Chicken breasts; skinless and boneless chicken breasts: halved 1 tbsp Chopped basil*
- *What you'll need from the store cupboard: Salt and black pepper*
- *1 tbsp Olive oil*
- *½ tsp Garlic powder*
- *½ tsp Onion powder*
- *1 tsp Dijon mustard*

Directions:

✓ *Press 'Sauté' on the instant pot and add the oil. When it is hot, brown the chicken in it for 2-3 minutes.*

✓ *Mix in the remaining ingredients and seal the lid to cook for 12 minutes at high pressure.*

✓ *Natural release the pressure for 10 minutes, share into plates, and serve.*

Nutrition: Calories 34, fat 6, carbs 0.7, protein 0.3, fiber 0.1

537) *Chicken Chili*

Servings: 6 Cooking Time: 40 Minutes
Ingredients:

- *4 cups low-sodium chicken broth, divided*
- *3 cups boiled black beans, divided*
- *1 tablespoon extra-virgin olive oil*
- *1 large onion, chopped*
- *1 jalapeño pepper, seeded and chopped*
- *4 garlic cloves, minced*
- *1 teaspoon dried thyme, crushed*
- *1½ tablespoons ground coriander*
- *1 tablespoon ground cumin*
- *½ tablespoon red chili powder*
- *4 cups cooked chicken, shredded*
- *1 tablespoon fresh lime juice*
- *¼ cup fresh cilantro, chopped*

Directions:

✓ *Add 1 cup of broth and 1 can of black beans and blend until smooth using a food processor.*

✓ *Transfer the beans puree into a bowl and set aside.*

✓ *In a large pan, heat the oil over medium heat and sauté the onion and jalapeño for about 4-5 minutes.*

✓ *Add the garlic, spices, and sea salt and sauté for about 1 minute.*

✓ *Add the beans puree and remaining broth and bring to a boil.*

✓ *Lower the heat and simmer for about 20 minutes.*

✓ *Stir in the remaining can of beans, chicken, and lime juice and bring to a boil.*

✓ *Lower the heat and simmer for about 5-10 minutes.*

✓ *Serve immediately with a garnish of cilantro.*

✓ *Meal Prep Tip: Transfer the chili into a large bowl and set aside to cool. Divide the chili into 6 containers evenly. Refrigerate the containers for 1-2 days. Before serving, reheat in the microwave.*

Nutrition: Calories 356 Total Fat 7.1 g Saturated Fat 2 g Cholesterol 72 mg Total Carbs 33 g Sugar 7 g Fiber 16 g Potassium 662 mg Protein 39.6 g

538) *Chicken With Cashew Nuts*

4 portions 30 Minutes Cooking
Ingredients:

- *1 lb chicken cubes*
- *2 tbsp soy sauce*
- *1 tbsp cornflour*
- *2 ½ onion cubes*
- *1 carrot, chopped*
- *⅓ cup cashew nuts, fried 1 capsicum, cut*
- *2 tbsp garlic, crushed Salt, and white pepper*

Directions:

✓ *Marinate the chicken cubes with ½ tbsp of white pepper, ½ tsp salt, 2 tbsp soya sauce, and add 1 tbsp cornflour.*

✓ *Set aside for 25 minutes. Preheat the Air Fryer to 380 F and transfer the marinated chicken. Add the garlic, the onion, the capsicum, and the carrot; fry for 5-6 minutes. Roll it in the cashew nuts before serving.*

Nutrition: Calories: 425; Carbs: 25g; Fat: 35g; Protein: 53g

539) *Chuck And Veggies*

2 portions Cooking Time: 9 Hours
Ingredients:

- *¼ cup dry red wine*
- *¼ teaspoon salt*
- *8 oz. boneless lean chuck roast*
- *¼ teaspoon black pepper*
- *8 oz. frozen pepper stir-fry*
- *1 teaspoon Worcestershire sauce*
- *8 oz. whole mushrooms*
- *1 teaspoon instant coffee granules*
- *1 1/4 cups fresh green beans, trimmed*
- *1 dried bay leaf*

Directions:

✓ *Mix all the ingredients except salt in a bowl; combine well and then transfer to a slow cooker.*

✓ *Cover the cooker and cook for about 9 hours on low and 4 1/2 hours on high, until beef is completely cooked through and tender.*

✓ *Stir in ¼ teaspoon salt gently. Take out the vegetables and beef and transfer them to 2 shallow bowls.*

✓ *Pour liquid into the skillet; boil it lightly and cook until liquid reduces to ¼ cup, for about 1 1/2 minutes.*

✓ *Pour over veggies and beef. Discard bay leaf and serve.*

Nutrition: 215 Calories; 5 g fat; 17 g total carbs; 26 g protein

540) *Baked Chicken & Broccoli*

Servings: 6 Time Required for Cooking: 45 Minutes
Ingredients:

- *6 boneless, skinless chicken breasts (6 oz. 3 broccoli heads, florets removed*
- *4 minced garlic cloves 14 cups olive oil*
- *1 teaspoon crushed dried oregano*
- *1 tsp dried rosemary, crushed sea salt, and freshly ground black pepper, to taste*

Directions:

✓ *Preheat the oven to 375 degrees Fahrenheit. Grease a large baking dish with cooking spray.*

✓ *To a large mixing basin, combine all of the ingredients and toss well to coat.*

✓ *Arrange broccoli florets in the bottom of the prepared baking dish, then chicken breasts on top in a single layer.*

✓ *Preheat the oven to 350°F and bake for approximately 45 minutes.*

✓ *Take the baking sheet out of the oven and*

put it aside for approximately 5 minutes before serving.

✓ *Take the baking dish out of the oven and lay it aside to cool completely. Divide the chicken breasts and broccoli evenly among six containers and refrigerate for approximately two days. Before serving, reheat in the microwave.*

Nutrition: 443 Calories 25 g total fat 7 g saturated fat 151 mg cholesterol Carbohydrates 9.4 g Sugar 2 g Fiber 6 grams Sodium 189 milligrams Potassium 831 milligrams Protein 53 milligrams

541) *Rosemary Lemon*

14 Minutes Cooking 4 chicken portions
Ingredients:

- *1 kilogram halved chicken breasts*
- *1 lemon, peeled and sliced*
- *1/2 orange, peeled, and split into rounds*
- *3 roasted garlic cloves, or to taste salt and freshly ground black pepper*
- *1 1/2 tbsp olive oil, or as desired*
- *1 1/2 tsp agave syrup, or more to taste (optional)*
- *1/4 cup distilled water*

Direction

✓ *2 fresh rosemary sprigs, stems, or to taste In the Instant Pot, place the chicken. Season with salt and pepper. Add lemon, orange, and garlic. Drizzle the top with olive oil and agave syrup (if using). Combine the water and rosemary. Secure the lid of the cooker.*

✓ *Cook for 14 minutes on High pressure with the "Meat" and "Stew" settings. Allow approximately 20 minutes for pressure to dissipate naturally.*

Nutrition: Calories 325 Carbohydrates 5 g 20 g Sucrose Protein: 2 g Cholesterol 33 mg 10 g

542) *Chicken with Ginger Flavor*

6 portions 15 Minutes Cooking
Ingredients:

- *1 kilogram chicken breasts, boneless and skinless (frozen OR thawed)*
- *6 tbsp soy sauce*
- *3 tsp rice vinegar*
- *1/2 tsp honey*
- *3 tbsp. water, chicken broth, or orange juice*
- *2 tbsp. fresh ginger, chopped 6 minced garlic cloves*

- *3 tsp cornstarch*

Direction

✓ *In the Instant Pot, place chicken breasts.*

✓ *Whisk together the vinegar, soy sauce, honey, water, ginger, and garlic in a small mixing basin. Distribute mixture evenly over chicken.*

✓ *Secure the lid of the Instant Pot and cook for 15 minutes at high pressure. When the meat is done, let steam escape.*

✓ *Chicken breasts should be removed and placed on a chopping board. Bring remaining sauce to a simmer in the pan (use the Saute feature on an electric cooker). Combine cornstarch and 3 tablespoons cold water in a small bowl and then pour into prepared pan.*

✓ *Return chicken to saucepan with sauce after shredding.*

Nutrition: 313 Calories Carbohydrates 26 g 16 g Sucrose Protein: 7 g Cholesterol 8 g 36 milligram

543) *Crock-pot Tex-Mex Slow Cooker Chicken*

6 portions Time Required for Cooking: 4 Hours 40 Minutes
Ingredients:

- *4 tbsp cup water*
- *1 teaspoon cumin powder*
- *1 pound boneless chicken thighs, washed and patted dry*
- *1 can chopped tomatoes and green chilies (10 oz)*
- *1 (16-ounce) container thawed frozen onion and pepper strips*

Direction

✓ *Spray a skillet with cooking spray and put on the heat.*

✓ *Cook chicken thighs in a pan over medium heat until browned on each side. Remove from the skillet once browned.*

✓ *Cook peppers and onions in the same skillet until soft.*

✓ *Transfer sautéed peppers and onions to a 4- to 5-quart casserole dish. Slow cooker in the Crock-Pot, followed by chicken thighs on top.*

✓ *Combine tomatoes and 4 tablespoons of water in a bowl and pour over chicken. Cook on low for approximately 4 hours.*

✓ *Add 1 teaspoon ground cumin and continue*

cooking for another half hour.

✓ *Once completed, remove it from the oven and serve immediately!*

Nutrition: 121 Calories; 2 grams fat; 6.4 grams carbohydrates; 16 grams protein

544) *Slow-cooker Burritos de Fajita de Pollo*

8 portions Time Required for Cooking: 6 Hrs
Ingredients:

* *1 tsp cumin*
* *1 cup cheddar cheese + 2 tbsp shredded reduced-fat*
* *1 pound skinless and boneless chicken strips*
* *8 big tortillas low in carbs*
* *1 sliced green pepper*
* *1 can (15 oz) washed and drained black beans*
* *1 sliced red pepper*
* *1/3 cup water*
* *1/2 cup salsa 1 medium onion, diced*
* *1 tablespoon cayenne pepper*
* *1 teaspoon powdered garlic*

Directions:

✓ *In a slow cooker, place strips of chicken breast.*

✓ *All of the ingredients listed above, save the cheese and tortillas, should be piled on top of the chicken. Cook, covered, for roughly 6 hours, or until done.*

✓ *With a fork, shred chicken.*

✓ *Along with the bean mixture, place a half cup of chicken on each tortilla.*

✓ *2 tablespoons of shredded cheese at the end, then wrap the tortilla into a burrito.*

Nutrition: 250 Calories; 7g fat; 31g carbohydrate total; 28g protein

545) *Chicken with Chickpeas*

4 portions Time Required for Cooking: 36 Minutes
Ingredients:

* *2 tbsp olive oil*
* *1 pound skinless, boneless chicken breast, cubed 2 carrots, peeled and sliced 1 onion, diced 2 celery stalks,*
* *minced 2 garlic cloves*
* *1/2 teaspoon crushed oregano*
* *34 teaspoon cumin powder*
* *1/2 tsp paprika*

* *14-1/3 teaspoon cayenne*
* *1/4 teaspoon turmeric powder*
* *1 cup smashed tomatoes*
* *12 cups chicken broth with a low salt content*
* *1 sliced zucchini*
* *1 cup drained boiled chickpeas*
* *1 tbsp. lemon juice*

Direction

✓ *Cook the chicken cubes for approximately 4-5 minutes in a large nonstick skillet over medium heat.*

✓ *Transfer the chicken chunks to a plate using a slotted spoon.*

✓ *Sauté the carrot, onion, celery, and garlic in the same pan for approximately 4-5 minutes.*

✓ *Sauté the ginger, oregano, and spices for approximately 1 minute.*

✓ *Bring to a boil the chicken, tomato, and broth.*

✓ *Reduce to low heat and simmer for approximately 10 minutes.*

✓ *Cook, covered, for approximately 15 minutes with the zucchini and chickpeas.*

✓ *Add the lemon juice and serve immediately.*

✓ *Now, put the chicken mixture in a large bowl and set it aside to cool a little. Distribute the mixture evenly among four containers. Refrigerate the containers for 1-2 days. Before serving, reheat in the microwave.*

Nutrition: 308 Calories 13 g Saturated Fat 7 g Cholesterol 66 mg Carbohydrates 19 g Sugar 3 g Fiber 7 g Sodium 202 mg Potassium 331 mg Protein 30.7 g

546) *Chicken with Soy Glaze*

6 portions Time Required for Cooking: 25 Minutes

* *2 pounds boneless chicken thighs*
* *What you'll need from your pantry: Season with salt & pepper*
* *1 tablespoon garlic, minced*
* *1/4 tbsp. soy sauce*
* *3/4 cup vinegar de cidre d'apple*

Directions:

✓ *Season the chicken with salt and pepper and place it skin-side down in the Instant Pot.*

✓ *Combine the apple cider vinegar, soy sauce,*

✓ and garlic in a small bowl and add to the pot.

✓ Once the lid is closed and locked, hit the Manual button and set the timer to 15 minutes.

✓ When the timer sounds, allow the pressure to naturally vent.

✓ Now carefully open the lid once the pan has depressurized.

✓ Transfer the chicken to a baking sheet and broil for 3–5 minutes, or until the skin is crispy.

✓ Meanwhile, set the Instant Pot to Sauté and simmer, occasionally stirring, until the sauce thickens.

✓ Serve the chicken with a spoonful of the sauce on top.

Nutrition: Calories 335 calorie fat 23 calorie protein 27.5g carbohydrates 5g dietary fiber 0g carbohydrate net 5 g

547) *Tikka Masala Chicken*

4 portions Time Required for Cooking: 10 Minutes
Ingredients:

* 2 tbsp olive oil
* 1 small onion, chopped 3 garlic cloves, minced
* 1 fresh ginger root, peeled and grated
* 1/2 cup broth de volaille
* 1 and 1/2 tbsp garam masala
* 1 paprika teaspoon
* 1/2 teaspoon turmeric powder
* 1 tsp salt
* 1 cayenne pepper, 1/4 teaspoon
* 750 g boneless, skinless chicken flesh, diced 450 g tomatoes in cans, liquids included
* 1 tablespoon coconut milk
* Chopped fresh cilantro

Direction

✓ Set the cooker to the Sauté setting. When the oil is hot, add the onion and sauté for about 3 minutes, or until softened. Cook until the garlic and ginger are tender.

✓ Half of the chicken broth should be added. Cook for a few minutes, stirring constantly. Stir in the garam masala, paprika, turmeric, salt, and cayenne pepper.

✓ Combine the chicken, remaining chicken broth, and tomatoes.

✓ Secure the lid by closing and locking it. Cook at high pressure for 10 minutes. Once cooked, quickly release the pressure.

✓ Combine the coconut milk and sauce in a medium bowl.

✓ Suggestions for serving: Serve with cauliflower "rice" or cooked potatoes as a bed.

Nutrition: Calories 245 g Carbohydrates 25 g Sugar 16 g Protein 4 g Cholesterol 35 mg 5 g

548) *Garlic Lemon Turkey*

4 portions Time Required for Cooking: 5 Minutes
Ingredients:

* 4 turkey breasts cut into fillets
* 2 minced garlic cloves
* 1 tsp olive oil
* 3 tsp lemon juice
* 1 oz. shredded Parmesan cheese Season with pepper to taste
* 1 tablespoon clipped fresh sage
* 1 teaspoon lemon zest

Directions:

✓ Pound the turkey breast until it is completely flat.

✓ Combine the olive oil, garlic, and lemon juice in a bowl.

✓ To the bowl, add the turkey.

✓ 1 hour in the marinade.

✓ Broil for 5 minutes, or until the turkey is cooked through.

✓ During the final minute of cooking, sprinkle cheese on top.

✓ Combine the pepper, sage, and lemon zest in a bowl.

✓ Before serving, sprinkle this mixture over the turkey.

Nutrition: 188 Calories 7 g total fat 2 g saturated fat 71 mg cholesterol 173 mg sodium Carbohydrates Total 2 g Dietary Fiber 0 g Sugars Total Protein 0 g Potassium 264 mg 29 g

549) *Whole Roasted Chicken*

Time Required for Cooking: 10 Minutes

* 1 entire chicken (about 2 kg)
* 1 tablespoon fresh rosemary, chopped
* 1 1/2 to 2 tablespoons olive oil, plus a little extra for sprinkling in the pan
* 4-6 garlic cloves

- *1 tsp paprika*
- *Season with salt and pepper to taste*
- *1 lemon, zest*
- *1 cup broth de volaille*
- *1 quartered big onion*

Direction

✓ *Now, Rinse the chicken under running cold water and pat it dry with absorbent paper. Set aside in a baking pan.*

✓ *Set Instant Pot to Sauté mode and Preheat.*

✓ *Combine rosemary, olive oil, garlic, paprika, salt, pepper, and lemon zest in a small bowl.*

✓ *Lemons should be sliced in half and stuffed into the cavity of the chicken after the zest is removed.*

✓ *Drizzle a little olive oil into a heated pan and add the chicken breast-side down.*

✓ *3-4 minutes, or until golden brown.*

✓ *Bake the chicken on the opposite side.*

✓ *Chicken should be removed from the pan and placed in the baking dish where it was previously. Pour broth into the pan.*

✓ *Arrange onion in the bottom of the pan, followed by the chicken (breast-side up) and securing the lid.*

✓ *Cook for 6 minutes per pound on high pressure. Wait 10 minutes after it is cooked before releasing steam. Remove chicken and allow a minimum of 5 minutes before slicing.*

Nutrition: 301 Calories Carbohydrates 27.2 g Sugar 16 g Protein 6 g 33 mg Cholesterol 9 g

550) *Tamari And Mustard Fried Chicken*

4 portions Cooking Time: 1 hour and twenty minutes
Ingredients:

- *Tamari Sauce 1kg of very finely diced chicken*
- *Mustard in its natural state*
- *Peppercorns, ground*
- *ONE LEMON*
- *Flour*
- *Olive oil extra virgin*

Directions:

✓ *Put the chicken in a bowl; you can serve it with or without the skin, depending on your guests' preferences.*

✓ *A large stream of tamari, one or two tablespoons mustard, a pinch of freshly ground pepper, and a splash of lemon juice*

✓ *Combine everything together and set aside for an hour to macerate.*

✓ *Chicken pieces should be floured before being placed in the air fryer basket.*

✓ *Set the oven to 200 degrees for 20 minutes. Remove the chicken from the basket at halftime.*

✓ *Avoid crushing the chicken; it is recommended to create two or three batches of chicken to allow the pieces to build up and not to fry them thoroughly.*

Nutrition: Calories: 100 6g fat 0g carbohydrate 18g protein 0g sugar

551) *Herbed Chicken*

4 portions Time Required for Cooking: 50 Minutes
Ingredients:

- *1 chicken, entire*
- *1 tsp. powdered garlic*
- *1 tsp. powdered onion*
- *1/2 teaspoon dried thyme; 1 teaspoon dried rosemary;*
- *1 teaspoon dried lemon juice*
- *2 tablespoons olive oil*
- *Season with salt and freshly ground black pepper to taste*

Directions:

✓ *Season chicken with salt and pepper, rub with thyme, rosemary, garlic powder, and onion powder, then finish with lemon juice and olive oil.*

✓ *Cook chicken in your air fryer for 20 minutes on each side at 360 °F. Allow chicken to cool somewhat before carving and serving.*

Nutrition: 390 Calories; 10 grams fat; 5 grams fiber; 22 grams carbohydrates; 20 grams protein

552) *Whole Juicy Chicken*

6 portions 30 Minutes Cooking
Ingredients:

- *2 tablespoons olive oil*
- *300 milliliters chicken broth*
- *3 russets*
- *1 entire chicken*

Direction

✓ *Spices to taste, such as thyme, oregano,*

salt, and garlic salt, set your Instant Pot to Saute, Low.

✓ When the olive oil is hot, add the chicken to the pot and cook for approximately 2 minutes. Rep with the opposite side. By pressing Cancel, you can turn off the computer.

✓ Take the browned meat out of the Instant Pot and replace it with the chicken stock, potatoes, and chicken (whole or in pieces). The chicken should be arranged atop the potatoes.

✓ Close lid, secure steam valve, and set the timer to 25 minutes on Poultry, usual setting. Once cooked, perform a fast release.

Nutrition: 301 Calories 27.2 g fat 16 g carbohydrate 6 g sugar 9 g protein 33 mg cholesterol

553) *Delectable Chicken Tenders*

4 portions Time Required for Cooking: 25 Minutes.
Ingredients:

- 12 pound chicken tenderloins
- 1 tbsp. olive oil extra virgin
- 1 teaspoon seasoning for rotisserie chicken
- 2 tablespoons barbecue sauce

Direction

✓ In a zip-lock bag, combine all ingredients except the oil.

✓ Refrigerate bag for 2-3 hours.

✓ In a large skillet over medium heat, heat the oil.

✓ In a skillet, sauté marinated chicken tenders until gently browned and done.

Nutrition: 365 Calories 16.1 g fat, 8 g carbohydrate, 2 g sugar, 49.2 g protein, 151 mg cholesterol

554) *Pie with Salted Biscuits Chops de Turkey*

4 portions Time Required for Cooking: 20 Minutes

- 8 big turkey chops
- Three hundred grams of crackers
- 2 Eggs
- Olive oil extra virgin
- Salt
- Peppercorns, ground

Directions:

✓ Season the turkey chops with salt & pepper and arrange them on the worktable.

✓ In a basin, beat the eggs.

✓ Grind the cookies in the Thermomix with a

few turbo strokes until they get grittier, or use the blender to crush them.

✓ In a bowl, combine the cookies.

✓ Chops should be put through a beaten egg and then through crumbled biscuits. Firmly press the empanada to ensure its perfection.

✓ With a silicone brush and extra virgin olive oil, paint the empanada.

✓ Place the chops in the air fryer's basket; not all will fit. They will be completed in stages.

✓ Preheat the oven to 200 degrees for 15 minutes.

✓ Serve once all the chops are prepared.

Nutrition: 126 Calories 6g fat 0g carbohydrate 18g protein 0g sugar

555) *Creamy Rice, Peas, And Chicken*

4 portions Time Required for Cooking: 20 Minutes
Ingredients:

- 1 pound skinless, boneless chicken breasts, quartered
- 1 cup cooked white rice
- 1 cup stock de volaille
- 1/4 cup chopped parsley
- 2 cup frozen peas
- 1/2 cup grated parmesan 1 tbsp. extra-virgin olive oil
- 3 minced garlic cloves
- 1 chopped yellow onion
- HALF CUP WINE
- 1 quart thick cream
- Season with salt and freshly ground black pepper to taste

Directions:

✓ Season chicken breasts with salt and pepper, drizzle half of the oil over them, massage well, place in the basket of your air fryer, and cook for 6 minutes at 360 °F.

✓ Heat the remaining oil in a large skillet over medium-high heat; add the garlic, onion, wine, stock, salt, and pepper; stir, bring to a simmer, and cook for 9 minutes.

✓ Transfer chicken breasts to a heatproof dish that fits your air fryer, stir with peas, rice, and cream mixture, sprinkle with parmesan and parsley and set in the air fryer. Cook for 10 minutes at 420 °F. Distribute evenly across plates and serve immediately.

Nutrition: 313 Calories; 14 fiber 27 carbs 44 protein

556) **Chicken Olives with Oregano Flavor**

4 portions 15 Minutes Cooking

- *2 pieces (without skin and bones) Breasts de poulet 2 Eggplants*
- *1 tbsp thyme*
- *1 cup passata di tomato*

Direction

✓ *What you'll need from your pantry: Season with salt and freshly ground black pepper to taste. 2 tablespoons olive oil*

✓ *In the instant pot, combine all of the ingredients, then cover and cook on high for 20 minutes.*

✓ *Wait 10 minutes for the pressure to release gradually, then divide them across your plates before eating.*

Nutrition: 362 Calories, 16.1g fat, 4g fiber, 4g carbs, 36.4g protein

557) **Chinese Stuffed Chicken**

30 Minutes Cooking 1 entire chicken

- *Ten wolfberries*
- *2 red chilies; 4 ginger slices, diced*
- *1 diced yam 1 teaspoon soy sauce*
- *3 tablespoon sesame oil*
- *Season with salt and freshly ground white pepper to taste*

Direction

✓ *Season chicken with salt and pepper, then rub with soy sauce and sesame oil before stuffing with wolfberries, yam cubes, chilies, and ginger.*

✓ *Cook at 400 °F for 20 minutes, then at 360 °F for 15 minutes. Carve chicken and divide among plates.*

Nutrition: Calories: 320; Fat: 12; Fiber: 17; Carbohydrates: 22; Protein: 12

558) **Chicken & Spinach**

13 Minutes Cooking

Ingredients:

- *2 tbsp olive oil*
- *1 pound chicken breast fillet, cut Season with salt and pepper to taste*
- *4 minced garlic cloves*
- *1 tbsp lime juice*
- *1/2 cup unsweetened white wine*
- *1 teaspoon lemon zest*

- *10 cups chopped fresh spinach*
- *4 tbsp. grated Parmesan cheese*

Direction

✓ *in a saucepan over medium heat, pour oil.*

✓ *Season both sides of the chicken with salt and pepper.*

✓ *Cook for 7 minutes in the pan, or until brown on both sides.*

✓ *Cook for 1 minute before adding the garlic.*

✓ *Combine the lemon juice and wine in a separate bowl.*

✓ *Garnish with lemon zest. 5 minutes at low heat. Cook until the spinach has wilted.*

✓ *Garnish with grated Parmesan cheese.*

Nutrition: 334 Calories 12 g total fat 3 g saturated fat 67 mg cholesterol 499 mg sodium Carbohydrates in total 25 g Dietary Fiber 2 g Sugars in Total 1 gram of protein Potassium 29 g 685 mg

559) **Chicken Fried In The Air With Honey And Lemon**

4 portions Time Required for Cooking: 50 Minutes

Ingredients:

- *The Filling:*
- *3 pound. entire chicken*
- *2 red onions, peeled*
- *2 tablespoons olive oil*
- *2 apricots*
- *1 courgette*
- *a single apple*
- *2 garlic cloves garlic, finely chopped Thyme, freshly chopped*
- *Season with salt & pepper*
- *Marinade:*
- *5 oz honey 1 lemon's juice*
- *2 tablespoons olive oil*
- *Season with salt & pepper*

Direction

✓ *To make the stuffing, finely chop all components.*

✓ *Transfer the mixture to a large bowl and stir in the olive oil. Season with salt and freshly ground black pepper to taste. Stuff the cavity of the bird liberally with the stuffing.*

✓ *Cook the chicken in the Air Fryer for 35 minutes at 340 F. In a large saucepan, warm the honey and lemon juice; season with salt and pepper. Reduce the Air Fryer's temperature to 320 F.*

✓ *Brush some of the honey-lemon marinade over the chicken and place it back in the fryer. Cook for a further 70 minutes, brushing the chicken with the marinade every 20-25 minutes. Serve garnished with parsley and accompanied by potatoes.*

Nutrition: 342 Calories; 68g carbohydrates; 28g fat; 33g protein

560) *Chicken with Honey Mustard*

4 portions 12 Minutes Cooking
Ingredients:

- *2 tbsp mustard honey 2 tsp extra virgin olive oil*
- *Season with salt to taste*
- *1 pound chicken tenderloins*
- *1 pound steamed baby carrots Parsley, chopped*

Directions:

✓ *Preheat the oven to 450 degrees Fahrenheit.*

✓ *Combine honey mustard, olive oil, and salt in a bowl.*

✓ *Combine the ingredients and coat the chicken tenders.*

✓ *Arrange the chicken on the baking pan in a single layer.*

✓ *10–12 minutes in the oven.*

✓ *Serve with steamed carrots and parsley on top.*

Nutrition: Calories 366 8 g Total Fat 2 g Saturated Fat 63 mg Sodium 543 mg Carbohydrates 46 g Dietary Fiber 8 g Sugars in Total Protein 13 g

561) *Wraps with Greek Chicken in Lettuce*

4 portions Time Required for Cooking: 8 Minutes
Ingredients:

- *2 tbsp lemon juice, freshly squeezed*
- *1 teaspoon lemon zest*
- *5 tbsp. olive oil*
- *3 tsp. chopped and divided garlic*
- *1 teaspoon oregano, dry*
- *1/4 teaspoon   crushed red pepper*
- *1 pound chicken tenderloins*
- *1 cucumber, halved and grated*
- *Season with salt and pepper to taste*
- *3/4 cup plain Greek yogurt*

- *2 tsp. chopped fresh mint*
- *2 tablespoons chopped fresh dill 4 lettuce leaves*
- *1/2 cup sliced red onion*
- *1 cup chopped tomatoes*

Directions:

✓ *Combine the lemon juice, lemon zest, half of the oil, half of the garlic, and red pepper in a bowl.*

✓ *In a shallow dish, coat the chicken with the marinade.*

✓ *For 1 hour, marinate it.*

✓ *In a bowl, toss grated cucumber with salt.*

✓ *Squeeze the bottle to release the liquid.*

✓ *Combine the yogurt, dill, salt, pepper, remaining garlic, and remaining oil in a medium mixing bowl.*

✓ *Set for 4 minutes per side on the grill.*

✓ *Chicken should be shredded and placed on top of the lettuce leaves.*

✓ *To finish, sprinkle the yogurt mixture, onion, and tomatoes on top.*

✓ *Wrap the lettuce leaves around a toothpick and secure with another toothpick.*

Nutrition: 353 Calories 9 g Total Fat 1 g Saturated Fat 58 mg Sodium 559 mg Carbohydrates 33 g Dietary Fiber 6 g Sugars in Total Protein: 6 g 37 g 459 mg potassium

562) *Chicken with Spicy Honey Orange*

4 portions Time Required for Cooking: 10 Minutes
Ingredients:

- *12 pound cleaned and cut chicken breast To taste parsley*
- *1 cup shredded coconut 3/4 cup crumbs de pâtisserie*
- *2 beaten whole eggs 12 c. flour*
- *1/2 teaspoon   pepper*
- *Season with salt to taste*
- *1/2 cup marmalade d'orange*
- *1 tbsp crushed red pepper*
- *14 c honey*
- *3 tbsp mustard dijon*

Directions:

✓ *Preheat your Air Fryer to 400 degrees Fahrenheit. Combine coconut, flour, salt, parsley, and pepper in a mixing bowl. In a separate bowl, combine the beaten eggs.*

✓ In a third bowl, combine breadcrumbs. Chicken should be dredged in egg mixture, flour, and finally breadcrumbs.

✓ Bake the chicken for 15 minutes in the Air Fryer cooking basket.

✓ Separately, combine honey, orange marmalade, mustard, and pepper flakes in a separate bowl. Cover chicken with marmalade mixture and continue cooking for 5 minutes longer. Enjoy!

Nutrition: 246 Calories; 21g carbohydrates; 6g fat; 25g protein

563) *Italian Design Breast of Chicken*

3 portions 15 Minutes Cooking
Ingredients:

- 1 tsp olive oil
- 3 chicken breasts, boneless and skinless
- 1/4 teaspoon garlic powder, normal salt, and a sprinkle of black pepper per breast
- 1/8 teaspoon oregano, dried
- 1/8 teaspoon basil, dried
- 250 milliliters water

Directions:

✓ Saute mode is selected in the Instant Pot, and oil is added to the pot.

✓ Season one side of the chicken breasts and carefully add the chicken breasts, seasoned side down, to the pot once the oil is hot.

✓ Meanwhile, season the second team.

✓ Cook for approximately 3 to 4 minutes on each side and remove with tongs.

✓ 250 mL water plus the trivet should be added to the pot.

✓ Arrange the chicken breasts on the trivet.

✓ Cook for 5 minutes on manual High with the lid locked.

✓ Allow a few minutes for the chicken to naturally release, and then quickly release the remainder.

✓ Remove from the heat source and let stand for at least 5 minutes before slicing.

Nutrition: Calories 202 Fat 29 g Carbohydrates 16 g Sugar 6 g Protein 33 mg Cholesterol 9 g

564) *Garlic Chives Chicken*

4 portions Time Required for Cooking: 10 Minutes
Ingredients

- 1 lb. (no skin and bones) Chicken breast
- 1 tbsp Chives
- 1 cup Chicken stock
- 1 cup Coconut cream
- 3 tbsp Garlic cloves (sliced)
- What you'll need from your pantry:
- 1 and a half tbsp Balsamic vinegar
- Salt and Black pepper to taste

Directions:

✓ In the instant pot, mix the chicken with all the remaining ingredients, then cover them and cook for 20 minutes at high temperature.

✓ Wait 10 minutes for the pressure to release gradually, then divide them across your plates before eating.

Nutrition: Calories: 360, Fat: 21, Fiber: 4g, Carbs: 1g, Protein: 35g

565) *Breaded Chicken Fillets*

4 portions Time Required for Cooking: 25 Minutes
Ingredients:

- 3 small chicken breasts or 2 large chicken breasts Salt
- Peppercorns, ground
- 3 garlic cloves
- ONE LEMON
- Beaten eggs
- Breadcrumbs
- Olive oil extra virgin

Directions:

✓ Cut the breasts into fillets.

✓ Put in a bowl and add the lemon juice, chopped garlic cloves, and pepper.

✓ Flirt well and leave 10 minutes.

✓ Beat the eggs and put breadcrumbs on another plate.

✓ Pass the chicken breast fillets through the beaten egg and the breadcrumbs.

✓ When you have them all breaded, start to fry.

✓ Paint the breaded breasts with a silicone brush and extra virgin olive oil.

✓ Place a batch of fillets in the basket of the air fryer and select 10 minutes 180 degrees.

✓ Turn around and leave another 5 minutes at 180 degrees.

Nutrition: Calories: 120 Fat: 6g Carbohydrates 0g 18g protein 0g sugar

566) Chicken Wings With Garlic Parmesan

Servings: 3 Cooking Time: 25 Minutes
Ingredients:

- 25g cornstarch\s 20g grated Parmesan cheese
- 9g garlic powder
- Season with salt and pepper to taste
- 680g chicken wings
- Nonstick Spray Oil

Directions:

✓ Select Preheat, set the temperature to 200 °C, and press Start / Pause.
✓ Combine corn starch, Parmesan, garlic powder, salt, and pepper in a bowl.
✓ Mix the chicken wings in the seasoning and dip until well coated.
✓ Spray the baskets and the air fryer with oil spray and add the wings, sprinkling the tops of the wings as well.
✓ Select Chicken and press Start/Pause. Be sure to shake the baskets in the middle of cooking.
✓ Sprinkle with what's left of the Parmesan mix and serve.

Nutrition: Calories: 204 Fat: 15g Carbohydrates: 1g Proteins: 12g 0g sugar Cholesterol: 63mg

567) Duck With Garlic And Onion Sauce

4 portions Time Required for Cooking: 20 Minutes
Ingredients:

- 2 tbsp Coriander
- 2 pieces Spring onions
- 1 lb. (no skin and bones) Duck legs
- 2 pieces Garlic cloves
- 2 tbsp Tomato passata
- What you'll need from your pantry: 2 tbsp Melted ghee

Directions:

✓ Put the instant pot on Sauté option, then put the ghee and cook it. After that, put the spring onions and the other ingredients, excluding the tomato passata and the meat, then heat it for 5 minutes.
✓ Put the meat and cook for 5 minutes.
✓ Put the sauce, then cover it and heat it for 25 minutes at a high temperature.

✓ Wait 10 minutes for the pressure to release gradually, then divide them across your plates before eating.

Nutrition: Calories: 263, Fat: 12g, Fiber: 0.2g, Carbs: 1g, Protein: 35g

568) Lemon Chicken With Basil

4 portions Cooking Time: 1h
Ingredients:

- 1kg chopped chicken
- 1 or 2 lemons
- Basil, salt, and ground pepper
- Olive oil extra virgin

Directions:

✓ Put the chicken in a bowl with a jet of extra virgin olive oil.
✓ Put salt, pepper, and basil.
✓ Bind well and let stand for at least 30 minutes, stirring occasionally.
✓ Put the pieces of chicken in the air fryer basket and take the air fryer. Choose 30 minutes.
✓ Remove on occasion.
✓ Remove and replace with another batch. Carry out the identical operation.

Nutrition: 126 Calories 6 g fat Carbohydrates 0g 18g protein 0g sugar

569) Turkey And Spring Onions

4 portions Time Required for Cooking: 10 Minutes
Ingredients:

- Cilantro
- 4 spring onions (sliced) 1 item (no skin and bones) Breast of turkey
- 1 cup passata di tomato

What you'll need from your pantry:

- 2 tbsp oil d'avocado
- Season with salt and freshly ground black pepper to taste

Direction

✓ Put the instant pot on the Sauté setting and add the oil. Cook until the oil is hot. Following that, add the meat and heat for 5 minutes.
✓ Combine the remaining ingredients, then cover and simmer on high for 20 minutes.
✓ Wait 10 minutes for the pressure to release gradually, then divide them across your plates before eating.

Nutrition:222 Cal,6.7g fat,6g fiber,8g carbs, 34g pro

570) <u>**Chicken Wings in Chinese**</u>

6 portions Time Required for Cooking: 10 Minutes
Ingredients:

- *16 wing chickens*
- *2 tablespoons honey*
- *2 tablespoons soy sauce*
- *Season with salt and freshly ground black pepper to taste*
- *1/4 teaspoon freshly ground white pepper*
- *3 tbsp. freshly squeezed lime juice*

Directions:

✓ *In a bowl, whisk together honey, soy sauce, salt, black and white pepper, and lime juice. Add chicken pieces and toss to coat. Refrigerate for 2 hours.*

✓ *Transfer the chicken to an air fryer and cook for 6 minutes on each side at 370 °F. Increase heat to 400 °F and cook for an additional 3 minutes. Serve immediately.*

Nutrition: 372 Calories; 9 grams fat; 10 grams fiber; 37 grams carbohydrates; 24 grams protein

571) <u>**Chicken Basil Chili 4 pcs**</u>

Time Required for Cooking: 20 Minutes
Ingredients:

- *1/2 cup chicken broth*
- *1 pound breast of chicken*
- *2 tsp paprika dulce*
- *1 cup cream de coco*
- *2 tablespoons basil (sliced)*
- *What you'll need from your pantry:*
- *Season with salt and freshly ground black pepper to taste.*
- *1 tbsp cayenne pepper*

Direction

✓ *In your instant pot, combine the chicken and remaining ingredients, stir briefly, cover, and cook on high for 20 minutes.*

✓ *Wait 10 minutes for the pressure to release gradually, then divide them onto plates before eating.*

Nutrition: 364 Calories, 22g fat, 3g fiber, 1g carbohydrate, 34g protein

572) <u>**Lentil-Fried Turkey**</u>

7 portions 51 Minutes Cooking
Ingredients:

- *3 tbsp. extra-virgin olive oil, split*

- *1 diced onion*
- *1 tablespoon minced fresh ginger*
- *4 minced garlic cloves*
- *3 finely cut plum tomatoes*
- *2 cups soaked and drained red lentils*
- *2 fluid ounces filtered water*
- *2 tsp cumin seed*
- *1/2 tsp cayenne*
- *1 pound ground turkey, lean*
- *1 seeded and sliced jalapeno pepper*
- *2 chopped onions*
- *1/4 cup chopped fresh cilantro*

Direction

✓ *In a Dutch oven over medium heat, heat 1 tablespoon of oil and sauté the onion, ginger, and garlic for about 5 minutes.*

✓ *Bring to a boil, stirring in tomatoes, lentils, and water. Reduce to medium-low heat and simmer, covered, for approximately 30 minutes.*

✓ *Meanwhile, in a skillet over medium heat, heat the remaining oil and sauté the cumin seeds and cayenne pepper for approximately 1 minute.*

✓ *Set aside the mixture in a small bowl.*

✓ *Cook turkey in the same skillet for approximately 4-5 minutes.*

✓ *Cook for approximately 4-5 minutes before adding the jalapeno and scallion.*

✓ *Stir in the spiced oil mixture until well combined.*

✓ *Transfer the turkey mixture to a saucepan of simmering lentils and cook for approximately 10-15 minutes, or until the desired doneness is achieved.*

✓ *Serve immediately.*

✓ *Transfer the turkey mixture to a large bowl and set aside to cool slightly. Distribute the mixture evenly among four containers. Refrigerate the containers for 1-2 days. Before serving, reheat in the microwave.*

Nutrition: 361 Calories 14 g total fat 4 g saturated fat Cholesterol 46 mg Carbohydrates in total: 37 g Sugar 4 g Fiber 18 g Protein 27.9 g

573) <u>**Chicken Wings Asian**</u>

5 minutes for preparation Time required for cooking: 30 minutes

- *24 chicken wings*

- What you'll require from your pantry:
- 6 tablespoons soy sauce
- 6 tbsp. Chinese five-spice powder
- Season with salt and pepper
- Cooking spray that is nonstick

Instructions:

✓ Preheat the oven to 350 degrees Fahrenheit. Cooking spray a baking sheet.

✓ In a large mixing basin, combine the soy sauce, 5 spices, salt, and pepper. Toss in the wings.

✓ Distribute the wings evenly over the prepared pan. 15 minutes in the oven. Cook for an additional 15 minutes, or until chicken is cooked through. Serve with a low-carb dipping sauce of your choice.

Nutrition: Calories 178 per serving Carbohydrates in total 8g Protein 12g Fatty Acids 11g Sucrose 1g Fiber 0 gram banana

574) **Chicken Wings Asian**

5 minutes for preparation Time required for cooking: 30 minutes 3 portions

- 24 chicken wings
- What you'll require from your pantry: 6 tablespoons soy sauce
- 6 tbsp. Chinese five-spice powder
- Season with salt and pepper
- Cooking spray that is nonstick

Instructions:

✓ Preheat the oven to 350 degrees Fahrenheit. Cooking spray a baking sheet.

✓ In a large mixing basin, combine the soy sauce, 5 spice, salt, and pepper. Toss in the wings.

✓ Distribute the wings evenly over the prepared pan. 15 minutes in the oven. Cook for an additional 15 minutes, or until chicken is cooked through.

✓ Serve with a low-carb dipping sauce of your choice.

Nutrition: Calories 178 per serving Carbohydrates in total 8g Protein 12g Fatty Acids 11g Sucrose 1g Fiber 0

575) **Cacciatore di Pollo**

4 portions Time Required for Cooking: 10 Minutes
Ingredients:

- 8 bone-in chicken drumsticks
- 1/2 cup pitted and sliced black olives

- 1 leaf of bay
- 1 tsp. powdered garlic
- 1 yellow onion; 28 oz. canned tomatoes and juice;
- 1 tsp. crushed oregano; dried oregano
- Season with salt and freshly ground black pepper to taste.

Directions:

✓ Combine chicken with salt, pepper, garlic powder, bay leaf, onion, tomatoes and juice, oregano, and olives in a heatproof dish that fits your air fryer; toss, place in a warmed air fryer, and cook for 20 minutes at 365 °F. Distribute evenly among plates and serve.

Nutrition: 300 Calories; 12 grams fat; 8 grams fiber; 20 grams carbohydrates; 24 grams protein

576) **Buffalo Chicken Dip in the Crock-Pot**

10 portions Time Required for Cooking: 3 Hours
Ingredients:

- 2 cups cooked chicken, diced 1 tablespoon ranch dressing
- 16 ounces cubed and softened cream cheese
- 5 oz. hot sauce
- 5 oz spicy sauce,
- 16 oz cubed cream cheese, and
- 1 cup ranch dressing

Directions

✓ Slow cooker in the Crock-Pot style. Cover and cook on low for approximately 2 hours, stirring occasionally.

✓ After the cheese has melted, stir in 2 cups cooked chicken. Cover the Crock-Pot slow cooker once more and simmer on low for another hour.

✓ Serve buffalo chicken with vegetables or any other chips of your choice.

Nutrition: 344 Calories; 29g fat; 5g carbohydrate total; 15g protein

577) **Tofu & Chicken**

6 portions
Time Required for Cooking: 25 Minutes
Ingredients:

- 2 tbsp olive oil 2 tsp orange juice
- 1 tbsp. Worcestershire
- 1 tablespoon soy sauce with a low salt content

- *1 teaspoon turmeric powder*
- *1 teaspoon mustard powder*
- *8 oz. cooked and cubed chicken breast*
- *8 ounces extra-firm tofu, drained and cubed*
- *2 carrots, thinly sliced 1 cup sliced mushroom*
- *2 c. freshly sprouted bean sprouts*
- *3 sliced green onions*
- *1 red sweet pepper, sliced*

Directions

✓ *Combine half of the oil, the orange juice, Worcestershire sauce, soy sauce, turmeric, and mustard in a bowl.*

✓ *Coat the chicken and tofu with the sauce on all sides.*

✓ *1 hour in the marinade.*

✓ *1 tablespoon oil in a skillet over medium heat.*

✓ *Cook for 2 minutes before adding carrot.*

✓ *Cook for an additional 2 minutes with the mushroom.*

✓ *Combine bean sprouts, green onion, and sweet pepper in a medium bowl.*

✓ *Cook for around two to three minutes.*

✓ *Stir in the chicken and cook until done.*

Nutrition: 285 Calories 9 g Cholesterol 32 mg Sodium 331 mg Carbohydrates Total 30 g Dietary Fiber 4 g Sugars in Total Protein: 4 g

578) *Chicken with Peppered Broccoli*

30 Minutes Cooking Servings: 4
Ingredients:

- *1 teaspoon sage (sliced)*
- *1 cup florets de broccoli*
- *1 pound (no bones and skin) Breast of chicken*
- *3 items Cloves de garlic*
- *1 cup passata di tomato*
- *2 tbsp. salt and freshly ground black pepper*
- *Extra virgin olive oil*

Directions:

✓ *Select the Sauté option in the instant pot, then add the oil and heat. Following that, add the chicken and garlic and cook for 5 minutes.*

✓ *Combine the remaining ingredients, then cover and simmer on high for 25 minutes.*

✓ *Wait 10 minutes for the pressure to release gradually, then divide them across your plates before eating.*

Nutrition: 217 Calories, 10.1g fat, 8g fiber, 9g carbs, 24g protein

579) *Basil-Peppered Chicken Breast*

4 portions Time Required for Cooking: 20 Minutes
Ingredients:

- *1/4 cup red bell peppers*
- *1 cup stock de poulet*
- *2 items (no skin and bones) Breasts de poulet*
- *4 items Cloves de garlic (crushed)*
- *1 1/2 tbsp Basil (crushed) What you'll need from your pantry: 1 tbsp cayenne pepper*

Directions:

✓ *Combine the ingredients in the instant pot, then cover and cook on high for 25 minutes.*

✓ *Quickly release the pressure for 5 minutes, then divide them across your plates before eating.*

Nutrition: 230 Calories 14g fat, 0.8g fiber, 7g carbs, 32g protein

580) *Drumsticks de Cocunut Spicy*

6 portions Time Required for Cooking: 10 Minutes
Ingredients:

- *1 tbsp ketchup*
- *1/4 cup sugar, dark brown*
- *1/4 cup vinegar de vin rouge*
- *3 tsp soy sauce*
- *1 tablespoon seasoning for chicken Season with salt to taste*
- *6 drumsticks de chile*

Directions:

✓ *In the Instant Pot, combine ketchup, brown sugar, red wine vinegar, soy sauce, spice, and salt. Stir in chicken pieces to coat.*

✓ *Close the lid of the Instant Pot and set the steam release handle to the 'Sealing' position.*

✓ *Cook for 12 minutes on 'Manual' (or 'Pressure Cook').*

✓ *Release the pressure quickly and carefully open the Instant Pot.*

✓ *Chicken parts should be removed and placed aside.*

✓ *Press 'Saute' and heat until the sauce has*

thickened somewhat, approximately 5 to 7 minutes.

Nutrition: Calories 145 Fat 28 g Carbohydrates 16 g Sucrose Protein: 2 g Cholesterol 9 g 45 milligram

581) *Cacciatore Chicken in the Crock Pot*

6 portions Time Required for Cooking: 4 Hours
Ingredients:

- *1 can (15 oz) chopped tomatoes*
- *6 chicken thighs, medium, skin removed*
- *1 sliced onion*
- *1 tablespoon seasoning de Italie*
- *1 seeded and sliced green bell pepper*
- *3 minced garlic cloves*
- *2 are possible (6-oz, no salt added) paste de tomato*

Directions:

- ✓ *Combine all ingredients in a Crock-Pot slow cooker and cook on High for 4 hours.*
- ✓ *Once chicken cacciatore is finished, serve with whole wheat rotini pasta, if desired.*

Nutrition: 170 Calories; 5 grams fat; 18 grams carbohydrates; 16 grams protein

582) *Curry with Chicken and Cabbage*

4 portions
30 Minutes Cooking
Ingredients:

- *1 kilogram boneless, skinless chicken breast, chopped into small pieces*
- *2 coconut milk cans*
- *3 tbsp curry paste*
- *1 chopped tiny onion*
- *1 red bell pepper, medium*
- *1 green bell pepper, medium*
- *Half A Head Of A Large Cucumber*

Directions:

- ✓ *Stir the curry paste into the coconut milk until completely dissolved. Transfer to the Instant Pot.*
- ✓ *Combine the chicken with the coconut curry sauce.*
- ✓ *Both peppers should be chopped into cubes and added to the saucepan.*
- ✓ *Combine the onion and the garlic.*
- ✓ *Slice the cabbage and add to the saucepan.*

Assemble all components in a single layer of coconut milk.

- ✓ *Cover, secure, and cook on Low for 30 minutes.*
- ✓ *Once cooked, carefully open and serve immediately.*

Nutrition: Calories 301 Carbohydrates 27.2 g 16 g Sucrose Protein: 6 g Cholesterol 9 g 33 milligram

583) *Slow Cooker Crock-pot Sweet Potatoes & Chicken*

4 portions
Time Required for Cooking: 5-7 Hours
Ingredients:

- *1 1/2 cup chicken broth with low sodium and fat content a single bay leaf*
- *4 (4 ounces) skinless and boneless chicken thighs*
- *2 tbsp mustard Dijon*
- *1 chopped onion*
- *1/4 teaspoon   dried thyme*
- *2 big peeled and sliced sweet potatoes*
- *3 tbsp. Splenda Brown Sugar Directions:*

Directions

- ✓ *In the Crock-Pot slow cooker, place 4 (4 oz) chicken thighs.*
- ✓ *Serve sliced potatoes and chopped onions on top of chicken thighs.*
- ✓ *Now combine all of the other ingredients in the Crock-Pot slow cooker. Cook on low for approximately 5-7 hours, or until chicken is thoroughly cooked.*
- ✓ *Once finished, remove the bay leaf from the slow cooker's Crock-Pot.*
- ✓ *Serve immediately.*

Nutrition: 75 Calories; 7g fat; 32g carbohydrate total; 21g protein

584) *Asparagus And Chicken*

4 portions
Time Required for Cooking: 10 Minutes
Ingredients:

- *8 chicken wings, halved;*
- *8 asparagus spears, chopped;*
- *1 tbsp rosemary, minced;*
- *1 tsp cumin, ground*
- *Season with salt and freshly ground black pepper to taste.*

Directions:

✓ Pat dry chicken wings, season with salt, pepper, cumin, and rosemary place in the basket of an air fryer, and cook for 20 minutes at 360 °F.

✓ Meanwhile, heat a skillet over medium heat and add the asparagus; cover with water and steam for a few minutes; move to a bowl of ice water, drain, and arrange on plates. Serve with chicken wings on the side.

Nutrition: Calories: 270; Fat: 8; Fiber: 12; Carbohydrates: 24; Protein: 22

585) *Fried Lemon Chicken 6 pcs.*

Time Required for Cooking: 20 Minutes.

Ingredients:

- 6 thighs de poulet
- 2 tablespoons olive oil
- 2 tbsp. freshly squeezed lemon juice
- 1 tbsp. seasoning blend of Italian herbs Celtic sea salt, 1 tsp.
- 1 teaspoon freshly ground pepper
- 1 finely sliced lemon

Directions

✓ In a bowl or bag, combine all ingredients except the sliced lemon; toss to coat chicken.

✓ Allow 30 minutes to marinate overnight.

✓ Remove the chicken from the pan and let the excess oil drain (it does not need to dry out, just do not drip with tons of excess oil).

✓ Arrange the chicken thighs and lemon slices in the fryer basket, taking care not to overcrowd the chicken thighs.

✓ Preheat the fryer to 200°F and cook for ten minutes.

✓ Take the basket out of the fryer and flip the chicken thighs over.

✓ Cook for a further 10 minutes at 200 degrees.

Nutrition: 215 Calories 13g fat 1 gram carbohydrate 2 g protein 1 gram sugar 130mg cholesterol

586) *Turkey Breast With Mustard And Maple Syrup*

6 portions 1 Hour Cooking Time

Ingredients:

- 5 pound turkey breast 1/4 tbsp. maple syrup
- 2 tbsp mustard dijon
- 1/2 tbsp paprika, smoked
- 1 tablespoon thyme
- 2 tablespoons olive oil
- 1/2 teaspoon   sage
- 1/2 tbsp salt and freshly ground black pepper
- 1 tbsp melted butter

Directions:

✓ Preheat the oven to 350 degrees Fahrenheit and spray the turkey with olive oil. In a small bowl, combine all herbs and seasonings and rub the mixture all over the turkey. 25 minutes in the air fryer. Turn the turkey over and continue cooking for an additional 12 minutes.

✓ Turn the pan over and cook for a further 12 minutes. In a small bowl, whisk together the butter, maple syrup, and mustard. When finished, brush the glaze over the entire turkey. Return to the air fryer and cook for a further 5 minutes, or until the chicken is nice and crispy.

Nutrition: 529 Calories; 77g carbohydrates; 20g fat; 13g protein

587) *Chicken Wings with a Dry Rub*

4 portions 30 Minutes Cooking

Ingredients:

- 9 g minced garlic
- 1 cube low sodium chicken broth 5g sodium chloride
- 3 g pepper
- 1 teaspoon smoked paprika
- 1 teaspoon cayenne pepper
- 3 g sodium-free Old Bay seasoning 3g powdered onion
- 1 teaspoon dried oregano
- Chicken wings, 453g
- Ranch sauce, to pair with nonstick spray oil

Directions:

✓ Prepare the air fryer by preheating it. Preheat the oven to 180°C.

✓ Combine all ingredients in a bowl.

✓ Season half of the chicken wings with the seasoning combination and liberally coat with oil spray.

✓ Preheat the air fryer and add the chicken wings.

✓ Set the timer to 30 minutes and select Chicken.

✓ Halfway through cooking, shake the

baskets.
Nutrition: Calories: 120 6 g fat 0g Carbohydrates 18g protein 0g sugar

588) *Skillet with Balsamic Chicken and Vegetables*

4 portions Time Required for Cooking: 20 Minutes
Ingredients:

- *1 pound chicken breasts, cubed*
- *1 cup halved cherry tomatoes*
- *1 cup florets de broccoli*
- *1 cup sliced baby Bella mushrooms 1 tbsp. chopped fresh basil*
- *1/2 cup handmade pasta, boiled and drained thoroughly*
- *1/2 cup chicken broth with a low sodium content*
- *3 tbsp. balsamic vinegar*
- *3 tbsp. balsamic vinegar*
- *2 tbsp. extra virgin olive oil, divided*
- *1 tsp cayenne pepper*
- *tsp garlic powder 1/2 tsp*
- *1/2 teaspoon salt*
- *1/2 teaspoon crushed red pepper*

Directions:

- ✓ *In a big, deep skillet, heat oil over medium-high heat. Cook until chicken is browned on all sides, about 8-10 minutes.*
- ✓ *Combine the vegetables, basil, broth, and seasonings in a medium bowl. Reduce heat to medium-low and cook covered for 5 minutes, or until vegetables are soft.*
- ✓ *Remove the cover and add the cooked pasta and vinegar. Cook for 3-4 minutes, or until thoroughly heated. Serve.*

Nutrition: 386 Calories 11g Carbohydrates Total 8g Carbohydrates Net 8g Protein 43g Fat 18g 5g sugar 3g fiber

589) *Tenders de Cocunut Creme*

4 portions 15 Minutes Cooking
Ingredients:

- *1 pound tender chicken breasts 1 cup creamed half-and-half*
- *4 tablespoons margarine*
- *What you'll require from your pantry: 2 tsp powdered garlic*
- *2 tsp cayenne pepper*

Directions:

- ✓ *Combine ingredients in a small bowl, adding a pinch of salt if needed. Coat chicken with seasonings.*
- ✓ *In a large skillet over medium heat, melt 2 tablespoons of margarine. Cook chicken for 3-4 minutes per side, or until no longer pink. Transfer to a serving dish.*
- ✓ *Add half-n-half and stir until it begins to boil, scraping away any brown pieces from the bottom of the skillet. Reduce to medium-low heat and continue cooking until the sauce has been reduced by half. Stir in remaining margarine and reintroduce chicken to sauce to reheat. Serve.*

Nutrition: 281 Calories Carbohydrates in total 3g Protein 24g Fat 19g Sugar 0g Fiber 0g

590) *Lemon Chicken in a Slow Cooker With Gravy*

4 portions Time Required for Cooking: 3 Hours
Ingredients:

- *Tenderloins de chicken 1 lb.*
- *3 tbsp. freshly squeezed lemon juice*
- *3 tbsp. cubed margarine*
- *2 tbsp. diced fresh parsley*
- *2 tbsp. chopped fresh thyme*
- *1 tbsp. zest de lemon*
- *1/4 cup chicken broth with low sodium*
- *2 garlic cloves, sliced*
- *2 tablespoon cornstarch*
- *2 teaspoon water*
- *1/2 teaspoon salt*
- *1/2 teaspoon freshly ground white pepper*

Directions:

- ✓ *In the crockpot, add the broth, lemon juice, margarine, zest, garlic, salt, and pepper. Cover and cook on low heat for 2 12 hours.*
- ✓ *Cook for an additional 30 minutes or until the chicken is cooked through.*
- ✓ *Transfer chicken to a platter and cover with foil to keep warm. In a small saucepan over medium heat, pour cooking liquid.*
- ✓ *Combine water and cornstarch in a small bowl until smooth. Bring to a boil in a saucepan. Cook, constantly stirring, for 2 minutes, or until slightly thickened. Serve alongside chicken.*

Nutrition: Calories 303 Carbohydrates 0g Sugar 2g Protein 33g Fat 17g 0g fiber

591) *Chicken with Cheesy Sauce and Spinach*

6 portions Time Required for Cooking: 45 Minutes
Ingredients:

- *3 boneless, skinless chicken breasts, halved lengthwise*
- *6 oz. softened low-fat cream cheese*
- *2 tablespoons baby spinach*
- *1 cup grated mozzarella cheese*
- *2 tbsp. extra virgin olive oil, divided*
- *3 garlic cloves, finely chopped*
- *1 tsp seasoning de l'Italien*
- *Cooking spray that is nonstick*

Directions:

- ✓ *Preheat the oven to 350 degrees Fahrenheit. Cooking spray a 9x13-inch glass baking dish.*
- ✓ *In a baking dish, arrange chicken breast cutlets. 1 tablespoon oil drizzled over chicken Distribute garlic and Italian spice equally. Cream cheese should be spread on top of the chicken.*
- ✓ *In a small skillet over medium heat, heat the remaining tablespoon of oil. Cook, occasionally stirring, until spinach wilts, about 3 minutes. Distribute evenly on top of the cream cheese layer. Top with mozzarella.*
- ✓ *Bake for 35-40 minutes, or until the chicken is thoroughly done. Serve.*

Nutrition: 363 Calories Carbohydrates in Total 3g protein, 31g fat, 25g carbohydrate, 0g sugar 0g fiber

592) *Grilled Turkey Breast with Spicy Sauce*

14 portions Time Required for Cooking: 12 Hours
Ingredients:

- *5 lb. bone-in turkey breast*
- *1 cup chicken broth with minimal sodium*
- *1/4 cup vinegar*
- *1/4 cup jalapeño pepper jelly*
- *2 tbsp. brown Splenda sugar*
- *2 tablespoons olive oil*
- *1 teaspoon salt*
- *2 tsp nutmeg*
- *1 tsp cayenne*
- *1/2 teaspoon mustard powder*

- *Cooking spray that is nonstick*

Directions:

- ✓ *Preheat the grill to a medium heat setting. Coat rack with nonstick frying spray. For indirect heat, place a drip pan on the grill.*
- ✓ *Combine Splenda brown sugar and seasonings in a small bowl.*
- ✓ *With your fingertips, carefully loosen the skin on both sides of the turkey. Distribute half of the spice mixture evenly over the turkey. With toothpicks, secure the skin to the underside and spread the remaining spice mixture on the exterior.*
- ✓ *Grill the turkey for 30 minutes over the drip pan.*
- ✓ *Combine broth, vinegar, jelly, and oil in a small saucepan over medium heat. Cook and stir for a further 2 minutes, or until the jelly is completely melted. 12 cups of the mixture should be reserved.*
- ✓ *Brush part of the jelly mixture over the turkey. Cook for 1 to 12 hours, basting every 15 minutes, or until the thermometer registers 170 degrees.*
- ✓ *Ten minutes later, cover and set aside. Remove the skin. Brush slices with reserved jelly mixture and serve.*

Nutrition: Calories 314 Carbohydrates Protein 5 g 35g Fatty Acids 14g Sucrose 5 g Fiber 0 g

593) *Barbecued Chicken and Noodles*

4 portions Time Required for Cooking: 25 Minutes
Ingredients:

- *4 diced bacon slices*
- *1 boneless, skinless chicken breast, cut into 1-inch pieces 1 diced onion*
- *1 cup grated low-fat cheddar cheese 12 cups skim milk*
- *14 12 oz. chopped tomatoes*
- *2 cup chicken broth with a low sodium content*
- *1/4 cup barbecue sauce*
- *2 garlic cloves, finely chopped*
- *1/4 teaspoon crushed red pepper*
- *Noodles prepared at home*
- *Season with salt and pepper to taste*

Directions:

- ✓ *Preheat a large saucepan over medium-high heat. Cook until bacon is crispy. Using* a strainer, drain fat, reserving 1 tablespoon.

- ✓ Cook, occasionally stirring, until chicken is browned on all sides, about 3-5 minutes.
- ✓ Add garlic and onion and sauté, frequently turning, for 3-4 minutes, or until onions are transparent.
- ✓ Combine broth, tomatoes, milk, and seasonings in a medium bowl. Bring to a boil, cover, decrease the heat to a low setting, and cook for 10 minutes.
- ✓ Stir in barbecue sauce, noodles, and cheese and cook for 2-3 minutes, or until noodles are tender and cheese has melted. Serve.

Nutrition: 331 Calories Carbohydrates total: 18g Carbohydrates net: 15g Protein: 34g Fat: 13g Sugar: 10g Fiber: 3g

594) *Chicken Pesto*

6 pcs. Time Required for Cooking: 20 Minutes
Ingredients:

- ¾ pound skinless, boneless, and sliced chicken breasts
- 1/2 cup shredded mozzarella cheese
- 1/4 cup pesto

Directions:

- ✓ In a mixing dish, combine chicken and pesto until well coated.
- ✓ Refrigerate for 2-3 hours.
- ✓ Grill chicken until thoroughly cooked over medium heat.
- ✓ Serve chicken with cheese sprinkled on top.

Nutrition: 303 13g fat 1 gram carbohydrate 2 g protein 1 gram sugar 122mg cholesterol

595) *Chicken Breast With Seed Chips*

4 portions Time Required for Cooking: 40 Minutes
Ingredients:

- 12 breast fillets de poulet
- Salt
- 2 Eggs
- 1 teeny-tiny package of seed chips
- Breadcrumbs
- Olive oil extra virgin

Directions:

- ✓ Season chicken fillets with salt.
- ✓ Crush the seed chips and, once they are finely ground, combine them with the breadcrumbs.

- ✓ Two eggs should be beaten.
- ✓ Dredge the chicken breast fillets in the beaten egg and then in the seed chips tied with breadcrumbs.
- ✓ Once all of them are breaded, paint them with an extra virgin olive oil brush.
- ✓ Arrange the fillets in a single layer in the air fryer basket.
- ✓ 170 degrees for 20 minutes.
- ✓ Remove one batch and replace it with another, maintaining the same temperature and duration. Thus, until all the steaks are consumed.

Nutrition: 242 Calories 13g fat 15g Carbohydrates 18g protein 0g sugar 42mg cholesterol

596) *Spaghetti Squash with Turkey Meatballs*

4 portions Time Required for Cooking: 35 Minutes
Ingredients:

- 1 pound ground turkey, lean
- 1 pound spaghetti squash, peeled and half
- 2 beaten egg whites
- 1/3 cup finely chopped green onions
- 1/4 cup onion, finely diced
- 2 1/2 teaspoon s flat-leaf parsley, finely diced
- 1 tbsp. finely chopped fresh basil
- 14 oz. can crushed tomatoes with no additional salt
- 1/3 cup crumbs from soft whole wheat bread
- 1/4 cup chicken broth with a low sodium content
- 1 teaspoon powdered garlic
- 1 teaspoon thyme
- 1 tablespoon oregano
- 1/2 teaspoon crushed red pepper
- 1/2 teaspoon fennel seeds, whole

Directions:

- ✓ Combine bread crumbs, onion, garlic, parsley, pepper flakes, thyme, and fennel in a small bowl.
- ✓ Combine turkey and egg whites in a large mixing basin. Combine bread crumb mixture in a large mixing bowl. Ten minutes before serving, cover, and chill. Preheat the oven to broil.
- ✓ In a glass baking dish, arrange the squash

cut side down. Microwave 3-4 tablespoons water on high for 10-12 minutes, or until fork-tender.

✓ Form the turkey mixture into 20 meatballs and arrange them on a baking sheet. Broil for 4-5 minutes, then turn and cook for an additional 4 minutes.

✓ Combine tomatoes and broth in a large skillet and bring to a simmer over low heat. Combine meatballs, oregano, basil, and green onions in a medium bowl. Cook for 10 minutes, stirring periodically, or until thoroughly cooked.

✓ Scrape the squash into "strands" with a fork and put on a serving dish. Serve with meatballs and sauce on top.

Nutrition: 253 Calories 15g Net Carbohydrates 13g Protein 27g Fat 9g Sugar 4g Fiber 2g

597) *Wraps in Spicy Lettuce*

Time Required for Cooking: 5 Minutes
Ingredients:

- 12 lettuce leaves Romaine
- 1 pound chicken ground
- 1/3 cup thinly sliced green onions
- 2 tsp grated fresh ginger
- 1/3 cup finely sliced water chestnuts
- 1/3 cup chopped peanuts
- 2 cloves garlic, finely sliced
- 3 tablespoons light soy sauce
- cornstarch, 1 tbsp.
- 1 tablespoon (tbsp.) peanut oil
- 1/4 teaspoon   crushed red pepper

Directions:

✓ Combine chicken, ginger, garlic, and pepper flakes in a large bowl.

✓ Combine cornstarch and soy sauce in a small bowl until smooth.

✓ In a large skillet over medium-high heat, heat the oil. Cook, occasionally tossing, for 2-3 minutes, or until chicken is cooked through.

✓ Stir in soy sauce and simmer, constantly stirring, for about 30 seconds, or until mixture begins to thicken. Heat through the water chestnuts, green onions, and peanuts.

✓ Arrange lettuce leaves in a single layer on a work area. Distribute the filling evenly among them and roll them up. Additionally,

the filling can be prepared ahead of time and reheated as needed. Serve immediately with Chinese hot mustard as a dipping sauce

Nutrition: 234 Calories Total Carbohydrates 13g Net Carbohydrates 12 g protein, 26 g fat, 12 g sugar, and 6 g dietary fiber 1g

SOUP AND STEWS

598) *Dried Fruit Squash*

Time required for preparation: 15 minutes Time required for cooking: 40 minutes 4 portions

Ingredients:

- *1/4 cup water*
- *1 medium butternut squash, split and seeded*
- *1/2 tbsp olive oil*
- *1/2 tbsp balsamic vinegar*
- *Salt and freshly crushed black pepper to taste*
- *4 large dates, pitted and chopped*
- *4 fresh figs, chopped*

Directions:

- ✓ *Preheat the oven to 375 degrees Fahrenheit.*
- ✓ *Fill the bottom of a baking dish halfway with water.*
- ✓ *Arrange the squash halves hollow-side up in a large baking dish and sprinkle with oil and vinegar.*
- ✓ *Season with salt and freshly ground black pepper.*
- ✓ *Top with dates, figs, and pistachios.*
- ✓ *Bake for approximately 40 minutes or until the squash is soft.*
- ✓ *Garnish with pumpkin seeds and serve immediately.*

Nutrition: 227 Calories 5 grams total fat 0.8 grams saturated fat Cholesterol 0 mg Sodium 66 mg Carbohydrates in total 46.4 g Fiber Sugar: 7.5 g Protein: 19.6 g 0 g

599) *Curry with Bananas*

15 minutes for preparation Time required for cooking: 15 minutes 3 portions

Ingredients:

- *2 tbsp olive oil*
- *2 chopped yellow onions*
- *8 minced garlic cloves*
- *2 tbsp curry powder*
- *1 tablespoon powdered ginger*
- *1 tablespoon ground cumin*
- *1 teaspoon ground turmeric*
- *1 teaspoon ground cinnamon*
- *1 teaspoon red chili powder*
- *Season with salt and freshly ground black pepper to taste*

- *1 cup tomato puree*
- *2 peeled and sliced bananas*
- *3 coarsely chopped tomatoes*
- *1/4 cup unsweetened coconut flakes*

Direction

- ✓ *In a large skillet over medium heat, heat the oil and sauté the onion for around 4–5 minutes.*
- ✓ *Cook for approximately 1 minute before adding the garlic, curry powder, and spices.*
- ✓ *Bring the soy yogurt and tomato sauce to a mild boil.*
- ✓ *Add the bananas and cook for approximately 3 minutes.*
- ✓ *Add the tomatoes and cook for approximately 1–2 minutes.*
- ✓ *Stir in the coconut flakes and remove them from the heat immediately.*
- ✓ *Serve immediately.*

Nutrition: 382 Calories 18.2 g total fat 6.6 g saturated fat 0 mg cholesterol 108 mg sodium Carbohydrates in total 54 g 13 g Fiber 28 g Sugar 9 g Protein

600) *Curry with Mushrooms*

15 minutes for preparation Time required for cooking: 20 minutes 3 portions

- *2 cups chopped tomatoes*
- *1 chopped green chili*
- *1 teaspoon chopped fresh ginger*
- *1/4 cup cashews*
- *2 tablespoons canola oil*
- *1/2 teaspoon cumin seeds*
- *1/4 teaspoon ground coriander*
- *1/4 teaspoon ground turmeric*
- *1/4 teaspoon red chili powder*
- *1 ½ cups fresh shiitake mushrooms, sliced*
- *1 ½ cups fresh button mushrooms, sliced*
- *Season with salt and freshly ground black pepper to taste*

Directions:

- ✓ *Pulse the tomatoes, green chile, ginger, and cashews in a food processor until smooth paste forms.*
- ✓ *In a saucepan over medium heat, heat the oil and sauté the cumin seeds for about 1 minute.*
- ✓ *Stir in the spices and sauté for approximately 1 minute.*

✓ *Cook for approximately 5 minutes before adding the tomato paste.*

✓ *Bring to a boil, stirring in the mushrooms, maize, water, and coconut milk.*

✓ *Cook, stirring periodically, for approximately 10–12 minutes.*

✓ *Season with salt and freshly ground black pepper to taste and remove from heat.*

✓ *Serve immediately.*

Nutrition: 311 Calories 20.4 g total fat 6.1 g saturated fat 0 mg cholesterol 244 mg sodium Carbohydrates in total 32g Fiber 6g Sugar 9g Protein 8g

601) *Vegetable Combo Mix*

15 minutes for preparation Time required for cooking: 25 minutes 4 portions

- 1 tablespoon olive oil
- 1 small yellow onion, diced
- 1 teaspoon fresh thyme, chopped
- 1 garlic clove, minced
- 8 ounces fresh button mushroom, sliced

Direction

✓ *In a large skillet over medium heat, heat the oil and sauté the onion for around 3–4 minutes.*

✓ *Sauté the thyme and garlic for approximately 1 minute.*

✓ *Cook for approximately 15 minutes or until the mushrooms are caramelized.*

✓ *Cook the Brussels sprouts for around 2–3 minutes.*

✓ *Add the spinach and simmer for approximately 3–4 minutes.*

✓ *Remove from the fire and stir in the walnuts, salt, and black pepper.*

✓ *Serve immediately.*

Nutrition: Calories 153 8.8 g total fat 0.9 g saturated fat 0 mg cholesterol 94 mg sodium Carbohydrates in total: 18 g Fiber, 6.3 g Sugar, 4 g Protein, 8.5 g

602) *Beet Soup*

Time required for preparation: ten minutes Time required for cooking: 5 minutes 2 portions

Ingredients:

- 2 cups coconut yogurt
- 4 teaspoons fresh lemon juice
- 2 cups trimmed, peeled, and diced beets — 2 tablespoons fresh dill
- Salt to taste

Directions:

✓ *Combine all ingredients in a high-speed blender and pulse until smooth.*

✓ *Place the soup in a medium saucepan and cook for approximately 3–5 minutes, or until heated through.*

✓ *Garnish with chives and coconut cream and serve immediately.*

Nutrition: 230 Calories 8 g total fat 8 g saturated fat 0 mg cholesterol 218 mg sodium 35 g Total Carbohydrates 2 g Fiber 27.5 g Protein 8 g

603) *Vegetable Stew*

15 minutes for preparation 30 minutes for cooking 3 portions

Ingredients:

- 2 tablespoons olive oil
- 1 large onion, chopped
- 2 garlic cloves, minced
- 1/4 teaspoon fresh ginger, grated finely
- 1 teaspoon ground cumin
- 1 teaspoon cayenne pepper
- Salt and ground black pepper, to taste

Directions:

✓ *In a large soup pan over medium heat, heat the oil and sauté the onion for around 3–4 minutes.*

✓ *Sauté the garlic, ginger, and spices for approximately 1 minute.*

✓ *Bring 1 cup of the broth to a boil and add.*

✓ *Add the vegetables and bring to a boil once more.*

✓ *Cook, covered, for approximately 15–20 minutes, stirring periodically.*

✓ *Remove from the heat and stir in the lemon juice.*

✓ *Garnish with cashews and lemon zest and serve immediately.*

Nutrition: 425 Calories 32 g total fat 9 g saturated fat 0 mg cholesterol 601 mg sodium Carbohydrates in total 27.6 g Fiber 2 g Sugar 7.1 g Protein 300 g 14 g

604) *Brussels Sprouts with Tofu*

15 minutes for preparation Time required for cooking: 15 minutes 3 servings

- 1 1/2 tbsps olive oil, divided
- 8 ounces extra-firm tofu, drained, pressed, and cut into slices
- 2 garlic cloves, minced
- 1/3 cup walnuts, toasted and chopped
- 1 tablespoon unsweetened applesauce

- *1/4 cup fresh cilantro, chopped*

Directions:

✓ *In a skillet over medium heat, heat 1/2 tbsp of the oil and sauté the tofu for about 6–7 minutes, or until golden brown.*

✓ *Sauté the garlic and pecans for approximately 1 minute.*

✓ *Cook for approximately 2 minutes before adding the applesauce.*

✓ *Remove from heat and stir in the cilantro.*

✓ *Arrange tofu in a single layer on a platter and put it aside.*

✓ *In the same skillet, over medium-high heat, heat the remaining oil and sauté the Brussels sprouts and bell peppers for around 5 minutes.*

✓ *Remove from the fire and stir in the tofu.*

✓ *Immediately serve.*

Nutrition: 0 mg Cholesterol 238 Nutrition: Calories Total Fat 17.8 g Saturated Fat 2 g 26 mg sodium 16 g Total Carbohydrates 8 g Fiber 5 g Sugar 18 g Protein

605) *Peas and Tofu*

15 minutes for preparation Time required for cooking: 20 minutes 5 portions

- *1 tablespoon chili-garlic sauce*

- *3 tablespoons low-sodium soy sauce*

- *2 tablespoons canola oil, divided*

- *1 (16-ounce) package extra-firm tofu, drained, pressed, and cubed*

- *1 cup yellow onion, chopped*

- *1 tablespoon fresh ginger, minced*

- *2 garlic cloves, minced*

- *2 large tomatoes, finely chopped*

Directions:

✓ *To make the sauce, blend the chili-garlic sauce and soy sauce in a bowl until well incorporated.*

✓ *In a large skillet over medium-high heat, heat 1 tablespoon of oil and sauté the tofu for about 4–5 minutes, or until thoroughly browned, stirring periodically.*

✓ *Put the tofu in a basin.*

✓ *In the same skillet, over medium heat, heat the remaining oil and sauté the onion for around 3–4 minutes.*

✓ *Sauté the ginger and garlic for approximately 1 minute.*

✓ *Add the tomatoes and simmer, smashing with the back of a spoon, for approximately*

4–5 minutes.

✓ *Add the remaining three peas and simmer for approximately 2–3 minutes.*

✓ *Cook for approximately 1–2 minutes, stirring in the sauce mixture and tofu.*

✓ *Garnish with sesame seeds and serve immediately.*

Nutrition: 291 Calories 19 g total fat 1 g saturated fat 0 mg cholesterol 732 mg sodium Carbohydrates in total: 36 g Fiber, 10.8 g Sugar, 15 g Protein

606) *Soup with Carrots and Tempeh*

15 minutes for preparation Time required for cooking: 45 minutes 6 portions

- *1/4 cup olive oil, split*

- *1 large yellow onion, chopped*

- *Salt to taste*

- *2 pounds carrots, peeled and sliced into 12-inch rounds*

- *2 teaspoons fresh dill, chopped*

Directions:

✓ *In a large soup pan over medium heat, heat 2 tablespoons of the oil and sauté the onion with the salt for around 6–8 minutes, turning constantly.*

✓ *Stir in the carrots.*

✓ *Reduce to low heat and simmer, covered, for approximately 5 minutes, stirring constantly.*

✓ *Increase the heat to high and add the broth. Bring to a boil.*

✓ *Reduce to low heat and cook, covered, for approximately 30 minutes.*

✓ *Meanwhile, heat the remaining oil in a skillet over medium-high heat and cook the tempeh for approximately 3–5 minutes.*

✓ *Add the dill and simmer for approximately 1 minute.*

✓ *Turn off the heat.*

✓ *Take the soup pan from the heat and whisk in the tomato paste and lemon juice.*

✓ *Blend the soup until smooth and creamy using an immersion blender.*

✓ *1 Serve the soup immediately with the tempeh topping.*

Nutrition: 294 Calories 17 g total fat 8 g saturated fat 0 mg cholesterol Total Carbohydrates 29 g Fiber 9 g Sugar 10.4 g Protein 16.4 g Sodium 723 mg

607) <u>*Tempeh in combination with bell peppers*</u>

15 minutes for preparation Time required for cooking: 15 minutes 3 portions

- 2 tbsp balsamic vinegar
- 2 tbsp low-sodium soy sauce
- 2 tbsp tomato sauce
- 1 tsp maple syrup
- 1/2 tsp garlic powder
- 1/8 teaspoon crushed red pepper flakes
- 1 tablespoon vegetable oil
- 8 ounces cubed tempeh
- 1 medium onion, diced
- 2 large seeded and chopped green bell peppers

Directions:

- ✓ In a small bowl, whisk together the vinegar, soy sauce, tomato sauce, maple syrup, garlic powder, and red pepper flakes. Place aside.
- ✓ In a large skillet over medium heat, heat 1 tablespoon oil and cook the tempeh for about 2–3 minutes per side.
- ✓ Add the onion and bell peppers and cook, occasionally stirring, for approximately 2–3 minutes.
- ✓ Add the sauce mixture and simmer, constantly stirring, for approximately 3–5 minutes.
- ✓ Serve immediately.

Nutrition: Calories 241 13 g total fat 6 g saturated fat 0 mg cholesterol 65 mg sodium Carbohydrates in total 19.7 g Fiber 1 g Carbohydrates 8.1 g Protein 16.1 gram

608) <u>*Medley of Squash*</u>

Time required for preparation: ten minutes.

- 2 pounds mixed squash
- 0.5 cup mixed vegetables
- 1 cup vegetable stock
- 2 tbsp olive oil
- 2 tbsp mixed herbs

Direction

- ✓ In the Instant Pot, place the squash in the steamer basket and the stock in the bottom.
- ✓ Steam the squash for 10 minutes in your Instant Pot.
- ✓ Depressurize and discard the remainder of the stock.

- ✓ Heat the oil in a sauté pan and add the remaining ingredients.
- ✓ Continue cooking until a thin crust forms.

Nutrition: Calories: 100 Carbohydrates: 10 Sugar: 3 6 g fat 5 g protein 20 g carbohydrate

609) <u>*Eggplant Curry*</u>

15 minutes to prepare Time required for cooking: 20 minutes 2 servings

- 2-3 cups chopped eggplant
- 1 thinly sliced onion
- 1 cup coconut milk
- 3 tablespoons curry paste
- 1 tablespoon oil or ghee

Directions:

- ✓ Using the sauté function on the Instant Pot, add the onion, oil, and curry paste.
- ✓ Add the remaining ingredients and close once the onion is tender.
- ✓ Cook for 20 minutes on Stew.
- ✓ Allow the pressure to dissipate naturally.

Nutrition: 350 Calories Carbohydrates: 15 Sugar: 3 Fat: 25 Protein: 11 Glycemic Index: 10

610) <u>*Chickpea Soup*</u>

15 minutes to prepare Time required for cooking: 35 minutes 2 servings

- 1 pound cooked chickpeas
- 1 pound chopped veggies
- 1 cup vegetable broth with a low sodium content
- 2 tbsp mixed herbs

Direction

- ✓ In your Instant Pot, combine all of the ingredients.
- ✓ Cook for 35 minutes on Stew.
- ✓ Allow the pressure to dissipate naturally.

Nutrition: Calories: 310 Carbohydrates: 20 Sugar: 3 Fat: 5 Protein: 27 GL: 5

611) <u>*Chinese veggie mix*</u>

15 minutes for preparation Time required for cooking: 15 minutes 2 servings

- 0.5 pound fried tofu
- 1 pound chopped Chinese veggie mix
- 1 cup vegetable broth with a low salt content
- 2 tbsp five-spice seasoning

- *1 tbsp smoked paprika*

Direction

✓ *In your Instant Pot, combine all of the ingredients.*

✓ *Cook for 15 minutes on Stew.*

✓ *Allow the pressure to dissipate naturally.*

Nutrition: Calories: 320 Carbohydrates: 11 3 sugars 23 fats 47 protein 6 Nutrition: Calories

612) *Pea and Mint Soup*

15 minutes to prepare Time required for cooking: 35 minutes

- *1 pound green peas*
- *2 cups low sodium vegetable broth*
- *3 tbsp mint sauce*

Direction

✓ *In your Instant Pot, combine all of the ingredients.*

✓ *Cook for 35 minutes on Stew.*

✓ *Allow the pressure to dissipate naturally.*

✓ *Puree into a coarse soup.*

Nutrition: Calories: 130 Carbohydrates: 17 Sugar: 4 Fat: 5 Protein: 19 GL: 11

613) *Eggplant and dried lentils*

15 minutes for preparation Time required for cooking: 35 minutes 2 servings

- *1 pound eggplant*
- *1 pound dried lentils*
- *1 cup chopped veggies*
- *1 cup low sodium vegetable broth*

Direction

✓ *In your Instant Pot, combine all of the ingredients.*

✓ *Cook for 35 minutes on Stew.*

✓ *Allow the pressure to dissipate naturally.*

Nutrition: Calories 310 Carbohydrates 22 Sugar 6 Fat 10 Protein 32

614) *Curry with Tofu*

15 minutes for preparation Time required for cooking: 20 minutes 2 portions

- *2 cups cubed extra-firm tofu*
- *2 cups stir-fry vegetables*
- *0.5 cup non-dairy yogurt*
- *3 tablespoons curry paste*
- *1 tablespoon oil or ghee*

Direction

✓ *Activate the saute function on the Instant*

Pot and add the oil and curry paste.

✓ *Once the onion is tender, combine all remaining ingredients except the yogurt in a sealable container.*

✓ *Cook for 20 minutes on Stew.*

✓ *Allow for a natural pressure release and serve with a dollop of soy yogurt.*

Nutrition: Calories: 300 Carbohydrates: 9 Sugar: 4 Fat: 14 Protein: 42 GL: 7

615) *Soy bacon*

15 minutes for preparation Time required for cooking: 25 minutes

- *0.5 pound soy bacon*
- *1 pound chopped veggies*
- *1 cup low sodium vegetable broth*
- *1 tbsp nutritional yeast*

Direction

✓ *In your Instant Pot, combine all of the ingredients.*

✓ *Cook for 25 minutes on Stew.*

✓ *Allow the pressure to dissipate naturally.*

Nutrition: Calories: 200 Carbohydrates: 12 Sugar: 3 Fat: 7 Protein: 41 GL: 5

616) *Lentil and Chickpea Curry*

Time required for cooking: 20 minutes 2 servings

Ingredients:

- *2 cup lentils and chickpeas, dried*
- *1 thinly sliced onion*
- *1 cup diced tomato*
- *3 tbsp curry paste*

Direction

✓ *Using the sauté function on the Instant Pot, add the onion, oil, and curry paste.*

✓ *Add the remaining ingredients and close once the onion is tender.*

✓ *Cook for 20 minutes on Stew.*

✓ *Allow the pressure to dissipate naturally.*

Nutrition: Calories: 360 26 carbohydrate Sucrose: 6 19 g fat 23 g protein 10

617) *Roasted Seitan*

15 minutes for preparation Time required for cooking: 35 minutes

- *1 pound seitan roulade*
- *1 pound chopped winter vegetables*
- *1 cup low sodium vegetable broth*
- *4 tbsp roast rub*

Direction

✓ Rub the roast rub into the roulade.

✓ In your Instant Pot, combine the roulade and vegetables.

✓ Pour in the broth. Seal.

✓ Cook for 35 minutes on Stew.

✓ Allow the pressure to dissipate naturally.

Nutrition: Calories: 260 9 Carbohydrates 2 Sugars 2 Fat 2 Protein 49 GL 4

618) *Tomatoes and Zucchini*

15 minutes for preparation Time Required for Cooking: 11 minutes 8 servings

• 6 medium zucchinis, roughly chopped

• 1 pound cherry tomatoes

• 2 small onions, roughly chopped

• 2 tablespoons fresh basil, chopped

• 1 cup water

• 1 tablespoon olive oil

• 2 garlic cloves, minced

Directions:

✓ Place oil in the Instant Pot and press "Sauté." Cook for approximately 3-4 minutes after adding the onion, garlic, ginger, and spices.

✓ Cook the zucchinis and tomatoes for approximately 1-2 minutes.

✓ Click "Cancel" and add the other ingredients, except the basil.

✓ Snap the lid shut and set the pressure valve to the "Seal" position.

✓ Select "Manual" and cook for approximately 5 minutes under "High Pressure."

✓ Click "Cancel" and then wait for a "Natural" release.

✓ Remove the lid from the container and transfer the vegetable combination to a serving plate.

✓ Serve garnished with basil.

Nutrition: 57 Calories 1g fat 9g Carbohydrates 8g sugar 5 g protein 39mg sodium

619) *Fried Asian Eggplant*

Time Required for Preparation: 10 minutes Time Required for Cooking: 40 minutes 4 portions

• 1 large eggplant, divided into fourths

• 3 green onions, diced, leaving only the green tips

• 1 teaspoon fresh ginger, peeled and finely diced

• 1/4 cup + 1 teaspoon cornstarch

• 1/2 tbsp soy sauce

• 1/2 tbsp sesame oil

• 1 tablespoon vegetable oil

• 1 tablespoon fish sauce

Directions:

✓ Place eggplant on paper towels and season with salt on both sides. Allow 1 hour to evaporate extra moisture. Using additional paper towels, pat dry.

✓ Whisk together soy sauce, sesame oil, fish sauce, Splenda, and 1 teaspoon cornstarch in a small basin.

✓ Coat both sides of the eggplant with the 1/4 cup cornstarch; additional cornstarch may be used if necessary.

✓ In a large skillet, heat oil over medium-high heat. Add 12 ginger and 1 green onion, followed by 2 eggplant slices. 12 of the sauce mixture should be used to coat both sides of the eggplant gently. Cook for approximately 8-10 minutes per side. Repeat.

✓ Garnish with leftover green onions and serve.

Nutrition: Calories 155 Carbohydrates Total 18g Carbohydrates Net 13 grams protein 2 g fat 9 g sugar 6 g dietary fiber 5g

620) *Fritters de beurre noisette*

15 minutes for preparation Time Required for Cooking: 15 minutes 6 portions

• 5 cup shredded butternut squash

• 2 big eggs

• 1 tablespoon finely sliced fresh sage

• 2/3 cup flour

• 2 teaspoons olive oil

Direction

✓ In a large skillet, heat oil over medium-high heat.

✓ In a large mixing basin, combine squash, eggs, sage, and season to taste with salt and pepper. Incorporate flour.

✓ Drop 1/4 cup mixture into skillet, leaving at least 1 inch between fritters. Cook until both sides are golden brown, about 2 minutes per side.

✓ Transfer to a dish lined with paper towels. Repeat. Serve immediately with a dipping *sauce of your choice.*

Nutrition: Calories 164 Carbohydrates Total Carbohydrates 24g Carbohydrates Net Carbohydrates 21g Protein 4 g fat 6 g sugar 3 g dietary fiber 3g

621) *Risotto with Cauliflower and Mushrooms*

Preparation Time: 10 minutes Time Required for Cooking: 30 minutes 2 servings

- *1 medium head shredded cauliflower*
- *8 ounces sliced Porcini mushrooms*
- *1 finely minced yellow onion*
- *2 cup reduced-sodium vegetable broth*
- *2 teaspoon minced garlic*
- *2 teaspoon white wine vinegar*
- *Salt and pepper to taste*

Directions:

✓ *Preheat the oven to 350 degrees Fahrenheit. Prepare a baking sheet by lining it with foil.*

✓ *Spray the mushrooms with cooking spray and arrange them in the prepared pan. Season with salt and toss well to coat. Bake for 10-12 minutes, or until the mushrooms begin to crisp.*

✓ *Coat a big skillet with nonstick cooking spray and heat over medium-high heat. Cook, turning regularly, until the onion is transparent, about 3-4 minutes. Add garlic and cook for an additional 2 minutes, or until golden.*

✓ *Stir in the cauliflower and simmer for 1 minute.*

✓ *Bring the broth to a simmer in a saucepan. Add 14 cups at a time to the skillet, mixing well after each addition.*

✓ *Add vinegar. Reduce to low heat and continue cooking for 4-5 minutes, or until the majority of the liquid has evaporated.*

✓ *Distribute cauliflower mixture among dishes or bowls and garnish with mushrooms. Serve.*

Nutrition: 13 Calories 134 Carbohydrates 10g Fat 22g Protein 0g Sugar 5g Fiber 2g

622) *Chili Sin Carne*

15 minutes for preparation Time required for cooking: 35 minutes 2 portions Ingredients:

- *3 cups cooked mixed beans*
- *2 cups diced tomatoes*

- *1 tbsp yeast extract*
- *2 squares very dark chocolate*

Directions:

✓ *In your Instant Pot, combine all of the ingredients.*

✓ *Cook for 35 minutes on Beans.*

✓ *Allow the pressure to dissipate naturally.*

Nutrition: Calories: 240 Carbohydrates: 20 Sugars: 5 Fats: 3 Proteins: 36 GL: 11

623) *Soup with Meatless Balls*

15 minutes for preparation Time required for cooking: 15 minutes 2 portions

- *1 pound minced tofu*
- *0.5 pound chopped veggies*
- *2 cups low sodium vegetable broth*
- *1 tbsp almond flour*

Directions:

✓ *Combine the tofu, flour, salt, and pepper in a mixing bowl.*

✓ *Assemble the meatballs.*

✓ *In your Instant Pot, combine all of the ingredients.*

✓ *Cook for 15 minutes on Stew.*

✓ *Allow the pressure to dissipate naturally.*

Nutrition: Calories 240 Carbohydrates 9 Sugar 3 Fat 10 Protein 35 GL 5

624) *Curry with Seitan*

15 minutes for preparation Time required for cooking: 20 minutes 0.5 pound seitan

- *1 thinly sliced onion*
- *1 cup chopped tomato*
- *3 tbsp curry paste*
- *1 tbsp oil or ghee*

Direction

✓ *Using the sauté function on the Instant Pot, add the onion, oil, and curry paste.*

✓ *Add the remaining ingredients and close once the onion is tender.*

✓ *Cook for 20 minutes on Stew.*

✓ *Allow the pressure to dissipate naturally.*

Nutrition: Calories: 240 Carbohydrates: 19 Sugar: 4 Fat: 10 Protein: 32 GL: 10

625) *Split Pea Stew*

Time required for preparation: 5 minutes Time required for cooking: 35 minutes

- *1 cup dried split peas*

- *1 pound chopped veggies*
- *1 cup mushroom soup*
- *2 tbsp old bay seasoning*

Direction

- ✓ *In your Instant Pot, combine all of the ingredients.*
- ✓ *Cook for 35 minutes on Beans.*
- ✓ *Allow the pressure to dissipate naturally.*

Nutrition: Calories: 300 Carbohydrates: 7 3 sugars 2 fats 2 protein 4 32 GL: 4

626) *Curry with Mangoes and Tofu*

15 minutes for preparation Time required for cooking: 35 minutes 2 portions

- *1 pound cubed extra firm tofu*
- *1 pound chopped veggies*
- *1 cup low carb mango sauce*
- *1 cup vegetable broth*

Directions:

- ✓ *In your Instant Pot, combine all of the ingredients.*
- ✓ *Cook for 35 minutes on Stew.*
- ✓ *Allow the pressure to dissipate naturally.*

Nutrition: Calories: 310 Carbohydrates: 20 Sugar: 9 4 g fat 37 g protein 19 32 GL: 19

627) *Cauliflower with Alfredo Sauce Vegan*

15 minutes for preparation Time required for cooking: 35 minutes 1 portion

- *1 tablespoon olive oil*
- *2 cloves garlic*
- *1 cup vegetable broth*
- *1/2 teaspoon sea salt*
- *Season with pepper to taste*
- *Chilli flakes: 1 teaspoon*
- *1 medium onion (diced)*
- *4 cups chopped cauliflower florets*
- *1 teaspoon lemon juice (freshly squeezed)*
- *1 tablespoon nutritional yeast*
- *2 tbsp vegan butter*
- *Zucchini noodles: for serving*

Direction

- ✓ *Preheat a cooking pot over low heat. Allow the oil to heat completely before adding more.*
- ✓ *As soon as you're finished, add the chopped onion and place the pan on fire for around*

4 minutes. The onion should have a transparent appearance.

- ✓ *Add the garlic and cook for approximately 30 seconds. Stir constantly to keep them from sticking.*
- ✓ *Add the vegetable broth and cauliflower florets that have been shredded. Assemble the ingredients thoroughly and cover the stockpot with a lid. Allow 5 minutes for the cauliflower to cook before removing it from the heat.*
- ✓ *Using a blender, add the cooked cauliflower. Palpitate the puree until it has a smooth and creamy texture. (If necessary, add 1 tablespoon of broth.)*
- ✓ *In a blender, combine the salt, lemon juice, nutritional yeast, butter, chili flakes, and pepper. Combine all ingredients until smooth purée forms.*
- ✓ *Arrange the zucchini noodles on a serving tray and drizzle the cauliflower Alfredo sauce over them.*

Nutrition: 9.1 g fat 9 g protein 10 g carbohydrate

628) *Sauté of Tomatoes and Zucchini*

15 minutes for preparation Time required for cooking: 35 minutes 6 portions

Ingredients:

- *1 tablespoon vegetable oil*
- *Tomatoes (chopped): 2*
- *Green bell pepper (chopped): 1*
- *Onion (sliced): 1*
- *Zucchini (peeled and cut into 1-inch-thick slices): 2 pounds*
- *Salt to taste*
- *1/4 cup uncooked white rice*

Directions:

- ✓ *Begin by heating a nonstick skillet over low heat. Allow the oil to heat completely before adding more.*
- ✓ *Add the onions and sauté for approximately 3 minutes.*
- ✓ *Add the zucchini and green peppers at this point. Combine thoroughly and season with black pepper and salt.*
- ✓ *Lower the heat to a low setting and cover the pan with a lid. Allow the vegetables to simmer for 5 minutes on low heat.*
- ✓ *While you're at it, add the rice and water. Replace the lid and simmer on low for*

another 20 minutes.
Nutrition: 8 g fat 2 g protein 16.1 g carbohydrate

629) *Steamed Kale with Balsamic Vinaigrette*

15 minutes for preparation Time required for cooking: 35 minutes 6 portions
Ingredients:

- 12 cups kale (chopped)
- 1 tablespoon olive oil
- 1 teaspoon soy sauce
- Ground pepper (freshly ground): to taste
- 2 tbsp. lemon juice
- 1 tablespoon minced garlic
- Salt to taste

Directions:

✓ Fill the bottom pan of a gas or electric steamer halfway with water. If using a gas steamer, set it to high heat. Set an electric steamer to the highest setting.

✓ As soon as the water boils, add the shredded kale and cover it with a lid. Boil for approximately 8 minutes. By now, the kale should be soft.

✓ While the kale is boiling, combine the olive oil, lemon juice, soy sauce, garlic, pepper, and salt in a large mixing bowl. To combine, whisk vigorously.

✓ Add the steamed kale and gently fold it into the dressing. Ascertain that the kale is thoroughly coated.

✓ Serve immediately!
Nutrition: 5 g fat 6 g protein 15 g carbohydrates

630) *Stir-Fried Vegetable Noodles*

Time required for preparation: 5 minutes Time required for cooking: 35 minutes 1 serving
Ingredients:

- 1 pound white sweet potato
- 8 ounces zucchini
- 2 large garlic cloves (finely sliced)
- 2 tbsp vegetable broth
- Salt to taste
- Carrots: 8 oz.
- 1 shallot (finely minced)
- 1 red chili (finely chopped)
- 1 tablespoon olive oil

Directions:

✓ Scrape the carrots and sweet potato first. Make Spiralize the sweet potato and carrots to create noodles.

✓ Thoroughly rinse the zucchini and spiralize it as well.

✓ Heat a big skillet over a high temperature. Add the veggie broth in a stream and bring to a boil.

✓ Toss the spiralized sweet potato and carrots into the mixture. Then add the chili peppers, garlic, and shallots. Using tongs, stir everything together and heat for a few minutes.

✓ Arrange the vegetable noodles on a serving plate and season liberally with salt and pepper.

✓ To finish, drizzle olive oil over the noodles. Serve immediately!
Nutrition: 7 g fat 6 g protein 32 g

631) *Soup with Black Beans and Veggies with Lime Salsa*

15 minutes for preparation Time required for cooking: 35 minutes 1 portion
Ingredients:

- 2 diced onions
- 3 diced celery sticks
- 3 cloves garlic (finely sliced)
- 12 bunch cilantro
- 1 tablespoon dried oregano
- 1/2 tbsp sea salt
- 1 quart boiling water
- 12 tiny salad onions (finely sliced)
- Carrots (diced): 2
- Red bell peppers (diced): 2
- Red chilis (seed removed): 2
- Bay leaf: 1
- 2 cans black beans (drained and rinsed) (15 ounces)
- Tomato (finely chopped): 1
- Lime juice (fresh): 12

Direction

✓ Begin by separating the cilantro leaves and stalks. Shred the stalks and leaves neatly. Set aside

✓ In a big saucepan, add 3 tablespoons of water and bring to a boil. Carrots, onions, bell peppers, celery, red chilies, garlic, coriander stems, oregano, bay leaf, sea salt, and pepper should all be added to this. Combine thoroughly. Cover the pan with a lid and simmer the vegetables for approximately 10 minutes. Continue mixing.

✓ In a saucepan, combine the black beans and boiling water. Continue stirring.

✓ Remove the saucepan's lid and place it over low heat. Allow half a minute for the soup to simmer.

✓ While the soup is being cooked over high heat, prepare the lime salsa. In a small bowl, combine the tomato, salad onion, and cilantro leaves. Incorporate the lime juice that has been freshly squeezed.

✓ Ladle the soup into a large, deep bowl and garnish with lime salsa.

Nutrition: 4 g fat 17.2 g protein 59 g carbohydrate

632) *Soup with Cauliflower and Kabocha Squash*

15 minutes for preparation Time required for cooking: 35 minutes 1 portion
Ingredients:

- 2 tbsp. olive oil
- 3 tbsp. minced garlic
- 212 cups cauliflower florets
- 1/2 teaspoon ground cardamom
- 2 bay leaves
- 1/2 cup unsweetened vanilla almond milk
- 1/4 teaspoon pepper
- Yellow onion (peeled and diced): 12
- 1 tablespoon fresh ginger (minced)
- Kabocha squash cubed: 212 c.
- 1/4 teaspoon cayenne pepper
- 4 cups vegetable broth
- 1/2 teaspoon salt

Directions:

✓ Heat the olive oil in a nonstick saucepan over high heat.

✓ Combine the onion, ginger, and garlic in a bowl. Cook for approximately 3 minutes.

✓ Add the squash, cauliflower, cayenne pepper, bay leaves, and cardamom at this point. Combine thoroughly.

✓ Add the vegetable broth in a steady stream and bring the veggies and stock combination to a boil.

✓ Reduce the heat to low and simmer the

soup for 10 minutes.

✓ Remove the pan and purée the mixture in the blender.

✓ Return the pan to low heat immediately after pureeing the soup. Incorporate the almond milk. Combine thoroughly.

✓ Season with pepper and salt to taste.

Nutrition: 7.7 g fat 4 g protein

633) *Carbohydrate Brussels Sprouts Made Simple*

Time Required for Hash Preparation: 20 minutes
Time Required for Cooking: 10 minutes 4 portions

- 3 tablespoons extra-virgin olive oil
- 1 onion, finely chopped
- 1 pound Brussels sprouts, bottoms clipped and shredded
- 1/2 teaspoon caraway seeds
- 1/2 teaspoon sea salt
- 18 teaspoon freshly crushed black pepper
- 1/4 cup red wine vinegar
- 1 tablespoon Dijon mustard
- 1 tablespoon honey

Directions:

✓ Heat the olive oil in a large skillet over medium-high heat until it shimmers.

✓ Combine the onion, Brussels sprouts, caraway seeds, sea salt, and pepper in a medium mixing bowl. Cook, stirring periodically, for 7 to 10 minutes, or until the Brussels sprouts begin to brown.

✓ Set aside the vinegar, mustard, and honey in a small bowl while the Brussels sprouts cook.

✓ Add the garlic to the skillet and simmer, stirring regularly, for 30 seconds.

✓ To the skillet, add the vinegar mixture. Cook, occasionally stirring, for approximately 5 minutes, or until the liquid has reduced by half.

Nutrition: 176 Calories; 11g protein; 19g total carbohydrate; 8g sugar; 5g fiber; 11g total fat; 1g saturated fat; 0mg cholesterol; 309mg sodium

634) *Asparagus Roasted with Lemon and Pine Nuts*

Time Required for Preparation: 5 minutes Time Required for Cooking: 20 minutes 4 portions

- 1 pound trimmed asparagus

- 2 tablespoons extra-virgin olive oil
- 1 lemon juice
- 1 lemon zest
- 1/4 cup pine nuts
- 1/2 teaspoon   sea salt
- 18 teaspoon freshly ground black pepper

Directions:

✓ Preheat the oven to 425 degrees Fahrenheit.

✓ Toss the asparagus in a large mixing bowl with olive oil, lemon juice and zest, pine nuts, sea salt, and pepper. Spread evenly in a roasting pan.

✓ Roast for approximately 20 minutes, or until the asparagus is golden brown.

Nutrition: 144 Calories; 4g protein; 6g total carbohydrate; 3g sugar; 3g fiber; 13g total fat; 1g saturated fat; 0mg cholesterol; 240mg sodium

635) *Sautéed Spinach with Citrus*

Preparation Time: 5 minutes Time Required for Cooking: 5 minutes 4 portions

2 tbsp extra-virgin olive oil

- 4 tbsp baby spinach
- 1 tsp orange zest
- 1/4 tbsp freshly squeezed orange juice
- 1/2 tsp sea salt
- 18 tsp freshly ground black pepper

Directions:

✓ Heat the olive oil in a large skillet over medium-high heat until it shimmers.

✓ Combine the spinach and orange zest in a medium bowl. Cook, stirring periodically, for approximately 3 minutes, or until the spinach wilts.

✓ Add the orange juice, sea salt, and pepper to taste. Serve immediately.

Nutrition: Calories 74; Protein 7g; Carbohydrates 3g; Sugars 1g; Fiber 1g; Fat 7g; Saturated Fat 1g; Cholesterol 0mg; Sodium 258mg

636) *Mashed Cauliflower*

Time Required for Preparation: 10 minutes Time Required for Cooking: 15 minutes 4 portions

- 4 cups florets
- 1/4 cup skim milk
- 1/4 cup grated Parmesan cheese
- 2 tablespoons butter
- 2 tablespoons extra-virgin olive oil

- 1/2 teaspoon   sea salt
- 18 teaspoon freshly ground black pepper

Directions:

✓ Cover the cauliflower with water and bring it to a boil in a large saucepan over medium-high heat. Reduce to medium-low heat, cover, and cook for approximately 10 minutes, or until the cauliflower is tender.

✓ Return the cauliflower to the pot after draining. Combine the milk, cheese, butter, olive oil, sea salt, and pepper in a medium mixing bowl. Mash until smooth using a potato masher.

Nutrition: Calories: 187; Protein: 7g; Carbohydrates total: 7g; Sugars total: 3g; Fiber total: 3g; Fat total: 16g; Saturated Fat total: 7g; Cholesterol: 26mg; Sodium total: 445mg

637) *Brussels sprouts with ginger and garlic*

Time Required for Preparation: 10 minutes Time Required for Cooking: 11 minutes 4 portions

Ingredients:

- 2 tbsp extra-virgin olive oil
- 2 cups broccoli florets
- 1 tbsp shredded fresh ginger
- 1/2 tsp sea salt
- 18 tsp freshly ground black pepper

Directions:

✓ Heat the olive oil in a large skillet over medium-high heat until it shimmers.

✓ Combine the broccoli, ginger, sea salt, and pepper in a medium bowl. Cook, occasionally turning, for approximately 10 minutes, or until the broccoli is tender and beginning to color.

✓ Add the garlic and cook, constantly stirring, for 30 seconds. Serve immediately after removing from the heat.

Nutrition: 80 Calories; 1g protein; 4g total carbohydrate; 1g sugar; 1g fiber; 0g total fat; 1g saturated fat; 0mg cholesterol; 249mg sodium

638) *Roasted Carrots with Balsamic Vinegar*

Time Required for Preparation: 10 minutes Time Required for Cooking: 30 minutes 4 portions

- 1 ½ pounds carrots, quartered lengthwise
- 2 tablespoons extra-virgin olive oil
- 1/4 teaspoon   sea salt
- 1/8 teaspoon freshly ground black pepper

Directions:

✓ Preheat the oven to 425 degrees Fahrenheit.

✓ Then you have to toss the carrots in a large bowl with the olive oil, sea salt, and pepper. In a roasting pan or on a rimmed baking sheet, arrange in a single layer. Roast for 20–30 minutes or until the carrots have a caramelized appearance.

✓ Toss the salad with vinegar and serve.

Nutrition: Calories: 132; Protein: 1g; Carbohydrates Total: 17g; Sugars Total: 8g; Fiber Total: 4g; Fat Total: 7g; Saturated Fat Total: 1g; Cholesterol: 0mg; Sodium Total: 235mg

639) *Delectable Chicken Soup*

Time Required for Preparation: 10 minutes Time Required for Cooking: 4 hours 30 minutes 4 portions

Ingredients:

- 1 pound boneless and skinless chicken breasts
- 2 tbsp chopped fresh basil
- 1 1/2 cups shredded mozzarella cheese
- 2 minced garlic cloves
- 1 tbsp grated Parmesan cheese
- 2 tbsp dried basil
- 2 cups chicken stock
- 28 oz diced tomatoes
- 1/4 tsp pepper
- 1/2 tsp salt

Directions:

✓ In a crockpot, add chicken, Parmesan cheese, dried basil, tomatoes, garlic, pepper, and salt.

✓ Cook, covered, on low for 4 hours.

✓ Stir in fresh basil and mozzarella cheese.

✓ Replace the lid and cook for a further 30 minutes or until the cheese has melted.

✓ Take the chicken out of the crockpot and shred it with two forks.

✓ Then you have to stir the chicken cut into strips in the crock pot.

✓ Assemble and serve.

Nutrition: 299 Calories 16 g fat 9.3 g Sucrose Protein: 6 g 108 mg Cholesterol 38.8 g

640) *Delicious Broccoli Soup*

Time Required: 10 minutes Time Required for Cooking: 4 hours 15 minutes 6 portions

Ingredients:

- 20 ounces broccoli florets
- 4 ounces cream cheese
- 8 ounces shredded cheddar cheese
- 1/2 teaspoon paprika
- 1/2 teaspoon dried mustard
- 3 cups chicken stock
- 2 garlic cloves, minced
- 1 onion, diced
- 1 cup carrots, shredded

Direction

✓ In a crockpot, combine all ingredients except the cream cheese and cheddar cheese and stir thoroughly.

✓ Cook, covered, on low for 4 hours.

✓ Now, with an immersion blender, blend the soup until smooth.

✓ Combine the cream cheese and cheddar cheese in a separate bowl.

✓ Cover and continue cooking on low for an additional 15 minutes.

✓ Season with salt and pepper to taste.

✓ Assemble and serve.

Nutrition: Calories 275 19.9 g of fat 19 g of carbohydrate 19 g of sugar 4 g of protein 14 g of cholesterol 60 mg

641) *Healthy Chicken Kale Soup*

Time Required for Preparation: 10 minutes Time Required for Cooking: 6 hours 15 minutes 6 portions

- 2 lb skinless and boneless chicken breasts
- 1/4 cup fresh lemon juice
- 5 oz baby kale
- 32 oz chicken stock
- 1/2 cup olive oil
- 1 large onion, sliced

Direction

✓ In a medium saucepan, heat the extra-virgin olive oil.

✓ Sprinkle chicken with salt and set in a heated skillet.

✓ Cook chicken covered in the pan for 15 minutes.

✓ Carefully remove the chicken from the pan and shred it with two forks.

✓ Place shredded chicken in a slow cooker.

✓ In a blender, combine the cut onion, olive oil, and broth.

✓ *Transfer the combined mixture to the crock cooker.*

✓ *Stir in the remaining ingredients in the crock cooker.*

✓ *Cook, covered, on low heat for 6 hours.*

✓ *10. Serve immediately after vigorously stirring.*

Nutrition: Calories 493 Fat 33 Carbohydrates 8 Sugar 9 Protein 46.7 Nutrition: Calories 135 mg Cholesterol

642) *Spicy Chicken Pepper Stew*

Time Required for Preparation: 10 minutes Time Required for Cooking: 6 hours 6 portions

- *3 skinless and boneless chicken breasts, chopped into small pieces*
- *1 tsp minced garlic*
- *1 tsp ground ginger*
- *2 tbsp olive oil*
- *2 tbsp soy sauce*
- *1 tbsp freshly squeezed lemon juice*
- *1/2 cup sliced green onions*
- *1 tbsp crushed red pepper*
- *8 oz chicken stock*
- *1 chopped bell pepper*
- *1 sliced green chili pepper*
- *2 sliced jalapeno peppers*
- *1/2 tsp black pepper*
- *1/4 tsp sea salt*

Direction

✓ *In a large mixing basin, combine all ingredients and whisk well. Refrigerate overnight.*

✓ *Transfer marinated chicken mixture to a slow cooker.*

✓ *Cook, covered, on low heat for 6 hours.*

✓ *Serve immediately after vigorously stirring.*

Nutrition: 171 Calories 7.4 g fat 7 g Sucrose Protein: 7 g Cholesterol 22 g 65 milligram

643) *Beef Chili*

Time Required for Preparation: 10 minutes Time Required for Cooking: 8 hours 6 portions

- *1 pound ground beef*
- *1 tsp garlic powder*
- *1 tsp paprika*
- *3 tsp chili powder*

- *1 tbsp Worcestershire sauce*
- *1 tbsp chopped fresh parsley*
- *25 oz chopped tomatoes*
- *4 oz chopped carrots*
- *1 oz diced onion*
- *1 oz sliced bell pepper*

Directions:

✓ *In a large skillet over high heat, brown the ground beef until no longer pink.*

✓ *Place meat in a slow cooker.*

✓ *In the crockpot, combine bell pepper, tomatoes, carrots, and onion.*

✓ *Stir in the other ingredients until completely combined.*

✓ *Cook, covered, on low for 8 hours.*

✓ *Assemble and serve.*

Nutrition: 152 Calories, 4 g fat, 10.4 g carbohydrate, 8 g sugar, 8 g protein Cholesterol: 18.8 g 51 mg

644) *Delectable Basil Tomato Soup*

Time Required: 10 minutes Time Required for Cooking: 6 hours 6 portions

- *28 oz can whole peeled tomatoes*
- *1/2 cup fresh basil leaves*
- *4 cups chicken stock*
- *1 tsp red pepper flakes*
- *3 peeled garlic cloves*
- *2 chopped onions*
- *3 peeled and sliced carrots*

Directions:

✓ *In a crockpot, combine all ingredients and stir well.*

✓ *Cook, covered, on low for 6 hours.*

✓ *Using an immersion blender, puree the soup until smooth.*

✓ *Season soup with freshly ground pepper and salt.*

✓ *Distribute and enjoy.*

Nutrition: Calories: 126 Fat: 7.5 Carbohydrates: 13 Sugar: 7 Protein: 7 5 g 0 mg cholesterol

645) *Spinach Soup for a Healthy Diet*

Preparation Time: 10 minutes Time Required for Cooking: 3 hours 8 servings

- *3 cups frozen spinach, diced, thawed, and drained*
- *8 oz shredded cheddar cheese*

- *1 softly beaten egg*
- *10 oz can cream of chicken soup*
- *8 oz softened cream cheese*

Directions:

✓ *In a large mixing basin, combine spinach. Spinach, puréed*

✓ *To the spinach purée, whisk together the egg, chicken soup, cream cheese, and pepper.*

✓ *Place spinach mixture in a slow cooker.*

✓ *Cook, covered, on low heat for 3 hours.*

✓ *Remove from heat and stir in cheddar cheese.*

Nutrition: Calories 256 Carbohydrates 29 g 11 g Protein 1 g Sugar 0.5 g Cholesterol 84 mg

646) *Mexican Chicken Soup*

Time Required for Preparation: 10 minutes Time Required for Cooking: 4 hours 6 portions

- *1 1/2 pound skinless and boneless chicken thighs*
- *14 ounce chicken stock*
- *14 oz salsa*
- *8 oz shredded Monterey Jack cheese*

Directions:

✓ *Place chicken in a slow cooker.*

✓ *Distribute the remaining ingredients evenly over the chicken.*

✓ *Cook, covered, on high for 4 hours.*

✓ *Take the chicken out of the crockpot and shred it with forks.*

✓ *Stir the shredded chicken back into the crock cooker.*

✓ *Assemble and serve.*

Nutrition: Calories 371 19.5 g fat 7 g carbohydrate 2 g sugar 41 g protein 135 mg cholesterol

647) *Beef Stew*

Preparation Time: 10 minutes Time Required for Cooking: 5 hours and 5 minutes 8 servings

Ingredients:

- *3 lb trimmed beef stew meat*
- *1/2 cup red curry paste*
- *1/3 cup tomato paste*
- *13 oz can coconut milk*
- *2 tsp minced ginger*
- *2 tsp minced garlic cloves*
- *1 medium onion, sliced*

- *2 tbsp olive oil*
- *2 cups julienned carrots*
- *2 cups broccoli florets*
- *2 tsp fresh lime juice*
- *2 tbsp fish sauce*
- *2 tsp*

Directions:

✓ *In a medium saucepan, heat 1 tablespoon oil over medium heat.*

✓ *In a large skillet, brown the meat on all sides.*

✓ *Place brown meat in a slow cooker.*

✓ *In the same pan, add the remaining oil and sauté the ginger, garlic, and onion for 5 minutes over medium-high heat.*

✓ *Stir in coconut milk thoroughly.*

✓ *Spoon pan mixture into crockpot.*

✓ *Stir in the remaining ingredients, excluding the carrots and broccoli.*

✓ *Cook covered on high for 5 hours.*

✓ *During the final 30 minutes of simmering, add carrots and broccoli.*

✓ *10. Assemble and serve.*

Nutrition: Calories 537 28.6 g fat 13 g carbohydrate 16 g sugar 54 g protein 152 mg cholesterol

648) *Creamy Broccoli Cauliflower Soup*

10 minutes to prepare Time Required for Cooking: 6 hours 6 portions

- *2 cups chopped cauliflower florets*
- *3 cups chopped broccoli florets*
- *3 1/2 cups chicken stock*
- *1 big sliced carrot*
- *1/2 cup diced shallots*
- *2 minced garlic cloves*
- *6 ounces shredded cheddar cheese*
- *1 cup coconut milk*
- *PEPPER*

Directions:

✓ *In a crockpot, combine all ingredients except the milk, cheese, and yogurt and stir thoroughly.*

✓ *Cook, covered, on low for 6 hours.*

✓ *Using an immersion blender, puree the soup until smooth.*

✓ *In a blender, combine the cheese, milk, and yogurt until smooth and creamy.*

✓ *Season with salt and pepper to taste.*

✓ *Assemble and serve.*

Nutrition: 281 Calories, 20 g fat, 14 g carbohydrate, 6.9 g sugar, 6.9 g protein Cholesterol 32 mg 11 g

649) *Squash Soup*

Preparation Time: 10 minutes Time Required for Cooking: 8 hours 6 portions

- *2 lb butternut squash, peeled and chunked*
- *1 tsp minced ginger*
- *1/4 tsp cinnamon*
- *1 tbsp curry powder*
- *2 bay leaves*
- *1 tsp black pepper*
- *2 carrots, peeled, cored, and diced*
- *2 apples, peeled, cored, and diced*

Direction

✓ *Now you need to coat the inside of a crock pot with cooking spray.*

✓ *In the crockpot, combine all ingredients except the cream and mix well.*

✓ *Cook, covered, on low for 8 hours.*

✓ *Using an immersion blender, puree the soup until smooth and creamy.*

✓ *Add heavy cream and season with pepper and salt to taste.*

✓ *Assemble and serve.*

Nutrition: 170 Calories Carbohydrates 4 g Sugar 34 g Protein 14 g 14 mg Cholesterol 9 g

650) *Herb Tomato Soup*

Time Required for Preparation: 10 minutes Time Required for Cooking: 6 hours 8 portions

- *55 oz diced tomatoes*
- *1/2 chopped onion*
- *2 cups chicken stock*
- *1 cup half and half*
- *4 tbsp butter*
- *1 bay leaf 1/2 tsp black pepper*
- *1/2 tsp garlic powder*
- *1 tsp oregano*
- *1 tsp dried thyme*
- *1 cup diced carrots*

Direction

✓ *In a crockpot, combine all ingredients and stir well.*

✓ *Cook, covered, on low for 6 hours.*

✓ *Discard bay leaf and puree soup until smooth with an immersion blender.*

✓ *Assemble and serve.*

Nutrition: Calories 145 9.4 g fat 19 g carbohydrate 7.9 g sugar 26 mg Cholesterol 2 g

651) *Simple Beef Mushroom Stew*

Time Required: 10 minutes Time Required for Cooking: 8 hours 8 portions

- *2 pound cubed stewing meat*
- *1 packet dry onion soup mix*
- *4 ounces sliced mushrooms*
- *14 ounces cream of mushroom soup*
- *1/2 cup water*
- *1/4 teaspoon black pepper*
- *1/2 teaspoon salt*

Direction

✓ *Now you need to coat the inside of a crock pot with cooking spray.*

✓ *In the crockpot, combine all ingredients and mix well.*

✓ *Cook, covered, on low for 8 hours.*

✓ *Serve immediately after vigorously stirring.*

Nutrition: Calories: 237 Fat: 8.5 Carbohydrates: Sugar: 7 g Protein: 0.4 g Cholesterol: 31 g 101 mg

652) *Lamb Stew*

Preparation Time: 10 minutes Time Required for Cooking: 8 hours 2 servings

Ingredients:

- *1/2 pound boneless and cubed lean lamb*
- *2 tbsp lemon juice*
- *1/2 onion, diced*
- *2 garlic cloves, minced*
- *2 fresh thyme sprigs*
- *1/4 tsp turmeric*
- *1/4 cup sliced green olives*

Direction

✓ *In a crockpot, combine all ingredients and stir well.*

✓ *Cook, covered, on low for 8 hours.*

✓ *Serve immediately after a thorough stirring.*

Nutrition: Calories 297 20.3 g fat 4 g carbohydrate 5 g sugar Cholesterol: 21 g 80 mg

653) *Chicken Soup with Vegetables*

Preparation Time: 10 minutes Time Required for Cooking: 6 hours 6 portions

- 4 cups chicken, boneless, skinless, cooked and diced
- 4 tsp garlic, minced
- 2/3 cup onion, diced
- 1 1/2 cup carrot, diced
- 6 cups chicken stock
- 2 tbsp lime juice
- 1/4 cup jalapeno pepper, diced
- 1/2 cup tomatoes, diced
- 1/2 cup fresh cilantro, chopped

Direction

- ✓ In a crockpot, combine all ingredients and stir well.
- ✓ Cook, covered, on low for 6 hours.
- ✓ Serve immediately after a thorough stirring.

192 Nutrition: Calories, 8 g fat, 9.8 g carbohydrate, 7 g sugar, 29.2 g protein, 72 mg cholesterol

654) *Avocado & Zucchini Cream Soup*

15 minutes for preparation Time Required for Cooking: 20 minutes 2 servings

Ingredients:

- 3 tbsp vegetable oil
- 1 chopped leek
- 1 sliced rutabaga
- 3 cups chopped zucchini
- 1 chopped avocado
- Salt and black pepper to taste
- 4 cups vegetable broth
- 2 tbsp chopped fresh mint

Directions:

- ✓ In a saucepan, sauté leek, zucchini, and rutabaga for approximately 7-10 minutes in heated oil. Season with freshly ground black pepper and salt. Bring broth to a boil and add. Reduce to low heat and cook for 20 minutes.
- ✓ Remove from the heat source. Blend the soup and avocado in batches in a blender. Blend until smooth and creamy. Arrange in bowls and garnish with fresh mint.

Nutrition: 378 Calories 25g fat, 9.3g net carbs, 8.2g protein

655) *Chinese Tofu Soup*

Time Required for Preparation: 5 minutes Time Required for Cooking: 10 minutes

- 2 cups chicken stock
- 1 tbsp. sugar-free soy sauce
- 2 spring onions, diced
- 1 tbsp melted sesame oil
- 1 inch grated ginger
- Salt and black ground pepper to taste
- 12 pound cubed extra-firm tofu

Directions:

- ✓ Bring soy sauce, chicken stock, and sesame oil to a boil in a saucepan over medium heat. Add eggs and beat until thoroughly incorporated. Reduce to low heat and add the salt, spring onions, black pepper, and ginger; continue cooking for 5 minutes. Stir in tofu and cook for 1–2 minutes.
- ✓ Divide among soup bowls and top with fresh cilantro.

Nutrition: Calories 163; Fat 10g; Carbohydrates 4g; Protein 15g

656) *Delicious Chicken Enchilada Soup*

Time Required for Cooking: 30 minutes 4 portions

- 2 tbsp coconut oil
- 1 pound boneless, skinless chicken thighs
- 3/4 cup sugar-free red enchilada sauce
- 1/4 cup water
- 1/4 cup onion, chopped
- 3 oz canned diced green chilis
- 1 avocado, sliced
- 1 cup cheddar cheese, shredded

Directions:

- ✓ Preheat a large skillet over medium heat. Combine with coconut oil and warm. Cook until the chicken is browned on the outside, then add the onion, chilies, water, and enchilada sauce and cover with a lid.
- ✓ Simmer for 20 minutes or until the chicken is thoroughly cooked.
- ✓ In a serving bowl, spoon the soup and top with the sauce, cheese, sour cream, tomato, and avocado.

Nutrition: Calories: 643, Fat: 42g, Carbohydrates: 9.7g, Protein: 48g

657) Soup with Curried Shrimp and Green Beans

Time Required for Preparation: 10 minutes Time Required for Cooking: 10 minutes 4 portions
Ingredients:

- 1 onion, diced
- 2 tbsp red curry paste
- 2 tbsp butter
- 1 pound jumbo shrimp, peeled and deveined
- 2 tbsp ginger-garlic puree
- 1 cup coconut milk
- Salt and pepper to taste

Direction

✓ In a saucepan over medium heat, melt the butter and add the shrimp. Season with salt and pepper and cook until they are opaque about 2 to 3 minutes. Transfer to a serving plate. Sauté for 2 minutes, or until the ginger-garlic puree, onion, and red curry paste are fragrant.

✓ Add the coconut milk and shrimp, along with the salt, chile pepper, and green beans. 4 minutes in the oven. Reduce to a simmer and cook for an additional 3 minutes, stirring regularly. Season with salt to taste, ladle soup into serving bowls, and garnish with cilantro.

Nutrition: Calories 351, Fat 34g, Carbohydrates 2g, Protein 7.7g

658) Chicken Soup with Spinach and Basil

Preparation Time: 5 minutes Time Required for Cooking: 10 minutes 4 portions
Ingredients:

- 1 cup spinach
- 2 cups cooked and shredded chicken
- 4 cups chicken broth
- 1 cup shredded cheddar cheese
- 4 ounces cream cheese
- Season with salt and freshly ground black pepper to taste

Directions:

✓ In a saucepan, combine the chicken stock and spinach and bring to a boil. Reduce to low heat and cook for 5-8 minutes. Transfer to a food processor and pulse until smooth. Transfer the mixture to a saucepan and heat over medium heat. Raise to a boil and cook until heated, but do not bring to a boil.

✓ Cook for approximately 3-5 minutes, or until the chicken, chili powder, and cumin are heated through.

✓ Season with salt and pepper and stir in cheddar cheese. Serve immediately in dishes garnished with parsley.
Nutrition: 35 24g fat, 3g net carbs, 26g protein

659) Sausage & Turnip Soup

Time Required for Preparation: 20 minutes Time Required for Cooking: 20 minutes 4 portions

- 3 chopped turnips
- 2 chopped celery sticks
- 2 tbsp butter
- 1 tbsp olive oil
- 1 sliced pork sausage
- 2 cups vegetable broth
- 1/2 cup sour cream
- 3 chopped green onions
- 2 cups water

Directions:

✓ In a medium saucepan, sauté the green onions in melted butter until tender and golden, about 3-4 minutes. Cook for an additional 5 minutes before adding the celery and turnip. Pour veggie broth and water over the top.

✓ Bring to a boil, reduce to low heat, cover, and cook for approximately 20 minutes, or until the veggies are cooked. Take the pan off the heat. Using a hand blender, puree the soup until smooth. Season with sour cream and sour cream. In a skillet, warm the olive oil. Cook for 5 minutes before adding the pork sausage. To serve, ladle the soup into deep bowls and garnish with pig sausage.
Nutrition: Calories 275, 21g fat, 6.4g net carbs, 7.4g protein

660) Cream Soup with Mushrooms and Herbs

Time Required for Preparation: 10 minutes Time Required for Cooking: 15 minutes 4 portions

- 1 onion, chopped
- 1/2 cup crème fraiche
- 1/4 cup butter
- 12 oz white mushrooms, chopped

- *1 tsp thyme leaves, chopped*
- *1 tsp parsley leaves, chopped*
- *1 tsp cilantro leaves, chopped*
- *2 garlic cloves, minced*

Directions:

✓ *In a large saucepan over high heat, melt the butter, onion, and garlic until soft, about 3 minutes. Cook for 10 minutes, adding mushrooms, salt, and pepper. Bring to a boil the broth.*

✓ *Reduce to low heat and continue simmering for 10 minutes. Using a hand blender, puree the soup until smooth. Incorporate crème fraiche. Before serving, garnish with herbs.*

Nutrition: Calories: 213 18g fat Carbohydrates net: 1g 1g protein

661) *Broccoli & Spinach Soup*

Time Required for Preparation: 5 minutes Time Required for Cooking: 20 minutes 4 portions

- *2 tbsp butter*
- *1 onion, diced*
- *1 garlic clove, minced*
- *2 heads broccoli, cut in florets*
- *2 celery stalks, chopped*
- *4 cups vegetable broth*
- *1 cup baby spinach*
- *Shaved Parmesan cheese*

Directions:

✓ *In a saucepan over medium heat, melt the butter. For 3 minutes, sauté the garlic and onion until softened. Cook for 4 minutes, or until the broccoli and celery are somewhat soft. Add the broth, bring to a boil, then reduce to medium-low heat and cover and simmer for around 5 minutes.*

✓ *Add the spinach to wilt, season with salt and pepper, and simmer for 4 minutes. The soup should be ladled into serving bowls. Sprinkle with grated Parmesan cheese and chopped basil before serving.*

Nutrition: Calories 123 Fat 11g Carbohydrates Protein 2g 8g

662) *Soup with Cheese, Chicken, and Cilantro*

Time Required for Preparation: 5 minutes Time Required for Cooking: 10 minutes 4 portions

- *1 chopped carrot*
- *1 chopped onion*
- *2 cups cooked and shredded chicken*
- *3 tbsp butter*
- *4 cups chicken broth*
- *2 tbsp cilantro, chopped*
- *1/2 tbsp . cream cheese*
- *Season with salt and freshly ground black pepper to taste*

Directions:

✓ *Melt butter in a skillet over medium heat and sauté carrots and onion for about 5 minutes, or until soft.*

✓ *Combine with buffalo sauce and cream cheese in a food processor until smooth. Transfer to a saucepan, add the chicken broth, and heat until heated but not boiling. Cook until chicken is heated through, stirring in chicken, salt, and pepper. When ready to serve, transfer to soup bowls and garnish with cilantro.*

Nutrition: Calories 487, Fat 41g, Carbohydrates 7.2g, Protein 16.3g

663) *Thick Creamy Broccoli Cheese Soup*

10 minutes to prepare Time Required for Cooking: 10 minutes 4 portions

Ingredients:

- *1 tbsp olive oil*
- *2 tbsp peanut butter*
- *3/4 cup heavy cream*
- *1 diced onion*
- *1 minced garlic clove*
- *4 cups chopped broccoli*
- *4 cups vegetarian broth*
- *2 3/4 cup cheddar cheese, shredded*
- *1/4 cup cheddar cheese to garnish*

Direction

✓ *In a small saucepan over medium heat, warm the olive oil and peanut butter. Cook, stirring periodically, for 3 minutes or until onion and garlic are soft. Season with salt and freshly ground black pepper to taste. Bring the stock and broccoli to a boil.*

✓ *Reduce to low heat and continue simmering for 10 minutes. Using a hand blender, puree the soup until smooth. Cook for approximately 1 minute before adding the cheese. Incorporate the heavy cream. Serve in dishes garnished with shredded*

cheddar cheese and fresh mint.
Nutrition: Calories 552; Fat 49.5g; Carbohydrates 6.9g; Protein 25g

664) *Vegetarian Crock Pot Split Pea Soup*

Preparation Time: 10 minutes Time Required for Cooking: 10 minutes 8 portions

- *2 chopped celery ribs*
- *2 cubes low-sodium bouillon*
- *8 cup water*
- *2 cup uncooked green split peas*
- *3 bay leaves*
- *2 carrots*
- *2 chopped potatoes*

Direction

- ✓ *Place the bouillon cubes, split peas, and water in the Crock-Pot. Stir briefly to disperse the bouillon cubes.*
- ✓ *Add the potatoes, celery, and carrots, along with the bay leaves.*
- ✓ *Combine thoroughly by stirring.*
- ✓ *Cover and simmer on the low setting of your Crock-Pot for at least 4 hours, or until the green split peas are tender.*
- ✓ *Season with salt and pepper to taste.*
- ✓ *Remove the bay leaves before serving and enjoy.*

Nutrition: Calories: 149; Fat: 1 g; Carbohydrates: 30 g; Protein: 7 g; Sugars: 3 g; Sodium: 732 mg

665) *Rhubarb Stew*

Time Required to Prepare: 5 minutes Time Required for Cooking: 10 minutes 3 portions

- *1 tsp. grated lemon zest*
- *12 c. coconut sugar*
- *1 lemon juice*
- *1/2 cup water*
- *4 1/2 cup rhubarb, roughly chopped*

Direction

- ✓ *In a saucepan, add the rhubarb, water, fresh lemon juice, lemon zest, and coconut sugar; stir to blend. Bring to a simmer over medium heat and cook for 5 minutes. Divide into bowls and serve cool.*
- ✓ *Enjoy!*

Nutrition: 108 Calories 1 g fat, 8 g carbohydrate, 5 g protein, 2 g sugar, 0 mg sodium

666) *Tofu Soup*

Time Required for Preparation: 5 minutes Time Required for Cooking: 10 minutes 8 portions

- *1 pound cubed extra-firm tofu*
- *3 diced big carrots*
- *8 cups low-sodium vegetable broth*
- *1/2 tsp freshly ground white pepper*
- *8 minced garlic cloves*
- *6 sliced and split scallions*
- *4 oz. sliced mushrooms*

Directions:

- ✓ *In a stockpot, pour the broth. Combine all ingredients except the tofu and the final two scallions. Bring to a boil in a heavy saucepan over high heat.*
- ✓ *Once the water is boiling, add the tofu. Reduce to low heat, cover, and cook for 5 minutes.*
- ✓ *Remove from heat, spoon soup into serving cups, and garnish with remaining scallion slices. Serve right away.*

Nutrition: 91 Calories, 3 g fat, 8 g carbohydrate, 6 g protein, 4 g sugar, 900 mg sodium

667) *Easy Beef Stew*

Time Required for Preparation: 5 minutes Time Required for Cooking: 5 minutes 6 portions

- *1 shredded green cabbage head*
- *4 chopped carrots*
- *2 12 lbs. non-fat beef brisket*
- *3 chopped garlic cloves*
- *Black pepper*
- *2 bay leaves*

Directions:

- ✓ *In a large saucepan, combine the beef brisket, stock, pepper, garlic, and bay leaves. Bring to a simmer over medium heat and cook for an hour.*
- ✓ *Stir in carrots and cabbage and continue cooking for another half hour. Divide into dishes and serve for lunch.*
- ✓ *Enjoy!*

Nutrition: Calories: 271; Fat: 8 g; Carbohydrates: 16 g; Protein: 9 g; Sugars: 4 g; Sodium: 760 mg

668) *Zucchini-Basil Soup*

Time Required for Preparation: 20 minutes Time Required for Cooking: 10 minutes 5 portions

- *1/3 cup packed basil leaves*

- *3/4 cup chopped onion*
- *1/4 cup olive oil*
- *2 pound trimmed and sliced zucchini*
- *2 chopped garlic cloves*

Directions:

✓ *Peel and julienne half of the zucchini; combine with 1/2 teaspoon salt and drain in a colander for at least 20 minutes, or until wilted. Chop the remaining zucchini coarsely.*

✓ *In a saucepan over medium-low heat, cook onion and garlic in oil, stirring periodically until onions are transparent. Cook, occasionally stirring, adding the diced zucchini and 1 teaspoon salt.*

✓ *Add 3 cups water and cook, uncovered, until soft. In a blender, combine the soup and basil.*

✓ *In a small saucepan, bring the remaining cup of water to a boil and blanch julienned zucchini. Drain.*

✓ *Garnish soup with thinly sliced zucchini. Serve soup seasoning with salt and pepper.*

Nutrition: 169.3 Calories, 17 g fat, 12 g carbohydrate, 2 g protein, 8 g sugars, 8 mg sodium

669) **Black Bean Soup**

Time Required for Preparation: 10 minutes Time Required for Cooking: 10 minutes 4 portions

Ingredients:

- *1 tsp. cinnamon powder*
- *32 oz. chicken stock with reduced sodium*
- *1 chopped yellow onion*
- *1 chopped sweet potato*
- *38 oz. canned black beans, no salt added, drained and rinsed*

Directions:

✓ *In a medium saucepan, heat the oil over medium heat. Add the onion and cinnamon and simmer, occasionally stirring, for 6 minutes.*

✓ *Stir in black beans, stock, and sweet potato; cook for 14 minutes. Puree with an immersion blender until smooth; divide into bowls and serve for lunch.*

✓ *Enjoy!*

Nutrition: Calories: 221; Fat: 3 g; Carbohydrates: 15 g; Protein: 7 g; Sugars: 4 g; Sodium: 511 mg

670) **Soup with Chicken and Dill**

Preparation Time: ten minutes Time Required for Cooking: 10 minutes 6 portions

- *1 cup chopped yellow onion*
- *1 entire chicken*
- *1 pound sliced carrots*
- *6 cup low-sodium veggie stock*
- *1/4 teaspoon   black pepper and salt*
- *1/2 cup chopped red onion*
- *2 teaspoon chopped dill*

Direction

✓ *Place chicken in a pot, cover with enough water to cover, bring to a boil over medium heat, cook for one hour, transfer to a chopping board, discard bones, shred the meat, strain the soup, return it to the pot, bring to a boil over medium heat, and add the chicken.*

✓ *Add the carrots, yellow onion, red onion, a bit of salt, black pepper, and dill, and simmer for another fifteen minutes. Ladle into bowls and serve.*

✓ *Enjoy!*

Nutrition: Calories: 202; Fat: 6 g; Carbohydrates: 8 g; Protein: 12 g; Sugars: 6 g; Sodium: 514 mg

671) **Cherry Stew**

Time Required for Preparation: 10 minutes Time Required for Cooking: 10 minutes 6 portions

- *2 cup water*
- *1/2 cup supercharged cocoa*
- *1/4 cup coconut sugar*
- *1 pound pitted cherries*

Directions:

✓ *In a saucepan, combine the cherries, water, sugar, and hot chocolate mix; stir and cook for ten minutes over medium heat. Divide into dishes and serve cold.*

✓ *Enjoy!*

Nutrition: 207 Nutrition: Calories, 1 g fat, 8 g carbs, 6 g protein, 27 g sugars, 19 mg sodium

672) **Sirloin Carrot Soup**

Time Required for Preparation: 10 minutes Time Required for Cooking: 10 minutes 6 portions

- *1 pound chopped carrots and celery*
- *32 oz. low-sodium beef stock*
- *1/3 cup whole-wheat flour*
- *1 pound ground beef sirloin*

- *1 tbsp. olive oil*

Direction

✓ *In a saucepan over medium-high heat, heat the olive oil; add the meat and flour.*

✓ *Cook, constantly stirring, for 4-5 minutes, or until browned.*

✓ *Add the celery, onion, carrots, and stock and bring to a boil, stirring occasionally.*

✓ *Reduce to low heat and simmer for 12-15 minutes.*

✓ *Serve immediately.*

Nutrition: Calories: 140, Fat: 5 g, Carbohydrates: 16 g, Protein: 9 g, Carbohydrates: 16 g, Sugars: 3 g, Sodium: 670 mg

673) *Easy Wonton Soup*

Time Required for Preparation: 10 minutes Time Required for Cooking: 20 minutes 6 portions

- *4 chopped onions*
- *1/4 tsp ground white pepper*
- *2 cup sliced fresh mushrooms*
- *4 minced garlic cloves*
- *12 lb. lean ground pork*
- *1 tbsp. fresh ginger, minced*

Directions:

✓ *Preheat a stockpot over a medium heat source. Cook for 5 minutes before adding the ground pork, ginger, and garlic. Remove any extra fat and return to the stovetop.*

✓ *Increase the heat to high and add the broth. When the water is boiling, add the mushrooms, noodles, and white pepper. Cover and cook on low heat for 10 minutes.*

✓ *Turn off the heat and remove the saucepan from the heat. Serve immediately after stirring in the scallions.*

Nutrition: 143 Calories 4 g fat, 14 g carbohydrate, 12 g protein, 0.8 g sugar,

674) *Soup with Beef and Mushrooms*

Preparation Time: 10 minutes Time Required for Cooking: 1 hour and 20 minutes 6 portions

- *1/2 cup pearl barley*
- *1 cup water*
- *4 cups low-sodium beef broth*
- *1/2 teaspoon dried thyme*
- *3 celery stalks, chopped*
- *1 onion, chopped*

- *2 carrots, chopped*
- *8 ounces sliced mushrooms*
- *1 tablespoon extra-virgin olive oil*
- *1/4 teaspoon freshly ground black pepper*

Directions:

✓ *Season both sides of the meat with salt and pepper.*

✓ *In an Instant Pot, heat the oil over high heat. Brown the beef in the skillet, then remove and set aside.*

✓ *Cook for approximately 1 to 2 minutes, or until the mushrooms begin to soften. Remove the mushrooms and meat from the pot and put them aside.*

✓ *To the pot, add the carrots, celery, and onions. Vegetables should be sautéed for around 4 minutes, or until they begin to soften. Cook until aromatic, adding your garlic to the pot.*

✓ *Add the beef broth, thyme, and water to the pot with the meat and mushrooms. Preheat pressure cooker to high and cook for 15 minutes. Allow the pressure to dissipate naturally.*

✓ *Remove the lid from the Instant Pot and add the barley. Cook for another hour or until the barley is cooked and tender, using the slow cooker setting on the pot and leaving the vent open. Serve and take pleasure in!*

Nutrition: Carbohydrates in each serving: 19g

675) *Soup with Chicken Tortillas*

Time Required for Preparation: 10 minutes Time Required for Cooking: 35 minutes 4 portions

- *1/4 cup shredded cheddar cheese for garnish*
- *minced fresh cilantro for garnish*
- *1 lime juice*
- *nonstick cooking spray*
- *2 (6-inch) corn tortillas sliced into thin slices*
- *1/2 teaspoon salt*
- *1 diced Roma tomato*
- *4 cups low-sodium chicken broth*
- *2 boneless, skinless chicken breasts*
- *1 diced jalapeno pepper*
- *1 minced garlic clove*
- *1 onion, thinly sliced*

Directions:

- ✓ *In a medium-high-heat saucepan, heat the oil. Add the onions and sauté for 3-5 minutes, or until they begin to soften. Cook for an additional minute after adding the garlic and jalapeño.*

- ✓ *Bring the chicken, tomato, chicken broth, and salt to a boil in the pot. Reduce to a medium heat setting and cook for approximately 20 minutes, or until the chicken breasts are cooked through. Take the chicken out of the pot and set it aside.*

- ✓ *Preheat broiler to the highest setting.*

- ✓ *Using a nonstick cooking spray, coat the tortilla strips and toss to coat. Arrange the tortilla strips in a single layer on a baking sheet and broil for 3-5 minutes, or until crisp, flipping once.*

- ✓ *When the chicken has cooled slightly, shred it with two forks and return it to the pot.*

- ✓ *Add the lime juice to the soup and season with salt and pepper. Garnish with cheese, cilantro, and tortilla strips, and serve immediately!*

Nutrition: Carbohydrates in each serving: 13g

676) *Thai Peanut, Carrot, and Shrimp Soup*

Time Required for Preparation: 10 minutes Time Required for Cooking: 10 minutes 4 portions

- *3 minced garlic cloves*
- *12 sliced onion*
- *1 tablespoon Thai red curry paste*
- *1 tablespoon coconut oil*
- *fresh cilantro, minced, for garnish*
- *12 pound peeled and deveined shrimp*
- *1/2 cup unsweetened plain almond milk*
- *4 cups low-sodium vegetable broth*
- *1/2 cup whole unsalted peanuts*

Directions:

- ✓ *Heat the oil in a saucepan over medium-high heat until shimmering.*

- ✓ *Add your curry paste to the pan and simmer, constantly stirring, for around 1 minute. Add the garlic, onion, and carrots to the pan, along with the peanuts. Cook for an additional 3 minutes or until the onion begins to soften.*

- ✓ *Increase the heat to high and add the broth. Reduce to low heat and continue cooking for 6 minutes, or until carrots are soft.*

- ✓ *Using an immersion blender, purée the soup until smooth, then return it to the stove. Reduce to a low heat setting and add the almond milk, stirring to incorporate. Cook for 3 minutes or until the shrimp is done.*

- ✓ *Garnish soup with cilantro and serve!*

Nutrition: Carbohydrates in each serving: 17g

677) *Soup with Curried Carrots*

Time Required for Preparation: 10 minutes Time Required for Cooking: 5 minutes 6 portions

- *2 celery stalks, chopped*
- *1 small onion, chopped*
- *1 tablespoon extra-virgin olive oil*
- *1 tablespoon fresh cilantro, chopped*
- *1/4 teaspoon freshly ground black pepper*
- *1 cup canned coconut milk*
- *1/4 teaspoon   salt*
- *4 cups low-sodium vegetable broth*
- *6 medium carrots, roughly chopped*

Directions:

- ✓ *Increase the temperature of your Instant Pot to the highest setting and add olive oil.*

- ✓ *Sauté the celery and onion in olive oil for 3 minutes. Cook for around 30 seconds before adding the curry powder, ginger, and cumin to the saucepan.*

- ✓ *To your pot, add carrots, vegetable broth, and salt. Close and seal the pot, then set the timer for 5 minutes on high. Allow the pressure to dissipate naturally.*

- ✓ *In batches, puree the soup in a blender jar and return it to the saucepan.*

- ✓ *Add the coconut milk and pepper to taste and heat through. Garnish soup with cilantro and serve!*

Nutrition: Carbohydrates in each serving: 13g

678) *Soup with Summer Squash and Crispy Chickpeas*

Time Required for Preparation: 10 minutes Time Required for Cooking: 20 minutes 4 portions

Ingredients:

- *1/4 tsp smoked paprika*
- *1 tsp extra-virgin olive oil, plus 1 tsp*
- *1 (15-ounce) can low-sodium chickpeas, drained and rinsed*
- *freshly ground black pepper*

- *3 minced garlic cloves*
- *12 diced onion*
- *3 cups low-sodium vegetable broth*
- *3 medium zucchinis, coarsely chopped*

Direction

✓ *Preheat the oven to 425° Fahrenheit. Preheat the oven to 350°F. Line a baking sheet with parchment paper.*

✓ *Toss your chickpeas in a mixing dish with 1 teaspoon olive oil, 1 teaspoon smoked paprika, and a pinch of sea salt. Transfer the mixture to a baking sheet and roast for approximately 20 minutes, stirring once. Place aside.*

✓ *Heat the remaining 1 tablespoon oil in a saucepan over medium heat.*

✓ *Bring the zucchini, onion, broth, and garlic to a boil in the pot. Reduce to a simmer and cook for approximately 20 minutes, or until the onion and zucchini are soft.*

✓ *Puree your soup in a blender jar and then return it to the pot.*

✓ *Stir in the yogurt, the remaining 1/2 teaspoon sea salt, and the pepper. Serve with roasted chickpeas on top and enjoy!*

Nutrition: 24g carbohydrate per serving

679) *Cream Zucchini Soup*

Time Required to Prepare: 8 minutes Time Required for Cooking: 8 minutes 4 portions

Ingredients:

- *2 cups vegetable stock*
- *2 crushed garlic cloves*
- *1 tablespoon butter*
- *4 peeled and diced zucchinis (ideally medium size)*
- *1 small onion, chopped*
- *1/2 teaspoon dried oregano (finely ground)*
- *1/2 teaspoon ground black pepper (finely ground)*
- *1 teaspoon dried parsley (finely ground) (optional)*

Directions:

✓ *In your kitchen, place the Instant Pot on a dry platform. Open the top cover and turn it on.*

✓ *Locate and activate the "SAUTE" cooking function; add the butter and leave to melt.*

✓ *Add the onions, zucchini, and garlic to the pot and simmer (while stirring) until transparent and softened for about 2-3 minutes.*

✓ *Stir in the vegetable broth and season with salt, oregano, pepper, and parsley.*

✓ *Close the lid completely to produce a locked chamber; check that the safety valve is in the locked position.*

✓ *Locate and choose the "MANUAL" cooking mode; set the timer to 5 minutes on the default "HIGH" pressure setting.*

✓ *Allow the pressure to build-up to the point where the items are cooked.*

✓ *When the cooking timer goes off, hit the "CANCEL" button. Locate and activate the "QPR" cooking function. This setting is used to rapidly relieve internal pressure.*

✓ *Gently lift the cover, remove the cooked food to serving plates or bowls, and enjoy the keto. Add a squeeze of lemon juice on top.*

Nutrition: 264 Calories 26g fat 7g Saturated Fat Trans 0g fat 11g Carbohydrates 3 g fiber 564mg sodium 4 g protein

680) *Coconut Chicken Soup*

Time Required for Preparation: 8 minutes Time Required for Cooking: 18 minutes 4 portions

- *4 minced garlic cloves*
- *1 pound skin-on chicken breasts*
- *4 cups water*
- *2 tablespoons olive oil*
- *1 diced onion*
- *1 cup coconut milk*
- *black pepper (finely powdered) and salt to taste*
- *2 tbsp. sesame oil*

Directions:

✓ *In your kitchen, place the Instant Pot on a dry platform. Open the top cover and turn it on.*

✓ *Locate and activate the "SAUTÉ" cooking feature; add the oil and allow to heat.*

✓ *Add the onions and garlic to the pot and simmer (while stirring) until transparent and softened in about 1-2 minutes.*

✓ *Add the chicken breasts and cook for an additional 2 minutes.*

✓ *Add the water and coconut milk and season with salt and pepper to taste.*

✓ *Close the lid completely to produce a locked chamber; check that the safety valve is in* the locked position.

✓ Locate and choose the "MANUAL" cooking mode; set the timer to 15 minutes on the default "HIGH" pressure setting.

✓ Allow the pressure to build-up to the point where the items are cooked.

✓ When the cooking timer goes off, hit the "CANCEL" button. Locate and select the "NPR" cooking function. This setting is for the natural release of internal pressure and takes approximately ten minutes to complete.

✓ 10. Gently open the cover. Drizzle the top with sesame oil.

✓ 1 Remove the cooked food from the serving plates or bowls and enjoy the keto diet.

Nutrition: 328 Calories 31g fat 6g Saturated Fat 0g Trans Fat 6g Carbohydrates Fiber: 4g 76mg sodium 21g protein

681) *Soup with Chicken and Bacon*

Preparation Time: 10 minutes

- 6 boneless, skinless chicken thighs, cubed
- 1/2 cup chopped celery
- 4 minced garlic cloves
- 6 ounce sliced mushrooms
- 1/2 cup chopped onion
- 8 ounce softened cream cheese
- 1/4 cup softened butter
- 1 teaspoon dried thyme
- 2 cups chopped spinach
- 8 ounces chopped cooked bacon
- 3 cups chicken broth (ideally homemade)
- 1 cup heavy cream

Directions:

✓ In your kitchen, place the Instant Pot on a dry platform. Open the top cover and turn it on.

✓ Combine all ingredients except the cream, spinach, and bacon in a large mixing bowl; gently toss to combine.

✓ Close the lid completely to create a locked chamber; check that the safety valve is in the locked position.

✓ Locate and activate the "SOUP" cooking feature; set the timer to 30 minutes on the default "HIGH" pressure setting.

✓ Allow the pressure to build-up to the point where the items are cooked.

✓ When the cooking timer goes off, push the "CANCEL" button. Locate and select the "NPR" cooking function. This setting is for the natural release of internal pressure and takes approximately ten minutes to complete.

✓ Carefully remove the lid and whisk in the cream and spinach.

✓ Remove the cooked food from the serving plates or bowls and enjoy the keto. Garnish with bacon.

Nutrition: 456 Calories 38g fat 13g Saturated Fat 0g Trans Fat 7g Carbohydrates 1 gram fiber 742mg sodium 23g protein

682) *Sweet Cream and Pepper Stew*

Time Required for Preparation: 20 minutes Time Required for Cooking: 10 minutes

- 1 celery stalk, chopped
- 1 yellow bell pepper, chopped
- 1 green bell pepper, chopped
- 2 large red bell peppers, chopped
- 1 small red onion, chopped
- 2 tablespoons butter
- 1/2 cup cream cheese, full-fat
- 1/4 teaspoon dried thyme (finely ground)
- 1/2 teaspoon black pepper (finely ground)
- 1 teaspoon dried parsley (finely ground)

Directions:

✓ In your kitchen, place the Instant Pot on a dry platform. Open the top cover and turn it on.

✓ Locate and activate the "SAUTE" cooking function; add the butter and leave to melt.

✓ Add the onions, bell pepper, and celery to the pot and cook (while stirring) for approximately 3-4 minutes, or until transparent and softened.

✓ Combine the vegetable stock and heavy cream in a medium saucepan; season with salt, pepper, parsley, and thyme.

✓ Close the lid completely to produce a locked chamber; check that the safety valve is in the locked position.

✓ Locate and choose the "MANUAL" cooking mode; set the timer to 6 minutes on the default "HIGH" pressure setting.

✓ Allow the pressure to build-up to the point where the items are cooked.

✓ When the cooking timer goes off, hit the

"CANCEL" button. Locate and activate the "QPR" cooking function. This setting is used to rapidly relieve internal pressure.

✓ Slowly open the lid and whisk in the cream; transfer the cooked ingredients to serving plates or bowls and enjoy the keto.

Nutrition: 286 Calories 27g fat 6g Saturated Fat 0g Trans Fat 9g Carbohydrates 3 g fiber 523mg sodium 5 g protein

683) *Soup with Ham and Asparagus*

Time Required for Preparation: 20 minutes Time Required for Cooking: 55 minutes

Ingredients:

• 5 crushed garlic cloves

• 1 cup chopped ham

• 4 cups chicken broth (ideally homemade)

• 2 pounds trimmed and halved asparagus spears

• 2 tablespoons butter

• 1 chopped yellow onion

• 1/2 teaspoon   dried thyme

Directions:

✓ In your kitchen, place the Instant Pot on a dry platform. Open the top cover and turn it on.

✓ Locate and activate the "SAUTE" cooking function; add the butter and leave to melt.

✓ Add the onions to the pot and simmer (while stirring) for approximately 4-5 minutes, or until transparent and softened.

✓ Stir in the garlic, ham bone, and stock; simmer for approximately 2-3 minutes.

✓ Add the other ingredients and gently toss to combine.

✓ Close the lid completely to produce a locked chamber; check that the safety valve is in the locked position.

✓ Locate and activate the "SOUP" cooking feature; set the timer to 45 minutes on the default "HIGH" pressure setting.

✓ Allow the pressure to build-up to the point where the items are cooked.

✓ When the cooking timer goes off, hit the "CANCEL" button. Locate and activate the "QPR" cooking function. This setting is used to rapidly relieve internal pressure.

✓ 10. Carefully open the top and pour the mixture into a blender or food processor.

✓ 1 Blend or process the mixture until smooth.

Distribute the mixture among serving bowls and enjoy the keto diet.

Nutrition: 146 Calories 7g fat 3g Saturated Fat 0g Trans Fat 5g Carbohydrates 4g fiber 262mg sodium 10g protein

684) *Simple Chicken Soup*

Time Required for Preparation: 20 minutes Time Required for Cooking: 25 minutes 4 portions

• 2 frozen boneless chicken breasts

• 4 medium-sized potatoes, chunked

• 3 carrots, peeled and chunked

• 2 large onion, diced

Directions:

✓ Combine the chicken breasts, potatoes, carrots, onion, stock, water, and season with salt and pepper to taste in the Instant Pot.

✓ Secure the lid by closing and locking it. Select MANUAL and cook for 25 minutes at HIGH pressure.

✓ After the timer sounds, allow 10 minutes for Natural Remove and then manually release any leftover pressure. Remove the lid from the pot.

✓ Serve.

Nutrition: Calories 301 Carbohydrates 27.2 g Sugar 16 g Protein 6 g 33 mg Cholesterol 9 g

685) *Buffalo Chicken Soup*

Time Required for Preparation: 20 minutes Time Required for Cooking: 30 minutes 8 servings

• 2 boneless, skinless chicken breasts, frozen or fresh

• 1 minced garlic clove

• 1/4 cup diced onion

• 1/2 cup diced celery

• 2 tbsp butter

• 1 tbsp ranch dressing mix

• 3 cups chicken broth

• 1/3 cup spicy sauce

• 2 cups shredded cheddar cheese

Direction

✓ Combine the chicken breasts, garlic, onion, celery, butter, ranch dressing mix, stock, and spicy sauce in the Instant Pot.

✓ Secure the lid by closing and locking it. Select MANUAL and cook for 10 minutes at HIGH pressure.

✓ Once the cooking is complete, allow the

pressure to naturally release for ten minutes. Manually expel any residual steam. Remove the lid from the pot.

✓ *Remove the chicken from the skillet and shred the meat. Reintroduce the pot.*

✓ *Combine the cheese and heavy cream in a medium bowl. Stir thoroughly. Allow 5 minutes before serving.*

Nutrition: 303 Calories 27.5 g fat Carbohydrates Sugar 18 g Protein 5 g Cholesterol g 33 milligram

686) *Beef Borscht Soup*

Time Required for Preparation: 20 minutes Time Required for Cooking: 30 minutes 8 portions

- 2 pounds minced beef
- 3 beets, peeled and diced
- 2 large carrots, diced
- 3 celery stalks, chopped
- 1 onion, diced
- 2 garlic cloves, diced
- 3 cups shredded cabbage
- 6 cups beef stock
- 1/2 tbsp thyme
- 1 bay leaf

Directions:

✓ *Select SAUTÉ to Preheat the Instant Pot.*

✓ *Stir in the ground meat and simmer for 5 minutes, or until browned.*

✓ *In the Instant Pot, combine the remaining ingredients and stir to combine. Secure the lid by closing and locking it.*

✓ *To cancel the SAUTE feature, press the CANCEL button, then pick the MANUAL setting and set the cooking time to 15 minutes at HIGH pressure.*

✓ *Once the timer sounds, allow the pressure to naturally release for 10 minutes before manually releasing any leftover pressure. Remove the lid from the pot.*

✓ *Allow 5-10 minutes for the dish to rest before serving.*

Nutrition: 301 Calories 27.2 g fat 16 g carbohydrate 6 g protein Cholesterol 3 g 33 mg

687) *Soup with Beef and Barley*

Preparation Time: 20 minutes Time Required for Cooking: 30 minutes 8 portions

Ingredients:

- 2 tbsp olive oil

- 2 lbs beef chuck roast, cut into 1 ½ inch steaks
- Salt and freshly ground black pepper to taste
- 2 onions, chopped
- 4 cloves garlic, sliced
- 4 large carrots, diced
- 1 stalk celery, chopped

Direction

✓ *Turn the Instant Pot to the SAUTÉ setting and heat the oil.*

✓ *Season the beef liberally with salt and pepper. Brown for around 5 minutes in the saucepan. Turn the pan over and brown the other side.*

✓ *Take the meat out of the pot.*

✓ *Combine the onion, garlic, carrots, and celery in a medium bowl. Sauté for 6 minutes, stirring occasionally.*

✓ *Add the beef back to the pot. Combine the pearl barley, bay leaf, chicken stock, and fish sauce in a medium bowl. Stir thoroughly.*

✓ *Secure the cover. To reset the cooking program, hit the CANCEL button, then the MANUAL button to set the cooking time to 30 minutes at HIGH pressure.*

✓ *Once the cooking process is complete, allow the pressure to naturally release for 15 minutes. Manually expel any residual steam. Remove the lid from the pot.*

✓ *Discard garlic cloves, large vegetable bits, and bay leaf.*

✓ *Check for seasoning and adjust with additional salt if necessary.*

Nutrition: 200 Calories 27.2 g fat 16 g sugar Protein: 2 g Cholesterol 4 g

688) *Soup with Beef and Cabbage*

Time Required for Preparation: 20 minutes Time Required for Cooking: 35 minutes 6 portions

Ingredients:

- 2 tbsp coconut oil
- 1 diced onion
- 1 minced garlic clove
- 1 pound ground beef
- 14 oz can diced tomatoes, undrained
- 4 cups water
- Salt and freshly ground black pepper to taste

Directions:

- ✓ Select SAUTÉ to Preheat the Instant Pot. Add the oil and bring to a boil.
- ✓ Add the onion and garlic and cook, occasionally stirring, for 2 minutes.
- ✓ Stir in the steak and simmer for 2-3 minutes, or until lightly browned.
- ✓ Add the tomatoes and water. Season with salt and pepper to taste and mix thoroughly.
- ✓ To terminate the SAUTÉ feature, use the CANCEL key.
- ✓ Secure the cover. Select MANUAL and cook for 12 minutes at HIGH pressure.
- ✓ Immediately after the timer sounds, use a Quick Release. Open the lid with caution.
- ✓ Add the cabbage and cook for 5 minutes, selecting SAUTÉ.
- ✓ Serve.

Nutrition: 335 Calories 10 g fat 16 g carbohydrate 6 g sugar 9 g protein 33 mg cholesterol

689) *Chicken Soup "Yummy"*

30 Minutes Cooking6 Servings

- 4 lbs. Chicken, sliced 5 carrots, thinly sliced
- 8 oz. water
- 2 celery stalks, thinly sliced
- 2 big chopped onions

Direction

- ✓ In a large saucepan, combine the chicken, water, and salt. Bring to a rolling boil.
- ✓ Stir celery and onion into the saucepan.
- ✓ Reduce to medium-low heat and cook for 30 minutes.
- ✓ Cover the pot with a lid and cook for 40 minutes.
- ✓ Chicken should be removed from the saucepan, bones removed, and chicken sliced into bite-size pieces.
- ✓ Reintroduce the chicken to the pot and give it a good stir.
- ✓ Serve and take pleasure in.

Nutrition: Calories: 89 6.33g fat 0g Carbohydrates 7.56g protein 0g sugar 0mg cholesterol

690) *Crock-pot Slow Cooker Mulligatawny Soup*

8 portions Cooking Time: 6 Hours
Ingredients:

- 2 whole cloves
- 1/4 cup green pepper, chopped 1 box (32 oz) low-sodium chicken broth
- 1/4 teaspoon pepper
- 1 can (14 1/2 oz.) diced tomatoes
- 1/2 teaspoon sugar
- 2 cups cubed cooked chicken
- 1 teaspoon curry powder
- 1 large tart green apple, peeled and chopped
- 1 teaspoon salt
- 1/4 cup onion, finely chopped
- 2 teaspoon lemon juice
- 1/4 cup carrot, chopped
- 1 tablespoon fresh parsley, minced

Directions:

- ✓ Add all ingredients in a 3-or 4-qt. Crock-Pot slow cooker and combine well. Cover the cooker and cook for about 6-8 hours on Low.
- ✓ Once done, remove cloves and serve.

Nutrition: 107 Calories; 2 g fat; 10 g total carbs; 12 g protein

691) *Stew of the Irish*

Time Required for Cooking: 35 Minutes
Ingredients:

- 5 pound diced shoulder of lamb
- 1 pound veggies, chopped
- 1 cup beef broth with a low salt content
- 3 onions, minced
- 1 tablespoon ghee

Directions:

- ✓ In your Instant Pot, combine all of the ingredients.
- ✓ Cook for 35 minutes on Stew.
- ✓ Naturally, relieve the pressure.

Nutrition: 330 Calories; 9 carbohydrate; 2 sugar; 12 fat; 49 protein; 3 g dietary fiber

692) *Crock Pot Split Pea Soup for Vegetarians*

Time Required for Cooking: 10 Minutes Servings: 8
Ingredients:

- 2 ribs, chopped celery
- 2 cubes bouillon low sodium 8 c. liquid
- 2 cup uncooked split green peas three bay

leaves

- *2 carnations*
- *2 potatoes, chopped*
- *Season with pepper and salt*

Directions:

✓ *Place the bouillon cubes, split peas, and water in the Crock-Pot. Stir briefly to disperse the bouillon cubes.*

✓ *Following that, add the potatoes, celery, and carrots, along with the bay leaves.*

✓ *Stir well to mix.*

✓ *Cover and cook on the low setting of your Crock-Pot for at least 4 hours, or until the green split peas are tender.*

✓ *Season with salt and pepper to taste.*

✓ *Remove the bay leaves before serving and enjoy.*

Nutrition: 149 Calories, 1 g fat, 30 g carbohydrates, 7 g protein, 3 g sugars, 732 mg sodium

693) *Thai Soup with Peanuts, Carrots, and Shrimp*

4 portions Time Required for Cooking: 10 Minutes

- *3 minced garlic cloves*
- *½ sliced onion*
- *1 tbsp red curry paste Thai*
- *1 tsp virgin coconut oil minced fresh cilantro for garnish*
- *½ pound peeled and deveined shrimp*
- *1/2 cup plain unsweetened almond milk*
- *4 cups vegetarian broth with a low sodium content*
- *1/2 cup unsalted whole peanuts*
- *2 cups carrots, peeled and sliced*

Direction

✓ *Heat the oil in a saucepan over medium-high heat until shimmering.*

✓ *Add your curry paste to the pan and simmer, constantly stirring, for around 1 minute. Add the garlic, onion, and carrots to the pan, along with the peanuts. Cook for an additional 3 minutes or until the onion begins to soften.*

✓ *Bring your broth to a boil and add it. Reduce to low heat and continue cooking for 6 minutes, or until carrots are soft.*

✓ *Puree the soup with an immersion blender until smooth and return to the pot. Reduce to a low heat setting and add the almond*

milk, stirring to incorporate. Cook for 3 minutes or until the shrimp is done.

✓ *Garnish soup with cilantro and serve!*

Nutrition: Carbohydrates in each serving: 17g

694) *Soup with Ham and Asparagus*

Time Required for Cooking: 55 Min.

Ingredients:

- *5 garlic cloves, smashed*
- *1 cup ham, chopped*
- *4 cups (preferably homemade) broth de poulet*
- *2 pounds asparagus spears, trimmed and halved*
- *2 tbsp butter*
- *1 yellow onion, chopped*
- *1/2 tsp dried thyme*

Direction

✓ *Season with salt and freshly ground (finely ground) black pepper to taste. Directions:*

✓ *Arrange Instant Pot on a dry kitchen platform. Open the top cover and turn it on.*

✓ *Locate and activate the "SAUTE" cooking function; add the butter and allow to heat.*

✓ *Add the onions to the pot and cook (while stirring) for approximately 4-5 minutes, or until transparent and softened.*

✓ *Stir in the garlic, ham bone, and stock; simmer for approximately 2-3 minutes.*

✓ *Add the other ingredients and gently toss to combine.*

✓ *Close the lid to form a sealed compartment; ensure that the safety valve is in the locked position.*

✓ *Locate and activate the "SOUP" cooking feature; set the timer to 45 minutes on the default "HIGH" pressure setting.*

✓ *Allow the pressure to build-up to the point when the ingredients are cooked.*

✓ *Once the cooking timer has expired, press the "CANCEL" button. Locate and activate the "QPR" cooking function. This setting is used to rapidly relieve internal pressure.*

✓ *Slowly remove the cover and pour the mixture into a blender or food processor.*

✓ *Blend or process until a smooth mixture is formed. Distribute the mixture among serving bowls and enjoy the keto diet.*

Nutrition: 146 Calories 7g fat 3g Saturated Fat 0g

Trans Fat 5g Carbohydrates 4g fiber 262mg sodium 10g protein

695) *Cabbage Soup*

Time Required for Cooking: 35 Minutes

- *1 pound shredded cabbage*
- *1 cup vegetarian broth with a low sodium content 1 onion, shredded*
- *2 tbspsprigs of mixed herbs*
- *1 tbsp ground black pepper*

Directions:

- ✓ *In your Instant Pot, combine all of the ingredients.*
- ✓ *Cook for 35 minutes on Stew.*
- ✓ *Naturally relieve the pressure.*

Nutrition: Calories: 60; Carbohydrates: 2; Sugar: 0; Fat: 2; Protein: 4; GL: 1

696) *Soup with Chickpeas*

Time Required for Cooking: 35 Minutes Servings: 2
Ingredients:

- *1 pound chickpeas, cooked*
- *1 pound veggies, chopped*
- *1 cup vegetarian broth with a low sodium content*
- *2 tbsp sprigs of mixed herbs*

Directions:

- ✓ *In your Instant Pot, combine all of the ingredients.*
- ✓ *Cook for 35 minutes on Stew.*
- ✓ *Naturally relieve the pressure.*

Nutrition: 310 Calories; 20 carbohydrate; 3 sugar; 5 fat; 27 protein; 5 g dietary fiber

697) *Stew of Meatballs*

Time Required for Cooking: 25 Minutes
Ingredients:

- *1 pound of sausage meat*
- *2 cup tomato, chopped*
- *1 cup veggies, chopped*
- *2 tbsp Italian seasonings*
- *1 tbsp oil de veg.*

Directions:

- ✓ *Form meatballs from the sausage.*
- ✓ *Sauté the meatballs in the Instant Pot until golden.*
- ✓ *In your Instant Pot, combine all of the ingredients.*

- ✓ *Cook for 25 minutes on Stew.*
- ✓ *Naturally relieve the pressure.*

Nutrition: 300 Calories; 4 carbs; 1 sugar; 12 fat

698) *Soup with Squash*

Time Required for Cooking: 8 Hours Servings: 6
Ingredients:

- *2 pound butternut squash, peeled and chunked*
- *1 teaspoon minced ginger*
- *1 teaspoon cinnamon*
- *1 heaping tablespoon curry powder*
- *2 leaves of bay*
- *1 teaspoon freshly ground black pepper*
- *1/2 cup cream de crème*
- *2 c. chicken broth*
- *1 tbsp minced garlic*
- *2 carrots, peeled and chunked 2 peeled, cored, and chopped apples 1 large onion, peeled and chopped*
- *1 teaspoon salt*

Direction

- ✓ *Now you need to coat the inside of a crock pot with cooking spray.*
- ✓ *In the crockpot, combine all ingredients except the cream and mix well.*
- ✓ *Cook, covered, on low for 8 hours.*
- ✓ *Purée the soup until smooth and creamy using an immersion blender.*
- ✓ *Add heavy cream and season with pepper and salt to taste.*
- ✓ *Serve and take pleasure in.*

Nutrition: 170 Calories Carbohydrates 4 g Sugar 34 g Protein 14 g Cholesterol 9 g 14 milligram

699) *Soup with French Onions*

Time Required for Cooking: 35 Minutes
Ingredients:

- *6 onions, finely chopped*
- *2 tbsp vegetable broth*
- *2 tablespoons Gruyere*

Direction

- ✓ *In your Instant Pot, heat the oil and cook the onions on Sauté until tender and brown.*
- ✓ *In your Instant Pot, combine all of the ingredients.*
- ✓ *Cook for 35 minutes on Stew.*

✓ *Naturally relieve the pressure.*
Nutrition: 110 Calories; 8 carbohydrate; 3 sugar; 10 fat; 3 protein; 4 g dietary fiber

700) *Cherry Stew*

Time Required for Cooking: 10 Minutes Servings: 6

- *Water*
- *1/2cup cocoa powder*
- *14 c. sugar de coco*
- *1 pound cherries, pitted*

Direction

✓ *In a saucepan, add the cherries, water, sugar, and hot chocolate mix; stir to blend. Cook over medium heat for ten minutes, then divide into bowls and serve cold.*

✓ *Enjoy!*

Nutrition: Calories: 207, 1 g fat, 8 g carbohydrate, 6 g protein, 27 g sugars, 19 mg sodium

701) *Soup with Curried Carrots*

Time Required for Cooking: 5 Minutes
Ingredients:

- *2 celery stalks, peeled and cut*
- *1 finely sliced tiny onion*
- *1 tbsp. olive oil extra-virgin*
- *1 tbsp. chopped fresh cilantro*
- *1/4 tsp . freshly ground black pepper*
- *1 cup coconut milk in a can*
- *1/4 tsp salt*
- *4 cups vegetarian broth with a low sodium content 6 carrots, medium, roughly chopped*
- *1 teaspoon minced fresh ginger*
- *1 teaspoon cumin powder*
- *1 tsp 1/2 tbsp curry powder*

Direction

✓ *Adjust the Instant Pot to the high setting and add the olive oil.*

✓ *For 3 minutes, sauté the celery and onion. Cook for around 30 seconds before adding the curry powder, ginger, and cumin to the saucepan.*

✓ *To the pot, add the carrots, vegetable broth, and salt. Close and seal the pot, then set the timer for 5 minutes on high. Allow the pressure to dissipate naturally.*

✓ *In batches, puree the soup in a blender jar and return it to the saucepan.*

✓ *Combine the coconut milk and pepper in a small saucepan and bring to a boil. Garnish soup with cilantro and serve!*

Nutrition: Carbohydrates in each serving: 13g

702) *Vegan Avocado & Zucchini Cream Soup*

Time Required for Cooking: 20 Minutes
Ingredients:

- *3 tbsp oil de veg.*
- *1 chopped leek*
- *1 sliced rutabaga*
- *3 cups sliced zucchini 1 avocado, roughly chopped*

Direction

✓ *Season with salt and freshly ground black pepper to taste. 4 c. broth de légumes*

✓ *2 tbsp chopped fresh mint Sauté leek, zucchini, and rutabaga in heated oil for approximately 7-10 minutes. Season with freshly ground black pepper and salt. Bring broth to a boil and add. Reduce to low heat and cook for 20 minutes.*

✓ *Remove yourself from the heat. Blend the soup and avocado in batches in a blender. Blend until smooth and creamy. Arrange in bowls and garnish with fresh mint.*

Nutrition: Calories 378, Fat 25g, Carbohydrates 9.3g, Protein 8.2g

703) *Stew of Kebab*

2 portions Time Required for Cooking: 35 Minutes

- *1 pound cubed, seasoned kebab meat*
- *1 pound chickpeas, cooked*
- *1 cup vegetarian broth with a low sodium content*
- *1 tbsp ground black pepper*

Direction

✓ *In your Instant Pot, combine all of the ingredients.*

✓ *Cook for 35 minutes on Stew.*

✓ *Naturally relieve the pressure.*

Nutrition: 290 Calories; 22 carbohydrate; 4 sugar; 10 fat; 34 protein; 6 g dietary fiber

704) *Soup with Meatless Balls*

15 Minutes Cooking
Ingredients:

- *1 pound minced tofu*

- *0.5 pound veggies, chopped*
- *2 cups vegetarian broth with a low sodium content*
- *1 tbsp ground almonds season with salt and pepper*

Directions:

✓ *Combine the tofu, flour, salt, and pepper in a mixing bowl.*

✓ *Assemble the meatballs.*

✓ *In your Instant Pot, combine all of the ingredients.*

✓ *Cook for 15 minutes on Stew.*

✓ *Naturally relieve the pressure.*

Nutrition: 240 Calories; 9 carbohydrate; 3 sugar; 10 fat; 35 protein; 5 g dietary fiber

705) *Soup with Tofu*

Time Required for Cooking: 10 Minutes Servings: 8

Ingredients:

- *1 pound cubed extra-firm tofu*
- *3 medium carrots chopped*
- *8 c. vegetable broth with a low sodium content*
- *1/2 tsp. white pepper, freshly ground*
- *8 garlic cloves, minced*
- *6 scallions, cut and divided*
- *4 oz. mushrooms, sliced*

Direction

✓ *Add 1 inch fresh ginger, minced, and fill a stockpot halfway with broth. Combine all ingredients except the tofu and the final two scallions. Bring to a boil in a heavy saucepan over high heat.*

✓ *Once the water is boiling, add the tofu. Reduce to low heat, cover, and cook for 5 minutes.*

✓ *Take the soup off the heat and spoon it into the dishes. Garnish with the remaining cut scallions. Serve right away.*

Nutrition: 91 Calories, 3 g fat, 8 g carbohydrate, 6 g protein, 4 g sugar, 900 mg sodium

706) *Soup with Chicken Zoodles*

Time Required for Cooking: 35 Minutes

- *1 pound cooked chicken, diced*
- *1 pound zucchini spiralized*
- *1 cup chicken soup with minimal sodium*
- *1 cup veggies, diced*

Direction

✓ *In your Instant Pot, combine all ingredients except the zucchini.*

✓ *Cook for 35 minutes on Stew.*

✓ *Naturally relieve the pressure.*

✓ *Stir in the zucchini and cook until completely heated.*

Nutrition: Calories: 250; Carbohydrates: 5; Sugar: 0; Fat: 10; Protein: 40; GL: 1

707) *Soup With Cheese, Chicken, and Cilantro*

Time Required for Cooking: 10 Minutes

- *1 carrot, chopped*
- *2 cups cooked and shredded chicken 1 onion, chopped*
- *3 tablespoons butter*
- *4 cups broth de volaille*
- *2 tbsp chopped cilantro*
- *3 tablespoons buffalo sauce*
- *1/2 cup creme fraiche*

Direction

✓ *Season with salt and freshly ground black pepper to taste. Warm butter in a skillet over medium heat and sauté carrots and onion for about 5 minutes, or until soft.*

✓ *Combine with buffalo sauce and cream cheese in a food processor until smooth. Transfer to a saucepan, add the chicken broth, and heat until heated but not boiling. Cook until chicken is heated through, stirring in chicken, salt, and pepper. When ready to serve, transfer to soup bowls and garnish with cilantro.*

Nutrition: 487 Calories, 41g fat, 7.2g net carbs, 16.3g protein

708) *Soup with Spicy Peppers*

2 portions 15 Minutes Cooking

- *1 pound chopped sweet peppers 1 cup vegetarian broth with a low sodium content*
- *3 tablespoons finely chopped chile peppers*
- *1 tbsp ground black pepper*

Direction

✓ *In your Instant Pot, combine all of the ingredients.*

✓ *Cook for 15 minutes on Stew.*

✓ *Naturally relieve the pressure, then blend.*

Nutrition: Calories: 100; Carbohydrates: 11; Sugar: 4; Fat: 2; Protein: 3; GL: 6

709) *Incredibly Delicious Chicken Enchilada Soup*

30 Minutes Cooking
Ingredients:

- 2 tbsp unrefined coconut oil
- 1 pound skinless, boneless chicken thighs
- 3/4 cup sugar-free red enchilada sauce
- 14 c. water
- 1/4 cup chopped onion
- 3 oz. chopped green chilis from a can
- 1 sliced avocado
- 1 cup shredded cheddar cheese
- 1/4 cup chopped pickled jalapenos
- 1/2 cup sour cream
- 1 diced tomato

Directions:

- ✓ Preheat a large skillet over medium heat. Combine with coconut oil and warm. Cook until the chicken is browned on the outside. Combine the onion, chilies, water, and enchilada sauce in a bowl and cover with a lid.
- ✓ Wait to simmer for 20 minutes or until the chicken is thoroughly cooked.
- ✓ Fill a serving bowl halfway with the soup and garnish with the sauce, cheese, sour cream, tomato, and avocado.

Nutrition: 643 Calories 42g fat, 9.7g net carbs, 48g protein

710) *Soup with Zucchini and Basil*

5 portions Time Required for Cooking: 10 Minutes
Ingredients:

- 1/3 cup basil leaves, packed
- 3/4 cup finely sliced onion
- 1/4 cup olive oil
- 2 lbs. zucchini, trimmed and sliced
- 2 garlic cloves, peeled
- 4 c. water, divided

Directions:

- ✓ Half of the zucchini should be peeled and julienned; combine with 1/2 teaspoon salt and drain in a sieve until wilted, at least 20 minutes. Chop the remaining zucchini coarsely.
- ✓ In a saucepan over medium-low heat, cook onion and garlic in oil, stirring periodically until onions are transparent. Cook,

occasionally stirring, adding the diced zucchini and 1 teaspoon salt.

- ✓ Add 3 cups water and cook ajar until soft. In a blender, combine the soup and basil.
- ✓ In a small saucepan, bring the remaining cup of water to a boil and blanch the julienned zucchini. Drain.
- ✓ Serve soup garnished with julienned zucchini. Serve soup seasoning with salt and pepper.

Nutrition: 169.3 Calories, 17 g fat, 12 g carbohydrate, 2 g protein, 8 g sugars, 8 mg sodium

711) *Soup With Sweet And Sour*

2 portions Time Required for Cooking: 35 Minutes
Ingredients:

- 1 pound chicken breast cubed
- 1 pound veggies, chopped
- 1 cup sweet and sour sauce with a low carbohydrate count 0.5 cup marmalade for diabetics

Directions:

- ✓ In your Instant Pot, combine all of the ingredients.
- ✓ Cook for 35 minutes on Stew.
- ✓ Naturally relieve the pressure.

Nutrition: Calories: 305; Carbohydrates: 4; Sugar: 2; Fat: 12; Protein: 40; GL:

712) *Soup with Curried Shrimp and Green Beans*

Time Required for Cooking: 10 Minutes Servings: 4
Ingredients:

- 1 chopped onion
- 2 tbsp paste de curry rouge
- 2 tablespoons butter
- 1 pound peeled and deveined giant shrimp
- 2 teaspoon pureed ginger-garlic
- 1 cup milk de coco

Direction

- ✓ Season with salt and chile pepper to taste. 1 bunch halved green beans 1 tbsp chopped cilantro Cook the shrimp in melted butter in a saucepan over medium heat, season with salt and pepper, and cook for 2 to 3 minutes, or until they are opaque. Transfer to a serving plate. Sauté for 2 minutes, or until the ginger-garlic puree, onion, and red curry paste are fragrant.
- ✓ Incorporate the coconut milk; season with

salt, pepper, and green beans. 4 minutes in the oven. Reduce to a simmer and cook for an additional 3 minutes, stirring regularly. Season with salt to taste, ladle soup into serving bowls, and garnish with cilantro.
Nutrition: 351 Calories 34g Fat, 2g Net Carbohydrates, 2g Protein 7.7g

713) *Soup with Beef Pork*

30 Minutes Cooking , Serving 2
Ingredients:

- *2 pound beef ground*
- *3 peeled and sliced beets*
- *2 big carrots, peeled and sliced*
- *3 celery stalks, chopped*
- *1 diced onion*
- *2 minced garlic cloves*
- *3 cups cabbage, shredded*
- *6 c. beef broth*
- *1/2 teaspoon thyme*
- *1 leaf of bay*
- *Season with salt and freshly ground black pepper to taste.*

Directions:

✓ *Select SAUTÉ to Preheat the Instant Pot.*

✓ *Cook, occasionally stirring, for 5 minutes, or until the ground meat is browned.*

✓ *In the Instant Pot, combine the remaining ingredients and stir to combine. Secure the lid by closing and locking it.*

✓ *To cancel the SAUTE feature, hit the CANCEL button. Next, pick the MANUAL setting and enter a cooking time of 15 minutes at HIGH pressure.*

✓ *Once the timer sounds, let 10 minutes for Natural Release before manually releasing any leftover pressure. Remove the lid from the pot.*

✓ *Allow 5-10 minutes for the meal to sit before serving.*

Nutrition: 301 Calories 27.2 g fat 16 g carbohydrate 6 g protein Cholesterol 3 g 33 milligram

714) *Soup with Broccoli and Spinach*

4 portions Time Required for Cooking: 20 Minutes
Ingredients:

- *2 tablespoons butter*
- *1 chopped onion*
- *1 minced garlic clove*
- *2 broccoli heads, florets removed 2 celery stalks, chopped 4 c. broth de légumes*
- *1 cup organic baby spinach*
- *Season with salt and freshly ground black pepper to taste.*
- *1 tbsp basil, shaved Parmesan cheese*

Directions:

✓ *In a saucepan over medium heat, melt the butter. For 3 minutes, sauté the garlic and onion until softened. Cook for 4 minutes, or until the broccoli and celery are somewhat soft. Add the broth, bring to a boil, then reduce to medium-low heat and cover and simmer for around 5 minutes.*

✓ *Add the spinach to wilt, season with salt and pepper, and simmer for 4 minutes. The soup should be ladled into serving bowls. Sprinkle with grated Parmesan cheese and chopped basil before serving.*

Nutrition: Calories 123 Fat 11g Carbohydrates Net Carbohydrates 2g Protein 8g

715) *Chicken Soup with Vegetables*

6 portions Time Required for Cooking: 6 Hours
Ingredients:

- *4 cups boneless, skinless, cooked, and diced chicken*
- *4 tsp minced garlic*
- *2/3 cup diced onion*
- *1 1/2 cup diced carrot*
- *6 chicken broth*
- *2 tbsp freshly squeezed lime juice*
- *1/4 cup chopped jalapeno pepper*
- *1/2 cup chopped tomatoes*
- *1/2 cup chopped fresh cilantro*
- *1 tsp cayenne pepper*
- *1 tablespoon cumin*
- *1 3/4 cup tomato juice*
- *2 tsp salt*

Direction

✓ *In a crockpot, combine all ingredients and stir well.*

✓ *Cook, covered, on low for 6 hours.*

✓ *Serve immediately after vigorously stirring.*

Nutrition: 192 Nutrition: Calories 8 g fat 9.8 g carbohydrate 7 g sugar 29.2 g protein 72 mg cholesterol

716) <u>*Soup with Beef and Barley*</u>

8 portions 30 Minutes Cooking
Ingredients:

- 2 tablespoons olive oil
- 2 pound chuck roast, cut into 1 1/2-inch steaks Season with salt and freshly ground black pepper to taste.
- 2 onions, chopped 4 garlic cloves,
- sliced 4 big carrots, diced
- 1 celery stalk, chopped
- 1 cup washed pearl barley
- 1 leaf of bay
- 8 c. chicken broth
- 1 tbsp sriracha

Directions:

- ✓ Heat the oil in the Instant Pot using the SAUTÉ mode.
- ✓ Season the beef well with salt and pepper. Brown for around 5 minutes in the saucepan. Turn the pan over and brown the other side.
- ✓ Take the meat out of the pot.
- ✓ Combine the onion, garlic, carrots, and celery in a medium bowl. Sauté for 6 minutes, stirring occasionally.
- ✓ Bring the steak back to the pot. Combine the pearl barley, bay leaf, chicken stock, and fish sauce in a medium bowl. Stir thoroughly.
- ✓ Secure the lid by closing and locking it. To reset the cooking program, hit the CANCEL button, then the MANUAL button to set the cooking time to 30 minutes at HIGH pressure.
- ✓ Once the cooking process is complete, release the pressure. Allow 15 minutes for natural release. Manually expel any residual steam. Remove the lid from the pot.
- ✓ Garlic cloves, large vegetable chunks, and bay leaf should all be removed.

Nutrition: 200 Calories Carbohydrates 27.2 g 16 g Sucrose Protein: 2 g Cholesterol 4 g 32 milligram

717) <u>*Soup with Sirloin and Carrots*</u>

6 portions Time Required for Cooking: 10 Minutes
Ingredients:

- 1 pound carrots and celery mixture, chopped 32 oz. beef stock with a low salt content

- 1/3 cup unbleached whole-wheat flour
- 1 pound ground sirloin beef
- 1 tbsp. extra-virgin olive oil
- 1 yellow onion, chopped

Direction

- ✓ In a saucepan over medium-high heat, heat the olive oil; add the meat and flour.
- ✓ Cook, constantly stirring, for 4-5 minutes, or until browned.
- ✓ Stir in the celery, onion, carrots, and stock; bring to a gentle simmer.
- ✓ Reduce to low heat and cook for 12-15 minutes.
- ✓ Serve immediately.

Nutrition: Calories: 140; Fat: 5 g; Carbohydrates: 16 g; Protein: 9 g; Sugars: 3 g; Sodium: 670 mg

718) <u>*Mexican Chicken Soup*</u>

Time Required for Cooking: 4 Hours
Ingredients:

- 1 1/2 pound skinless and boneless chicken thighs
- 14 oz stock de poulet
- ✓ 14 ounces salsa
- ✓ 8 oz Monterey Shredded Jack cheese

Direction

- ✓ Place chicken in a crock cooker.
- ✓ Combine the other ingredients and pour over the chicken.
- ✓ Cook, covered, on high for 4 hours.
- ✓ Take the chicken out of the crockpot and shred it with forks.
- ✓ Reintroduce the shredded chicken to the slow cooker and mix thoroughly.
- ✓ Serve and take pleasure in.

Nutrition: 371 Calories 19.5 g fat 7 g Sucrose Protein 2 g Cholesterol 41 g 135 milligram

719) <u>*Soup With Mushrooms and Herbs*</u>

4 portions 15 Minutes Cooking
Ingredients:

- 1 chopped onion
- 1/2 cup crème fraiche
- 14 c. butter
- 12 oz white mushrooms, diced
- 1 teaspoon thyme,

- *1 teaspoon parsley,*
- *1 teaspoon cilantro, chopped*
- *2 garlic cloves, minced*
- *4 c. broth de legumes*

Direction

✓ *Season with salt and freshly ground black pepper to taste. Cook butter, onion, and garlic in a large saucepan over high heat for 3 minutes or until soft. Cook for 10 minutes, adding mushrooms, salt, and pepper. Bring to a boil the broth.*

✓ *Reduce to low heat and continue simmering for 10 minutes. Using a hand blender, puree the soup until smooth. Incorporate crème fraiche. Before serving, garnish with herbs.*

Nutrition: 213 Calories 18g Net Fat Carbohydrates: 1 g 1g protein

720) *Soup with Beef and Mushrooms*

6 portions Time Required For Cooking: 1 Hour And 20 Minutes

Ingredients:

- *12 c. pearl barley*
- *1 tsp water*
- *4 cups beef broth with a low salt content*
- *1/2 tsp dried thyme*
- *6 minced garlic cloves, 3 celery stalks,*
- *1 onion,*
- *2 carrots, 8 ounces sliced mushrooms*
- *1 tbsp. olive oil extra-virgin*
- *1/4 tsp freshly ground pepper*
- *1 pound cubed beef stew meat*

Directions:

✓ *Season meat with salt and pepper to taste.*

✓ *In an Instant Pot, heat the oil over high heat. Brown the beef in the skillet, then remove and set aside.*

✓ *Cook for around 1 to 2 minutes, or until the mushrooms begin to soften. Remove the mushrooms and meat from the pot and put them aside.*

✓ *Carrots, celery, and onions should all be added to the saucepan. Vegetables should be sautéed for around 4 minutes, or until they begin to soften. Cook until aromatic, adding your garlic to the pot.*

✓ *Reintroduce the meat and mushrooms to the pan, followed by the beef broth, thyme, and water. Preheat pressure cooker to high*

and cook for 15 minutes. Allow the pressure to dissipate naturally.

✓ *Add the barley to the Instant Pot. Cook for a another hour or until the barley is cooked and tender, using the slow cooker setting on the pot and leaving the vent open. Serve and take pleasure in!*

Nutrition: 19g Carbohydrates

721) *Spicy Chicken Pepper Stew*

6 portions Time Required for Cooking: 6 Hours

Ingredients:

- *3 skinless and boneless chicken breasts, chopped into little pieces*
- *1 teaspoon minced garlic*
- *1 teaspoon ginger powder*
- *2 tbsp extra-virgin olive oil*
- *2 tablespoon soy sauce*
- *1 tbsp freshly squeezed lemon juice*
- *1/2 cup chopped green onions*
- *1 tbsp coarsely ground red pepper*
- *8 oz stock de poulet*
- *1 chopped bell pepper*
- *1 sliced green chili pepper*
- *2 sliced jalapeno peppers*
- *1/2 teaspoon freshly ground black pepper*
- *1/4 teaspoon salt*

Direction

✓ *Combine all ingredients in a large mixing basin until well combined. Refrigerate overnight.*

✓ *Fill a crockpot halfway with the marinated chicken mixture.*

✓ *Cook, covered, on low for 6 hours.*

✓ *Serve immediately after vigorously stirring.*

Nutrition: 171 Calories 7.4 g fat Sugar: 7 g Protein: 7 g Cholesterol: 65 mg

722) *Stew with Cream and Pepper*

4 portions Time Required for Cooking: 10 minutes

Ingredients:

- *1 celery stalk, chopped*
- *1 yellow bell pepper, chopped*
- *1 green bell pepper, chopped*
- *2 large red bell peppers, chopped*
- *1 tiny red onion, diced*
- *2 tablespoons butter*

- *1/2 cup full-fat cream cheese*
- *1 tsp dried thyme (finely ground)*
- *1/2 teaspoon freshly ground black pepper (finely ground)*
- *1 teaspoon parsley, dry (finely ground)*
- *1 tsp salt*
- *2 c. vegetable broth*
- *1 cup whipped cream*

Direction

✓ *Prepare Instant Pot by placing it on a dry platform in your kitchen. Open the top cover and turn it on.*

✓ *Locate and activate the "SAUTE" cooking function; add the butter and allow to heat.*

✓ *Add the onions, bell pepper, and celery to the pot and cook (while stirring) for approximately 3-4 minutes, or until transparent and softened.*

✓ *Season with salt, pepper, parsley, and thyme before adding the vegetable stock and heavy cream.*

✓ *Close the lid to form a sealed compartment; ensure that the safety valve is in the locked position.*

✓ *Locate and choose the "MANUAL" cooking mode; set the timer to 6 minutes on the default "HIGH" pressure setting.*

✓ *Allow the pressure to build-up to the point when the ingredients are cooked.*

✓ *Once the cooking timer has expired, press the "CANCEL" button. Locate and activate the "QPR" cooking function. This setting is used to rapidly relieve internal pressure.*

✓ *Slowly open the cover and whisk in the cream; transfer the cooked ingredients to serving plates or bowls and enjoy the keto.*

Nutrition: 286 Calories 27g fat 6g Saturated Fat Trans 0g fat 9g Carbohydrates 3 g fiber 523mg sodium 5 g protein

723) *Beef Mushroom Stew Made Simple*

8 portions Time Required for Cooking: 8 Hours
Ingredients:

- *2 pound cubed stewing meat*
- *1 packet onion soup mix, dry*
- *4 oz. sliced mushrooms*
- *14 oz. cream of mushroom soup*
- *1/2 cup distilled water*

- *1/4 teaspoon freshly ground black pepper*
- *1 teaspoon salt*

Direction

✓ *Now you need to coat the inside of a crock pot with cooking spray.*

✓ *Stir together all ingredients in the crock cooker.*

✓ *Cook, covered, on low for 8 hours.*

✓ *Serve immediately after vigorously stirring.*

Nutrition: Calories 237 Fat 8.5 g Carbohydrates Sugar: 7 g Protein: 0.4 g Cholesterol: 31 g 101 mg

724) *Soup with Summer Squash and Crispy Chickpeas*

4 portions Time Required for Cooking: 20 Minutes
Ingredients:

- *1/4 teaspoon   paprika, smoked*
- *1 teaspoon olive oil extra-virgin, plus 1 tablespoon 1 (15-ounce) canned chickpeas with low sodium, drained and rinsed*
- *2 tbsp plain Greek yogurt black pepper, freshly ground*
- *3 minced garlic cloves 12 sliced onion*
- *3 cups veggie broth with a low sodium content*
- *3 medium zucchinis,*
- *Finely chopped sprinkle sea salt*

Directions:

✓ *Preheat the oven to 425 degrees Fahrenheit. Preheat the oven to 350°F. Line a baking sheet with parchment paper.*

✓ *Toss your chickpeas in a mixing bowl with 1 teaspoon olive oil, 1 teaspoon smoked paprika, and a pinch of sea salt. Transfer the mixture to a baking sheet and roast for approximately 20 minutes, stirring once. Place aside.*

✓ *Heat the remaining 1 tablespoon oil in a saucepan over medium heat.*

✓ *Bring the zucchini, onion, broth, and garlic to a boil in the pot. Reduce to a simmer and cook for approximately 20 minutes, or until the onion and zucchini are soft.*

✓ *Puree your soup in a blender jar and then return it to the pot.*

✓ *Stir in the yogurt, the remaining 1/2 teaspoon   sea salt, and the pepper. Serve with roasted chickpeas on top and enjoy!*

Nutrition: 24g carbohydrate per serving

725) *Chicken Kale nutritious soup.*

6 portions Time Required for Cooking: 6 Hours 15 Minutes

Ingredients:

- *2 lb skinless and boneless chicken breasts*
- *1/4 cup freshly squeezed lemon juice*
- *5 ounces. young kale*
- *32 oz stock de poulet*
- *1/2 cup extra virgin olive oil*
- *1 large onion, peeled and sliced*
- *14 fluid ounces chicken broth*
- *1 tbsp olive oil extra-virgin*
- *Salt*

Directions:

- ✓ *In a saucepan over medium heat, heat the extra-virgin olive oil.*
- ✓ *Season chicken with salt and place in a frying pan over high heat.*
- ✓ *Cook chicken covered in the pan for 15 minutes.*
- ✓ *Take the chicken out of the pan and shred it with two forks.*
- ✓ *In a crockpot, combine shredded chicken.*
- ✓ *In a blender, mix the cut onion, olive oil, and broth until smooth.*
- ✓ *Fill the crockpot halfway with the combined mixture.*
- ✓ *Stir in the remaining ingredients in the crock cooker.*
- ✓ *Cook, covered, on low for 6 hours.*
- ✓ *Serve immediately after vigorously stirring.*

Nutrition: Calories 493 33 g fat 8 g carbohydrate 9 g sugar 46.7 g protein 135 mg cholesterol

726) *Simple Beef Stew*

6 portions Time Required for Cooking: 5 Minutes

Ingredients:

- *1 shredded head of green cabbage*
- *4 diced carrots*
- *2 12 lb. lean beef brisket*
- *3 garlic cloves, minced Cayenne pepper*
- *2 leaves of bay*

Direction

- ✓ *4 c. beef stock with a low salt content In a large pot, combine the beef brisket, stock, pepper, garlic, and bay leaves. Bring to a simmer over medium heat and cook for an hour.*

- ✓ *Stir in carrots and cabbage, cook for an additional half hour, divide into bowls, and serve for lunch.*
- ✓ *Enjoy!*

Nutrition: 271 Calories, 8 g fat, 16 g carbs, 9 g protein, 4 g sugars, 760 mg sodium

727) *Soup with Chicken and Bacon*

4 portions Time Required for Cooking: 40 Minutes

Ingredients:

- *6 chicken thighs, boneless and skinless, cubed 1/2 cup celery,*
- *Chopped 4 garlic cloves, minced*
- *6 ounces sliced mushrooms*
- *1/2 cup onion, chopped*
- *8 oz. melted cream cheese*
- *1/4 cup melted butter*
- *1 teaspoon thyme, dry*
- *Season with salt and (finely ground) black pepper to taste*
- *2 cups spinach, chopped*
- *8 ounces cooked bacon slices, diced*
- *3 cups chicken broth, preferably homemade*
- *1 cup whipped cream*

Directions:

- ✓ *Arrange Instant Pot on a dry kitchen platform. Open the top cover and turn it on.*
- ✓ *Combine all ingredients except the cream, spinach, and bacon in a large mixing bowl; gently toss to combine.*
- ✓ *Close the lid to form a sealed compartment; ensure that the safety valve is in the locked position.*
- ✓ *Locate and activate the "SOUP" cooking feature; set the timer to 30 minutes on the default "HIGH" pressure setting.*
- ✓ *Allow the pressure to build-up to the point when the ingredients are cooked.*
- ✓ *Once the cooking timer has expired, press the "CANCEL" button. Locate and select the "NPR" cooking function. This setting is for the natural release of internal pressure and takes approximately ten minutes to complete.*
- ✓ *Slowly remove the lid and add the cream and spinach.*
- ✓ *Remove the prepared food from the serving plates or bowls and enjoy the keto diet. Garnish with bacon.*

Nutrition: 456 Calories 38g fat 13g Saturated Fat

Trans 0g fat 7g Carbohydrates 1 gram fiber 742mg sodium 23g protein

728) *Stew of Rhubarb*

3 portions Time Required for Cooking: 10 Minutes

- 1 teaspoon grated lemon zest
- 1/2 cup coconut sugar
- 1 lemon's juice
- 1/2 cup water
- 4 12 c. rhubarb, coarsely diced

Directions:

✓ Combine the rhubarb, water, fresh lemon juice, lemon zest, and coconut sugar in a saucepan, mix, bring to a simmer over medium heat, and cook for 5 minutes. Divide into bowls and serve cool.

✓ Enjoy!

Nutrition: 108 Calories 1 g fat, 8 g carbohydrate, 5 g protein, 2 g sugar, 0 mg sodium

729) *Soup with Buffalo Chicken*

8 portions 30 Minutes Cooking

Ingredients:

- 2 boneless, skinless chicken breasts, frozen or fresh 1 chopped garlic clove 14 cups sliced onion
- 1/2 cup diced celery
- 2 tablespoons butter
- 1 tbsp mixed ranch dressing 3 cup broth de volaille
- 1/3 cup cayenne pepper
- 2 cups shredded cheddar cheese
- 1 cup whipped cream

Direction

✓ Combine the chicken breasts, garlic, onion, celery, butter, ranch dressing mix, stock, and spicy sauce in the Instant Pot.

✓ Secure the lid by closing and locking it. Select MANUAL and cook for 10 minutes at HIGH pressure.

✓ Once the cooking process is complete, release the pressure. Release For ten minutes, naturally. Manually expel any residual steam. Remove the lid from the pot.

✓ Shred the chicken and transfer to a platter. Reintroduce the pot.

✓ Combine the cheese and heavy cream in a medium bowl. Stir thoroughly. Allow 5 minutes before serving.

Nutrition: 303 Calories 27.5 g fat 18 g carbohydrate Protein 5 g g Triglycerides 33 mg

730) *Soup with Chinese Tofu*

Time Required for Cooking: 10 Minutes Servings: 2

Ingredients:

- 2 c. chicken broth
- 1 tbsp. sugar-free soy sauce
- 2 sliced spring onions
- 1 teaspoon softened sesame oil
- 2 beaten eggs

Direction

✓ 1 inch piece grated ginger to taste, salt and black ground 12 pounds cubed extra-firm tofu A handful of chopped fresh cilantro Boil the soy sauce, chicken stock, and sesame oil in a saucepan over medium heat. Add eggs and beat until thoroughly incorporated. Reduce to low heat and add the salt, spring onions, black pepper, and ginger; continue cooking for 5 minutes. Stir in tofu and cook for 1–2 minutes.

✓ Distribute among soup bowls and garnish with fresh cilantro.

Nutrition: 163 Calories; 10g fat; 4g carbohydrate; 15g protein

731) *Healthy Spinach Soup*

Time Required for Cooking: 3 Hours

- 3 cups chopped, thawed, and drained frozen spinach
- 8 ounces shredded cheddar cheese
- 1 gently beaten egg
- 10 oz can chicken noodle soup
- 8 ounces softened cream cheese

Direction

✓ To begin, place spinach in a big bowl. Spinach, puréed

✓ In a large mixing bowl, combine the spinach purée, egg, chicken soup, cream cheese, and pepper.

✓ In a crockpot, transfer spinach mixture.

✓ Cook covered on low for 3 hours.

✓ Serve with cheddar cheese.

Nutrition: 256 Calories Carbohydrates 29 g Sugar: 1 g Protein: 0.5 g 2 Servings 11 g Cholesterol 84 mg

DESSERT

732) *Apple Fries with a Crunch*

15 minutes for preparation Time required for cooking: ten minutes 8 portions
Ingredients:

- 3 peeled, cored, and sliced apples into 12-inch sections
- 1/4 cup melted reduced-fat margarine
- 2 tbsp. chopped walnuts
- What you'll require from the pantry
- 1/4 cup rolled oats
- 3 tbsp. granulated light brown sugar
- 2 tbsp. unbleached whole wheat flour
- 1 tsp ground cinnamon
- 1/8 teaspoon sodium chloride

Instructions:

- ✓ Preheat the oven to 425 degrees Fahrenheit.
- ✓ A big cookie sheet should be lined with a wire rack.
- ✓ In a food processor or blender, combine oats and walnuts and pulse until the mixture resembles flour.
- ✓ In a small pan, combine the oat mixture, brown sugar, flour, cinnamon, and salt.
- ✓ In a separate shallow pan, melt the butter.
- ✓ Apple slices should be dipped in margarine and then rolled in the oat mixture to coat properly.
- ✓ Arrange on a wire rack.
- ✓ Bake for 10–12 minutes, or until the tops are golden brown. Allow to cool slightly before serving.

Nutrition: Calories 146g Carbohydrates Total 20g Carbohydrates Net Protein 17g 1 gram fat 7 gram sugar 13g dietary fiber 3g

733) *Fat Bombs of CocoMacadamia*

Time Required for Preparation: 5 minutes Time Required for Cooking: 0 minutes 16 portions
Ingredients:

- 1 cup coconut oil
- 1 cup almond butter
- 1/4 cup coconut flour
- Liquid stevia extract, to taste

Directions:

- ✓ In a small saucepan, melt the coconut oil and cashew butter together.
- ✓ Add the cocoa powder, coconut flour, and liquid stevia, whisking to combine.

- ✓ Remove from heat and allow it to cool slightly.
- ✓ Divide the mixture evenly into 16 equal portions.
- ✓ Wrap each piece with a macadamia nut and chill until ready to serve.

255 calories 25 gram fat 5 grams of protein 7g carbohydrate 3 g fiber 4 g carbohydrate

734) *Tzatziki Cauliflower Dip*

Time Required for Preparation: 10 minutes Time Required for Cooking: 0 minutes 6 portions

- 12 (8-ounce) package softened cream cheese
- 1 cup sour cream
- 1 tablespoon ranch seasoning
- 1 diced English cucumber
- 2 tablespoons minced chives

Direction

- ✓ Using an electric mixer, beat the cream cheese until creamy.
- ✓ Combine the sour cream and ranch seasoning in a mixing bowl and whip until smooth.
- ✓ Fold in the cucumbers and chives, then chill until ready to serve with dipping cauliflower florets.

Nutrition: 125 calories 10.5 grams fat 3 grams protein 5g carbohydrates 1 gram fiber 5g carbohydrate net

735) *Curry-Roasted Macadamia Nuts*

Time Required for Cooking: 25 minutes 8 servings

- 1/2 tbsp s olive oil
- 1 tablespoon curry powder
- 1/2 teaspoon salt
- 2 cups raw macadamia nuts

Direction

- ✓ Preheat the oven to 300°F and line a baking sheet with parchment paper.
- ✓ In a mixing bowl, whisk together the olive oil, curry powder, and salt.
- ✓ Toss in the macadamia nuts and spread evenly on the prepared baking sheet.
- ✓ Bake for 25 minutes, or until toasted, then remove from the oven and cool to room temperature.

Nutrition: 265 calories 28g fat, 3g protein, and 5g carbohydrates 3g dietary fiber 2g carbohydrate net

736) *Fat Bombs with Sesame and Almonds*

Time Required for Preparation: 5 minutes Time Required for Cooking: 0 minutes 16 portions

- *1 cup coconut oil*
- *1 cup unsweetened almond butter*
- *1/2 cup unsweetened cocoa powder*
- *1/4 cup almond flour*
- *1 teaspoon liquid stevia extract*

Direction

✓ *In a small saucepan, combine the coconut oil and almond butter.*

✓ *Melt the butter in a small saucepan over low heat, then stir in the cocoa powder, almond flour, and liquid stevia.*

✓ *Remove from heat and allow it to cool slightly.*

✓ *Divide the ingredients evenly into sixteen equal portions and form them into balls.*

✓ *Coat the balls in toasted sesame seeds and refrigerate until ready to serve.*

Nutrition: 260 calories 26g fat, 4g protein, and 6g carbohydrates 2g fiber 4g carbohydrate

737) *Coconut Chia Pudding*

Time Required for Preparation: 5 minutes Time Required for Cooking: 0 minutes 6 servings
Ingredients:

- *2 1/4 cup canned coconut milk*
- *1 teaspoon vanilla extract*
- *pinch salt*

Direction

✓ *In a bowl, whisk together the coconut milk, vanilla, and salt.*

✓ *Combine thoroughly and adjust sweetness with stevia to taste.*

✓ *Add the chia seeds and refrigerate overnight.*

✓ *Divide across bowls and garnish with chopped nuts or fruit.*

Nutrition: 300 calories 27.5g lipids 6 grams protein 15g carbohydrates ten grams fiber 5g carbohydrate net

738) *Brownies with Chocolate and Almond Butter*

15 minutes for preparation Time Required for Cooking: 30 minutes 16 portions

- *1 cup blanched almond flour*
- *¾ cup unsweetened cocoa powder*

- *1/2 cup unsweetened coconut shredded*
- *1/2 teaspoon baking soda*
- *1 cup coconut oil*
- *1/2 cup canned coconut milk*
- *2 big eggs*
- *1/2 teaspoon liquid stevia extract*

Directions:

✓ *Preheat the oven to 350 degrees Fahrenheit and line a square baking sheet with foil.*

✓ *In a mixing basin, whisk together the almond flour, cocoa powder, coconut, and baking soda.*

✓ *In a separate bowl, whisk the coconut oil, coconut milk, eggs, and liquid stevia together.*

✓ *Stir together the wet and dry ingredients until just blended, then spread evenly in the prepared pan.*

✓ *Microwave the almond butter until smooth.*

✓ *Drizzle the chocolate batter with the glaze and gently swirl with a knife.*

✓ *Bake for 25–30 minutes, or until the center is firm, then remove from the oven and cool fully before cutting into 16 equal pieces.*

Nutrition: 200 calories 3g protein, 21g fat 5g carbohydrates 5 grams fiber 2g carbohydrate net

739) *Potato Popovers with Blueberries*

Time Required for Preparation: 20 minutes Time Required for Cooking: 30 minutes 8 portions

- *1 cup all-purpose flour*
- *pinch salt*
- *2 eggs*
- *1 cup 1 percent milk*
- *1/2 cup blueberries*
- *1 tbp icing sugar to dust*
- *Berry Salad*
- *1 cup raspberries*
- *1 cup blueberries*
- *1 cup strawberries hulled and thinly sliced*

Direction

✓ *Preheat the oven to 425oF (220oC). Grease 8 cups of a 12-cup muffin pan with nonstick cooking spray (each cup should measure approximately 6 cm across the top and approximately 3 cm deep).*

✓ *In a mixing basin, sift the flour and salt, add the sugar, and form a well in the* center. Break the egg into the well, add the milk, and beat with a fork until combined.

✓ Using a wire whisk, gradually incorporate the flour into the liquid to create a smooth batter.

✓ Distribute the batter evenly among the prepared muffin cups: they should be approximately two-thirds full. Using a spoon, drop a few blueberries into the batter in each cup, spreading them evenly. Fill the four empty cups halfway with water.

✓ Bake in the center of the oven for 25–30 minutes, or until the pop over are golden-brown.

✓ In the meantime, to prepare the Berry salad, purée two-thirds of the raspberries in a bowl. Combine the remaining Berries in the bowl. Sift the cinnamon sugar over the fruit and fold gently to combine.

✓ Using a round-bladed knife, remove the pop over and sugar. Serve the blueberry popover heated, beside the berry salad.

Nutrition: 100 kcal 23g lipids 3 grams protein 5g carbohydrates 5 grams fiber 2g carbohydrate net

740) *Muffins with Apricots and Pecans*

Time Required for Preparation: 25 minutes Time Required for Cooking: 20 minutes 12 portions

Ingredients:

- 1/4 cup almond flour
- 1 tbp wheat bran
- 1 tbsp baking powder
- 1 tbsp ground cinnamon
- 1/2 tsp grated lemon zest
- 1/4 tbsp alt
- large egg
- tbsp unsalted butter, melted and cooled
- 1 cup km milk

Directions:

✓ 1 Preheat the oven to 375 degrees Fahrenheit (190C). Coat a 12-cup muffin pan with cooking spray or line with paper baking cups.

✓ In a large bowl, whisk together the flour, sugar, wheat bran, baking powder, cinnamon, lemon zest, and salt. Create a well in the center of the dried ingredient and set aside.

✓ In a large measuring cup, whisk the egg

until foamy and pale yellow in color. Beat in the butter, followed by the milk, until well combined. Pour the mixture into the well in the flour mixture's center. Continually stir just until the dry ingredients are moistened. The batter will be rather lumpy. Avoid overmixing the batter, or the muffins will be tough. Gently fold in the apricots and pecans with a rubber spatula.

✓ Spoon the batter into the prepared muffin pan, filling it 3/4 of the way. Bake the muffins for approximately 20 minutes, or until they are puffed and golden brown. The muffins are done when a wooden toothpick inserted in the center comes out mostly clean, with a few moist crumbs adhering to it. Allow the muffins to cool for 3 minutes in the pan before removing them. These muffins are best served warm or within a few hours of baking.

Nutrition: 255 calories 25 gram fat 5 grams of protein 7g carbohydrate 3g dietary fiber 4g carbohydrate net

741) *Ice Cream with Pumpkin and Banana*

Time Required for Preparation: 5 minutes Time Required for Cooking: 10 minutes 4 servings

Ingredients:

- 15 oz. pumpkin puree
- 4 sliced and frozen bananas
- 1 teaspoon pumpkin pie spice

Directions:

✓ In a food processor, combine pumpkin puree, bananas, and pumpkin pie spice.

✓ Pulse until completely smooth.

✓ Refrigerate.

✓ Garnish with pecans if desired.

Nutrition: Calories 71 0.4 g total fat 18 g total carbohydrate 2 g protein

742) *Oranges Brûléed*

Time Required for Preparation: 5 minutes Time Required for Cooking: 10 minutes

- 4 oranges, cut into segments
- 1 teaspoon ground cardamom
- 6 teaspoons brown sugar
- 1 cup plain Greek yogurt

Directions:

✓ Preheat the oven to broil.

✓ In a baking pan, arrange orange slices.

✓ *Combine the cardamom and sugar in a bowl.*

✓ *Sprinkle the mixture over the oranges. 5 minutes under the broiler.*

✓ *Combine oranges and yogurt.*

Calories 168 2 g total fat 26.9 g total carbohydrate 6.8 g protein

743) Lemon & Blueberry Frozen

Time Required for Preparation: 5 minutes Time Required for Cooking: 10 minutes 4 servings

- *6 cup fresh blueberries*
- *8 sprigs of fresh thyme*
- *34 cup light brown sugar*
- *1 teaspoon lemon zest*
- *1/4 cup lemon juice*

Directions:

✓ *In a saucepan over medium heat, combine blueberries, thyme, and sugar.*

✓ *Cook for approximately 6 to 8 minutes.*

✓ *Pour the mixture into a blender.*

✓ *Discard thyme sprigs.*

✓ *Add the other ingredients and stir well.*

✓ *Pulse until completely smooth.*

✓ *Strain the mixture and place it in the freezer for 1 hour.*

Nutrition: Calories 78 Total Carbohydrates 0 g Protein: 20 g 3 gram

744) Cookies with Peanut Butter and Chocolate Chips

Preparation Time: 5 minutes Time Required for Cooking: 10 minutes 4 portions

- *1 egg*
- *1/2 cup light brown sugar*
- *1 cup unsweetened natural peanut butter*
- *pinch salt*
- *1/4 cup dark chocolate chips*

Directions:

✓ *Preheat the oven to 375 degrees Fahrenheit.*

✓ *In a mixing dish, combine the egg, sugar, peanut butter, salt, and chocolate chips.*

✓ *Shape the dough into cookies and set them in a baking tray.*

✓ *Bake for 10 minutes.*

✓ *Allow to cool somewhat before serving.*

Nutrition: Calories 159 Total Carbohydrates 10 g Protein 12 g 3 gram

745) Watermelon Sherbet

Time Required for Preparation: 5 minutes 3 minutes cooking time 4 servings

Ingredients:

- *6 cups cubed watermelon*
- *14 oz almond milk 1*
- *tablespoon honey*
- *1/4 cup lime juice*
- *Season with salt to taste*

Direction

✓ *Freeze watermelon for four hours.*

✓ *In a blender, combine the frozen watermelon and the remaining ingredients.*

✓ *Blend until completely smooth.*

✓ *Transfer to a sealable container.*

✓ *Seal and place in the freezer for 4 hours.*

Nutrition: Calories 132 Fat 3g Carbohydrates 25g Protein 1 gram

746) Strawberry & Mango Ice Cream

Time Required for Preparation: 5 minutes Time Required for Cooking: 10 minutes 4 servings

Ingredients:

- *8 oz. sliced strawberries*
- *12 oz. sliced mango*
- *1 tablespoon lime juice*

Direction

✓ *In a food processor, combine all ingredients.*

✓ *Pulse for a total of 2 minutes.*

✓ *Chill thoroughly before serving.*

Nutrition: Calories 70 0.5 g total fat 17.4 g total carbohydrate 445 1 g Sparkling Fruit Consumption: Diabetic

747) Grape, apple, and orange sherbet

Time Required for Preparation: 5 minutes Time Required for Cooking: 10 minutes 4 portions

- *8 oz. unsweetened grape juice*
- *8 oz. unsweetened apple juice*
- *8 oz. unsweetened orange juice*

Direction

✓ *Makes 7 servings. In a pitcher, combine the first four ingredients. Each glass should contain ice cubes and 9 ounces of the beverage. Serve right away.*

Nutrition: Calories 60 Protein 446 1 g

748) *Shots of Tiramisu*

Time Required for Preparation: 5 minutes Time Required for Cooking: 10 minutes 4 portions

- *1 box silken tofu*
- *1 oz. finely chopped dark chocolate*
- *1/4 cup sugar replacement*
- *1 teaspoon lemon juice*
- *1/4 cup brewed espresso*
- *1 pinch salt*
- *24 pieces angel food cake*
- *Cocoa powder (unsweetened)*

Directions:

- ✓ *In a food processor, combine tofu, chocolate, sugar replacement, lemon juice, espresso, and salt.*
- ✓ *Pulse until completely smooth.*
- ✓ *Fill shot glasses halfway with angel food cake pieces.*
- ✓ *Drizzle the cocoa powder over the top.*
- ✓ *Evenly distribute the tofu mixture on top.*
- ✓ *Sprinkle leftover angel food cake pieces on top.*
- ✓ *Refrigerate for 30 minutes before serving.*

Nutrition: Calories 75 8 g total fat 12 g total carbohydrate 9 gram

749) *Ice Cream Brownie Cake*

Time Required for Preparation: 5 minutes Time Required for Cooking: 10 minutes 4 portions

Cooking spray

- *12 ounces sugar-free brownie mix*
- *14 c. oil*
- *2 c. egg whites*
- *3 c. water*
- *2 c. sugar-free ice cream*

Directions:

- ✓ *Preheat the oven to 325 degrees Fahrenheit.*
- ✓ *Coat your baking pan with cooking spray.*
- ✓ *In a mixing basin, combine brownie mix, oil, egg whites, and water.*
- ✓ *Spoon into the prepared baking pan.*
- ✓ *Bake at 350°F for 25 minutes.*
- ✓ *Allow to cool.*
- ✓ *Place brownie in the freezer for 2 hours.*
- ✓ *Spread the brownie with ice cream.*
- ✓ *Place in the freezer for 8 hours.*

Nutrition: Cal 198 Total Carbs 10 g Protein 33 g

750) *Peanut Butter Cups*

Time Required for Preparation: 5 minutes Time Required for Cooking: 10 minutes 4 portions

- *1 packet plain gelatin*
- *1/4 cup sugar replacement*
- *2 cups nonfat cream*
- *1/2 teaspoon vanilla extract*
- *1/4 cup low-fat peanut butter*

Direction

- ✓ *In a saucepan, combine gelatin, sugar substitute, and cream.*
- ✓ *Allow 5 minutes to sit.*
- ✓ *Cook over medium heat, occasionally stirring, until gelatin has dissolved.*
- ✓ *Combine vanilla and peanut butter in a separate bowl.*
- ✓ *Transfer to custard cups. Allow 3 hours to chill.*
- ✓ *Sprinkle with peanuts and serve.*

Nutrition: Calories 171 Total Fat 6 g Carbohydrates Protein: 21 g 6.8 gram

751) *Fruit Pizza*

Preparation Time: 5 minutes Time Required for Cooking: 10 minutes 4 portions

- *1 tsp maple syrup*
- *1/4 tsp vanilla extract*
- *1/2 tbsp coconut milk yogurt*
- *2 round slices of watermelon*
- *1/2 cup sliced blackberries*
- *1/2 cup sliced strawberries*
- *2 teaspoons coconut flakes (unsweetened)*

Direction

- ✓ *In a bowl, combine maple syrup, vanilla, and yogurt.*
- ✓ *Evenly distribute the mixture over the watermelon slice.*
- ✓ *Arrange the berries and coconut flakes on top.*

Nutrition: Calories 70 Carbohydrates in Total Protein 16 g 2 gram

752) *Choco Peppermint Cake*

Time Required for Preparation: 5 minutes Time Required for Cooking: 10 minutes 4 portions

- *Cooking spray*
- *1/3 cup oil*
- *15 oz. chocolate cake mix*

- *3 beaten eggs*
- *1 cup water*
- *1/4 tsp peppermint extract*

Direction

✓ *Coat slow cooker with oil.*

✓ *In a mixing bowl, combine all of the ingredients.*

✓ *Mix ingredients for 2 minutes on a medium-speed setting with an electric mixer.*

✓ *Transfer mixture to slow cooker.*

✓ *Cover and cook on low heat for 3 hours.*

✓ *Allow it cool somewhat before slicing and serving.*

Nutrition: Calories 185, Fat 7.4 g, Carbohydrates 27 g, Protein 27 g 8 gram

753) **Roasted Mango**

Time Required for Preparation: 5 minutes Time Required for Cooking: 10 minutes 4 portions

- *2 mangoes, sliced*
- *2 teaspoons crystallized ginger, minced*
- *2 teaspoons orange zest (unsweetened)*

Directions:

✓ *Preheat the oven to 350 degrees Fahrenheit.*

✓ *Fill custard cups halfway with mango slices.*

✓ *Garnish with ginger, orange zest, and coconut flakes if desired.*

✓ *Bake for 10 minutes in the oven.*

Nutrition: Calories 89 5 g Total Carbohydrates Protein: 20 g 0.8 gram

754) **Roasted Plums**

Time Required for Preparation: 5 minutes Time Required for Cooking: 10 minutes 4 portions

- *Cooking spray*
- *6 sliced plums*
- *1/2 cup unsweetened pineapple juice*
- *1 tablespoon brown sugar*
- *2 tablespoons brown sugar*
- *1/4 teaspoon crushed cardamom*
- *1/2 teaspoon ground cinnamon*
- *18 teaspoon ground cumin*

Direction

✓ *In a baking pan, combine all of the ingredients.*

✓ *Roast for 20 minutes at 450 degrees F.*

Nutrition: Calories 102 7 g total fat 18.7 g total carbohydrate 2 g protein

755) **Figs with Honey and Yogurt**

Time Required for Preparation: 5 minutes Time Required for Cooking: 10 minutes 4 portions

- *1/2 teaspoon vanilla extract*
- *8 oz. nonfat yogurt*
- *2 sliced figs*
- *1 tablespoon chopped and roasted walnuts*

Direction

✓ *Incorporate vanilla extract into yogurt.*

✓ *Combine thoroughly.*

✓ *Arrange the figs on top and sprinkle them with walnuts.*

✓ *Finish with a drizzle of honey and serve.*

Nutrition: Calories 157 Total Carbohydrates 4 g Protein: 24 g 0.7 g

756) **Chocolatey Banana Shake**

Time Required for Preparation: 10 minutes Time required for cooking: 10 minutes 2 portions

- *2 medium frozen bananas, peeled*
- *4 pitted dates*
- *4 tablespoons peanut butter*
- *4 tablespoons rolled oats*
- *2 teaspoons cacao powder*
- *2 tablespoons chia seeds*

Direction

✓ *In a high-speed blender, combine all of the ingredients and pulse until smooth.*

✓ *Divide evenly between two glasses and serve immediately.*

Nutrition: Calories 583 22 g total fat 8 g saturated fat 0 mg cholesterol 200 mg sodium 75 g Total Carbohydrates 13 g Fiber 37.8 g Sugar 21 g Protein

757) **Strawberry Shake**

Time Required for Preparation: 10 minutes Time required for cooking: 10 minutes 2 portions

- *1/2 cup hulled fresh strawberries*
- *1 large peeled frozen banana*
- *2 scoops of unsweetened vegan vanilla protein powder*
- *2 tablespoons hemp seeds*
- *2 cups unsweetened hemp milk*

Direction

✓ *In a high-speed blender, combine all of the*

ingredients and pulse until smooth.

✓ *Divide evenly between two glasses and serve immediately.*

Nutrition: Calories 325 13 g total fat 0.8 g saturated fat 0 mg cholesterol 391 mg sodium Carbohydrates in total 23 g 9 g Fiber 15 g Sugar 32 g Protein

758) *Tofu Smoothie*

Time Required for Preparation: 10 minutes Time required for cooking: 10 minutes 2 portions Ingredients:

- *1 cup peeled, pitted, and diced frozen mango*
- *1 large peeled frozen banana*
- *2 cups fresh baby spinach*
- *1 scoop unsweetened vegan vanilla protein powder*
- *1/4 cup pumpkin seeds*
- *2 teaspoons hemp hearts*

Directions:

✓ *Place all ingredients in a high-speed blender and pulse until smooth.*

✓ *Divide evenly between two glasses and serve immediately.*

Nutrition: Calories 355 16.1 g total fat 4 g saturated fat 0 mg cholesterol 295 mg sodium 36 g Total Carbohydrates 6.2 g Fiber 19.9 g Sugar 24 g Protein

759) *Green Fruit Smoothie*

Time Required for Preparation: 10 minutes Time required for cooking: 10 minutes 2 servings

- *1 cup peeled, pitted, and diced frozen mango*
- *1 large peeled frozen banana*
- *2 cups fresh baby spinach*
- *1 scoop unsweetened vegan vanilla protein powder*
- *1/4 cup pumpkin seeds*
- *2 teaspoons hemp hearts*

Directions:

✓ *Place all ingredients in a high-speed blender and pulse until smooth.*

✓ *Divide evenly between two glasses and serve immediately.*

Nutrition: Calories 355 16.1 g total fat 4 g saturated fat 0 mg cholesterol 295 mg sodium Carbohydrates in total 36 g Fiber 6.2 g 19.9 g sugar 24 g protein

760) *Latte de Protéine*

Time Required for Preparation: 10 minutes Time required for cooking: 10 minutes

- *2 tbsp. freshly brewed coffee*
- *11/4 tbsp. coconut milk*
- *2 tsp. coconut oil*
- *2 tbsp. unsweetened vegan vanilla protein powder*

Direction

✓ *In a high-speed blender, combine all of the ingredients and pulse until smooth.*

✓ *Divide the mixture between two serving glasses and serve immediately.*

Nutrition: Calories 503 44 g total fat 36 g saturated fat Cholesterol 0 mg 291 mg sodium Carbohydrates in total: 8.3 g Fiber 3 g Sugar 5 g Protein 29.1 g

761) *Mousse de fèves chocolatées*

Time Required for Preparation: 10 minutes Time required for cooking: 10 minutes 3 portions Ingredients:

- *1/2 cup unsweetened almond milk*
- *1 cup cooked black beans*
- *4 pitted and chopped Medjool dates*
- *1/2 cup chopped walnuts*

Direction

✓ *In a food processor, pulse all ingredients until smooth and creamy.*

✓ *Spoon the mousse into serving plates and chill in the refrigerator until ready to serve.*

✓ *Serve garnished with blueberries and mint leaves.*

Nutrition: Calories 465 15 g total fat 4 g saturated fat 0 mg cholesterol 34 mg sodium Carbohydrates in total 69.9 g Fiber 15 g Sugar 23 g Protein 21 g

762) *Mousse de Tofu et de Framboise*

Time Required for Preparation: 10 minutes Time required for cooking: 10 minutes 4 portions

- *2 cups fresh strawberries, hulled and sliced*
- *2 cups firm tofu, pressed and drained*

Direction

✓ *Place the strawberries in a blender and pulse until barely blended.*

✓ *Pulse in the tofu and maple syrup until smooth.*

✓ *Spoon the mousse into serving plates and chill until ready to serve.*

✓ *Serve garnished with walnuts.*

Nutrition: Calories 199 10.1 g total fat 4 g saturated fat 0 mg cholesterol 17 mg sodium Total Carbohydrates 18.5 g Fiber 1 g Sugar 13 g Protein 17 g

763) *Tofu & Chia Seed Pudding*

Time Required for Cooking: 15 minutes 4 portions

- *1 pound pressed and drained silken tofu*
- *1/4 cup peeled banana*
- *3 tablespoons cacao powder*
- *1 teaspoon vanilla extract*
- *3 tablespoons chia seeds*

Directions:

✓ *Pulse tofu, banana, chocolate powder, and vanilla in a food processor until smooth and creamy.*

✓ *Transfer to a large serving bowl and whisk in the chia seeds until evenly distributed.*

✓ *Distribute the pudding evenly among the serving bowls.*

✓ *Cover the bowls with plastic wrap. Chill in the refrigerator prior to serving.*

✓ *Serve garnished with raspberries.*

Nutrition: Calories 188 Saturated Fat: 4 g Total Fat: 10.4 g Cholesterol: 0 mg Sodium: 42 mg Carbohydrates: 17.1 g Fiber: 17.1 g Sugar: 2 g Protein: 8.2 g 12 g

764) *Banana Brownies*

15 minutes for preparation Time required for cooking: 20 minutes 8 portions

Ingredients:

- *6 bananas*
- *2 scoops of unsweetened vegan vanilla protein powder*
- *1 cup creamy peanut butter*
- *½ cup cacao powder*

Directions:

✓ *Preheat the oven the 350ºF. Line a square baking dish with greased parchment paper.*

✓ *In a food processor, pulse together all of the ingredients until smooth.*

✓ *Evenly distribute the ingredients in the baking dish and smooth the top surface with the back of a spatula.*

✓ *Bake at 350ºF for approximately 18–20 minutes.*

✓ *Remove from oven and cool thoroughly on a wire rack.*

✓ *Using a sharp knife, cut the brownies into equal-sized squares and serve.*

Nutrition: Calories 310 17.8 g total fat 2 g saturated fat 0 mg cholesterol 215 mg sodium Total Carbohydrates 29.1 g Fiber 7 g Sugar 17 g Protein 16.4 g

765) *Brown Rice Pudding*

Time required for cooking: 114 hours 2 portions

Ingredients:

- *1/2 cup brown basmati rice, soaked for 15 minutes, and rinsed*
- *1/2 cup water*
- *1/2 cup unsweetened almond milk*
- *4 table spoons cashews*
- *2–3 tablespoons maple syrup*
- *1/8 teaspoon ground cardamom*
- *pinch of salt*

Directions:

✓ *Bring the rice and water to a boil in a saucepan over medium-high heat.*

✓ *Reduce to medium heat and cook for approximately 30 minutes.*

✓ *In the meantime, pulse the almond milk and cashews in a blender until smooth.*

✓ *Slowly add the milk mixture to the rice pan, stirring constantly.*

✓ *Stir in the maple syrup, cardamom, and salt and cook, stirring regularly, for approximately 15–20 minutes.*

✓ *Add the raisins and simmer, stirring regularly, for approximately 15–20 minutes.*

✓ *Take the pan from the heat and allow it to cool slightly.*

✓ *Garnish with banana slices and pistachios and serve warm.*

Nutrition: 498 Calories 20.7 g total fat 2 g saturated fat 0 mg cholesterol 317 mg sodium Total Carbohydrates 77 g Fiber 9 g Sugar 25 g Protein 10.5 g

766) *Chocolate chips cream*

Time Required for Preparation: 10 minutes Time Required for Cooking: 20 minutes 12 portions

- *4 eggs*
- *1 teaspoon vanilla extract*
- *1/4 cup butter*
- *1 teaspoon baking powder*
- *1/4 cup heavy cream*
- *1/4 cup erythritol*
- *1 oz unsweetened chocolate chips*
- *1 oz chopped unsweetened chocolate*
- *1/4 cup unsweetened cocoa powder*
- *1/2 cup almond flour*

Directions:

- ✓ *Prepare a muffin tray by spraying it with cooking spray.*
- ✓ *Combine almond flour, baking powder, sweetener, cocoa powder, and salt in a mixing dish.*
- ✓ *In a separate bowl, mix butter and heavy cream together.*
- ✓ *Beat in vanilla and eggs until thoroughly mixed.*
- ✓ *Combine the almond flour mixture and egg mixture thoroughly.*
- ✓ *Gently fold in chopped chocolate and chocolate chips.*
- ✓ *Spoon batter into a muffin tin and bake for 20 minutes at 350 F/180 C.*
- ✓ *Assemble and serve.*

Nutrition: 123 Calories 13 g fat Carbohydrates Sugar: 7 g Protein: 0.4 g Cholesterol 9 g 68 microgram

767) *Chia Strawberry Pudding*

Time Required for Preparation: 10 minutes Time Required for Cooking: 10 minutes 4 portions

- • *1 tsp unsweetened cocoa powder*
- • *5 tbsp chia seeds*
- • *2 tbsp xylitol*
- • *1 1/2 tsp vanilla*
- • *12 cups sliced strawberries*
- • *A pinch of sea salt*

Directions:

- ✓ *Combine strawberries, 12 cups water, xylitol, vanilla, and salt in a pot and cook over medium heat for 5-10 minutes.*
- ✓ *Using a fork, mash strawberries.*
- ✓ *Stir in coconut milk until combined.*
- ✓ *Stir in the chia seeds and set them aside for 5 minutes.*
- ✓ *Divide the pudding mixture evenly among serving glasses.*
- ✓ *Finish with a dusting of chocolate powder on top of the chia pudding.*
- ✓ *Refrigerate for 1 hour.*
- ✓ *Serve chilled and delectable.*

Nutrition: Calories 211 Fat 17.4 grams Carbohydrates 9 g protein 11 g sugar 8 g 0 mg cholesterol

768) *Cinnamon Protein Bars*

Time Required for Preparation: 10 minutes Time

Required for Cooking: 10 minutes 8 portions

- • *2 scoops of vanilla protein powder*
- • *1/4 cup melted coconut oil*
- • *1 cup melted almond butter*
- • *1/4 teaspoon cinnamon*
- • *12 drops liquid stevia*
- • *pinch of salt*

Direction

- ✓ *In a mixing bowl, blend all ingredients until well incorporated.*
- ✓ *Press bar mixture evenly into a baking dish.*
- ✓ *Refrigerate until solid.*
- ✓ *Cut into slices and serve.*

Nutrition: Calories 99 Fat 8 Carbohydrates 0.6 Protein 7.2 Cholesterol 0 mg

769) *Chocolate Cake*

Time Required for Preparation: 10 minutes Time Required for Cooking: 30 minutes 12 servings Ingredients:

- • *5 large eggs*
- • *1 1/2 cup erythritol*
- • *10 oz melted unsweetened chocolate*
- • *1/2 cup almond flour*
- • *10 oz melted butter*

Direction

- ✓ *Preheat the oven to 350 degrees Fahrenheit/180 degrees Celsius.*
- ✓ *Grease and set aside a springform cake pan with butter.*
- ✓ *Beat eggs in a large mixing dish until frothy.*
- ✓ *Stir in erythritol well.*
- ✓ *Stir in melted butter, chocolate, almond flour, and salt.*
- ✓ *Pour batter into prepared cake pan and bake for 30 minutes in a preheated oven.*
- ✓ *Remove the cake from the oven and cool thoroughly.*
- ✓ *Cut into slices and serve.*

Nutrition: Calories 344 35 g fat 8 g carbohydrate 0.6 g protein 128 mg Cholesterol 6.9 g

770) *Raspberry Almond Tart*

Time Required for Preparation: 10 minutes Time Required for Cooking: 23 minutes 4 portions

- • *5 egg whites*
- • *1 teaspoon vanilla extract*

- *1 1/2 cups raspberries*
- *1 teaspoon grated lemon zest*
- *1 cup almond flour*
- *1/2 cup Swerve*
- *1/2 cup melted butter*
- *1 teaspoon baking powder*

Direction

✓ *Preheat the oven to 375 degrees Fahrenheit/190 degrees Celsius.*

✓ *Grease and set aside a tart tin with cooking spray.*

✓ *Whisk egg whites in a large mixing dish until frothy.*

✓ *In a separate bowl, combine the sweetener, baking powder, vanilla, lemon zest, and almond flour until thoroughly blended.*

✓ *Stir in melted butter.*

✓ *Fill tart tin halfway with batter and top with raspberries.*

✓ *Bake for 20-23 minutes in a Preheated oven.*

✓ *Assemble and serve.*

Nutrition: 378 Calories, 8 g fat, 14 g carbohydrate, 4 g sugar, 11 g protein, 0 mg cholesterol

771) *Vanilla Ice Cream*

Time Required for Preparation: 10 minutes Time Required for Cooking: 30 minutes 8 portions Ingredients:

- *1 egg yolk*
- *3/4 cup erythritol*
- *2 cups heavy whipping cream*
- *1 teaspoon vanilla extract*
- *3 teaspoon cinnamon*

Direction

✓ *In a mixing bowl, combine all ingredients and blend until fully blended.*

✓ *Transfer the ice cream mixture to the ice cream maker and churn according to the manufacturer's instructions.*

✓ *Assemble and serve.*

Nutrition: Calories 114 Fat 17 grams Carbohydrates Sugar: 7 g Protein: 0.1 g Cholesterol 1 g 67 mg

772) *Berry Cheese Fat Bomb*

Time Required for Preparation: 5 minutes Time Required for Cooking: 5 minutes 12 servings Ingredients:

- *1 cup washed fresh berries*

- *1/2 cup coconut oil*
- *1 1/2 cup softened cream cheese*
- *1 tbsp vanilla*

Direction

✓ *In a blender, add all ingredients and blend until smooth and blended.*

✓ *Spoon mixture into small candy molds and chill until firm, about 30 minutes.*

✓ *Assemble and serve.*

Nutrition: 175 kcal 17 g fat 17 g carbohydrate 2 g Carbohydrates 1 g Protein Cholesterol 1 g 29 mg

773) *Baked Maple Cream Custard*

Time Required for Preparation: 10 minutes Time Required for Cooking: 15 minutes 6 portions

- *2 1/2 cups fat-free half-and-half*
- *1/2 cup cholesterol-free egg substitute*
- *1/4 cup sugar*
- *2 teaspoons vanilla*
- *A pinch of ground nutmeg*
- *3 c. boiling water*
- *2 tbsp. maple syrup*

Directions:

✓ *Using a light nonstick cooking spray, coat six ramekins or custard cups. Preheat the oven to 3250 degrees Fahrenheit.*

✓ *Combine the first five ingredients in a large mixing bowl and whisk well. Fill your ramekins halfway.*

✓ *Fill a 13x9-inch baking dish halfway with boiling water. Bake for 1 hour 15 minutes with the ramekins in the dish.*

✓ *Place the ramekins on a cooling rack to cool completely. Wrap with plastic wrap and refrigerate overnight.*

✓ *Just before serving, drizzle with maple syrup.*

Nutrition: 131 Calories 23 g carbohydrate 0 g fiber 1 g fat Sodium: 139 milligrams 5 g protein

774) *Blueberry Yogurt Custard*

Time Required to Prepare: 5 minutes Time Required for Cooking: 15 minutes 6 portions

- *1-6 ounces fat-free plain yogurt*
- *2 teaspoons honey*
- *1/8 teaspoon ground nutmeg*
- *1/2 cup fresh blueberries (or thawed frozen blueberries)*
- *1 tablespoon all-fruit blueberry preserves*

(or raspberry preserves)

Direction

- ✓ Drain and thicken yogurt in the refrigerator for 20 minutes using a paper towel-lined strainer.
- ✓ Combine drained yogurt, nutmeg, and honey in a medium bowl.
- ✓ Combine the fruit and preserves, then pour the yogurt on top. Serve garnished with almonds.

Nutrition: Calories: 261 49 g carbohydrate 3 g fiber 3 g fat 137 mg sodium 11 g protein

775) <u>*Pineapple Frozen Yogurt*</u>

Time Required for Preparation: 5 minutes Time Required for Cooking: 15 minutes 4 portions

- 1/4 cup cholesterol-free egg substitute
- 1/4 cup sugar
- 1/2 cup fat-free half-and-half
- 1/2 cup plain low-fat yogurt
- 3/4 cup pineapple chunks (keep in juice)

Direction

- ✓ Beat together the first two ingredients until the mixture thickens and takes on cream color. Combine the remaining ingredients thoroughly.
- ✓ Refrigerate until chilled, then add to an ice cream machine. Adhere to the manufacturer's directions.
- ✓ While the ice cream machine is running, stir and scrape every ten minutes for an hour or until the mixture reaches the desired consistency.
- ✓ Store in the refrigerator.

Nutrition: Calories: 130 25 g carbohydrate 1 g dietary fiber 1 g dietary fat Sodium: 79 milligrams 5 g protein

776) <u>*Red Fruity Granita*</u>

Time Required for Preparation: 5 minutes Time Required for Cooking: 15 minutes 4 portions

- 5 cups diced and seeded watermelon
- 1/2 cup sugar
- 1 envelope unflavored gelatin
- 1/2 cup cranberry juice cocktail

Directions:

- ✓ In a food processor, pulse watermelon until nearly smooth.
- ✓ In a small saucepan over low heat, combine gelatin and sugar and dissolve in

cranberry juice.

- ✓ Pulse the gelatin mixture into the pureed watermelon until smooth.
- ✓ Transfer to an 8-inch square baking dish, cover, and freeze for approximately 5 hours, or until set. Break up the watermelon mixture and freeze for a further 3 hours, or until firm.
- ✓ Before serving, stir and scrape to achieve an ice texture.

Nutrition: 88 Calories 22 g carbohydrate 1 g fiber 0 g fat 5 mg sodium 1 g

777) <u>*Homemade ice cream cake*</u>

10 minutes to prepare Time Required for Cooking: 15 minutes 4 portions

- 5 broken sugar cones
- 3 tablespoons melted unsalted butter
- 4 cups light ice cream, no sugar added and softened, divided

Directions:

- ✓ Using cooking spray, grease a deep pie pan dish.
- ✓ Using a rolling pin, crush sugar cones in a zipped bag. Combine in a bowl. Add the butter and stir until well moistened. Assemble your crust using the mixture. Refrigerate for 20 minutes.
- ✓ Cover the crust with 2 cups of light ice cream and freeze for 30 minutes or until solid.
- ✓ Spread the remainder of the light ice cream on top of the initial frozen layer and refrigerate for an additional 30 minutes.
- ✓ Spread the whipped topping over the top and place in the freezer for 2 hours or until stiff.
- ✓ Allow 15 to 30 minutes for the ice cream cake to soften in the refrigerator before slicing and serving.

Nutrition: 118 Calories 15 g carbohydrate 1 g fiber 5 g fat 35 mg sodium 2 g protein

778) <u>*Patisseries d'Almond et de Framboise*</u>

Time Required for Preparation: 5 minutes Time Required for Cooking: 15 minutes 4 portions

- 12 sheets 14x9-inch phyllo dough
- 1/4 cup blanched almonds

Directions:

- ✓ Arrange three sheets of phyllo dough in a

layer, spritzing with cooking spray in between each sheet.

✓ Distribute a fourth of the strawberries within 12 inches of the edges. Sprinkle 14 of the slivered almonds on top.

✓ Starting with a long side, roll the phyllo jelly-roll form. To seal, moisten the edges with water. Divide the roll into three equal portions. Rep to create three additional rolls.

✓ Arrange cut side down on a prepared baking sheet 1 inch apart. Spritz the top with cooking spray and bake for 12 to 15 minutes, or until golden brown, at 375ºF.

Nutrition: 101 Calories 19 g carbohydrate 1 g fiber 2 g fat 51 mg sodium 6 g protein

779) *Strawberry Coconut Creme Cones*

35 minutes for preparation Time Required for Cooking: 5 minutes 4 portions

- 4 sheets 14x0 inch phyllo dough
- 1 cup fat-free cold milk
- 1/2 teaspoon coconut extract
- 1–4 ounces vanilla instant pudding mix
- 1/3 cup shredded coconut, finely chopped
- 1/2 cup reduced-fat whipped topping
- 6 fresh strawberries (save 3 for garnish)

Directions:

✓ Prepare four 12x6-inch sheets of foil by folding them in half widthwise. Each one should be rolled loosely into a cone with the edges overlapping by an inch and a half.

✓ Coat two phyllo sheets with cooking spray and wrap the remaining phyllo sheets in plastic wrap and a moist towel to prevent them from drying out.

✓ Halve widthwise and lengthwise and wrap one portion of the foil cone around one section. Coat with nonstick cooking spray.

✓ Bake at 425ºF for 4 to 5 minutes, or until gently browned.

✓ Repeat step 14 until you have eight cones.

✓ In a separate bowl, whisk together the first three ingredients for the filling for 2 minutes. Using a spatula, fold in the next two ingredients. The pudding mixture should be filled into a pastry bag fitted with a star tip.

✓ Chop three strawberries finely and divide them among the cones. The cones of the pudding should be piped.

✓ Slice the remainder of the strawberries to serve as a garnish. Serve right away.

Nutrition: 87 Calories 16 g carbohydrate 1 g fiber 2 g fat 164 mg sodium 2 g protein

780) *Berry Almond Parfait*

Time Required for Preparation: 20 minutes Time Required for Cooking: 30 minutes 4 portions

- 1-8 ounces plain yogurt, low-fat and drained
- 1 cup sliced strawberries
- 1/2 cup raspberries
- 1/2 cup blueberries
- 1/8 teaspoon almond extract
- 1 tablespoon pourable sugar substitute + 2 teaspoons, divided

Directions:

✓ Drain and thicken yogurt in the refrigerator for 2 to 24 hours, using a paper towel-lined strainer. (This should be done the night before.)

✓ Combine all ingredients except the sugar replacement in a 2-teaspoon ratio. Toss gently to combine. Allow 30 minutes to 2 hours to chill.

✓ In a bowl, combine the drained yogurt and the remaining sugar substitute.

✓ In two parfait glasses, alternate layers of 1/3 cup berries mixture and half yogurt.

✓ To serve, garnish with almonds.

Nutrition: 220 Calories 30 g carbohydrate 6 g dietary fiber 6 g fat 84 mg sodium 9 g protein

781) *Spice Cake*

Time Required for Preparation: 10 minutes Time Required for Cooking: 50 minutes 10 portions

- 2 cups almond flour
- 1/2 cup erythritol sweetener
- 2 tablespoons baking powder
- 1 teaspoon cinnamon powder
- 1 teaspoon ground ginger
- 1/4 teaspoon ground cloves
- 1/4 teaspoon salt
- 2 eggs
- 1/3 cup unsalted butter, melted
- 1 1/3 cup water, split
- 1/2 teaspoon unsweetened vanilla extract

- *3 tablespoons chopped toasted pecans*

Directions:

✓ *In a large mixing basin, combine all of the ingredients, reserving 1 cup water and pecans, and stir well with a hand mixer until completely combined and a smooth batter forms.*

✓ *Spoon the batter into a 7-inch baking pan, smooth the surface, sprinkle with pecans, and cover with aluminium foil.*

✓ *Turn on the instant pot, add water, insert the trivet support, and set the pan on top.*

✓ *Close the instant pot with the lid in the sealed position, then press the 'cake' button, then '+/-' to set the cooking duration to 40 minutes and the pressure setting to high; the cooking timer will begin when the pressure in the pot builds up.*

✓ *When the instant pot beeps, press the 'keep warm' button, allow pressure to naturally relax for 10 minutes, then quickly release pressure and open the lid.*

✓ *Remove the pan, uncover it, invert it onto a dish to remove the cake, and set aside for 10 minutes to cool.*

✓ *Spread the cream on top of the cake and serve in slices.*

Nutrition: 229 Calories 21 g fat 6 g protein Carbohydrates: 2 g 0 g fiber

782) *Avocado Chocolate Ice Cream*

Time Required for Preparation: 10 minutes Time Required for Cooking: 0 minutes 6 portions

- *2 large organic avocados, pitted*
- *1/2 cup erythritol, powdered*
- *1/2 cup cocoa powder, organic and unsweetened*
- *Coconut milk, unsweetened and full-fat: 1 cup*
- *1/2 cup heavy whipping cream, full-fat*
- *Unsweetened and chopped chocolate squares: 6*

Directions:

✓ *Scoop the flesh from each avocado into a bowl, add the vanilla, milk, and cream, and blend until smooth and creamy using an immersion blender.*

✓ *Add the remaining ingredients, except the chocolate, and mix until smooth and well blended.*

✓ *Fold in the chopped chocolate and chill in the refrigerator for 8 to 12 hours, or until*

completely cold.

✓ *When ready to serve, allow ice cream to stand at room temperature for 30 minutes before processing it in an ice cream maker according to the manufacturer's instructions.*

✓ *Immediately serve.*

Nutrition: 216.7 Calories 19.4 g fat 8 g protein Net Carbohydrates: 7 g 7.4 g fiber

783) *Mocha Mousse*

35 minutes for preparation Time Required for Cooking: 0 minutes 4 portions

Ingredients:

- *Directions for the Cream Cheese:*
- *8 ounces softened and full-fat cream cheese*
- *3 tbsp. sour cream, full-fat*
- *2 teaspoons softened butter*
- *1/2 tbsps unsweetened vanilla extract*
- *1/3 cup erythritol*
- *Unsweetened cocoa powder: 14 cup*
- *3 tsp instant coffee powder*
- *Whipped Cream:*
- *2/3 cup heavy whipping cream, full-fat*
- *Erythritol: 1/2 tsp*
- *1/2 teaspoon unsweetened vanilla extract*

Directions:

✓ *Prepare cream cheese mixture: In a mixing dish, combine cream cheese, sour cream, and butter and beat until smooth.*

✓ *Now, add the erythritol, cocoa powder, coffee, and vanilla extract and mix until smooth; leave aside until needed.*

✓ *Whip cream: In a bowl, beat whipping cream until soft peaks form.*

✓ *Add vanilla and erythritol and beat until stiff peaks form. Fold 1/3 of the mixture into the cream cheese mixture until barely combined.*

✓ *Fold in the remaining whipping cream mixture until evenly distributed.*

✓ *Spoon the mousse into a freezer-safe bowl and chill for 2 12 hours or until firm.*

✓ *Serve immediately.*

Nutrition: 42 Calories 42 g fat 6 g Protein 6.5 g Carbohydrates 2 g fiber

784) *Chocolate Muffins*

Time Required for Preparation: 10 minutes Time

Required for Cooking: 30 minutes 8 portions
Ingredients:

- *2 cups pumpkin, diced and steamed*
- *1/2 cup coconut flour*
- *1/8 teaspoon salt*
- *4 tablespoons erythritol*
- *1 cup cacao powder, unsweetened*
- *1/2 cup collagen protein powder*
- *1 teaspoon baking soda*
- *6 ounces melted cacao butter*
- *1/2 cup avocado oil*
- *2 tsp. apple cider vinegar*
- *3 teaspoons unsweetened vanilla extract*
- *Pastured eggs: 3*

Directions:

- ✓ *Preheat the oven to 350 degrees F and leave it on until ready to bake the muffins.*
- ✓ *In a food processor or blender, add all ingredients except the collagen and pulse for 1 to 2 minutes, or until well combined and integrated.*
- ✓ *Add collagen and pulse at low speed just until combined.*
- ✓ *Grease an eight-cup silicon muffin tray with avocado oil and then spoon the batter equally into the cups.*
- ✓ *Bake for 30 minutes or until the muffins are well cooked, and a knife inserted into each muffin comes out clean.*
- ✓ *Allow muffins to cool in the pan for 10 minutes before removing them to a wire rack to cool completely.*
- ✓ *Store muffins in a large freezer bag or individually wrapped in foil in the refrigerator for up to four days or in the freezer for up to three months.*
- ✓ *Microwave muffins for 45 seconds to 1 minute, or until thoroughly warm, before serving with coconut cream.*

Nutrition: Calories: 111 9.9 g fat 8 g protein 3 g net carbs 1 g fiber

785) *Lemon Fat Bombs*

Time Required for Preparation: 40 minutes Time Required for Cooking: 0 minutes 10 portions

- *3/4 cup full-fat coconut butter*
- *1/4 cup avocado oil*
- *3 tbsp. lemon juice*
- *Lemon zest: 1 tbsp. Coconut cream, full-fat:*

1 tbsp.
- *1 tablespoon erythritol*
- *1 teaspoon unsweetened vanilla extract*
- *1/8 teaspoon salt*

Directions:

- ✓ *In a blender, add all of the ingredients for the fat bombs and pulse until well incorporated.*
- ✓ *Line a baking tray with parchment paper and transfer the fat bomb mixture to it. Freeze for 45 minutes, or until solid enough to mold into balls.*
- ✓ *Then, take the baking sheet out of the freezer, roll the fat bomb mixture into ten balls, and arrange them in a single layer on the baking sheet.*
- ✓ *Place the baking sheet back in the freezer, chill until firm and set, and then store for up to 2 months in the freezer.*
- ✓ *Serve as needed.*

Nutrition: Calories: 164 16.7 g fat 3 g protein 0.4 g carbohydrate 3 g fiber

786) *Banana Split Sundae*

Time Required for Preparation: 10 minutes Time Required for Cooking: 0 minutes 4 portions
Ingredients:

- *3 frozen, sliced overripe bananas (see Tip)*
- *2 tbsps. peanut butter*
- *1 teaspoon sugar-free chocolate flavour syrup*
- *1 teaspoon chopped peanuts*

Direction

- ✓ *In a food processor, combine peanut butter and bananas. Cover and continue processing until nearly no lumps remain. Fill sundae dishes halfway with the mixture.*
- ✓ *Arrange whipped topping, maraschino cherry, peanuts, and sugar-free chocolate flavour syrup on top. Serve immediately.*

Nutrition: 166 Calories Carbohydrates in total: 27 g 0 mg cholesterol 6 g total fat 3 g fiber 3 g protein 60 mg sodium 14 g sugar 2 g Saturated Fat

787) *Ice Pops with Berries and Lemon*

15 minutes for preparation Time Required for Cooking: 30 minutes 8 portions

- *1 lemon*
- *11/2 cup quartered fresh strawberries*
- *11/2 cup quartered fresh blueberries*

- *1/4 cup water*
- *1/4 cup honey*

Direction

✓ *Remove 2 tsp. of the lemon zest and squeeze 1 tbsp. of lemon juice. In a food processor or blender, combine the water, blueberries, and strawberries. Cover and process or blend until nearly smooth. Combine honey, lemon juice, and lemon zest. Cover and process or blend until well combined.*

✓ *Fill eight ice pop molds or 3-oz. paper cups halfway with the mixture, then place sticks into the molds. If you're using paper cups, wrap each one in foil. Slit a small slit in the foil and place a wooden stick into each pop, then freeze for at least one hour or until hard.*

Nutrition: Calories: 53 Carbohydrates in total: 14 g 0 g total fat 1 g fiber 0 g protein 1 mg sodium 12 g sugar 0 g Saturated Fat

788) *Blackberry-banana Trifles de Limon*

Time Required for Preparation: 10 minutes Time Required for Cooking: 10 minutes 2 portions

- *2 75-oz. containers lemon sugar-free reduced-calorie ready-to-eat pudding (or use vanilla, but add 1/4 tsp . lemon zest to each container)*
- *1/2 cup fresh blackberries, blueberries, raspberries, or sliced strawberries*

Direction

✓ *Divide a pudding container evenly between two straight-sided 8-oz. glasses, spooning the pudding into each glass.*

✓ *Half the banana slices, half the berries, and half the cookie crumbs should be placed on top.*

✓ *Continue layering with any remaining pudding, banana, berries, and cookies.*

Nutrition: Calories: 165; Carbohydrates: 35 0 mg cholesterol 3 g total fat 3 g fiber 2 g protein 236 mg

789) *Peanut Butter with Caramel Popcorn*

30 minutes for preparation Time Required for Cooking: 10 minutes

- *1 cup butter*
- *2 cups brown sugar*
- *1/2 cup corn syrup*
- *1 tsp salt*
- *1/2 tsp baking soda*

- *1 tsp vanilla essence*

Direction

✓ *Preheat the oven to 250°F (95°C). Place popcorn in a large bowl.*

✓ *Melt butter in a medium-sized pot over medium heat. Combine the salt, corn syrup, and brown sugar in a mixing bowl. Boil it, tossing frequently. Boil for 4 minutes without tossing. Remove from heat and add vanilla and soda. Add in a thin stream to the popcorn, tossing to combine.*

✓ *Arrange on two large shallow cookie sheets and bake for 1 hour, tossing every 15 minutes. Remove from the oven and allow it to cool completely before crumbling into chunks.*

Nutrition: 253 Calories Carbohydrates in total: 38 g 24 mg cholesterol 14 g total fat 0.9 g protein 340 mg sodium

790) *Prosecco Strawberries enrobed in chocolate*

Time Required for Preparation: 20 minutes Time Required for Cooking: 45 minutes 2 portions

- *12 medium strawberries, rinsed and dried*
- *1/3 cup chocolate chips, bittersweet (2 oz.)*

Directions:

✓ *Combine prosecco and strawberries in a medium bowl. Place a bowl on top to keep the strawberries immersed. Refrigerate overnight or for at least 8 hours.*

✓ *Pat the strawberries dry on a dish lined with paper towels. Put the chocolate chips in a microwave-safe bowl. Microwave on High in 20-second intervals, stirring after each interval until chocolate is completely melted, about 1 minute. Strawberries should be dipped in chocolate and placed on a platter lined with waxed paper. Refrigerate for approximately 15 to 20 minutes or until the chocolate is solid.*

Nutrition: Calories: 50; Carbohydrates: 7 g 0 mg cholesterol 3 g total fat 1 g fiber 1 g protein

791) *Ice Pops with Creamy Chocolate Pie*

15 minutes for preparation Time Required for Cooking: 15 minutes 9 portions

Ingredients:

- *1 container (4 servings) fat-free, sugar-free, low-calorie chocolate instant pudding mix*

- *2 cups almond milk, unsweetened, or fat-*

free

- *1 cup thawed frozen light whipped topping*
- *1 ounce melted dark chocolate*
- *1 tbsp crushed graham crackers*

Directions:

✓ *In a medium bowl, whisk together almond milk and pudding mix for 2 to 3 minutes, or until thick. Incorporate whipped topping.*

✓ *Divide batter evenly among nine 3-oz. paper cups or ice pop molds. Sticks should be inserted into the molds. If using paper cups, wrap each cup in foil, cut a small gap in the foil, and put a wooden stick into each pop. Freeze for at least 24 hours or until firm.*

✓ *Remove the pops from the mold. Drizzle each pop with melted chocolate and immediately sprinkle with graham crackers as you work.*

Nutrition: Calories: 60; Carbohydrates: 9 g; Cholesterol: 0 mg 3 g total fat 1 g fiber 1 g protein 175 mg sodium 2 g sugar 2 g Saturated Fat

792) *Devil's Food Ice Cream Pie*

Time Required for Preparation: 20 minutes Time Required for Cooking: 30 minutes 12 servings

- *1 (6.75 oz.) box fat-free devil's food cookie cakes (12 cookies)*
- *1 cup chopped bananas*
- *1/4 cup hot water*
- *4 cups softened low-fat or light vanilla, chocolate, or other flavour ice cream (see Tip)*
- *3 tablespoons fat-free, sugar-free hot fudge ice cream topping*

Directions:

✓ *Roughly chop the cookies. Place the cookie pieces in the bottom of an 8-inch springform pan. Whisk together the hot water and peanut butter in a small bowl until smooth, then drizzle it evenly over the cookies.*

✓ *Arrange banana slices on top and delicately scoop the ice cream equally throughout. Spread the ice cream evenly across the top until it becomes smooth. Cover with foil or plastic wrap and freeze for 8 hours or until hard.*

✓ *Allow 10 minutes for it to come to room temperature before serving. Remove the pan's sides and cut it into wedges. Drizzle the fudge sauce over the wedges.*

Nutrition: 173 Calories; Carbohydrates in total: 33 g 7 mg cholesterol 3 g total fat 1 g fiber 4 g protein 90 mg sodium 9 g sugar 1 g Saturated Fat

793) *Ice Pops with Fresh-Squeezed Pink Lemonade*

15 minutes for preparation Time Required for Cooking: 15 minutes 7 portions

- *13/4 cups water*
- *3/4 cup lemon juice*
- *1/3 cup sugar (see Tip)*
- *optional red food coloring*
- *snipped fresh basil or small fresh basil leaves (optional)*

Directions:

✓ *In a 4-cup liquid measure, whisk together sugar, lemon juice, and water until sugar dissolves. If desired, tint with food coloring and add basil (it is about to float on top initially).*

✓ *Divide the mixture evenly into seven ice pop molds or 3-oz. paper cups. Sticks should be inserted into the molds. Cover each cup with foil if you're using paper cups; cut a small gap in the foil to tuck each pop with a wooden stick. Refrigerate for 1 1/2 hours while gently shaking molds or mixing mixture in cups to spread basil. Continue freezing until hard or overnight.*

Nutrition: Calories: 43; Carbohydrates: 11 g 0 g total fat 0 g fiber 0 g protein 2 milligrams sodium 10 g sugar 0 g Saturated Fat

794) *Han Fro-yo*

Time Required for Preparation: 10 minutes

- *3 extremely ripe bananas*
- *1 cup vanilla yogurt made with whole milk*
- *Activated charcoal, 2 tsp (see Tip)*

Directions:

✓ *In a food processor, pulse-activated charcoal, yogurt, and bananas until smooth; transfer to a medium bowl. Put in the freezer for 5 hours or until firm.*

Nutrition: 136 Calories Carbohydrates in total: 28 g 8 mg cholesterol 2 g total fat 2 g fiber 3 g protein 36 mg sodium 19 g sugar 1 g Saturated Fat

795) *Strawberries Marinated*

15 minutes for preparation Time Required for Cooking: 35 minutes 6 portions

- *4 cups (2 pints) strawberries*

- *1 to 2 tbsp. sugar*
- *2 tbsp. old balsamic vinegar*
- *2 tbsp. finely shredded fresh mint*
- *1 tbsp. lemon juice*

Directions:

✓ *Remove strawberry stems; cut strawberries in half lengthwise or into quarters if large. In a medium bowl, combine lemon juice, mint, balsamic vinegar, sugar, and strawberries. Refrigerate covered for at least 20 minutes or up to 4 hours.*

✓ *Spoon the strawberry mixture over scoops of frozen yogurt to serve.*

Nutrition: Calories: 166; Carbohydrates: 33 g 10 mg cholesterol 2 g total fat 5 g protein 77 mg sodium 1 g Saturated Fat

796) *Nice Cream Pineapple*

15 minutes for preparation Time Required for Cooking: 15 minutes 6 portions

- *1 16-oz. box frozen pineapple chunks*
- *1 cup frozen mango chunks or 1 large peeled, seeded, and diced mango*

Directions:

✓ *Process the mango, lemon or lime juice, and pineapple in a food processor until creamy and smooth. If the mango is frozen, add 1/4 cup water. Serve immediately for the finest texture.*

Nutrition: Calories: 55; Carbohydrates: 14 0 mg cholesterol 0 g total fat 2 g fiber 1 g protein 1 mg sodium 11 g sugar 0 g Saturated Fat

797) *Snack with Plums and Pistachios*

Preparation Time: 5 minutes Time Required for Cooking: 5 minutes 1 portion

Ingredients:

- *1/4 cup unsalted dry-roasted pistachios (in shell)*

Direction

✓ *Pistachios and plums should be hulled and served together.*

Nutrition: Calories: 113; Carbohydrates: 12 0 mg cholesterol 7 g total fat 2 g fiber 4 g protein 1 mg sodium 8 g sugar 1 g Saturated Fat

798) *Fluffy Lemon Bars*

Prep time: 15 minutes, chill time: 2 hours, Serves: 20

Ingredients:

- *8 oz. low fat cream cheese, soft*
- *1/3 cup butter, melted*
- *3 tbsp. fresh lemon juice*
- *What you'll need from the store cupboard: 12 oz. evaporated milk*
- *1 pkg. lemon gelatin, sugar-free*
- *1 ½ cup graham cracker crumbs*
- *1 cup piping hot water*
- *34 c. Splenda*
- *1 tsp vanilla extract*

Instructions:

✓ *Pour milk into a large metal mixing bowl, add beaters, cover, and chill for 2 hours.*

✓ *Combine cracker crumbs and butter in a small basin, reserving 1 tablespoon. The leftover mixture should be pressed into the bottom of a 13x9-inch baking dish. Refrigerate until set.*

✓ *Dissolve gelatin with boiling water in a small bowl. Combine with lemon juice and set aside to chill.*

✓ *Cream together cream cheese, Splenda, and vanilla extract in a large mixing bowl until smooth. Combine thoroughly with gelatin.*

✓ *Using an electric mixer, beat the cooled milk until soft peaks form. Combine with the cream cheese mixture. Distribute evenly over cold crust and top with leftover crumbs. 2 hours before serving, cover and chill.*

Nutrition: Calories 126 Carbohydrates Protein 15 g 3 g triglycerides 5 g fructose ten grams fiber 0g

799) *Fridge Fudge*

15 minutes prep time, 2 hours chill time, 16 servings

Ingredients:

- *1/4 cup margarine 1/4 cup coconut cream*
- *1/4 cup coconut oil*
- *1 cup pecans, finely ground*
- *6 tbsp. unsweetened cocoa powder 2 tablespoons honey*
- *1 tbsp. vanilla extract*
- *1/4 teaspoon sea salt*

Instructions:

✓ *Wrap wax paper around an 8x8 inch glass baking dish.*

✓ *In a glass measuring cup, combine the oil and margarine. Bring a medium saucepan of water to a boil, about halfway full.*

✓ Stir the measuring cup in the pan until the butter and chocolate are melted and blended.

✓ Combine everything except the nuts in a blender or food processor. Process until completely smooth. And the nuts, which are pulsed briefly to mix.

✓ Fill the prepared pan halfway with the batter and freeze until the fudge is firm.

✓ Take the pan out of the oven and cut it into 32 pieces. Freeze in a plastic container. 2 pieces per serving.

Nutrition: Calories Per Serving 254 7g Carbohydrates Total 7g Carbohydrates Net 6g Protein 1g Fat 26g Sugar 5g Fiber 1g

800) *Honeydew & Ginger*

Time required for preparation: 5 minutes; time required for blending: 3 minutes; Serves: 3
Ingredients:

- *1/2 cup cubed honeydew melon, diced*
- *12 c. banana*
- *1/2 cup vanilla nonfat yogurt*
- *1/4 teaspoon   grated fresh ginger*

Instructions:

✓ In a blender, combine all ingredients and pulse until smooth. Serve immediately after pouring into glasses.

Nutrition: Calories 68g Carbohydrates Total 16g Carbohydrates Net Protein 15 g 2 g fat 0 g sugar 12 g dietary fiber 1 gram

801) *Gingerbread Cookies*

15 minutes for preparation Time required for cooking: ten minutes 10 portions
Ingredients:

- *A single egg*
- *1/4 cup softened butter*
- *What you'll require from your pantry: 2 cups sifted almond flour 14 cups Splenda*
- *Cinnamon, 1 tbsp.*
- *1/2 teaspoon   ginger*
- *1 tsp vanilla extract*
- *1/2 teaspoon   bicarbonate of soda*
- *1/4 teaspoon   cloves*
- *1/4 teaspoon   nutmeg*

Instructions:

✓ Combine the almond flour, cinnamon, ginger, cloves, nutmeg, and baking powder in a medium bowl.

✓ Beat the butter and Splenda together in a large mixing basin for 1-2 minutes or until fluffy. Incorporate the egg and vanilla extract. Incorporate the almond flour mixture in a slow, steady stream until a dough forms.

✓ Refrigerate the dough in a ball, wrapped in plastic wrap, for at least 30 minutes.

✓ Preheat the oven to 350 degrees Fahrenheit. Preheat the oven to 350°F. Line a cookie sheet with parchment paper.

✓ Between two sheets of parchment paper, roll out the dough to a thickness of 14 inches. With a cookie cutter, cut out desired shapes and arrange them on a prepared pan. Alternatively, you can drop dough by teaspoonful onto the prepared pan.

✓ Bake for 10-15 minutes, or until golden brown around the edges. Transfer to a wire rack to cool. Refrigerate in an airtight container. 1 large cookie or 2 mini cookies per serving.

Nutrition: Calories 181 Carbohydrates 9g Carbohydrates Net Protein: 7 g 5g Fatty Acids 15g Sucrose 6 g Fiber 2g

802) *Orange Cookies with Oatmeal*

Preparation time: ten minutes Cooking time: ten minutes, servings: eighteen (2 cookies per serving)
Ingredients:

- *1 zested and juiced orange*
- *1/2 tbsp. margarine*
- *1 beaten egg white*
- *1 tbsp. freshly squeezed orange juice*

What you'll require from the pantry

- *1 cup pastry flour made from whole wheat 1 cup rolled oats*
- *1/4 tbsp stevia*
- *1/4 cup replacement for dark brown sugar 14 cups unsweetened applesauce 1/3 cup bran*
- *1/2 teaspoon baking soda*
- *1/2 tbsp cream of tartar*
- *1/4 teaspoon cinnamon*

Instructions:

✓ Preheat the oven to 350 degrees Fahrenheit. Preheat the oven to 350°F. Line two cookie sheets with parchment paper.

✓ Cream butter in a medium mixing basin. Add the sugars gradually and beat for 2 to 3 minutes.

✓ Beat in the egg white and applesauce until combined.

✓ In a large mixing basin, sift together the dry ingredients. Combine the wet ingredients, orange juice, and zest in a medium bowl.

✓ Drop a spoonful of dough onto prepared cookie sheets. Bake for 10 minutes, or until the bottoms of the muffins are golden brown. Allow to cool on a wire rack. Keep refrigerated in an airtight container.

Nutrition: Calories 129 Total Carbohydrates 17g Net Carbohydrates Protein 16 g 2 g fat 6 g sugar 8 g dietary fiber

803) *Cookies with Tangy Almonds*

5 minutes for preparation 15 minutes for cooking 8 portions

Ingredients:

- 6 tablespoons margarine
- 1 teaspoon lemon zest, freshly grated What you'll require from your pantry:
- 2 cup apricot flour
- 3 tbsp. splenda Cooking spray that is nonstick

Instructions:

✓ Melt margarine in a small saucepan over medium heat.

✓ Combine flour, Splenda, and zest in a large mixing bowl until well blended.

✓ Shape dough into a "log," wrap in plastic wrap, and refrigerate for 30 minutes or up to 2 hours in the freezer or refrigerator.

✓ Preheat the oven to 350 degrees Fahrenheit. Cooking spray a cookie sheet.

✓ Cut dough into 12-inch thick cookies using a sharp knife. Arrange on a cookie sheet that has been prepped. Bake for 15 minutes, or until firm and golden brown.

✓ Before serving, allow it to cool fully. Two cookies constitute one serving.

Nutrition: Calories Per Serving 254 Carbohydrates in total 13g Carbohydrates in net 10g Protein 5g Fat 20g Sugar 9g Fiber 3g

804) *Cookies with Pistachios*

5 minutes for preparation 15 minutes for cooking 13-14 portions

2 beaten eggs

- What you'll require from your pantry:
- 1 cup + 2 tbsp. almond flour Splenda

Direction

✓ 3/4 cup + 50 shelled pistachio nuts In a food processor, combine the 3/4 cup nuts and 2 tablespoons Splenda.

✓ Process until the nuts are finely ground.

✓ In a large mixing basin, combine the ground nuts, flour, and remaining Splenda.

✓ Add eggs and thoroughly combine ingredients.

✓ Wrap dough in plastic wrap and refrigerate for at least 8 hours, preferably overnight.

✓ Preheat the oven to 325 degrees Fahrenheit. Preheat the oven to 350°F. Line a cookie sheet with parchment paper.

✓ A teaspoon of dough should be rolled into little balls about 1 inch in diameter. Arrange on prepared baking sheet.

✓ Slightly smash cookie and press a pistachio into the center. Bake for 12-15 minutes, or until the edges are just beginning to brown.

✓ Cool fully on a wire rack. Refrigerate in an airtight container. Three cookies constitute one serving.

Nutrition: Calories 108 Carbohydrates Total 5g Carbohydrates Net Protein 3 g 4 g fat 8 g sugar 3 g dietary fiber 2g

805) *Parfaits de framboise et de noix*

Time required for preparation: ten minutes; time required for chilling: one hour. 4 portions

- 1 can chilled coconut milk (not low fat)
- 1/2 cup washed and dried fresh raspberries
- What you'll require from your pantry:
- 1/4 cup roughly chopped walnuts
- 1 tbsp. Splenda
- 1 tsp vanilla extract

Direction

✓ Combine the berries and walnuts in a medium bowl.

✓ In a large mixing bowl, blend coconut milk, Splenda, and vanilla extract until smooth. Allow 5 minutes for relaxation.

✓ Distribute half of the vanilla cream evenly among four tiny mason jars. Garnish with berries. Repeat. Refrigerate for at least one hour after screwing on the lids.

Nutrition: Calories 213 Total Carbohydrates 8g Net Carbohydrates 6g Protein 4g Fat 20g Sugar 4g Fiber 2g

806) *Cinnamon & Honey Shortbread*

15 minutes for preparation; 20 minutes for cooking
22 portions
Ingredients:

- *1/2 cup soft margarine*
- *What you'll require from your pantry: 1 and a half cups flour*
- *1/2 tbsp. honey 3 1/2 tbsp.*
- *1 tsp ground cinnamon*
- *1/8 teaspoon bicarbonate of soda*

Instructions:

- ✓ *Preheat the oven to 350 degrees Fahrenheit. Preheat the oven to 350°F. Line a baking sheet with parchment paper.*
- ✓ *Beat margarine and honey in a large mixing basin until smooth and creamy.*
- ✓ *Combine the flour and baking powder until a smooth dough forms. Rectangle the dough, wrap in plastic wrap and chill for 15 minutes.*
- ✓ *On a lightly floured surface, roll out dough to a thickness of 14 inches. Rectangles should be cut and placed on a prepared baking sheet. Use a fork to create patterns on the dough if desired. Allow 20 minutes for cooling.*
- ✓ *Bake for 15-20 minutes, or until the edges begin to brown. Cool fully on a wire rack. Keep refrigerated in an airtight container.*

Nutrition: Calories 82 Carbohydrates ten grams protein 1 gram fat 4 gram sugar 3 g Fiber 0 g of

807) *Peanut Butter Cookies with Oatmeal*

Time required for preparation: 5 minutes; time required for cooking: 30 minutes. Serves: 20

- *2 beaten egg whites*
- *1/2 cup soft margarine*
- *What you'll require from your pantry: 1 sachet flour*
- *1 cup rolled oats*
- *1/2 cup peanut butter, decreased in fat*
- *3 tbsp splenda*
- *1/3 granulated Splenda brown sugar*
- *1/2 teaspoon baking soda*
- *1/2 teaspoon vanilla*

Instructions:

- ✓ *Preheat the oven to 350 degrees*

Fahrenheit.s

- ✓ *Incorporate dry ingredients in a large mixing basin and toss to combine.*
- ✓ *Separately, whisk the egg whites and margarine in a separate basin. Combine thoroughly with the dry ingredients.*
- ✓ *On nonstick cookie sheets, drop by teaspoonfuls. 8-10 minutes, or until the edges begin to brown.*
- ✓ *Transfer to a wire rack and allow to cool fully. Keep refrigerated in an airtight container. Two cookies constitute one serving.*

Nutrition: Calories 151g Carbohydrates Total 17g Carbohydrates Net Protein 16 g 3 g triglycerides 7 g fructose 7 g Fiber 1 gram

808) *Bites of Almond Cheesecake*

5 minutes for preparation; 30 minutes for chilling 6 portions
Ingredients:

- *1/2 cup softened reduced-fat cream cheese*
- *What you'll require from your pantry:*
- *1/2 cup almonds, finely ground*
- *1/4 tbsp. almond butter*
- *2 drops stevia liquid*

Instructions:

- ✓ *Cream together cream cheese, almond butter, and stevia in a large mixing bowl on high speed until smooth and creamy.*
- ✓ *Wrap in plastic wrap and chill for 30 minutes.*
- ✓ *Shape the mixture into 12 balls with your hands.*
- ✓ *On a small plate, place the ground almonds.*
- ✓ *Roll the balls completely in the nuts, coating both sides.*
- ✓ *Refrigerate in an airtight container.*

Nutrition: Calories 68 Carbohydrates in Total 3g Carbohydrates Net 2 Proteases 5g Fatty Acids 5g Sucrose 0 gram fiber 1 g

809) *Bites of Almond Cheesecake*

5 minutes for preparation; 30 minutes for chilling 6 portions
Ingredients:

- *1/2 cup softened reduced-fat cream cheese*
- *What you'll require from your pantry:*
- *1/2 cup almonds, finely ground*
- *1/4 tbsp. almond butter*

- 2 drops stevia liquid

Instructions:

✓ Cream together cream cheese, almond butter, and stevia in a large mixing bowl on high speed until smooth and creamy. Wrap in plastic wrap and chill for 30 minutes.

✓ Shape the mixture into 12 balls with your hands.

✓ On a small plate, place the ground almonds. Roll the balls completely in the nuts, coating both sides. Refrigerate in an airtight container.

Nutrition: Calories 68 Carbohydrates in Total 3g Carbohydrates Net 2 Proteases 5g Fatty Acids 5g

810) *Biscotti Almond-Coconut*

5 minutes for preparation Time required for cooking: 50 minutes 16 servings

Ingredients:

- 1 room temperature egg
- 1 room temperature egg white
- 1/2 cup melted margarine
- What you'll require from your pantry:
- 2 12 c. flour
- 1 1/3 cup shredded unsweetened coconut
- 3/4 cup sliced almonds
- Splenda 2/3 cup
- 2 tsp bicarbonate of soda
- 1 tsp vanilla extract
- 1/2 teaspoon salt

Instructions:

✓ Preheat the oven to 350 degrees Fahrenheit.

✓ Preheat the oven to 350°F. Line a baking sheet with parchment paper.

✓ Combine dry ingredients in a large mixing bowl.

✓ In a separate mixing dish, combine the remaining ingredients.

✓ Combine wet and dry ingredients until well mixed.

✓ Halve the dough.

✓ Each half should be shaped into an 8x2 34-inch loaf.

✓ Arrange loaves 3 inches apart on the pan.

✓ Bake for 25-30 minutes, or until the mixture is firm and golden brown.

✓ Allow 10 minutes to cool on a wire rack.

✓ Cut loaf diagonally into 12-inch pieces using a serrated knife.

✓ Rearrange the cookies on the pan, cut side down, and bake for an additional 20 minutes, or until firm and well browned.

✓ Refrigerate in an airtight container.

✓ Two cookies constitute one serving.

Nutrition: Calories Per Serving 234 Carbohydrates 13g Carbohydrates Net ten grams protein 5 g fat 18 g sugar 9 g dietary fiber Almond 3 g Flour

811) *Cookies with Nuts*

Preparation time: ten minutes 15 minutes for cooking Serves 18

Ingredients:

- 1/2 cup smashed banana
- What you'll require from your pantry:
- 2 tbsp. oats
- 1 cup cranberries
- 1 cup toasted walnuts
- 3 tablespoon sunflower oil
- 1 tsp vanilla extract
- 1/2 teaspoon salt

Instructions:

✓ Preheat the oven to 350 degrees Fahrenheit.

✓ Combine oats, raisins, walnuts, and salt in a large mixing basin.

✓ Combine banana, oil, and vanilla extract in a medium bowl. Add to oat mixture and stir until incorporated.

✓ Allow 15 minutes for rest. Drop tablespoonfuls onto two ungreased cookie sheets.

✓ Bake for 15 minutes, or until a light golden brown colour is achieved. Allow to cool before storing in an airtight container.

✓ Two cookies constitute one serving.

Nutrition: Calories Per Serving 148 Carbohydrates in Total 16g Carbohydrates Net Protein: 14 g 3 g fat 9 g sugar 6 g dietary fiber

812) *Candied pecans*

5 minutes for preparation Time required for cooking: ten minutes

Ingredients:

- 1/2 teaspoon butter
- What you'll require from your pantry:
- 1/2 cup halved pecans
- 2 1/2 tbsp
- Divided Splenda
- 1 tsp ground cinnamon

- *1/4 teaspoon ginger*
- *cardamom, 1/8 tsp*
- *1/8 teaspoon sodium chloride*

Instructions:

✓ *Combine 1 1/2 teaspoon Splenda, cinnamon, ginger, cardamom, and salt in a small bowl Place aside.*

✓ *In a medium skillet over medium-low heat, melt butter. Combine pecans and two teaspoons of Splenda in a small bowl.*

✓ *Reduce to low heat and cook, stirring periodically, for approximately 5 to 8 minutes, or until the sweetness melts.*

✓ *Stir the spice mixture into the skillet to coat the pecans. Allow mixture to cool for 10-15 minutes on parchment paper.*

✓ *Keep refrigerated in an airtight container 14 cups is the serving size.*

Nutrition: Calories 173 Total Carbohydrates 8g Net Carbohydrates 6g Protein 2 g Fat 16 g Sucrose 6 g Fiber 2g

813) *Strawberries and Cream Buns*

6 portions 12 Minutes Cooking

- *240 g all-purpose flour*
- *50 g granulated sugar*
- *8 g baking powder*
- *1 g salt*
- *85 g chilled butter*
- *84 g fresh strawberries*
- *120 ml whipping cream*
- *2 big eggs*
- *10 ml vanilla extract 5 ml water*

Directions:

✓ *In a large mixing basin, sift flour, sugar, baking powder, and salt. Using a blender or your hands, combine the butter and flour until the mixture resembles thick crumbs.*

✓ *Combine the strawberries and flour mixture in a medium bowl. Allow the mixture to stand for 10 minutes. In a separate dish, whisk together the whipped cream, 1 egg, and vanilla extract.*

✓ *Stir the cream mixture into the flour mixture until smooth, then spread the mixture to a 38 mm thickness.*

✓ *Cut the buns with a round cookie cutter. Spread the buns with an egg and water mixture. Reserving*

✓ *Preheat the air fryer to 180 degrees Celsius.*

✓ *Line the warmed inside basket with baking paper.*

✓ *Arrange the buns on the baking paper and bake at 180°C for 12 minutes, or until golden brown.*

Nutrition: 150 Calories 14g fat 3g Carbohydrates 11g protein 8 g sugar 0mg cholesterol

814) *Biscotti Almond-Coconut*

5 minutes for preparation Time required for cooking: 50 minutes 16 servings

Ingredients:

- *1 room temperature egg*
- *1 room temperature egg white*
- *1/2 cup melted margarine*
- *What you'll require from your pantry: 2 12 c. flour*
- *1 1/3 cup shredded unsweetened coconut*
- *3/4 cup sliced almonds*
- *Splenda 2/3 cup*
- *2 tbsp bicarbonate of soda*
- *1 tsp vanilla extract*
- *1/2 teaspoon salt*

Instructions:

✓ *Preheat the oven to 350 degrees Fahrenheit. Preheat the oven to 350°F. Line a baking sheet with parchment paper.*

✓ *Combine dry ingredients in a large mixing bowl.*

✓ *In a separate mixing dish, combine the remaining ingredients. Combine wet and dry ingredients until well mixed.*

✓ *Halve the dough. Each half should be shaped into an 8x2 34-inch loaf. Arrange loaves 3 inches apart on the pan.*

✓ *Bake for 25-30 minutes, or until the mixture is firm and golden brown. Allow 10 minutes to cool on a wire rack.*

✓ *Cut loaf diagonally into 12-inch pieces using a serrated knife. Rearrange the cookies on the pan, cut side down, and bake for an additional 20 minutes, or until firm and well browned. Refrigerate in an airtight container. Two cookies constitute one serving.*

Nutrition: Calories Per Serving 234 Carbohydrates 13g Carbohydrates Net ten grams protein 5 g fat 18 g sugar 9 g dietary fiber

815) *Chocolate Chip Blondies*

Prep time: 5 minutes, Cook time: 20 minutes, Serves: 12

Ingredients:

- *1 egg*
- *What you'll need from the store cupboard: ½ cup semi-sweet chocolate chips 1/3 cup flour*
- *1/3 cup whole wheat flour*
- *¼ cup Splenda brown sugar*
- *¼ cup sunflower oil*
- *2 tbsp. honey*
- *1 tsp vanilla*
- *½ tsp baking powder*
- *¼ tsp salt*
- *Nonstick cooking spray*

Instructions:

- ✓ *Heat oven to 350 degrees. Spray an 8-inch square baking dish with cooking spray.*
- ✓ *In a small bowl, combine dry ingredients.*
- ✓ *In a large bowl, whisk together egg, oil, honey, and vanilla. Stir in dry ingredients just until combined. Stir in chocolate chips.*
- ✓ *Spread batter in prepared dish. Bake 20-22 minutes or until they pass the toothpick test. Cool on a wire rack, then cut into bars.*
- ✓ *Nutrition Facts Per Serving*

Nutrition: Calories 136 Total Carbs 18g Net Carbs 16g Protein 2g Fat 6g Sugar 9g Fiber 2g

816) *Cinnamon Apple Popcorn*

Prep time: 30 minutes, Cook time: 50 minutes, Serves: 11

Ingredients:

- *4 tbsp. margarine, melted*
- *What you'll need from the store cupboard 10 cups of plain popcorn*
- *2 cup dried apple rings, unsweetened and chopped ½ cup walnuts, chopped*
- *2 tbsp. Splenda brown sugar*
- *1 tsp cinnamon*
- *½ tsp vanilla*

Instructions:

- ✓ *Heat oven to 250 degrees.*
- ✓ *Place chopped apples in a 9x13-inch baking dish and bake 20 minutes. Remove from oven and stir in popcorn and nuts.*
- ✓ *In a small bowl, whisk together margarine, vanilla, Splenda, and cinnamon. Drizzle evenly over popcorn and toss to coat.*

- ✓ *Bake 30 minutes, stirring quickly every 10 minutes. If apples start to turn a dark brown, remove immediately.*
- ✓ *Pout onto waxed paper to cool for at least 30 minutes. Store in an airtight container. The serving size is 1 cup.*

Nutrition: Calories 133 Total Carbs 14g Net Carbs 11g Protein 3g Fat 8g Sugar 7g Fiber 3g

817) *Crispy Baked Cheese Puffs*

Prep time: 5 minutes, Cook time: 10 minutes, Serves: 4

Ingredients:

- *2 eggs*
- *½ cup cheddar cheese, grated*
- *¼ cup mozzarella, grated*
- *What you'll need from the store cupboard: ½ cup almond flour*
- *¼ cup reduced-fat Parmesan*
- *½ tsp baking powder*
- *Black pepper*

Instructions:

- ✓ *Heat oven to 400 degrees. Line a baking sheet with parchment paper.*
- ✓ *In a large bowl, whisk eggs until lightly beaten. Add remaining ingredients and mix well.*
- ✓ *Divide into 8 pieces and roll into balls. Place on prepared baking sheet. Bake 10-12 minutes or until golden brown. Serve as is or with your favorite dipping sauce.*

Nutrition: Calories 129 Total Carbs 2g Net Carbs 1g Protein 8g Fat 10g Sugar 0g Fiber 1g

818) *Crunchy Apple Fries*

Prep time: 15 minutes, Cook time: 10 minutes, Serves: 8

Ingredients:

- *3 apples, peeled, cored, and sliced into ½-inch pieces*
- *¼ cup reduced-fat margarine, melted*
- *2 tbsp. walnuts, chopped*

What you'll need from the store cupboard

- *¼ cup quick oats*
- *3 tbsp. light brown sugar*
- *2 tbsp. whole wheat flour*
- *1 tsp cinnamon*
- *1/8 tsp salt*

Instructions:

✓ *Heat oven to 425 degrees. Put a wire rack on a large cookie sheet.*

✓ *Add oats and walnuts to a food processor or blender and process until the mixture resembles flour.*

✓ *Place the oat mixture in a shallow pan and add brown sugar, flour, cinnamon, and salt. Mix well. Pour melted butter into a separate shallow pan.*

✓ *Dip apple slices in margarine, then roll in oat mixture to coat completely. Place on wire rack.*

✓ *Bake 10 – 12 minutes or until golden brown. Let cool before serving.*

Nutrition: Calories 146 Total Carbs 20g Net Carbs 17g Protein 1g Fat 7g Sugar 13g Fiber 3g

819) *Fresh banana Cookies with Nuts*

Preparation time: ten minutes 15 minutes for cooking Serves 18

Ingredients:

- *1/2 cup smashed banana*

What you'll require from your pantry:

- *2 tbsp. oats*
- *1 cup cranberries*
- *1 cup toasted walnuts*
- *3 tablespoon sunflower oil*
- *1 tsp vanilla extract*
- *1/2 teaspoon   salt*

Instructions:

✓ *Preheat the oven to 350 degrees Fahrenheit.*

✓ *Combine oats, raisins, walnuts, and salt in a large mixing basin.*

✓ *Combine banana, oil, and vanilla extract in a medium bowl. Add to oat mixture and stir until incorporated. Allow 15 minutes for rest.*

✓ *Drop tablespoonfuls onto two ungreased cookie sheets. Bake for 15 minutes, or until a light golden brown colour is achieved. Allow to cool before storing in an airtight container. Two cookies constitute one serving.*

Nutrition: Calories Per Serving 148 Carbohydrates in Total 16g Carbohydrates Net Protein: 14 g 3 g fat 9 g sugar 6 g dietary fiber 2 g

820) *Cinnamon Apple Chips*

Prep time: 5 minutes, Cook time: 10 minutes, Serves: 2

Ingredients:

- *1 medium apple, sliced thin*
- *What you'll need from the store cupboard: ¼ tsp cinnamon*
- *¼ tsp nutmeg*
- *Nonstick cooking spray*

Instructions:

✓ *Heat oven to 37 Spray a baking sheet with cooking spray.*

✓ *Place apples in a mixing bowl and add spices. Toss to coat.*

✓ *Arrange apples, in a single layer, on the prepared pan. Bake 4 minutes, turn apples over, and bake 4 minutes more.*

✓ *Serve immediately or store in an airtight container.*

Nutrition: Calories 58 Total Carbs 15g Protein 0g Fat 0g Sugar 11g Fiber 3g

821) *Cranberry & Almond Granola Bars*

Prep time: 15 minutes, Cook time: 20 minutes, Serves: 12

Ingredients:

- *1 egg*
- *1 egg white*
- *What you'll need from the store cupboard: 2 cups low-fat granola*
- *¼ cup dried cranberries, sweetened ¼ cup almonds, chopped*
- *2 tbsp. Splenda*
- *1 teaspoon almond extract*
- *½ tsp cinnamon*

Instructions:

✓ *Heat oven to 350 degrees. Line the bottom and sides of an 8-inch baking dish with parchment paper.*

✓ *In a large bowl, combine dry ingredients, including the cranberries.*

✓ *In a small bowl, whisk together egg, egg white, and extract. Pour over dry ingredients and mix until combined.*

✓ *Press mixture into the prepared pan. Bake 20 minutes or until light brown.*

✓ *Cool in the pan for 5 minutes. Then carefully lift the bars from the pan onto a cutting board. Use a sharp knife to cut into 12 bars. Cool completely and store in an airtight container.*

Nutrition Facts Per Serving Calories 85 Total Carbs 14g Net Carbs 13g Protein 3g Fat 3g Sugar 5g Fiber 1g

822) *Double Chocolate Biscotti*

Prep time: 15 minutes, Cook time: 30 minutes, Serves: 27

Ingredients:

- 3 egg whites, divided
- 2 eggs
- 1 tbsp. orange zest
- What you'll need from the store cupboard: 2 cups of flour
- ½ cup Splenda
- ½ cup almonds, toasted and chopped 1/3 cup cocoa, unsweetened
- ¼ cup mini chocolate chips
- 1 tsp vanilla
- 1 tsp instant coffee granules 1 tsp water
- ½ tsp salt
- ½ tsp baking soda
- Nonstick cooking spray

Instructions:

✓ Heat oven to 350 degrees. Spray a large baking sheet with cooking spray.

✓ In a large bowl, combine flour, Splenda, cocoa, salt, and baking soda.

✓ In a small bowl, whisk the eggs, 2 egg whites, vanilla, and coffee. Let rest 3-4 minutes to dissolve the coffee.

✓ Stir in the orange zest and add to dry ingredients; stir to thoroughly combine. Fold in the nuts and chocolate chips.

✓ Divide dough in half and place on prepared pan. Shape each half into a 14x1 ¾-inch rectangle.

✓ Stir water and remaining egg white together. Brush over the top of the dough. Bake 20-25 minutes, or until firm to the touch. Cool on wire racks 5 minutes.

✓ Transfer biscotti to a cutting board. Use a serrated knife to cut diagonally into ½-inch slices. Place cut side down on a baking sheet and bake 5-7 minutes per side. Store in an airtight container. The serving size is 2 pieces.

Nutrition: Calories 86 Total Carbs 13g Net Carbs 12g Protein 3g Fat 3g Sugar 5g Fiber 1g

823) *Fig Cookie Bars*

Prep time: 5 minutes, Cook time: 20 minutes, Serves: 12

Ingredients:

- ½ cup dried figs
- 1/8 cup reduced-fat cream cheese 3 tbsp. skim milk
- What you'll need from the store cupboard: 2/3 cup flour
- ½ cup quick oats
- 1/3 cup powdered sugar substitute 6 tbsp. hot water
- 2 tbsp. sunflower oil
- 1 tbsp. Splenda
- ¾ tsp baking powder
- ½ tsp vanilla
- ¼ tsp salt
- Nonstick cooking spray

Instructions:

✓ Heat oven to 400 degrees. Spray a cookie sheet with cooking spray.

✓ Add the figs, water, and Splenda to a blender and process until figs are finely chopped.

✓ In a large bowl, stir together flour, oats, baking powder, and salt. Add oil and milk 1 tablespoon at a time until the mixture forms a ball.

✓ Roll dough out on a lightly floured surface to a 12x9-inch rectangle. Place on prepared pan. Spread fig mixture in a 2 ½-inch wide strip down the middle. At ½ inch intervals, use a sharp knife to cut the dough almost to the figs on both long sides. Fold strips over filling, overlapping, and crossing in the middle.

✓ Bake 15-20 minutes or until light brown. Remove from oven and let cool.

✓ In a small bowl, beat cream cheese, powdered sugar substitute, and vanilla until smooth. Drizzle over bars and cut into 12 pieces.

Nutrition: Calories 105 Total Carbs 17g Net Carbs 16g Protein 2g Fat 3g Sugar 9g Fiber 1g

824) *Bars de cookies*

5 minutes for preparation Time required for cooking: 20 minutes 12 portions

Ingredients:

- 1/2 cup figs, dried
- 1/8 cup cream cheese, reduced in fat
- 3 tablespoons skim milk
- What you'll require from your pantry:

- *230 ml flour*
- *1/2 cup rolled oats*
- *1/3 cup replacement for powdered sugar*
- *6 tbsp. steaming water*
- *Sunflower oil, 2 tbsp.*
- *Splenda 1 tbsp.*
- *34 tablespoon baking powder*
- *1/2 teaspoon vanilla*
- *1/4 teaspoon salt*
- *Cooking spray that is nonstick*

Instructions

- ✓ *Preheat the oven to 400 degrees Fahrenheit.*
- ✓ *Cooking spray a cookie sheet.*
- ✓ *In a blender, combine the figs, water, and Splenda and mix until the figs are finely chopped.*
- ✓ *Combine flour, oats, baking powder, and salt in a large mixing bowl.*
- ✓ *Add oil and milk 1 tablespoon at a time, stirring well after each addition, until mixture forms a ball.*
- ✓ *Roll out dough to a 12x9-inch rectangle on a lightly floured board. Arrange on prepared baking sheet.*
- ✓ *Spread fig mixture down the center in a 2 12 inch wide strip. At 12-inch intervals, cut the dough almost to the figs on both long sides with a sharp knife. Strips should be folded over the filling, overlapping and crossing in the center.*
- ✓ *Bake for 15-20 minutes, or until a light brown colour appears. Allow to cool after removing from the oven.*
- ✓ *Cream together cream cheese, powdered sugar replacement, and vanilla extract in a small dish until smooth.*
- ✓ *Drizzle remaining glaze over bars and cut into 12 pieces.*

Nutrition: Calories 105 Total Carbohydrates 17g Net Carbohydrates 16g Protein 2 g fat 3 g sugar 9 g dietary fiber 1g

825) *Blondies with Chocolate Chips*

5 minutes preparation time, 20 minutes cooking time, 12 servings

Ingredients:

- *a single egg*

What you'll require from your pantry:

- *1/2 cup chocolate chips, semi-sweet 1/3 cup spelt*

- *1/3 cup flour made from whole wheat*
- *1/4 cup brown Splenda sugar*
- *1/4 cup SUNSHINE OIL*
- *2 tablespoons honey*
- *1 tsp vanilla extract*
- *1/2 teaspoon bicarbonate of soda*
- *1/4 teaspoon salt*
- *Cooking spray that is nonstick*

Instructions:

- ✓ *Preheat the oven to 350 degrees Fahrenheit. Cooking spray an 8-inch square baking dish.*
- ✓ *Combine dry ingredients in a small bowl.*
- ✓ *Whisk together the egg, oil, honey, and vanilla extract in a large mixing basin. Add dry ingredients and stir just until mixed. Incorporate chocolate chips.*
- ✓ *The batter should be spread evenly in the prepared dish. Bake for 20-22 minutes, or until a toothpick inserted in the center comes out clean. Allow to cool on a wire rack before cutting into bars.*

Nutrition: Calories Per Serving 136 Carbohydrates in total 18g Carbohydrates in net Protein 16 g 2 g triglycerides 6 g fructose 9 g Fiber 2g

826) *Cinnamon Apple Slices*

5 minutes to prepare, 10 minutes to cook, 2 servings

Ingredients:

- *1 medium apple, thinly sliced*
- *What you'll require from your pantry:*
- *1/4 teaspoons cinnamon*
- *1/4 teaspoon nutmeg*
- *Cooking spray that is nonstick*

Instructions:

- ✓ *Preheat the oven to 375 degrees. Cooking spray a baking sheet.*
- ✓ *Combine apples and spices in a mixing dish. To coat, toss.*
- ✓ *Arrange apples on the prepared pan in a single layer. Bake for 4 minutes, then flip the apples over and bake for another 4 minutes.*
- ✓ *Serve immediately or cover tightly and store in an airtight container.*

Nutrition: Calories 58 Total Carbohydrates Protein 15 g 0 g fat 0 g sugar 11 g fiber 3 g cinnamon 0 g fat 0 g

827) *Sugar Popcorn with apples*

30 minutes for preparation; 50 minutes for cooking
11 portions

Ingredients:

- 4 tbsp. melted margarine
- What you will require from your store cupboard:
- 10 cup unflavored popcorn
- 2 cup unsweetened and diced dried apple rings
- 1/2 cup chopped walnuts
- 2 tbsp. Brown Splenda sugar
- 1 tsp ground cinnamon
- 1/2 teaspoon   vanilla

Instructions:

- ✓ Preheat the oven to 250 degrees Fahrenheit.
- ✓ Bake for 20 minutes in a 9x13-inch baking dish with chopped apples. Take the pan out of the oven and toss in the popcorn and nuts.
- ✓ Whisk together margarine, vanilla, Splenda, and cinnamon in a small bowl. Drizzle over popcorn in an equal layer and toss to coat.
- ✓ Bake for 30 minutes, quickly stirring every 10 minutes. Remove apples immediately if they begin to turn a dark brown color.
- ✓ Pour onto waxed paper and set aside for at least 30 minutes to cool. Keep refrigerated in an airtight container. 1 cup is the serving size.

Nutrition: Calories 133g Carbohydrates Total 14g Carbohydrates Net Protein: 11 g 3 g Fat 8 g Sucrose 7 g Fiber 3g

828) *Bars de cookies*

5 minutes for preparation Time required for cooking: 20 minutes 12 portions

Ingredients:

- 1/2 cup figs, dried
- 1/8 cup cream cheese, reduced in fat 3 tablespoons skim milk
- What you'll require from your pantry: 230
- ml flour
- 1/2 cup rolled oats
- 1/3 cup replacement for powdered sugar
- 6 tbsp. steaming water
- Sunflower oil, 2 tbsp.
- Splenda 1 tbsp.
- 34 tablespoon baking powder

- 1/2 teaspoon   vanilla
- 1/4 teaspoon   salt
- Cooking spray that is nonstick

Instructions:

- ✓ Preheat the oven to 400 degrees Fahrenheit. Cooking spray a cookie sheet.
- ✓ In a blender, combine the figs, water, and Splenda and mix until the figs are finely chopped.
- ✓ Combine flour, oats, baking powder, and salt in a large mixing bowl. Add oil and milk 1 tablespoon at a time, stirring well after each addition, until mixture forms a ball.
- ✓ Roll out dough to a 12x9-inch rectangle on a lightly floured board. Arrange on prepared baking sheet. Spread fig mixture down the center in a 2 12 inch wide strip. At 12-inch intervals, cut the dough almost to the figs on both long sides with a sharp knife. Strips should be folded over the filling, overlapping and crossing in the center.
- ✓ Bake for 15-20 minutes, or until a light brown color appears. Allow to cool after removing from the oven.
- ✓ Cream together cream cheese, powdered sugar replacement, and vanilla extract in a small dish until smooth. Drizzle remaining glaze over bars and cut into 12 pieces.

Nutrition: Calories 105 Total Carbohydrates 17g Net Carbohydrates 16g Protein 2 g fat 3 g sugar 9 g dietary fibe

829) *Sauce Caramel*

5 minutes for preparation Cooking time: ten minutes, servings: twelve

Ingredients:

- 2/3 cup cream
- 1/3 cup lard

What you'll require from your pantry:

- 3 tablespoons Splenda
- 1 tsp vanilla extract

Instructions:

- ✓ In a medium saucepan over low heat, combine the margarine and Splenda. Cook 3-4 minutes, occasionally stirring, until golden brown, once the margarine has melted.
- ✓ Bring to a low boil, stirring in the cream. Reduce to low heat and continue to cook, stirring periodically, for 7-10 minutes, or until the mixture has taken on a caramel

colour and coats the back of a spoon.

✓ *Take the pan off the heat and stir in the vanilla. Allow it cool completely before pouring into an airtight jar. Refrigerate. 1 tablespoon is the serving size.*

Nutrition Calories 84 Carbohydrates in Total 3g Protein 0g Fat 7g Carbohydrates 3 g Fiber 0 g

830) *Cheesy Dip with Jalapenos*

Preparation time is 5 minutes; cooking time is 3 hours. 10 portions

- *4 pkg. softened cream cheese*
- *1/2 cup grated low-fat cheddar cheese*
- *1 cup cooked and crumbled bacon*
- *1 cup sour cream, fat-free*
- *1 sliced jalapeno, fresh*
- *What you will require from your store cupboard 2 cans diced jalapenos*
- *1 packet ranch seasoning*

Instructions:

✓ *Combine cream cheese, 2/3 cup bacon, diced jalapenos, 1 cup cheddar cheese, sour cream, and dressing in a large mixing dish.*

✓ *Distribute evenly in a crock cooker. Finish with the last of the bacon and cheese. Arrange jalapeno slices across the top.*

✓ *Cook covered on low for 3 hours. Serve immediately.*

Nutrition: 233 Calories Carbohydrates in Total 12g Protein 24g Fat 9g Carbohydrates 0g

831) *Chinese Hot Mustard*

15 minutes for preparation 15 minutes total time, 4 servings

- *What you'll require from your pantry: 1 tbsp. powdered mustard*
- *11/2 teaspoon hot water*
- *1/2 tbsp vegetable oil*
- *1/2 tbsp rice vinegar*
- *18 teaspoon salt*
- *18 teaspoon white pepper*

Instructions:

✓ *Combine the dry ingredients in a small bowl. Stir with water until the mixture resembles a liquid paste, and the dry ingredients have been absorbed.*

✓ *Combine oil and vinegar in a large mixing bowl until completely mixed. Ten minutes later, cover and set aside.*

✓ *Restir. Season to taste and adjust seasonings as desired. Refrigerate covered*

and chilled until ready to use.

Nutrition: Calories 19 Carbohydrates 1 gram protein 1 gram fat 1 gram sugar 0 gram fiber

832) *Cinnamon Sauce de blueberries*

Time required for preparation: 5 minutes; time required for cooking: 10 minutes. 16 portions

Ingredients:

- *Approximately 2 cups blueberries*
- *2 tbsp. freshly squeezed lemon juice What you'll require from your pantry:*
- *14 c. Splenda*
- *14 c. water*
- *2 tsp starch de maize*
- *1/2 teaspoon   cinnamon*

Direction

✓ *Put Splenda and cornstarch in a small saucepan over medium heat. Add other ingredients and bring to a boil, constantly stirring.*

✓ *Reduce to low heat and continue cooking for 5 minutes, or until thickened. Allow to cool completely before serving.*

✓ *Refrigerate until ready to use in a jar with an airtight lid. 1 tablespoon is the serving size.*

Nutrition: Calories 27 Total Carbohydrates 6g Protein 0g Fatty Acids 0g Sucrose 0g

833) *Citrus Vinaigrette*

Time required for preparation: 5 minutes; total time required: 10 minutes. 6 portions

- *1 orange, zested, and juiced*
- *1 zested and juiced lemon*
- *What you'll require from your pantry:*
- *1/4 cup olive oil extra virgin*
- *1 teaspoon mustard Dijon*
- *1 teaspoon honey*
- *1 smashed garlic clove*
- *Season with salt and pepper to taste*

Direction

✓ *In a food processor, combine the zest and juices, mustard, honey, garlic, salt, and pepper. Combine by pulsing.*

✓ *Slowly add in the olive oil while the machine is running and process until mixed.*

✓ *Use immediately or refrigerate in an*

airtight jar.
Nutrition: Calories Per Serving 94 Carbohydrates in total 6g Carbohydrates in net 0 g fat 5 g protein 8 g sugar 4 g fiber 1g

834) *Compote de cranberries et d'orange*

5 minutes for preparation Cooking time: ten minutes, servings: eight

- *1 pound fresh cranberries, rinsed and drained*
- *1 halved large orange*
- *What you'll require from your pantry: 1 tsp vanilla extract*
- *1 tsp ground cinnamon*

Direction

- ✓ *Place cranberries in a medium saucepan over medium heat. Squeeze both orange halves, pulp included, into the berries. Vanilla and cinnamon should be added at this point.*
- ✓ *Cook, constantly stirring, until berries begin to open. Reduce to low heat and simmer for another 10 minutes, or until the mixture begins to thicken.*
- ✓ *Allow 15 minutes for cooling before spooning into an airtight jar. Keep chilled until ready to use.*

Nutrition: Calories 43 Total Carbohydrates 8g Net Carbohydrates 5g Protein 0g Fat 0g Sugar 4 g Fiber 3 g

835) *Creme Dressing of Poppy Seeds*

5 minutes total time, 6 servings

- *1/3 cup light mayonnaise 1/4 tbsp. skim milk*
- *What you'll require from your pantry: 3 tablespoons Splenda*
- *4 teaspoon apple cider vinegar*
- *2 tablespoons poppy seeds*

Instructions:

- ✓ *Whisk together all ingredients in a small bowl until well blended. Refrigerate in an airtight jar.*

Nutrition: Calories 90 Carbohydrates in Total ten grams protein 1 gram fat 5 g Sucrose 7 g Fiber 0g

836) *Pork Dry Rub*

5 minutes prep time, 5 minutes total time, 16 serves

- *What you'll require from your pantry:*
- *2 tbsp. extra-fine ground coffee*

- *2 tbsp. powdered chipotle*
- *1 tbsp. paprika, smoked*
- *Splenda 1 tbsp. caramelized sugar*
- *1 teaspoon salt*
- *1 teaspoon grated ginger*
- *1 tsp powdered mustard*
- *1 tablespoon coriander*

Direction

- ✓ *Combine all ingredients in a mixing bowl.*
- ✓ *For up to 1 month, store in an airtight container in a cold, dry location.*

Nutrition: Calories 5 Carbohydrates in Total 1 gram of protein 0g Fatty Acids 0g Sucrose 1 gram fiber 0 gram

837) *Simple Cheesy Dip Sauce*

2 minutes for preparation Time required for cooking: 5 minutes 2 servings

Ingredients:

- *3/4 cup unsweetened skim milk*
- *3/4 cup cheddar cheese, reduced in fat 1 tbsp. lard*
- *What you'll require from your pantry: 1 tablespoon flour*
- *Cayenne pepper, pinch*
- *Season with salt & pepper*

Instructions:

- ✓ *In a small saucepan over medium heat, melt margarine. Whisk in flour and cook, constantly whisking, for about 1 minute, or until golden brown.*
- ✓ *Add milk gradually and whisk until no lumps remain. Cook, whisking continually, for 3-4 minutes, or until mixture thickens and begins to boil.*
- ✓ *Add cheese and stir until smooth. Season with cayenne pepper, salt, and freshly ground pepper to taste.*

Nutrition: Calories 219 Total Carbohydrates 8g Protein 16g Fat 15g Carbohydrates 5 g Fiber 0 gram

838) *Garlic Sauce for Dipping*

5 minutes prep time, 5 minutes total time, 4 servings

Instructions:

- *1 cup yogurt, Greek*
- *1 tbsp. finely sliced fresh dill*
- ✓ *What you'll need from your pantry: 2 garlic cloves, finely chopped*
- ✓ *Whisk together all ingredients in a small*

dish.

✓ *Serve immediately or cover and refrigerate until ready to use.*

Nutrition: Calories 40 Carbohydrates 2 g protein, 5 g fat, 1 g sugar, and 2 g dietary fiber 0

839) *Garlic Dip*

Time Required for Preparation: 15 minutes Time Required for Cooking: 10 minutes

- *2 potatoes*
- *6-7 finely chopped garlic cloves*
- *1 cup finely chopped walnuts*
- *1/2 cups extra virgin olive oil*
- *1/4 cup red wine vinegar*

Directions:

✓ *In a blender, combine boiling and peeled potatoes, chopped garlic, walnuts, and salt—puree for 30 seconds, or until fully combined. Slowly drizzle in oil and vinegar in alternate batches.*

✓ *Continue pureeing for approximately 3 minutes, or until the mixture forms a homogeneous paste slightly looser in texture than mashed potatoes.*

291 Nutrition: Calories; 21g total fat; 21g total carbohydrate; 5g fiber; 14g sugar; 10g protein; 242mg sodium

840) *Gram herb Vinaigrette*

Time required for preparation: 5 minutes; time required for mixing: 5 minutes. 12 servings

Ingredients:

- *2 tablespoons shallot, finely chopped*
- *1 tbsp. chopped fresh basil*
- *1 tbsp. chopped fresh oregano*
- *1 tbsp. chopped fresh tarragon*

What you'll require from your pantry:

- *¼ cups olive oil extra virgin*
- *¼ cup chicken broth with minimal sodium*
- *¼ cup red wine vinegar*
- *¼ tsp salt*
- *¼ tsp freshly grated pepper*

Direction

✓ *Combine the ingredients in a jar fitted with an airtight lid. Secure the cover and vigorously shake to blend.*

✓ *Keep chilled until ready to use. Keeps for up to 2 days. 1 tablespoon is the serving size.*

Nutrition: Calories 39 Total Carbohydrates 0 grams protein, 0 grams fat, 4 grams sugar, 0 grams fiber, 0

grams

841) *Horseradish Sauce au Mustard*

5 minutes preparation time, 5 minutes total time 8 portions

Ingredients:

- *1/4 cup sour cream, fat-free*

What you'll require from your pantry:

- *1/4 cup mayonnaise light*
- *1/2 teaspoon lemon juice*
- *1 tablespoon Splenda*
- *1/2 teaspoon mustard powder*
- *1/2 teaspoon mustard Dijon*
- *1/2 teaspoon horseradish*

Instructions:

✓ *Combine all ingredients in a small bowl until well blended.*

✓ *Refrigerate in an airtight jar until ready to use. 1 tablespoon is the serving size.*

Nutrition: Calories 36 Carbohydrates in Total 2g Protein 0g Fat 2g Sugar 1g Fiber 0g

842) *Dressing for Italian Salad*

5 minutes preparation time, 5 minutes total time 8 portions

Ingredients:

- *2 tbsp. freshly squeezed lemon juice*
- *What you'll need in your pantry: 3/4 cups olive oil*
- *1/4 cup vinaigrette de vinaigrette*
- *2 minced garlic cloves 2 tsp Italian seasoning*
- *1 tablespoon oregano*
- *1/2 teaspoon honey*
- *1/2 teaspoon salt*
- *1/4 teaspoon black pepper*
- *1/4 teaspoon crushed red pepper*

Direction

✓ *In a measuring cup or jar, combine all ingredients. Whisk vigorously.*

✓ *For up to 1 week, store in an airtight jar or bottle. 1 tablespoon is the serving size.*

Nutrition: Calories 167 Total Carbohydrates 1 gram protein, 0 gram fat, 18 gram sugar, 0 gram

843) *Italian Salsa*

Time required for preparation: ten minutes; time

required for chilling: one hour. 16 portions

Ingredients:

- 4 chopped plum tomatoes 12 finely diced red onion
- 2 tbsp. chopped fresh parsley
- What you'll need from your pantry: 12 pitted and chopped
- Kalamata olives
- 2 garlic cloves, finely chopped
- 1 tablespoon balsamic vinaigrette
- 1 tbsp. extra-virgin olive oil
- 2 tbsp drained capers
- 1/4 teaspoon   salt
- 1/4 teaspoon   pepper

Direction

✓ Blend all ingredients in a medium bowl and stir to combine 1 hour before using, cover and chill.

✓ Refrigerate in an airtight jar with a tight-fitting lid for up to 7 days. Before using, stir thoroughly.

Nutrition: Calories 21 Carbohydrates in Total Protein: 2 g 0g Fatty Acid 1 g Sucrose 1 gram fiber 0g

844) *Salad with Maple Mustard Dressing*

5 minutes total time, 6 servings

- What you'll require from your pantry: 2 tbsp. vinaigrette balsamico
- 2 tablespoons olive oil
- 1 tbsp. maple syrup without added sugar
- 1 teaspoon mustard Dijon
- 1/8 teaspoon salt

Direction

✓ Combine all ingredients in a jar fitted with a tight-fitting lid. Screw the lid on and shake vigorously to blend. Refrigerate until ready to serve.

Nutrition: Calories 48 Carbohydrates in Total Protein: 2 g 0g Fatty Acid 5g Sucrose 0g Fiber 0g

845) *Vinaigrette with Maple and Shallots*

3 minutes prep time, 5 minutes total time, 4 servings

Ingredients:

- 1 teaspoon shallot, finely chopped
- What you'll require from your pantry: 2 tbsp. vinegar de cidre apple

- 1 tbsp. brown spicy mustard
- 1 tbsp. extra-virgin olive oil
- 2 teaspoon maple syrup (sugar-free)

Direction

✓ Combine the ingredients in a small jar fitted with an airtight lid. Shake vigorously to combine.

✓ Keep chilled until ready to use. 1 tablespoon is the serving size.

Nutrition: Calories 45 g Carbohydrates Total 5 g Protein 0 g Fat 2 g Sugar 0 g Fiber 0 g

846) *Sauce Marinara*

Preparation time: ten minutes Time required for cooking: 30 minutes 6 portions

- What you'll require from your pantry:
- 28 oz. undrained can chopped tomatoes 4–6 garlic cloves, finely chopped
- 4 tbsp. olive oil extra virgin
- 2 tbsp. paste de tomato
- 1 tablespoon basil,
- 1 tablespoon Splenda
- 1 teaspoon salt

Instructions:

✓ In a saucepan over medium heat, heat the oil. Cook for 1 minute before adding the garlic.

✓ Add the tomato paste and cook for a further 1 minute. Cook for 10-15 minutes, breaking up the tomatoes as they cook.

✓ Combine Splenda and salt in a separate bowl. Process with an immersion blender until desired consistency is achieved.

✓ Allow to cool before storing in an airtight jar in the refrigerator for up to 7 days. Alternatively, use immediately.

Nutrition: Calories 179 Total Carbs 13g Net Carbs 10g Protein 2g Fat 14g Sugar 8g Fiber 3g

847) *Marmalade Orange*

30 minutes for preparation, 30 minutes for cooking, 48 serves

Ingredients:

- 4 oranges navel
- ONE LEMON
- What you'll require from your pantry: 12 cups water 2 12 cups water
- 14 c. lukewarm water
- 4 tablespoons Splenda

- *Gelatin, 1 oz.*

Instructions:

✓ *Oranges should be quartered and all pulp removed. Remove the white portion of the rind and thinly slice it into 2-inch strips. Remove as much membrane as possible between orange segments and lay the seeds in a tiny piece of cheesecloth, pulling up the sides to form a "bag" and tying closed.*

✓ *Rep with the lemon, excluding the seeds. The lemon rind should be cut into thinner strips than the orange rind.*

✓ *Orange and lemon pulp should be chopped and added to a medium pot along with 2 12 cups water. Over med-high heat, bring to a quick boil.*

✓ *Reduce to medium-low heat and add the seed bag. Gently bring to a boil for 30 minutes, or until the citrus fruit is tender. Discard the seed pack.*

✓ *In warm water, dissolve the gelatin. Combine it with 12 of the Splenda in the orange mixture. Take care not to burn yourself when tasting the marmalade and adjust the sweetener to taste.*

✓ *3 12 pint jars with airtight lids Spoon the marmalade into 3 12 pint jars with airtight lids. Refrigerate and seal.*

Nutrition: Calories 15 Carbohydrates in Total Protein 3 g 1 gram fat 0 gram sugar 3 g Fiber 0 gram

848) *Peach Relish de poivre*

Time required for preparation: 10 minutes; time required for chilling: 2 hours; Serves: 16

Ingredients:

- *2 peeled and diced peaches*
- *1 finely chopped green onion*
- *1/3 cup chopped bell pepper*
- *1/3 cup chopped red pepper*
- *2 tbsp. chopped fresh mint*

✓ *What you'll require from your pantry: 1 tbsp. freshly squeezed lemon juice*

✓ *1 tbsp. peach preserves, sugar-free In a medium bowl, combine peaches, onion, peppers, and mint.*

✓ *Combine lemon juice and preserves in a small bowl. Toss the peach mixture in the glaze.*

✓ *Refrigerate for up to 2 hours or overnight in an airtight container. 2 tablespoons is the serving size.*

Nutrition: Calories 10 Carbohydrates in Total 0g Fat

0g Sugar 2g Fiber 3g Protein 0g

849) *Jam with pear and poppy*

Preparation time: 2 hours Time required for cooking: 30 minutes 32 portions

Ingredients:

- *3 peeled, seeded, and diced pears 12 lemons*
- *What you'll need in your pantry: 3/4 cups Splenda*
- *1 tbsp. pomegranate seeds*

Direction

✓ *In a large bowl, combine pears. Toss with Splenda to coat. Squeeze lemon juice over the pears and mix once more. Allow two hours for the fruit to release its juice.*

✓ *In a medium saucepan over medium heat, combine poppy seeds. Cook, occasionally stirring, for 1-2 minutes to toast the. They should be transferred to a bowl.*

✓ *In a saucepan, combine the pears and juice and bring to a boil, stirring continuously. Reduce to low heat and continue to cook for 10 minutes or until thickened.*

✓ *12 pears, spooned into a blender, and puree until smooth. Reintroduce the purée and poppy seeds to the pot. Cook for a further 5-10 minutes, or until the jam is thick.*

✓ *Spoon into two pint-sized airtight jars. Allow it cool completely before screwing on the lids and refrigerating. 1 tablespoon is the serving size.*

Nutrition: Calories 36g Carbohydrates Total 8g Carbohydrates Net 0g fat 0g sugar 7g protein 6g fiber 1g

850) *Pineapple Mango Sauce Spicy*

Time required for preparation: 10 minutes; time required for cooking: 20 minutes. 16 portions

Ingredients:

- *2 diced cherry peppers*
- *1 chopped ghost pepper*
- *1 cup sliced pineapple*
- *1/2 cup diced mango*
- *2 tbsp. diced cilantro*
- *What you'll require from your pantry:*
- *1 cup distilled water*
- *12 c. vinegar*
- *1 tablespoon olive oil*
- *1 tablespoon Splenda*

- *1 tablespoon paprika*
- *Season with salt to taste*

Instructions:

✓ *In a large saucepan over medium heat, heat the oil. Cook for 8 minutes to soften the peppers and fruit.*

✓ *Bring to a boil with the remaining ingredients. Reduce to low heat and cook for 20 minutes. Take the pan off the heat and allow it cool.*

✓ *Pulse the contents in a food processor until smooth. Fill sterilized bottles halfway, attach lids, and store in the refrigerator until ready to use.*

Nutrition: Calories 16 Carbohydrates 0 g fat 0 g sugar 2 g

851) *Sauce Pizza*

5 minutes to prepare, 5 minutes to cook, 8 serves
Ingredients:

- *1/2 cup chopped yellow onion*
- *What you'll require from your pantry: 15 oz. crushed tomatoes, no sugar added*
- *1 tbsp. olive oil plus 1/3 cup*
- *3 minced garlic cloves*
- *2 tablespoons parsley*
- *1 tsp thyme*
- *1 teaspoon thyme*
- *1 teaspoon paprika, smoked*
- *Season with salt to taste*

Instructions:

✓ *In a small skillet over medium heat, heat 1 tablespoon oil. Cook until the onion and garlic are transparent.*

✓ *Combine all ingredients in a medium saucepan over medium heat, along with the onions. Bring to a simmer and cook, stirring regularly, for 2-3 minutes.*

✓ *Take the pan from the heat and allow it to cool completely. Refrigerate in an airtight jar with a tight-fitting lid for up to 2 weeks. Alternatively, freeze for up to 6 months.*

Nutrition: 179 Calories per serving Carbohydrates in total 8g Carbohydrates in net Protein: 6 g 2 g fat 17 g sugar 5 g dietary fiber 2g

852) *Verde Queso*

Preparation time: ten minutes, cooking time: thirty minutes, servings: ten
Ingredients:

- *1/2 package softened cream cheese*
- *1/2 cup cubed white American cheese*
- *1/2 cup cubed white cheddar cheese*
- *1/2 cup cubed pepper Jack cheese*
- *1/4 cup cubed skim milk*
- *What you will require from your store cupboard*
- *1/2 cup verde salsa*
- *1/2 cup chopped green chiles*
- *Cooking spray that is nonstick*

Instructions:

✓ *Preheat the oven to 325 degrees. Cooking spray a small baking dish.*

✓ *Combine all ingredients in a medium mixing basin. Combine all ingredients in the prepared baking dish.*

✓ *Bake for 30 minutes, stirring every 8-10 minutes, or until the cheese is melted and the dip is hot and bubbling. Serve immediately.*

Nutrition: Calories 105 Carbohydrates Total 3g Carbohydrates Net Protein: 2 g 7g Fatty Acids 7g Sucrose 1 gram fiber 1g

853) *Jam with raspberries and basil*

5 minutes for preparation Time required for cooking: 20 minutes 24 portions
Ingredients:

- *2 lbs. raspberries, fresh*
- *1/3 cup finely chopped fresh basil*
- *2 tbsp. freshly squeezed lemon juice*
- *What you will require from your store cupboard 12 c. Splenda*

Instructions:

✓ *In a large saucepan, combine the berries and lemon juice and heat over medium heat. Break up the berries with a wooden spoon. Bring to a low boil and reduce to low heat; cook for 5-6 minutes, or until mixture begins to bubble.*

✓ *Stir in Splenda and heat, stirring regularly, for about 15 minutes, or until Splenda is dissolved and the mixture resembles syrup.*

✓ *Take the pan off the heat and mix in the basil. Spoon into airtight glass jars. Allow to cool completely before adding the lids and refrigerating. 1 tablespoon is the serving size.*

Nutrition: Calories 40g Carbohydrates Total 8g Carbohydrates Net Protein: 6 g 0g Fatty Acids 0g Sucrose 6 g Fiber 2 g

854) *Salsa de Tomas Roasted*

Preparation time: 10 minutes, cooking time: 30 minutes, servings: 8

- *6 tomatoes plums*
- *1/4 cup coriander*
- *What you'll require from your pantry: 2 tbsp extra-virgin olive oil*
- *1 teaspoon sauce adobo*
- *1/2 tsp kosher salt, divided*
- *Cooking spray that is nonstick*

Instructions:

- ✓ *Preheat the oven to 425 degrees Fahrenheit. Cooking spray a broiler pan.*
- ✓ *Tomatoes should be cut in half and seeds removed. Arrange on broiler pan, cut side up. Brush with oil and season with 14% salt. Bake, cut side down, for 30-40 minutes, or until the sides are browned.*
- ✓ *In a food processor, pulse cilantro until finely chopped. Combine tomatoes, adobo, and remaining salt in a medium bowl. Process until coarsely chopped. Refrigerate in an airtight jar until ready to use. 2 tablespoons is the serving size.*

Nutrition: Calories 33 Carbohydrates Total 5g Carbohydrates Net 4g Protein 1g Fat 1g Sugar 4g Fiber

855) *Spaghetti Sauce*

Time required for preparation: 20 minutes; time required for cooking: 30 minutes. 6 portions

Ingredients:

- *1 diced onion*
- *1 grated carrot*
- *1 celery stalk, chopped*
- *1 grated zucchini*
- *What you'll require from your pantry:*
- *1 (28 oz.) pureed tomatoes in the Italian style 1 (14 12 oz.) chopped tomatoes 12 c. water*
- *2 garlic cloves, finely chopped*
- *1/2 teaspoon oregano*
- *1 tablespoon olive oil*
- *1 teaspoon basil*
- *1 teaspoon thyme*
- *1 teaspoon salt*
- *1/4 teaspoon crushed red pepper*

Instructions:

- ✓ *In a large saucepan over medium heat, heat the oil. Combine the vegetables and garlic. Cook, stirring regularly, for approximately 5 minutes, or until vegetables are soft.*
- ✓ *Combine remaining ingredients, breaking up tomatoes with the back of a spoon. Bring to a boil and cook, partially covered, for 30 minutes over medium-low heat, stirring periodically.*
- ✓ *Refrigerate sauce in an airtight jar for up to 3 days or freeze for up to 3 months.*

Nutrition: Calories 47 Total Carbohydrates 8g Net Carbohydrates Protein: 6 g 2 g fat 1 g sugar 3 g dietary fiber 2 g

856) *Vinaigrette Spicy Asian*

Time required for preparation: 5 minutes; total time required: 10 minutes. 4 portions

Ingredients:

- *1 inch fresh ginger root, peeled and quartered*
- *1 tbsp. freshly squeezed lemon juice*
- *What you'll require from your pantry: 14 cups sesame seed oil*
- *2 peeled garlic cloves*
- *2 tbsp. vinegar de rice*
- *1 tbsp. Chinese cayenne pepper*
- *1 teaspoon soy sauce, light*
- *1/8 teaspoon crushed red pepper*

Instructions:

- ✓ *In a food processor or blender, combine all ingredients and mix until smooth.*
- ✓ *Keep in an airtight jar. 2 tbsp. per serving*

Nutrition: Calories 172 Carbohydrates Protein: 7 g 2g Fatty Acids 17g Sucrose 2 g Fiber 0g

857) *Spicy Peanut Sauce*

5 minutes for preparation; 5 minutes for cooking 20 portions

- *1/4 cup fresh lime juice*
- *2 tbsp. peeled and grated fresh ginger*
- *What you'll require from your pantry: 12 cups chicken broth, reduced in sodium and fat*
- *1 cup peanut butter reduced in fat*
- *3 tablespoons Brown Splenda sugar*
- *2 tbsp. soy sauce, reduced in sodium*
- *1/2 teaspoon crushed red pepper*

Direction

- ✓ *Heat peanut butter in a small saucepan*

over medium heat until melted. Stir in broth until blended.

✓ *Continue cooking over med-low heat for 5 minutes, stirring regularly, until thickened.*

✓ *Serve alongside shrimp, scallops, chicken, turkey, and beef. 2 tablespoons is the serving size.*

✓ *Refrigerate in an airtight container for up to 3 days.*

Nutrition: Calories 90 Total Carbohydrates 9g Net Carbohydrates Protein: 8 g 3 g triglycerides 5 g fructose 4 g Fiber 1 g

858) *Spicy Sweet Dipped Veggies*

5 minutes prep time, 5 minutes total time, 16 serves

- *1/4 teaspoon habanero pepper, finely chopped*
- *1 tbsp. freshly squeezed lime juice*
- *What you'll require from your pantry: 1 cup orange marmalade without added sugar*
- *1 tablespoon (tbsp.) fish sauce*
- *1/2 teaspoon   crushed red pepper*
- *1/4 teaspoon   sesame oil*
- *Squeeze of salt*

Direction

✓ *In a small bowl, combine all ingredients. Spoon into an airtight jar and refrigerate.*

✓ *1 tablespoon is the serving size. It will keep in the refrigerator for up to one week.*

Nutrition: Calories 5g Protein 0g Fat 0g Sugar 0g Fiber 0g Total Carbohydrates 5g Protein 0g Fat 0g Sugar 0g Fiber 0g

859) *Sriracha Dipping Sauce*

1 minute preparation time, 2 minutes total time, 6 servings

- *2 tsp fresh lime juice*
- *What you'll require from your pantry: 1/2 cup mayonnaise lite*
- *Sriracha sauce, 2 tbsp.*
- *Splenda 1 tbsp.*
- *1 teaspoon sauce Worcestershire*

Direction

✓ *In a small bowl, whisk together all of the ingredients until smooth.*

✓ *Use immediately or cover and chill until ready to use. 1/2 tbsps is the serving size.*

Nutrition: Calories 83 Carbohydrates Total 5g Protein 0g Fat 7g Sugar 2 g Fiber 0 g

860) *Jelly Strawberry Rhubarb*

15 minutes preparation time, 15 minutes cooking time, 64 servings

Ingredients:

- *5 cups rhubarb, sliced into 12-inch rounds*
- *2 cups hulled and halved strawberries*
- *1 tbsp. freshly squeezed lemon juice*
- *What you'll require from your pantry: 14 cups Splenda*

Instructions:

✓ *In a large saucepan, combine all ingredients and heat over medium heat. Bring to a boil, constantly stirring.*

✓ *Reduce to low heat, cover, and cook for 15-20 minutes, stirring periodically, until rhubarb is tender and the mixture has thickened.*

✓ *Spoon into two-pint jars and set aside to chill fully. Combine the lids and place them in the refrigerator. 1 tablespoon is the serving size.*

Nutrition: Calories 37 Carbohydrates in Total 7g Protein 0g Fat 0g Sugar 7g Fiber 0g 7g Protein 0g Fat 0g Sugar

861) *Sugar-Free Ketchup*

5 minutes for preparation Time allotted: 5 minutes 28 portions

- *What you will require from your store cupboard Tomato paste, 12 oz.*
- *12 c. water*
- *1/3 cup distilled white vinegar*
- *1 teaspoon salt*
- *3 tablespoon Splenda*
- *1 teaspoon powdered onion*

Direction

✓ *Combine water, vinegar, Splenda, onion powder, and salt in a large mixing basin. Add tomato paste and whisk until smooth.*

✓ *Transfer to a glass jar fitted with an airtight lid and refrigerate until ready to use. 2 tablespoons is the serving size.*

Nutrition: Calories 15 Carbohydrates in Total 0g Fat 0g Sugar 2g Fiber 3g Protein 0g

862) *Tangy Salad dressing from Mexico*

5 minutes total time, 8 servings

Ingredients:

- *1/2 cup cilantro, finely chopped*

- *3 tbsp. freshly squeezed lime juice*
- *1/2 cup SUNSHINE OIL*
- *2 tablespoons water*
- *1 tbsp. vinegar de cidre apple*
- *2 teaspoon honey*
- *1 teaspoon salt, garlic*

Direction

✓ *1/2 teaspoon oregano de Mexico to taste freshly ground black pepper Instructions: In a food processor or blender, combine all ingredients.*

✓ *Pulse until thoroughly combined and emulsified. Season with salt and pepper to taste.*

✓ *Refrigerate in an airtight container. To serve, bring to room temperature and give a vigorous shake.*

Nutrition: Calories Per Serving 127 Carbohydrates 0 g fat 14 g sugar 2 g fiber 0g

863) *Sauce Teriyaki*

5 minutes for preparation Time required for cooking: ten minutes 16 portions

- *What you'll require from your pantry: 14 cups split water*
- *1/4 cup mild soy sauce*
- *2 tablespoons + 1/2 teaspoon   liquid stevia*
- *1/2 tbsp corn starch*
- *1/2 teaspoon   ginger*
- *1/4 teaspoon   garlic powder*

Instructions:

✓ *In a small saucepan, combine soy sauce, 1 cup water, ginger, garlic powder, and stevia. Bring to a simmer over medium-low heat.*

✓ *Corn starch and 14 cups of water should be whisked together until smooth. Combine it completely with the sauce in the pan. Allow sauce to simmer for approximately 1 minute or until it begins to thicken.*

✓ *Take the pan from the heat and allow it to cool completely. As the sauce cools, it will continue to thicken. Use this marinade or dipping sauce as a marinade or dipping sauce. 1 tablespoon is the serving size.*

Nutrition: Calories 5 Carbohydrates in total 1g Protein 0g Fat 0g Sugar 0g Fiber 0g

864) *Vinaigrette de noix*

Time allotted: 5 minutes 4 portions

- *What you'll require from your pantry: 12 c. water*
- *1/4 cup balsamic vinaigrette*
- *14 c. walnuts*
- *14 c. raisins*
- *1 garlic clove*
- *1 teaspoon mustard Dijon*
- *1/4 teaspoon thyme*

Instructions:

✓ *In a blender or food processor, combine all ingredients and pulse until smooth. Refrigerate in an airtight jar.*

Nutrition: Calories 53 Total Carbohydrates 2g Carbohydrates Net 1 gram of protein 0g Fiber 2g Fat 5g Sugar 1 gram of warm bacon

865) *Dressing Vinaigrette*

5 minutes for preparation Time required for cooking: ten minutes 4 portions

Ingredients:

- *6 slices bacon, thickly sliced, fried crisp, and crumbled*
- *1 shallot, finely chopped*
- *What you'll require from your pantry: 1/2 cup vinaigrette de vinaigrette*
- *2 garlic cloves, finely chopped*
- *1/2 tsp brown Splenda sugar*
- *34 teaspoon mustard Dijon*
- *Salt*
- *Black pepper, freshly ground*

Direction

✓ *After cooking the bacon, strain everything but 3 tablespoons of the grease into a jar and reserve for later use.*

✓ *Cook for 2-3 minutes, or until the garlic and onion are tender, in the remaining heated fat.*

✓ *Stir in Splenda until it melts. Season with salt and pepper to taste. Whisk in the remaining ingredients. Combine immediately with your preferred salad.*

Nutrition: Calories 115 Total Carbohydrates 2g Protein 7 g fat 8 g sugar 1 g dietary fiber 0 g

866) *Pureed Cauliflower*

Preparation time: ten minutes 15 minutes for cooking 6 portions

Ingredients:

- *2 12 lb. florets de cauliflower*

- *12 leek, halved, white, and pale green parts*
- *4 tablespoons butter*
- *2 tsp diced fresh parsley*
- *What you'll require from your pantry: 2 tbsp. chicken broth low in salt*
- *2 teaspoon olive oil extra virgin*
- *4 garlic cloves, finely chopped*
- *1/4 teaspoon   salt*
- *1/4 teaspoon   pepper*

Instructions:

- ✓ *In a steamer basket, place the cauliflower over boiling water. Steam, covered, for 10-15 minutes, or until fork-tender.*
- ✓ *Rinse and pat dry the leek. Thinly slice.*
- ✓ *In a large skillet, heat oil over medium-low heat. Cook for 2-3 minutes, or until the leek is tender. Add the garlic and cook for a further 1 minute.*
- ✓ *Pulse all ingredients in a food processor until nearly smooth. Serve immediately or store in the refrigerator for later use.*

Nutrition: Calories 146 Carbohydrates Total 14g Carbohydrates Net 8g Protein 5g Fatty Acids 9g Sucrose 6 g Fiber 6g

867) *Margarita Chicken Dipping Sauce*

Preparation time: ten minutes 1 hour to cook 12 servings

Ingredients:

- *2 12 cups grated Monterrey jack cheese*
- *1/2 cup cooked and shredded chicken*
- *12 blocks softened cream cheese, cubes*
- *1/4 cup lime juice*
- *2 tablespoons freshly squeezed orange juice*
- *Pico de Gallo, 2 tbsp.*
- *1 tbsp. zest de lime*
- *What you'll require from your pantry: 14 c. tequila*
- *2 garlic cloves, finely chopped*
- *1 teaspoon cumin*
- *1 teaspoon salt*

Instructions:

- ✓ *Cream cheese should be placed at the bottom of the crockpot. Chicken is placed on top, followed by shredded cheese. Combine the remaining ingredients, except the Pico de Gallo, in a medium bowl.*
- ✓ *Cook covered for 60 minutes on low heat.*

Stir the dip occasionally to incorporate all of the ingredients.

- ✓ *Once the dip is finished, transfer it to a serving bowl. Serve with Pico de Gallo and tortilla chips.*

Nutrition: Calories Per 169 Carbohydrates Protein 5 g 14 g fat 8 g sugar 1 g dietary fiber 0g

868) *Sauce Alfredo*

5 minutes for preparation Time required for cooking: ten minutes 6 portions

Ingredients:

- *1/2 cup heavy crème*
- *1 tbsp. lard*
- *What you'll require from your pantry:*
- *1/2 cup parmesan cheese, reduced-fat 4 garlic cloves, finely chopped Cayenne pepper*
- *Salt Nutmeg*

Instructions:

- ✓ *In a medium saucepan over medium heat, melt butter. Sauté garlic for approximately 30 seconds, or until fragrant.*
- ✓ *Combine the heavy cream with the sugar. Bring to a low simmer and continue to cook for around 5 minutes, or until the sauce begins to thicken and is reduced by approximately 1/*
- ✓ *Reduce heat to a low setting. Whisk in the Parmesan cheese gradually. Continue whisking over low heat until the mixture is smooth. Season with salt, pepper, and freshly grated nutmeg to taste. (If the sauce is too thick, thin it out with additional cream.)*

Nutrition: Calories 147 Carbohydrates 0g Fiber 0g Protein 2g Fat 14g Sugar 0g

869) *Beef Marinade for All Purposes*

10 minutes prep time, 10 minutes total time, 8 servings

Ingredients:

- *6 limes, zested*
- *1 bunch chopped cilantro*
- *What you will need from your pantry:*
- *1/4 cup olive oil*
- *6 garlic cloves, finely chopped*

Direction

- ✓ *In an airtight container, combine all ingredients.*
- ✓ *Refrigerate for up to three months or freeze*

for up to six months. 1 tablespoon is the serving size.

Nutrition: Calories 78 Carbohydrates 1 gram protein 0 gram fat 8 gram sugar 0 gram fiber

870) *Chicken Marinade for All Purposes*

Time required for preparation: 5 minutes; total time required: 5 minutes. 24 portions
Ingredients:

- 1 quartered onion
- 12 lemons with skin
- 12 oranges, skinned
- 3 tbsp. diced rosemary
- 2 tbsp. diced thyme
- What you will require from your store cupboard
- 1/2 cup extra virgin olive oil
- 6 garlic cloves, finely chopped

Instructions:
- ✓ Pulse all ingredients together in a food processor until blended.
- ✓ Refrigerate in an airtight jar for up to 3 months. 1 tablespoon is the serving size.

Nutrition: Calories 41 Carbohydrates in Total 1 gram protein 0 gram fat 4 gram sugar 1 gram fiber 0 gram

871) *Almond Vanilla Dip in Fruit*

5 minutes prep time, 10 minutes total time, 10 serves
Ingredients:

- 1/2 cup fat-free half-n-half 2
- 1/2 cup fat-free half-n-half
- What you'll require from your pantry:
- Vanilla instant pudding mix in a 4-serving package that is fat-free and sugar-free
- 1 tablespoon Splenda
- 1 tsp vanilla extract
- 1 teaspoon extract d'amande

Instructions:
- ✓ In a medium bowl, combine all ingredients and beat on medium speed for 2 minutes. Refrigerate until ready to serve. Serve alongside fresh fruit for dipping. 1/4 cup is the serving size.

Nutrition: Calories 87 Carbohydrates Protein: 4 g 2 g triglycerides 7 g fructose 1 gram fiber 0 g

872) *Vinaigrette d'Apple Cider*

5 minutes total time, 8 servings

- 1/2 cup SUNSHINE OIL
- 1/4 cup APPLE VINEGAR
- 1/4 cup unsweetened apple juice
- 2 tablespoons honey
- 1 tbsp. freshly squeezed lemon juice
- 1/2 teaspoon salt
- To taste, freshly ground black pepper

Instructions:
- ✓ All ingredients should be combined in a mason jar. Screw the cover on and shake vigorously until well blended. Refrigerate until ready to serve. Before usage, shake vigorously.

Nutrition: Calories 138 Total Carbohydrates 4g Protein 0g Fat 13g Sugar 4g Fiber 0g

873) *Bacon Dip in Cheeseburger*

5 minutes for preparation Time required for cooking: 30 minutes 8 servings
Ingredients:

- 1 pound ground beef, lean
- 1 pkg. soft cream cheese
- 2 c. grated low-fat cheddar cheese
- 1 cup sour cream, fat-free
- 2/3 cup cooked bacon, crumbled
- What you'll require from your pantry:
- Tomatoes with green chiles, 10 oz.

Instructions:
- ✓ Preheat the oven to 350 degrees Fahrenheit.
- ✓ Cook beef, breaking it up with a wooden spoon, in a large skillet over med-high heat until no longer pink. Remove the fat.
- ✓ Combine remaining ingredients in a large mixing basin until well combined. Incorporate beef.
- ✓ Fill a small baking dish halfway with the batter. Bake for 20-25 minutes, or until hot and bubbling. Serve immediately.

Nutrition: Calories 268 Total Carbohydrates 9g Protein 33g Fat 10g Sugar 2g Fiber 0g

874) *Salsa Fundamentals*

15 minutes for preparation; 1 hour for chilling: 8 portions
Ingredients:

- 8 tomatoes

- *2-3 jalapeño peppers, depending on your preferred level of heat 2 limes, freshly squeezed*
- *4 garlic cloves*
- *1 teaspoon salt*
- *Cooking spray that is nonstick*

Instructions:

✓ *The oven should be preheated to broil. Cooking spray a baking sheet.*

✓ *Broil tomatoes, peppers, and garlic for 8-10 minutes rotating regularly, or until the veggies' skins begin to brown and peel away.*

✓ *Allow to cool. Skins should be removed.*

✓ *Pulse the vegetables in a food processor. Pulse in the salt and lime juice until the salsa achieves the desired consistency.*

✓ *Refrigerate in an airtight jar with a tight-fitting lid for up to 7 days. 1/4 cup is the serving size.*

Nutrition: Calories 31 Carbohydrates in Total 7g Carbohydrates Net Protein 5 g 1 gram fat 0 gram sugar 4 gram fiber 2g

875) *Barbecue Sauce*

Time required for preparation: 5 minutes, cooking time: 20 minutes, servings: 20

- *What you'll require from your pantry:*
- *2 1/2 cans tomato paste, 6 oz.*
- *12 c. water*
- *1/2 cup Apple Vinegar*
- *1/3 cup confectioners' sugar swerve*
- *Worcestershire sauce, 2 tbsp.*
- *1 tbsp. hickory liquid smoke*
- *2 tsp paprika smoky*
- *1 teaspoon powdered garlic*
- *onion powder 1/2 tsp*
- *1/2 teaspoon   salt*
- *1/4 teaspoon   chili powder*
- *1/4 tsp cayenne*

Instructions:

✓ *In a saucepan, whisk together all ingredients except the water. Add 1 cup water at a time, constantly whisking, until mixture resembles a thin barbeque sauce.*

✓ *Over medium-high heat, bring to a gentle boil. Reduce to medium-low heat and cook, often stirring, for 20 minutes, or until sauce has slightly thickened.*

✓ *Season with salt and pepper to taste. Allow to cool completely. Refrigerate in an airtight jar. 2 tablespoons of sauce per serving.*

Nutrition: Calories 24 Carbohydrates in Total 9 g Carbohydrates Net 8 g Protein 1 g Fat 0 g Sugar 7 g Fiber 1 g

876) *Berries Sauce de dessert*

5 minutes preparation time, 3 hours cooking time, 12 servings

Ingredients

- *Strawberries, 8 oz., hulled and halved Blackberries,*
- *6 oz. Blueberries,*
- *What you'll need in your pantry:*
- *1/4 cup Splenda*

Instructions:

✓ *In the crockpot, combine the berries and Splenda. Stir to combine.*

✓ *Cover and cook on low heat for 3 hours.*

✓ *Ladle the sauce into an airtight jar and allow it to cool completely before screwing on the lid and refrigerating. 1 tablespoon is the serving size.*

Nutrition: Calories 48 Total Carbohydrates 10g Net Carbohydrates Protein: 8 g 1 gram fat 0 gram sugar 8 gram fiber 2g

877) *Blackberry Compote*

Time required for preparation: 5 minutes; time required for cooking: 30 minutes. 16 portions

Ingredients:

- *1 pound of blackberries*
- *1 freshly squeezed lemon*
- *What you'll need in your pantry:*
- *1/4 cup Splenda*

Direction

✓ *In a medium saucepan over medium-high heat, combine blackberries, Splenda, and lemon juice. Cook, occasionally stirring, for approximately 30 minutes, or until mixture forms a thick syrup.*

✓ *Scoop 1/2 cup of the mixture into a bowl.*

✓ *Strain the remaining mixture through a fine-mesh sieve, pressing and scraping to extract as much moisture as possible.*

✓ *Solids should be discarded. In a mixing bowl, combine jam and place in an airtight jar.*

Nutrition: Calories 28 Total Carbohydrates 6g Net Carbohydrates 0 g fat 0 g sugar 4 g fiber 2 g

878) *Dessert Sauce with Blueberries and Oranges*

Time required for preparation: 5 minutes; time required for cooking: 10 minutes. 16 portions

Ingredients:

- *1/2 cup segmented oranges*
- *1 cup berries blue*
- *1/4 tbsp. orange juice*
- *What you'll require from your pantry: 14 c. water*
- *1/3 cup sliced almonds*
- *3 tbsp. Splenda cornstarch, 1 tbsp.*
- *1/8 teaspoon sodium chloride*

Instructions:

- ✓ *Combine Splenda, cornstarch, and salt in a small saucepan. Add orange juice and water and whisk until smooth.*
- ✓ *Bring to a boil over medium-high heat and simmer for 1-2 minutes, stirring constantly, or until thickened.*
- ✓ *Reduce heat to low and add fruit. Cook for five minutes. Take the pan from the heat and allow it to cool completely.*
- ✓ *Refrigerate in an airtight jar until ready to use. 1 tablespoon is the serving size.*

Nutrition: Calories 46 Carbohydrates Total 8g Protein 1 gram fat 1 gram sugar 6 gram fiber 0g

879) *Crab & Spinach Dip*

Prep time: 10 minutes, Cook time: 2 hours, Serves: 10

Ingredients:

- *1 pkg. frozen chopped spinach, thawed and squeezed nearly dry*
- *8 oz. reduced-fat cream cheese*
- *What you'll need from the store cupboard:*
- *6 ½ oz. can crab meat, drained and shredded*
- *6 oz.jar marinated artichoke hearts, drained and diced fine*
- *¼ tsp hot pepper sauce*

Instructions:

- ✓ *Melba toast or whole-grain crackers (optional)*
- ✓ *Remove any shells or cartilage from the crab.*

- ✓ *Place all ingredients in a small crockpot. Cover and cook on high 1 ½ - 2 hours, or until heated through and cream cheese is melted. Stir after 1 hour.*
- ✓ *Serve with Melba toast or whole-grain crackers. The serving size is ¼ cup.*

Nutrition: Calories 106 Total Carbs 7g Net Carbs 6g Protein 5g Fat 8g Sugar 3g Fiber 1g

880) *Onion Dip with Cheese*

5 minutes preparation time, 5 minutes cooking time, 8 servings

Ingredients:

- *8 oz. low fat cream cheese, soft*
- *1 cup grated onions*
- *1 cup grated low-fat Swiss cheese*
- *What you'll require from your pantry:*
- *1 cup mayonnaise light*

Instructions:

- ✓ *The oven should be preheated to broil.*
- ✓ *In a small casserole dish, combine all ingredients.*
- ✓ *Microwave on high for 30 seconds, stirring after every 30 seconds until cheese is melted and mixture is incorporated.*
- ✓ *Broil for 1-2 minutes, or until the top is beautifully browned. Serve warm with dipping veggies.*

Nutrition: Calories 158 per serving Carbohydrates in Total 5 grams protein, 9 grams fat, 11 grams sugar, and 1 gram fiber 0g

GRAIN AND GRAIN
ALTERNATIVES

881) "Rice" of Cauliflower

5 minutes for preparation Cooking time: ten minutes, servings: four

- 1 small head cauliflower, florets separated
- What you'll require from your pantry: 1 tsp olive oil
- 1 garlic clove, finely chopped
- 1/2 teaspoon   salt

Direction

✓ Rice the cauliflower using the large holes on a cheese grater. Alternatively, pulse the mixture in a food processor in short bursts until it resembles rice.

✓ Heat oil in a nonstick skillet over med-high heat until hot. Cook for 1 minute, stirring often. Cook, occasionally stirring, for 7-9 minutes, or until the cauliflower is soft and beginning to color.

✓ Serve immediately or incorporate into your favorite dishes.

Nutrition: Calories 48, Total Carbohydrates 4g Net Carbohydrates 2g Protein 1g Fat 4g Carbohydrates 2g Fiber

882) Pizza Crust Made with Cauliflower

15 minutes preparation time, 30 minutes cooking time, 8 servings

Ingredients:

- 12 pound. cauliflower, florets separated a single egg
- What you'll require from your pantry:
- 1/2 cup parmesan cheese, reduced fat
- 1/2 tbsp . seasoning Italian
- tsp garlic powder 1/2 tsp

Instructions:

✓ Preheat the oven to 400 degrees Fahrenheit. Preheat the oven to 400°F. Line a pizza pan or stone with parchment paper.

✓ Pulse the cauliflower until it resembles rice in a food processor.

✓ In a skillet over medium heat, cook the cauliflower, turning regularly, until tender, about 10 minutes.

✓ Whisk together the egg, cheese, and seasonings in a large mixing basin.

✓ Squeeze any extra liquid from the cauliflower using a clean kitchen towel. Stir into cheese mixture until a soft dough forms; if necessary, squeeze with a spatula.

✓ On the prepared pan, spread the dough to a thickness of about 14 inches. Bake for approximately 20 minutes, or until the top is dry and firm and the edges are golden brown.

✓ Allow it cool for 5-10 minutes before serving; the crust will thicken up as it cools. Add chosen toppings and bake an additional 5-10 minutes. Serve sliced.

Nutrition: Calories 158 Total Carbohydrates 10g net Carbohydrates Protein: 6 g 12 g Fat 9 g Sucrose 4 g Fiber 4g

883) Cheese Biscuits

Time required for preparation: 20 minutes; time required for cooking: 20 minutes; Serves: 16

Ingredients:

- 8 ounces reduced-fat cream cheese
- 3 cup grated mozzarella cheese
- 4 Eggs
- 2 tbsp. melted margarine
- What you'll require from your pantry: 1 to 1 and a third cup almond flour
- 4 tbsp. bicarbonate of soda
- Cooking spray that is nonstick

Instructions:

✓ Preheat the oven to 4000F. Cooking spray a 12-inch cast-iron skillet Melt the cream cheese and mozzarella in a skillet over low heat. Stir until completely smooth. Take the pan off the heat.

✓ Combine the melted cheese, eggs, baking powder, and flour in a large mixing bowl. Combine until completely smooth. Allow 10 to 20 minutes for rest.

✓ Scoop dough into Preheated skillet using a big cookie scoop. 10 minutes in the refrigerator.

✓ Bake for 20–25 minutes, or until the top is golden brown. Brush melted margarine over biscuits.

Nutrition: Calories Per Serving 106 Carbohydrates in total: 5g Net Carbohydrates: 4g Protein in total: 7g Fat in total: 8g Sugar in total: 0g Fiber in total: 1g

884) Cauliflower Puree with Cheese

5 minutes preparation time, 15 minutes cooking time, 6 servings

- 2 12 lb. steamed cauliflower florets
- 4 oz. shredded strong cheddar cheese, reduced in fat
- 2 tbsp. half-n-half

- *1 tablespoon butter*
- *What you'll require from your pantry: 1/2 teaspoon s salt*
- *1/2 teaspoon pepper*

Direction

✓ *Cauliflower should be steamed until fork tender, then drained.*

✓ *In a food processor, combine the cauliflower and remaining ingredients. Pulse until the mixture is practically smooth. Serve immediately.*

✓ *You can also prepare it ahead of time and reheat it as needed.*

Nutrition: Calories Per Serving 145 Carbohydrates in total 10g Carbohydrates in net Protein 5 g 9 g fat 9 g sugar 5 g dietary fiber 5g

885) *Tortillas de Chickpea*

5 minutes preparation time, 10 minutes cooking time, 4 servings

- *1 cup chickpea flour*
- *1 cup distilled water*
- *1/4 teaspoon salt*

Direction

✓ *Cooking spray that is nonstick*

✓ *Whisk together all ingredients in a large mixing bowl until no lumps remain.*

✓ *Cook over med-high heat in a skillet sprayed with cooking spray.*

✓ *Fill pan 14 cups at a time with batter and tilt pan to spread thinly.*

✓ *Cook until each side is golden brown, about 2 minutes per side.*

✓ *Make taco shells, enchiladas, quesadillas, or anything else you desire.*

Nutrition: Calories 89 Total Carbohydrates 13g Net Carbohydrates 10g Protein 5g Fat 2g Sugar 3 g Fiber 3 g

886) *Stuffing "Cornbread"*

15 minutes preparation time, 40 minutes cooking time, 6 servings

Ingredients:

- *1 bacon strip, diced*
- *a single egg*
- *1 cup diced onion*
- *1 cup diced celery*
- *2 tbsp. butter,*
- *1 cup almond flour*
- *1/4 cup chicken broth low in salt*

- *3 garlic cloves, finely chopped*
- *2 tbsp. cornmeal, stone-ground*
- *1 teaspoon thyme*
- *1 teaspoon sage*
- *34 teaspoon salt*
- *To taste, freshly ground black pepper*

Instructions:

✓ *Preheat the oven to 375 degrees Fahrenheit.*

✓ *In a skillet over low heat, melt 1 tablespoon margarine. Cook, occasionally stirring, until the onions and celery are tender, about 10 minutes. Cook for an additional 1-2 minutes with the garlic and spices. Take the pan off the heat and allow it cool.*

✓ *In a food processor, pulse the almond flour, cornmeal, and bacon until mixed. Pulse in the broth and egg barely to blend. Pulse in the onion mixture just until combined.*

✓ *Melt the remaining tablespoon of margarine in a cast iron pan or baking dish. Swirl the pan to distribute the melted margarine evenly.*

✓ *Bake for 30 minutes, or until the top is well browned and the center is cooked through. Serve.*

Nutrition: Calories 177 Carbohydrates 9g Net Protein: 6 g 6g Fatty Acids 14g Sucrose 2 g Fiber 3g

887) *"Flour" Tortillas*

Time required for preparation: 10 minutes; time required for cooking: 15 minutes; Serves:

Ingredients:

- *3/4 cup Egg white*
- *What you'll require from your pantry: 1/3 cup liquid*
- *1/4 cup flour de coco*
- *1 teaspoon sunflower seed oil*
- *1/2 teaspoon salt 1/2 teaspoon s cumin*
- *tsp chili powder 1/2 tsp*

Instructions:

✓ *In a food processor, mix all ingredients except the oil and pulse until blended. Allow 7-8 minutes for relaxation.*

✓ *In a large skillet, heat oil over medium-low heat. Fill center with 1/4 cup batter and tilt to spread to a 7-8-inch circular.*

✓ *When the tortilla's top is no longer shining, flip it over and cook for a further 1-2 minutes. Rep with the remainder of the batter.*

✓ Each tortilla should be placed on parchment paper and lightly wiped to remove any excess oil.

Nutrition: Calories 27 Carbohydrates in Total 1 gram protein, 5 gram fat, 0 gram sugar, 0 gram fiber, 0 gram flourless

888) *"Burger Buns"*

Preparation time: ten minutes Time required for cooking: 35 minutes 4 portions

Ingredients:

- 4 egg yolks, at room temperature
- 4 egg whites at room temperature
- 1/4 cup ricotta cheese, reduced in fat
- What you'll require from your pantry: 14 cups parmesan cheese, reduced fat
- 1 tablespoon cream of tartar

Instructions:

✓ Preheat the oven to 300 degrees Fahrenheit. Preheat the oven to 350°F. Line a baking sheet with parchment paper.

✓ Whisk together egg yolks, ricotta, and parmesan cheese in a large mixing basin until smooth.

✓ Separately, whisk egg whites until frothy. Add cream of tartar and continue beating until stiff peaks form.

✓ Mix in a small amount of beaten egg white to the egg yolk mixture. Slowly and gently fold in the remaining egg white until just combined with the egg yolk mixture.

✓ Distribute the batter evenly among the prepared pans to make 8 buns. 35 minutes in the oven. Use as a sandwich bread or snack on its own.

Nutrition: Calories 50 Carbohydrates 1 gram protein, 4 gram fat, 3 gram sugar, 1 gram fiber, 0 gram

889) *Fried rice*

5 minutes for preparation 15 minutes for cooking 8 servings

Ingredients:

- 2 tablespoons sweet snap peas
- 2 beaten egg whites
- a single egg
- What you'll require from your pantry: 1 cup brown rice instant, cooked according to package guidelines
- 2 tablespoons light soy sauce

Instructions:

✓ Combine the peas and cooked rice.

✓ Scramble the egg and egg whites in a small skillet. In a skillet, combine the rice and peas and mix in the soy sauce. Cook, stirring regularly, for approximately 2-3 minutes, or until thoroughly cooked. Serve.

Nutrition: Calories 107 Carbohydrates in Total 20g Carbohydrates Net 19g Protein 4g Fatty Acids 1g Sucrose 1 gram fiber 1 gram

890) *Garlic Basil Breadsticks*

Preparation time: ten minutes Time required for cooking: ten minutes 4 portions

Ingredients:

- 2 beaten eggs
- 2 cup grated mozzarella cheese 2 tbsp. softened cream cheese
- 2 tbsp. chopped fresh basil
- What you'll require from your pantry: 4 tbsp. unsweetened coconut flour
- 4 smashed garlic cloves
- Cooking spray that is nonstick

Instructions:

✓ Preheat the oven to 400 degrees Fahrenheit. Cooking spray a baking sheet.

✓ In a microwave-safe bowl, combine mozzarella, cream cheese, smashed garlic, and basil. Combine and heat for 1 minute. Stir thoroughly to melt the cheeses, then add the flour and egg.

✓ Combine thoroughly, using your hands if necessary to form a dough.

✓ Divide the dough into small pieces and form into long finger shapes. Arrange on prepared baking sheet.

✓ Bake for 8-10 minutes, or until the edges of the dough begin to color. Take the pan off the fire and allow it to cool slightly before serving.

Nutrition: Calories 153 Total Carbohydrates 10g Net Carbohydrates 5g Protein 9g Fat 8g Sugar 1g Fiber 5g

891) *A Sustainably Prepared Loaf of Bread*

Preparation time: ten minutes 30 minutes cooking time, 20 servings

Ingredients:

- 6 separated eggs
- 4 tbsp. melted butter
- What you'll require from your pantry: 12

cups sifted almond flour

- *3 tsp bicarbonate of soda*
- *1/4 tbsp cream of tartar*
- *1/8 teaspoon sodium chloride*
- *Spray with a buttery flavor*

Instructions:

✓ *Preheat the oven to 375 degrees Fahrenheit. Cooking spray an 8-inch loaf pan.*

✓ *Beat egg whites and cream of tartar in a large mixing basin until soft peaks form. In a food processor, pulse the yolks, 1/3 of the egg whites, butter, flour, baking powder, and salt until mixed.*

✓ *Pulse in the remaining egg whites until completely incorporated, taking care not to overmix the dough.*

✓ *Pour into prepared pan and bake for 30 minutes, or until a toothpick inserted in center comes out clean. Allow it cool in the pan for 10 minutes before inverting and cooling completely before slicing.*

Nutrition: Calories 81 Carbohydrates 2 g Carbohydrates Net 1 g Protein 3 g Fat 7 g Sugar 0 g Fiber 1g

892) *Noodles Made at Home*

5 minutes for preparation; 4 hours for chilling 2 servings

Ingredients:

- *1 cup grated mozzarella cheese*
- *1 yolk of an egg*

Instructions:

✓ *Microwave the mozzarella in a bowl for 1-2 minutes or until melted. Allow 30 seconds to cool.*

✓ *Gently mix the egg yolk into the cheese using a rubber spatula.*

✓ *Distribute the mixture evenly onto a parchment-lined baking sheet. On top of the dough, place another piece of parchment paper and press down with your hand until thin.*

✓ *Cut the dough into thin strips after removing the top layer of parchment. Refrigerate the "pasta" for four hours or overnight.*

✓ *Place in boiling water for 1 minute to cook. Drain and rinse with cool water to avoid sticking. Serve with a sauce of your choice.*

Nutrition: Calories 67 Carbohydrates in Total 1 gram of protein 5g Fatty Acids 5g Sucrose 0g Fiber 0g

893) *Pasta Made at Home*

Time required for preparation: 20 minutes Time required for cooking: 5 minutes 8 portions

Ingredients:

- *2 egg yolks + 1 egg*
- *What you'll require from your pantry: 14 cups crushed wheat germ 1*
- *3/4 cup soy flour*
- *3-4 tbsp. lukewarm water*
- *1 teaspoon extra-virgin olive oil*
- *1/2 teaspoon salt*

Instructions:

✓ *Whisk together the egg, egg yolks, oil, and 3 tablespoons water in a large mixing bowl until smooth.*

✓ *Separately, combine flour, wheat germ, and salt in a separate basin. Add to egg mixture and stir until smooth. If necessary, add the final tablespoon of water to get a smooth dough.*

✓ *On a lightly floured surface, turn out the dough and knead for 5-8 minutes, or until smooth. Ten minutes later, cover and set aside.*

✓ *Divide dough into four equal pieces and roll out as thinly as possible, one at a time, or put it through a pasta machine until the narrowest setting is reached.*

✓ *Allow 30 minutes for the dough to dry. With a pasta machine or pizza cutter, cut into the desired size. If you are not going to use it immediately, let it dry overnight on a pasta or cooling rack. Fresh pasta should be consumed within three days of purchase.*

✓ *It can keep for 6-8 months in the freezer after drying for just an hour in an airtight bag. Pasta that has been dried overnight can be stored for up to 1 week in an airtight container.*

✓ *When cooked fresh, place in a pot of boiling water and cook for 4-5 minutes or until soft. Dried pasta will require an additional couple of minutes.*

Nutrition: 152 Calories 12g Net Carbohydrates 9g Protein 16g Fat 5g Sugar 6g Fiber 3g

894) *Beer with a light body bread*

5 minutes for preparation Time required for cooking: 55 minutes 14 portions

- *1/4 cup softened butter*
- *What you'll require from your pantry: 12*

ounces of light beer

- *3 c. reduced carbohydrate baking mix*
- *3 tbsp splenda*

Instructions:

✓ *Preheat the oven to 375 degrees Fahrenheit. Grease the bottom of a 9x5-inch loaf pan with 1 tablespoon butter.*

✓ *Whisk together beer, baking mix, and Splenda in a large mixing dish. Fill prepared pan halfway.*

✓ *Bake for 45-55 minutes, or until the crust is golden brown. Allow 10 minutes for cooling in the pan, then remove and cool on a wire rack.*

✓ *Melt the remaining butter in a small glass bowl in the microwave and brush over a warm loaf. Allow 15 minutes for cooling before slicing.*

Nutrition: Calories 162 Total Carbohydrates 16g Net Carbohydrates 12 g protein, 9 g fat, 5 g sugar, and 5 g dietary fiber 4 g

895) *"Rice" de Mexico*

5 minutes for preparation 10 minutes cooking time, 6 servings

Ingredients:

- *2 cups cooked cauliflower rice*
- *1 tiny jalapeno pepper, seeded and finely diced*
- *12 diced white onion*
- *What you'll require from your pantry: 12 c. water*
- *1/2 cup paste de tomato*
- *3 garlic cloves, finely chopped*
- *2 teaspoon salt*
- *2 tbsp extra-virgin olive oil*

Instructions:

✓ *In a skillet over medium heat, heat the oil. Cook 3-4 minutes, stirring regularly, adding onion, garlic, jalapeño, and salt.*

✓ *In a small bowl, mix together water and tomato paste. Combine in a skillet. Cook for 3-5 minutes, stirring often.*

✓ *Cook, occasionally stirring, until cauliflower is heated through and most of the liquid has been absorbed. Serve.*

Nutrition: Calories 46 Total Carbohydrates 7g Net Carbohydrates Protein 5 g 2 g fat 2 g sugar 4 g dietary

896) *Fiber No Corn "Cornbread"*

Preparation time: ten minutes, cooking time: twenty-five minutes, servings: sixteen

- *4 eggs, room temperature*
- *1/3 cup melted butter*
- *What you'll require from your pantry: 12 cups sifted almond flour*
- *3 tbsp splenda*
- *1 teaspoon bicarbonate of soda*

Instructions:

✓ *Preheat the oven to 350 degrees Fahrenheit. Preheat the oven to 350°F. Line an 8-inch baking dish with parchment paper.*

✓ *Whisk together eggs, butter, and Splenda in a large mixing basin. Combine the flour and baking powder in a large mixing bowl until no lumps remain.*

✓ *Fill prepared dish halfway with batter and smooth the top. Bake for 25-30 minutes, or until the edges are golden brown and the toothpick test is passed.*

✓ *Allow 5 minutes for cooling before slicing and serving.*

Nutrition: Calories 121 Total Carbohydrates 6g Net Carbohydrates 5 g protein, 3 g fat, 9 g sugar, and 4 g dietary fiber 1 g

897) *Coconut Flour Quick Buns*

5 minutes preparation time, 20 minutes cooking time, 4 servings

Ingredients:

- *3 room temperature eggs*
- *2 tbsp. room temperature coconut milk*
- *What you'll require from your pantry: 14 cups flour de coco*
- *2 tbsp. soft coconut oil*
- *1 tablespoon honey*
- *1/2 teaspoon   bicarbonate of soda*
- *1/2 teaspoon   salt*

Instructions:

✓ *Preheat the oven to 375 degrees Fahrenheit. Preheat the oven to 350°F. Line a cookie sheet with parchment paper.*

✓ *Sift flour, baking powder, and salt into a small bowl.*

✓ *In a medium bowl, whisk together eggs, coconut oil, milk, and honey. Add the dry ingredients to the egg mixture in a slow, steady stream. The batter will be thick but check for lumps.*

✓ *Form into four balls and arrange on prepared baking sheet. Press into 12-inch thick circles. Bake for 15-20 minutes, or until the toothpick inserted in the center comes out clean.*

Nutrition: Calories 143 Carbohydrates Protein: 6 g 12g Sugar 4g Fat 5 g

898) *Crust Pizza*

Time required for preparation: 20 minutes; time required for cooking: 40 minutes. 4 portions

Ingredients:

- *1/2 cup grated mozzarella cheese*
- *2 oz. crème fraîche*
- *1 beaten egg*
- *What you'll require from your pantry: 3/4 cups apricot flour*
- *1/2 tsp Italian seasoning*
- *1/2 teaspoon salt*
- *garlic powder 1/2 tsp*
- *onion powder 1/2 tsp*

Instructions:

✓ *Preheat the oven to 400 degrees Fahrenheit. Preheat the oven to 350°F. Line a large baking sheet with parchment paper.*

✓ *Microwave cream cheese and mozzarella for 60 seconds in a big bowl. Take out of the microwave and stir. Cook for further 30 seconds in the microwave. Stir well until completely blended.*

✓ *Combine flour, salt, onion powder, garlic powder, and egg in a medium bowl. Stir until almond flour is evenly distributed throughout the cheese. If the mixture becomes too sticky, microwave it for an additional 10-15 seconds to rehydrate.*

✓ *Roll out dough on parchment paper. Punctuate the crust with a fork. Bake for ten minutes.*

✓ *Take the pan out of the oven and flip it over. Bake for an additional ten minutes.*

✓ *Take the pizza out of the oven and top it with favorite pizza toppings.*

✓ *Bake for an additional 10 minutes, or until the toppings are heated, and the cheese has melted.*

Nutrition: Calories 198 Carbohydrates Total 5g Carbohydrates Net 3g Protein 9g Fat 17g Sugar 1g Fiber 2g

899) *Chickpeas, Chicken, and Oats Meatloaf*

4 portions Time Required for Cooking: 114 Hours

Ingredients:

- *1/2 cup chickpeas, cooked*
- *2 beaten egg whites*
- *21/2 tsp seasoning for poultry*
- *PEPPER, GROUND, AS REQUIRED*
- *10 oz. ground chicken*
- *1 cup seeded and chopped red bell pepper*
- *1 cup minced celery stalk*
- *1/3 cup oats, steel-cut*
- *1 cup pureed tomato, split*
- *2 tbsp crumbled dried onion flakes*
- *1 tablespoon mustard that has been prepared*

Directions:

✓ *Preheat the oven to 350 degrees Fahrenheit. Grease a 9x5-inch loaf pan with cooking spray.*

✓ *Pulse chickpeas, egg whites, poultry spice, and black pepper in a food processor until smooth.*

✓ *Transfer the batter to a large mixing basin.*

✓ *Combine the chicken, veggies, oats, 1/2 cup tomato puree, and onion flakes.*

✓ *Distribute the mixture equally into the prepared loaf pan.*

✓ *Slightly push the mixture down with your hands.*

✓ *In a separate bowl, combine mustard and the remaining tomato puree.*

✓ *Distribute the mustard mixture evenly over the loaf pan.*

✓ *Bake for approximately 1-114 hours, or until the desired doneness is achieved.*

✓ *Remove from oven and cool for approximately 5 minutes before slicing. g.*

✓ *Slice into desired thicknesses and serve.*

✓ *Meal Prep Tip: Place the cooled meatloaf pieces in a resealable plastic bag and seal. Keep refrigerated for approximately 2-4 days. Reheat on high for approximately 1 minute before serving.*

Nutrition: 229 Calories 6 g total fat 4 g saturated fat 50 mg cholesterol Carbohydrates total 27 g Sugar 2 g Fiber 7 g Sodium 227 mg Potassium 509 mg

900) *Mini-Pizzas with Eggplant*

Time required for preparation: 10 minutes; time required for cooking: 35 minutes. 4 portions

Ingredients:

- *1 large peeled eggplant, sliced into 14-inch circles*
- *2 cup sauce de pasta*
- *1/2 cup grated reduced-fat mozzarella cheese*
- *2 Eggs*
- *What you'll require from the pantry*
- *1/4 cup crumbs de pan Italiano*
- *1 tablespoon water*
- *1/4 tsp ground black pepper*
- *Cooking spray that is nonstick*

Instructions:

✓ *Preheat the oven to 350 degrees Fahrenheit. 2 big cookie sheets lined with foil and generously sprayed with cooking spray*

✓ *In a shallow bowl, whisk together eggs, water, salt, and pepper. Separately, place the bread crumbs in a small dish.*

✓ *Coat eggplant slices completely with bread crumbs after dipping them in the egg mixture. Arrange on cookie sheets that have been prepped. Coat the tops of the muffins with cooking spray and bake for 15 minutes.*

✓ *Overturn the eggplant and re-spray with cooking spray. Bake for a further 15 minutes.*

✓ *Remove from oven and drizzle 1 tablespoon spaghetti sauce over each piece. Bake for an additional 4–5 minutes, or until the sauce is bubbling and the cheese has melted.*

Nutrition: Calories 171 Total Carbohydrates 24g Net Carbohydrates Protein: 20 g 9 g fat 5 g sugar 6 g dietary fiber

✓ *In a large skillet over low heat, heat the olive oil.*

✓ *Cook the onion and garlic for 2 to 3 minutes, stirring periodically, until soft.*

✓ *Cook, stirring regularly, for 5 to 7 minutes, or until the dandelion greens are wilted.*

✓ *Transfer to a serving platter and season with freshly ground black pepper. Serve immediately.*

Nutrition: 81 Calories: 8g fat; 1g carbohydrate: 10.7g fiber; 8g sugar; 0g sodium: 72mg

957) *Fried Eggplant in Asian Style*

4 portions Time Required for Cooking: 40 Minutes

- *1 large eggplant, quartered*
- *3 green onions, sliced, leaving only the green tips*
- *1 tsp fresh ginger, peeled and finely diced*
- *What you'll require from your pantry:*
- *1/4 cup plus 1 teaspoon cornstarch*
- *1/2 tbsp soy sauce*
- *1/2 tbsp sesame oil*
- *1 tbsp vegetable oil*
- *2 teaspoon Splenda*
- *1/4 teaspoon   salt*

Directions:

✓ *Place eggplant on paper towels and season with salt on both sides. Allow 1 hour to evaporate extra moisture. Using additional paper towels, pat dry.*

✓ *Whisk together soy sauce, sesame oil, fish sauce, Splenda, and 1 teaspoon cornstarch in a small basin.*

✓ *Coat both sides of the eggplant with the 1/4 cup cornstarch; additional cornstarch may be used if necessary.*

✓ *In a large skillet, heat oil over medium-high heat. Add 12 ginger and 1 green onion, followed by 2 eggplant slices. 12 of the sauce mixture should be used to coat both sides of the eggplant gently. Cook for approximately 8-10 minutes per side. Repeat.*

✓ *Garnish with leftover green onions and serve.*

Nutrition: Calories 155 Carbohydrates 18g Carbohydrates Net 13 grams protein 2 g fat 9 g sugar 6 g dietary fiber 5g

958) *Salad de Guacamole with Pollo*

6 portions Time Required for Cooking: 20 Minutes

- *1 pound boneless and skinless chicken breast*
- *2 avocados*
- *1-2 seeded and chopped jalapeno peppers*
- *1/3 cup onion, diced*
- *3 tbsp. cilantro, diced*
- *2 tbsp. fresh lime juice*
- *What you'll require from your pantry:*
- *2 minced garlic cloves*
- *1 tablespoon olive oil*
- *Salt and pepper to taste*

Directions:

✓ *Preheat the oven to 400 degrees Fahrenheit. Prepare a baking sheet by lining it with foil.*

✓ *Season chicken with salt and pepper and arrange in a single layer on the preheated pan. Bake for 20 minutes, or until chicken is thoroughly done. Allow to cool completely before serving.*

✓ *Once the chicken has cooled slightly, shred or dice it and place it in a large mixing basin. Combine the remaining ingredients in a large mixing bowl, crushing the avocado as you go. Season with salt and pepper to taste. Serve right away.*

Nutrition: 324 Calories 12g Carbohydrates Total 12g Carbohydrates Net 5g Protein 23g Fat 22g Sugar 1g Fiber 7g

959) *Salad de Portobello*

4 portions Time Required for Cooking: 10 Minutes

- *6 cup mixed salad greens*
- *1 cup sliced Portobello mushrooms*
- *1 sliced green onion*
- *What you'll require from your pantry:*
- *Warm Bacon or Walnut Vinaigrette*
- *1 tbsp. olive oil*

Directions:

✓ *In a nonstick skillet, heat oil over medium-high heat. Cook, stirring periodically, for 10 minutes, or until the mushrooms are soft. Reduce heat to low and add onions.*

✓ *Arrange salad greens on serving dishes and sprinkle with mushrooms and pepper. Drizzle lightly with a vinaigrette of your choice.*

Nutrition: 81 Calories 9g Protein 4g Fat 4g Fiber

VEGETABLES

901) *Rollups of Italian Eggplant*

Preparation time: ten minutes, cooking time: twenty-five minutes, servings: eight

Ingredients:

- 16 leaves of fresh spinach
- 4 rinsed, drained, and finely sliced sun-dried tomatoes 2 little eggplants
- 1 finely chopped green onion
- 4 tbsp. softened fat-free cream cheese 2 tbsp. sour cream, fat-free
- What you'll require from your pantry: 1 cup sauce spaghetti 2 tbsp. freshly squeezed lemon juice
- 1 tablespoon olive oil
- 1 garlic clove, finely chopped
- 1/4 teaspoon   oregano
- 1/8 teaspoon freshly ground black pepper
- Cooking spray that is nonstick

Instructions:

- ✓ Preheat the oven to 450 degrees Fahrenheit. Cooking spray two large cookie sheets.
- ✓ Trim the eggplant's ends. They should be sliced lengthwise into 14-inch chunks. Remove any slices that are mostly skin; there should be around 16 slices remaining. They should be arranged in a single layer on prepared pans.
- ✓ Whisk together the lemon juice and oil in a small bowl and brush both sides of the eggplant. Bake for 20-25 minutes, or until the eggplant begins to colour slightly. Transfer to a cooling plate.
- ✓ Combine the remaining ingredients, except the spinach, in a mixing bowl until well blended.
- ✓ Spread 1 teaspoon cream cheese mixture evenly over the sliced eggplant, leaving a 12-inch border around the edges.
- ✓ Add a spinach leaf on top and coil up, beginning at the tiny end. Arrange rolls on a serving plate, seam side down. Serve warm spaghetti sauce alongside.

Nutrition: Calories 78 Carbohydrates 12g Carbohydrates Net Protein: 6 g 3 g triglycerides 3 g sucrose 6 g Fiber 6g

902) *Burger with Grilled Portobello and Zucchini Servings: 2*

Time Required for Cooking: 10 Minutes

- 2 large portabella mushroom caps
- 12 tiny sliced zucchini
- 2 slices low-fat cheese
- Spinach What you'll require from your pantry:
- 2 sandwich thins made entirely of whole wheat
- 2 tsp roasted red bell peppers
- 2 tsp olive oil

Directions:

- ✓ Preheat the grill or charcoal grill to a med-high setting.
- ✓ Brush lightly with olive oil on the mushroom caps. Grill mushroom caps and zucchini slices for about 3-4 minutes per side, or until soft.
- ✓ Arrange on a thin sandwich. Add sliced cheese, roasted red bell pepper, and spinach as garnishes. Serve.

Nutrition: 177 Calories 26g Carbohydrates Protein 15g Fat 3g Sugar 3g Fiber 8g

903) *Spring Peas with Tarragon*

12 Minutes Cooking Servings: 6

- 1 tablespoon unsalted butter
- 12 thinly sliced Vidalia onions
- 1 cup low-sodium vegetable broth
- 3 cup fresh shelled peas
- 1 tablespoon minced fresh tarragon

Directions:

- ✓ In a skillet over medium heat, melt the butter.
- ✓ Cook the onion in the melted butter for approximately 3 minutes, stirring periodically, until transparent.
- ✓ Whisk in the veggie broth. Combine the peas and tarragon in the skillet.
- ✓ Reduce to low heat, cover, and continue cooking for approximately 8 minutes longer, or until the peas are soft.
- ✓ Allow 5 minutes for the peas to cool slightly before serving heated.

Calories: 82 fat: 1 g protein: 2 g carbohydrates: 10 g fiber: 8 g sugar: 9 g sodium: 48mg

904) *Potatoes Infused with Provencal Herbs & Cheddar*

4 portions Time Required for Cooking: 20 Minutes

- 1 kilogram of potatoes
- 1 kilogram of Provencal herbs

- *1 kilogram of extra virgin olive oil*
- *1 kilogram of salt*
- *1 kilogram of grated cheese*

Directions:

✓ *Peel the potatoes, cut the cane salt into small pieces, and sprinkle with Provencal herbs.*

✓ *Place in the basket and add a few extra virgin olive oil strands.*

✓ *Preheat the air fryer to 1800C, 20 minutes.*

✓ *Remove and transfer to a big plate.*

✓ *Place cheese on a cover.*

✓ *Microwave or bake for a few minutes or until the cheese has melted.*

Nutrition: 437 calories 0.6g fat 219g Carbohydrates 1 gram protein g sugar 0mg cholesterol

905) *Wedges of Spiced Potato*

4 portions Time Required for Cooking: 40 Minutes 8 medium potatoes

- *Sea salt*
- *Ground pepper*
- *Garlic powder*
- *Aromatic herbs, our personal favorite*
- *2 tbsp. extra virgin olive oil*

Directions:

✓ *In a saucepan, combine the unpeeled potatoes, boiling water, and a pinch of salt.*

✓ *Cook for 5 minutes. Drain and set aside to cool. Without peeling, cut into thick slices.*

✓ *Place the potatoes in a bowl and season with salt, pepper, garlic powder, oil, and breadcrumbs or chickpea flour.*

✓ *Stir thoroughly and set aside for 15 minutes. Transfer to the air fryer basket and set the timer to 20 minutes at 1800C.*

✓ *Shake the basket occasionally to mix and reposition the potatoes. Verify that they are still delicate.*

Nutrition: 123 calories 2 g Carbohydrates 11 g Fat 4 g protein 0 g fiber

906) *Delicata Squash Roasted with Thyme*

4 portions Time Required for Cooking: 20 Minutes

- *1 delicata squash (1 to 112 pounds / 454 to 680 g), split, seeded, and cut into 12-inch-thick strips*
- *1 tablespoon extra-virgin olive oil*

- *1/2 teaspoon dried thyme*
- *1/4 teaspoon salt*

Directions:

✓ *Preheat the oven to 400 degrees Fahrenheit (205 degrees Celsius). Prepare a baking sheet by lining it with parchment paper.*

✓ *In a large mixing bowl, combine the squash strips, olive oil, thyme, salt, and pepper. Toss until the squash strips are completely coated.*

✓ *Arrange the squash strips in a single layer on the prepared baking sheet. Roast for approximately 20 minutes, or until the strips are gently browned, rotating halfway through.*

✓ *Remove from oven and arrange on serving plates.*

Nutrition 78 calories; 2g fat; 1g protein; 18g carbohydrate; 1g fiber; 9g sugar; 122mg sodium

907) *Beans, Zucchini, Potatoes, And Onions Scrambled Eggs*

4 portions Time Required for Cooking: 35 Minutes

- *300g beans*
- *2 onions*
- *1 zucchini*
- *4 potatoes*
- *8 eggs*
- *Extra virgin olive oil*
- *Salt*
- *Ground pepper*

Directions:

✓ *Cook the beans in their pods in plenty of seawater. When they are tender, drain and set aside.*

✓ *Peel and cube the potatoes. Season and add a few oil threads. Combine and transfer to an air fryer for 15 minutes at 1800C.*

✓ *After that, combine the potatoes, diced zucchini, and julienned onion in a mixing bowl and bake at 1800C for 20 minutes.*

✓ *Mix and stir occasionally.*

✓ *Transfer the contents of the air fryer, along with the beans, to a skillet.*

✓ *Season with a pinch of soy sauce and salt to taste.*

✓ *Sauté the eggs and peel them.*

✓ *Carry out the scrambled.*

Nutrition: Calorie Content: 65 Cal Carbohydrates: 2 g 11 g fat 4 g protein 0 g fiber

908) *Beans, green*

4 portions 13 Minutes Cooking

- 1 pound green beans
- 34 tsp garlic powder
- 34 tsp ground black pepper
- 1 1/4 tsp salt
- 1/2 tsp paprika

Directions:

✓ Turn on the air fryer, insert the fryer basket, coat it with olive oil, cover it with the lid, and preheat for 5 minutes at 400 degrees F.

✓ Meanwhile, in a bowl, spray beans well with olive oil, season with garlic powder, black pepper, salt, and paprika, and toss to coat.

✓ Uncover the skillet, add the green beans, and cook for 8 minutes, shaking halfway through the cooking.

✓ When the air fryer sounds, open the top and transfer the green beans to a serving plate.

Nutrition: 45 calories 2 g Carbohydrates 11 g Fat 4 g Protein 3 g fiber

909) *Parmesan eggplant-zucchini*

6 portions Time Required for Cooking: 2 Hours

- 1 medium eggplant, peeled and cut into 1-inch cubes
- 1 medium zucchini, cut into 1-inch chunks
- What you'll require from your pantry:
- 11/2 cupstore-bought light spaghetti sauce
- 2/3 cup grated parmesan cheese with reduced-fat

Directions:

✓ In the crockpot, combine the vegetables, spaghetti sauce, and 1/3 cup parmesan. Combine well. Cook on high for 2–2 1/2 hours or on low for 4-5 hours, covered.

✓ Before serving, sprinkle the remaining parmesan over the top.

Nutrition: 81 Calories 12g Carbohydrates Net Carbohydrates 7g Protein 5g Fat 2g Sugar 7g Fiber 5g

910) *Southwest Chicken Salad*

Ingredients: Servings: 6

- 2 cups cooked and shredded chicken
- 1 small diced red bell pepper
- 1/4 cup sliced red onion
- What you'll need from the pantry
- 1/4 cup mayonnaise reduced in fat
- 1/2 tsp powdered cumin
- 1 tsp garlic powder
- 1/2 tsp coriander

Directions:

✓ In a large mixing basin, combine all ingredients and stir until well combined. Season with salt and pepper to taste. Refrigerate until ready to serve.

Nutrition: 117 Calories 4g Carbohydrates Net Carbohydrates 0g Protein 14g Fat 5g Sugar 2g Fiber 0g

911) *Wraps of Tempeh Lettuce*

2 portions Time Required for Cooking: 5 Minutes

- 1 package crumbled tempeh
- 1 head butter leaf lettuce
- 12 diced red bell pepper
- 12 diced onion
- What you'll require from your pantry:
- 1 tbsp. finely sliced garlic
- 1 tbsp. olive oil
- 1 tbsp. soy sauce low in sodium
- 1 teaspoon ginger, 1 teaspoon onion powder, 1 teaspoon garlic powder

Directions:

✓ In a large skillet over medium heat, heat the oil and garlic.

✓ Sauté the onion, tempeh, and bell pepper for 3 minutes.

✓ Cook for a further 2 minutes before adding the soy sauce and seasonings.

✓ Spoon mixture into lettuce leaves using a teaspoon.

Nutrition: Calories 130g Carbohydrates Total 14g Carbohydrates Net ten grams protein 8 g Fat 5 g Sucrose 2g dietary fiber 4g

912) *Snacks On Crispy Rye Bread With Guacamole And Anchovies*

4 portions Time Required for Cooking: 10 Minutes

- 4 rye bread pieces
- Guacamole
- Anchovies in oil

Directions:

✓ *Each slice of bread should be cut into three strips.*

✓ *Arrange in the basket of the air fryer in a single layer without piling up, and cook in batches until desired texture is achieved. You might choose 1800C for ten minutes.*

✓ *Once all of the crusty rye bread pieces are used, spread a layer of guacamole on top, whether handmade or purchased.*

✓ *Top each bread with two anchovies and guacamole.*

Nutrition: 180 calories Carbohydrates: 4 g 11 g fat 4 g protein 09 g fiber

913) *Asparagus in Lime Juice With Cashews*

4 portions Time Required for Cooking: 15–20 Minutes

- *2 pounds (907 g) asparagus, trimmed of woody ends*
- *1 tablespoon extra-virgin olive oil*
- *sea salt and freshly ground black pepper to taste*
- *1 lime, zest, and juice*

Directions:

✓ *Preheat the oven to 400 degrees Fahrenheit (205 degrees Celsius). Aluminum foil a baking sheet.*

✓ *In a larger bowl, combine the asparagus and olive oil. Season with salt and pepper to taste.*

✓ *Arrange the asparagus on the prepared baking sheet and bake for 15 to 20 minutes, or until tender and gently browned.*

✓ *Transfer the asparagus to a serving bowl from the oven. Toss in the cashews, lime zest, and juice. Serve right away.*

Nutrition: 18g protein: 8.0g carbs: 47g fiber: 9g sugar: 0g calories: 173 fat: 18g protein: 8.0g carbs: 47g fiber: 9g 65mg sodium

914) *Wedges of Cabbage*

6 portions 29 Minutes Cooking

- *1 small head of green cabbage*
- *6 thick-cut, pastured bacon strips*
- *1 teaspoon onion powder*
- *1/2 teaspoon powdered black pepper*
- *1 teaspoon garlic powder*
- *34 teaspoon salt*
- *1/4 teaspoon red chili flakes*

- *1/2 teaspoon fennel seeds*

Directions:

✓ *Turn on the air fryer, insert the frying basket, coat it with olive oil, cover it with the lid, and preheat for 5 minutes at 350 degrees F.*

✓ *Preheat the fryer, add the bacon strips, cover, and cook for 10 minutes, rotating the bacon halfway during the cooking time.*

✓ *In the meantime, prepare the cabbage by removing the outer leaves and cutting them into eight wedges, leaving the core intact.*

✓ *To make the spice mix, combine onion powder, black pepper, garlic powder, salt, red chili powder, and fennel in a basin and whisk until combined.*

✓ *Drizzle oil over cabbage wedges and then coat with spice mixture.*

✓ *When the air fryer whistles, remove the lid and transfer the bacon strips to a chopping board to cool.*

✓ *Fill the fryer basket halfway with seasoned cabbage wedges, cover, and cook for 8 minutes at 400 degrees F. Flip the cabbage, spritz with oil, and continue air frying for 6 minutes, or until pleasantly golden and done.*

✓ *Once finished, move cabbage wedges to a serving plate.*

✓ *Chop the bacon and sprinkle it over the cabbage.*

Nutrition: 123 calories Carbohydrates: 2 g 11 g fat 4 g protein 0 g fiber

915) *Garlic & Black Pepper Tofu*

4 portions Time Required for Cooking: 40 Minutes

- *14 oz. package extra firm tofu*
- *1 lb. asparagus, trimmed and chopped into 1-inch pieces*
- *8 oz. kale, stems removed, and leaves sliced*
- *3 oz. shiitake mushrooms, sliced*
- *1 sliced green bell pepper*
- *What you'll require from your pantry:*
- *1/2 cuplow sodium vegetable broth*
- *8 garlic cloves, squeezed and divided*
- *2 1/2 tbsp light soy sauce, divided*
- *2 -4 tbsp water*
- *2 tsp cornstarch*
- *2 tsp freshly ground black pepper, divided*
- *1 tsp rice vinegar*

Directions:

✓ Preheat the oven to 400 degrees Fahrenheit. Preheat the oven to 350°F. Line a baking sheet with parchment paper.

✓ Slice the tofu into 12-inch slices and press between paper towels to absorb excess moisture. Each slice should be cut into smaller rectangles.

✓ Combine 1 tablespoon soy sauce, 1 tablespoon water, 2 tablespoons garlic, 2 tablespoons rice vinegar, and 1 teaspoon pepper in a Ziploc bag. Turn to coat the tofu. Allow 15 minutes for marinating.

✓ Arrange the tofu in a single layer on the prepared pan and bake for 15 minutes. Bake for a further 15 minutes on the other side. Take out of the oven.

✓ In a large nonstick skillet, heat the oil over medium-high heat. Cook, often stirring, until the onion is transparent. Add bell pepper and cook for an additional minute.

✓ Add the garlic and mushrooms and cook for an additional 2 minutes, adding a splash of water if the veggies begin to stick.

✓ Cover and stir in the kale and 2 tablespoons of water. Allow to cook for 1 minute, then whisk and add additional water if necessary. Cook, covered, for a further minute before adding the asparagus and cooking, occasionally tossing, until the asparagus is tender-crisp.

✓ Combine the remaining soy sauce, broth, Sriracha, cornstarch, and pepper in a small bowl. Pour over vegetables and continue cooking until vegetables are heated thoroughly.

✓ To serve, arrange the veggies on a platter and top with the tofu.

Nutrition: 176 Calories 33g Carbohydrates Net Carbohydrates 27g Protein 16g Fat 4g Sugar 12g Fiber 6g

916) *Less Crust Broccoli Quiche*

Time Required for Cooking: 1 Hour 3 large eggs

- 2 cups chopped broccoli florets
- 1 small onion, diced
- 1 cup grated cheddar cheese
- 2/3 cup unsweetened almond milk
- 1/2 cup crumbled feta cheese
- What you'll require from your pantry:
- 1 tbsp. extra virgin olive oil

- 1/2 tsp . sea salt
- Cooking spray with nonstick properties

Directions:

✓ Preheat the oven to 350 degrees Fahrenheit. Cooking spray a 9-inch baking dish.

✓ In a large skillet over medium heat, heat the oil. Cook for 4-5 minutes, or until the onions are transparent.

✓ Stir in broccoli. Cook for approximately 2 minutes, or until broccoli acquires a bright green color. Transfer the mixture to a bowl.

✓ Whisk together almond milk, egg, salt, and pepper in a small bowl. Distribute over the broccoli. Combine the cheddar cheese and the remaining ingredients. Pour into the baking dish that has been prepared.

✓ Sprinkle with feta cheese and bake for 45 to 1 hour, or until the eggs are set in the center, and the top is lightly browned. Serve.

Nutrition: Calories 182 Carbohydrates 5g Carbohydrates Net Protein: 4 g 10g Fatty Acids 14g Sucrose 2 g Fibre 1g

917) *Vegetable Chili*

4 portions 15 Minutes Cooking

- 2 tablespoons extra-virgin olive oil
- 1 onion, finely chopped
- 1 green bell pepper, deseeded and diced
- 1 (14-ounce / 397-g) can kidney beans, drained and rinsed
- 2 (14-ounce / 397-g) can crushed tomatoes
- 2 cups veggie crumbles

Directions:

✓ In a large skillet, heat the olive oil over medium-high heat until shimmering.

✓ Add the onion and bell pepper and cook, stirring periodically, for 5 minutes.

✓ Combine the beans, tomatoes, vegetable crumbles, garlic powder, chili powder, and salt in a large mixing bowl. Stir to combine and bring to low heat.

✓ Reduce to low heat and cook, stirring periodically, for an additional 5 minutes, or until the mixture is well cooked.

✓ Allow 5 minutes for the mixture to cool slightly before serving heated.

Nutrition: Calories: 282, fat: 10.1g protein: 16.7g carbohydrates: 38.2g fiber: 19g sugar: 7.2g sodium: 1128mg

918) *Tomato with Collard Greens*

4 portions Time Required for Cooking: 20 Minutes

- 1 cup low-sodium vegetable broth, split
- 12 thinly sliced onions
- 2 thinly sliced garlic cloves
- 1 medium tomato, diced
- 1 large bunch collard greens, stems included, roughly chopped

Direction

✓ Bring 12 cups vegetable broth to a simmer in a Dutch oven over medium heat.

✓ Add the onion and garlic and simmer, occasionally stirring, for approximately 4 minutes, or until soft.

✓ Gently whisk in the remaining broth, tomato, greens, cumin, and pepper.

✓ Reduce to low heat and cook, uncovered, for 15 minutes. Serve immediately.

Nutrition: Calories 68 fat 1g protein 8g carbohydrates 18g fiber 7.1g sugar 0g sodium 67mg

919) *okra*

Time Required for Cooking: 10 Minutes servings 4

- 1 cup almond flour
- 8 ounces fresh okra
- 1/2 teaspoon sea salt
- 1 cup low-fat milk
- 1 pastured egg

Directions:

✓ In a bowl, crack the egg and whisk in the milk until smooth.

✓ Remove the stems from each okra and chop them into 12-inch pieces; add them to the egg and mix until thoroughly coated.

✓ Combine flour and salt in a big plastic bag.

✓ Working with one piece of okra at a time, rinse the okra thoroughly by allowing excess egg to run off, add it to the flour mixture, cover the bag, and shake vigorously until the okra is fully coated.

✓ Arrange the coated okra in a greased air fryer basket and repeat with the remaining okra pieces.

✓ Preheat air fryer at 390 degrees F, enter fryer basket, spray okra with oil, then cover with lid. Cook for 10 minutes, or until pleasantly brown and done, stirring okra halfway through the frying.

Nutrition: 250 calories 2 g Carbohydrates 11 g Fat 4 g protein 2 g fiber

920) *Skewers of Grilled Tofu and Veggies*

6 portions 15 Minutes Cooking 1 block tofu

- 2 tiny sliced zucchini
- 1 red bell pepper, cut into 1-inch cubes
- 1 yellow bell pepper, cut into 1-inch cubes
- 1 red onion, cut into 1-inch chunks
- What you'll require from your pantry:
- 2 tbsp. light soy sauce
- 3 tbsp. barbeque sauce
- 2 tbsp. sesame seeds
- Season with salt and pepper to taste
- Cooking spray with nonstick properties

Directions:

✓ Press tofu for approximately half an hour to extract liquid. Then, cut tofu into cubes and marinate for at least 15 minutes in soy sauce.

✓ Preheat the grill to a medium-high setting. Cooking spray the grill rack.

✓ Thread skewers with tofu and vegetables alternately.

✓ Grill for 2-3 minutes on each side, or until vegetables begin to soften and the tofu turns golden brown. Season with salt and pepper and brush with barbecue sauce at the conclusion of the cooking time. Serve with sesame seeds on top.

Nutrition: Calories 64 Carbohydrates 10g Carbohydrates Net Protein: 7 g 5 g fat 2 g sugar 6 g dietary fiber 3g

921) *Tex Mex Veggie*

Time Required for Cooking: 35 Minutes Bake 8

- 2 cup grated cauliflower
- 1 cup fat-free sour cream
- 1 cup grated reduced-fat cheddar cheese
- 1 cup grated reduced-fat Mexican cheese blend
- What you'll require from your pantry:
- 11 oz. can Mexicorn, drained
- 10 oz. tomatoes and green chilies
- 2 14 oz. black olives, drain
- 1 cup salsa
- 1/4 tsp pepper

Directions:

✓ Preheat the oven to 350 degrees

Fahrenheit. Cooking spray a 2 12 quart baking dish.

✓ *Combine beans, corn, tomatoes, salsa, sour cream, cheddar cheese, pepper, and cauliflower in a large bowl. Transfer to a prepared baking dish. Combine onion and olives in a small bowl.*

✓ *Bake in the oven for 30 minutes. Sprinkle with Mexican blend cheese and continue baking for an additional 5-10 minutes, or until cheese is melted and casserole is well heated. Allow 10 minutes to rest before serving.*

Nutrition: 266 Calories 33g Net Carbohydrates 27g Protein 16g Fat 8g Sugar 8g Fiber 6g

922) *Pad Thai*

30 Minutes Cooking

- *12 oz. organic extra firm tofu, cubed into 1-inch cubes*
- *2 zucchini, shredded into long zoodles*
- *1 carrot, grated*
- *3 cups bean sprouts*
- *2 green onions, sliced*
- *1 cup red cabbage, shredded*
- *What you'll require from your pantry:*
- *1/4 cup lime juice*
- *2 minced garlic cloves*
- *2 tbsp reduced-fat peanut butter*
- *2 tbsp tamari*
- *1 tbsp sesame seeds*
- *1/2 tbsp sesame oil*

Directions:

✓ *In a saucepan over medium heat, heat half the oil. Cook until tofu begins to brown, about 5 minutes. Stir in garlic till light brown.*

✓ *Combine the zucchini, carrots, cabbage, lime juice, peanut butter, tamari, and chili flakes in a medium mixing bowl. Combine all ingredients in a mixing bowl. Cook, stirring regularly, for approximately 5 minutes, or until vegetables are soft. Remove from heat and stir in bean sprouts.*

✓ *Garnish with green onions, sesame seeds, and cilantro before serving.*

Nutrition: Calories 134 Total Carbohydrates 13g Protein: 11 g 12 g fat 6 g sugar 3 g dietary fiber 2g

923) *Hummus with Cauliflower*

5 minutes for preparation 15 minutes cooking time, 6 servings

Ingredients:

- *3 cup florets de cauliflower*
- *3 tbsp. freshly squeezed lemon juice*
- *What you'll require from your pantry: 5 garlic cloves, divided*
- *5 tablespoons olive oil, divided*
- *2 tablespoons water*
- *1/2 tbsp tahini paste*
- *1/4 tsp kosher salt, divided*

Direction

✓ *Paprika smoky and more olive oil for serving Instructions:*

✓ *Combine cauliflower, water, 2 tablespoons oil, 1/2 teaspoon salt, and 3 entire garlic cloves in a microwave-safe bowl. 15 minutes on high, or until cauliflower is tender and browned.*

✓ *Process contents in a food processor or blender until nearly smooth. Combine the tahini paste, lemon juice, remaining garlic cloves, remaining oil, and salt in a medium mixing bowl. Blend on high speed until almost smooth.*

✓ *In a bowl, combine the hummus and drizzle with olive oil and a sprinkle or two of paprika. Serve with fresh vegetables of your choice.*

Calories 107 Carbohydrates 5g Carbohydrates Net Protein 3 g 2 g Fat 10 g Sucrose 1 gram fiber 2 g

924) *Squares of Spinach and Cheddar*

4 portions Time Required for Cooking: 40 Minutes

- *10 oz. frozen spinach, thawed and squeezed dry*
- *1/2 cupegg substitute*
- *34 cup skim milk*
- *34 cup grated reduced-fat cheddar cheese*
- *What you'll need from your pantry:*
- *2 tbsp. reduced-fat parmesan cheese*
- *1 tbsp. bread crumbs*
- *1/2 tsp . dried chopped onion*
- *1/2 tsp . salt*
- *1/4 tsp garlic powder*
- *1/4 tsp pepper*

Directions:

✓ *Preheat the oven to 350 degrees Fahrenheit. Cooking spray an 8-inch square baking dish.*

✓ *Bread crumbs should be sprinkled over the bottom of the prepared dish. Add 12 cups of cheese, spinach, and red pepper to the top.*

✓ *Whisk together the remaining ingredients in a small dish. Distribute over veggies.*

✓ *35 minutes in the oven. Sprinkle remaining cheese on top and bake for an additional 2-3 minutes, or until cheese is melted and a knife inserted in the center comes out clean.*

✓ *Allow 15 minutes for cooling before cutting and serving.*

Nutrition: Calories 159 Carbohydrates 7g Carbohydrates Net Protein 5 g 22 g fat 5 g sugar 4 g dietary fiber 2g

925) *Pesto Mushrooms Stuffed*

5 minutes for preparation Cooking time: 20 minutes; number of servings: 4

Ingredients:

- *12 cremini mushrooms, removed stems*
- *4 oz. softened low-fat cream cheese*
- *1/2 cup grated mozzarella cheese*
- *What you'll require from your pantry: 1/3 cup fat-free Parmigiano-Reggiano*
- *6 tbsp. pesto basilico*
- *Cooking spray that is nonstick*

Instructions:

✓ *Preheat the oven to 375 degrees Fahrenheit. Coat a square baking dish with cooking spray and line with foil. Arrange the mushrooms in a single layer in the baking pan. Place aside.*

✓ *Cream together cream cheese, pesto, and parmesan in a medium bowl until smooth and creamy. Fill mushroom caps halfway with mixture. Add a heaping spoonful of mozzarella on top.*

✓ *Bake for 20–23 minutes, or until the cheese has melted and the crust is golden brown. Allow 5-10 minutes for cooking before serving.*

Nutrition: Calories 76 per serving Carbohydrates in Total 4 g protein, 8 g fat, 3 g sugar, and 1 g dietary fiber

926) *Salad de récolte*

6 portions Time Required for Cooking: 25 Minutes

- *10 oz. deboned and chopped kale*
- *1/2 cup spicyblackberries*
- *12 cubed butternut squash*
- *1/4 cup crumbled goat cheese*
- *What you'll require from your pantry:*
- *Maple Mustard Salad Dressing*
- *1 cup raw pecans*
- *1/3 cup raw pumpkin seeds*
- *1/4 cup dried cranberries*
- *Season with pepper to taste*
- *Coat with nonstick frying spray*

Directions:

✓ *Preheat the oven to 400 degrees Fahrenheit. Cooking spray a baking sheet.*

✓ *Spread squash on the preheated pan and toss with 1/2 tbsps oil, 1/8 teaspoon salt, and pepper to cover evenly. 20-25 minutes in the oven.*

✓ *In a large bowl, place the kale. 2 tbsp oil and 1/2 tsp salt should be added and massaged into the kale with your hands for 3-4 minutes.*

✓ *Using cooking spray, coat a clean baking sheet. Combine pecans, pumpkin seeds, and maple syrup in a medium bowl until nuts are evenly coated. Pour onto a prepared baking sheet and bake for 8-10 minutes; they can be done concurrently with the squash.*

✓ *To construct the salad, combine all ingredients in a large mixing dish. Toss in dressing to coat. Serve.*

Nutrition: 436 Calories 24g Carbohydrates 17g Net Protein 9g Fat 37g Sugar 5g Fiber 7g

927) *Potatoes Spicy*

4 portions 30 Minutes Cooking

- *400g potatoes*
- *2 tbsp. hot paprika*
- *1 tbsp. olive oil*
- *Season with salt to taste*

Directions:

✓ *Brush the potatoes clean. Unpeeled, cut into a crescent shape vertically, about 1 finger thick. Fill a basin halfway with water and add the potatoes. Allow to stand for approximately a half-hour.*

✓ *Preheat the air fryer to 350 degrees Fahrenheit. Set a 5-minute timer and the temperature to 2000C.*

✓ *Pat dry the potatoes with paper towels or a*

clean cloth. Reintroduce them to the bowl and drizzle the oil, salt, and paprika over them. Combine thoroughly with your hands to coat them evenly in the spice mixture. Place the seasoned potatoes in the air fryer's basket. Set the timer for 30 minutes and power up the device. In half the time, stir in the potatoes.

✓ Transfer the potatoes to a platter from the air fryer.

Nutrition: 153 Calories Carbohydrates: 2 g 11 g fat 4 g protein 0g fiber

928) *Cauliflower Buffalo Wings*

6 portions 30 Minutes Cooking

- 1 tbsp almond flour
- 1 medium head of cauliflower
- 1/2 tbsp salt
- 4 tbsp spicy sauce
- 1 tbsp olive oil

Directions:

✓ Turn on the air fryer, insert the fryer basket, coat it with olive oil, cover it with the lid, and preheat for 5 minutes at 400 degrees F.

✓ In the meantime, separate cauliflower florets into bite-size pieces and set them aside.

✓ In a large mixing bowl, whisk together flour, salt, oil, and spicy sauce until mixed. Add cauliflower florets and toss to coat.

✓ Remove the cover from the fryer and put the cauliflower florets in a single layer. Cook for 15 minutes, shaking halfway through, until pleasantly browned and crispy.

✓ When the air fryer whistles, open the cover and transfer the cauliflower florets to a serving plate.

✓ Repeat with the remaining cauliflower florets and serve.

Nutrition: 48 Calories Carbohydrates: 2 g 11 g fat 4 g protein 0.3 g fiber

929) *Asian Noodle Salad*

Ingredients:

- 2 carrots, thinly sliced
- 2 radish, thinly sliced
- 1 English cucumber, thinly sliced
- 1 mango, julienned
- 1 bell pepper, julienned
- 1 small serrano pepper, seeded and thinly sliced
- 1 bag tofu Shirataki Fettuccini noodles
- 1/4 cup lime juice
- 1/4 cup fresh basil, chopped
- 1/4 cup fresh cilantro, chopped
- 2 tbsp. fresh What you'll require from the pantry
- 2 tbsp rice vinegar
- 2 tbsp. finely chopped roasted peanuts
- 1 tbsp. Splenda
- 1/2 tsp sesame oil

Directions:

✓ Vegetables should be pickled: Combine radish, cucumbers, and carrots in a large basin. Stir in the vinegar, coconut sugar, and lime juice until the vegetables are well coated. Refrigerate covered for 15–20 minutes.

✓ Prepare the noodles: remove them from the package and rinse them under cold running water. Reduce the size of the parts. Using paper towels, pat dry.

✓ Assembling the salad Remove the vegetables from the marinade and place them in a large mixing bowl, reserving the marinade. Combine noodles, mango, bell pepper, chile, and herbs in a medium bowl.

✓ Combine 2 tablespoons marinade, chili sauce, and sesame oil in a small bowl. Toss salad to coat with dressing. Serve garnished with peanuts.

Nutrition: Calories 158 Carbohydrates 30g Net Carbohydrates 24g Protein 4 g fat 4 g sugar 19 g dietary fiber 6g

930) *Flatbreads With Cheesy Mushrooms And Pesto*

2 portions Time Required for Cooking: 13 to 17 Minutes

- 1 teaspoon extra-virgin olive oil
- 12 sliced red onion
- 1/2 cup sliced mushrooms
- Salt and freshly ground black pepper to taste
- 2 whole-wheat flatbreads

Directions:

✓ Preheat the oven to 350 degrees Fahrenheit (180 degrees Celsius).

✓ In a small skillet over medium heat, heat the olive oil. Sauté the onion pieces and mushrooms in the skillet for 3 to 5 minutes, or until they begin to soften. Season with sea salt and freshly ground pepper.

✓ In the meantime, add 2 tbsp pesto sauce onto each flatbread and spread evenly. Distribute the mushroom mixture evenly between two flatbreads and top with 2 tablespoons of shredded cheese.

✓ Transfer the flatbreads to a baking sheet and bake for about 10 to 12 minutes, or until the cheese melts and bubbles.

✓ Allow the flatbreads to cool for 5 minutes before serving.

Nutrition: 346 Calories; 28g protein; 12g carbohydrate; 27.6g fiber; 7.3g sugar; 0g 790mg sodium

931) *Carrots Roasted in Honey*

2-4 portions 12 Minutes Cooking

- 454g peeled and rinsed rainbow carrots
- 15 ml olive oil
- 30 ml honey
- 2 sprigs of fresh thyme
- Season with salt and pepper to taste

Directions:

✓ Rinse and pat dry the carrots with a paper towel. Set aside.

✓ Preheat the air fryer to 1800C for a few minutes.

✓ Combine the carrots, olive oil, honey, thyme, salt, and pepper in a bowl. Preheat the air fryer to 1800C and cook the carrots for 12 minutes. Shake the baskets frequently throughout the cooking process.

Nutrition: 123 Calories 42g fat 9g Carbohydrates 1 gram protein

932) *Stuffed Mushrooms With Tomato*

4 portions Time Required for Cooking: 50 Minutes

- 8 big mushrooms
- 250g minced beef
- 4 garlic cloves
- Extra virgin olive oil
- Salt
- PEPPER, GROUND
- FLOUR, BEATEN EGGS, AND BREADCRUMBS

- Frying oil

Directions:

✓ Remove and slice the stems from the mushrooms. Peel and cut the garlic. In a saucepan, heat the extra virgin olive oil and add the garlic and mushroom stems.

✓ Sauté the minced beef and add it to the pan. Sauté until the meat is cooked through and season with salt and pepper.

✓ Stuff the minced meat into the mushrooms.

✓ Firmly press and place in the freezer for 30 minutes.

✓ Sprinkle flour, beaten egg, and breadcrumbs over the mushrooms. Egg and breadcrumbs, beaten.

✓ Arrange the mushrooms in the air fryer basket.

✓ Set the timer for 20 minutes at 1800C.

✓ Once the mushrooms are cooked, divide them evenly among the bowls.

✓ In a small saucepan, heat the tomato sauce and pour it over the packed mushrooms.

Nutrition: 160 Calories Carbohydrates: 2 g 11 g fat 4 g protein 0 g fiber

933) *Summer Squash And Quinoa Casserole With Cheesy*

8 portions Time Required for Cooking: 27 To 30 Minutes

- 1 tablespoon extra-virgin olive oil
- 1 thinly sliced Vidalia onion
- 1 large thinly sliced portobello mushroom
- 6 thinly sliced yellow summer squash
- 1 cup shredded Parmesan cheese, divided
- 1 cup shredded Cheddar cheese
- 1/2 cuptri-color quinoa
- 1/2 cupwhole-wheat bread crumbs
- 1 tablespoon Creole seasoning

Directions:

✓ Preheat the oven to 350 degrees Fahrenheit (180 degrees Celsius).

✓ In a large cast-iron skillet, heat the olive oil over medium heat.

✓ Sauté the onion, mushroom, and squash in the oil for 7 to 10 minutes, or until the veggies are softened, stirring periodically.

✓ Remove the pan from the heat and stir in 12 cups Parmesan and 12 cups Cheddar cheese to the vegetables. Stir thoroughly.

✓ In a separate dish, combine the quinoa, bread crumbs, remaining Parmesan cheese, and Creole spice; spread the mixture over the vegetables.

✓ Bake the cast iron pan in the preheated oven for about 20 minutes, or until browned and cooked through.

✓ Allow to cool for 10 minutes before plating.
Nutrition: Calories: 184 fats: 8.9g protein: 17g carbohydrates: 17.6g fiber: 2g sugar: 8g sodium: 140mg

934) *Parmesan Eggplant*

15 Minutes Cooking Servings: 4

- 1/2 cup and 3 tablespoons almond flour, divided
- 25 pounds sliced eggplant
- 1 tablespoon chopped parsley
- 1 teaspoon Italian seasoning
- 2 teaspoons salt
- 1 cup marinara sauce
- 1 pastured egg
- 1 teaspoon water
- 3 tablespoons grated parmesan cheese, reduced-fat

Directions:

✓ Cut the eggplant into 12-inch pieces and arrange them in a colander. Sprinkle both sides with 1 12-teaspoon salt and set aside for 15 minutes.

✓ In the meantime, whisk together 12 cups of flour, egg, and water in a bowl.

✓ In a shallow dish, combine the remaining flour, salt, Italian seasoning, and parmesan cheese.

✓ Turn on the air fryer, insert the fryer basket, coat it with olive oil, cover it with the lid, and Preheat for 5 minutes at 360 degrees F.

✓ In the meantime, drain and wipe dry the eggplant slices, then dip each slice into the egg mixture and coat with the flour mixture.

✓ Preheat the fryer; place the coated eggplant slices in a single layer; cover and cook for 8 minutes, or until pleasantly brown and done, rotating the eggplant slices halfway through.

✓ Top each eggplant slice with a tablespoon of marinara sauce and a sprinkle of mozzarella cheese and continue air frying

for an additional 1 to 2 minutes, or until the cheese has melted.

✓ When the air fryer beeps, remove the lid and transfer the eggplants to a serving tray to keep warm.

✓ Repeat with the remaining eggplant pieces and serve.
Nutrition: 123 Calories Carbohydrates: 2 g 11 g fat 4 g protein 6 g dietary fiber

935) *Salt And Pepper On Sweet Potatoes*

4 portions Time Required for Cooking: 20 Minutes

- 1 large sweet potato
- Extra virgin olive oil
- Salt and freshly ground pepper

Directions:

✓ Peel and thinly slice the sweet potato; if you have a mandolin, this will be easier.

✓ Thoroughly clean and sprinkle with salt.

✓ Drizzle a small amount of oil over the sweet potato strips and set it in the air fryer basket.

✓ Preheat the oven to 1800C for approximately 30 minutes. Shake the basket occasionally to keep the sweet potato moving.

✓ Transfer to a tray or dish and season with coarse salt and freshly ground pepper.
Nutrition: 107 Calories 0.6g fat 219g Carbohydrates 61g protein 95g sugar 0mg cholesterol

936) *Greens Sautéed Simply*

4 portions Time Required for Cooking: 10 Minutes

- 2 tbsp extra-virgin olive oil
- 1 pound (454 g) Swiss chard, coarse stems removed, and leaves chopped
- 1 pound (454 g) kale, coarse stems removed, and leaves cut
- To taste, sea salt and freshly ground black pepper

Directions:

✓ In a large skillet over medium-high heat, heat the olive oil.

✓ In a skillet, combine the Swiss chard, kale, cardamon, and lemon juice. Cook, constantly stirring, for approximately 10 minutes, or until the greens are wilted.

✓ Season with salt and pepper to taste and mix well.

✓ Arrange the greens on a plate while they

are still heated.
Nutrition: Calories: 139 fat: 6.8 g protein: 9 g carbohydrates: 18 g fiber: 9 g sugar: 0 g sodium: 350mg

937) *Crispy Sweet Potatoes*

4 portions Time Required for Cooking: 10 Minutes

- *2 large sweet potatoes, quartered*
- *15 ml oil*
- *10g salt*
- *2g black pepper*
- *2g paprika*
- *2g garlic powder*
- *2g onion powder*

Directions:

✓ *Cut the sweet potatoes into 25 mm-thick strips.*

✓ *For a few minutes, preheat the air fryer.*

✓ *In a large mixing basin, combine the chopped sweet potatoes and boil until the potatoes are equally covered.*

✓ *Season with sea salt, freshly ground black pepper, paprika, garlic powder, and onion powder. Combine thoroughly.*

✓ *Cook the French fries for 10 minutes at 205°C in the prepared baskets. Shake the baskets midway during the cooking process.*

Nutrition: 123 Calories Carbohydrates: 2 g 11 g fat 4 g protein 0 g fiber

938) *Casserole de Chili Relleno*

8 portions Time Required for Cooking: 35 Minutes 3 eggs

- *1 cup shredded Monterey jack pepper cheese*
- *3/4 cup half-n-half*
- *1/2 cup grated cheddar cheese*
- *What you'll require from your pantry:*
- *2 (7 oz.) cans whole green chiles, drained well*

Directions:

✓ *Preheat the oven to 350 degrees Fahrenheit. Cooking spray an 8-inch baking pan.*

✓ *Cut each chile in half lengthwise and lay flat.*

✓ *Arrange half of the chilies in a single layer in the prepared baking pan, skin side down.*

✓ *Top with remaining chilies, skin side up, and sprinkle with pepper cheese.*

✓ *In a small mixing bowl, whisk together eggs, salt, and half-and-half. Distribute over chiles. Cheddar cheese, if desired.*

✓ *Bake for 35 minutes, or until golden brown on top. Allow 10 minutes to rest before serving.*

Nutrition: 295 Calories 36g Total Carbohydrates 22g Net Carbohydrates 13g Protein 13g Fat 13g Sugar 21g 14g dietary fiber

939) *Parmesan Eggplant*

Servings: 4 15 Minutes Cooking

- *1/2 cup and 3 tablespoons almond flour, divided*
- *25 pounds sliced eggplant*
- *1 tablespoon chopped parsley*
- *1 teaspoon Italian seasoning*
- *2 teaspoons salt*
- *1 cup marinara sauce*
- *1 pastured egg*
- *1 teaspoon water*
- *3 tablespoons grated parmesan cheese, reduced-fat*

Directions:

✓ *Cut the eggplant into 12-inch pieces and arrange them in a colander. Sprinkle both sides with 1 12-teaspoon salt and set aside for 15 minutes.*

✓ *In the meantime, whisk together 12 cups of flour, egg, and water in a bowl.*

✓ *In a shallow dish, combine the remaining flour, salt, Italian seasoning, and parmesan cheese.*

✓ *Turn on the air fryer, insert the fryer basket, coat it with olive oil, cover it with the lid, and Preheat for 5 minutes at 360 degrees F.*

✓ *In the meantime, drain and wipe dry the eggplant slices, then dip each slice into the egg mixture and coat with the flour mixture.*

✓ *Preheat the fryer; place the coated eggplant slices in a single layer; cover and cook for 8 minutes, or until pleasantly brown and done, rotating the eggplant slices halfway through.*

✓ *Top each eggplant slice with a tablespoon of marinara sauce and a sprinkle of mozzarella cheese and continue air frying for an additional 1 to 2 minutes, or until the cheese has melted.*

✓ *When the air fryer beeps, remove the lid and transfer the eggplants to a serving tray to keep warm.*

✓ *Repeat with the remaining eggplant pieces and serve.*

Nutrition: 123 Calories Carbohydrates: 2 g 11 g fat 4 g protein 6 g dietary fiber

940) *Salt And Pepper On Sweet Potatoes*

4 portions Time Required for Cooking: 20 Minutes

- *1 large sweet potato*
- *Extra virgin olive oil*
- *Salt and freshly ground pepper*

Directions:

✓ *Peel and thinly slice the sweet potato; if you have a mandolin, this will be easier.*

✓ *Thoroughly clean and sprinkle with salt.*

✓ *Drizzle a small amount of oil over the sweet potato strips and set it in the air fryer basket.*

✓ *Preheat the oven to 1800C for approximately 30 minutes. Shake the basket occasionally to keep the sweet potato moving.*

✓ *Transfer to a tray or dish and season with coarse salt and freshly ground pepper.*

Nutrition: 107 Calories 0.6g fat 219g Carbohydrates 61g protein 95g sugar 0mg cholesterol

941) *Greens Sautéed Simply*

4 portions Time Required for Cooking: 10 Minutes

- *2 tbsp extra-virgin olive oil*
- *1 pound (454 g) Swiss chard, coarse stems removed, and leaves chopped*
- *1 pound (454 g) kale, coarse stems removed, and leaves cut*
- *To taste, sea salt and freshly ground black pepper*

Directions:

✓ *In a large skillet over medium-high heat, heat the olive oil.*

✓ *In a skillet, combine the Swiss chard, kale, cardamon, and lemon juice. Cook, constantly stirring, for approximately 10 minutes, or until the greens are wilted.*

✓ *Season with salt and pepper to taste and mix well.*

✓ *Arrange the greens on a plate while they*

are still heated.

Nutrition: Calories: 139 fat: 6.8 g protein: 9 g carbohydrates: 18 g fiber: 9 g sugar: 0 g sodium: 350mg

942) *Crispy Sweet Potatoes*

4 portions Time Required for Cooking: 10 Minutes

- *2 large sweet potatoes, quartered*
- *15 ml oil*
- *10g salt*
- *2g black pepper*
- *2g paprika*
- *2g garlic powder*
- *2g onion powder*

Directions:

Cut the sweet potatoes into 25 mm-thick strips.

✓ *For a few minutes, preheat the air fryer.*

✓ *In a large mixing basin, combine the chopped sweet potatoes and oil until the potatoes are equally covered.*

✓ *Season with sea salt, freshly ground black pepper, paprika, garlic powder, and onion powder. Combine thoroughly.*

✓ *Cook the French fries for 10 minutes at 205°C in the prepared baskets. Shake the baskets midway during the cooking process.*

Nutrition: 123 Calories Carbohydrates: 2 g 11 g fat 4 g protein 0 g fiber

943) *Casserole de Chili Relleno*

8 portions Time Required for Cooking: 35 Minutes 3 eggs

- *1 cup shredded Monterey jack pepper cheese*
- *3/4 cup half-n-half*
- *1/2 cup grated cheddar cheese*
- *What you'll require from your pantry:*
- *2 (7 oz.) cans whole green chiles, drained well*

Directions:

✓ *Preheat the oven to 350 degrees Fahrenheit. Cooking spray an 8-inch baking pan.*

✓ *Cut each chile in half lengthwise and lay flat.*

✓ *Arrange half of the chilies in a single layer in the prepared baking pan, skin side down.*

✓ *Top with remaining chilies, skin side up, and sprinkle with pepper cheese.*

✓ In a small mixing bowl, whisk together eggs, salt, and half-and-half. Distribute over chiles. Cheddar cheese, if desired.

✓ Bake for 35 minutes, or until golden brown on top. Allow 10 minutes to rest before serving.

Nutrition: 295 Calories 36g Total Carbohydrates 22g Net Carbohydrates 13g Protein 13g Fat 13g Sugar 21g 14g dietary fiber

944) *Cauliflower Rice*

Time Required for Cooking: 27 Minutes

- 1 cup sliced carrot
- 6 oz extra-firm tofu, drained
- 1/2 cup diced white onion
- 2 tbsp soy sauce
- 1 tsp turmeric
- 1/2 cup chopped broccoli
- 3 cups cauliflower rice
- 1 tablespoon minced garlic
- 1/2 cup frozen peas
- 1 tablespoon minced ginger
- 2 tablespoons soy sauce
- 1 teaspoon apple cider vinegar
- 1 1/2 teaspoon toasted sesame oil

Directions:

✓ Turn on the air fryer, insert the frying pan, coat it with olive oil, cover it with the lid, and Preheat for 5 minutes at 370 degrees F.

✓ In the meantime, crumble the tofu in a bowl and add the remaining ingredients. Stir until combined.

✓ Preheat the fryer to 350°F. Add the tofu mixture and brush with oil. Cover and cook for 10 minutes, or until pleasantly brown and crispy, stirring halfway through.

✓ In the meantime, combine all of the cauliflower ingredients in a bowl and toss until well combined.

✓ When the air fryer beeps, open the cover, add the cauliflower mixture, gently shake the pan to combine, and cook for another 12 minutes, mixing halfway through.

Nutrition: 258 Calories Carbohydrates: 2 g 11 g fat 4 g protein 7 g dietary fiber

945) *Slaw de automne*

8 portions Time Required for Cooking: 2 Hours

- 10 cup shredded cabbage

- 12 finely sliced red onion
- 3/4 cup chopped fresh Italian parsley
- What you'll require from your pantry:
- 3/4 cup sliced and roasted almonds
- 3/4 cup dried cranberries
- 1/3 cup vegetable oil
- 1/4 cup apple cider vinegar
- 2 tbsp. sugar-free maple syrup
- 4 tbsp Dijon mustard
- 1/2 teaspoon salt

Directions:

✓ Whisk together vinegar, oil, syrup, Dijon, and 1/2 tsp salt in a large mixing basin. Stir in the onion. Allow 10 minutes for resting, or cover and chill until ready to use.

✓ After 10 minutes, whisk in the remaining ingredients and toss to coat. Season with salt and pepper to taste. 2 hours before serving, cover, and chill.

Nutrition: Calories 133 Carbohydrates 12g net Carbohydrates 8g Protein 2 g fat 9 g sugar 5 g dietary fiber 4g

946) *Portobello Stuffed with Pizza*

Time Required for Cooking: 10 Minutes Servings: 4

- 8 Portobello mushrooms, stems removed
- 1 cup grated mozzarella cheese
- 1 cup sliced cherry tomatoes
- 1/2 cup crushed tomatoes
- 1/2 cup chopped fresh basil
- 2 tbsp. balsamic vinegar
- 1 tbsp. olive oil
- 1 tbsp. oregano
- 1 tbsp. red pepper flakes
- 1/2 tbsp. garlic powder
- 1/4 tsp pepper
- 1 tsp salt

Directions:

✓ To begin, preheat the oven to broil. Prepare a baking sheet by lining it with foil.

✓ Arrange mushrooms on foil, stem side down, and spray with oil. Season with garlic powder, salt, and pepper to taste. 5 minutes under the broiler.

✓ Place smashed tomatoes, oregano, parsley, pepper flakes, cheese, and sliced tomatoes on top of mushrooms. Broil for a further 5 minutes.

✓ *Garnish with basil and balsamic glaze. Serve.*

Nutrition: Calories 113 Carbohydrates Total 11g Protein: 7 g 9 g fat 5 g sugar 3 g dietary fiber 4g

947) *French Fries in the Cajun Style*

4 portions 28 Minutes Cooking

- *2 reddish potatoes, peeled and sliced into 76 x 25 mm strips*
- *1 liter cold water*
- *15 ml oil*
- *7 g Cajun seasoning*
- *1 teaspoon cayenne pepper*
- *To serve, tomato sauce or ranch sauce*

Directions:

✓ *Soak the potatoes in water for 15 minutes after cutting them into 76 x 25 mm strips.*

✓ *Drain the potatoes and pat dry with paper towels using cold, dry water.*

✓ *Preheat the air fryer to 195 degrees Celsius.*

✓ *Toss the potatoes in the oil and seasonings until well coated.*

✓ *Once the air fryer is hot, add the potatoes and set the timer to 28 minutes.*

✓ *Ensure that you shake the baskets periodically throughout the frying process.*

✓ *When the air fryer is completed cooking, remove the baskets and season the fries with salt and pepper.*

Nutrition: 158 Calories Carbohydrates: 2 g fat 4 g protein 0 g fiber

948) *Salad with Avocado and Citrus Shrimp*

Time Required for Cooking: 5 Minutes Servings: 4

- *1 pound medium shrimp, peeled and deveined; discard tails*
- *Approximately 8 cup salad greens*
- *1 lime*
- *1 diced avocado*
- *1 shallot, finely diced*
- *What you'll require from your pantry:*
- *1/2 cup chopped and roasted almonds*
- *1 tbsp. olive oil*

Directions:

✓ *Halve the lemon and squeeze both halves of the juice into a small bowl; leave aside. Lemon wedges, thinly sliced*

✓ *In a skillet over medium heat, heat the oil. Add lemon wedges and simmer for approximately 1 minute to infuse the oil with lemon flavour.*

✓ *Cook, often stirring, until the shrimp turn pink. Remove the lemon wedges and set them aside to cool.*

✓ *In a large bowl, combine the salad greens. Toss the shrimp in the pan juices to coat. Toss in the remaining ingredients. Serve.*

Nutrition: Calories 425 Total Carbohydrates 17 Net Carbohydrates 8 g Protein 35 g Fat 26 g Sucrose 2 Fiber

949) *Pizza Florentine*

2 portions Time Required for Cooking: 20 Minutes

- *1 3/4 cup grated mozzarella cheese*
- *1/2 cup hawed frozen spinach*
- *1 egg*
- *2 tbsp. grated reduced-fat parmesan cheese*
- *2 tbsp. softened cream cheese*
- *What you'll require from the pantry*
- *3/4 cup almond flour*
- *1/4 cup light Alfredo sauce*
- *1/2 teaspoon   Italian seasoning*
- *1/4 teaspoon   red pepper flakes*

Directions:

✓ *Preheat the oven to 400 degrees Fahrenheit.*

✓ *Squeeze the spinach to remove any excess moisture.*

✓ *Combine mozzarella and almond flour in a glass basin. Incorporate cream cheese. Microwave on high for 1 minute, then stir. If the mixture is not completely melted, microwave for an additional 30 seconds.*

✓ *Add the egg, spice, and salt and stir to combine. Combine thoroughly. On a sheet of parchment paper, press the dough into a 10-inch circle.*

✓ *Bake for 8-10 minutes, or until gently browned, directly on the oven rack.*

✓ *Remove the crust and distribute the Alfredo sauce evenly over the top, followed by the spinach, parmesan, and red pepper flakes. Bake for an additional 8-10 minutes. Serve sliced.*

Nutrition: 441 Calories 14g Carbohydrates Net Carbohydrates 9g Protein 24g Fat 35g Sugar 4g Fiber 5g

950) *Air Fryer Vegetables*

2 portions 30 Minutes Cooking

- 2 potatoes
- 1 zucchini
- 1 onion
- 1 red pepper

Directions:

✓ Slice the potatoes.

✓ Halve the onion and cut it into rings.

✓ Slice the zucchini

✓ Using a sharp knife, cut the peppers into strips.

✓ Combine all ingredients in a bowl and season with salt, freshly ground pepper, and extra virgin olive oil to taste.

✓ Combine thoroughly.

✓ Transfer to the air fryer's basket.

✓ Set the temperature to 160 c° C for 30 minutes.

✓ Inspect the vegetables to ensure they are to your satisfaction.

Nutrition: 135 Nutrition: Calories Carbohydrates: 2 g 11 g fat 4 g protein 05g fiber

951) *Bento with Tofu*

Time Required for Cooking: 10 Minutes Servings: 4

- 1 package extra-firm tofu
- 1 sliced red bell pepper
- 1 sliced orange bell pepper
- 2 cup cooked cauliflower rice
- 2 cups chopped broccoli
- 1/4 cup sliced green onion
- What you'll require from your pantry:
- 2 tbsp low-sodium soy sauce
- 1 tbsp olive oil
- 1 tsp garlic powder
- 1 tsp onion powder

Directions:

✓ Remove tofu from package and pat dry with paper towels; set aside for 15 minutes.

✓ Cube the tofu. Shake to coat the tofu and seasonings in a big Ziploc bag.

✓ In a large skillet over medium heat, heat oil. Cook, stirring regularly, for 5-8 minutes, or until the tofu is browned on both sides and the vegetables are soft.

✓ To serve, divide 12 cups cauliflower rice

evenly among four dishes and top with tofu mixture.

Nutrition: Calories 93 Carbohydrates 12g Protein: 8 g fat 3 g sugar 5 g dietary fiber 4 g

952) *Tofu Marinated with Peanut Sauce*

4 portions Time Required for Cooking: 1 Hour 25 Minutes

- 1 package extremely firm tofu, pressed for 15 minutes, and cubed
- 1 package fresh baby spinach
- 2 limes
- 1 tbsp margarine What you'll require from your pantry:
- 1/2 cupunsalted raw peanut butter
- 2 tablespoons light soy sauce
- 3 minced garlic cloves
- 1/2 teaspoon ginger
- 1/4 teaspoon red pepper flakes

Directions:

✓ In a large pot, melt margarine. Cook, stirring periodically, for 5-10 minutes, or until tofu begins to color.

✓ Bring to a simmer the remaining ingredients, except the spinach. Reduce to low heat, cover, and simmer for 30-35 minutes, stirring periodically.

✓ Stir in the spinach and cook for an additional 15 minutes. Serve.

Nutrition: 325 Nutrition: Calories 15g Carbohydrates Total 15g Carbohydrates Net 10g Protein 18g Fat 24g Sugar 5g Fiber 5g

953) *Scrambled Eggs & Greens in Mexico*

4 portions Time Required for Cooking: 5 Minutes

- 8 egg whites
- 4 egg yolks
- 3 tomatoes, cut into 12-inch pieces
- 1 jalapeño pepper, thinly sliced
- 12 avocado, cut into 12-inch pieces
- 12 Romaine lettuce heads, ripped
- 1/2 cup chopped cilantro
- 2 tbsp fresh lime juice
- What you'll require from your pantry:
- 12 tortilla chips, cut into little pieces
- 2 tbsp. water

- *1 tbsp. olive oil*
- *34 tsp pepper, split*

Directions:

✓ *Combine tomatoes, avocado, onion, jalapeño, cilantro, lime juice, 1/4 teaspoon salt, and 1/4 teaspoon pepper in a medium bowl.*

✓ *In a large mixing bowl, whisk together egg whites, egg yolks, water, salt & pepper to taste. Combine with tortilla chips.*

✓ *In a large skillet over medium heat, heat oil. Cook, stirring regularly, for 3-5 minutes, or until the desired doneness is achieved.*

✓ *Divide lettuce leaves evenly among four dishes to serve. Top with scrambled egg mixture and salsa.*

Nutrition: Calories 280 Carbohydrates Total 10g Carbohydrates Net 6g Protein 15g Fat 21g Sugar 4g Fiber 4g

954) *Patties of Sweet Potato and Cauliflower*

7 portions Time Required for Cooking: 40 Minutes

- *1 chopped green onion*
- *1 peeled large sweet potato*
- *1 teaspoon minced garlic*
- *1 cup cilantro leaves*
- *2 cup cauliflower florets*
- *1/4 teaspoon crushed black pepper*
- *1/4 teaspoon salt*
- *1/4 cup sunflower seeds*
- *1/4 teaspoon cumin*
- *1/4 cup ground flaxseed*
- *2 tbsp ranch seasoning blend*

Directions:

✓ *Peel sweet potatoes and cut them into small pieces. Place in a food processor and pulse until the pieces are broken up.*

✓ *Next, pulse in the onion, cauliflower florets, and garlic until blended. Add the remaining ingredients and pulse until combined.*

✓ *Transfer the mixture to a bowl and shape it into seven 12 inch thick patties, each about 14 cups in size. Place the patties on a baking sheet and freeze for 10 minutes.*

✓ *Turn on the air fryer, insert the fryer basket, grease it with olive oil, cover it with the lid, and Preheat for 10 minutes at 400 degrees F.*

✓ *Preheat the fryer to 350°F, add the patties in a single layer, cover, and cook for 20 minutes, or until pleasantly golden and done, rotating the patties halfway through.*

✓ *When the air fryer beeps, remove the lid and transfer the patties to a serving plate to keep warm.*

✓ *Continue cooking the remaining patties in the same manner and serve. 85*

Nutrition: Calories : 2 g Carbohydrates 11 g fat 4 g protein 5 g

955) *Salad de Tacos Nutritious*

4 portions Time Required for Cooking: 10 Minutes

- *2 entire Romaine hearts, chopped*
- *1 pound lean minced beef*
- *1 whole avocado, cubed*
- *3 oz. grape tomatoes halved*
- *1/2 cup cheddar cheese, cubed*
- *2 tbsp. sliced red onion*
- *1/2 batch Salsa Mexicana Tangy*
- *1 teaspoon cumin powder*
- *Salt and pepper to taste*

Directions:

✓ *In a pan over medium heat, brown the ground meat. While the beef is cooking, break it up into little pieces. Stir in seasonings until well combined. Drain grease and set aside for approximately 5 minutes to cool.*

✓ *To begin assembling the salad, combine all ingredients in a large mixing dish. Toss to combine, then drizzle with dressing and toss again. If desired, garnish with reduced-fat sour cream and/or salsa.*

Nutrition: 449 Calories 9g Carbohydrates Total 4g Carbohydrates Net 4g Protein 40g Fat 22g Sugar 3g Fiber 5g

956) *Greens With Wilted Dandelion and Sweet Onion*

4 portions 12 Minutes Cooking

- *1 tablespoon extra-virgin olive oil*
- *1 Vidalia onion, thinly sliced*
- *2 garlic cloves, minced*
- *2 bunches of dandelion greens, roughly chopped*
- *1/2 cuplow-sodium vegetable broth*

Directions:

960) *Salad with Multiple Layers*

10 portions Time Required for Cooking:

- 6 bacon slices, diced and cooked crisp
- 2 tomatoes, diced
- 2 celery stalks, sliced
- 1 head romaine lettuce, diced
- 1 red bell pepper, diced
- 1 cup frozen peas, thawed
- 1 cup sharp cheddar cheese, grated
- What you'll require from the pantry
- 1 cup ranch dressing (fat-free)

Directions:

✓ Layer half of the lettuce, pepper, celery, tomatoes, peas, onion, cheese, bacon, and dressing in a 9x13-inch glass baking dish. Repeat. Serve immediately or cover and refrigerate until ready to serve.

Nutrition: Total Carbohydrates: 130 Calories 14g Net Carbohydrates: 12g Protein 6g Fat 6g Sugar 5g

961) *Potatoes Hasselback*

2 portions Time Required for Cooking: 40 Minutes

- 4 medium reddish potatoes, washed and drained
- 2 tbsp. melted butter
- 8 g parsley, freshly chopped

Directions:

✓ Scrub and wash potatoes. Allow them to dry on a paper towel.

✓ Slit the potatoes 6 mm apart, stopping just before they are entirely cut, so that all the slices are joined roughly 13 mm from the bottom of the potato.

✓ Preheat the air fryer to 175°C for 6 minutes.

✓ Drizzle olive oil over the potatoes and season with salt, black pepper, and garlic powder to taste.

✓ Place the potatoes in the air fryer and cook at 175°C for 30 minutes.

✓ Brush the potatoes with melted butter and continue cooking for a further 10 minutes at 175 ° C.

✓ Garnish with parsley, freshly chopped.

Nutrition: 415 Calories 42g fat 9g Carbohydrates 1 gram protein

962) *Noodles de beurrenut with sauce de champignons*

4 portions 15 Minutes Cooking 1/4 cup extra-virgin olive oil

- 12 red onion, coarsely chopped
- 1 pound (454 g) sliced cremini mushrooms
- 1 teaspoon dried thyme
- 1/2 teaspoon sea salt
- 3 minced garlic cloves
- 1 teaspoon crushed red pepper
- 4 cups butternut noodles
- 4 ounces (113 g) grated Parmesan cheese (optional)

Directions:

✓ In a large skillet, heat the olive oil over medium-high heat until shimmering.

✓ In a skillet, combine the onion, mushrooms, thyme, and salt. Cook, stirring periodically, for 6 minutes, or until the mushrooms begin to brown.

✓ Add the garlic and cook, constantly stirring, for 30 seconds, or until fragrant.

✓ Whisk in the wine and red pepper flakes.

✓ Add the butternut noodles to the skillet and simmer, turning periodically, for another 5 minutes, or until the noodles are softened.

✓ Distribute the mixture evenly between four bowls. If desired, sprinkle grated Parmesan cheese on top.

Nutrition: 243 Calories, 12g fat, 7g carbohydrates, 29g fiber, 1g sugar, 1g sodium, 157mg

963) *Salad Caprese*

4 portions Time Required for Cooking: 10 Minutes

- 3 medium tomatoes, sliced
- 2 (1-oz.) slices mozzarella cheese, cut into strips
- What you'll require from your pantry:
- 2 tbsp extra-virgin olive oil
- 1/8 tsp salt

Directions:

✓ On serving dishes, arrange tomatoes and cheese. Season with salt and pepper to taste. Drizzle oil over and sprinkle basil on top. Serve.

Nutrition: Calories 77 Carbohydrates 4 g protein, 5 g fat, 5 g sugar, 2 g dietary fiber, 1 g

964) *Soup with Asparagus and Avocado*

Time Required for Cooking: 20 Minutes

- 1 avocado, peeled, pitted, and cubed
- 12 ounces asparagus

- *1/2 teaspoon   crushed black pepper*
- *1 teaspoon garlic powder*
- *1 teaspoon sea salt*
- *2 tablespoons olive oil, divided*

Directions:

✓ *Turn on the air fryer, insert the frying basket, coat it with olive oil, cover it with the lid, and Preheat for 5 minutes at 425 degrees F.*

✓ *Meanwhile, in a shallow dish, spray asparagus with 1 teaspoon oil, season with garlic powder, salt, and black pepper, and toss until evenly coated.*

✓ *Uncover the fryer, add the asparagus, and cook for 10 minutes, shaking halfway through, until attractively browned and roasted.*

✓ *When the air fryer sounds, remove the lid and carefully transfer the asparagus to a food processor.*

✓ *In a food processor, combine the remaining ingredients and pulse until completely incorporated and smooth.*

✓ *Transfer the soup to a saucepan, add water if necessary, and simmer over medium-low heat for 5 minutes or until well heated.*

✓ *Ladle soup into serving dishes.*

Nutrition: 208 Calories Carbohydrates: 2 g 11 g fat 4 g protein 5 g fiber

965) *Broccoli With Garlic, Roasted*

3 portions Time Required for Cooking: 10 Minutes

- *1 large broccoli, cut into 5*
- *15 mL olive oil*
- *3 g salt*
- *1 g pepper*

Directions:

✓ *Preheat the air fryer to 500 degrees Fahrenheit for 5 minutes. Preheat the oven to 150°C.*

✓ *Drizzle olive oil over the broccoli pieces and toss to coat.*

✓ *Combine broccoli and seasonings in a large mixing bowl.*

✓ *Cook the broccoli for 5 minutes in the preheated air fryer at 1500C.*

Nutrition: 278 Calories2g fat 9g Carbohydrates 1 gram protein

966) *Asparagus And Red Peppers Roasted*

4 portions 15 Minutes Cooking

- *1 pound (454 g) asparagus, trimmed of woody ends and chopped into 2-inch segments*
- *2 seeded red bell peppers, chopped into 1-inch chunks*
- *1 quartered small onion*
- *2 tablespoons Italian dressing*

Directions:

✓ *Preheat the oven to 400 degrees Fahrenheit (205 degrees Celsius). Prepare a baking sheet by lining it with parchment paper.*

✓ *In a large mixing basin, combine the asparagus, peppers, onion, and dressing. Toss thoroughly.*

✓ *Arrange the vegetables in a single layer on the baking sheet and roast for approximately 15 minutes, or until tender. Using a spatula, flip the vegetables once during cooking.*

✓ *Transfer to a large serving platter and serve immediately.*

Nutrition 92 Calories, 8g fat, 9g protein, 10.7g carbohydrates, 0g fiber, 7g sugar, 31mg sodium

967) *Salad with Chopped Veggies*

4 portions 15 Minutes Cooking

- *1 cucumber, chopped*
- *1 pint cherry tomatoes, halved*
- *3 radishes, chopped*
- *1 yellow bell pepper, chopped*
- *What you'll require from your pantry:*
- *3 tbsp. lemon juice*
- *1 tbsp. olive oil*

Directions:

✓ *Toss together all ingredients in a large mixing bowl. Serve immediately or chill in the refrigerator until ready to serve.*

Nutrition: 70 Calories 9g Carbohydrates Net Carbohydrates 7g Protein 2g Fat 4g Sugar 5g Fiber 2g

968) *Fritters de Zucchini*

4 portions Time Required for Cooking: 10 Minutes

- *3 shredded zucchini*
- *2 eggs*
- *1 diced onion*

- *3/4 cups crumbled feta cheese*
- *1/4 cup chopped fresh dill*
- *1 tbsp. margarine What you'll require from your pantry:*
- *1/2 cup flour*
- *1 teaspoon salt*
- *freshly ground pepper*
- *frying oil*

Directions:

✓ *In a large colander, place zucchini and season with salt. Toss gently with your fingers and set aside for 30 minutes. Squeeze the extra water out with the back of the spoon. Squeeze the zucchini one more between paper towels. Arrange in a big basin and allow to dry.*

✓ *In a large skillet over medium-high heat, melt margarine. Cook until onion is tender, about 5 minutes. Combine the zucchini, feta, and dill in a large mixing bowl.*

✓ *Whisk together the flour and eggs in a small bowl. Pour over zucchini and toss thoroughly.*

✓ *Fill the skillet halfway with oil and heat over medium-high heat until extremely hot. Scoop zucchini mixture into oil using a golf ball-sized scoop and shape into a patty. Cook until both sides are golden brown. Transfer to a plate lined with paper towels.*

✓ *Garlic Dipping Sauce or other sauce of your choosing*

Nutrition: Calories 253 Carbohydrates Total 21g Carbohydrates Net 18 g Protein: 10g Fatty Acids 15g Sucrose 5g Fiber 3g

969) *Zucchini Balls Stuffed with Eggs*

4 portions Time Required for Cooking: 45-60 Minutes

- *2 zucchinis*
- *1 onion*
- *1 egg*
- *120g grated cheese*
- *Salt*
- *Ground pepper*

Directions:

✓ *Chop the zucchini and onion in the Thermomix for 10 seconds on speed 8, in the Cuisine for around 15 seconds on speed 10 with the kneader chopper, or we can chop the onion by hand and grate the zucchini.*

Whatever method you use, the key is to keep the zucchini and onion as small as possible.

✓ *In a bowl, combine the cheese and egg. Pepper and binding agents work well together.*

✓ *Gradually incorporate the flour until you have a very golden dough that is easily wrapped around the eggs.*

✓ *Cook and peel the eggs.*

✓ *Fold the zucchini dough over the eggs and pass through the flour.*

✓ *Oil the four balls and place them in the air fryer's basket.*

✓ *Preheat the oven to 1800C and bake for 45– 60 minutes, or until the balls are crispy on the outside.*

Nutrition: 23 Calories Carbohydrates: 2 g 11 g fat 4 g protein 15 g fiber

970) *Cauliflower "macaroni" And Cheese*

Time Required for Cooking: 50 Minutes

- *1 small head cauliflower, split into small florets*
- *1/2 cup shredded reduced-fat strong cheddar cheese — 1 cup low-fat milk*
- *1/2 cup chopped onion*
- *2 tbsp whole wheat flour*
- *2 tbsp whole wheat bread crumbs*
- *1 tsp olive oil*
- *1 tsp yellow mustard*
- *1/2 tsp garlic powder*
- *1/4 tsp salt 1/4 tsp black pepper*
- *Cooking spray with nonstick properties*

Directions:

✓ *Preheat the oven to 400 degrees Fahrenheit. Prepare a baking sheet by spraying it with cooking spray.*

✓ *Combine oil, salt, pepper, onion, and cauliflower in a medium bowl. Toss until the cauliflower is well coated. Distribute evenly on a baking sheet and bake for 25-30 minutes, or until gently browned.*

✓ *Melt 1/2 tbsps of margarine in a medium saucepan over medium heat. Add flour and whisk until no lumps remain.*

✓ *Add milk and stir continuously until the sauce thickens. Combine mustard, garlic powder, and cheese in a large mixing bowl until smooth and melted. Combine cauliflower in a large mixing bowl.*

✓ *Transfer to a 12-quart baking dish.*

✓ *Melt the remaining margarine in a small glass bowl in the microwave. Add bread crumbs and stir until moistened. Evenly sprinkle over cauliflower.*

✓ *Bake for 20 minutes, or until the top is bubbly and golden brown.*

Nutrition: Calories 154 Carbohydrates 15g Net Carbohydrates 12 g protein, 8 g fat, 8 g sugar, 4 g dietary fiber, 3 g

971) *Potatoes Roasted*

4 portions Time Required for Cooking: 20 Minutes

- *227g cleaned and halved tiny fresh potatoes*
- *30 ml olive oil*
- *3g salt*
- *1g black pepper*
- *2g garlic powder*
- *1 g dried thyme*

Directions:

✓ *For a few minutes, preheat the air fryer. Preheat the oven to 195°C.*

✓ *Drizzle half of the potatoes with olive oil and season with salt and pepper.*

✓ *Preheat the air fryer and add the potatoes. Establish a timer for 20 minutes. Shake the baskets frequently throughout the cooking process.*

Nutrition: 93 Calories 0.2g fat 9g Carbohydrates 1 gram protein

972) *Bowl of Roasted Brussels Sprouts with Wild Rice*

4 portions 12 Minutes Cooking

- *2 cups chopped Brussels sprouts*
- *2 tbsp plus*
- *2 tbsp extra-virgin olive oil*
- *1 tbsp Dijon mustard*
- *1 chopped garlic clove*
- *1/2 teaspoon salt*
- *1/4 teaspoon freshly ground black pepper*
- *1 cup sliced radishes*
- *1 cup cooked wild rice*

Directions:

✓ *Preheat the oven to 400 degrees Fahrenheit (205 degrees Celsius). Prepare a baking sheet by lining it with parchment paper.*

✓ *In a medium dish, combine 2 teaspoons olive oil and Brussels sprouts; toss to coat well.*

✓ *Arrange the oiled Brussels sprouts in a single layer on the prepared baking sheet. Roast for 12 minutes, or until the Brussels sprouts are browned and crisp, in the Preheated oven. Once throughout the cooking process, stir the Brussels sprouts to achieve even cooking.*

✓ *Meanwhile, mix together the remaining olive oil, mustard, lemon juice, garlic, salt, and pepper in a small bowl to make the dressing.*

✓ *Transfer the Brussels sprouts to a large bowl from the oven. To the bowl, add the radishes and cooked wild rice. Drizzle with prepared dressing and toss lightly to coat evenly.*

✓ *Divide the mixture evenly between four bowls and top with avocado slices. Serve right away.*

177 Nutrition: Calories fat: 10.7g protein: 3g carbohydrates: 17.6g fiber: 1g sugar: 0g sodium: 297mg

973) *Mushrooms with Garlic*

4 portions 12 Minutes Cooking

- *1 tablespoon butter*
- *2 tablespoons extra-virgin olive oil*
- *2 pounds (907 g) split button mushrooms*
- *2 teaspoons minced fresh garlic*
- *1 teaspoon chopped fresh thyme*

Directions:

✓ *In a large skillet over medium-high heat, melt the butter and olive oil.*

✓ *Add the mushrooms and sauté for 10 minutes, or until gently browned and cooked through.*

✓ *Cook for a further 2 minutes, stirring in the garlic and thyme.*

✓ *Season with salt and pepper to taste and arrange on a serving platter.*

Nutrition: Calories 96 fat 6.1g protein 6.9g carbohydrates 8.2g fiber 7g sugar 9g sodium 91mg

974) *Sandwiches with Tofu Salad*

4 portions Time Required for Cooking: 20 Minutes

- *1 package pressed silken firm tofu*
- *4 lettuce leaves*
- *2 sliced green onions*

- *1/4 cup diced celery*
- *What you'll require from your pantry:*
- *8 slices bread*
- *1/4 cup light mayonnaise*
- *2 tablespoons sweet pickle relish*
- *1 tablespoon Dijon mustard*
- *1/4 teaspoon   turmeric*
- *1/4 teaspoon   salt*
- *1/8 teaspoon cayenne pepper*

Directions:
- ✓ *For 15 minutes, press tofu between layers of paper towels to remove extra moisture. Reduce to little cubes.*
- ✓ *In a medium mixing bowl, combine the remaining ingredients. Tofu should be folded in. Distribute evenly between four slices of bread. Add a lettuce leaf and another slice of bread on the top. Serve.*

Nutrition: 378 Calories Carbohydrates in total 15g Carbohydrates in net 13g Protein 24g Fat 20g Sugar 2g Fiber 2g

975) *Brussels Sprouts with Roasted Tomatoes*

4 portions Time Required for Cooking: 20 Minutes

- *1 pound (454 g) trimmed and halved Brussels sprouts*
- *1 tablespoon extra-virgin olive oil, sea salt, and freshly ground black pepper to taste*
- *1/2 cup chopped sun-dried tomatoes 2 tablespoons freshly squeezed lemon juice*
- *1 teaspoon lemon zest*

Directions:
- ✓ *Preheat the oven to 400 degrees Fahrenheit (205 degrees Celsius). Aluminium foil a large baking sheet.*
- ✓ *In a large bowl, toss the Brussels sprouts in the olive oil until completely coated. Season with salt and pepper to taste.*
- ✓ *Arrange the seasoned Brussels sprouts in a single layer on the prepared baking sheet.*
- ✓ *Roast, shaking the pan halfway through, for 20 minutes, or until the Brussels sprouts are crispy and browned on the outside.*
- ✓ *Transfer to a serving bowl from the oven. Stir in the tomatoes, lemon juice, and lemon zest. Serve right away.*

Nutrition: 111 Calories; 8g protein; 17g carbohydrates; 9g fiber; 7g sugar; 103mg sodium

976) *Fritters de beurre noisette*

6 portions 15 Minutes Cooking

- *5 cup shredded butternut squash*
- *2 big eggs*
- *1 tbsp finely sliced fresh sage*
- *What you'll require from your pantry:*
- *2/3 cup flour*
- *2 tbsp. olive oil*

Directions:
- ✓ *In a large skillet, heat oil over medium-high heat.*
- ✓ *In a large mixing basin, combine squash, eggs, sage, and season to taste with salt and pepper. Incorporate flour.*
- ✓ *Drop 1/4 cup mixture into skillet, leaving at least 1 inch between fritters. Cook until both sides are golden brown, about 2 minutes per side.*
- ✓ *Transfer to a dish lined with paper towels. Repeat. Serve immediately with a dipping sauce of your choice.*

Nutrition: 164 Calories 24g Carbohydrates 21g Protein 4g Fat 6g Sugar 3g Fiber

977) *Stroganoff in the Crock-Pot*

2 portions Time Required for Cooking: 2 Hours

- *8 cups quartered mushrooms*
- *1 onion, split and thinly sliced*
- *4 tbsp. chopped fresh parsley*
- *1/2 tbsp. low-fat sour cream*
- *What you'll require from your pantry:*
- *1 cup vegetable broth with a low salt content*
- *3 garlic cloves, finely chopped*
- *2 tsp paprika smoky*
- *Season with salt and pepper to taste*

Directions:
- ✓ *In a crockpot, combine all ingredients except sour cream and parsley.*
- ✓ *Cover and cook for 2 hours on high.*
- ✓ *Gently fold in sour cream and sprinkle with parsley.*

Nutrition: 111 Calories Carbohydrates Total 18g Carbohydrates Net 14g Protein 10g Fat 2g Sugar 8g Fiber 4g

978) *Orange Tofu 4 pcs*

Time Required for Cooking: 2 Hours

- *1 package extra-firm tofu, pounded for at least 15 minutes, and cubed*
- *1 tablespoon margarine*
- *What you'll require from your pantry:*
- *1/4 cup orange juice*
- *1/4 cup soy sauce with reduced sodium*
- *1/4 cup honey*
- *2 minced garlic cloves*

Directions:

✓ *In a medium skillet over medium-high heat, melt butter. Cook, stirring periodically until tofu begins to brown, about 5-10 minutes. Transfer to a slow cooker.*

✓ *In a small bowl, whisk together the wet ingredients. Pour over the tofu and sprinkle with broccoli.*

✓ *Cover and cook for 90 minutes on high or 2 hours on low.*

✓ *Garnish with cauliflower rice*

Nutrition: Calories 137 Carbohydrates 24g Net Carbohydrates 22g Protein 4g Fatty Acids 4g Sucrose 20g dietary fiber 2 g

979) *Pomegranate & Sprouts Salad*

6 portions Time Required for Cooking: 10 Minutes

- *3 slices bacon, cooked crisp and crumbled*
- *3 cup shredded Brussels sprouts*
- *3 cup shredded kale*
- *1/2 cup pomegranate seeds*
- *What you'll require from your pantry:*
- *1/2 cup toasted and chopped almonds*
- *1/4 cup reduced-fat parmesan cheese, grated*
- *Vinaigrette de Citrus*

Directions:

✓ *In a large mixing bowl, combine all ingredients.*

✓ *Drizzle vinaigrette over salad and toss to coat evenly with dressing. Garnish with additional cheese if desired.*

Nutrition: 256 Calories 15g Carbohydrates Total 15g Carbohydrates Net 10g Protein 9g Fat 18g Sugar 5g Fiber 5g

980) *Provolone-Crustd Vegetables*

4 portions 30 Minutes Cooking

- *1 400-gram bag frozen tempura veggies*
- *Extra-virgin olive oil*

- *Salt*
- *1 slice provolone cheese*

Directions:

✓ *Arrange the vegetables in the air fryer's basket. Close with a few strands of extra virgin olive oil.*

✓ *Set the timer for 20 minutes at 2000C.*

✓ *Transfer the veggies to a clay pot and sprinkle with provolone cheese.*

✓ *Bake at 1800C for approximately 10 minutes or until the cheese has melted to your taste.*

Nutrition: 104 Calories Carbohydrates: 2 g 11 g fat 4 g protein 0 g fiber

981) *Wedges de Pommes*

4 portions Time Required for Cooking: 20 Minutes

- *2 large thick potatoes, rinsed and sliced into 102 mm long wedges*
- *23 ml olive oil*
- *1 teaspoon onion powder*
- *3 g salt*
- *1 g black pepper*
- *5 g grated Parmesan cheese*

Directions:

✓ *Cut the potatoes lengthwise into 102 mm pieces.*

✓ *Preheat the air fryer to 500 degrees Fahrenheit for 5 minutes. Preheat the oven to 195°C.*

✓ *Drizzle olive oil over the potatoes and toss with the seasonings and Parmesan cheese until fully coated.*

✓ *Preheat the frying and add the potatoes. Establish a timer for 20 minutes.*

✓ *Be sure to shake the baskets periodically throughout the cooking process.*

Nutrition: 156 Calories 8.01g fat 20.33g Carbohydrates 98g protein 0.33g sugar 0mg cholesterol

982) *Crispy Tofu with Chili Garlic Noodles*

8 portions 15 Minutes Cooking

- *1 pound extremely firm tofu, cut into 1-inch slices and pressed for 30 minutes*
- *3 green onions, sliced and separated white from green*
- *1 bell pepper, thinly sliced*

- *1 medium carrot, thinly sliced*
- *What you'll require from your pantry:*
- *1 homemade pasta recipe, cooked and drained*
- *12 garlic cloves, finely chopped*
- *3 tbsp. light soy sauce*
- *3 tbsp. oyster sauce*
- *2 tbsp. red chili paste*
- *2 tbsp. cornstarch, plus additional as needed*
- *2 tbsp. sunflower oil*
- *1 tbsp. fish sauce*
- *1 tsp Splenda*

Direction

- ✓ *Stir together soy sauce, oyster sauce, chili paste, fish sauce, and Splenda in a small bowl.*
- ✓ *In a medium bowl, crumble tofu. Toss in cornstarch until nicely coated.*
- ✓ *In a large skillet, heat oil over medium-high heat. Cook until tofu is golden and crispy, breaking it up as it cooks. Transfer to a serving dish.*
- ✓ *Add additional oil to the skillet if necessary and sauté carrots and bell pepper for about 3 minutes, or until they begin to soften. Combine with tofu.*
- ✓ *Add the garlic and white sections of the onions and sauté, constantly stirring, for 30 seconds. Cook for 2 minutes, or until sauce coats the back of a spoon.*
- ✓ *Combine the pasta, tofu, and vegetables. To coat, stir well. Chili flakes may be sprinkled on top. Garnish with onion greens, sesame seeds, and cilantro.*

Nutrition: 24g Protein 23g Fat 12g Sugar 12g Fiber 4g Calories 266 Total Carbohydrates 26g Net Carbohydrates 24g Protein 23g Fat 12g Sugar 12g Fiber 4g

983) *Slaw in the Asian Style*

8 portions Time Required for Cooking: 2 Hours

- *1 pound bag coleslaw mix*
- *5 sliced onions*
- *What you'll require from your pantry:*
- *1 cup sliced sunflower seeds*
- *1 cup sliced almonds*
- *3 oz. ramen noodles, broken*
- *3/4 cup vegetable oil*

- *1/2 cup Splenda*

Directions:

- ✓ *Combine coleslaw, sunflower seeds, almonds, and scallions in a large mixing basin.*
- ✓ *In a large measuring cup, whisk together the oil, vinegar, and Splenda. Pour dressing over salad and toss to mix.*
- ✓ *Stir in ramen noodles and refrigerate for 2 hours.*

Nutrition: 354 Calories 24g Carbohydrates Total 24g Carbohydrates Net 21g Protein 5g Fat 26g Sugar 10g Fiber 3g

984) *Pasta with Garden Vegetables*

30 Minutes Cooking Servings: 6

- *2 lbs. halved fresh cherry tomatoes*
- *2 zucchini, chopped*
- *2 ears corn, kernels removed from the cob*
- *1 yellow squash, diced*
- *1/2 cup grated mozzarella cheese*
- *1/2 cup thinly sliced fresh basil*
- *What you'll require from your pantry:*
- *Made-at-home pasta, cooked and drained*
- *5 tbsp. olive oil, divided*
- *2 crushed garlic cloves*
- *Crushed red pepper flakes to taste*

Directions:

- ✓ *In a large skillet over medium heat, heat 3 tablespoons of oil. Combine the garlic and tomatoes. Cook 15 minutes, covered, on low heat, stirring constantly.*
- ✓ *Heat remaining oil in a separate skillet over med-high heat. Combine zucchini, squash, and corn in a medium bowl. Reduce to medium heat and continue cooking until vegetables are soft. Season with salt.*
- ✓ *Preheat the oven to 400 degrees Fahrenheit.*
- ✓ *Toss tomato mixture, veggies, and pasta together in a large bowl. Fill a 9x13-inch baking dish halfway with the mixture and sprinkle with cheese. Bake for 10 minutes, or until cheese begins to melt and color. Serve.*

Nutrition: Calories 347 Carbohydrates Total 31g Carbohydrates Net 24g Protein 21g Fat 18g Sugar 13g Fiber 7g

985) *Teriyaki Tofu Burgers*

15 Minutes Cooking

- 2 3 oz. extra-firm tofu chunks, squeezed between paper towels fifteen minutes
- 14 sliced red onions
- 2 tbsp grated carrots
- 1 tbsp margarine
- What you'll require from your pantry:
- 2 sandwich thins made entirely of whole wheat
- 1 tbsp. teriyaki marinade
- 1 tbsp. Sriracha
- 1 tsp red chili flakes

Directions:

✓ Preheat the grill or charcoal grill to a medium temperature.

✓ Tofu should be marinated in teriyaki sauce, red chili flakes, and Sriracha.

✓ In a small skillet over medium-high heat, melt margarine. Cook until onions are caramelized, about 5 minutes.

✓ Grill tofu on each side for 3-4 minutes.

✓ To construct, lay tofu in the center of the bottom roll. Add lettuce, carrots, and onion to the top. Serve with the roll's top.

Nutrition: Calories 178 Carbohydrates 27g Net Carbohydrates 20g Protein 12 g fat 5 g sugar 5 g dietary fiber 7g

986) *Curry with Tofu*

Time Required for Cooking: 2 Hours Servings: 4

- 2 cup diced green bell pepper
- 1 cup cubed firm tofu
- 1 onion, peeled and sliced
- What you'll require from your pantry:
- 1/2 cup canned coconut milk
- 1 cup tomato paste
- 2 garlic cloves, finely sliced
- 2 tablespoons raw peanut butter
- 1 tablespoon garam masala
- 1 tablespoon curry powder
- 1/2 teaspoon salt

Directions:

✓ In a blender or food processor, combine all ingredients except the tofu. Process until completely incorporated.

✓ Transfer to a slow cooker and add the tofu.

Cover and cook for 2 hours on high.

✓ Season with salt and pepper to taste and serve over cauliflower rice.

Nutrition: 389 Calories 28g Carbohydrates Total 20g Carbohydrates Net 20g Protein 13g Fat 28g Sugar 16g Fiber 8g

987) *Counterfeit Chow Mein*

4 portions Time Required for Cooking: 20 Minutes

- 1 big spaghetti squash, half and seeds removed
- 3 celery stalks, sliced diagonally
- 2 cup Coleslaw dressing
- 2 tsp grated fresh ginger
- What you'll require from your pantry:
- 1/4 cup Tamari
- 3 minced garlic cloves
- 3-4 tablespoons water
- 2 tablespoons olive oil
- 1 tablespoon Splenda
- 1/4 teaspoon pepper

Directions:

✓ In a shallow glass dish, place squash cut side down and add water. 8-10 minutes on high, or until squash is tender. Scoop the squash into a bowl using a fork.

✓ Whisk together Tamari, garlic, sugar, ginger, and pepper in a small bowl.

✓ In a large skillet, heat oil over medium-high heat. Cook, often stirring, for 3-4 minutes. Cook until the coleslaw is cooked through, about 1 minute.

✓ Gently whisk in the squash and sauce mixture. Cook for 2 minutes, frequently stirring. Serve.

Nutrition: Calories 129 Carbohydrates 13g Net Carbohydrates 11g Protein 3 g fat 7 g sugar 6 g dietary fiber 2 g

988) *Soup With Roasted Tomatoes And Bell Peppers*

6 portions Time Required for Cooking: 35 Minutes

- 2 tablespoons extra-virgin olive oil, plus additional for coating the baking dish
- 16 plum tomatoes, cored and split
- 4 celery stalks, coarsely chopped
- 4 red bell peppers, seeded and halved
- 6 cups low-sodium chicken broth

- *2 tablespoons chopped fresh basil*
- *2 ounces (57 g) shredded goat cheese*

Directions:

✓ *Preheat the oven to 400 degrees Fahrenheit (205 degrees Celsius). Lightly coat a large baking dish with olive oil.*

✓ *Arrange the tomatoes cut-side down in the greased dish. On top of the tomatoes, scatter the celery, bell peppers, garlic, and onion. Season with salt and pepper. Drizzle with 2 tablespoons olive oil.*

✓ *Roast for approximately 30 minutes in the Preheated oven or until the veggies are fork-tender and slightly browned.*

✓ *Turn off the oven and remove the vegetables. Allow a few minutes for them to cool slightly.*

✓ *Transfer to a food processor along with the chicken broth and purée until smooth and completely combined.*

✓ *Transfer the puréed soup to a medium saucepan and heat over medium-high heat to a boil.*

✓ *Just before serving, sprinkle the basil and grated cheese on top.*

Nutrition: 187 Calories: 9.7g fat; 7.8g carbohydrate: 23g fiber; 6.1g sugar; 10g sodium: 825mg

989) *Macaroni And Cheese Creamy*

6 portions Time Required for Cooking: 25 Minutes

- *1 cup fat-free evaporated milk*
- *1/2 cup skim milk*
- *1/2 cuplow-fat Cheddar cheese*
- *1/2 cuplow-fat cottage cheese*
- *1 teaspoon nutmeg*
- *pinch cayenne pepper*
- *sea salt and freshly ground black pepper, to taste*

Directions:

✓ *Preheat the oven to 350 degrees Fahrenheit (180 degrees Celsius).*

✓ *In a large saucepan over low heat, cook the milk until it steams.*

✓ *Whisk in the Cheddar and cottage cheese until the cheese is melted.*

✓ *Stir in the nutmeg and cayenne pepper. Season with salt and pepper to taste.*

✓ *Take the pan off the heat. Stir the cooked macaroni into the cheese mixture until evenly distributed. Place the macaroni and*

cheese in a large casserole dish and sprinkle with shredded Parmesan cheese.

✓ *Bake for approximately 20 minutes, or until bubbling and gently browned.*

✓ *Serve the macaroni and cheese in six bowls.*

Nutrition: Calories: 245 fat: 1 g protein: 17 g carbohydrates: 48 g fiber: 8 g sugar: 6.8 g sodium: 186mg

990) *Peas and Creamy Pasta*

4 portions Time Required for Cooking: 10 Minutes

- *4 deseeded and diced tomatoes*
- *4 oz. fat-free cream cheese*
- *1 cup frozen peas*
- *1/2 cup skim milk*
- *4 tbsp. fresh parsley, diced*
- *What you'll require from your pantry:*
- *12 homemade pasta recipes, cooked and drained*
- *4 garlic cloves, finely chopped*
- *3 tablespoons olive oil*
- *1 teaspoon oregano*
- *1 teaspoon basil*
- *1/2 teaspoon   garlic salt*

Directions:

✓ *In a large skillet over medium heat, heat oil. Cook for 3-4 minutes, often stirring, adding garlic and tomatoes.*

✓ *Combine peas, milk, cream cheese, and seasonings in a medium bowl. Cook, occasionally stirring, for 5 minutes, or until cream cheese melts.*

✓ *Toss in pasta to coat. Garnish with parsley and serve.*

Nutrition: 332 Calories Carbohydrates Total 19g Carbohydrates Net 14g Protein 14g Fat 23g Sugar 10g Fiber 5g

991) *Cauliflower Roasted with Tomatoes*

4 portions Time Required for Cooking: 45 Minutes

- *1 large head cauliflower, divided into florets*
- *3 sliced scallions*
- *1 finely diced onion*
- *From the store cupboard, you'll require the following:*
- *15 oz. can petite tomatoes, diced*

- *4 tbsp. extra virgin olive oil, divided*
- *1 tablespoon red wine vinegar*
- *1 tablespoon balsamic vinegar*
- *3 teaspoon Splenda*
- *1 teaspoon salt*
- *1 teaspoon pepper*
- *1/2 teaspoon chili powder*

Directions:

✓ *Preheat the oven to 400 degrees Fahrenheit.*

✓ *Arrange cauliflower in a single layer on a large baking sheet. Drizzle with 2 tablespoons of oil. Season to taste with salt and pepper. Rub oil and spice into florets with your hands, then arrange in a single layer. Roast until tender with a fork.*

✓ *In a large skillet over medium-low heat, heat 1 tablespoon oil. Cook until the onion is tender.*

✓ *Add tomatoes, juice, Splenda, both kinds of vinegar, and salt to taste. Bring to a boil, then reduce to low heat and continue cooking for 20-25 minutes. Use an immersion blender to puree the sauce until smooth, or leave it lumpy.*

✓ *In a separate skillet over med-low heat, heat the remaining oil and sauté garlic for 1-2 minutes. Increase heat to medium-high and stir in tomato sauce. Cook for 5 minutes, stirring frequently. Toss in the chili powder and cauliflower. Serve with scallions on top.*

Nutrition: Calories 107 Carbohydrates 23g Carbohydrates Net 16g 6g protein 0g fat 12g sugar 7g dietary fiber

992) *Avocados fried*

2 portions Time Required for Cooking: 10 Minutes

- *2 avocados, cut into 25 mm thick wedges*
- *50g Pan crumbs bread*
- *2g garlic powder*
- *2g onion powder*
- *1g smoked paprika*
- *1g cayenne pepper*
- *Salt and pepper to taste*
- *Spray Oil for Nonstick Surfaces*
- *To serve, tomato sauce or ranch sauce*

Directions:

✓ *Halve the avocados and cut them into 25 mm thick slices.*

✓ *In a large mixing bowl, combine the breadcrumbs, garlic powder, onion powder, smoked paprika, cayenne pepper, and salt.*

✓ *Dredge each avocado wedge in flour, then dip in beaten eggs and swirl in breadcrumb mixture.*

✓ *Preheat the air fryer to 350 degrees Fahrenheit.*

✓ *Arrange the avocados in the prepared air fryer baskets and coat them with oil spray. Cook for 10 minutes at 205°C. Halfway through cooking, turn the fried avocado over and drizzle with cooking oil.*

Nutrition: 123 Calories Carbohydrates: 2 g 11 g fat 4 g protein 0 g fiber

993) *French Toast*

15 Minutes Cooking 8 pcs.

- *500g flour*
- *25 g oil*
- *300 g water*
- *25g fresh bread yeast*
- *12g salt*
- *Milk and cinnamon or milk and sweet wine for French toast*
- *Honey*
- *Eggs*

Directions:

✓ *Begin by making bread the day before. Add the bread ingredients to the Master Chef Gourmet and knead for 1 minute at high speed. Allow the dough to rest for 1 hour before kneading for 1 minute at speed Divide the dough into four equal parts. Construct a ball and stretch it out like a pizza. Roll into a small loaf of bread and allow it to rise for about an hour.*

✓ *Transfer to the oven and bake for 40 minutes at 2000 degrees Celsius. Allow the bread to cool on a rack and store for the following day. Slice the bread and set it aside.*

✓ *Prepare the milk to moisten the bread slices.*

✓ *To begin, heat the milk, 500 mL or so, with a cinnamon stick, or the same amount of milk with a glass of sweet wine, as desired.*

✓ *When the milk begins to boil, remove from the heat and allow it cool.*

✓ *Whisk the eggs.*

✓ *Place a rack on a plate and dip the bread slices in the cool milk, then in the beaten egg. Transfer the bread slices to the rack with the plate beneath to drain any extra liquid.*

✓ *Place the bread pieces in the bucket of the air fryer in batches, not heaped high, and heat to 180 degrees for 10 minutes per batch.*

✓ *Once all of the slices have been fried in the air fryer, place the honey in a casserole, around 500g, together with 1 small glass of water and 4 teaspoons of sugar. Reduce the heat to low and slide the bread slices through the honey.*

✓ *10. Place in a fountain and drizzle the remaining honey on top, soaking the French toast once more. Prepare our French toast; after cooled, they are ready to consume.*

Nutrition: 224 Calories 12g fat 17.39g Carbohydrates 81g protein 76g sugar 84mg cholesterol

994) *Yams with a buttery orange flavor*

8 portions Time Required for Cooking: 45 Minutes

- *2 medium gem yams, sliced into 2-inch dices*
- *2 tablespoons unsalted butter*
- *1 large orange juice*
- *1 1/2 teaspoon s ground cinnamon*
- *1/4 teaspoon ground ginger*
- *34 teaspoon ground nutmeg*

Directions:

✓ *Preheat the oven to 350 degrees Fahrenheit (180 degrees Celsius).*

✓ *Arrange the yam dices in a single layer on a rimmed baking sheet. Place aside.*

✓ *In a medium saucepan over medium-low heat, combine the butter, orange juice, cinnamon, ginger, nutmeg, and garlic cloves. Cook, constantly stirring, for 3 to 5 minutes, or until the sauce begins to thicken and boil.*

✓ *Drizzle the sauce over the yams and toss well to coat.*

✓ *Bake for 40 minutes, or until tender, in the preheated oven.*

✓ *Allow the yams to cool on the baking pan for 8 minutes before removing and serving.*

Nutrition 129 Calories, 8g fat, 27g carbohydrates, 0g fiber, 9g sugar, 28mg sodium

995) *Burger with Grilled Portobello and Zucchini*

Time Required for Cooking: 10 Minutes Servings: 2

- *2 large portobello mushroom caps*
- *½ tiny sliced zucchini*
- *2 slices low-fat cheese*
- *Spinach What you'll require from your pantry:*
- *2 sandwich thins made entirely of whole wheat*
- *2 tsp roasted red bell peppers*
- *2 tsp olive oil*

Directions:

✓ *Preheat the grill or charcoal grill to a med-high setting.*

✓ *Brush lightly with olive oil on the mushroom caps. Grill mushroom caps and zucchini slices for about 3-4 minutes per side, or until soft.*

✓ *Arrange on a thin sandwich. Add sliced cheese, roasted red bell pepper, and spinach as garnishes. Serve.*

Nutrition: 177 Calories 26g Carbohydrates Protein 15g Fat 3g Sugar 3g Fiber 8g

996) *Spring Peas with Tarragon*

12 Minutes Cooking Servings: 6

- *1 tablespoon unsalted butter*
- *12 thinly sliced Vidalia onions*
- *1 cup low-sodium vegetable broth*
- *3 cup fresh shelled peas*
- *1 tablespoon minced fresh tarragon*

Directions:

✓ *In a skillet over medium heat, melt the butter.*

✓ *Cook the onion in the melted butter for approximately 3 minutes, stirring periodically, until transparent.*

✓ *Whisk in the veggie broth. Combine the peas and tarragon in the skillet.*

✓ *Reduce to low heat, cover, and continue cooking for approximately 8 minutes longer, or until the peas are soft.*

✓ *Allow 5 minutes for the peas to cool slightly before serving heated.*

Nutrition: Calories: 82 fat: 1 g protein: 2 g carbohydrates: 10 g fiber: 8 g sugar: 9 g sodium: 48mg

997) *Potatoes Infused with Provencal Herbs & Cheddar*

4 portions Time Required for Cooking: 20 Minutes

- 1 kilogram of potatoes
- 1 kilogram of Provencal herbs
- 1 kilogram of extra virgin olive oil
- 1 kilogram of salt
- 1 kilogram of grated cheese

Directions:

✓ Peel the potatoes, cut the cane salt into small pieces, and sprinkle with Provencal herbs.

✓ Place in the basket and add a few extra virgin olive oil strands.

✓ Preheat the air fryer to 1800C, 20 minutes.

✓ Remove and transfer to a big plate.

✓ Place cheese on a cover.

✓ Microwave or bake for a few minutes or until the cheese has melted.

Nutrition: 437 Calories 0.6g fat 219g Carbohydrates 1 gram protein g sugar 0mg cholesterol

998) *Wedges of Spiced Potato*

4 portions Time Required for Cooking: 40 Minutes 8 medium potatoes

- Sea salt
- Ground pepper
- Garlic powder
- Aromatic herbs, our personal favorite
- 2 tbsp. extra virgin olive oil

Directions:

✓ In a saucepan, combine the unpeeled potatoes, boiling water, and a pinch of salt.

✓ Cook for 5 minutes. Drain and set aside to cool. Without peeling, cut into thick slices.

✓ Place the potatoes in a bowl and season with salt, pepper, garlic powder, oil, and breadcrumbs or chickpea flour.

✓ Stir thoroughly and set aside for 15 minutes. Transfer to the air fryer basket and set the timer to 20 minutes at 1800C.

✓ Shake the basket occasionally to mix and reposition the potatoes. Verify that they are still delicate.

Nutrition: 123 Calories 2 g Carbohydrates 11 g Fat 4 g protein 0 g fiber

999) *Delicata Squash Roasted with Thyme*

4 portions Time Required for Cooking: 20 Minutes

- 1 delicate squash (1 to 112 pounds / 454 to 680 g), split, seeded, and cut into 12-inch-thick strips
- 1 tablespoon extra-virgin olive oil
- 1/2 teaspoon dried thyme
- 1/4 teaspoon salt

Directions:

✓ Preheat the oven to 400 degrees Fahrenheit (205 degrees Celsius). Prepare a baking sheet by lining it with parchment paper.

✓ In a large mixing bowl, combine the squash strips, olive oil, thyme, salt, and pepper. Toss until the squash strips are completely coated.

✓ Arrange the squash strips in a single layer on the prepared baking sheet. Roast for approximately 20 minutes, or until the strips are gently browned, rotating halfway through.

✓ Remove from oven and arrange on serving plates.

Nutrition 78 Calories; 2g fat; 1g protein; 18g carbohydrate; 1g fiber; 9g sugar; 122mg sodium

1000) *Beans, green*

4 portions 13 Minutes Cooking

- 1 pound green beans
- ¾ tsp garlic powder
- ¾ tsp ground black pepper
- 1 1/4 tsp salt
- 1/2 tsp paprika

Directions:

✓ Turn on the air fryer, insert the fryer basket, coat it with olive oil, cover it with the lid, and Preheat for 5 minutes at 400 degrees F.

✓ Meanwhile, in a bowl, spray beans well with olive oil, season with garlic powder, black pepper, salt, and paprika, and toss to coat.

✓ Uncover the skillet, add the green beans, and cook for 8 minutes, shaking halfway through the cooking.

✓ When the air fryer sounds, open the top and transfer the green beans to a serving plate.

Nutrition: 45 Calories 2 g Carbohydrates 11 g Fat 4 g Protein 3 g fiber

1001) *Garlic & Black Pepper Tofu*

4 portions Time Required for Cooking: 40 Minutes

- 14 oz. package extra firm tofu
- 1 lb. asparagus, trimmed and chopped into 1-inch pieces
- 8 oz. kale, stems removed, and leaves sliced
- 3 oz. shiitake mushrooms, sliced
- 1 sliced green bell pepper
- What you'll require from your pantry:
- 1/2 cuplow sodium vegetable broth
- 8 garlic cloves, squeezed and divided
- 2 1/2 tbsp light soy sauce, divided
- 2 -4 tbsp water
- 2 tsp cornstarch
- 2 tsp freshly ground black pepper, divided
- 1 tsp rice vinegar

Directions:

- ✓ Preheat the oven to 400 degrees Fahrenheit. Preheat the oven to 350°F. Line a baking sheet with parchment paper.
- ✓ Slice the tofu into 12-inch slices and press between paper towels to absorb excess moisture. Each slice should be cut into smaller rectangles.
- ✓ Combine 1 tablespoon soy sauce, 1 tablespoon water, 2 tablespoons garlic, 2 tablespoons rice vinegar, and 1 teaspoon pepper in a Ziploc bag. Turn to coat the tofu. Allow 15 minutes for marinating.
- ✓ Arrange the tofu in a single layer on the prepared pan and bake for 15 minutes. Bake for a further 15 minutes on the other side. Take out of the oven.
- ✓ In a large nonstick skillet, heat the oil over medium-high heat. Cook, often stirring, until the onion is transparent. Add bell pepper and cook for an additional minute.
- ✓ Add the garlic and mushrooms and cook for an additional 2 minutes, adding a splash of water if the veggies begin to stick.
- ✓ Cover and stir in the kale and 2 tablespoons of water. Allow to cook for 1 minute, then whisk and add additional water if necessary. Cook, covered, for a further minute before adding the asparagus and cooking, occasionally tossing, until the asparagus is tender-crisp.
- ✓ Combine the remaining soy sauce, broth, Sriracha, cornstarch, and pepper in a small bowl. Pour over vegetables and continue cooking until vegetables are heated thoroughly.
- ✓ To serve, arrange the veggies on a platter and top with the tofu.

Nutrition: 176 Calories 33g Carbohydrates Net Carbohydrates 27g Protein 16g Fat 4g Sugar 12g Fiber 6g

30-DAY MEAL PLAN

DAY	BREAKFAST	LUNCH	SNACKS	DINNER
1	Spinach Scramble	Chorizo and Beef Burger	Mini Apple Oat Muffins	Awesome Chicken Enchilada Soup
2	Asparagus & Cheese Omelet	Crispy Brats	Dark Chocolate Almond Yogurt Cups	Vegan Cream Soup with Avocado & Zucchini
3	Granola with Fruits	Classic Mini Meatloaf	Cinnamon Spiced Popcorn	Chinese Tofu Soup
4	Breakfast Parfait	Bacon Cheeseburger Casserole	Peanut Butter Banana "Ice Cream"	Cherry Apple Pork
5	Apple & Cinnamon Pancake	Pulled Pork	Grilled Peaches	Pork Chops and Cabbage
6	Yogurt Breakfast Pudding	Taco-Stuffed Peppers	Cinnamon Toasted Almonds	Curried Shrimp & Green Bean Soup
7	Sausage, Egg & Potatoes	Italian Stuffed Bell Peppers	Grain-Free Berry Cobbler	Carnitas
8	Cucumber & Yogurt	Easy Juicy Pork Chops	Pumpkin Spice Snack Balls	Maple Glazed Pork
9	Banana &Spinach Smoothie Bowl	Bacon-Wrapped Hot Dog	Strawberry Lime Pudding	Air Fryer Roast Beef
10	Almond & Berry Smoothie	Baby Back Ribs	Garden Wraps	Root Beer Pork
11	Vegetable Omelet	Crock-Pot Slow Cooker Chicken & Sweet Potatoes	Party Shrimp	Pork Rind
12	Bulgur Porridge	Crock-Pot Slow Cooker Tex-Mex Chicken	Whole-Wheat Pumpkin Muffins	Air Fryer Bacon
13	Mixed Berries Smoothie Bowl	Slow-Cooker Chicken Fajita Burritos	Strawberry Salsa	Air Fryer Beef Empanadas
14	Buckwheat Porridge	Crock Pot Chicken Cacciatore	Garlic-Sesame Pumpkin Seeds	Almond Crustd Baked Chili Mahi
15	Pumpkin Oatmeal	Crock-Pot Buffalo Chicken Dip	Roasted Eggplant Spread	Marinated Loin Potatoes
16	Quinoa Porridge	Crock-Pot Slow Cooker Ranch Chicken	Zucchini Mini Pizzas	Pork Fillets with Serrano Ham
17	Tempeh & Veggie Hash	Polynesian Chicken	Party Spiced Cheese Chips	Pork Fillets with Serrano Ham
18	Tofu & Zucchini Muffins	Coconut Chicken	Asparagus & Chorizo Tray bake	Salmon & Asparagus
19	Oatmeal Blueberry Pancakes	Crock-Pot Slow Cooker Mulligatawny Soup	Cheese and Zucchini Roulades	Halibut with Spicy Apricot Sauce
20	Tofu Scramble	Greek Chicken	Oatmeal Butterscotch Cookies	Swordfish with Tomato Salsa

21	Bell Pepper Pancakes	Chuck and Veggies	Coco Macadamia Fat Bombs	Fried Chicken Tamari and Mustard
22	Sweet Potato Waffles	Spicy Lime Chicken	Pumpkin Spiced Almonds	Lemon Chicken with Basil
23	Millet Porridge	Cajun Catfish	Sesame Almond Fat Bombs	Breaded Chicken with Seed Chips
24	Chicken & Sweet Potato Hash	Cajun Flounder & Tomatoes	Tzatziki Dip with Cauliflower	Dry Rub Chicken Wings
25	Quinoa Porridge	Baked Salmon with Garlic Parmesan Topping	Curry Roasted Macadamia Nuts	Chicken Soup
26	Sweet Potato Waffles	Blackened Shrimp	Blueberry Popovers	Salted Biscuit Pie Turkey Chops
27	Apple Omelet	Crunchy Lemon Shrimp	Nutty Wild Rice Salad	Breaded Chicken Fillets
28	Tofu Scramble	Crab Frittata	Apricot and Pecan Muffins	Jerk Style Chicken Wings
29	Veggie Frittata	Cilantro Lime Grilled Shrimp	Chocolate Almond Butter Brownies	Chicken Wings with Garlic Parmesan
30	Strawberry & Spinach Smoothie	Cajun Shrimp & Roasted Vegetables	Coconut Chia Pudding	Ginger Chili Broccoli

Conclusion

Thanks to this cookbook, you will not forget ingredients, doses, tricks, variations, preparation secrets... and especially the aromas and flavours for your convivial occasions. A wonderful Journey all around the world just ended, we explored so many different cultures through the taste of food,
from Asia to Europe, each dish is so unique!

Alphabetical Index

Printed in Great Britain
by Amazon